Open Strategic Autonomy in EU Trade Policy

This book analyses whether the recent reorientation of EU trade policy towards stronger enforcement and more robust representation of interests, resulting in a series of new or amended legislative tools, is in conformity with the EU's international commitments, particularly WTO, FTA, environmental, and general international law, and with its multilateralist stance and underlying constitutional obligations. The analysis is also set against the consequences that would flow from within the EU legal order, providing readers with a comprehensive view of the external and internal constraints on trade policy that the EU should respect, as well as the leeway it enjoys. In case of potential tensions, it submits changes that would better balance the EU's new ambitions and international obligations. Furthermore, the book looks beyond the possible legal repercussions to consider the broader political implications of these instruments on the credibility of the EU's commitment to multilateralism and international law.

Wolfgang Weiß is Full Professor and Chair Holder of Public Law, European Law and Public International Law at the German University of Administrative Sciences Speyer. His main research areas are EU, WTO, and international economic law. He regularly contributes to article-by-article commentaries on EU law and publishes books and articles in both English- and German-language journals. Two of his books won academic book prizes. His most recent monographs are *WTO Law and Domestic Regulation: Exploring the Determinants for the Impact of the WTO on Domestic Regulatory Autonomy* (2020) and a treatise on WTO law (published in German: *Welthandelsrecht*, 3rd ed. 2022, co-authored with Christoph Ohler and Marc Bungenberg). He is also a co-editor of *Global Politics and EU Trade Policy* (2020).

Cornelia Furculita is a postdoctoral researcher at the Chair for Public Law, European Law and Public International Law at the German University of Administrative Sciences Speyer. Cornelia's research interests lie in international trade law, especially the intersection of WTO, FTAs, and EU trade law. She is the author of *The WTO and the New Generation EU FTA Dispute Settlement Mechanisms* (2021) and a co-editor of *Global Politics and EU Trade Policy* (2020).

Cambridge Studies in European Law and Policy

The focus of this series is European law broadly understood. It aims to publish original monographs in all fields of European law, from work focusing on the institutions of the EU and the Council of Europe to books examining substantive fields of European law as well as examining the relationship between European law and domestic, regional and international legal orders. The series publishes works adopting a wide variety of methods: comparative, doctrinal, theoretical and inter-disciplinary approaches to European law are equally welcome, as are works looking at the historical and political facets of the development of European law and policy. The main criterion is excellence, i.e. the publication of innovative work, which will help to shape the legal, political and scholarly debate on the future of European law.

Books in the Series

Reimagining Prosperity: Toward a New Imaginary of Law and Political Economy in the EU
Marija Bartl

Open Strategic Autonomy in EU Trade Policy: Assessing the Turn to Stronger Enforcement and More Robust Interest Representation
Wolfgang Weiß and Cornelia Furculiță

Trilogues: The Democratic Secret of European Legislation
Giacomo Rugge

The European Union, Emerging Global Business and Human Rights
Aleydis Nissen

The European Central Bank and the European Macroeconomic Constitution
Klaus Tuori

The Procedural and Organisational Law of the European Court of Justice: An Incomplete Transformation
Christoph Krenn

The New Economic Governance of the Eurozone: A Rule of Law Analysis
Paul Dermine

Digital Constitutionalism in Europe: Reframing Rights and Powers in the Algorithmic Society
Giovanni De Gregorio

Can the European Court of Human Rights Shape European Public Order?
Kanstantsin Dzehtsiarou

The Constitutional Boundaries of European Fiscal Federalism
Brady Gordon

Private Selves: Legal Personhood in European Privacy Protection
Susanna Lindroos-Hovinheimo

Fissures in EU Citizenship: The Deconstruction and Reconstruction of the Legal Evolution of EU Citizenship
Martin Steinfeld

The Boundaries of the EU Internal Market: Participation without Membership
Marja-Liisa Öberg

The Currency of Solidarity: Constitutional Transformation during the Euro Crisis
Vestert Borger

Empire of Law: Nazi Germany, Exile Scholars and the Battle for the Future of Europe
Kaius Tuori

In the Court We Trust: Cooperation, Coordination and Collaboration between the ECJ and Supreme Administrative Courts
Rob van Gestel and Jurgen de Poorter

Beyond Minimum Harmonisation: Gold-Plating and Green-Plating of European Environmental Law
Lorenzo Squintani

The Court of Justice of the European Union as an Institutional Actor: Judicial Lawmaking and its Limits
Thomas Horsley

The Politics of Justice in European Private Law: Social Justice, Access Justice, Societal Justice
Hans-W Micklitz

The Transformation of EU Treaty Making: The Rise of Parliaments, Referendums and Courts Since 1950
Dermot Hodson and Imelda Maher

Redefining European Economic Integration
Dariusz Adamski

Human Rights in the Council of Europe and the European Union: Achievements, Trends and Challenges
Steven Greer, Janneke Gerards and Rosie Slowe

Core Socio-Economic Rights and the European Court of Human Rights
Ingrid Leijten

Green Trade and Fair Trade in and with the EU: Process-based Measures within the EU Legal Order
Laurens Ankersmit

New Labour Laws in Old Member States: Trade Union Responses to European Enlargement
Rebecca Zahn

The Governance of EU Fundamental Rights
Mark Dawson

The International Responsibility of the European Union: From Competence to Normative Control
Andrés Delgado Casteleiro

Frontex and Non-Refoulement: The International Responsibility of the EU
Roberta Mungianu

Gendering European Working Time Regimes: The Working Time Directive and the Case of Poland
Ania Zbyszewska

EU Renewable Electricity Law and Policy: From National Targets to a Common Market
Tim Maxian Rusche

European Constitutionalism
Kaarlo Tuori

Brokering Europe: Euro-Lawyers and the Making of a Transnational Polity
Antoine Vauchez

Services Liberalization in the EU and the WTO: Concepts, Standards and Regulatory Approaches
Marcus Klamert

Referendums and the European Union: A Comparative Enquiry
Fernando Mendez, Mario Mendez and Vasiliki Triga

The Allocation of Regulatory Competence in the EU Emissions Trading Scheme
Jospehine van Zeben

The Eurozone Crisis: A Constitutional Analysis
Kaarlo Tuori and Klaus Tuori

International Trade Disputes and EU Liability
Anne Thies

The Limits of Legal Reasoning and the European Court of Justice
Gerard Conway

New Governance and the Transformation of European Law: Coordinating EU Social Law and Policy
Mark Dawson

The Lisbon Treaty: A Legal and Political Analysis
Jean-Claude Piris

The European Union's Fight Against Corruption: The Evolving Policy Towards Member States and Candidate Countries
Patrycja Szarek-Mason

The Ethos of Europe: Values, Law and Justice in the EU
Andrew Williams

State and Market in European Union Law: The Public and Private Spheres of the Internal Market before the EU Courts
Wolf Sauter and Harm Schepel

The European Civil Code: The Way Forward
Hugh Collins

Ethical Dimensions of the Foreign Policy of the European Union: A Legal Appraisal
Urfan Khaliq

Implementing EU Pollution Control: Law and Integration
Bettina Lange

European Broadcasting Law and Policy
Jackie Harrison and Lorna Woods

The Transformation of Citizenship in the European Union: Electoral Rights and the Restructuring of Political Space
Jo Shaw

The Constitution for Europe: A Legal Analysis
Jean-Claude Piris

The European Convention on Human Rights: Achievements, Problems and Prospects
Steven Greer

Social Rights and Market Freedom in the European Constitution: A Labour Law Perspective
Stefano Giubboni

EU Enlargement and the Constitutions of Central and Eastern Europe
Anneli Albi

Open Strategic Autonomy in EU Trade Policy

Assessing the Turn to Stronger Enforcement and More Robust Interest Representation

Wolfgang Weiß
University Speyer

Cornelia Furculita
University Speyer

CAMBRIDGE
UNIVERSITY PRESS

CAMBRIDGE
UNIVERSITY PRESS

Shaftesbury Road, Cambridge CB2 8EA, United Kingdom

One Liberty Plaza, 20th Floor, New York, NY 10006, USA

477 Williamstown Road, Port Melbourne, VIC 3207, Australia

314–321, 3rd Floor, Plot 3, Splendor Forum, Jasola District Centre, New Delhi – 110025, India

103 Penang Road, #05–06/07, Visioncrest Commercial, Singapore 238467

Cambridge University Press is part of Cambridge University Press & Assessment, a department of the University of Cambridge.

We share the University's mission to contribute to society through the pursuit of education, learning and research at the highest international levels of excellence.

www.cambridge.org
Information on this title: www.cambridge.org/9781009196536

DOI: 10.1017/9781009196529

When citing this work, please include a reference to the DOI 10.1017/9781009196529

First published 2024

A catalogue record for this publication is available from the British Library

Library of Congress Cataloging-in-Publication Data
Names: Weiss, Wolfgang, 1966– author. | Furculiță, Cornelia, author.
Title: Open strategic autonomy in EU trade policy : assessing the turn to stronger enforcement and more robust interest representation / Wolfgang Weiss, University Speyer; Cornelia Furculita, University Speyer.
Other titles: Open strategic autonomy in European Union trade policy
Description: Cambridge, United Kingdom ; New York, NY : Cambridge University Press, 2024. | Series: Cambridge studies in European law and policy | Includes bibliographical references and index.
Identifiers: LCCN 2024008596 (print) | LCCN 2024008597 (ebook) | ISBN 9781009196536 (hardback) | ISBN 9781009196543 (paperback) | ISBN 9781009196529 (epub)
Subjects: LCSH: Trade regulation–European Union countries. | Foreign trade regulation–European Union countries. | Autonomy (Philosophy)–European Union countries. | World Trade Organization. | Arbitration (International law)
Classification: LCC KJE6791 .W45 2024 (print) | LCC KJE6791 (ebook) | DDC 382.094–dc23/eng/20240224
LC record available at https://lccn.loc.gov/2024008596
LC ebook record available at https://lccn.loc.gov/2024008597

ISBN 978-1-009-19653-6 Hardback

Contents

Preface

The EU of the 2020s is beset by a number of challenges. High among them, however, is the place of the EU in the wider world. Since its birth, the EU has been seen as part of a broader process of globalization that includes the internationalization of law itself. The opening of national law to the law of the EU could thus be conceptualized as a broader opening of European states to international legal obligations, which EU law might underpin and support.

What, however, does EU law do in an increasingly *closed* world? The rise of China and the seeming return of geopolitical 'blocks' increasingly threaten the integrity of the international legal order and the multilateral institutions which underpin it. This is most marked in the area of trade policy, where decades of openness seem to be coming to an abrupt close, and where a historical pioneer of global free trade, the United States, has been accused of domestic protectionism. In response, the EU has seen a need to take a more sovereigntist stance not just in trade policy but in a host of other areas, often grouped together under the infamous term 'strategic autonomy'. The Union has entered a brave new world, in which it must use (and potentially misuse) legal tools to level the competitive playing field.

This book, written by Cornelia Furculita and Wolfgang Weiß, is devoted to understanding how EU trade law and policy are adapting to this world. As the book charts, the EU faces a fundamental dilemma. On the one hand, it must meet the new geopolitical reality and its associated challenges (particularly to the EU's environmental and social objectives). On the other, it must not lose its fundamental 'DNA' in the process, namely its commitment to respect international law (a commitment embedded in the Treaty itself). EU trade law and policy must thus chart an increasingly narrow path.

Furculita and Weiß's book takes great care in leading us along precisely this path, assessing the compatibility of important new EU initiatives developed in the name of strategic autonomy with a complex web of international trade obligations. It is therefore not only a book with useful scholarly lessons but a wonderful resource for practitioners interested both in important recent EU initiatives (such as on procurement and sustainability) and in specialized fields of law such as competition, dispute resolution, and, of course, trade. The book is not afraid to make strong normative conclusions, pointing to important inconsistencies between EU legislative initiatives and commitments embedded in international and EU constitutional law (with clear ideas on how to remedy them, drawing on public international law scholarship). As a book tackling one of the Union's (and world's) foremost challenges, it deserves to be widely read. We are delighted to welcome it to the *Cambridge Studies in European Law and Policy* series.

Mark Dawson
Laurence Gormley
Jo Shaw

Abbreviations

AA	Association Agreement
AB	Appellate Body
ACI	Anti-Coercion Instrument
ADA	Anti-Dumping Agreement
AG	Advocate General
AJIL	*American Journal of International Law*
ASCM	Agreement on Subsidies and Countervailing Measures
ASEAN	Association of Southeast Asian Nations
BASR	Basic Anti-Subsidy Regulation
BTA	Border Tariff Adjustment
CARIFORUM	The Caribbean Forum
CBAM	Carbon Border Adjustment Mechanism
CBDR	Common But Differentiated Responsibilities
CEPR	Centre for Economic Policy Research
CETA	EU–Canada Trade Agreement
CJEU	Court of Justice of the European Union
CMLRev	*Common Market Law Review*
CPTPP	Comprehensive and Progressive Agreement for Trans-Pacific Partnership
CTEI	Centre for Trade and Economic Integration
CTEO	Chief Trade Enforcement Officer
DAG	Domestic Advisory Group
DG	Director General
DSB	Dispute Settlement Body
DSU	Dispute Settlement Understanding
ECT	Treaty Establishing the European Community
EEA	European Economic Area
EECT	Treaty Establishing the European Economic Community

EFARev	*European Foreign Affairs Review*
EC	European Communities
ECHR	European Convention on Human Rights
EEA	The Agreement on the European Economic Area
EEC	European Economic Community
EFTA	European Free Trade Association
EJIL	*The European Journal of International Law*
ELJ	*European Law Journal*
ELRev	*European Law Review*
EP	European Parliament
EPA	Economic Partnership Agreement
EPRS	European Parliamentary Research Service
ETS	Emissions Trading System
EU	European Union
EUI	European University Institute
EU–UA AA	EU–Ukraine Association Agreement
EuZW	*Europäische Zeitschrift für Wirtschaftsrecht*
FSR	Foreign Subsidies Regulation
FTA	Free Trade Agreement
GATS	General Agreement on Trade in Services
GATT	General Agreement on Tariffs and Trade
GBER	General Block Exemption Regulation
GC	General Court
GHG	Greenhouse Gas
GPA	Agreement on Government Procurement
GSP	Generalized Scheme of Preferences
GTCJ	*Global Trade and Customs Journal*
ICJ	International Court of Justice
ICLQ	*International & Comparative Law Quarterly*
IELP	*International Economic Law and Policy*
ILC	International Law Commission
ILO	International Labour Organization
ILSA	International Law Students Association
INTA	European Parliament Committee on International Trade
IPI	International Procurement Instrument
JCMS	*Journal of Common Market Studies*
JEPA	EU–Japan Economic Partnership Agreement
JEPP	*Journal of European Public Policy*
JEI	*Journal of European Integration*
JIEL	*Journal of International Economic Law*
JWIT	*Journal of World Investment & Trade*

JWT	*Journal of World Trade*
LDC	Least Developed Country
LIEI	*Legal Issues of Economic Integration*
LSE	London School of Economics and Political Science
MAS	Mutually Agreed Solution
MFN	Most Favored Nation
MPIA	Multi-Party Interim Appeal Arbitration Arrangement
NAFTA	North American Free Trade Agreement
NAP	No Appeal Pact
NDC	Nationally Determined Contribution
NT	National Treatment
OECD	Organisation for Economic Co-operation and Development
OJ	*Official Journal*
PCIJ	Permanent Court of International Justice
QMV	Qualified Majority Vote
RCEP	Regional Comprehensive Economic Partnership
RSCAS	Robert Schuman Centre for Advanced Studies
SAA	Stabilisation and Association Agreement
SDT	Special and Differential Treatment
SIDS	Small Island Developing States
SME	Small and Medium-Sized Enterprise
TBT	Technical Barriers to Trade
TCA	Trade and Cooperation Agreement
TEU	Treaty on European Union
TFEU	Treaty on the Functioning of the European Union
TRIPS	Agreement on Trade-Related Aspects of Intellectual Property Rights
TSD	Trade and Sustainable Development
UN	United Nations
UNCTAD	United Nations Conference on Trade and Development
UNFCCC	United Nations Framework Convention on Climate Change
USMCA	United States–Mexico–Canada Agreement
VCLT	Vienna Convention on the Law of Treaties
WP	Working Party
WTI	World Trade Institute
WTO	World Trade Organization
WTRev	*World Trade Review*
ZEuS	*Zeitschrift fuer Europarechtliche Studien*

1 Introduction

1.1 The Mission of This Book: Scrutinizing the New EU Trade Policy against Its Legal Constraints

This book analyses the EU trade policy's turn towards stronger enforcement and ensuring a level playing field, which the European Commission adopted in its most recent trade policy review communication of February 2021 on an 'open, sustainable and assertive trade policy'.[1] Thereby, the EU redefined its trade policy based on the model of 'open strategic autonomy', which, in the eyes of the Commission, is meant to combine benefitting from a rules-based trade system with protecting against unfair and abusive practices. The reorientation undertakes to assertively enforce the EU's existing bilateral and multilateral trade rights against its trade partners, as well as to level the playing field of competition between domestic and foreign undertakings in the internal market, and externally as regards labour rights and sustainability. Admittedly, the trade policy review indicates more policy objectives than the one on increasing the EU's capacity to enforce its trading rights, and lists six areas of action.[2] But the last one, on stronger implementation and enforcement, is particularly explicit and elaborate, much more than the others, and clearly sets out a detailed programme of policy initiatives and legislative action[3] (for a detailed analysis of the communication, see Section 2.1). What is really new according to our assessment is that the Commission places a new and determined focus on implementation and enforcement of trading rights, including strengthened powers to

[1] European Commission, Trade Policy Review – An Open, Sustainable and Assertive Trade Policy (Trade Policy Review), COM(2021) 66 final, 18 February 2021.

[2] ibid, pp. 10 f. [3] ibid. pp. 19–21.

advocate its interests more forcefully, and wants to ensure the EU's actorness in trade relations in order to justify continued, albeit conditioned, openness. Thus, the trade policy review not only takes up an evolving awareness in the EU for a greater need for trade enforcement and transfers the EU Global Strategy's pragmatist turn into trade policy with a new impetus, but also comes as a response to most recent fundamental changes in trade politics of its trading partners (for a more detailed discussion, see Sections 1.2 and 2.2). The new trade policy extends the EU's capacities of responding effectively to trade measures of others, and so will increase its deterrence power. It is embedded in its search for strategic autonomy in its external relations with a view to expand the EU's ability for autonomous determination of its common foreign policy. Gaining more 'sovereignty' – that is, independence and self-determination – also in its external economic presence is an expression of a new global, geostrategic orientation of the EU and its policies which intends to address current world challenges.[4]

In implementing the ensuing new trade policy, the EU tabled several legislative proposals to amend or adopt enforcement tools in order to ward off what it perceives as unfair treatment.[5] The legislative projects and new approaches to sustainability, labour, and dispute settlement (which will be dealt with in detail in Parts II and III) grant the EU new powers and instruments to defend itself against unfair trade practices and, if necessary, to restore a level playing field, particularly in terms of competition in the EU's internal market. The projects and initiatives envisioned in the trade policy review communication, however, trigger internal and external reservations. Internally, the consequences of the new approach for the EU internal separation and balance of powers and the institutional balance between the EU institutions are debated. The new legislation will give the Commission considerable new powers which not only lead to trade restrictions but may imply considerable

[4] Milan Babić, Adam Dixon, and Imogen Liu, 'Geoeconomics in a Changing Global Order', in Milan Babić, Adam Dixon, and Imogen Liu (eds.), *The Political Economy of Geoeconomics* (Cham: Palgrave Macmillan, 2022), pp. 12 f; Luuk Schmitz and Timo Seidl, 'As Open as Possible, as Autonomous as Necessary' (2023) 61(3) JCMS 834–852 at 841; Tobias Gehrke, 'EU Open Strategic Autonomy and the Trappings of Geoeconomics' (2022) *European Foreign Affairs Review* Special Issue 61–78 at 68 ff.

[5] Frank Hoffmeister, 'Do Ut Des oder Tit For Tat? – Die Europäische Handelspolitik Angesichts Neuer Herausforderungen aus den USA und China', in Christoph Herrmann (ed.), *Die Gemeinsame Handelspolitik im Europäischen Verfassungsverbund* (Baden-Baden: Nomos, 2020), p. 94.

consequences for trade and even beyond, specifically general foreign relations with third countries, whereas it actually is for the Council to determine foreign policy and, in cooperation with the European Parliament, to shape trade policy so that it should be their competence to decide about the use of instruments that could produce considerable foreign trade and policy effects.[6] Given its enlarged policy leeway, demands for more accountability and democratic control of the Commission rise. Externally, the EU could be blamed for neglecting its multilateral, rule-oriented policy stance and imitating power politics in the US or Chinese style.[7] It could be seen to start merely paying lip service to multilateralism by picking and choosing those commitments that are in its interest while preparing tools for disrespecting the others. The new robustness of the EU's trade policy approach entails increased capacities for autonomous, even unilateral behaviour which might be perceived as a threat undermining the credibility of the EU's support for multilateralism, its compliance with international law, and its reform efforts in the WTO,[8] going 'against previously dominant ideas of free trade and multilateralism'.[9] It might put at risk EU trading interests in the long run, as other countries might emulate what the EU does. The EU could be blamed for adding to the current severe contestation of multilateral trade rules, and international law in general, thus exposing the international rules-based trade order to additional stress and contributing to a further demise of rule of law in international relations.[10] The 'last big defender of rules-based open trade' may be seen to fall and 'give

[6] See e.g. the results of the open public consultation on a EU anti-coercion instrument (https://web.archive.org/web/20220712213138/https://trade.ec.europa.eu/doclib/docs/2021/september/tradoc_159792.pdf), replies to question 18.

[7] For the 'Trumpian Turn', see Gabriel Felbermayr, 'A Trumpian Turn in EU Trade Politics and the Silence of Germany', 2018 EconPol Opinion 6 (www.econpol.eu/opinion_6), with regard to the modernization of anti-dumping rules.

[8] For these, see Jan Wouters and Akhil Raina, 'The European Union and Global Economic Governance: A Leader without a Roadmap?', in Julien Chaisse (ed.), *Sixty Years of European Integration and Global Power Shifts: Perceptions, Interactions and Lessons* (London: Hart Publishing, 2020), pp. 198 ff.

[9] Sjorre Couvreur, et al., 'The Good Geopolitical Trade Actor? The European Union's Discursive Justification of the Anti-Coercion Instrument' (2022) *Journal of Political Science* Special Issue 133–147 at 136.

[10] For the current contests of multilateralism in the WTO as a challenge to the international rule of law, see Vineet Hegde, Jan Wouters, and Akhil Raina, 'The Demise of the Rules-Based International Economic Order?' (2020) Leuven Centre for Global Governance Studies, Working Paper 224, 8 ff.

up on the concept of free trade' with the new trade policy.[11] The EU appears to be aware of this criticism as it tries to juxtapose its new trade policy orientation on the weaponization of trade by other countries.[12] With regard to its new Anti-Coercion Instrument (ACI),[13] for example, which allows the Commission to impose sanctions on third countries allegedly coercing the EU or a Member State to adopt or stop policies which is their own sovereign choice to determine, the European Commission justifies the new legislation by claiming that it allegedly preserves EU autonomy in policymaking from third countries that use trade as a weapon to unduly, even illegally, interfere with the sovereignty of others.[14] The EU represents itself as a victim of other states' protectionism and interventionism in the EU's policy choices and presents its new ACI as a legitimate response, with it being portrayed as a protection against breaches of international law. Thus, the EU claims to respond only to illegalities of others, and to do so merely in a defensive approach using lawful means.[15] It defends its self-perception as a good actor. One may, however, contest this presentation of the ACI, as this instrument has at least the capacity also to be used in an offensive way, all the more so considering that the assessment of what a coercive practices by a third country actually implies is far from simple, because the concept is vague.[16] The EU commitment to multilateralism and international law has a long tradition in political terms, and is also a constitutional obligation for the EU by virtue of Articles 3 (5), 21 (2) TEU, and 216 (2) TFEU, which the CJEU appears to be willing to enforce,

[11] Barbara Moens and Hans van der Burchard, 'Europe First: Brussels Gets Ready to Dump Its Free Trade Ideals', www.politico.eu/article/ursula-von-der-leyen-joe-biden-trade-europe-first-brussels-gets-ready-to-dump-its-free-trade-ideals/.

[12] Commission Proposal for a Regulation on the protection of the Union and its Member States from economic coercion by third countries, COM(2021) 775 final, pp. 1–3, 26; Impact Assessment Report Accompanying the document Proposal for a Regulation of the European Parliament and of the Council on the protection of the Union and its Member States from economic coercion by third countries (Impact Assessment Report), 8 December 2021, SWD(2021) 371 final, 5, p. 14.

[13] See Regulation (EU) 2023/2675 of the European Parliament and of the Council of 22 November 2023 on the protection of the Union and its Member States from economic coercion by third countries, OJ EU 2023 No. L 2675, 7 December 2023.

[14] Impact Assessment Report, SWD(2021) 371 final, 9, p. 49 f.

[15] See Couvreur, et al., 'The Good Geopolitical Trade Actor?' (2022), 141 f.

[16] See ibid, 143. Article 2 ACI Regulation 2023/2675 defines economic coercion to refer to a situation 'where a third country applies or threatens to apply a third-country measure affecting trade or investment in order to prevent or obtain the cessation, modification or adoption of a particular act by the Union or a Member State, thereby interfering in the legitimate sovereign choices of the Union or a Member State'.

particularly in trade policy.[17] The new robustness may jeopardize this, as the new tools, much more than ever, seek not only to emphasize the EU's interests but also to enforce them more assertively, and could, therefore, conflict with the EU's obligations also under international law. These internal and external concerns are interrelated, as parliamentary scrutiny allows for greater transparency of EU politics and increased control of the EU executive. Intensified Commission accountability may be a useful way of ensuring that the new powers in EU trade policy are not employed for measures that represent violations of international obligations, in particular with regard to the rules-based international trade order, or even amount to blatant protectionism. As the internal concerns have been dealt with elsewhere, albeit briefly,[18] the book's focus will be on evaluating and assessing the new turn in the EU's trade policy towards a more assertive enforcement of its trade rights and more robust representation of its interests (the last, as will be shown in Chapter 2, is actually what signifies what EU calls safeguarding 'a level playing field') in view of its impact on the EU's obligations deriving from its multilateral stance and its international legal obligations.

Even though the EU confirms its intention to abide within the limits of international law in its new trade policy legislation, whether the EU has succeeded insofar deserves closer inspection and is far from trivial. The reason for this is that the new legislation introduces quite novel tools such as an instrument against coercion, a monitoring mechanism regarding the competition distortion caused by third-country subsidies, or a carbon border mechanism intended to compensate for the burden on intra-Union trade resulting from carbon tax, all of which represent instruments for adopting countermeasures in response to other states' behaviour for which there hardly is an international example. Furthermore, these novel tools raise complex questions as to their compatibility with WTO law in particular. Also, there currently are no international precedents or clear pertinent rules having been worked out by international institutions or courts. And even if the black letter of the new provisions is in conformity with international law (due to sometimes rather general disclaimers of compatibility with international law

[17] See CJEU, Cases C-104/16 P, *Council v Front Polisario* [2017] ECLI:EU:C:2016:973; C-266/16, *Western Sahara Campaign UK* [2018], ECLI:EU:C:2018:118; C-66/18, *Commission v Hungary (Enseignement supérieur)* [2020] ECLI:EU:C:2020:792, and Chapter 3 for more details.

[18] Wolfgang Weiß, 'The EU's Strategic Autonomy in Times of Politicization of International Trade: The Future of Commission Accountability' (2023) *Global Policy* (Suppl. 3) 54–64.

present in the new legislation, reflecting the intention of the EU not to intentionally breach international law), its implementation and application in concrete cases might have to observe certain limits to avoid sliding into protectionism, besides the political problem of escalation and counteraction by trade partners. The new tools may bring to the fore an inherent contradiction embodied in the new trade policy review: While the Commission confessed to the significance of multilateralism and confirmed the EU trade policy's openness and engagement on the international scene and support for cooperation,[19] the new tools give the Commission the capacity to behave autonomously and even unilaterally (i.e. without considering trade partners' interests), if not protectionist, which puts its openness and cooperative approach hitherto in serious question. Concepts such as resilience or security, which feature prominently in the 2021 trade policy review,[20] have previously been associated with protectionist tendencies.[21] Thus, the policy review induces concerns for the EU's future credibility with regard to its defence of multilateralism. As has been observed, there is a 'fine line' between more robust and assertive representation and enforcement of own interests on the one hand and protectionism on the other; whether this line is crossed will also depend on the assessment of the reaction of trade partners and on the broader, still developing economic and security policy context of EU trade policy.[22]

Therefore, the present book takes up the research question of whether the implementation of the new trade policy reorientation of the EU resulting in the adoption of new legislation and approaches is compliant with its international legal commitments, and beyond, with its multilateral orientation rooted in constitutional obligations. It pursues a comprehensive legal analysis and assessment of the new EU tools developing novel or amending existing enforcement and level playing field legislation and of the related legal constraints to EU trade policy flowing from EU constitutional law and international law (i.e. WTO, EU FTA, climate protection rules, and general international law on treaties and countermeasures). The book exemplifies the inherent tensions the EU as a

[19] Trade Policy Review, COM(2021) 66 final, p. 6.

[20] Resilience is referred to sixteen times, and security nine times, in the Trade Policy Review.

[21] Thomas Jacobs, et al., 'The Hegemonic Politics of Strategic Autonomy and Resilience' (2023) *JCMS* 3–19 at 5.

[22] Sophie Meunier, 'The End of Naivety: Assertiveness and New Instruments in EU Trade and Investment Policy' (2022) *EUI Global Governance Programme*, Policy Brief issue 2022/55, p. 8.

principled pragmatist in external relations has to face, and analyses the limits, flexibilities, and broader implications of the new EU trade policy. In this way, it adds to the broader discussion of the demise (or not) of the rule of law in international relations,[23] with a view to EU trade policy. Thereby, it contributes to identifying solutions in conformity with the EU's support for a multilateral rules-based order and commitment to respect public international law. The results allow to determine the legal scope for a more robust EU trade policy in line with international law and deepen the understanding of how trade policy can evolve in the light of the challenges it faces.

1.2 Roots, Causes, Context: From 'A Stronger Europe' via 'Open Strategic Autonomy' towards an 'Open, Sustainable and Assertive Trade Policy'

The turn towards more robustness in trade policy did not begin in 2021; it has recent roots, current causes, and contemporary context, which will be briefly recalled here. First of all, the turn reflects a more pragmatic, realist, and resilient policy approach which started in the EU's Global Strategy on Foreign and Security Policy of June 2016 for a 'Stronger Europe' that reflected a conflict-prone external policy environment and fed geopolitical thinking into the EU's external relations approaches.[24] The EU's Global Strategy, while paying tribute to promoting a 'rules-based global order' with multilateralism as a key principle, amidst existential crises around the globe, complemented its more traditional value-based approach with geopolitical realism and flexibility. Hence, the EU initiated a pragmatist turn[25] and became a 'principled pragmatist'.[26] The Global Strategy used the term *strategic autonomy* several times, particularly with

[23] See Heike Krieger, Georg Nolte, and Andreas Zimmermann (eds.), *The International Rule of Law: Rise or Decline?* (Oxford: Oxford University Press, 2019); Luis M. Hinojosa-Martínez and Carmela Pérez-Bernárdez (eds.), *Enhancing the Rule of Law in the EU's External Action* (Cheltenham, Northampton: Elgar Publishing, 2023).

[24] Heather Conley, 'The Birth of a Global Strategy Amid Deep Crisis' (2016) 51(3) *The International Spectator* 12–14.

[25] Shared Vision, Common Action: A Stronger Europe – A Global Strategy for the European Union's Foreign and Security Policy, 2016, pp. 7 f, 39 ff, https://eeas.europa.eu/archives/docs/top_stories/pdf/eugs_review_web.pdf.

[26] Ana Juncos, 'Resilience as the New EU Foreign Policy Paradigm: A Pragmatist Turn' (2017) 26(1) *European Security* 1; Nathalie Tocci, 'The Making of the EU Global Strategy' (2016) 37 *Contemporary Security Policy* 461–472.

regard to the required EU independence in security and defense issues; soon, discussions about European sovereignty developed,[27] with the recent initiative of Commission President Ursula von der Leyen for a European Sovereignty Fund.[28]

This more realist and tentatively geopolitical approach first became translated into trade policy at the highest level in a statement of the European Council in June 2019 on the New Strategic Agenda 2019–2024 which called for 'an ambitious and robust trade policy ensuring fair competition, reciprocity and mutual benefits' both at the WTO and in bilateral relations,[29] from which emerged the more geopolitical new 'open, sustainable and assertive trade policy' .[30]

Secondly, of pivotal significance to date was the advent of the new European Commission under von der Leyen striving for being more geopolitical.[31] In her political guidelines for the European Commission 2019–2024,[32] and her first mission letter to the Trade Commissioner,[33] strengthening the enforcement of trade rules features prominently. At the start of the discussion and consultation on the new direction of EU's trade policy in June 2020, the central leitmotif of 'open strategic autonomy' (which was used for the first time by the then Trade Commissioner Phil Hogan in a speech at a G20 meeting on 14 May 2020[34] and then again on 27 May 2020 in a Commission

[27] Scott Lavery, Sean McDaniel, and Davide Schmid, 'European Strategic Autonomy', in Babić, Dixon, and Liu (eds.), *The Political Economy of Geoeconomics* (2022), pp. 60 ff.

[28] Thierry Breton, 'A European Sovereignty Fund for an industry "Made in Europe"', Blog of Commissioner Thierry Breton, 15 September 2022, https://ec.europa.eu/commission/presscorner/detail/en/statement_22_5543.

[29] European Council, 'A New Strategic Agenda 2019–2024', pp. 4, 6 (www.consilium.europa.eu/media/39914/a-new-strategic-agenda-2019-2024.pdf).

[30] For its greater geopolitical inclination compared to previous more normative trade policy, see Couvreur, et al., 'The Good Geopolitical Trade Actor?' (2022), 134 f.

[31] For the 'geopolitical Commission', see Ursula von der Leyen, Speech in the European Parliament Plenary Session, Strasbourg, 27 November 2019, https://ec.europa.eu/commission/presscorner/detail/en/SPEECH_19_6408.

[32] Ursula von der Leyen, Political Guidelines for the Next European Commission 2019–2024, 'A Union That Strives for More', https://data.europa.eu/doi/10.2775/101756.

[33] See Ursula von der Leyen, 'Mission Letter to Phil Hogan, Commissioner for Trade', 1 December 2019, https://commissioners.ec.europa.eu/system/files/2022-12/mission-letter-phil-hogan-2019_en.pdf.

[34] Intro Remarks by Commissions Phil Hogan at Second G20 Extraordinary Trade and Investment Ministers Meeting. See also Patrick Holden, 'Regional Integration and Trade in the Era of COVID-19: A First Look', UNU-CRIS Working Paper Series, September 2020, p. 11, https://cris.unu.edu/sites/cris.unu.edu/files/WP20.3%20-%20Holden.pdf.

Communication[35]) was coined in order to signify that the EU should continue reaping the benefits of the international rules-based trade order by focusing on implementation and enforcement issues, while having the right tools in place to protect itself from unfair, hostile, or uncompetitive practices.[36] The 'open strategic autonomy' (which will be looked at more closely in Section 2.1.3). is intended to balance and combine the fundamental openness of the EU's markets with protection for its people and businesses. This implies the EU's ability to take the enforcement of trade rules into its own hands even more than it has done before and to assert the EU's rights to enforce greater reciprocity. Adding the adjective 'open' to the existing term 'strategic autonomy' might have meant to underline that the new policy was not intended to develop into protectionism.[37]

Thirdly, the shift towards a more robust policy formulation, oriented toward the assertive representation of the EU's own economic as well as non-economic (regarding sustainability and labour rights) interests, was strongly stimulated in the area of trade relations by the EU's need to respond to far-reaching changes in the trade environment in recent years. Trade relations and trade governance, while being subject to NGO, trade union, and (parts of) civil society criticism already since the 1990s in view of the WTO and since around 2013 with regard to EU FTA negotiations,[38] lately have been facing an unprecedented level of simultaneous economic, institutional, political, and technological challenges such as the contested state of the WTO and its rules; the rise of unilateralism and protectionism; the greater salience of climate change, public health, and digitalization for trade governance; and the increasing geoeconomic orientation of trade powers such as China and the United States (for more, see Section 2.2). The most recent of these challenges to international trade regulation, before the trade policy review was formulated, was the COVID-19 pandemic in 2020–2021, which gave additional weight to public health issues and supply security in regulating international trade. The variety, severity, and simultaneity of the current challenges to the global environment for trade and the current pace of change appear

[35] European Commission, 'Europe's Moment: Repair and Prepare for the Next Generation', COM(2020) 456 final, 13.

[36] European Commission, 'A renewed trade policy for a stronger Europe. Consultation Note', 16 June 2020, 3, 8.

[37] See Lavery, McDaniel, and Schmid, 'European Strategic Autonomy' (2022), p. 71 f.

[38] Sangeeta Khorana and Maria Garcia, 'Introduction', in Sangheta Khorana and Maria Garcia (eds.), *Handbook on the EU and International Trade* (Cheltenham, Northampton: Edward Elgar Publishing 2018), pp. 7 f.

unprecedented compared to the last seventy years. The global economic order, the whole world order actually, as we know it is changing drastically as the transatlantic US hegemony in political, technological, and economic terms comes to an end, in particular with China rising to an almost equal power.[39] The liberal economic order faces unprecedented hurdles and contests, and so does the EU trade policy, which has to find ways to respond to them.[40] The multilateral trading system has regulated international trade relationships and provided relative stability for decades since World War II with the establishment of the Bretton Woods institutions and the reform of GATT 1947 by the introduction of the WTO in 1994. The order established by these institutions currently is under severe threat, in particular the functioning of the WTO. Multilateral trade institutions have been put in profound danger. As multilateral negotiations are stalled, by and large, bilateral or plurilateral trade agreements appear as the only propelling force. The WTO dispute settlement mechanism, the former 'jewel of the crown', has been strangled by the US blockage of appointment of new Appellate Body members.[41] Protectionist measures are rising, not least as a consequence of the economic nationalism of 'Trumponomics',[42] alleged national security reasons, and the economic turmoil following the spread of coronavirus.[43] A further challenge to the present system of multilateral trade regulation is posed by the enormous and still rising economic importance of China and its more recent global aspirations that gained new momentum with the Russian war against Ukraine as China instigates attempts to install an alternative to the Western-driven international order.[44] World trade is confronted with systemic challenges

[39] G. John Ikenberry, 'The End of Liberal International Order?' (2018) 94(1) *International Affairs* 7; John J. Mearsheimer, 'Bound to Fail: The Rise and Fall of the Liberal International Order' (2019) 43(4) *International Security* 7; Dilip Hiro, *After Empire: The Birth of a Multipolar World* (New York: National Books, 2010), pp. 13 ff.

[40] Antonina Bakardjieva Engelbrekt, et al., *The European Union in a Changing World Order* (Cham: Palgrave Macmillan, 2020).

[41] Geraldo Vidigal, 'Living without the Appellate Body: Multilateral, Bilateral and Plurilateral Solutions to the WTO Dispute Settlement Crisis' (2019) 20(6) *JWIT* 862–890.

[42] Stephen Moore and Arthur B. Laffer, *Trumponomics: Inside the America First Plan to Revive Our Economy* (New York: St. Martin's Press, 2018).

[43] See WTO, 'Report on G20 Trade Measures', June 2020, pp. 2, 32 ff.; WTO, 'Report on G20 Trade Measures', November 2020, pp. 3, 31 ff.; Louise Curran, Jappe Eckhardt, and Jaemin Lee, 'The Trade Policy Response to COVID-19 and Its Implications for International Business' (2021) 17(2) *Critical Perspectives on International Business* 252–320.

[44] See the declaration to the 2023 XV BRICS Summit Johannesburg, https://brics2023.gov.za/2023/07/05/summit-declarations/.

caused by the Chinese form of state capitalism and state-led economic system allegedly leading to unfair competition. Concerns about the systemic issues raised by China are widespread among nations. China's conscious geostrategic and geoeconomic behaviour systematically expands its world market position and exerts pressure on WTO members to respond by behaving geostrategically and geoeconomically themselves. China's specific economic model affects the very foundations of the international trade order. With the advent of the WTO and in particular its judicialized dispute settlement with an ensuing compulsory implementation phase, trade relations and resulting disputes had been perceived – quite commonly – as legalized and depoliticized, but this perception of trade rules is changing fundamentally nowadays. In this context, the new EU trade policy seeks to significantly expand the EU's room for manoeuvre in this area of policy and to gain more autonomy by strengthening the enforcement of its trade rights within both multilateral and bilateral settings and by ensuring more assertively, including unilaterally, the representation of its interests in order to protect its economy from unfair trade practices. Furthermore, the new turn aligns trade policy with the EU's general political priorities in the areas of sustainability, climate change, the digital economy, and economic and political security. The European Commission is thus outlining the trade policy consequences of its central political projects, first and foremost the European Green Deal.[45]

Finally, the recent reorientation of trade policy echoes a longer-standing trend. The new EU trade policy redefinition summarizes and confirms a reorientation of trade policy practice already present since several years before 2019, as trade policy had been refocused on a more effective implementation and enforcement of trade rules and the benefits they bring to market access for the EU industry. After enforcement had not been a priority in EU trade policy,[46] things started changing as of 2012 when what later became the so-called Trade Enforcement Regulation 654/2014[47] was proposed, which regulates the exercise of EU

[45] European Commission, Communication on the European Green Deal, COM(2019) 640 final.

[46] Simon J. Evenett, 'Paper Tiger? EU Trade Enforcement as If Binding Pacts Mattered' (2016) New Direction, The Foundation for European Reform, pp. 17–39; Marise Cremona, 'A Quiet Revolution: The Common Commercial Policy Six Years after the Treaty of Lisbon' (2017) Report No. 2, Swedish Institute for European Policy Studies, p. 56.

[47] Regulation (EU) 654/2014 of the European Parliament and of the Council of 15 May 2014 concerning the exercise of the Union's rights for the application and enforcement of

rights for the enforcement of international trade rules under WTO law and bilateral trade agreements and provides for the 'appropriate instruments to ensure the effective exercise of the Union's rights under international trade agreements'[48] and when a reform of trade defence instruments was initiated with a view to their greater effectivity.[49] In 2015, the European Commission's Communication 'Trade for All' announced that it will step up the enforcement and implementation of the EU trade rights and ensure that its partners live up to their promises, including for the benefit of small businesses, consumers, and workers.[50] In this Communication, effectiveness of trade policy was identified as one of its three key objectives, alongside transparency and value orientation,[51] and the Commission committed itself to producing annual FTA implementation reports, six of which have already been published since 2016.[52] Effective implementation of trade policy then became one of four strategic objectives of the European Commission for 2016–2020.[53] Strengthening the enforcement of trade rules also was and still is a core issue in the debate on how to improve the implementation of trade and sustainable development (TSD) chapters in EU FTAs, that the EU had negotiated since 2010 into its FTAs and whose improvement was already part of a 2018 '15 point action plan'.[54] The policy shift also engendered changes on institutional level, as, for example, since 2018, the

international trade rules and amending Council Regulation (EC) No 3286/94 laying down Community procedures in the field of the common commercial policy in order to ensure the exercise of the Community's rights under international trade rules, in particular those established under the auspices of the World Trade Organization (Trade Enforcement Regulation), OJ EU 2014 No. L 189/50, 27 June 2014.

48 See Trade Enforcement Regulation, Preamble, recital 2.

49 Modernisation of Trade Defence Instruments. Adapting trade defence instruments to the current needs of the European economy, COM(2013) 191. See also Section 2.1.2.

50 European Commission, Trade for All: Towards a More Responsible Trade and Investment Policy, COM(2015) 497 final, 15-17.

51 ibid, p. 10 ff.

52 FTA Implementation Report 2016, COM(2017) 654 final; FTA Implementation Report 2017, COM(2018) 728 final, FTA Implementation Report 2018, COM(2019) 455 final, FTA Implementation Report 2019, COM(2020) 705 final; FTA Implementation Report 2021, COM(2021) 654 final. Since 2022, the Report is called Implementation and Enforcement Report, COM (2022) 730 final.

53 European Commission, DG Trade, 'Strategic Plan 2016-2020', 12 https://commission.europa.eu/system/files/2018-01/trade_sp_2016_2020_revised_en.pdf.

54 FTA Implementation Report 2017, p. 39; For the Action Plan see NonPaper of the Commission Services, Feedback and Way Forward on Improving the Implementation and Enforcement of Trade and Sustainable Development Chapters in EU Free Trade Agreements, 26 February 2018; FTA Implementation Report 2018, p. 26.

Commission has been making use of bilateral dispute settlement mechanisms on several occasions,[55] including for solving a labor dispute under the EU–Korea FTA. In July 2020 finally, a Chief Trade Enforcement Officer was appointed on a position officially created already at the end of 2019. This position is in particular responsible for monitoring and enforcing trade agreements, including sustainable development (i.e. environmental and labour) obligations, overseeing EU trade defence work, and coordinating dispute settlement procedures.[56]

All in all, the most recent reorientation of trade policy points to a more geopolitical EU trade policy than ever before. The geopolitical thinking of the Global Strategy for a 'Stronger Europe' became implemented and expanded in trade policy,[57] and new instruments thereof were put in place which also reflect a turn towards a geoeconomic stance.[58]

1.3 Methodology

The present analysis of the new turn in the EU trade policy focuses on an exploration and assessment of its consequences for the EU's multilateral stance and commitment to international law and respect for its international, in particular trade law, obligations. Hence the research is pivotally approaching its topic from a legal point of view. Consequently the research methods used are legal doctrinal ones that survey and assess the

[55] For more on these disputes, see European Commission, 'Disputes under Bilateral Trade Agreements' https://policy.trade.ec.europa.eu/enforcement-and-protection/dispute-settlement/bilateral-disputes_en /; Cornelia Furculita, 'The Time of PTA Dispute Settlement Mechanisms Might Have Come', in Manfred Elsig, Rodrigo Polanco, and Peter Van den Bossche (eds.), *International Economic Dispute Settlement: Demise or Transformation?* (New York: Cambridge University Press, 2021), pp. 442–469; Cornelia Furculita, *The WTO and the New Generation EU FTA Dispute Settlement Mechanisms: Interacting in a Fragmented and Changing International Trade Law Regime* (Cham: Springer, 2021), pp. 20 ff.

[56] See European Commission, 'Chief Trade Enforcement Officer', https://policy.trade.ec.europa.eu/enforcement-and-protection/chief-trade-enforcement-officer_en/.

[57] See also Couvreur, et al., 'The Good Geopolitical Trade Actor?' (2022), p. 137 f; Jan Orbie, 'EU Trade Policy Meets Geopolitics' (2021) 26(2) *EFARev* 197–202; Sophie Meunier and Kalypso Nicolaidis, 'The Geopoliticization of European Trade and Investment Policy' (2019) *JCMS* 103–113 at 106 ff; Schmitz and Seidl, 'As Open as Possible' (2023) 841.

[58] For more on this, see Sections 2.1.3 and 2.2, and Henrique Choer Moraes and Mikael Wigell, 'Balancing Dependence: The Quest for Autonomy and the Rise of Corporate Geoeconomics', in Babić, Dixon, and Liu (eds.), *The Political Economy of Geoeconomics* (2022), p. 39 f; Lavery, McDaniel, and Schmid, 'European Strategic Autonomy' (2022), pp. 69 ff; Clara Weinhardt, Karsten Mau, and Jens Hillebrand Pohl, 'The EU as a Geoeconomic Actor? A Review of Recent European Trade and Investment Policies', in Babić, Dixon, and Liu (eds.), *The Political Economy of Geoeconomics* (2022), p. 109 f.

legal content of the new EU rules adopted in the implementation of the trade policy review 2021, with a view to tensions, even collision and conflicts between EU legislation/legal acts and international law, particularly WTO law.[59] The legal interpretive doctrinal methodology for such endeavour is reflected in the customary rules of interpretation of public international law, which have been codified in Article 31 Vienna Convention on the Law of Treaties (VCLT)[60] and which are applicable also to WTO law and its dispute settlement (see Article 3.2 DSU[61]). Accordingly, international rules are to be interpreted in good faith in accordance with the ordinary meaning to be given to the terms of the treaty in their context and in the light of its object and purpose. Thus, grammatical-textual, contextual-systematic, and teleological approaches must be employed to the interpretation of international rules,[62] and these approaches also apply to the interpretation of EU law. For EU, primary law stems from international legal instruments. The founding treaties of what is today is EU, and all subsequent reforms, took the legal form of an international agreement entered into by the EU Member States. Even though EU law has developed considerably and establishes a genuine multi-level system of exercising public powers, which is detached and autonomous from both general international and domestic law, these rules on interpretation still apply, all the more as they also reflect the interpretive methodology within domestic legal orders.[63] There are, nevertheless, differences, first, with regard to the exact weight given to the different interpretative approaches, and second, with regard to the specific aspects of an interpretative approach. Whereas in domestic systems, preparatory texts might play an important role as they inform about the legislator's intent, and hence are the basis for a historic interpretation of rules in consideration of the legislator's intention, preparatory documents in international law only play a minor role. Under Article 32 VCLT, preparatory work is a supplementary means of interpretation

[59] For the notion of conflict of rules, see Erich Vranes, 'The Definition of "Norm Conflict" in International Law and Legal Theory' (2006) 17(2) *EJIL* 395–411.

[60] Vienna Convention on the Law of Treaties, Vienna, 23 May 1969, in force 27 January 1980, 1155 U.N.T.S. 331; (1969) 8 ILM 679; UKTS (1980) 58.

[61] Understanding on Rules and Procedures Governing the Settlement of Disputes (DSU), Marrakesh Agreement Establishing the World Trade Organization, Annex 2, 1869 U.N.T.S. 401, 33 I.L.M. 1226 (1994).

[62] For more detail, see Andrea Bianchi, Daniel Peat, and Matthew Windsor (eds.), *Interpretation in International Law* (New York: Oxford University Press, 2015).

[63] Stefan Vogenauer, *Die Auslegung von Gesetzen in England und auf dem Kontinent* (Tübingen: Mohr Siebeck, 2001), pp. 1295 ff.

only. In EU law, the preparatory documents for EU Treaties initially had no relevance in the CJEU case law in their interpretation, but this has changed in more recent times.[64] The Court, for example, relied on preparatory work of the Maastricht Treaty for the interpretation of Article 125 TFEU.[65] As the deliberations in the Convention that drafted the EU Constitutional Treaty (that became the basis for the subsequent Lisbon Reform Treaty) were made publicly available, there is even more room now for considering *travaux preparatoires*. As regards the interpretation of EU secondary law, consideration of preparatory documents is interpretive practice, and this practice by the CJEU appears to use preparatory documents merely for confirming an interpretation developed from terminological, systemic, and teleological approaches,[66] hence comparable to the legal value of *travaux preparatoires* under Article 32 VCLT. EU law has additional specific interpretive methods at its disposal. One important peculiarity of EU law interpretation is the method the CJEU developed with regard to the EU multilingualism setting out guidelines for the practical application of the principle of linguistic equality against the background of the requirement of uniform interpretation in case of linguistically divergent textual versions.[67] Another one is the highly purposive approach that gives the teleological interpretation a particular weight in interpreting EU law,[68] to which we will revert in a moment.

In order to correctly assess the new legal instruments and their capacity for conflict with international legal obligations, it is necessary for a legal review as undertaken in this book to consider the political developments and the legislator's intentions that led to their adoption, even

[64] Koen Lennaerts and José A. Gutiérrez-Fons, 'To Say What the Law of the EU Is: Methods of Interpretation and the European Court of Justice' (2013) EUI Working Papers AEL 2013/9, pp. 19 ff.

[65] CJEU, Case C-370/12, *Thomas Pringle v Government of Ireland and Others* [2012] ECLI:EU:C:2012:75, para. 135. Other examples are CJEU, Case C-583/11 P, *Inuit Tapiriit Kanatami and Others v Parliament and Council* [2013] ECLI:EU:C:2013:625, para. 50, 59; Case T-18/10, *Inuit Tapiriit Kanatami and Others v Parliament and Council* [2011] ECR II-05599, para. 49.

[66] CJEU, Case C-104/96, *Coöperatieve Rabobank "Vecht en Plassengebied" v Minderhoud* [1997] ECR I-07211 para. 25 ff; Karl Riesenhuber, '§ 10 Die Auslegung', in Karl Riesenhuber (ed.), *Europäische Methodenlehre*, 4th ed. (Berlin, München, Berlin: De Gruyter, 2021), para. 27 f.

[67] See CJEU, Case 283/81, *Srl CILFIT and Lanificio di Gavardo SpA v Ministry of Health* [1982] ECR 03415, para. 18; Lennaerts and Gutiérrez-Fons, 'To Say What the Law of the EU Is' (2013), pp. 8–13; for more specifics of interpreting EU law, see ibid 5.

[68] Admittedly, neither the CJEU recognizes a fixed hierarchy between the methods of interpretation, but there seems to be a certain preponderance of the teleological method. In comparison, see Vogenauer, *Die Auslegung von Gesetzen in England und auf dem Kontinent* (2001), pp. 388 f, 1297.

beyond the interpretative approach based on preparatory materials just mentioned. Otherwise, the legal appraisal of new rules in view of international obligations might be influenced from a wrong stance as to which intentions and motivations stand behind the new rules. This is all the more relevant in case of sometimes vague rules that may lend themselves to different interpretations. In order to assess the potential for conflict between EU rules and international obligations correctly, it is necessary not only to grasp the broadness of possible understandings from an analysis of a legal rules' textual formulation and context but also to consider the legislator's ideas and conceptions informative of the rules' rationale and purpose, as required by the interpretive methodology explained earlier in the chapter. Considering the purpose of a rule is particularly relevant in the interpretation of EU law because the CJEU's interpretations are considerably driven by a teleological, purposive approach taking care of the *effet utile* of EU rules, which is a methodical response to the EU's multi-level character and its autonomy.[69] The Court employs even a 'meta-teleological'[70] – that is, systemic – approach which not so much focuses on the particular objectives of a specific instrument or provision of EU law as takes much more account of the overall purpose, sometimes even the 'constitutional telos'[71] of the EU in light of which rules of EU law are conceptualized.[72] This specific interpretive approach thus may be particularly prone to induce tensions, even to give rise to conflict between EU provisions and EU's international legal obligations.

Taking account of the legislator's conceptions and motivations in the interpretation of EU law hence has two avenues in the legal interpretive methodology. First, it is part of the contextual interpretation insofar as the legislator's intentions are reflected in the preambular recitals to the

[69] See Stephen Brittain, 'Justifying the Teleological Methodology of the European Court of Justice: A Rebuttal' (2016) 55 *Irish Jurist* 134–165 at 135 ff; Lennaerts and Gutiérrez-Fons, 'To Say What the Law of the EU Is' (2013) p. 24; Duncan Pickard, 'Judicial Interpretation at the European Court of Justice as a Feature of Supranational Law' (2017) 20 European Union Law Working Papers.

[70] Miguel Poiares Maduro, 'Interpreting European Law: Judicial Adjudication in the Context of Constitutional Pluralism' (2007) 1(2) *European Journal of Legal Studies* 137–152 at 140 f.

[71] Poiares Maduro, 'Interpreting European Law' (2007) 140.

[72] See e.g. CJEU, Case C-583/11 P, *Inuit Tapiriit*, para. 50: 'in accordance with the Court's settled case-law, the interpretation of a provision of European Union law requires that account be taken not only of its wording and the objectives it pursues, but also its context *and the provisions of European Union law as a whole*' (emphasis added).

EU legislative act.[73] According to Article 31 (2) VCLT,[74] preambles form part of the context and also set forth the object and purpose of a treaty, thus helping in establishing the ordinary meaning of a provision.[75] Albeit the preambles do not establish obligations per se, their interpretative role reflecting the legislative intent has also been recognized in EU law.[76] Second, taking account of the legislator's conceptions and motivations is part of a historic approach insofar as preparatory documents can be considered in determining the legislator's intention. Proposals and similar preparatory work are not part of the context as they are not part of the law.[77] However, one must bear in mind that Commission documents such as proposals and White Books do not necessarily reflect EU legislators intentions fully.[78] Hence, these approaches will be employed with regard to each EU legal act adopted in implementing the new trade policy individually, but as they all have been enacted as an expression of the new trade policy reorientation, this reorientation and the idea and vision behind it has first to be introduced and explored, reflecting the background for the detailed analyses subsequently done in this book. That's why Chapter 2 of this book is dedicated to a brief analysis and description of the evolution of EU Trade policy, insofar as is relevant for the determination of the EU Open Strategic Autonomy's meaning and relevance for trade policy and its redirection in the trade policy review of 2021 (see Section 2.1.), as well as the external political, economic, technological, and institutional changes, developments, and challenges that had instigated the change in EU trade policy, and to which it intends to respond

[73] In contrast, Karl Riesenhuber, '§ 10 Die Auslegung' (2021) para. 35, sees them as part of the historic interpretative approach.

[74] Vienna Convention on the Law of Treaties, Vienna, 23 May 1969, in force 27 January 1980, 1155 U.N.T.S. 331; (1969) 8 ILM 679; UKTS (1980) 58.

[75] Makane Moïse Mbengue, 'Preamble', in Rüdiger Wolfrum (ed.), *The Max Planck Encyclopedia of Public International Law* (Oxford: Oxford University Press, 2008), https://opil.ouplaw.com/view/10.1093/law:epil/9780199231690/law-9780199231690-e1456.

[76] For more, see Tadas Klimas and Jīratė Vaičiukaitė, 'The Law of Recitals in European Community Legislation' (2008) 15(1) *ILSA Journal of International and Comparative Law* 1–33. According to Pechstein and Drechsler, preambles are an integral part of the legal act, providing information about the purpose of the legislation and do not fall under the scope of historical interpretation; Matthias Pechstein and Carola Drechsler, 'Die Auslegung und Fortbildung des Primärrechts', in Karl Riesenhuber (ed.), *Europäische Methodenlehre: Handbuch für Ausbildung und Praxis*, 4th ed. (Berlin, München, Boston: De Gruyter, 2015) 181–208, p. 197, para. 32.

[77] CJEU, Case C-441/93, *Panagis Pafitis and others v Trapeza Kentrikis Ellados A.E. and others* [1996] ECR I-01347, para. 43.

[78] Karl Riesenhuber, '§ 10 Die Auslegung' (2021), para. 28.

(see Section 2.2). As this chapter is based significantly on existing analyses in political science, economics, and international relations, it will be rather descriptive, but nevertheless it is necessary and unavoidable, as it paints the grand vision (giving context and rationale) standing behind the individual legislative instruments and legal acts, in which their interpretation must be embedded.

Admittedly, identifying the conception of the legislator in adopting certain rules and schemes is not an easy task. One may find diverse approaches, imaginations, and expectations among lawmakers when asked about the idea behind a legislative rule and the consequences thereof, even if there is a general agreement on the grand vision behind it. As the authors are lawyers, they prefer therefore to look at official documents, draft, proposals, and memoranda that accompanied a legislative process from the beginning until the adoption of the legal text, instead of asking individual representatives of the EU's institutions involved in lawmaking. Hence, this study is based – in addition to the legal methodology of interpreting statutory laws and conceptualizing the meaning of a legal rule (which may be based on preconceptions about its rationale; that's why Chapter 2 is so important) – on an exploration of official EU and WTO documents whichto understand, compare, and assess also lies within the research competence of legal scholars, as it is a text-based endeavour. This approach might be blamed for being rather descriptive, but we contend that even the study of mere official documents allows for assessments and findings about developments in a given policy field and for motivations and drivers standing behind them. This seemingly non-doctrinal approach is relevant in particular for the research presented in Chapter 2, and is part of the legal doctrinal research approach employed in this book insofar as rules have to be interpreted in view of their object and purpose, identifying which requires evaluation of the relevant documents.

1.4 Outline, Structure, and Core Results of the Book

The book explores the legal consequences of the new EU's trade policy focus (with a view also to their political implications) and determines the constraints and flexibilities available for the EU's search for Open Strategic Autonomy. This requires, first of all, as reasoned in earlier sections, setting the scene for such an analysis of the new turn by briefly recalling the evolution of the EU trade policy and the drivers behind the recent reorientation. Part I, consisting of Chapters 2 and 3, is dedicated to this. Chapter 2 deals with a look at the past, present, and prospect of the EU trade policy, which is a necessary starting point as a preparation for a correct understanding of what the EU intends and to what it responds in the trade policy review and the subsequently adopted legislative acts and other instruments. This is pivotal to fully grasp the comprehensive scope and breadth of the new approach and the correct perception of these acts and instruments will be relevant for the subsequent legal interpretation and analyses. Afterwards, as a second preliminary step undertaken in Chapter 3, one has to determine the internal and external constraints flowing from international law (derived in particular from WTO law, EU FTAs, and international law on countermeasures and climate protection) and EU constitutional law (in particular Articles 3 (5), 21 TEU, and 206 (2) TFEU). The latter also need to be analysed in view of the extent to which the EU Court of Justice might internalize the limits established by international law. International and EU constitutional rules are the legal benchmark and yardstick against which the new tools and instruments have to be assessed in order to identify the room of manoeuvre for EU trade policy flexibility strived for by the concept of Open Strategic Autonomy.

Then, considering the identified constraints and flexibilities, the new tools and instruments of the renewed trade policy to ensure more assertive enforcement and representation of EU's trade rights and interests will be introduced and analysed in detail. Additionally, their broader implications for the EU and the international trade system will be explored. For this reason, Part II is dedicated to a thorough analysis of the new tools for a stronger enforcement of the EU's trade rights and interest, whereas Part III deals with the tools for more assertive representation of EU interests and values.

Our analysis will show, as we finally conclude in Chapter 11, that even though the new instruments were generally designed with international obligations in mind, with some recognizing potential conflicts with international norms but relying on general customary rules on countermeasure or derogations and justifications, and others trying to limit the scope of application of the legislation, there are several instances where, for example, the amended Trade Enforcement, the International Procurement Instrument (IPI),[79] and the CBAM

[79] Regulation (EU) 2022/1031 of the European Parliament and of the Council of 23 June 2022 on the access of third-country economic operators, goods and services to the Union's public procurement and concession markets and procedures supporting negotiations on

Regulation[80] conflict 'as such' with procedural and substantive WTO norms, which prompts the need for legislative modifications. Even more cases were identified in which the instruments have the capacity for violating core WTO norms depending on the way they are applied. In other cases, non-application of the EU legislation is necessary to avoid conflict with specific rules of EU FTAs. Furthermore, the way the Commission applies the ACI could also be decisive in terms of its legality under customary international law on countermeasures, besides its legality under international trade rules. Thus, the Commission must pay utmost attention in its implementation of the new legislation and the new international approaches to ensure compliance with constitutional principles consecrating respect for EU's international obligations and its dedication to multilateralism. The majority of the instruments also bear such risks as the escalation of trade conflicts, deteriorating the competitiveness and market access of EU companies on external markets, or the emulation by other states of EU behaviour, which then contributes to further erosion of multilateral rules.

Regarding legislative modifications, generally, we propose that the instruments should be designed with respect to conditions required of countermeasures imposed under ILC Draft Articles, especially if those provisions are intended to be used as a justification for departure from multilateral and bilateral trade provisions as it is in the case of the Trade Enforcement Regulation. In case of the Anti-Coercion Instrument (ACI),[81] the instrument should be amended to specify not only in preambular language but also in the main text that response measures would be allowed only against serious cases of interferences to ensure that, in line with international customary norms and the ACI itself, the non-performance of EU international obligations takes place only against an internationally wrongful act. Second, the ACI should be amended to completely avoid the imposition of response measures in case of simultaneous alleged breaches of more special trade rules, unless trade justifications can be lawfully invoked in the bilateral context to justify

access of Union economic operators, goods and services to the public procurement and concession markets of third countries, OJ EU 2022 No. L 173/1.

80 Regulation (EU) 2023/956 of the European Parliament and of the Council of 10 May 2023 establishing a carbon border adjustment mechanism, OJ EU 2023 No. L 130/52, 16 May 2023.

81 Regulation (EU) 2023/2675 of the European Parliament and of the Council of 22 November 2023 on the protection of the Union and its Member States from economic coercion by third countries, OJ EU 2023 No. L 2675, 7 December 2023.

substantive violations. Furthermore, the ACI could be amended to explicitly allow the imposition of internationally lawful measures to provide an internal legal basis for doing so. The IPI's scope should be modified to reflect the conditions of the pertinent derogations contained in pertinent international trade rules. Furthermore, while advancing its climate ambitions, the EU legislators should not include additional CBAM rules on export rebates and should not disregard the EU´s related international commitments, such as the CBDR principle of *inter alia* the Paris Agreement.

Despite our critique, some of the analysed instruments may even contribute towards the credibility of the EU's multilateral stance. The MPIA might foster a solution to the WTO dispute settlement reform, and the EU action plan for TSD enforcement offers a valid legal basis for potential imposition of sanctions.

PART I

EU Trade Policy and Its Constraints

2 The EU's Trade Policy

Past and Prospect

In this chapter, the evolution of the EU's trade policy and the new focus on enforcement of international trade agreements and ensuring a level playing field will be analysed in more detail. Section 2.1 will trace how the EU's approach has changed from being mainly oriented towards a liberal trade paradigm of regulating trade and enforcing rights multilaterally, to combining multilateralism with an increased degree of bilateralism in the form of deep and comprehensive free trade agreements (FTAs) in order to meet EU interest in open markets, and finally arrived at a policy centred around a new robustness in the enforcement of trade rules and fair treatment ensuring a level playing field, including greater affirmation of EU interests in labour rights and sustainability. The section will present the model of 'Open Strategic Autonomy' as a basis of the renewed open, sustainable, and assertive trade policy (keeping the acronym OSA), which is to be understood in the broader context of the pragmatist turn of the Global Strategy, according to which the EU shall take more responsibility for its foreign affairs and be more flexible and active in reacting to new challenges. Section 2.2 of this chapter will briefly explore the simultaneous economic, institutional, political, and technological challenges the EU faces since several years, which induce the trade policy reorientation. Thus, the drivers and causes for the trade policy turn will be investigated. Section 2.3 highlights the new assertiveness in EU trade policy as reflected in the capabilities provided in the new instruments.

2.1 Evolution of the EU Trade Policy

2.1.1 Liberal Multilateralism: The Defining Feature

EU trade policy, or common commercial policy in EU parlance,[1] since the very beginning of EU integration was directed towards the harmonious development of world trade, the progressive abolition of restrictions on international trade, and the lowering of customs and other barriers to trade (see Article 206 Treaty on the Functioning of the European Union (TFEU), previous Article 110 Treaty Establishing the European Economic Community (EECT), and Article 131 Treaty Establishing the European Community (ECT)). The core instrument for implementing these objectives by liberalizing trade is the conclusion of international treaties, either bilaterally, plurilaterally, or multilaterally. According to the understanding of the EU, at least, multilateralism means international cooperation in the interest of mutually acceptable, rule-based solutions, in accordance with international values and legal requirements.[2] Multilateralism hence is a tool of organizing relations between as many states as possible, aiming for a global reach and based on common legal principles and values such as mutuality, respect, balancing of interests, and peaceful dispute settlement.[3] As a result of the lessons learned from the undesirable developments in world trade after the First World War, leading to the Great Depression, states recognized the need for a commonly agreed-upon open legal framework for monetary, economic, and trade issues that was as global as possible and counteracted protectionism and economic nationalism. The first substantive milestone for such an international economic order was the Atlantic Charter of 1941 agreed between Roosevelt and Churchill defining the core foundation by proclaiming a confession to 'the fullest collaboration between all nations in the economic field' to achieve free trade based on non-discrimination. Thus, the final phase of the Second World War was accompanied by efforts to create such a legal framework by establishing the so-called Bretton Woods Institutions.[4] Trade issues cannot be resolved

1 See Art. 207 (1) Consolidated version of the Treaty on the Functioning of the European Union (TFEU), OJ EU 2012 No. C 326/47, 26 October 2012.

2 See European Commission, 2021 Strategic Foresight. The EU's Capacity and Freedom to Act, COM(2021) 750 final, 8 September 2021, p. 1. For the EU's multilateralism generally, see Katie Verlin Laatikainen and Karen E. Smith (eds.), *The European Union at the United Nations: Intersecting Multilateralisms* (Hampshire: Palgrave Macmillan, 2006).

3 See James Scott, 'Multilateralism', in *Encyclopedia Britannica*, www.britannica.com/topic/multilateralism.

4 Raj Bhala, *Modern GATT Law: A Treatise on the Law and Political Economy of the GATT & Other W.T.O Agreements*, 2nd ed. (London: Sweet & Maxwell, Thomson Reuters, 2013), pp. 5 ff;

through unilateral action, but only through international cooperation within a fundamentally rules-based framework that allows for an open unhindered flow of goods and capital. Such type of cooperation, however, needs safety valves to balance negative outcomes (such as job losses, decrease of regulatory autonomy), and hence must make available domestic policy space for the pursuit of social purposes ('embedded liberalism'), among other things.[5] Accordingly, the General Agreement on Tariffs and Trade (GATT) 1947[6] was put into effect in 1948, which, through its secretariat, de facto transformed itself into a kind of international organization over the decades taking care of fundamental rules for goods trade. The international rule orientation in world trade was further expanded by the establishment of the World Trade Organization (WTO) with effect from 1995. Multilateral trade agreements, particularly as a result of the equal treatment obligations, lead to basically uniform rules in the interest of all participants, allow for balanced reciprocity and predictability in trade obligations, and ensure greater justice, since the powerful cannot push through their interests at the expense of smaller states.[7]

With the gradual transfer of the actual exercise of competencies in trade policy from the Member States to the European Communities (EC) institutions in the 1970s, after the expiry of the transition period and the completion of the customs union in 1968, the European Economic Community (EEC), EC, and later the EU have mainly relied on multilateralism in their external trade policy as the EEC stepped into exercising the Member States membership rights and obligations in the international trade institutions established by them before founding the EEC.[8] In this way, the EC adopted the underlying multilateral trade policy

Martin Daunton, 'The Inconsistent Quarte: Free Trade versus Competing Goals', in Amrita Narlikar, Martin Daunton, and Robert M. Stern (eds.), *Oxford Handbook on the World Trade Organization* (New York: Oxford University Press, 2012), pp. 49 ff.

[5] John Ruggie, 'International Regimes, Transactions, and Change: Embedded Liberalism in the Postwar Economic Order' (1982) 36(2) *International Organization* 379–415 at 393 ff.

[6] General Agreement on Tariffs and Trade, 30 October 1947, 61 Stat. A-11, 55 U.N.T.S. 194.

[7] For the benefits of a multilateral trade organization, see Peter Van den Bossche and Werner Zdouc, *The Law and Policy of the WTO*, 5th ed. (Cambridge: Cambridge University Press, 2022), pp. 36 ff; Robert E. Baldwin, 'The Case for a Multilateral Trade Organization' in Narlikar, Daunton, and Stern (eds.), *Oxford Handbook on the World Trade Organization* (2012), pp. 29 ff.

[8] A landmark statement insofar was made by the CJEU, Case 21/72, *International Fruit Company NV and others v Produktschap voor Groenten en Fruit* [1972] ECLI:EU:C:1972:115, paras. 13 ff. The EC's insertion into the membership obligations of its Member States in the GATT 1947 is an expression of a specific formation of customary law in this instance; see Ernst-Ulrich Petersmann, 'Participation of the EC in the GATT: International Law and

orientation that had underpinned not only its Member States' but a vast majority of states' approach to international trade regulation. At the heart of this move has been the EC/EU's participation in and development of international trade relations under the umbrella and according to the rules agreed by many states under the GATT 1947, in whose later rounds the EC played a leading role as regards tariff reduction,[9] before the EC later, with the advent of the WTO after the Uruguay Round, formally became a – even founding - member in its own right (Article XI WTO Agreement).[10] Since the 1970s, the EEC's external trade commitments have also been growing outside the GATT 1947 with regard to both the number of multilateral or bilateral agreements of trade relevance and the EC's genuine contribution and cooperation as a party in relevant multilateral arrangements, usually besides its Member States.[11] Hence, the EC concluded early association and trade agreements,[12] the selection of parties following political and development priorities instead of commercial ones.[13] The EU also became part of agreements within the OECD and the UN, and of specific agreements such as the International Sugar Agreement 1968[14] and the International Tin Agreement.[15] While the EEC's stance on international trade negotiations in the 1960s and 1970s, coined by protectionist national interests and the need to defend the protectionist common agricultural policy, was rather defensive, the political project of the completion of the EU Single Market from the mid-1980s on fostered an open, liberal free trade policy.[16] Thus,

Community Law Aspects', in David O'Keeffe and Henry G. Schermers (eds.), *Mixed Agreements* (Boston: Kluwer Law and Taxation Publishers, 1983), pp. 180 ff.

[9] For the EEC outcomes in the Kennedy and Tokyo Round, see www.wto.org/english/docs_e/gattbilaterals_e/indexbycountry_e.htm#EEC.

[10] Marrakesh Agreement Establishing the World Trade Organization (WTO Agreement), 15 April 1994, 1867 U.N.T.S. 154, 33 I.L.M. 1144 (1994).

[11] For more, see Rafael Leal-Arcas, *EU Trade Law* (Cheltenham: Edward Elgar Publishing, 2019), pp. 10 ff.

[12] A special role played the association under Part IV of the EECT with the overseas territories, which were granted only limited unilateral tariff reductions. The early agreements in this respect (Yaoundé I and II in 1963 and 1969) were in principle still based on reciprocity. See Lorand Bartels, 'The Trade and Development Policy of the European Union' (2007) 18(4) *EJIL* 715–756 at 717 ff.

[13] Billy Melo Araujo, *The EU Deep Trade Agenda: Law and Policy* (New York: Oxford University Press, 2016), p. 28 f; Stephen Woolcock, 'EU Policy on Preferential Trade Agreements in the 2000s: A Reorientation towards Commercial Aims' (2014) 20(6) *ELJ* 718–732.

[14] International Sugar Agreement 1968, New York, 3–24 December 1968, No. 9369 (1969); the Agreement expired in accordance with its provisions on 31 December 1973.

[15] Fifth International Tin Agreement, Geneva, 21 June 1975, No. 14851 (1976).

[16] Brian Hanson, 'What Happened to Fortress Europe? External Trade Policy Liberalization in the EU' (1998) 52(1) *International Organization*, 55–85 at 67 ff; Gabriel Siles-Brügge,

multilateral trade liberalization became the centerpiece of the EU (neo) liberal trade policy.[17] The trade policy agenda, which Pascal Lamy, then EU Trade Commissioner, initiated in 1999 under the motto of 'managing globalisation',[18] aiming at a 'new kind of global governance to manage the global economy and environment',[19] was based on the idea of mastering globalization by relying on multilateral rules and organizations and using trade policy to compensate for its deficits and negative consequences. The EU strived to employ the WTO for negotiating agreements on new regulatory issues such as investment, competition, environment, and labour in order to complement its advocacy for further liberalization of international trade.[20] The EU was expected to act confidently in this respect.[21] EU trade policy thus became based on an awareness of the capabilities of using trade policy instruments for achieving overriding societal goals such as social justice and sustainable development,[22] but allegedly mainly so in order to legitimize liberal trade policy.[23] As a result, EU trade policy became rather value driven and normative,[24] seeking to establish global rules and standards particularly within the WTO framework. This effort was again motivated by the EU commitment to multilateralism. The advancement of the multilateral trade rules entered into GATT 1947 and the WTO has continued to be the cornerstone of the EU's trade

Constructing European Union Trade Policy: A Global Idea of Europe (London: Palgrave Macmillan, 2014), pp. 59 ff.

17 Piet Eeckhout, *The European Internal Market and International Trade: A Legal Analysis* (New York: Oxford University Press, 1994), pp. 145 ff.

18 European Commission, Strategic Objectives 2000–2005: Shaping the New Europe, COM (2000) 154 final, OJ EU 2001 No. C 81/1, 9 February 2000, p. 4.

19 ibid., 2.

20 See e.g. European Commission, Promoting Core Labour Standards and Improving Social Governance in the Context of Globalisation, COM(2001) 416 final, 18 July 2001. Thomas Jacobs, et al., 'The Hegemonic Politics of "Strategic Autonomy" and "Resilience": COVID-19 and the Dislocation of EU Trade Policy' (2023) 61(1) *JCMS* 3–19 at 5 f.

21 Brigid Gavin, *The European Union and Globalization: Towards Global Democratic Governance* (Cheltenham: Edward Elgar, 2001), pp. 10 ff; Rawi Abdelal and Sophie Meunier, 'Managed Globalization: Doctrine, Practice and Promise' (2010) 17(3) *JEPP* 350–367; Dirk De Bièvre, 'EU Regulatory Trade Agenda and the Quest for WTO Trade Enforcement' (2006) 13(6) *JEPP* 851–866.

22 In 2002, the Commission underlined the trade policy´s contribution to sustainable development; see Communication from the Commission to the European Parliament, the Council, the Economic and Social Committee and the Committee of the Regions Towards a Global Partnership for Sustainable Development, COM (2002) 82 final, 13 February 2002.

23 Jacobs, et al., 'The Hegemonic Politics of "Strategic Autonomy" and "Resilience"' (2023) 6.

24 Ian Manners, 'Normative Power Europe: A Contradiction in Terms?' (2002) *JCMS* 235–258 at 238 ff.

policy even after the beginning of the twenty-first century. The EU not only was a very active proponent of the Uruguay Round but continued being an active actor within the WTO, contributing strongly to starting the Doha Round in 2001,[25] concluding several multilateral agreements such as the revised Government Procurement Agreement 2012[26] and the Trade Facilitation Agreement,[27] and being active in plurilateral trade negotiations within or outside the WTO in order to foster unhindered commerce with regard to, for example, services (the Trade in Services Agreement (TiSA)) or green goods (the Environmental Goods Agreements (EGA)),[28] besides being the most active user of WTO dispute settlement. That the EU is an enduring supporter of a rules-based and pro-trade multilateralism cannot be surprising given its own founding history and development; after all, its existence, its functioning and values, and the success of its internal market are lucid expressions of positive cooperation among numerous states for the sake of peace, prosperity, and regulatory approximation. Hence, the EU commitment to multilateralism and a rules-based international trade order does not only have a long political tradition and a constitutional foundation, as mentioned in Chapter 1, but forms the core of its essence. 'Multilateralism is in Europe's DNA.'[29] Thus, EU trade policy was also conceived as a reflection of its internal market logic.[30]

2.1.2 The Shift to Active Bilateralism

As a sign of its commitment to the Doha Round, the EU had dedicated itself to an informal moratorium on bilateral trade agreements from the beginning of the Round in 2001. In the autumn of 2006, however, the EU abandoned the moratorium, and already in April 2007 the Council mandated the Commission to negotiate free trade agreements with India, South Korea, and the Association of Southeast Asian Nations (ASEAN). Even though then–Trade Commissioner Peter Mandelson opined that FTAs would not contradict the Doha Round, but complement it, this course change clearly reflected a severe policy change which was brought

[25] Melo Araujo, *The EU Deep Trade Agenda* (2016), pp. 30 ff.

[26] Agreement on Government Procurement, as amended on 30 March 2012, 3009 U.N.T.S.

[27] The Agreement on Trade Facilitation, 22 February 2017, 3284 U.N.T.S.

[28] For negotiations on TiSA and, respectively, EGA, see www.europarl.europa.eu/legislative-train/theme-a-balanced-and-progressive-trade-policy-to-harness-globalisation/file-trade-in-services-agreement-(tisa) and www.wto.org/english/tratop_e/envir_e/ega_e.htm.

[29] Ursula von der Leyen, Political Guidelines for the Next European Commission 2019–2024, 'A Union That Strives for More', p. 17, https://data.europa.eu/doi/10.2775/101756.

[30] Siles-Brügge, *Constructing European Union Trade Policy* (2014) 62.

about by the Commission in its 2006 Communication 'Global Europe: Competing in the World',[31] which set out a globally oriented EU trade policy (referred to as the Global Europe Strategy) and brought to an end the EU's reluctance to enter into bilateral trade agreements, in reaction to the lack of progress within the WTO, the ineptitude of previous EU FTAs, and the advancement of globalization.[32] The Global Europe Strategy provided a new direction and placed more self-centered motives in the foreground. Trade policy became aimed at improving market access for EU goods and services. The Global Europe Strategy prescribed a trade policy that was more in tune with economic realities, was better tailored to specific EU trade issues, interests, and trade problems, and had a clearer orientation towards expanding market access for EU products on third-country markets and improving EU's competitiveness on the world market.[33] The EU's rejection of protectionism was supplemented by active efforts to ensure open markets and fair trading conditions on the globe. Free and fair trade was to serve not least also the commercial interests of the EU; thus, the Global Europe Strategy is considered – in a very pointed formulation – a 'radicalization of the EU's free trade approach'.[34]

The starting point for this reformulation was firstly the consideration that trade policy had to contribute to the then internal Lisbon Strategy of 2000 for Growth and Jobs.[35] It was also intended to merge trade policy with external policy and to contribute in particular to development and neighbourhood policy.[36] The embedding of trade policy and its re-contextualization within EU policies, in particular foreign policy by the subsequent Lisbon Treaty,[37] was already foreseeable, as Lisbon was based

[31] European Commission, Global Europe: Competing in the World, COM(2006) 567 final, 4 October 2006.

[32] Boris Rigod, 'Global Europe: The EU's New Trade Policy in Its Legal Context' (2012) 18 *Columbia Journal of European Law* 277–306 at 280 ff.

[33] Sophie Meunier, 'Managing Globalization? The EU in International Trade Negotiations' (2007) 45(4) *JCMS* 905–926 at 906, 910; Luuk Schmitz and Timo Seidl, 'As Open as Possible, as Autonomous as Necessary' (2023) 61(3) *JCMS* 834–852 at 840.

[34] Jacobs, et al., 'The Hegemonic Politics of "Strategic Autonomy" and "Resilience"' (2023) 6.

[35] This was adopted at the Lisbon European Council meeting of March 2000, see https://web.archive.org/web/20230429234810/https://www.consilium.europa.eu/uedocs/cms_data/docs/pressdata/en/ec/00100-r1.en0.htm.

[36] European Commission, Global Europe: Competing in the World, COM(2006) 567 final, p. 1.

[37] See Marise Cremona, 'A Quiet Revolution: The Changing Nature of the EU's Common Commercial Policy', in Marc Bungenberg, et al. (eds.), *European Yearbook of International Economic Law* (Cham: Springer, 2017), p. 16 f; Alessandra Asteriti, 'Article 21 TEU and the

on the preparatory work on the draft Constitutional Treaty. Secondly, the reassessment was made in light of the changes in world trade resulting from the rise of emerging markets such as China, Brazil, and India, which challenged not only the EU's strength in world trade but also its political influence in the WTO, and thus in the body within which the EU wanted to master globalization. Due to the increase both in numbers and diversity of WTO membership and a continued discourse about conflicting interests, it became ever more difficult to find agreement within the WTO whose political decision-making processes are hampered by the demand for consensus. Due to their inadequacies and failures, the normative option within the WTO thus lost its appeal, especially as the increase in regional trade alliances also seemed to weaken the importance of the WTO as a whole, and the EU was in danger of being disadvantaged by the increase of FTAs entered into by other trading nations that granted preferential market access to each other.[38]

As a consequence of the policy change, EU trade policy shifted towards an increased degree of bilateralism in the form of progressively deep and comprehensive FTAs. By entering into such type of FTAs, the EU could push through a broad agenda of trade issues that included topics that were identified as in need of regulation already in the previous managing globalization policy. In this way, the EU strives for deeper commitments going beyond WTO obligations, which are easier to enter into with preferred partners. The conclusion of bilateral agreements makes it possible to enter into additional obligations that either relate to matters not covered by the WTO (such as investment protection or competition law) (so-called WTO-X rules) or that entail liberalizations that go beyond WTO obligations, such as in the area of services or technical barriers to trade (known as WTO-plus obligations).[39] In almost two decades since then, plenty of new bilateral FTAs have been negotiated or are currently in the

EU's Common Commercial Policy: A Test of Coherence', in Marc Bungenberg, et al. (eds.), *European Yearbook of International Economic Law* (Cham: Springer, 2017), pp. 119 ff.

[38] Jan Wouters and Akhil Raina, 'The European Union and Global Economic Governance: A Leader without a Roadmap?' in Julien Chaisse (ed.), *Sixty Years of European Integration and Global Power Shifts: Perceptions, Interactions and Lessons* (London: Hart Publishing, 2020), p. 208. For the reasons of the strategy change, see Meunier, 'Managing Globalization?' (2007) 918–920; Stephen Woolcock, 'Trade Policy: Policy-Making after the Treaty of Lisbon', in Helen Wallace, Mark A. Pollack, and Alasdair R. Young (eds.), *Policy-Making in the European Union*, 7th ed. (New York: Oxford University Press, 2015), pp. 401 et seq.

[39] On WTO-X and WTO-plus obligations, see Henrik Horn, Petros C. Mavroidis, and André Sapir, 'Beyond the WTO? An Anatomy of EU and US Preferential Trade Agreements' (2010) 33(11) *The World Economy* 1565–1588 at 1567.

process of being negotiated, with emerging or established market countries mainly in Asia and Latin America (e.g. Korea, the Multi-Party Trade Agreement with Peru, Colombia, and later Ecuador, Singapore, the ASEAN states, but also Canada and Ukraine).[40] Many of these new-generation FTAs are already in force, either finally as, for example, with Korea since 2015, Singapore, Japan, and Vietnam, or provisionally, as is the case with EU–Canada Trade Agreement (CETA),[41] since 2017.[42] The EU succeeded in its objective to include FTA chapters on regulatory issues, intellectual property protection, or sustainable development.[43] Its new trade agreements deepened trade liberalization beyond WTO obligations and broadened the issues covered. This deepening and widening of trade relations[44] reflects its internal market development[45] and, to a lesser degree, its endeavour to export its norms and standards.[46]

[40] For the current state of play of EU trade or economic partnership agreements, see https://ec.europa.eu/trade/policy/countries-and-regions/negotiations-and-agreements/.

[41] Comprehensive Economic and Trade Agreement (CETA) between Canada, of the one part, and the European Union and its Member States, of the other part, OJ EU 2017 No. L 23/11, 14 January 2017.

[42] See Free Trade Agreement between the European Union and its Member States, of the one part, and the Republic of Korea, of the other part, OJ EU 2011 No. L 127/6, 14 May 2011; Agreement between the European Union and Japan for an Economic Partnership, OJ EU 2018 No. L 330/3, 27 December 2018; Free Trade Agreement between the European Union and the Republic of Singapore, OJ EU 2019 L No. 294/3, 14 November 2019; CETA, OJ EU 2017 No. L 1080/11.

[43] See European Commission, Trade, Growth and World Affairs: Trade Policy as a Core Component of the EU's 2020 Strategy, COM(2010) 612, 9 November 2010, p. 15 f. For a more recent analysis of Trade and Sustainable Development (TSD) Chapters in EU FTAs, which the EU succeeded to include in all FTA since 2011, see Jean Baptiste Velut, et al., 'Comparative Analysis of Trade and Sustainable Development Provisions in Free Trade Agreements' (2022) *Trade Policy Hub*, London School of Economics and Political Science Consulting, www.lse.ac.uk/business/consulting/assets/documents/TSD-Final-Report-Feb-2022.pdf.

[44] See Marise Cremona, 'The European Union and Regional Trade Agreements', in Christoph Herrmann and Jörg Philipp Terhechte (eds.), *European Yearbook of International Economic Law 2010* (Cham: Springer, 2010), p. 252.

[45] Nicholas Perdikis and Laurie Perdikis, 'The Establishment and Development of the European Union and Its Trade Policy', in Sangeeta Khorana and Maria Garcia (eds.), *Handbook on the EU and International Trade* (Cheltenham: Edward Elgar Publishing, 2018), p. 24 f.

[46] In former times, outside the context of associations and neighbourhood policy, the export of its *acquis* played a less eminent role, as the EU rather was oriented towards international standards, except in the area of protection of geographical indications and enforcement of intellectual property rights; see Melo Araujo, *The EU Deep Trade Agenda* (2016), pp. 227 ff. The open strategic autonomy has changed this, as the EU's 'first-mover global position' in standard-setting has become one of its top priorities for the next decades; see European Commission, 2021 Strategic Foresight, COM(2021) 750, 12.

The above exemplary list of treaty partners illustrates another new facet of the EU's trade policy since 2006, relating to the choice of parties to the agreements. They have been determined by the potential of the foreign market for the EU industry, but also by the extent of trade barriers and safeguards, and by the behaviour of other trading blocs, specifically competitors on world markets.[47] Thus, the EU has gone beyond the previous limitation mainly to developing and neighbouring countries as treaty partners in trade. The shift towards emerging and established market might also be explained by EU industry interests in establishing closer trade relations along their value chains.[48]

The reorientation of the EU trade policy through a more realistic and reciprocity-oriented approach and a softening of the focus on the WTO, however, was not a complete break, but rather a certain redirection and readjustment of the trade politics of 'managing globalisation' in view of changed realities.[49] Europe has been under increasing competitive pressure from other regions of the world, which has led it to pursue more mercantilist objectives of fostering competitive opportunities of EU products abroad, opening up markets, and strengthening its efforts of gripping globalization by establishing shared standards in the WTO. The EU hence started pursuing a dual strategy: While doing everything in its power to get the Doha Round back on track and bringing the WTO forward (the success of the Doha Round still was EU 'top priority'),[50] it equally insisted on the need for bilateral trade agreements complementing WTO rules and serving EU interests, and therefore, in order to sharpen its own profile, the EU cultivated active bilateralism in trade relations. In its bilateral approaches, the EU remained deeply committed to the WTO and its guiding values. The EU's switch to bilateral trade agreements hence was not a departure from the WTO. An analysis of the EU's more recent FTAs indeed demonstrates that they still are based on WTO rules and principles, and thus reaffirm their continued relevance.[51]

[47] European Commission, Global Europe: Competing in the World, COM(2006) 567 final; Woolcock, 'EU Policy on Preferential Trade Agreements' (2014), pp. 718 ff.

[48] For the trade policy impact of industry interests, see Song Kim and Iain Osgood, 'Firms in Trade and Trade Politics' (2019) *Annual Review of Political Science* 399–417.

[49] See Meunier, 'Managing Globalization?' (2007) 920 f; Schmitz and Seidl, 'As Open as Possible' (2023) 840 f.

[50] European Commission, Trade, Growth and World Affairs, COM(2010) 612.

[51] Michael Hahn, 'We'll Always Have Geneva: The Existential Crisis of the US-led Multilateral Trading System and the EU Reactions', in Inge Govaere and Sascha Garben (eds.), *The Interface between EU and International Law* (Oxford: Hart Publishing, 2019) p. 270. For an

Any new EU FTA can therefore be seen as a confirmation of the EU's commitment to a rules-based international trading system and, thus, ultimately as an endorsement of the WTO's fundamental mission to regulate world trade accordingly and to provide at least the most fundamental rules therefore.

While the EU incrementally expanded its bilateral trade policy and went forward on the path of mutual trade liberalization, its unilateral, autonomous trade policy, in particular its projects for the reform of trade defence instruments, that would allow the Commission to counteract negative outcomes of trade liberalization, slowed down and partly faced long delays, not least due to lack of agreement in the Council.[52] Also, in response to the Global Europe Strategy, some changes in the autonomous trade policy of the EU were pursued. After first deliberations by the Commission already in 2006 that attempted to stir a reform debate about the trade defence instruments[53] quickly failed, the Commission, in light of the growth of unfair practices since the economic crisis of 2008–2009 and of changing trade patterns, tabled proposals for a general legal framework for enforcing trade rights and for an anti-dumping reform which were quite balanced.[54] The former led to the adoption of the Trade Enforcement Regulation 654/2014.[55] The latter contained both improvements for making trade defence more effective and elements for taking better account of the effects of trade defence measures on consumers and

empirical affirmation, see Todd Allee, Manfred Elsig, and Andrew Lugg, 'The Ties between WTO and Preferential Trade Agreements' (2017) 20(2) *JIEL* 333–363.

52 Yelter Bollen, Ferdi de Ville, and Jan Orbie, 'EU Trade Policy: Persistent Liberalisation, Contentious Protectionism' (2016) 38(3) *JEI* 279–294 at 285.

53 European Commission Communication, Global Europe: Europe's trade defence instruments in a changing global economy: A Green Paper for public consultation, COM (2006) 763 final, 6 December 2006.

54 European Commission, Proposal for a Regulation of the European Parliament and of the Council concerning the exercise of the Union's rights for the application and enforcement of international trade rules, COM(2012) 773, 18 December 2012; European Commission Communication, Modernisation of Trade Defence Instruments Adapting trade defence instruments to the current needs of the European economy, COM(2013) 191, 10 April 2013.

55 Regulation (EU) 654/2014 of the European Parliament and of the Council of 15 May 2014 concerning the exercise of the Union's rights for the application and enforcement of international trade rules and amending Council Regulation (EC) No 3286/94, laying down Community procedures in the field of the common commercial policy in order to ensure the exercise of the Community's rights under international trade rules, in particular those established under the auspices of the World Trade Organization, OJ EU 2014 No. L 189/50, 27 June 2014.

importers.[56] Previously, the Trade Barriers Regulation had been extended to include a right of appeal in case of a violation of bilateral agreements.[57] Regarding anti-dumping, due to protracted debates in the Council, the reforms finally entered into force only in 2017 and 2018,[58] while the reform proposal on an International Procurement Instrument (IPI)[59] was still in the legislative machinery when the most recent Trade Policy Review was tabled in February 2021.

2.1.3 'Open Strategic Autonomy': The Turn to Stronger Enforcement and Ensuring a Level Playing Field Strengthens a More Geopoliticized EU Trade Policy

The previous brief exploration of the evolution of EU trade policy has shown that the drivers behind its developments and changing focuses are both internal and external, legal as well as economic and social, and that

[56] For more detail, see Frank Hoffmeister, 'The Devil Is in the Detail: A First Guide on the EU's New Trade Defence Rules', in Wolfgang Weiß and Cornelia Furculita (eds.), *Global Politics and EU Trade Policy: Facing the Challenges to a Multilateral Approach* (Cham: Springer, 2020), pp. 212 ff; Bollen, de Ville, and Orbie, 'EU Trade Policy' (2016) 284 f.

[57] Regulation (EC) 125/2008 amending Regulation (EC) 3286/94 laying down Community procedures in the field of the common commercial policy in order to ensure the exercise of the Community's rights under international trade rules, OJ EU 2008 No. L 40/1, 14 February 2008. See Art. 2 para. 1 lit. b Regulation (EU) 2015/1843 of the European Parliament and of the Council of 6 October 2015 laying down Union procedures in the field of the common commercial policy in order to ensure the exercise of the Union's rights under international trade rules, in particular those established under the auspices of the World Trade Organization, OJ EU 2015 J No. L 272, 16 October 2015.

[58] See the so-called new methodology Regulation (EU) 2017/2321, OJ EU 2017 No. L 338/3, 19 December 2017, and the modernisation Regulation (EU) 2018/825 OJ EU 2018 No. L 143/1, 7 June 2018, both amending Regulation (EU) 2016/1036 on protection against dumped imports from countries not members of the European Union, and Regulation (EU) 2016/1037 on protection against subsidised imports from countries not members of the European Union. For an assessment, also in view of WTO obligations, see Hoffmeister, 'The Devil Is in the Detail' (2020), p. 211; Edwin Vermulst and Juhi Dion Sud, 'Are the EU's Trade Defence Instruments WTO Compliant?', in Weiß and Furculita (eds.), *Global Politics and EU Trade Policy* (2020), p. 235 ff.

[59] For the first proposal, see European Commission, Proposal for a Regulation of the European Parliament and of the Council on the access of third-country goods and services to the Union's internal market in public procurement and procedures supporting negotiations on access of Union goods and services to the public procurement markets of third countries, COM(2012) 124 final, 21 March 2012, then an amended version, European Commission, Amended proposal for a Regulation of the European Parliament and of the Council on the access of third-country goods and services to the Union's internal market in public procurement and procedures supporting negotiations on access of Union goods and services to the public procurement markets of third countries, COM(2016) 34 final, 29 January 2016.

the internal and external drivers cannot be seen independently, but they interact. Trade policies intermingle with national policy fields that are concerned not only (if at all) with economic objectives but also with other general welfare interests such as environmental and climate protection, or fundamental rights. Trade policy is thus undergoing a fundamental qualitative change; it is becoming a rather domestic policy. In the same way, the Trade Policy Review of 2021 is a reflection of recent internal and external processes (see Section 1.2). As mentioned, trade relations for several years now face an unprecedented level of simultaneous political, institutional, economic, and technological challenges. In response to these tremendous contests to the current multilateral trade order posed inter alia by the crisis of the WTO and its rule-based order, US protectionism, China's state interventionist model of economy, the severe tensions between these two major global power houses, and the resulting increasingly geoeconomic approaches to trade policy, but also in view of grand domestic policy projects (for more, see Section 2.2), the Commission initiated a reform of its trade policy strategy under the motto of an 'Open Strategic Autonomy'. This process started with consultations on a trade policy review from June to November 2020.[60] According to the consultation documents, the review had two core objectives: (1) enabling recovery in the post–COVID-19 environment and (2) building a stronger and more resilient EU based on 'Open Strategic Autonomy'. The review of the EU's trade policy intends to ensure that trade policy works effectively despite the challenges; serves the EU's objectives and policy priorities in the areas of sustainability, climate change, the digital economy, and economic and political security; and contributes to the creation of quality jobs and new growth. The economy shall become more resilient, and the participation of small and medium-sized enterprises in external trade shall be facilitated. Open strategic autonomy aims to ensure that EU trade policy can operate effectively in the new global context and fully contribute to achieving the EU's priorities. The EU wants to continue reaping the benefits of international trade while being able to protect itself from unfair practices and assertively enforce its rights under international law and trade agreements. Hence, 'Open Strategic Autonomy' is proclaimed to combine the fundamental openness of the EU's markets with protection for its people and businesses. Thus, already from these

[60] See European Commission, Consultation Note, A renewed trade policy for a stronger Europe, 16 June 2020, www.astrid-online.it/static/upload/comm/0000/commue_trade-policy-review_consultation-note.pdf and the related Consultation Document.

explanations of the Commission one can infer that market openness is compromised in view of EU interests and values and comes under conditions.

The review resulted in the publication of a new trade policy communication by the Commission in February 2021, which brought about a reorientation of EU trade policy in accordance with the identified objectives.[61] The Commission now pursues a more assertive trade policy which is still grounded in the present rules-based trade order but merges this with a much more robust and assertive stance as regards enforcing the EU's trade rights and protecting its economy from unfair or abusive practices by trade partners. Furthermore, trade and investment policy should contribute more strongly to solving the most pressing global challenges of climate change, sustainable development, and digitalization. These notions of the new trade policy are reflected in the three core trade policy objectives: supporting the green and digital transformation of EU economy, shaping globalization for more sustainability and fairness, and 'increasing the EU's capacity to pursue its interest and enforce its rights, including autonomously where needed'.[62] These objectives are translated into six areas of action, three of which deal mainly with the reform of the WTO and the need for improved trade rules for greening the economy and making trade more sustainable and digital[63] (with only the second one on green transition mentioning an autonomous measure, i.e. the proposal for a carbon border adjustment mechanism (CBAM)). Another two focus on the increased global regulatory impact of the EU and strengthened relations with neighbours and Africa,[64] whereas the last one aims at strengthening implementation and enforcement of trade agreements and ensuring a level playing field.[65] To that extent, with the new 'open, sustainable and assertive trade policy' approach, the EU seeks to significantly expand its room for manoeuvre by unlocking the benefits of trade agreements and by taking a more assertive approach towards the enforcement of its trade rights as well as the representation of its interests, which is actually what the EU means when speaking about safeguarding a level playing field. This requires a strengthened capacity of the EU to take enforcement of trade rules into its own hands much more than before and to compel the EU's rights under multilateral and bilateral trade rules.

[61] European Commission, Trade Policy Review: An Open, Sustainable and Assertive Trade Policy (Trade Policy Review), COM(2021) 66 final, 18 February 2021.

[62] ibid, p. 9 f. [63] ibid, pp. 11–15. [64] ibid, pp. 16–18. [65] ibid, pp. 19–22.

Reforming the WTO is part of the EU's response in this multipolar, uncertain environment for international trade. It was mentioned as a segment of the Trade Policy Review already in May 2020.[66] In its Trade Policy Review communication the Commission reconfirms the continuing commitment to the WTO and its underlying idea of a multilateral rule-based, basically liberal trading system with its dispute settlement system that ensures a predictable framework for trade. The WTO shall be strengthened in its role as a forum for developing, implementing, and enforcing trade rules,[67] all the more as the new trade policy confirms its intention to protect EU interests and values 'in full compliance with its international commitments'.[68] Consequently, the new trade policy formulates an agenda for reforming the WTO, with the EU wanting to play an international leadership role in this regard. Besides developing further the substantive rules of the WTO, this includes the continuation of dispute settlement and, in particular, a reform of the Appellate Body (AB).[69] Hence, the new EU trade policy does not deny the continued relevance of the WTO.

While multilateralism continues to be part of the EU's commitment in external trade, it may, however, not be as clear in its meaning anymore, even though the Commission confirmed the salience of multilateral cooperation recently in its Strategic Foresight 2021. But in this document, the EU also stressed the need for multilateralism to 'adapt to remain fit for purpose [...] A truly inclusive, networked multilateralism is the only way forward.'[70] Multilateralism in trade policy therefore no longer may be just a matter of reforming the WTO, its decision-making and the interaction of states within it, and the restoration of its dispute settlement mechanism, which still is a 'pressing priority in the necessary

66 European Commission, Europe's Moment: Repair and Prepare for the Next Generation, COM(2020) 456 final, 2.

67 See the Annex to Trade Policy Review, COM(2021) 66 final.

68 Trade Policy Review, COM(2021) 66 final, p. 9.

69 See again the Annex to Trade Policy Review, COM(2021) 66 final. For earlier EU proposals for WTO reform, see https://ec.europa.eu/commission/presscorner/detail/en/IP_18_5786 and the Concept Paper, WTO Modernisation: Introduction to Future EU Proposals, www.wita.org/atp-research/eu-concept-paper-on-wto-reform/. On reform proposals of the EU, together with China, India, Canada, etc. regarding the AB, see the Communication from the European Union, China, Canada, India, Norway, New Zealand, Switzerland, Australia, Republic of Korea, Iceland, Singapore and Mexico, to the General Council WT/GC/W/752, 26 November 2018.

70 European Commission, 2021 Strategic Foresight Report, COM(2021) 750 final, p. 17.

modernisation of all of the WTO'.[71] Rather, multilateralism itself is described as in need of change, which may then also change the role of the EU in multilateralism. The adjustment is to bring about a network-type multilateralism that brings together international organizations under the leadership of the UN.[72] The EU's commitment to multilateralism in trade policy may therefore shift from its primary focus on the WTO.

The notion of Open Strategic Autonomy[73] in trade policy appears to have slightly developed in the above-mentioned steps towards defining a new trade policy. At first, the open strategic autonomy was meant to signify 'shaping the new [sic!] system of global economic governance and developing mutually beneficial bilateral relations, while protecting ourselves from unfair and abusive practices',[74] and was defined 'as the EU's commitment to open and fair trade, preserving the benefits of an open economy and supporting partners around the world to lead the renewed and reinvigorated form of multilateralism the world needs [sic!]' , while noting that 'the EU is aware of the need to reduce its dependency and strengthen its security of supply across key technologies and value chains'.[75] Later, open strategic autonomy was directed towards the 'EU's ability to make its own choices and shape the world around it through leadership and engagement, reflecting its strategic interest and values', and a 'reformed rules-based system of global trade governance'.[76] It seems that the Commission's initial reform zeal regarding multilateralism in the WTO has become more sober, whereas the strategic dimension of the Open Strategic Autonomy has been invigorated with respect to the EU's capacity for resilience, interest protection, and independence,[77] and this dimension appears to have even been extended and confirmed in the

[71] ibid. [72] ibid.

[73] For the development of the concept of EU strategic autonomy in defense and security policy and its subsequent more general diffusion, see Scott Lavery, Sean McDaniel, and Davide Schmid, 'European Strategic Autonomy', in Milan Babić, Adam Dixon, and Imogen Liu (eds.), *The Political Economy of Geoeconomics* (Cham: Palgrave Macmillan, 2022), pp. 59 ff.

[74] European Commission, Europe's Moment, COM(2020) 456 final, p. 13.

[75] European Commission, 2020 Strategic Foresight Report: Strategic Foresight – Charting the Course Towards a More Resilient Europe, COM(2020) 493, 9 September 2020, p. 14, fn. 63.

[76] Trade Policy Review, COM(2021) 66 final, 4.

[77] Suzana Anghel, et al., 'On the Path to "Strategic Autonomy"': The EU in an Evolving Geopolitical Environment' (2020) 652.096 EPRS Study; Milan Babić, Adam Dixon, and Imogen Liu, 'Geoeconomics in a Changing Global Order', in Babić, Dixon, and Liu (eds.), *The Political Economy of Geoeconomics* (2022), p. 11 f.

aftermath of the Russian war against Ukraine since 24 February 2022, which reinforces the need for Open Strategic Autonomy.[78] Hence, the notion of Open Strategic Autonomy in the end received an ameliorated, more outspoken dimension of trade policy capacity building by proposing several new trade policy tools and instruments which the trade policy review communication diligently enumerates (and which at the time of writing have been established). To that extent, the last of the six areas of action under the Trade Policy Review mentioned above – that is, the one on the stronger focus on implementation and enforcement of trade agreements and ensuring a level playing field – is much more explicit and elaborate in terms of a clear and detailed political programme for new initiatives than the other five (with the exception of the proposed CBAM under area two, as mentioned earlier). Besides promising to make full use of opportunities to implement trade agreements and monitoring their proper implementation, the trade policy review under its last heading lists very concrete plans: It starts with the recent amendment of the Trade Enforcement Regulation 654/2014[79] that improves the EU's capacity to respond to blocked dispute settlement mechanisms, and recalls the already adopted Foreign Direct Investment Screening Regulation 2019/452[80] to address risks to security and public order. The Commission then promises a row of new instruments. It will amend its Trade Defence Instruments in order to address foreign subsidies and the competition distortions caused by them in the internal market, propose a new Anti-Coercion Instrument (ACI) to protect the EU from coercive actions by third states that seek to coerce the Union and/or its Member States to take or withdraw particular policy measures, advance the already tabled International Procurement Instrument, and launch an EU export credit facility.[81] The proposal for a CBAM is to be named here, too. All of these new instruments meanwhile have been adopted and are subject to detailed analyses in the remainder of this book.

[78] See the European Commission, 2022 Strategic Foresight Report Twinning the green and digital transitions in the new geopolitical context, COM(2022) 289 final, 29 June 2022, pp. 8, 12.

[79] See Regulation (EU) 2021/167 amending Regulation (EU) No. 654/2014 concerning the exercise of the Union's rights for the application and enforcement of international trade rules, OJ EU 2021 No. L 49/1, 12 February 2021.

[80] Regulation (EU) 2019/452 establishing a framework for the screening of foreign direct investments into the Union, OJ EU 2019 No. L 79/1, 23 December 2021.

[81] See Trade Policy Review, COM(2021) 66 final, p. 20 f.

This list of projects set out in the trade policy review gives a clear indication towards what open, sustainable, and assertive trade policy actually means in operational practice[82] and illustrates that the move towards more effective implementation of trade rules and the creation of a level playing field represents a reorientation of trade policy that, on the one hand, integrates already present proposals and initiatives. Hence, the new trade policy takes up the already ongoing understanding of the Commission for a need for more effective trade enforcement, but, on the other hand, it goes far beyond. While being based on previously proposed initiatives for stronger enforcement of TSD Chapters and more reciprocity in government procurement (see Section 1.2), the new trade policy extends this policy insight considerably, takes care of its effective implementation by new legislative projects, expands it with a view to ensuring greater fairness also with regard to trade policy's impact on domestic competition, and embeds it within a more comprehensive trade policy vision that brings together multilateral, bilateral, unilateral, and even institutional[83] levels of trade policy. Trade policy turns to more assertive enforcement of the rules by the EU within both multilateral and bilateral settings and more effectively ensuring a fair playing field, even unilaterally. It transcends the enforcement objectives already mentioned in the 'Trade for All' communication in 2015.[84] The new legislative initiatives listed in the Trade Policy Review 2021 build EU capacities and affect trade policy with a distinct geopolitical notion at all levels: multilateral, bilateral, and unilateral. In consequence, the new trade policy engenders a new shift towards a more assertive and geostrategic EU in international trade relations, which shows a fresh determination in the robust enforcement of trade rules and an even and fairer treatment of the EU by its trade partners, in order to make space for a more geopolitical direction of EU trade policy in view of the new trade policy environment (see Sections 1.1 and 1.2).

Hence, even though one might blame the new trade policy review under the leitmotif of an open, sustainable, and assertive trade policy and the underlying motto of open strategic autonomy for neither being a strategy nor fully consistent in its approach (not least due to its vagueness

[82] Schmitz and Seidl, 'As Open as Possible' (2023) 847.

[83] The establishment of the new post of a Chief Trade Enforcement Officer is recalled in Trade Policy Review, COM(2021) 66 final, p. 19.

[84] European Commission, Trade for All: Towards a More Responsible Trade and Investment Policy, COM(2015) 497 final, 14 October 2015, p. 15. In this respect, see Section 1.2.

and ambiguity),[85] nor completely new,[86] one should accept that the focus towards greater assertiveness in trade enforcement is a new element which became considerably reaffirmed and extended and which received an explicit dimension of trade policy capacity building for more geopolitics in the area of trade policy. The new trade policy instruments indicate a clear direction in this respect, as mentioned. They also give witness to the increased awareness and concerns of the Commission about competition-distorting effects of third-country behavior within the internal market due to the EU's open market, which is reflected in the creation of instruments against third-country subsidies and the carbon border adjustment mechanism. The EU's capacity and scope for action to respond to third countries' behavior continues to be a core objective in the EU's subsequent Strategic Foresight 2021, adopted by the Commission in September 2021 and entitled 'The EU's capacity and freedom to act', in which the EU's ability to act more assertively in order to counter foreign coercive action or extraterritorial sanctions is stressed, and capacity building features prominently. In this context, the Strategic Foresight 2021 recalls exactly all the political initiatives enumerated in the trade policy review mentioned above: countering economic pressure; acting where dispute settlement mechanisms are blocked; strengthening trade defence instruments to protect EU operators from unfair trade; screening foreign direct investment; addressing distortive effects of foreign subsidies; and ensuring a level playing field in non-EU markets by EU export credits.[87]

That said, the trade policy review of 2021, of course, stands in the tradition of EU trade policy and its Commission communications as several topics are recurring: The need for reforming the WTO and in particular its dispute settlement mechanisms has been an object for EU trade policy since the Doha Round. The use of trade policy in the service of other EU policy objectives, in particular non-economic ones, has existed before the Lisbon reforms,[88] which not only made trade policy

[85] Schmitz and Seidl, 'As Open as Possible' (2023) 835, 838, 845. They illustrate, however, that the vagueness of the concepts expresses the compromise to be reached between different trade paradigms (free, fair, just) and contributes to appeasing critique by incorporating it and forming coalitions. See also Jacobs, et al., 'The Hegemonic Politics of "Strategic Autonomy" and "Resilience"' (2023) 13 f.

[86] Alaisdair Young, 'It's the End of EU Trade Policy as We Know It: The Commission's 2021 Trade Policy Review', Reconnect Online Workshop, 15 October 2021, https://reconnect-europe.eu/event/reconnect-online-workshop-eu-trade-policy/.

[87] European Commission, 2021 Strategic Foresight, COM(2021) 750 final, p. 17.

[88] See Opinion of Advocate General Wahl, Opinion 3/15, ECLI:EU:C:2016:657, 8 September 2016, paras. 69 ff.

an explicit part of the EU's overall external policy (see Article 207 (1) TFEU) but also requires trade policy to be compatible with internal policies and rules (Article 207 (3) TFEU). This re-contextualization and more general politicization of trade policy had already been emphasized by the Commission in in its 2015 Communication 'Trade for All',[89] so that the objectives of trade policy go beyond pure commercial objectives (set out in article 206 TFEU) and pertain to EU founding principles such as respect for democracy and human rights, and fundamental policy objectives such as sustainable development and a cooperative and just world order (Article 21(1) and (2) Treaty on European Union (TEU)[90]). Thus, EU trade policy is subject to multiple coherence requirements,[91] and it has been adjusted to the current grand policy projects of the Van der Leyen Commission, namely the European Green Deal and the Digital Strategy, by the new trade policy review in 2021 (see Section 1.2).

The implementation of the trade policy reorientation towards assertiveness and stronger enforcement is progressing quickly since the trade policy review published in February 2021. The EU is using its enforcement tools in bilateral dispute settlement in its FTAs with a new intensity.[92] It also initiated several WTO dispute settlement cases against China, Russia, and Egypt over intellectual property and trade practices.[93] With regard to WTO dispute settlement, the EU had already established an alternative multi-party interim appeal mechanism (MPIA) to enable WTO dispute settlement to go forward at an appeal stage as well,[94] despite the paralysis of the WTO AB, with those WTO members taking part. The Commission had since tabled proposals for its envisaged legislative instruments, all of which were finally – after sometimes very intense

[89] European Commission, Trade for All, COM(2015) 497 final, p. 3.

[90] Consolidated version of the Treaty on European Union, OJ EU 2012 No. C 326/13, 26 October 2010.

[91] Wolfgang Weiß, 'Enhancement of the European Parliament's Monitoring for Better Coherence between Trade Policy and Non-Trade Policy Objectives (NTPOs)' (2021) 2021/68 RSC Working Paper, p. 1.

[92] See Cornelia Furculita, 'The Time of PTA Dispute Settlement Mechanisms Might Have Come', in Manfred Elsig, Rodrigo Polanco, and Peter Van den Bossche (eds.), *International Economic Dispute Settlement: Demise or Transformation?* (New York: Cambridge University Press, 2021), pp. 442–469. For the cases, see https://policy.trade.ec.europa.eu/enforcement-and-protection/dispute-settlement/bilateral-disputes_en/.

[93] *China – IPRS Enforcement*, WT/DS611; *China – Goods (EU)*, WT/DS610; *Egypt – Import Registration Requirements (EU)*, WT/DS609; *Russia – Wood (EU)*, WT/DS608; *Russia – Domestic and Foreign Products and Services*, WT/DS604.

[94] Multi-Party Interim Appeal Arbitration Arrangement Pursuant to Article 25 of the DSU (MPIA), JOB/DSB/1/Add.12, 30 April 2020.

debates leading to considerable amendments – turned into legislative acts by the EU legislator in 2022 and 2023. After the successful amendment of the Trade Enforcement Regulation in the spring of 2021 towards stronger EU countermeasures, the Commission had presented a draft for a regulation on third-country subsidies in order to ensure a level playing field, designed to protect its economic operators against unfair, hostile, and uncompetitive practices,[95] which finally became Regulation 2022/2560 on foreign subsidies distorting the internal market.[96] The Commission's proposal for a CBAM that aims at ensuring equal market opportunities, by providing for the purchase of carbon certificates for certain imported goods in order to compensate for the cost disadvantages incurred in the EU as a result of CO_2 pricing through the Emissions Trading Scheme,[97] became the CBAM Regulation (EU) 2023/956 adopted in May 2023.[98] Finally, an ACI draft regulation was presented that improves the capacities of the EU to react to clear violations of international trade agreements by establishing a mechanism to deter and counteract coercive action (in the sense of trade or investment restrictions) by third states, which was enacted at the end of 2023.[99] The EU, furthermore, adopted the IPI Regulation 2022/1031.[100] The Commission's efforts to improve the enforcement of FTA TSD chapters were on their

[95] European Commission, Proposal for a Regulation of the European Parliament and of the Council on foreign subsidies distorting the internal market, COM(2021) 223 final, 5 May 2021.

[96] Regulation 2022/2560 of the European Parliament and the Council of 14 December 2022 on foreign subsidies distorting the internal market, OJ EU 2022 No. L 330/1, 23 December 2022.

[97] European Commission, Proposal for a Regulation of the European Parliament and of the Council establishing a carbon border adjustment mechanism, COM(2021) 564 final, 14 July 2021.

[98] Regulation (EU) 2023/956 of the European Parliament and of the Council of 10 May 2023 establishing a carbon border adjustment mechanism (CBAM Regulation), OJ EU 2023 No. L 130/52, 16 May 2023.

[99] European Commission, Proposal for a Regulation of the European Parliament and of the Council on the protection of the Union and its Member States from economic coercion by third countries, COM(2021) 775 final, 8 December 2021. See also Regulation (EU) 2023/2675 of the European Parliament and of the Council of 22 November 2023 on the protection of the Union and its Member States from economic coercion by third countries, OJ EU 2023 No. L 2675, 7 December 2023.

[100] Regulation (EU) 2022/1031 of the European Parliament and of the Council of 23 June 2022 on the access of third-country economic operators, goods and services to the Union's public procurement and concession markets and procedures supporting negotiations on access of Union economic operators, goods and services to the public procurement and concession markets of third countries (IPI Regulation), OJ EU 2022 No. L 173/1.

way first by conducting a consultation in the autumn of 2021.[101] The Commission's action plan on the TSD chapters meanwhile has been published in the summer of 2022.[102] The review of the TSD chapters will cover the scope, implementation, and enforcement of the TSD chapters in EU FTAs.

The rapidly advancing implementation of the new trade policy agenda is complemented and accompanied by increased efforts to develop a corresponding, more active industrial and competition policy to strengthen the EU as a business location and improve the competitive position of European companies on world markets against strong competitors, particularly from the United States and China. The EU has made it clear that it will increasingly put its competition rules at the service of trade policy in order to ensure a level playing field, including with competitors from third markets. In its New Strategic Agenda 2019–2024 it has stressed: 'In a world where common rules and standards are increasingly questioned, it will be vital to promote a level playing field, including in the area of trade.' It further emphasized that '[w]e will continue to update our European competition framework to new technological and global market developments. [. . .] An ambitious and robust trade policy ensuring fair competition, reciprocity and mutual benefits is a central element in that respect, both at the [. . .] WTO and in bilateral relations.'[103] Subsequently, the New Industrial Strategy for Europe 2020 started deliberation on how to strengthen EU anti-subsidies tools to counteract proliferation of subsidization in third countries,[104] leading to the above-mentioned proposal for a third-country subsidies regulation; furthermore, the EU intensifies its industry strategy with a view to correct the results of economic competition by fostering investment in certain technologies in order to bring forward EU's technological resilience and independence. This simultaneous reference and commission of future

[101] European Commission, Open public consultation on the Trade and Sustainable Development (TSD) Review, https://policy.trade.ec.europa.eu/consultations/open-public-consultation-trade-and-sustainable-development-tsd-review_en.

[102] European Commission Communication, The Power of Trade Partnerships: Together for Green and Just Economic Growth, COM(2022) 409, 22 June 2022.

[103] European Council, New Strategic Agenda 2019-2024, pp. 4, 6 (www.consilium.europa.eu/media/39914/a-new-strategic-agenda-2019-2024.pdf).

[104] European Commission, A New Industrial Strategy for Europe, COM(2020) 102, 10 March 2020, p. 6 f; European Commission, Updating the 2020 New Industrial Strategy: Building a Stronger Single Market for Europe's Recovery, COM(2021) 350 final, 5 May 2021, pp. 5, 15.

trade policy instruments and its industrial policy towards strategic goals testify to the EU's geoeconomic orientation in its new policies.[105]

2.2 Drivers behind the EU's Geoeconomic Reorientation towards Stronger Enforcement and Ensuring a Level Playing Field

This section briefly explores the challenging environment the EU faces in external trade in the past several years which led the EU to adjust its trade policy to address them and, accordingly, to move toward the greater robustness described in the earlier sections.[106] The analysis of the diverse developments that instigated the change in the EU's approach towards more assertive enforcement and representation of EU interests will allow discerning the drivers and causes behind this trade policy turn. As briefly mentioned (see Section 1.2), for several years now, trade relations and trade governance face an unprecedented level of simultaneous economic, institutional, political, and technological challenges, which led to a rise of unilateralism and protectionism. Multilateralism in the WTO, as multilateralism generally, became heavily contested;[107] digitization of the economy and the proliferation of global value chains challenged traditional patterns of economic wealth by novel business concepts; and trade powers such as China and the United States were increasingly and strategically subjecting their foreign trade relations to geoeconomic and geostrategic objectives, leading to a weaponization of trade and interdependence,[108] where, in its more recent version, trade policy is used not so much as a tool to enforce general foreign policy goals

[105] Henrique Choer Moraes and Mikael Wigell, 'Balancing Dependence: The Quest for Autonomy and the Rise of Corporate Geoeconomics', in Babić, Dixon, and Liu (eds.), *The Political Economy of Geoeconomics* (2022), pp. 39 ff; Lavery, McDaniel, and Schmid, 'European Strategic Autonomy', in ibid., pp. 57, 61 ff.

[106] Trade Policy Review, COM(2021) 66 final, p. 1.

[107] Vineet Hegde, Jan Wouters, and Akhil Raina, 'The Demise of the Rules-Based International Economic Order?' (2020) Leuven Centre for Global Governance Studies, Working Paper 224.

[108] Rebecca Harding and Jack Harding, *The Weaponization of Trade: The Great Unbalancing of Politics and Economics* (London: London Publishing Partnership, 2017); Daniel Drezner, Henry Farrell, and Abraham Newman (eds.), *The Uses and Abuses of Weaponized Interdependence* (Washington, DC: Brookings Institution Press, 2021); Henry Farrell and Abraham Newman, 'Weaponized Interdependence' (2019) 44(1) *International Security* 42–79. For the more frequent use of sanctions, see Bryan R. Early and Menevis Cilizoglu, 'Economic Sanctions in Flux: Enduring Challenges, New Policies, and Defining the Future Research Agenda' (2020) 21(4) *International Studies Perspectives* 438–477; Darren Lim and Victor Ferguson, 'Informal Economic Sanctions: The Political Economy of Chinese

(which would mean geopolitics and which already forms part of trade policy),[109] but rather more to influence economic processes in a targeted manner with regard to their results, with a view to enlarge the world market position of the domestic economy and/or to increase crisis resilience. These challenges to international trade were exacerbated by the COVID-19 pandemic in 2020–2021 and Russia's war on Ukraine since 2022.

2.2.1 The Crisis of Multilateralism and the Rise of Economic Nationalism

As already shown in the above analysis of the EU's trade policy development, which described a shift from a clear focus on multilateralism towards a more active bilateralism (Section 2.1.2), multilateralism in the WTO has incrementally become ever more difficult. While criticism of the prevailing liberal trade rules and of the WTO from civil society groups and developing countries has existed since the 1970s and 1990s, respectively, the functioning of the WTO's political task of being a forum for trade negotiations and reviewing domestic trade policies worsened considerably after the turn of the millennium, due to the rift between the different interests among its very heterogeneous membership. The emerging contestation of multilateralism in the WTO found its most visible expression in the inability of the WTO members to conclude the Doha Round in a meaningful way which would do justice to its designation as development round, and more generally to agree on new rules for current issues (for this see below Section 2.2.3). Also, numerous bi- or plurilateral trade agreements have been concluded outside the WTO, some of which even cover whole world regions or comprise huge trade blocs (so-called mega-regionals), like the Comprehensive and Progressive Agreement for Trans-Pacific Partnership (CPTPP)[110] or the Regional Comprehensive Economic Partnership (RCEP) that includes China.[111]

Coercion during the THAAD Dispute' (2022) 29(5) *Review of International Political Economy* 1525–1548.

[109] See Commission Staff Working Document, Impact Assessment Report Accompanying the document Proposal for a Regulation of the European Parliament and of the Council on the protection of the Union and its Member States from economic coercion by third countries, SWD(2021) 371 final, 8 December 2021, pp. 13 ff.

[110] The CPTPP was concluded between Australia, Brunei, Canada, Chile, Japan, Malaysia, Mexico, New Zealand, Peru, Singapore, and Vietnam.

[111] See https://rcepsec.org/. It entered into force on 1 January 2022 for Australia, Brunei, Cambodia, China, Japan, Laos, New Zealand, Singapore, Thailand, and Vietnam.

The worries about the WTO considerably accelerated with the advent of the Trump administration in the United States in 2017 and its 'America First' trade policy, and developed into a formidable crisis of multilateralism as Trump's nationalist economic policy[112] also affected international cooperation in general. The importance of the WTO as an institution was considerably diminished due to the blocking attitude of the US one-sided nationalist trade policy with regard to any agreement within the WTO. The United States resisted the appointment of AB members, which resulted in the paralysis of the WTO AB since 10 December 2019.[113] Even though US criticism of the AB's jurisprudence began long before Trump,[114] the blocking of appointments only came about under Trump.[115] Trump's challenges to the WTO have been posing a deeper threat to the multilateral trade regime than ever before because they come from a central actor and founding member of the WTO, which for the first time has been threatened of being destroyed from within.[116] The threats posed by Trump had and still have the capacity of fundamentally endangering the basic liberal consensus standing behind the WTO rules, and might deeply change the reality of the world trade order, as the WTO was and still is endangered on several levels. Besides damaging the WTO crown jewel of dispute settlement under the DSU, and together with it the compulsory implementing phase so important for enforcing compliance with WTO rules,[117] observance of very fundamental substantive trade rules was undermined. Trump even instigated trade wars, in

[112] Craig VanGrasstek, 'The Trade Policy of the United States under the Trump Administration' (2019) EUI Working Papers, RSCAS 2019/11; Stephen Moore and Arthur B. Laffer, *Trumponomics: Inside the America First Plan to Revive Our Economy* (New York: St. Martin's Press, 2018). For the consequences for the EU, see Frank Hoffmeister, 'Do Ut Des oder Tit for Tat? – Die Europäische Handelspolitik Angesichts Neuer Herausforderungen aus den USA und China', in Christoph Herrmann (ed.), *Die Gemeinsame Handelspolitik im Europäischen Verfassungsverbund* (Baden-Baden: Nomos, 2020), pp.78 ff.

[113] Rachel Brewster, 'WTO Dispute Settlement: Can We Go Back Again?' (2019) 113 *AJIL Unbound* 61–66; Caroline Glöckle and Aike Würdemann, 'Die Appellate Body-Krise der WTO – Eine Analyse der US-Kritikpunkte' (2018) 23 *EuZW* 976–982; Geraldo Vidigal, 'Living without the Appellate Body: Multilateral, Bilateral and Plurilateral Solutions to the WTO Dispute Settlement Crisis' (2019) 20(6) *JWIT* 862–890.

[114] Claude Barfield, *Free Trade, Sovereignty, Democracy: The Future of the World Trade Organization* (Washington, DC: AEI Press, 2001), pp. 38 ff.

[115] Joost Pauwelyn, 'WTO Dispute Settlement Post 2019: What to Expect?' (2019) *JIEL* 297–321; Glöckle and Würdemann, 'Die Appellate Body-Krise der WTO' (2018) 976.

[116] Geraldo Vidigal, 'Westphalia Strikes Back: The 2008 Trade Wars and Threat to the WTO Regime' (2018) 2018/31 Amsterdam Law School Legal Studies Research Paper.

[117] WTO members can avoid compliance with panel reports by appealing to the inactive AB, with the effect that the panel report cannot be adopted by the Dispute Settlement Body

particular with the EU and even more with China.[118] Trump's trade policy deviated from a multilateral trade policy to an extent going far beyond earlier tendencies in the United States,[119] and revealed another driving force of US trade policy already present under the Obama administration: the geostrategic goal of isolating China.[120] The latter became the target of particularly severe trade sanctions on grounds of alleged violations of intellectual property rights and accusations of technology theft and unfair competition, even coercion.[121] The US attempt to justify the tariffs against China as a defence of public morals was dismissed by the WTO panel, as the measures were not designed to protect the 'standards of right or wrong' invoked by the United States.[122] The US policy of arbitrary, differential 'additional tariffs' breached their WTO obligations under existing tariff bindings, the most-favoured-nation treatment and equal treatment requirement, being fundamental principles of international trade, all the more as they aimed at extracting unilateral concessions from trading partners, to which some have subjected.[123]

(DSB), which is a necessary condition for a report to become legally binding (i.e. 'appealing into the void').

118 See the detailed compilation of facts in Chad P. Bown and Melina Kolb, 'Trump's Trade War Timeline: An Up-to-Date Guide', 24 March 2023, www.piie.com/blogs/trade-investment-policy-watch/trump-trade-war-china-date-guide.

119 Cf. Craig VanGrasstek, *Trade and American Leadership: The Paradoxes of Power and Wealth from Alexander Hamilton to Donald Trump* (Cambridge: Cambridge University Press, 2019), pp. 142 ff, 195 f, 427 ff. For the history of US protectionism, see Nancy Williams, 'The Resilience of Protectionism in U.S. Trade Policy' (2019) *Boston University Law Review* 683–719; for the Art. 301 unilateralism in the 1980s and 1990s, see Jagdish Bhagwati and Hugh Patrick (eds.), *Aggressive Unilateralism: America's 301 Trade Policy and the World Trading System* (Ann Arbor: University of Michigan Press, 1991).

120 See VanGrasstek, 'The Trade Policy of the United States' (2019), pp. 2 ff, 12 ff.

121 Steve Charnovitz, 'Grading Trump's China Trade Strategy', in Marc Bungenberg, et al. (eds.) *European Yearbook of International Economic Law* 2019 (Cham: Springer, 2020), pp 217–256; Gabriel Felbermayr and Marina Steininger, 'Trump's Trade Attack on China – Who Will Have the Last Laugh?' (2019) 20(1) CesIfo Forum 1/2019, pp. 27–32; Caroline Glöckle and Aike Würdemann, 'The Atypical Fashion of the US-China 'Phase 1'-Deal: Context, Content and Perspectives' (2020) 23(2) *ZEuS* 347–370.

122 Panel Report, *US – Tariff Measures (China)*, WT/DS543/R, 15 September 2020, paras. 7.146 ff, 7.178 ff. In October 2020, the United States appealed into the void the panel report to the inactive AB.

123 Hegde, Wouters, and Raina, 'The Demise of the Rules-Based International Economic Order?' (2020), p. 14f; Bernard Hoekman and Laura Puccio, 'EU Trade Policy: Challenges and Opportunities' (2019) 2019/06 RSCAS Policy, pp. 1–7; Geraldo Vidigal, 'WTO Adjudication and the Security Exception: Something Old, Something New, Something Borrowed – Something Blue?' (2019) 46(3) *LIEI* 203–224 at 218 f; Wolfgang Weiß, 'EU Multilateral Trade Policy in a Changing, Multipolar World: The Way Forward', in Weiß and Furculita (eds.), *Global Politics and EU Trade Policy* (2020), pp. 19 ff.

The United States claimed these measures serve national security interests,[124] which fits into a more widespread current trend among WTO members to revive the national security exceptions (Article XXI GATT, Article XIVbis General Agreement on Trade in Services (GATS),[125] and Article 73 Agreement on Trade-Related Aspects of Intellectual Property Rights (TRIPS)[126]) for diverse kinds of security-related concerns.[127] The invocation of national security to justify trade barriers adopted in the pursuit of disguised economic objectives[128] adds another severe test to the multilateral trade order. National security exceptions may no longer be constrained to cover situations of regional conflicts or international terrorism, but may be invoked also in relation to measures adopted for the security of critical infrastructures and technologies, which adds another layer of contestation to the fragile accord behind these exceptions. An even more expanded scope of the national security exceptions might be applied in order to justify measures adopted in pursuit of economic security needs of states with regard to maintaining their particular socio-economic system and their economic position, as attempts to defend them are on the rise due to shifts in global trade. The economic interdependence resulting from open markets and effectuated by the prevailing liberal trade rules under the WTO, which until recently was seen as a guarantee for growing mutual prosperity and wealth, increasingly is assessed in a perspective of national security and economic resilience as a source of possible threats thereto because this interdependence is now perceived to undermine state control, self-sufficiency, and resilience and to become a source of

[124] Cf. Presidential Proclamation 9740 of 30 April 2018 on Adjusting Imports of Steel into the US, 27 December 2021, (www.whitehouse.gov/briefing-room/presidential-actions/2021/12/27/a-proclamation-on-adjusting-imports-of-steel-into-the-united-states/#:~:text=In%20Proclamation%209740%20of%20April,national%20security%20by%20imports%20of); Congressional Research Service, Section 232 Auto Investigation, IF10971, 31 January 2020, p. 2 (https://fas.org/sgp/crs/misc/IF10971.pdf).

[125] General Agreement on Trade in Services, 15 April 1994, Marrakesh Agreement Establishing the World Trade Organization, Annex 1B, 1869 U.N.T.S. 183, 33 I.L.M. 1167 (1994)

[126] Agreement on Trade-Related Aspects of Intellectual Property Rights, 15 April 1994, Marrakesh Agreement Establishing the World Trade Organization, Annex 1C, 1869 U.N.T.S. 299, 33 I.L.M. 1197 (1994).

[127] See the disputes between Russia and Ukraine, *Russia – Traffic in Transit*, WT/DS512, and Saudi-Arabia and Qatar, *Saudi Arabia – IPR*, WT/DS567.

[128] For the purely economic motivation of US additional tariffs, see Weiß, 'EU Multilateral Trade Policy' (2020), p. 20.

vulnerability.[129] Such a broad conceptualization of the notion of national security to even include economic security[130] would drastically increase its scope, open a grand door for escaping WTO obligations, and, consequently, de-legalize and re-politicize trade regulation.[131]

Although Trump has left office, the effects of his unilateralism in trade policy still linger, not least as some protectionist measures introduced by Trump against China still apply (against the EU, only some have been suspended), and as Trump's unilateralism still continues to have an impact on the Biden administration[132] and ruling Democrats as a result of broad support in the US Congress for action against China.

2.2.2 China's Systemic Challenges and the Proliferation of Geoeconomics

The political and institutional challenges to multilateralism are – to no lesser degree – also connected with the rise of China and its increasingly complex, even worrying role in the WTO and in world politics. China's economic output and share of world trade have sharply increased since the 1980s, in particular following its WTO accession in 2001.[133] China's annual trade surplus has been stable at over US$400 billion for several years now. Its economic output currently accounts for almost one-fifth of global economic output; in e-commerce the share is as high as 40 per cent.[134] In contrast, the EU has to face a halving of its share in the world

129 J. Benton Heath, 'The New National Security Challenge to the Economic Order' (2020) 129 (4) *Yale Law Journal* 1020–1098 at 1048; Anthea Roberts, Henrique Choer Moraes, and Victor Ferguson, 'Toward a Geoeconomic Order in International Trade and Investment' (2019) 22(4) *JIEL* 655–676 at, 659 f, 664 f; Schmitz and Seidl, 'As Open as Possible' (2023) 61 (3) *JCMS* 834–852 at 842.

130 Against such economic conceptualization of security exceptions, see Wolfgang Weiß, 'Interpreting Essential Security Exceptions in WTO Law in View of Economic Security Interests', in Weiß and Furculita (eds.), *Global Politics and EU Trade Policy* (2020), pp. 261 ff.

131 Roberts, Choer Moraes, and Ferguson, 'Toward a Geoeconomic Order' (2019) 672.

132 A most recent example of transatlantic trade struggles are the EU complaints about a discriminatory Inflation Reduction Act initiated by the Biden Administration. See the EU-US Joint Statement of the Trade and Technology Council, 5 December 2022, https://ec.europa.eu/commission/presscorner/detail/en/statement_22_7516, and the related EU press release 'EU-US Trade and Technology Council addresses common challenges and responds to global crises', 5 December 2022 confirming EU's concerns, https://ec.europa.eu/commission/presscorner/detail/en/ip_22_7433.

133 Kristen Hopeland, *Clash of Powers: US-China Rivalry in Global Trade Governance* (Cambridge: Cambridge University Press, 2020), pp. 40 ff.

134 WTO, World Trade Report 2018, The Future of World Trade: How Digital Technologies Are Transforming Global Commerce, www.wto.org/english/res_e/publications_e/world_trade_report18_e.pdf, p. 51 f.

economy from approximately 30 per cent in 2008 to a maximum of 16 per cent in 2050.[135] This reflects the fundamentally transformed realities of global trade, which the EU already takes into account with its Global Europe Strategy (Section 2.1.2). A significant shift of trading power from West to East, from America and Europe to Asia, can been observed for many years now and is continuing, as Asia has also weathered the coronavirus crisis better economically than Europe. Asia's economic expansion is most visibly reflected in the rise of China, which poses a fundamental challenge to the function of traditional multilateral trade rules and is about to change the discussion on globalization.[136] China currently is not explicitly opposing or even questioning the basic principles of international trade law. But Chinese exceptionalism[137] reveals an attitude no less dangerous for ensuring a reciprocal level playing field for trade than openly querying the traditional liberal rules of non-discrimination and reciprocity. China purposefully expands its market position in high technology and key raw materials. The 'Made in China 2025' plan represents a strategic orientation of the Chinese economy to become a world leader in key technology areas in a few years' time.[138] It is complemented by the Belt and Road Initiative,[139] which advances cross-border infrastructure projects and networks in Asia, Africa, and Europe. China strategically uses the advantages of its peculiar economic system of state-led capitalism, which, compared to a market economy, relies to a considerable extent on state guidance, control, and support of

[135] Anu Bradford, *The Brussels Effect: How the European Union Rules the World* (New York: Oxford University Press, 2020), p. 267.

[136] Cf. Hopeland, *Clash of Powers* (2020), pp. 18 ff; Joseph E. Stiglitz, *Making Globalization Work* (New York: W. W. Norton & Company, 2006), p. 22 f.

[137] Which stands for great reform power, benevolent pacifism, and harmonious inclusion of others, according to Feng Zhang, 'Chinese Exceptionalism in the Intellectual World of China's Foreign Policy' in Rosemary Foot (ed.), *China across the Divide: The Domestic and Global in Politics and Society* (New York: Oxford University Press, 2013), p. 64. China's recent policies in Southeast Asia and the conflict over the 'South China Sea' and Taiwan cast considerable doubt on its adherence to these maxims.

[138] Max J. Zenglein and Anna Holzmann, 'Evolving Made in China 2025: China's Industrial Policy in the Quest for Global Tech Leadership' (2019) No. 8 Merics Papers on China; Anton Malkin, 'The Made in China Challenge to US Structural Power: Industrial Policy, Intellectual Property and Multinational Corporations' (2018) No. 183 CIGI Papers.

[139] Julien Chaisse and Mitsuo Matsushita, 'China's "Belt and Road" Initiative: Mapping the World Trade Normative and Strategic Implications' (2018) 52(1) *JWT* 163–185; Peter Frankopan, *The New Silk Roads: The Present and Future of the World* (London: Bloomsbury Publishing, 2018), pp. 62 ff.

Chinese companies[140] and combines this with refusing to open up its own market in a way and to an extent adequate to its economic power. This strategic orientation, together with its peculiar type of state-capitalist economic model (while the latter is the condition for the former), is the origin of China's severe economic and systemic threats to the present liberal trade order.[141] This threat was not adequately reflected in China's terms of accession to the WTO, although early warnings were raised. Contrary to expectations, China's accession to the WTO did not lead to its transformation into a market economy. China's foreign policy in recent years has been geared towards securing a respected position by its own efforts and on its own terms, so China is developing from a rule-taker to an influential rule-maker that wants to shape the rules of globalization, even though only selectively,[142] according to its own ideas, interests, and values.[143] While the inherent contradiction between China's rather statist-mercantilist economic system on the one hand and its dependence on open world markets to maintain national economic growth on the other hand induced China's commitment to a rules-based liberal trade law, without which China's rise would not have been possible, it also provokes a particular challenge for China's implementation of trade rules and global economic governance.[144] Concerns about the systemic issues raised by China's peculiar

[140] See Wu (2016) 'The "China, Inc." Challenge', 264 ff; Seung-Youn Oh, 'China's Race to the Top: Regional and Global Implications of China's Industrial Policy' (2021) 20(2) *WTRev* 169–185 at 170 ff.

[141] See also Babić, Dixon, and Liu, 'Geoeconomics in a Changing Global Order' (2022), p. 14; Gregory Shaffer, *Emerging Powers and the World Tading System: The Past and Future of International Economic Law* (Cambridge: Cambridge University Press, 2021), pp. 174 ff.

[142] Chris Alden and Daniel Large, 'On Becoming a Norms Maker: Chinese Foreign Policy, Norms Evolution and the Challenges of Security in Africa' (2015) 221 *The China Quarterly* 123–142; Heng Wang, 'Selective Reshaping: China's Paradigm Shift in International Economic Governance' (2020) 23(3) *JIEL* 583–606 at 588 ff; Aniruddha Rajput, 'The BRICS as "Rising Powers" and the Development of International Law', in Heike Krieger, Georg Nolte, and Andreas Zimmermann (eds.), *International Rule of Law: Rise or Decline?* (New York: Oxford University Press, 2019), pp. 111 ff, 115 ff.

[143] William A. Callahan, 'Sino-Speak: Chinese Exceptionalism and the Politics of History' (2012) 71(1) *The Journal of Asian Studies* 33–55 at 34; Hegde, Wouters, and Raina, 'The Demise of the Rules-Based International Economic Order?' (2020), p. 16. For the contours of a possible sino-centric trade order, see Gregory Shaffer and Henry Gao, 'A New Chinese Economic Order?' (2020) 23(3) *JIEL* 607–635 at 614 ff.

[144] See WTO, World Trade Report 2017, Trade Technology and Jobs, www.wto.org/english/res_e/booksp_e/world_trade_report17_e.pdf, p. 14; VanGrasstek, 'Trade and American Leadership' (2019) 321 ff; Bas Hooijmaaijers, 'China, the BRICS and the Limitations of Reshaping Global Economic Governance' (2021) 34 *The Pacific Review* 29–55 at 35 ff.

type of state capitalism are widespread among nations and shared by the EU,[145] and have been highlighted early on.[146]

China's conscious geostrategic and geoeconomic endeavours to systematically expand its world market position, and the US attempts to change global trade by geoeconomically driven trade measures described above, put other WTO members under pressure to respond in the same way and to behave geoeconomically themselves. Thus, they no longer are willing to leave their world market position solely to the assertiveness of their economies' efficiency and to the justice of reciprocal multilateral trade rules (which often are deemed helpless against China's practices). Instead they may turn to a geoeconomic trade policy. At least, as we can observe in the EU's trade policy turn, being faced with geoeconomics by others will be answered with providing for greater robustness in presenting and enforcing EU trade rights and protecting genuine EU interests and values.[147] Geoeconomics denotes a policy approach that actively employs and combines, on the one hand, industrial and economic policy tools that aim at the promotion of domestic technology and innovation and may lead to protectionism[148] and, on the other hand, instruments of rather traditional trade policy, and in particular trade defence tools such as anti-dumping, anti-subsidy, or foreign investment control, in order to strategically develop and strengthen a domestic economy's (i.e. its leading companies') market position on regional and world markets and to create sectors of influence, not least for security purposes.[149] Thus, economic tools and novel economic instruments are used for rather geostrategic ends of an increase of both

[145] See Trade Policy Review, COM(2021) 66 final, p. 9, Annex, p. 2; European Commission, 2021 Strategic Foresight, COM(2021) 750, p. 18 f. European Parliament resolution of 16 September 2021 on a new EU-China strategy (2021/2037(INI)), OJ EU 2022 C No. 117/40, paras. 22 ff.

[146] Gary C. Hufbauer, 'China as an Economic Actor on the World Stage: An Overview', in Frederick M. Abbott (ed.), *China in the World Trading System: Defining the Principles of Engagement* (The Hague: Kluwer Law International, 1998), p. 50; Deborah Cass, Brett Williams, and George Barker (eds.), *China and the World Trading System: Entering the New Millennium* (Cambridge: Cambridge University Press, 2003), p. 5.

[147] See also Schmitz and Seidl, 'As Open as Possible' (2023) 844 f.

[148] WTO, World Trade Report 2020, Government Policies to Promote Innovation in the Digital Age, www.wto.org/english/res_e/booksp_e/wtr20_e/wtr20_e.pdf.

[149] See Roberts, Choer Moraes, and Ferguson, 'Toward a Geoeconomic Order' (2019) *JIEL* 655; Clara Weinhardt, Karsten Mau, and Jens Hillebrand Pohl, 'The EU as a Geoeconomic Actor? A Review of Recent European Trade and Investment Policies', in Babić, Dixon, and Liu (eds.), *The Political Economy of Geoeconomics* (2022), p. 107 f; Henrique Choer Moraes, 'The Turn to Managed Interdependence: A Glimpse into the Future of International Economic Law?' *EJIL:Talk!*, 14 August 2018, www.ejiltalk.org/the-turn-to-managed-interdependence-a-glimpse-into-the-future-of-international-economic-law/.

political and economic power.[150] This new strategy at least partly replaces the development of trade relations along the lines of economic efficiency and trust in market forces (as effectuated by the liberal trade order under WTO rules) with actively designing trade relations according to political prioritization and state intrusion in trade relations, not least by state capitalism and economic statecraft.[151] In consequence, the geoeconomic policy approach of deliberately shaping one's own world market position, not least in order to pursue geopolitical aims by other means, affects the very foundations of the international trade order because it is at odds with a basically reciprocal rules-based trade order where private individuals decide autonomously on their trade relations within a general, non-discriminatory legal framework. This may, in the long run, lead to a breakup of a globally coherent multilateral trade order into sectors of influence and polarization, where trade superpowers export their preferences, standards, and approaches.[152] Other WTO members then would come under pressure to choose sides. An explicit offspring of such approach are the US FTAs concluded under the Trump administration that bar their partners from entering into agreements with non-market economies.[153]

A solution to the specific, systemic challenges posed by China's state-centred economic model to WTO rules requires a new basic consensus on the role and extent of state influence on economic processes and on the application of existing rules to this economic model or their amendment,[154] which will be difficult to reach.[155] The legal and political problems of using, or even deliberately abusing, multilateral trade rules to enforce geostrategic goals to counter the systemic problems posed by China can be studied by analysing the US trade policy of the Trump administration, outlined earlier in the chapter.

[150] Choer Moraes and Wigell, 'Balancing Dependence' (2022), p. 34.

[151] On their role, see Geoffrey Gertz and Miles Evers, 'Geoeconomic Competition: Will State Capitalism Win?' (2020) 43(2) *The Washington Quarterly* 117–136 at 119 ff.

[152] Roberts, Choer Moraes, and Ferguson, 'Toward a Geoeconomic Order' (2019) 673 f; Babić, Dixon, and Liu, 'Geoeconomics in a Changing Global Order' (2022) 9 ff.

[153] Hegde, Wouters, and Raina, 'The Demise of the Rules-Based International Economic Order?' (2020), p. 20.

[154] For proposals, see Marco Bronckers, 'Trade Conflicts: Whither the WTO?' (2020) *LIEI* 221–244 at 236 ff; Mark Wu, 'The "China, Inc." Challenge to Global Trade Governance' (2016) 57(2) *Harvard International Law Journal* 261–324 at 295 ff, 308 ff.

[155] Roberts, Choer Moraes, and Ferguson, 'Toward a Geoeconomic Order' (2019) 670 f. For a critical assessment of allegedly more advanced rules on state-owned enterprises in most recent FTAs, see Weihuan Zhou, 'Rethinking the (CP)TPP as a Model for Regulation of Chinese State-Owned Enterprises' (2021) 24(3) *JIEL* 572–590 at 578 ff.

2.2.3 Trade Issues of Digitization of the Economy, Climate Change, and Resilience after COVID-19

The crisis of the WTO and the proliferation of economic nationalism and geoeconomic policy approaches are also linked to simultaneous economic, technological, and regulatory challenges to trade relations. The technological developments accompanying globalization and the resulting economic growth have raised the awareness for a need for international trade regulation to address regulatory challenges that emerge from new or revalued topics, such as the urgent importance of combatting climate change and addressing sustainability and global public health issues. The economic interdependences brought about by the proliferation of intertwined, diversified global supply chains – the second wave of globalization[156] – and underlying technological shifts, in particular the digitalization of the economy[157] and the associated trend towards servicification of trade,[158] which makes trade in services more salient,[159] add to the demand for new rules that could clearly regulate their trade-related issues. As interdependence is growing, trade becomes more vulnerable to shocks, as happened during the COVID-19 pandemic, which induced deliberations among WTO members about safeguards, diversification, and greater resilience. In the COVID-19 crisis, WTO members, including the EU, have introduced export controls and other protectionist measures.[160] Thus, besides bringing to the fore public health issues of international trade, the COVID-19 pandemic made the

[156] Richard Baldwin, 'Global Supply Chains: Why They Emerged, Why They Matter, and Where They Are Going' (2012) No. 9103 CEPR Discussion Paper. On the impact of global value chains on trade policy, see Andreas Dür, Jappe Eckhardt, and Arlo Poletti, 'Global Value Chains, the Anti-Globalization Backlash, and EU Trade Policy: A Research Agenda' (2020) 27 *Journal of European Public Policy* 944–956 at 947 ff.

[157] Christian Johannes Bluth, *Europe's Trade Strategy for the Age of Geoeconomic Globalization* (CEPR Press, 2020), pp. 64 ff.

[158] WTO, World Trade Report 2019, The Future of Services Trade, www.wto.org/english/res_e/booksp_e/00_wtr19_e.pdf, p. 67 f; Rainer Lanz and Andreas Maurer, 'Services and Global Value Chains: Some Evidence on Servicification of Manufacturing and Services Networks' (2015) No. ERSD-2015-03 WTO Staff Working Paper, www.wto.org/english/res_e/reser_e/ersd201503_e.pdf.

[159] WTO, World Trade Report 2019, pp. 14 ff.

[160] WTO, Report on G20 Trade Measures, June 2020, www.wto.org/english/news_e/news20_e/report_trdev_jun20_e.pdf, pp. 32 ff; WTO, Report on G20 Trade Measures, November 2020, www.wto.org/english/news_e/news20_e/report_trdev_nov20_e.pdf, pp. 31 ff; Louise Curran, Jappe Eckhardt, and Jaemin Lee, 'The Trade Policy Response to COVID-19 and Its Implications for International Business' (2021) 17(2) *Critical Perspectives on International Business* 252–320.

EU clearly realize how much the European economy depends on reliable trade relations and functioning global value chains. Consequently, EU resilience and security of supply became an issue for its open strategic autonomy in trade as well,[161] and with the war in Ukraine, this has even become more important.

With the climate-neutral, sustainable reorientation of at least some nations' trade policies, the ensuing need for room for manoeuvre for health, environmental, or data protection under the present legal framework of international trade pose fundamental legal and regulatory questions to national and international policy implementation, as does safeguarding human rights and social standards in value chains expected by consumers. In the absence of globally harmonized rules on these aspects, the realignment of national policies to address these issues domestically (in a kind of 'domesticization of international trade law')[162] – as, for example, the EU did with regard to safeguarding its data protection standard transnationally – will unavoidably affect international trade and may inevitably lead to trade restrictions. One may recall, for example, border adjustment measures for internal regulatory instruments, as being prepared by the EU with its carbon border adjustment mechanism, or the adoption of domestically defined data protection conditions for transnational digital trade.

Finding solutions to balance the regulatory objectives associated with these new issues and trade interests based on existing or new rules is becoming increasingly urgent. Nevertheless, the WTO was not in a position to present answers. It is not to be expected that globally uniform solutions for balancing climate, environment, or data protection and trade interests can be agreed upon anytime soon; this may succeed at best in the framework of bilateral or plurilateral trade agreements of like-minded states, as one can observe that bilateral trade agreements increasingly become linked to such non-commercial policy objectives.[163] Even

[161] See Trade Policy Review, COM(2021) 66 final, pp. 4 ff, 17; European Commission, Europe's Moment, COM(2020) 456 final, p. 12 f; Strategic European Commission, 2020 Strategic Foresight Report, COM(2020) 493 final, p. 14; Jacobs, et al., 'The Hegemonic Politics of "Strategic Autonomy" and "Resilience"' (2023) 13 f.

[162] Hegde, Wouters, and Raina, 'The Demise of the Rules-Based International Economic Order? (2020), p. 20 f.

[163] For EU trade agreements, see San Bilal and Bernard Hoekman, 'Introduction: EU Trade and External Policy in Troubled Waters', in San Bilal and Bernard Hoekman (eds.), *Perspectives on the Soft Power of EU Trade Policy* (CEPR Press, 2019), p. 9 f; Ingo Borchert, et al., 'The Pursuit of Non-Trade Policy Objectives in EU Trade Policy' (2020) EUI Working Papers, RSCAS 2020/26.

though the resulting challenges do not amount to a per se contestation of multilateralism but relate to the existing shape of the rules and their lack of clear guidance for the above-mentioned issues, the demands for new or amended trade rules and the lack of success in finding solutions to these challenges within the multilateralism in the WTO add to its crisis nevertheless. Against this background, it is urgently necessary that the EU, in creating autonomous instruments to expand its autonomy, remain within the confines established by the existing international rules, in line with its international and constitutional commitments.

2.3 Conclusion

The analysis of the development of EU trade policy could demonstrate that its new trade policy is embedded within an advancement from which the 'open, assertive and sustainable trade' policy does *not fundamentally* deviate. There is no deep ideational change[164] but a 'normative continuity',[165] and the EU tries its best to reconcile its new direction with its more traditional liberal and normative stance in trade politics (reflected in trade policy objectives set out in Article 206 TFEU) by presenting the new direction as a mere defensive response to third countries' behaviour and new global multipolar realities.[166] Still, the new trade policy sets markedly new directions and makes way for more geopolitics and geoeconomics in EU trade policy,[167] which might easily be seen by its trade partners as an aggressive turn of the EU towards considerable power politics in trade. One can agree with previous analyses that the new trade policy has 'not been a true paradigm shift'[168] and combines 'both continuity and change'.[169] However, it goes beyond a mere

[164] Patricia Garcia-Duran and Leif Johan Eliasson, 'Was the EU's 2021 Trade Strategy a Critical Juncture?' (2022) *EFARev* 563–584 at 574 ff, 583.

[165] Johan Eliasson and Patricia Garcia-Duran, 'New Is Old? The EU's Open, Sustainable and Assertive Trade Policy' (2023) 14(Suppl 3) *Global Policy* 9–18 at 16.

[166] Sjorre Couvreur, et al., 'The Good Geopolitical Trade Actor? The European Union's Discursive Justification of the Anti-Coercion Instrument' (2022) *Journal of Political Science* Special Issue 133–147 at 141.

[167] Schmitz and Seidl, 'As Open as Possible' (2023) 841; Tobias Gehrke, 'EU Open Strategic Autonomy and the Trappings of Geoeconomics' (2022) *EFARev* Special Issue 61–78 at 68 ff.

[168] Sophie Meunier, 'The End of Naivety: Assertiveness and New Instruments in EU Trade and Investment Policy' (2022) *EUI Global Governance Programme*, Policy Brief Issue 2022/55, p. 7; Garcia-Duran and Eliasson, 'Was the EU's 2021 Trade Strategy a Critical Juncture?' (2022) 566.

[169] Eliasson and Garcia-Duran, 'New Is Old?' (2023) 14. In their analysis, change is shown in increased realism and the end of dominance of a neoliberal trade approach in the new

continuation of traditional objectives in trade policy by new means. The new turn brings about a strong focus on assertiveness and autonomous capacities for implementation of trade rights and EU interests, namely enforcing reciprocity, increasing independence, and allowing more leeway in autonomous, novel ways of reaction to allegedly or truly unfair or illegal behaviour of trade partners. Not only can competition distortions now be more effectively addressed, but the idea of which behaviour by trade partners amounts to unfairness in trade relations has been significantly expanded by new concepts introduced, for example, by the ACI or the Foreign Subsidies Regulation. Trade policy is framed within a broader external policy context of and ongoing discussion about (more) EU 'sovereignty' to behave strategically and autonomously. Hence, the former openness of EU markets is now replaced by a sort of 'qualified openness'.[170]

Still, multilateralism and the WTO as its institutionalization in international trade relations has an important status in EU trade policy, even though its salience has diminished. The negotiation and conclusion of FTAs are continued. Yet, robust implementation and enforcement of trade rules and international rights of the EU form freshly enhanced directions of the EU's new trade policy which pertains in a comprehensive way to all levels of trade policy: multilateral, bilateral, and autonomous/unilateral. Robust assertiveness in trade policy goes beyond merely taking account of the contemporary context of an abundance of contests for the WTO and trade relations in general but also shifts the resulting challenges and consequences for the EU into the centre of trade policy. The EU's intention to respond to the challenges by enabling the Union to take corresponding measures and actions at all levels of trade policy and thus defend its interests and rights assertively stands at the centre of the new trade policy review and its accompanying documents, declarations, and resolutions of the EU institutions, and forms the core of its implementation by new instruments and legislation. The new trade policy addresses the challenges to international trade posed by the crisis of multilateralism, by the need for new rules due to technological and economic progress, and by the unilateral practices and geoeconomics approaches of the United States and China. The new trade policy, besides aiming at a reform of the functioning of the WTO, its decision-making

trade policy. For the neoliberal trade paradigm's loss of hegemony, see also Schmitz and Seidl, 'As Open as Possible' (2023) 849.

170 Schmitz and Seidl, 'As Open as Possible' (2023) 835 f, 845 f.

and dispute settlement mechanism, strives for new provisions on digital trade, services, and investment and broaches the issue of imbalances and lack of reciprocity between WTO members with regard to their markets' openness, in particular with a view to China.[171] The EU institutions share the conviction about the need for a multilateral approach and international cooperation for sustainable development and WTO reform.[172] They also share the intention to address trade, investment, or other actions by third countries that intend to coerce the EU or one of its Member States to adopt or not to adopt particular measures or policies.[173] Most significant for the new trade policy is the turn towards greater implementation and enforcement of EU's trade rights and interests and towards safeguarding a level playing field in terms of fair competition by establishing new legislative tools for unilateral measures in order to remedy the lack of suitable multilateral rules to counter the challenges. The new instruments will fill the existing or perceived regulatory gaps in this respect. For this purpose, the new trade policy makes available tools to enforce EU values and market access rights in order to create leeway for effective autonomous representation of own interests and establish broader capacities of the EU in this regard. The new trade policy includes current political EU priorities of climate change and digitization, as well as the concern about EU's economic resilience and dependence, which have found their way into EU trade policy most recently more than ever before as they became defining objectives at its core (see Section 2.1.3). The new tools will provide for mechanisms to unilaterally enforce the EU trade rights enshrined in WTO law or in FTAs even if pertinent dispute settlement mechanisms are blocked or unavailable. They will allow responding to geoeconomic behaviour by third states, in particular weaponization of trade relations, and establish instruments which enable redressive measures in case of competition distortion by subsidies granted by third states or an imbalance in market access in public procurement, in order to ensure a level playing field for EU companies in their competition with third-country companies in the internal

[171] Trade Policy Review, COM(2021) 66 final, Annex, 8, 10, 13.

[172] See Joint Declaration of the European Parliament, the Council and the Commission, OJ EU 2021 No. C 49/02. See also the Joint Statement of the European Parliament, the Council and the Commission on the occasion of the adoption of the Foreign Subsidies Regulation, OJ EU 2022 No. C 491/6.

[173] See Joint Declaration of the Commission, the Council and the European Parliament on an instrument to deter and counteract coercive actions by third countries, OJ EU 2021 No. C 49/1.

market. Ensuring a level playing field is also an important effect of a CBAM that aims at avoiding the effectiveness of EU climate policies being undermined by carbon leakage.[174] As this instrument requires imported goods to declare carbon certificates, it takes care for a balancing mechanism to level out cost disadvantages of the EU industry in the interest of competitive equality. Some of these instruments, in particular the Anti-Coercion and the Foreign Subsidies instrument, give the EU the capacity to behave geopolitically and geoeconomically itself, as the available measures might be used against certain trade partners in pursuit of specific (economic but also non-economic) objectives tailored to imbalances in their trade relations, or to defend or even impose EU regulatory preferences and policy choices. The use of competition and industrial policy also for trade policy objectives[175] is part of this.

[174] Trade Policy Review, COM(2021) 66 final, p. 13.

[175] See Section 2.1.3.

3 External and Internal Constraints for the EU's Open Strategic Autonomy in Trade Policy

3.1 Introduction

As shown in Chapter 2, while the EU's renewed trade policy is based on the idea of greater EU autonomy/sovereignty in its response to unfair practices of trade partners, in particular with a view that the EU should be able to pursue and enforce its own interests assertively and unilaterally, the EU's commitment to a multilateral rules-based system and international law still is part of its raison d'être. The concerns to that extent relate to whether the EU's credibility may be seen to be at risk with the new trade policy orientation. This chapter explores the legal causes and consequences of the multilateralist stance of the EU and compares them with the consequences of an autonomous approach in the enforcement of trade rights. It will be analyzed how a principled pragmatist like the EU faces tensions between its commitment to international rule of law and multilateralism on the one hand and the search for leeway for autonomously and unilaterally enforcing trade rules and assertively representing EU interests, strengthened by its striving for EU autonomy in its external relations as well, on the other hand. The analysis will show that for reasons of political credibility, but also for legal constitutional obligations, this tension can only be solved by a clear commitment to adhering to international law, the departure from which must be limited to truly exceptional situations. It will be argued that the EU's new approach to strengthen enforcement and more assertively represent EU interests can only operate within the limits set by international law and EU constitutional law. Unavoidably, this chapter has to re-engage with the long-lasting debate about the EU legal order's relationship to international law, an issue which has been the subject of various twists and turns, including in the case law of the Court of Justice of the European Union

(CJEU). While the Court in the beginning held that the EU (then EEC) legal order was a 'new order of international law',[1] decades later, in the *Kadi* case, the EU treaties were held to have created a 'municipal order' forming its 'basic constitutional charter' where the effect of international law is determined by conditions set by EU law,[2] and the General Court summarized the Court's *Kadi I* decision with the statement that EU law, at least with regard to the 'the principles that form part of the very foundations of the Community legal order', was 'a wholly autonomous legal order, not subject to the higher rules of international law'.[3] The linkage of Union law to international law appears to have been substantially consolidated and expanded most recently with the new provisions of primary law under the Lisbon Treaty,[4] most notably Articles 3 and 21 Treaty on European Union (TEU),[5] which also gave rise to new hopes in scholarly literature that respect for international law would now be seen as firmly established in the EU.[6] Due to the specific research questions addressed in this book, the multifaceted issue of the relationship between international and European law[7] cannot be developed here in its full breadth. The focus of the following analysis is on the constitutional justification of an obligation of the EU to respect international law, its internal relevance for the definition and legal implementation of EU policies and the assessment of EU legal acts, and its limits claimed from the autonomy of the Union legal order, as these are the core issues relevant to exploring the new trade policy's implementation acts in view of the EU's international obligations and its commitment to multilateralism. Hence, this chapter will demonstrate that there are – besides the obligation to abide by international law resulting from the EU's

[1] CJEU, Case 26/62, *Van Gend en Loos v Administratie der Belastingen* [1963] EU:C:1963:1.

[2] Advocate General (AG) Poiares Maduro in his Opinion, Case C-402/05 P and C-415/05 P, *Kadi and Al Barakaat International Foundation v Council and Commission* [2008] ECR I-06351, ECLI:EU:C:2008:11, paras. 21, 23.

[3] General Court (GC), Case T-85/09, *Kadi v Commission* [2010] ECR II-05177, EU:T:2010:418, para. 11.

[4] Treaty of Lisbon Amending the Treaty on European Union and the Treaty Establishing the European Community, OJ EU 2007 No. C 306/1, 13 December 2007.

[5] Consolidated version of the Treaty on European Union, OJ EU 2012 No. C 326/13, 26 October 2010.

[6] See, e.g. Mario Mendez, *The Legal Effects of EU Agreements: Maximalist Treaty Enforcement and Judicial Avoidance Techniques* (Oxford: Oxford University Press, 2013), p. 321.

[7] There are different dimensions to this large topic, such as exploring the general relationship in view of monism or dualism, the role of the EU in international lawmaking, reception and application of international law by the CJEU, and its role in assessing the legality of EU legal acts internally. The present chapter will concentrate on the latter issue.

international legal personality – also fundamental constitutional obligations under which the EU is bound to respect international law rules in defining and implementing its trade policy. The chapter will furthermore explore the inherent constraints with regard to the significance of international law within the EU legal order internally, as developed by the not wholly consistent CJEU case law over decades. It is in particular the relevance of the autonomy of the EU legal order in the most recent jurisprudential development which might be seen as a barrier to EU international legal obligations becoming relevant for its external actions. It will be shown, however, that the constitutionally grounded EU autonomy does not mitigate the relevance of the EU's international obligations in determining its policies, in particular in trade policy, and has no bearing on the EU's new trade policy assertiveness turn. Avoiding conflict with the EU's international legal obligations remains an important legal commitment for EU institutions in defining and implementing their trade policy and adopting trade legislation. This understanding confirms the need to determine the leeway international rules allow the EU to confer new robustness to its trade policy, even in the light of the current crisis at the WTO.

3.2 The Tensions of a Principled Pragmatist: Multilateralism versus Autonomy

3.2.1 The Commitment to Multilateralism and International Law Inscribed in the EU's DNA

The Introduction (see Section 1.1) briefly alluded to the possible negative consequences of the new trade policy approach. One of these caveats relates to the EU's credibility in its engagement for international cooperation and multilateralism, and its commitment to respect international law. The new approach is capable of undermining the quite widespread perception of the EU being the 'last truly committed defender of multilateralism', which is how many nations still see the EU.[8] The EU portrays itself as an international actor respecting its international legal commitments. The new approach, however, implies a shift towards increased self-centred autonomy, even unilateralism, which may not sufficiently

[8] David O'Sullivan, 'The European Union and the Multilateral System: Lessons from Past Experience and Future Challenges', EPRS Briefing PE 689.365, March 2021, p. 5, www.europarl.europa.eu/RegData/etudes/BRIE/2021/689365/EPRS_BRI(2021)689365_EN.pdf.

consider its broader consequences for external (trade) relations and the international community's dependence on cooperative approaches. The new legislative tools add to the arsenal of trade defence weapons and countermeasures the Commission has at its disposal, expanding the potential for threat available to the EU and its ability to behave geopolitically and geoeconomically. Compatibility of the new tools with international legal obligations, in particular flowing from WTO rules, cannot be taken for granted, as at least some of the instruments enter novel ground and encounter not always clear-cut stipulations from WTO law. The Commission is aware of the complexities inherent in formulating autonomous trade legislation compatible with international law. Regarding the project of an anti-coercion instrument, for example, the Commission promised to table 'a legislative proposal providing for a mechanism allowing to dissuade or offset such actions in a manner consistent with international law'.[9] Accordingly, the Commission's proposal contains Article 1 which recalls, 'consistent with the EU Treaties, that any action taken under the Regulation must comply with international law'.[10] The EU co-legislators in turn promised 'to consider the proposal in a timely manner, taking into account the Union's obligations under public international law and WTO law as well as relevant developments in international trade'.[11] Similarly, after the recent amendment of the Trade Enforcement Regulation 654/2014[12] was adopted by the EU co-legislators, the Commission stated that when 'adopting implementing acts pursuant to Article 3(aa) of the Regulation, the Commission will act in accordance with the requirements of the international law'.[13] Already

[9] See Joint Declaration of the Commission, the Council and the European Parliament on an instrument to deter and counteract coercive actions by third countries, OJ EU 2021 No. C 49/1, 12 February 2021.

[10] See the Proposal for a Regulation on the protection of the Union and its Member States from economic coercion by third countries, COM(2021) 775 final, and now recitals 8 and 12, and Article 1 (3), (4) Regulation (EU) 2023/2675 of the European Parliament and of the Council of 22 November 2023 on the protection of the Union and its Member States from economic coercion by third countries, OJ EU 2023 No. L 2675, 7 December 2023.

[11] See Joint Declaration of the Commission, the Council and the European Parliament on an instrument to deter and counteract coercive actions by third countries, OJ EU 2021 No. C 49/1.

[12] See Regulation 2021/167 amending Regulation 654/2014 concerning the exercise of the Union's rights for the application and enforcement of international trade rules, OJ EU 2021 No. L 49/1, 12 February 2021.

[13] Commission declaration on compliance with international law, OJ EU 2021 No. C 49/3, 12 December 2021.

in its proposal to the amendment of the Trade Enforcement Regulation, the Commission paid attention to compliance of its new rules with international law,[14] albeit in a contestable manner (for more detail, see Chapter 5). Even though the Commission in these and other statements and proposals confirms its willingness to obey to international law, maintaining compatibility with WTO and general international law both in drafting the new legislation and in their implementation raises complex issues (which will be explored in more detail in Parts II and III). The relevance of international law and of multilateralism for EU trade policy and its consequences for its implementation hence are an issue that shall be addressed here as a starting point for a more detailed analysis of the new instruments in the subsequent chapters.

As shown in Chapter 2, multilateralism for a long time has been the centrepiece of EU trade policy; the EU ultimately became a founding member of the WTO. This strong commitment to the WTO's significance is still relevant under the new trade policy approach. The Commission corroborates its dedication to strengthening the WTO as a forum for developing, implementing, and enforcing trade rules.[15] In its new trade strategy, the EU confirms its intention to protect EU interests and values 'in full compliance with its international commitments'.[16] The commitment to multilateralism and international law not only has a long tradition in the EU in political terms, reaffirmed in its Global Strategy. Multilateralism also has a deep institutional and constitutional entrenchment in the EU. As previously mentioned, '[m]ultilateralism is in Europe's DNA'.[17] The constitutional basis for this, which has been strengthened by the Lisbon Treaty, can be found in Article 3 (5), Article 21 (1) ('promote multilateral solutions to common problems'), (2) (b), (c), (h) TEU ('promote an international system based

[14] See Proposal for Amending Regulation 654/2014 concerning the Exercise of the Union's rights for the Application and Enforcement of International Trade Rules, COM(2019) 623 final, p. 4.

[15] See the Consultation Note, A renewed trade policy for a stronger Europe, 16 June 2020, www.astrid-online.it/static/upload/comm/0000/commue_trade-policy-review_consultation-note.pdf and the Annex to the Trade Policy Review: An Open, Sustainable and Assertive Trade Policy, COM(2021) 66 final.

[16] See Trade Policy Review: An Open, Sustainable and Assertive Trade Policy, COM(2021), p. 9.

[17] Ursula von der Leyen, 'A Union that wants to achieve more – my agenda for Europe', Political Guidelines for the Next European Commission 2019–2024, p. 17, https://commission.europa.eu/system/files/2020-04/political-guidelines-next-commission_en_0.pdf.

on stronger multilateral cooperation'), and Articles 205 and 207 (1) TFEU[18]. These provisions not only place EU trade policy fully in the context of the broader, more general political objectives of the EU, as trade policy has to be conducted in the context of the EU general external policy principles and objectives (Article 21 (1), (3) TEU; Articles 205, 207 (1) TFEU) and the EU's values (Articles 3 (5), 21 (2) TEU).[19] They also contain a clear commitment and EU primary law obligation to strictly observe international law and respect the principles of the UN Charter[20] and of international law (Articles 3 (5), 21 (1), (2) b) TEU), and to prevent conflicts (Article 21 (2) c) TEU). Article 21 (2) e) TEU even unfolds a specific policy aim for trade policy as it encourages the integration of all countries into the world economy, including through the progressive abolition of restrictions on international trade. As a consequence, a protectionist trade policy which does not respect WTO obligations would not only conflict with international law as flowing from WTO obligations but also breach Articles 205, 206 TFEU and Article 21 TEU. Thus, the principles and objectives of Article 21 TEU create a constitutional obligation for the EU to direct its trade policy accordingly.

The latter statement implies that said Articles – even though they at first glance only enshrine mere objectives of the EU for its external relations (which in itself already is quite unique compared to constitutions of states)[21] – are nevertheless legally binding provisions and give rise to an obligation for the EU institutions which they have to observe in their acts and policies. Thus, the premise is that these principles and objectives are neither purely political assertions or agendas[22] nor mere

[18] Consolidated version of the Treaty on the Functioning of the European Union (TFEU), OJ EU 2012 No. C 326/47, 26 October 2012.

[19] Angelos Dimopoulos, 'The Effects of the Lisbon Treaty on the Principles and Objectives of the Common Commercial Policy' (2010) *EFARev* 153–170; Marise Cremona, 'A Quiet Revolution: The Changing Nature of the EU's Common Commercial Policy', in Marc Bungenberg, et al. (eds.), *European Yearbook of International Economic Law 2017* (Cham: Springer, 2017), p. 15 f.

[20] United Nations, Charter of the United Nations, 24 October 1945, 1 UNTS XVI.

[21] The seminal treatise by Curtis A. Bradley, *The Oxford Handbook of Comparative Foreign Relations Law* (Oxford: Oxford University Press, 2019) does not even address the issue of foreign policy objectives, which confirms that this is not an issue in this field.

[22] Markus Krajewski, 'The Reform of the Common Commercial Policy', in Andrea Biondi and Piet Eeckhout (eds.), *EU Law after Lisbon* (Oxford: Oxford University Press, 2012), 292–311 at 295; Till Müller-Ibold, 'Die Externe Dimension der EU-Politiken', in Armin Hatje and Peter-Christian Müller-Graff (eds.), XXVIII. FIDE-Kongress 2018, Estoril: 'Die Deutschen Landesberichte', 2019/1 *Europarecht* Supplement 79–180 at 150.

declarations of intent.[23] Indeed the wording and context of provisions laying down principles and objectives such as Article 3 (5) TEU clearly speak in favour of granting them the same legal relevance, and particularly the binding force, as other EU primary law provisions. Additionally, Article 21 (3) TEU explicitly provides that the EU has to 'respect the principles and pursue the objectives set out in paragraphs 1 and 2 in the development and implementation' of its external policies and explicitly includes Part Five of the TFEU, which comprises trade policy. The terminological shift from 'values' to 'principles' is without relevance in that regard; it may be explained by the observation that values are related to defining the EU's identity, whereas the use of the term 'principles' denotes the shift of normative focus towards their relevance for EU policy determination and adoption of EU actions.[24] As mentioned, the relevance of these objectives for trade policy determination and implementation is expressly confirmed in Article 207 (1) sentence 2 TFEU, from which the Court derived the duty 'to integrate those objectives and principles into the conduct of its common commercial policy'.[25] Thus, the provisions of Articles 3 (5) and 21 TEU provide for trade policy direction and orientation, and they do so as legally binding obligations for the EU institutions.[26] Even a long time before the Lisbon Treaty, the Court had opined that EU Treaty objectives are implemented through the policies and actions of the EU.[27] Articles 3 (5) and 21 TEU lay down constitutional obligations to respect these objectives, and not mere policy choices.[28]

[23] Which was the Commission's position in CJEU, Opinion 1/78, *International Agreement on Natural Rubber* [1979] ECR 2871, 2884: 'it constitutes only a declaration of intent which cannot deprive the Community of the power to take commercial policy measures for other reasons related to the defence of its interests'.

[24] Marise Cremona, 'Values in Foreign Policy', in Malcolm Evans and Panos Koutrakos (eds.), *Beyond the Established Legal Orders* (Oxford: Hart Publishing, 2011), pp. 277, 280 f.

[25] CJEU, Opinion 2/15, *Free Trade Agreement between the European Union and the Republic of Singapore*, ECLI:EU:C:2017:376, 16 May 2017, para. 143.

[26] See also Eva Kassoti and Ramses A. Wessel, 'The Normative Effect of Article 3 (5) TEU: Observance and Development of International Law by the European Union', in Paula García Andrade (ed.) *Interacciones entre el Derecho de la Union Europea y el Derecho Internacional Público* (Valencia: Tirant lo Blanch, 2023), pp. 19–46; Joris Larik, *Foreign Policy Objectives in European Constitution* (Oxford: Oxford University Press, 2016), pp. 64 ff, 154 ff; Karl-Peter Sommermann, in Hermann-Josef Blanke and Stelio Mangiameli (eds.), *The Treaty on European Union: A Commentary* (Berlin: Springer, 2013), Art. 3, paras. 3–6.

[27] CJEU, Case C-149/96, *Portugal v Council* [1999] ECR I-08395, EU:C:1999:574, para. 86. Admittedly, the focus of said statement may rather be the political discretion of the EU institutions in implementing the objectives; see Section 3.2.2.2.

[28] See Pieter van Elsuwege, 'The Nexus between Common Commercial Policy and Human Rights', in Guillaume van der Loo and Michael Hahn (eds.) *The Law and Practice of Common*

Accordingly, the CJEU clearly held that compliance of the EU with the objectives set out in Article 21 TEU is required of all actions of the EU.[29]

Confirming the EU objectives' binding force and legal obligation, however, does not automatically clarify the resulting normative effect flowing from this obligation.[30] For, observing a legal stipulation can mean slightly different things: The normativity of a provision may require full compliance with it, but can also mean an obligation of mere consideration of it as an objective which has to be pursued in the determination of a policy that has to serve also other interests. The precise normative content differs according to the wording used, the vagueness of the terminology employed, and again also depending on the context. Regarding the wording, the objectives do not provide for means and ways in which they should be implemented. In that regard, the EU institutions have 'wide powers of assessment' in determining policies and their instruments, all the more as the formulations used in describing the objectives and principles of the EU may very often grant leeway when the objectives are formulated in generally quite vague terms with considerable openness.[31] In this respect, however, one must distinguish between rather abstract objectives of fostering or respecting democracy or the rule of law, as their substantive contents can be conceptualized quite differently, giving a considerable room for manoevre to the political process, and the objective of respecting international law that may require strict observance of international legal rules. This is because the concept of international law usually is very concrete, as international law consists of a set of international rules and norms prescribing specific obligations for the international legal subject. Therefore, respecting international law is not something that comes along with great discretion for

Commercial Policy: The First Ten Years after the Treaty of Lisbon (Leiden: Brill Nijhoff, 2021), p. 417; Eva Kassoti and Ramses A. Wessel, 'The Conclusion of Trade Agreements and the EU's Duty to Respect Human Rights Abroad', in Nuno Cunha Rodrigues (ed.) *Exterritoriality of EU Economic Law: The Application of EU Economic Law outside the Territory of the EU* (Cham: Springer, 2021), p. 244.

29 CJEU, C-263/14, *EU Tanzania Agreement on Transfer of Pirates* [2016] ECLI:EU:C:2106:435, para. 47.

30 Enzo Cannizarro, 'The Value of the EU International Values', in Wybe Douma, et al. (eds.). *The Evolving Nature of EU External Relations Law* (Berlin: T.M.C. Asser Press, Springer, 2021), p. 4; Kassoti and Wessel, 'The Normative Effect of Article 3 (5) TEU' (2023), sub. III.

31 See CJEU, Case C 5/73, *Balkan-Import-Export GmbH* [1973] ECR 01091, EU:C:1973:109, para. 27; Alessandra Asteriti, 'Article 21 TEU and the EU's Common Commercial Policy: A Test of Coherence', in Marc Bungenberg, et al. (eds.), *European Yearbook of International Economic Law 2017* (Cham: Springer, 2017), p. 130.

the political process, but international norms generally are rather clear-cut provisions that enshrine specific limits to the political process, in particular in case of international treaties, and thus do not come with considerable leeway for domestic state actors. One can observe, however, that in the wording of Articles 3 (5) and 21 TEU, the formulations used to describe the legal obligations with regard to international law offer some variation: While Article 21 (1) requires '*respect* for the principles of the United Nations Charter and international law', Article 21 (2) b) TEU merely stipulates to '*consolidate and support* [...] principles of international law', and Article 3 (5) TEU demands to 'contribute to peace, security, [...] free and fair trade [...], as well as to the *strict observance* and the *development* of international law, including *respect* for the principles of the United Nations Charter' (emphases added). These articles reflect a slight difference with regard to the required approach to international law, as Article 3 (5) postulates 'strict observance [...] of international law', whereas Article 21 (1) demands 'respect' for international law[32] and Article 21 (2) b) requires 'support' of the principles of international law. The differences in formulation, however, are not significant with regard to the binding force and legal nature of international law for the EU. The wording in Article 21 (1) and Article 3 (5) clearly expresses an obligation to '[strictly] observe' or 'respect' international law – that is, its rules (as the Articles do not relate only to 'principles') – which in any case first of all means that the EU has to avoid any violation of international law in its actions and, even more, must comply with its rules. Compliance with international law is also the ultimate way of supporting the principles of international law. Besides, the use of the term 'principle' in EU law may not necessarily indicate that the related norm or category thereof has less legal precision and grants broad leeway to the implementing institutions, but may rather indicate the fundamental nature of certain provisions and the resulting obligation.[33]

Hence, the EU is bound by international law not only by virtue of its existence as an international organization and legal person (Article 47 TEU) under international law but also by virtue of its constitutional prescription following from Articles 3 (5) and 21 TEU. As the EU values

[32] That Art. 21 (1) does not refer to the 'principles' of international law, but to 'international law' (i.e. all its rules without limitation to the principles only), can be derived from other language versions in more clarity than from the English one.

[33] CJEU, Case 43/75, *Defrenne v Sabena* [1976] ECR 455, EU:C:1976:56, paras. 28 f.

and objectives inform the exercise of the EU's competences,[34] this applies not only with regard to entering into international commitments but also with regard to autonomous, unilateral EU legal acts, in particular its autonomous trade policy. With regard to international agreements entered into by the EU, their binding nature for the EU institutions and the Member States is furthermore confirmed by Article 216 (2) TFEU. The reference to 'contribute to [. . .] the development of international law' in Article 3 (5) TEU, however, might be read as a very little caveat insofar as sometimes developing international law might imply at first a certain breach of international law.[35] An example of this may be seen in the *Kadi* case law of the CJEU (to which we will soon revert), which led to improvements in human rights and, particularly, judicial protection on the international (UN) level, as a consequence of the CJEU's judicial control over the EU's implementation of UN sanctions.[36]

This conceptualization of the EU objective's legal effect under Lisbon is in conformity with much earlier case law of the Court, starting long before the Lisbon Treaty, according to which the EU is bound by international law (not just the international agreements it entered into). The EU must respect international law in the exercise of its powers, because international law, even customary law, is binding upon the EU institutions and forms part of the EU legal order.[37] After Lisbon, the Court related this statement to Article 3 (5) TEU, as it held that due to this

[34] Ramses Wessel and Yuliya Kaspiarovich, 'The Role of Values in EU External Relations', in Elaine Fahey and Isabella Mancini (eds.), *Understanding the EU as a Good Global Actor: Ambitions, Values, and Metrics* (Cheltenham: Edward Elgar Publishing, 2022), p. 102.

[35] ibid, p. 98.

[36] CJEU, Case C-402/05 P and C-415/05 P, *Kadi I* [2008] ECR I-06351, ECLI:EU:C:2008:461. See Ernst-Ulrich Petersmann, 'Multilevel Judicial Protection of "Access to Justice" and the EU's Duty to Contribute to the "Strict Observance and Development of International Law"', in Matej Avbelj, Filippo Fontanelli, and Giuseppe Martinico (eds.), *Kadi on Trial: A Multifaceted Analysis of the Kadi Trial* (London: Routledge, 2014), pp. 187–217; Piet Eeckhout, 'The Integration of Public International Law in EU Law: Analytical and Normative Questions', in Piet Eeckhout and Manuel López-Escudero (eds.), *The EU's External Action in Times of Crisis* (Oxford: Hart Publishing, 2016), p. 197; Inge Govaere, 'Interconnecting Legal Systems and the Autonomous EU Legal Order', in Inge Govaere and Sacha Garben (eds.), *The Interface between EU and International Law: Contemporary Reflections* (Oxford: Hart Publishing, 2019), p. 36. This is true even though the CJEU, Case C-584/10 P, C-593/10 P and C-595/10 P, *Kadi II* [2013] ECLI:EU:C:2013:518, para. 163, opined that the implementation of the improvements (statement of reasons; submission of evidence) was not sufficient in the case before it.

[37] CJEU, Case C-286/90, *Poulsen and Diva Navigation* [1992] ECR I-06019, ECLI:EU:C:1992:453, para. 9 f; Case C-162/96, *Racke* [1998] ECR I-03655, ECLI:EU:C:1998:293, paras. 45 f; Case C-386/08, *Brita* [2010] ECR I-01289, ECLI:EU:C:2010:91, paras. 41 f.

provision, the EU, when adopting an act, is 'bound to observe international law in its entirety'.[38] Later, the Court confirmed the binding force of international law 'in its entirety, including not only the rules and principles of general and customary international law, but also the provisions of international conventions that are binding on it' in the context of Article 3 (5) TEU.[39]

In sum, we can conclude that the EU must respect international law in its external relations and when adopting any EU act or action related to it, and has to exercise its competencies accordingly. This is not only a consequence of the EU's actorness on international level, by virtue of which an international organization is bound to respect international law,[40] but derives from basic constitutional provisions on EU objectives and principles. This includes the EU's direction towards multilateralism as explicitly enshrined in the objectives set out in Article 21 TEU, for the implementation of which respect of international law is pivotal.

3.2.2 EU Internal Relevance of International Law: Respecting EU Autonomy

Being bound by international law as a constitutional obligation prompts the question of how exactly the normative effect of international law on EU legal acts can be understood and translated into the EU legal order. Respecting international law as a constitutional obligation might cause an understanding under which any EU legal act not in conformity with international law is illegal and invalid. A closer inspection of the pertinent case law of the Court, however, demonstrates that the legal value of international law in the EU legal order, and in particular in the implementation of international law, is subject to non-uniform trends in the Court's decisions, which shall be briefly explored here in order to analyze the internal constraints of the EU's promise of strict observance of international law in its legal order. Particular attention will be given to the Court's postulation of autonomy of the EU legal order from international law, first as it is in certain tension with the above clear confirmation of EU's strict observance of international law and its notion as a source of EU law as well, and second because the EU's drive for strategic autonomy

[38] CJEU, C-366/10, *Air Transport Association of America* [2011] ECR I-13755, ECLI:EU:C:2011:864, para. 101.

[39] CJEU, Case C-266/16, *Western Sahara Campaign UK* [2018] ECLI:EU:C:2018:118, para. 47.

[40] Jed Odermatt, *International Law and the European Union* (Cambridge: Cambridge University Press, 2021), pp. 19 ff.

in trade policy may deepen any autonomy of the EU from international law and could position the EU in a more conflictive role regarding its international commitments. Even though other EU institutions also play a role in determining the EU's approach to international law,[41] the subsequent analysis will focus on the Court's case law, as it is the Court that decides conclusively about the internal significance of international law for assessing the legality of EU acts within the EU, due to its task to ensure observance of the law in the EU (Article 19 (1) TEU).

3.2.2.1 International Law as a Constraint to the Validity of EU Legal Acts

As mentioned, Article 216 (2) TFEU, with regard to international treaties of which the EU is part, provides for a binding force of such treaties for all EU and domestic institutions,[42] which was extended to include customary law.[43] The consequence thereof is a primacy of international law over EU secondary law.[44] This reception of international law as superior to EU secondary law, however, in the CJEU case law is not automatically associated with legal invalidity of EU acts[45] violating international law. The 'primacy' of agreements concluded by the EU over EU legislation does not lead to the latter's (internal) unlawfulness in case of conflict[46] (but may cause international responsibility of the EU). Rather, the primacy was seen to merely demand harmonious, consistent interpretation; in other

[41] For a review of the EU legislator's approach, particularly in comparison to the Court's one, see Jan Wouters, Jed Odermatt, and Thomas Ramopoulos, 'Worlds Apart? Comparing the Approaches of the European Court of Justice and the EU Legislature to International Law', in Marise Cremona and Anne Thies (eds.), *The European Court of Justice and External Relations Law: Constitutional Challenges* (Oxford: Hart Publishing, 2014), pp. 249–279.

[42] In case of international agreements to which the EU is not party but the Member States are, the EU is bound only if the relevant powers have been assumed in their entirety by the EU; see Case C-366/10, *Air Transport Association of America*, para. 71.

[43] See CJEU, Case C-162/96, *Racke*, para. 46.

[44] CJEU, Case C-308/06, *Intertanko* [2008] ECR I-04057, ECLI :EU:C:2008:312, para. 42; CJEU, Case C-402/05 P and C-415/05 P, *Kadi I*, paras. 306 ff.

[45] With regard to national acts of EU member states, Art. 216 (2) TFEU is the basis for a legal obligation on them flowing from EU agreements, irrespective of their direct effect; see CJEU, Case C-66/18, *Commission v Hungary re Central European University* [2020] ECLI:EU:C:2020:792, para. 139. The relevance of Art. 216 (2) TFEU in that regard was much more clearly spelled out by AG Kokott in her Opinion, ECLI:EU:C:2020:172, paras. 86 ff.

[46] See Pieter Jan Kuijper, 'It Shall Contribute to [. . .] the Strict Observance and Development of International Law . . .', in Allan Rosas, Egils Levits, and Yves Bot (eds.), *The Court of Justice of the EU and the Construction of Europe: Analyses and Perspectives on Sixty Years of Case-law* (The Hague: T.M.C. Asser Press, 2013), pp. 601 ff; Katja Ziegler, 'Beyond Pluralism and Autonomy: Systemic Harmonization as a Paradigm for the Interaction of EU Law and International Law' (2016) 35(1) *Yearbook of European Law* 667–711 at 674 ff.

words, EU legal acts have to be interpreted so as to comply with international law as much as possible,[47] which includes delineating the EU acts' scope of application so as to bring them into compliance with international law.[48] Conflict between EU legal acts and international agreements does not automatically lead to the latter's relevance in assessing the former's unlawfulness, as CJEU's case law established quite early. This was decided by the Court at first with regard to the General Agreement on Tariffs and Trade (GATT)[49] rules, later confirmed with regard to WTO rules, and finally – after some turns, as the case law before 2008 was less reluctant to apply international treaties[50] – extended to other international agreements, with the UNCLOS[51] being the first one.[52]

The decisive litmus test for assessing an international treaty's capacity to function as a yardstick in reviewing EU acts' legality became the issue of direct effect (earlier, the Court rather used the notion of conferring individual rights).[53] Even though international law has been denoted as a source of EU law, international law's validity within the EU legal order does not necessarily imply direct effect and, hence, prevalence over conflicting EU or domestic acts. This legal situation may be compared to EU directives which are binding but whose provisions have direct

[47] For the early related case law, see CJEU, Case C-61/94, *Commission v. Germany* [1996] ECR I-03989, ECLI:EU:C:1996:313, para. 52; with regard to domestic application, see CJEU, Case C-53/96, *Hermes* [1998] ECR I-03603, ECLI:EU:C:1998:292, para. 28; more recent cases are CJEU, Case C-104/16 P, *Front Polisario* [2016] ECLI:EU:C:2016:973, paras. 93 ff, 100 ff; CJEU, Case C-363/18, *Organisation Juive Européenne* [2019] ECLI:EU:C:2019:954, paras. 28 ff. For parallel interpretation of the WTO ASCM and the EU Basic Anti-Subsidy Regulation as persistent practice of EU Courts, see GC, Case T-300/16, *Jindal Saw and Jindal Saw Italia v Commission* [2019] ECLI:EU:T:2019:235, para. 101; GC, Case T-480/20, *Hengshi Egypt Fiberglass Fabrics* [2023] ECLI:EU:T:2023:90, para. 100. The EU act can, however, not be interpreted *contra legem*; see AG Tamara Capeta, Opinion in Case C-123/21 P, *Changmao Biochemical Engineering* [2022] ECLI:EU:C:2022:890 para. 101,

[48] See CJEU, Case C-286/90, *Poulsen and Diva Navigation*, paras. 25–29; Case C-366/10, *Air Transport Association of America*, para. 123.

[49] General Agreement on Tariffs and Trade 1994, 15 April 1994, Marrakesh Agreement Establishing the World Trade Organization, Annex 1A, 1867 U.N.T.S. 187, 33 I.L.M. 1153 (1994).

[50] See Mario Mendez, 'The Application of International Law by the CJEU', in Curtis Bradly (ed.), *The Oxford Handbook of Comparative Foreign Relations Law* (New York: Oxford University Press, 2019), pp. 609, 611 ff. The year 2008 is singled out as a turning point in the Court's case law also by Rupert Dunbar, 'Article 3 (5) TEU a Decade On: Revisiting "Strict Observance of International Law" in the Text and Context of Other EU Values' (2021) 28 (4) *Maastricht Journal of European and Comparative Law* 479–497 at 480.

[51] Convention on the Law of the Sea, 10 December 1982, 1833 U.N.T.S.

[52] CJEU, Case C-308/06, *Intertanko*, paras. 54 ff.

[53] CJEU, Cases 21-24/72, *International Fruit Company* [1972] ECLI:EU:C:1972:115.

effect only under certain conditions. Accordingly, the validity of an international treaty for and in the EU (and its Member States) and its direct effect are separate issues. The direct effect of EU international treaty obligations depends on the preciseness of the content of the relevant provision and its unconditional legal force excluding flexibilities in its implementation,[54] but also on the general nature and structure of an agreement.[55] Consequently, international agreements become a yardstick for assessing the legality of EU acts only if their rules have direct effect[56] (even though in some early cases, the Court had adopted a different approach).[57] Where international agreements lack direct effect, which applies to WTO law and more recent bilateral trade agreements, for reasons of explicit exclusion of direct effect in the international treaty itself (as is general practice in the newer EU trade or association agreements)[58] or in the Council decision on the conclusion of the treaty, or due to their mainly reciprocal nature and flexibility in the implementation as in case of WTO rules,[59] an incompatibility of an EU legal act with these international rules does not give ground for the EU act's annulment. Even

[54] See Case C-363/12, Z. [2014] ECLI:EU:C:2014:159, paras. 87–90.

[55] See Case C-366/08, *Intertanko*, paras. 45, 54 ff; C-366/10, *Air Transport Association of America*, paras. 53–55. Theoretically, one may distinguish direct effect (the question as to whether a treaty provision is precise and unconditional) from applicability (related to structure and nature of a treaty with regard to its capacity to give rise to rights and obligations); see Koen Lenaerts, 'Direct Applicability and Direct Effect of International Law in the EU Legal Order', in Inge Govaere, et al. (eds.), *The EU in the World: Essays in Honour of Marc Maresceau* (Leiden: Brill Nijhoff, 2014), pp. 45–46. But this distinction is not logically sharp, as aspects of a treaty's structure and nature also impact the issue of conditionality.

[56] Kuijper, 'It Shall Contribute to [. . .] the Strict Observance and Development of International Law . . .' (2013), p. 605; Ziegler, 'Beyond Pluralism and Autonomy' (2016) 680.

[57] CJEU, Case C-377/98, *Netherlands v Parliament and Council* [2001] ECR I-07079, ECLI:EU:C:2001:523, paras. 53 f, where the Court reviewed an EU directive for its compatibility with the Convention on Biological Diversity, even though the Convention was seen not to have direct effect, nor to establish individual rights. See also Mendez, 'The Application of International Law by the CJEU' (2019), pp. 614–615.

[58] See e.g. Art. 30.6 Comprehensive Economic and Trade Agreement (CETA) between Canada, of the one part, and the European Union and its Member States, of the other part, OJ EU 2017 No. L 11/23, 14 January 2017, Art. 5 Trade and Cooperation Agreement between the European Union and the European Atomic Energy Community, of the one part, and the United Kingdom of Great Britain and Northern Ireland, of the other part (TCA), OJ EU 2021 No. L 149/1, 30 April 2021.

[59] See CJEU, Case C-149/96, *Portugal v. Council*, paras 39 ff; CJEU, C-135/10, *SCF* [2012] ECLI:EU:C:2012:140, paras. 43 ff. See with insightful clarity Pieter Jan Kuijper, 'From Dyestuffs to Kosovo Wine: From Avoidance to Acceptance by the European Community Courts of Customary International Law as Limit to Community Action', in Ige Dekker and Harry Post (eds.), *On the Foundations and Sources of International Law* (The Hague: T.M.C. Asser Press Institute, 2003), pp. 165 f.

though the CJEU identified a fundamental will of the Member States to ensure that the EU complies with GATT,[60] the Court allowed derogations from GATT (and later WTO) obligations and does not interpret the EU treaties as barring the EU from taking trade-restrictive measures against third countries if they are justified under EU law.[61] Besides the direct effect exception, the Court reviews EU acts for their conformity with WTO law in case an EU act was adopted in order to comply with WTO obligations[62] or directly refers to WTO rules.[63] These additional so-called Fediol and Nakajima exceptions are interpreted narrowly.[64] The Court held that the requirements of the Nakajima exception, namely that the EU legislator intended to implement a 'particular WTO obligation', are not satisfied where the 'preamble to an EU act support[s] only a general inference that the legal act in question was to be adopted with due regard for international obligations entered into by the European Union'.[65] Furthermore, these exceptions are not expanded to other international agreements; they only apply to WTO law.[66] Besides these exceptions, the above-mentioned case law clearly signals that even though an EU act does not conform to international treaty law, this does not affect its lawfulness, as international law in principle is not seen by the Court as a legal yardstick for assessing EU acts' legality under EU law.[67]

The situation with regard to assessing EU legal acts for their compliance with *customary international law* appears a bit different, as direct effect is not so much an issue for the Court: An individual may rely on rights derived from an international EU agreement and in this context invoke rules of customary international law to challenge the EU's competence or the validity of an EU regulation,[68] as it may be 'liable to affect

[60] CJEU, Joined Cases 21 to 24/72, *International Fruit*, paras. 10–13.

[61] CJEU, Case C-112/80, *Dürbeck* [1981] ECR 1095 ECLI:EU:C:1981:94, para 44; CJEU, Case C-245/81, *Edeka* [1982] ECR 2745, ECLI:EU:C:1982:277, para 24.

[62] CJEU, Case 69/89, *Nakajima* [1991] ECLI:EU:C:1991:186, paras. 29–31.

[63] CJEU, Case 70/87, *Fediol* [1989] ECLI:EU:C:1989:254, paras. 19–20, 22.

[64] See e.g. CJEU, Case C-377/02, *Van Parys* [2005] ECR I-01465, ECLI:EU:C:2005:121, paras. 41, 50 f; CJEU, C-351/04, *Ikea Wholesale* [2002] ECR I-07723, ECLI:EU:C:2007:547, paras. 29 ff; CJEU, Case C-533/10, *CIVAD* [2012] ECLI:EU:C:2012:347, para. 38 ff.

[65] CJEU, Case C-21/14 P, *Rusal Armenal* [2015] ECLI:EU:C:2015:494, paras. 45 ff.

[66] CJEU, Case C-401/12 P to C-403/12 P, *Vereniging Milieudefensie* [2015] ECLI:EU:C:2015:4, paras. 57, 59; CJEU, Case C-404/12 P and C-405/12 P, *Pesticide Action Network Europe* [2015] ECLI:EU:C:2015:5, paras. 49 ff.

[67] CJEU, Case C-280/93, *Germany v Council*, para. 112.

[68] CJEU, Case C-162/96, *Racke*, para. 51.

rights which the individual derives from EU law or to create obligations under EU law in this regard'.[69] The Court added that due to the complexity of international customary rules and their imprecision, judicial review on assessing the validity must be limited to the question whether the EU institution 'made manifest errors of assessment' in applying the international rules.[70] Thus, instead of denying review of conformity with international customary law as a consequence of its lack of direct effect, the Court applies a relaxed standard of review. Hence, one can observe a difference between customary rules of international law and international treaty law: Whereas the former appears to be always relevant for assessing EU legal acts when there is a link between a customary rule and an EU act influencing an individual legal position,[71] the latter is relevant only in the rare circumstance of having direct effect. This difference in effect translates into a higher legal relevance of international customary law in the EU legal order.[72] The resulting difference in the legal effect of different sources of international law of course appears inconsistent with Articles 3 (5), 21 TEU, since they do not distinguish between the sources of international law, and with Article 216 (2) TFEU generally transposing treaty but not customary law. Furthermore, granting a higher level of legal significance to customary rules is not compatible with the latter's lack of democratic legitimacy and interferes with the balance of power between the legislative and the judiciary.[73] In practice, harmonious interpretation appears to be the conflict avoidance tool of choice for the Court so that such differences may not become relevant. With regard to WTO law, it has been observed that even though the Court does not apply WTO rules, it appears that the Court strives for

[69] CJEU, Case C-366/10, *Air Transport Association of America*, paras. 107–109.

[70] CJEU, Case C-162/96, *Racke*, para. 52; CJEU, Case C-366/10, *Air Transport Association of America*, para. 110.

[71] See Lenaerts, 'Direct Applicability and Direct Effect of International Law in the EU Legal Order' (2014), p. 61.

[72] Eleftheria Neframi, 'Customary International Law and the EU from the Perspective of Article 3 (5) TEU', in Piet Eeckhout and Manuel López-Escudero (eds.) *The EU's External Action in Times of Crisis* (Oxford: Hart Publishing, 2016), p. 212 tries to justify this difference by referring to Art. 3 (5) TEU as a provision intended to limit the exercise of EU competences, in contrast to Art. 216 (2) TFEU as a particular transformation for international treaties. Nevertheless, it is still striking that the rules of customary law, lacking a specific transformation rule, in the end have a more assertive legal effect than those rules that are generally transformed into the EU legal order by virtue of an explicit provision of primary EU law.

[73] See Kuijper, 'From Dyestuffs to Kosovo Wine' (2003), pp. 162, 167 ff.

interpretive results that conform to WTO obligations.[74] As already mentioned, the Court confirms a duty-to-conform interpretation even if international legal commitments are not directly effective.[75] Similarly, the Court took pains to interpret EU acts in conformity with international customary law.[76]

The pronouncements of the Court in more recent decisions, after the entry into force of Lisbon, indicate a slightly different approach insofar as the Court after confirming the binding force of international law in its entirety in the context of Article 3 (5) TEU, assessed the legal validity of an EU act concluding an agreement in view of Article 3 (5) TEU with reference to international law norms.[77] The Court confirms, as before, that international agreements concluded by the EU form an integral part of EU law and must be in conformity with the EU primary law and its constitutional principles, but also with the rules of international law.[78] Consequently, the EU is obliged to respect international law in its entirety, for example when entering into agreements[79] or adopting other legal acts.[80] Recently, this seemingly more receptive approach led the General Court to annul a Council decision on the conclusion of an international agreement for reason of insufficient consideration and respect for customary international rules (i.e. on self-determination and the principle of relative effect of treaties), without granting a discretion to the Council in

[74] Jan Wouters, et al., *The Law of EU External Relations: Cases, Materials, and Commentary on the EU as an International Legal Actor*, 3rd ed. (New York: Oxford University Press, 2021), pp. 461 f.

[75] This distinction recently has been criticized by AG Tamara Capeta, Opinion in Case C-382/21 P, *EUIPO/KaiKai Company* [2023] ECLI:EU:C:2023:576 paras. 46 f, 73 ff. She contends that a conform interpretation leads to the same result as granting direct effect to international law. Her view, however, fails to recognize that a conforming interpretation is limited by the wording and only applies if an interpretable EU act exists at all. This limit and requirement do not exist in the case of direct application. Furthermore, the differentiation reflects the difference between an obligation under international law that applies to the EU and one whose legal effect also has a direct impact within the EU legal order. To the extent that Capeta wants to eliminate the distinction because of the undue impact on the legislature's discretion that exists even with a conforming interpretation, it must be countered that a conform interpretation has less impact and takes seriously the decision of the EU institutions to be bound by international law. She blurs the direct and indirect effects of the EU's international commitments.

[76] CJEU, C-104/16 P, *Front Polisario*, paras. 92 ff.

[77] CJEU, Case C-266/16, *Western Sahara Campaign UK*, paras. 47 ff.

[78] ibid, paras. 45 f, 63.

[79] CJEU, Case C-104/16 P, *Front Polisario*, paras. 86 ff.

[80] See C-366/10, *Air Transport Association of America*, para. 101. Theodore Konstadinides, 'Customary International Law as a Source of EU Law: A Two-Way Fertilization Route?' (2016) 35(1) *Yearbook of European Law* 513–532.

determining the resulting obligations.[81] This goes beyond previous statements where international law was used to determine the limits of EU competence and where the invocation of customary law depended on its relevance for individual rights.

The above brief exploration of the case law of the CJEU on the relevance of international law for EU acts also demonstrates, as had been observed, that the jurisprudence of the Court on the significance of international law has been varied and fragmented for quite some time[82] and does not appear to be based on a principled approach. It shows some flexibility and may be used by the Court to promote own ends.[83] The state of this case law, until recently, can be summarized as being coined by an approach of, by and large, irrelevance of a violation of international law by EU acts for their internal legality, subject to some narrow exceptions explained earlier in the chapter. Nevertheless, one can observe a certain development: The CJEU, even before Lisbon, confirmed the legal binding force of international law for the EU, and the related obligation to respect international law has been approved and even strengthened by the Lisbon rules and confirmed by the subsequent CJEU case law. A slight difference, however, may be observed in the Court's decisions with regard to the internal legal consequences of the EU institutions' duty to respect international law when adopting internal measures. The formulations used by recent case law can be understood to point towards a more receptive approach not only regarding customary law but also entire international law as to its legal significance in assessing the legal validity of EU acts.

All in all, one can summarize – as an interim conclusion – the consequences flowing from this state of case-law for the EU assessment of legal acts as follows: The constitutional obligation of international law compliance usually does not come with a contestability of EU legal acts' lawfulness for the mere reason of their lack of conformity with

[81] GC, Case T-279/19, *Front Polisario* [2021] ECLI:EU:T:2021:639, paras. 365 ff; Joined Cases T-344/19 and T-356/19, *Front Polisario* [2021] ECLI:EU:T:2021:640, paras. 276 ff. The decisions are subject to pending appeals, Case C-799/21 P.

[82] For the turns, see Violeta Moreno-Lax and Paul Gragl, 'Beyond Monism, Dualism, Pluralism: The Quest for a (Fully-Fledged) Theoretical Framework' (2016) 35(1) *Yearbook of European Law* 455–470 at 463 f; with regard to differentiations between customary international law and international treaty law in its internal effect, see Andreas Müller, 'The Direct Effect of Customary International Law', in Fernando Lusa Bordin, Andreas Th. Müller, and Francisco Pascual-Vives (eds.), *The EU and Customary International Law* (Cambridge: Cambridge University Press, 2022), pp. 221 ff, demanding a uniform direct effects test.

[83] Ziegler, 'Beyond Pluralism and Autonomy' (2016) 670 f.

international legal commitments of the EU, unless these international legal commitments meet the threshold of direct effect (which has been the case with some rules in former EU agreements but not with more recent ones). Still, even without international legal commitments being directly effective, EU acts should be interpreted in conformity with those commitments as much as possible. With regard to WTO law, which in general is not directly effective, EU legal acts that intentionally implement or explicitly refer to (particular) WTO obligations may, however, be unlawful in case of breach of international law, as the latter is relevant with respect to their legal validity under EU law. These are the abovementioned narrowly conceived exceptional situations (Nakajima and Fediol exception) where WTO agreements have a direct effect within EU law. With regard to customary international law, it may in any case serve as legal yardstick for EU's legislation and other legal acts, but in this respect the legal review by the CJEU over an EU act might be more restraint, as it may only employ a marginal review, granting the EU institutions some leeway depending on the vagueness of the international custom.

3.2.2.2 Constraints Flowing from Conflict with Other EU Primary Law

Another restraint on the implementation of a hard legal obligation of strict observance of international law results from the context in which an obligation is contained. Article 21 as well as Article 3 TEU enshrine diverse fundamental objectives and principles of the EU. As regards an obligation to respect different fundamental objectives and principles, the respect for them, even though clearly representing a hard legal obligation of full compliance, might nevertheless require a balancing exercise. The reason for this is that the legal obligation to respect or pursue an objective in determining trade policy also may be balanced against the obligation to respect other constitutional objectives indicated, if they are in tension, or even conflict, and thus not be easily compatible with each other. Respecting one objective cannot justify the complete disrespect of other constitutional objectives and values of the EU, and vice versa, so that the diverse constitutional EU objectives may be balanced against each other in their determinative force for EU policies by way of a practical concordance that attempts to realize conflicting objectives to the largest possible extent.

The political leeway and discretion of the EU institutions in balancing conflictive objectives that have to be pursued simultaneously have been expressed by the Court very early, in view of the presence of diverse policy objectives. The Court even held that provisions indicating EU objectives 'merely lay down a programme' so that their implementation must be employed by the determination of the EU policies and actions.[84] While the latter statement has been made with regard to the pursuance of the objectives enshrined in Articles 2 and 3 Treaty Establishing the European Community (ECT)[85] in view of the policy objective of strengthening the economic and social cohesion provided for in Articles 130a and 130e TEC (which can be said to not have a rank equal to the very foundational objectives of Article 3 Treaty on the European Union (TEU)), its rationale of confirming a leeway of the responsible EU institution in simultaneously observing different EU objectives is offering a suitable guideline for the requirement of the EU institutions under Lisbon rules to observe the diverse EU policy objectives concurrently when determining a specific policy such as trade policy. To give just one example of colliding principles: While the EU must safeguard its values and independence (Article 3(5) sentence 1, Article 21 (2) a) TEU), this may not always be in line with following what international law prescribes. As early as the 1980s, the Court had already confirmed that there might be tensions between different (then) EC objectives, as, for example, between trade policy objectives enshrined in Article 110 Treaty Establishing the European Economic Community (EECT)[86] (now Article 206 TFEU) and those of the Common Agricultural Policy in Article 39 EECT (now Article 39 TFEU), from which it inferred the need to 'maintain a reasonable balance' between the diverse objectives.[87] Therefore, depending on current problems and needs, the exact formulation of the EU's trade policy strategy must give weight to various objectives,[88] and the EU institutions have a certain discretion in that regard (see the mandate of the European Council in Article 22 TEU, and that of the Council and Commission in Article 207 (3) TFEU).[89] None of the EU objectives of Article 3 (5) and Article 21 TEU has legal priority over the other.[90]

[84] See Case C-149/96, *Portugal v Council*, para. 86.

[85] Treaty Establishing the European Community (Consolidated version 2002), OJ EU 2002 No. C325/33, 24 December 2002.

[86] Treaty establishing the European Economic Community, Rome, 25 March 1957.

[87] CJEU, Case 112/80, *Dürbeck*, para. 43.

[88] Krajewski, 'The Reform of the Common Commercial Policy' (2012), p. 298.

[89] Case C-150/94, *United Kingdom v Council* [1998] ECR I-07235, ECLI:EU:C:1998:547, paras. 67 f; For development policy and Art. 21 TEU, see CJEU, Case C-377/12, *Framework Agreement Philippines* [2014] EU:C:2014:1903, para. 37.

[90] Krajewski, 'The Reform of the Common Commercial Policy' (2012), p. 294.

3.2.2.3 *In Particular: Constraints Flowing from the 'Autonomy of the EU' Exception*

The case law of the CJEU on ensuring EU's autonomy is another constraint for the full implementation of international law, and it also can be perceived, by and large, as an expression of the above-mentioned constraint flowing from the need to simultaneously consider conflicting EU primary law objectives and provisions.[91] Autonomy of the EU legal order not only from national law of the Member States but also from international law is a stipulation the Court formulated at a very early stage to ensure the EU's independent development and to safeguard its constitutional identity.[92] As the autonomy of EU law safeguards essential constitutional characteristics of the EU legal order, the Court cannot link or base this jurisprudence on EU autonomy to/on the EU's independence required by Article 21 (2) a) TEU, even after Lisbon. While the latter relates to the independence of the EU's ability to determine its stance and policies in international relations from undue foreign impact (in other words, to the EU's sovereignty), the autonomy of the EU demanded by the Court is a fundamental constitutional principle identified at first in relation to the EU Member States (and in that regard the autonomy of EU legal order is a much broader concept, as it comprises the general direct effect and supremacy of almost all EU acts over domestic law). Nevertheless, the basic idea of ensuring the EU's independence and fundamental – that is, constitutional – essence can be seen as the common root.

In contrast to the aforementioned (Section 3.2.2.2) constraints resulting from the need to consider diverse, conflictive EU objectives simultaneously in the formulation of policies, protecting the autonomy of the EU legal order is considered by the Court to express a rather absolute constraint on the pursuit of objectives where there is no leeway for balancing conflicting interests. Consequently, in a situation where implementing international law leads to conflict with the requirements of autonomy of the EU legal order – for example, by entailing a breach of

[91] Also Ramses Wessel, 'The EU and International Law', in Ramses Wessel and Joris Larik (eds.), *EU External Relations Law: Text, Cases and Materials*, 2nd ed. (Oxford: Hart Publishing, 2020), p. 164 perceives the Kadi ruling as an expression of balancing constitutional principles.

[92] Case C-26/62, *van Gend en Loos*, para. 12; Case C-6/64, Costa v. E.N.E.L [1964] ECR 585, ECLI: EU:C:1964:66. For more on the external autonomy, see Loïc Azoulai, 'Structural Principles: Internal and External', in Marise Cremona (ed.), *Structural Principles in EU External Relations Law* (Oxford: Hart Publishing, 2018), p. 31.

EU fundamental rights – the implementation of international law has to cease.

Not every provision of EU primary law, however, forms part of the EU's autonomy. Safeguarding the EU's autonomy only pertains to the essential characteristics of the EU constitutional order, which is a second difference from the aforementioned constraints. One of the particular contents of EU autonomy, besides protection of the Court's own competencies, is the respect for fundamental rights. To that extent, the above principled statement that all objectives enshrined in Article 3 (5) TEU have the same rank needs a qualifier: The Court's case law on autonomy identifies core principles of the EU constitutional order which have the capacity to prevail over other primary EU law provisions.[93] Hence, full observance of international law may be compromised in case of conflict with core EU constitutional principles, as the latter demand full respect.

The resulting tension between respecting international law and ensuring the autonomy of the EU and its legal order can be studied in the already mentioned *Kadi* case law of the CJEU, where the Court held that 'an international agreement cannot affect the [...] the autonomy of the Community legal system' to which the respect for fundamental rights belongs and whose observance by EU actions the Court ensures. From this consideration, the Court inferred 'that the obligations imposed by an international agreement cannot have the effect of prejudicing the constitutional principles' of the EU, and the Court applied this even to UN Security Council Resolutions under Chapter VII UN Charter that postulate supremacy over any other international treaty (see Article 103 UN Charter).[94] Later, in the same vain, the Court disapproved the – yet to be – conclusion of the EU Canada Passenger Name Record (PNR) agreement[95] for reason of its incompatibility with EU fundamental rights.[96]

[93] Giuseppe Martinico, 'The Autonomy of EU Law: A Joint Celebration of Kadi II and Van Gend en Loos', in Matej Avbelj, Filippo Fontanelli, and Giuseppe Martinico (eds.), *Kadi on Trial: A Multifaceted Analysis of the Kadi Trial* (London: Routledge, 2014), p. 166.

[94] CJEU, C-402/05 P and C-415/05 P, *Kadi* I, paras. 281–286, 306–308.

[95] Agreement between Canada and the European Union on the transfer and processing of Passenger Name Record, 23 June 2014, https://data.consilium.europa.eu/doc/document/ST-12657-2013-REV-5/en/pdf.

[96] CJEU, Opinion 1/15, *PNR Agreements EU Canada* [2017] ECLI:EU:C:2017:592, paras. 125 ff, 167, 181. There are other cases in which the Court did not allow the conclusion of an international agreement, for reason of interferences with the Court's responsibilities by international courts foreseen in these agreements. See CJEU, Opinion 1/91, *EEA* [1991] ECR I-06079, ECLI:EU:C:1991:490, paras. 25 ff, 35; CJEU, Opinion 1/09, *European and Community Patents Court* [2011] ECR I-01137, ECLI:EU:C:2011:123, paras. 78 ff; or CJEU, Opinion 2/13,

Consequently, in effect, there is an exception to strict observance of international law if their implementation by an EU act (the Court clarified that its control does not pertain to the international obligation as such) would contradict the constitutional foundations of the EU.[97]

Also in recent decisions, the Court clearly upheld the EU's autonomy as a barrier to 'strict observance', or full conformity with international legal obligations. In these decisions, a key question for the compatibility of international agreements with EU primary law was the impact of the jurisdiction of an international tribunal or arbitration/dispute settlement mechanism on the EU legal order's autonomy – that is, the autonomy of EU law in its development. This has been addressed most clearly in Opinion 2/13 on the Draft Accession Agreement to the European Convention on Human Rights (ECHR),[98] and earlier with regard to the European Economic Area (EEA) Court, although at that time the CJEU had essentially confined its deliberations on autonomy to its relevance for the allocation of responsibilities and competencies in the EU treaties. It did so with a view to preserving the CJEU's ultimate responsibility for the interpretation of EU law, as part of the 'very foundations of the Community'.[99]

In its recent Opinion 1/17[100] on the EU–Canada Trade Agreement (CETA),[101] the Court set out in detail the significance of the autonomy of EU law for the (internal) legal validity of international law for the EU and explained the ensuing limitations on the EU's (external) competences. There the Court related the autonomy of EU law to be protected against international obligations to the 'essential characteristics of the

Accession to the ECHR [2014] ECLI:EU:C:2014:2454, paras. 182 ff on the conclusion of the EEA, the creation of a European Patent Court and the accession to the ECHR. A third line of case law restricts – even ex post – the conclusion of international agreements by the EU due to the Council having chosen the wrong EU legal basis for it; see CJEU, Case C-317/04, *PNR Agreement EC USA* [2006] ECR I-04721, ECLI:EU:C:2006:346, paras. 67 ff, regarding the EU US PNR agreement which had to be terminated thereafter.

97 CJEU, C-402/05 P and C-415/05 P, *Kadi* I, paras. 281–286. Joris Larik, 'The Kadi Saga as a Tale of "Strict Observance" of International Law' (2014) 61(1) *Netherlands International Law Review* 23–42 at 39 f, however, portrays the *Kadi* decision to be in line with the objective of strictly observing international law.

98 CJEU, Opinion 2/13, *Accession to the ECHR*, para. 158.

99 CJEU, Opinion 1/91, *EEA*, para. 35, 46.

100 CJEU, Opinion 1/17 *CETA* [2019] ECLI:EU:C:2019:341.

101 Comprehensive Economic and Trade Agreement (CETA) between Canada, of the one part, and the European Union and its Member States, of the other part, OJ EU 2017 No. L 11/23, 14 January 2017.

European Union and its law'.[102] The CJEU identified EU law being an independent source of law, characterized 'by its primacy over the laws of the Member States, and by direct effect of a whole series of provisions [...] Those characteristics have given rise to a structured network of principles, rules and mutually interdependent legal relations binding the European Union and its Member States'.[103] The CJEU refers to this as 'a constitutional framework' in its own right, encompassing the

> founding values set out in Article 2 TEU, [...] the general principles of EU law, the provisions of the Charter, and the provisions of the EU and FEU Treaties, which include, *inter alia*, rules on the conferral and division of powers, rules governing how the EU institutions and its judicial system are to operate, and fundamental rules in specific areas.[104]

Thus, autonomy of EU law after Opinion 1/17 goes far beyond safeguarding the jurisdiction of the CJEU but includes the central elements of the legal effects of EU law in the EU Member States as determined by the CJEU.[105] In addition, it includes fundamental procedural and substantive rules of EU primary law of constitutional dignity, such as the protection of fundamental rights, the institutional order, and the allocation of competences between the institutions.[106] Going beyond the self-referential standards of past CJEU decisions which focused on interferences with the jurisdiction of the CJEU in determining what the autonomy of the EU legal order actually implies,[107] the Court in its Opinion 1/17 even included into the rather broad definition of the EU's autonomy the requirement that international obligations must not have any effect on the operation of the EU institutions in accordance with the EU constitutional framework, which means that the competence and functioning of the democratic EU legislator as governed by the EU constitutional framework must be protected.[108] Hence, the CJEU for the very first time

[102] CJEU, Opinion 1/17, *CETA*, para. 109. [103] ibid. [104] ibid, para. 110.

[105] ibid, para. 111.

[106] Also, the function of the national courts as Union courts is one of these essential elements; see CJEU, Opinion 1/09, *European and Community Patents Court*, paras. 68 ff.; Opinion 2/13, *Accession to the ECHR*, para. 175.

[107] See Panos Koutrakos, 'More on Autonomy: Opinion 1/17 (CETA)' (2019) 3 *ELRev* 293–294 at 294. For criticism of the self-referential attitude of the CJEU in previous decisions on international courts, which in effect denies legal dialogue, see Bruno de Witte, 'A Selfish Court? The Court of Justice and the Design of International Dispute Settlement beyond the EU', in Marise Cremona and Anne Thies (eds.), *The European Court of Justice and External Relations Law* (Oxford: Hart Publishing, 2014), p. 46; Steve Peers, 'The EU's Accession to the ECHR: The Dream Becomes a Nightmare' (2015) 16(1) *German Law Journal* 213–222.

[108] Opinion 1/17, *CETA*, paras. 137–160.

declared the protection of EU political processes (limited to the definition of levels of protection)[109] from the effects of international court rulings as established under international law to be an element of the autonomy of EU law. This very peculiar statement may only pertain to the interference with EU law of international courts' rulings, not to international law as such, as the Court in Opinion 1/17 had to decide on the CETA Investment Court System (ICS). The exact consequence of this postulate nevertheless is far from clear. Furthermore, the reasons given by the Court for such a potentially wide-ranging statement, which could undermine the legal force of even though binding international court decisions for the EU generally, are meagre.[110]

From this case law on EU autonomy one can infer that the strict observance of international law is subject to the EU's autonomy, which the Court established as a constitutional principle of the EU legal order. While EU legislation that aims at implementing obligations resulting from international law may be void if it breaches international law (see Section 3.2.2.1), the implementing legislation also has to respect essential characteristics of the EU legal order, which prevail in case of conflict with international law. Thus, the constitutional obligation to comply with and hence implement international law is not an absolute one, in contrast to the respect for the EU's autonomy. This constraint on the relevance of international law within the EU legal order has to be added to the interim conclusion drawn at the end of Section 3.2.2.1. Accordingly, the Court's emphasis on EU autonomy was rightly perceived as an expression of the CJEU's defensiveness, even closure, towards international law.[111] Nevertheless, it must be pointed out that these restrictions to the internal relevance of EU's obligation under international law are only relevant insofar as their internal implementation and their legal effect on conflicting EU legislation is at stake. On the international level – that is, in its international relations – the EU is still fully bound by international law, as will be explained in more detail in the next section.

[109] See Opinion 1/17, *CETA*, paras. 148, 151 and Wolfgang Weiß, 'The CETA Investment Court and EU External Autonomy' (2020) (8) 1 *Hungarian Yearbook of International Law and European Law* 15–39 at 27 f.

[110] For a critical analysis, see Eva Kassoti and Jed Odermatt, 'The Principle of Autonomy and International Investment Arbitration: Reflections on Opinion 1/17' (2020) 73 *Questions of International Law* 5–20 at 17 ff; Weiß, 'The CETA Investment Court and EU External Autonomy' (2020) 29 ff.

[111] See e.g. Moreno-Lax and Gragl, 'Beyond Monism, Dualism, Pluralism' (2016) 457, 470.

3.2.3 Legal and Political Consequences of Respect for International Law and EU Autonomy for the Strategic Autonomy in Trade Policy

The foregoing analyses have made clear that international law must be respected by the EU not only by virtue of the international legal obligations following from them for the EU on the international, external level, as the EU is an international organization bestowed with treaty-making powers. For constitutional reasons, based on fundamental constitutional provisions on EU objectives and principles, international law that is binding on the EU has to be complied with internally, within the EU's legal order. As shown in Section 3.2.1, the EU has to respect international law in its external relations and when adopting any EU act or action falling under the purview of pertinent international rules, and must exercise its competencies accordingly and tailor its policies in a way that respects international law and complies with it. This includes the EU's direction towards multilateralism. The constitutional obligation does not, however, mean that a breach of international law, and hence a breach of this constitutional obligation, is automatically relevant for assessing the legal validity of an EU legal act. As analyzed in Section 3.2.2.1, EU legal acts still remain valid and effective despite their non-compliance with international legal obligations, apart from specific situations, where lack of respect of international law leads to illegality of EU acts.

Safeguarding the autonomy of the EU as a core constitutional principle even demands non-compliance with international law if essential characteristics of the EU's constitutional order are in conflict with the EU's domestic implementation of international legal obligations. In case of conflict, international commitments have to cease, and internal EU law prevails with regard to its effective application, as explored in Section 3.2.2.3. In effect, this means that international obligations then are not implemented within the EU for reasons of EU constitutional, thus internal, law.

As these consequences of the autonomy of the EU are severe, this subsection will first explore in more detail the international (as opposed to merely national) relevance of the constitutional requirement of protecting EU autonomy (Section 3.2.3.1) and its scope with regard to the recent trade policy reorientation (Section 3.2.3.2). Finally the consequence of the above exploration of the EU constitutional objective of respecting international law and multilateral approaches for the trade policy assertiveness turn will be summarized (Section 3.2.3.3).

3.2.3.1 *The EU Autonomy Exception and Article 46 Vienna Convention on the Law of Treaties*

Denying internal implementation of international legal obligations does not alter the EU's obligations under international law. If the application of the CJEU's doctrine of safeguarding the EU's autonomy leads to non-implementation of international legal commitments by EU institutions, this still amounts to a violation of international law and its fundamental rule of *pacta sunt servanda* on international level (see Articles 26 and 27 Vienna Convention on the Law of Treaties (VCLT)[112]/Vienna Convention on the Law of Treaties between States and International Organizations or between International Organizations (VCLTSIO),[113] which clarify that a party cannot invoke internal law as justification for its failure to perform treaty). This is so despite the fact that internally the violation of international law usually is not relevant for assessing the EU legal acts' legal force. International law only under very narrow conditions allows for deviation for internal reasons under Articles 46 of said Conventions on the Law of Treaties. Accordingly, an international organization is allowed to lawfully claim that it is not bound by a treaty if its consent has been expressed 'in violation of the rules of the organization regarding competence to conclude treaties [...] [if] that violation was manifest and concerned a rule of fundamental importance'. A manifest violation requires that the violation is 'objectively evident to any State or any international organization conducting itself in the matter in accordance with the normal practice of States and, where appropriate, of international organizations and in good faith' (see Article 46 (3) VCLTSIO). One might deliberate whether these conditions are met in the case of the CJEU's requirements of its EU autonomy exception which protects basic constitutional characteristics from being interfered with by international obligation. But this is highly unlikely. First, the obligation to safeguard the EU's autonomy may not represent a rule on EU's competence (or a related procedural provision) to enter into international treaties, for it is neither

[112] Vienna Convention on the Law of Treaties, Vienna, 23 May 1969, in force 27 January 1980, 1155 U.N.T.S. 331; (1969) 8 ILM 679; UKTS (1980) 58.

[113] Vienna Convention on the Law of Treaties between States and International Organizations or between International Organizations, 21 March 1986, not yet in force, 25 ILM 543 (1986), UN Doc. A/CONF.129/15. Even though the VCLTSIO has not yet entered into force, it is often referred to reflect customary law in the same way as the VCLT.

a rule in the sense of an explicit, written provision contained in EU primary law (but flows from a series of Court statements) nor a competence issue in the narrow sense of rules determining EU treaty-making competences (such as Article 3 TEU, Article 207 and Article 216 (1) TFEU, etc.) or prescribing the relevant procedures (such as Article 218 TFEU). Deliberations in the International Law Commission might indicate that Article 46 at least initially only was meant to refer to constitutional provisions that set out the rules governing the ways in which a state expressed its consent to be bound by a treaty. Later deliberations, however, indicate that competence provisions also may be relevant,[114] and in an even broader sense, some scholars opine that the exception enshrined in Article 46 is not limited to procedural or competence provisions in the narrow sense, but applies to any internal constitutional law provision, including substantive ones (such as fundamental rights obligations) relevant for lawfully entering into international treaties.[115]

But even if this stipulation could be met, there is the second requirement: The violation must be manifest – that is, objectively evident in the sense of Article 46 (3) cited above. Whether this can be said with regard to all aspects of EU autonomy appears highly doubtful, to say the least, all the more as the interpretation of the concept of autonomy of EU law in the academic literature is highly contested; hence the concept is not obvious even for those familiar with EU law. One surely can accept that a treaty entered into by the EU without necessary parliamentary approval would fall under the exception formulated by Article 46, as for a democratic polity such as the EU, parliamentary consent to important international treaties is a usual constitutional requirement.[116] But the postulated respect for the CJEU's competences in EU law, or for the rules governing the legal relations between EU and Member States, or EU primary law on the EU institutional order and the allocation of competences between the institutions, is far from being manifest, as it is not evident for treaty partners. This is because such or comparable requirements are not stipulated by other international actors. The standard required by Article 46 (3) for a constitutional limitation to be capable of making a consent null and void is one of notoriety. '[O]nly notorious constitutional limitations with which other States can reasonably be

[114] For a brief overview of the discussions in the ILC, see T. Rensmann, 'Article 46', in Oliver Dörr and Kirsten Schmalenbach (eds.), *Vienna Convention on the Law of Treaties: A Commentary*, 2nd ed. (Heidelberg: Springer, 2018), para. 34.

[115] ibid, paras. 62–63.

[116] ibid, para. 52.

expected to acquaint themselves should be taken into account.'[117] Violations of internal law are only manifest if the restriction to the treaty-making competence 'could have been established by any state without further investigation' or is 'easily ascertainable'.[118] This threshold is not met by the Court's determination of the content of EU autonomy. This applies even more to the protection of the 'level of protection of public interests' set up by the EU legislator in accordance with the EU constitutional rules, which was held to form part of EU autonomy in the most recent statement of the CJEU in Opinion 1/17.[119] If this formulation is taken to protect the EU regulatory autonomy[120] – that is, the policy choices it makes – against interference by international institutions or even rules, the EU autonomy exception not only would be particularly broad and very unique but would also mean that the EU could deny implementing any international obligation interfering with the EU's legislative choices. This would imply that by placing any international commitment under the reach of the EU autonomy exception, international law is subjected to any domestic rule, so that it would be possible for the Court to block implementation of any international commitment which the Court considers interfering with the policy choice expressed in EU regulation or legislation. International legal commitments (e.g. in the area of environmental protection or international economic law), however, are entered into and tailored exactly for the reason of restraining the parties' policy leeway, including legislative choices. In essence, such broad concept of EU autonomy would allow the EU to deny the bindingness of any international treaty for the EU. Such conception of EU autonomy would turn the EU into an international actor that could distance itself from international law at will – that is, at the discretion of the finally deciding EU Court. The constitutional obligation to comply with international law would in this way be completely emptied as well. It is therefore very likely that the Court cannot have meant a general protection of EU regulatory autonomy in Opinion 1/17 with the above-quoted phrase, as this would contradict the

[117] United Nations, 1966 Yearbook of International Law Commission II, A/CN.4/SER.A/1966/Add.l, p. 240.

[118] Rensmann, 'Article 46' (2018), para. 48; these thresholds also apply to rules of international organizations viewed from non-members; see ibid. para. 73.

[119] See Opinion 1/17, *CETA*, paras. 148, 151 and already above.

[120] In this direction, see Maria Fanou, 'The CETA ICS and the Autonomy of the EU Legal Order in Opinion 1/17' (2020) 22 *Cambridge Yearbook of European Legal Studies* 106–132 at 128.

overall endeavour of the Court in Opinion 1/17 to enlarge the external policy space of the EU and to broaden its capacity to enter into international treaties establishing international courts.[121] Instead, the Court may have formulated merely an imperative of non-interference into the constitutional operation of EU institutions.[122]

The above considerations make it clear that such a conception of EU autonomy cannot fall under the protection of Article 46, as they do not represent evident 'normal practice' of international actors. Besides, the facets of the CJEU's EU autonomy exception flow from a jurisprudence of the Court that is constantly evolving and, hence, far away from reflecting 'normal practice [. . .] in good faith', as this case law expresses an understanding of EU autonomy which is 'fluid and context-specific',[123] thus making it difficult to assess what it means for a specific international obligation. As the ICJ held, there is no legal obligation for states to keep themselves informed of constitutional developments in other international actors even if they are important for their international relations.[124] As a consequence thereof, the EU cannot escape its international legal obligations by invoking the CJEU's case law on safeguarding EU autonomy. The EU's commitments under the international treaties it consented to, in particular under the WTO agreement, bilateral trade agreements, or multilateral conventions on climate change and other relevant issues, still remain binding for the EU. That Article 46 of said Conventions may not apply here appears also to be the opinion of the CJEU itself, as it once held that the EU cannot rely on its own internal law as a justification for not fulfilling an international agreement (in that case, it was the PNR agreement between the EU and the United States, which was held to be incompatible with EU law for lack of legal basis for processing personal data for international security reasons).[125] Even though the Court neither commented on nor mentioned EU autonomy in this case, the dispute before the Court dealt with the requirements of

[121] See also Kassoti and Odermatt, 'The Principle of Autonomy and International Investment Arbitration' (2020) 19.

[122] Ibid, 13; but see Weiß, 'The CETA Investment Court and EU External Autonomy' (2020) 30 f, arguing that the two are different issues.

[123] Kassoti and Odermatt, 'The Principle of Autonomy and International Investment Arbitration' (2020) 5.

[124] ICJ, *Land and Maritime Boundary between Cameroon and Nigeria*, ICJ Reports 2002, 303, 430.

[125] CJEU, Case C-317/04, *PNR Agreement EC USA*, para. 73. Mario Mendez, 'The Application of International Law by the CJEU', in Curtis Bradly (ed.), *The Oxford Handbook of Comparative Foreign Relations Law* (New York: Oxford University Press, 2019), p. 605.

EU human rights protection in external relations, which nowadays is part of protecting the EU autonomy. Furthermore, in *Kadi*, the Court clearly stated that its reservations regarding international law in the EU legal order only pertain to its implementation, not to the legal commitment itself, and in this case the Court clearly addressed the requirements of EU autonomy.

3.2.3.2 The EU Autonomy Exception and the EU Trade Policy's Assertiveness Turn

Another issue one might deliberate as a consequence of the 'Autonomy of the EU' exception is the question of whether the protection of EU autonomy against stipulations flowing from international legal obligations might also cover the new legislation implementing the EU trade policy review. This is because the latter legislation is meant to transpose the EU vision of an Open Strategic *Autonomy* into the realm of trade policy (see Section 2.1.3) and make it become reality in the EU's trade relations with third countries. One might contend that – as a consequence of the EU autonomy exception – these legal instruments are bound not to implement and thus not to respect international law as a consequence of internal, albeit not international, law. One might even conclude that the whole of the new trade policy orientation is exempt from international legal obligations. However, the consonance of using the term *autonomy* must not be a cause for misunderstandings here. The endeavor of the EU trade policy's turn towards attaining more assertiveness, to which the motto of Open Strategic Autonomy was transformed in the EU's recent trade policy review, does not mean that the new assertiveness represents part and parcel of the constitutional level EU autonomy as defined in the CJEU case law. For, as shown in Section 2.1.3, where the notion of Open Strategic Autonomy in trade policy has been explored, the new trade policy aims at an autonomy of EU interest determination and enforcement, and does not pursue the implementation or protection of EU constitutional principles (such as EU human rights, democracy, and rule of law). There are no EU constitutional objectives or principles which would or could be pursued when adopting trade countermeasures or even raising trade barriers for the reason of stronger enforcement of EU trading rights. Possibly, one could deliberate justifying some of the new legislative instruments due to their contribution to fair trade and global sustainability (see for this EU objective Article 3 (5) TEU), but these are not part of those essential constitutional characteristics covered by the EU autonomy exception. The same applies to the EU independence as covered by Article 21 (2) a) TEU, as explained in Section 3.2.2.3. Generally, the EU's trade policy's strategic autonomy hardly is rooted in EU constitutional values, but rather is based on political determinations of EU interests in the present trade policy context, and these are not constitutionally demanded. The EU trade policy reorientation is guided by concerns for the EU's competitiveness, assertiveness (in the sense of its capacity to pursue and enforce its interests including sustainability and labour rights), and overall by its 'strategic interests and values'.[126] Even the sustainability branch of the reorientation is not derived from constitutional objectives but from a need for responsible action in the transformation of EU industry and its supply chains in the interest of social fairness, the environment, and climate neutrality.[127] Admittedly, part of the sustainability aspect of the new trade policy is the aim towards greater respect for 'core human and labour rights, as reflected in the UN fundamental conventions of the ILO', and particular mention is made of action against child labour.[128] But also in this respect, the driving force behind EU trade policy is not the respect for EU human rights such as those enshrined in the Fundamental Rights Charter[129] with a view to their internal realization within the EU. Instead, the EU intention to strengthen the respect for human rights in its trade policy is grounded in the need for fair market conditions globally, responsible business conduct, and the creation of jobs elsewhere, specifically in its trading partners, which are based on international, universal values and principles.[130] Thus, this aim does not reflect safeguarding EU constitutional autonomy, but rather – undeniably respectable and urgent – EU policy interests for strengthening the EU's worldwide value impact on domestic regulation and living conditions in foreign nations. The present assessment is in line with the observation that the paradigms of fair trade and sustainability feature considerably less prominently in the new EU trade policy than do liberal and geopolitical approaches to trade.[131]

Consequently, already from a legal point of view, the EU's constitutionally grounded obligation to comply with international law cannot be

[126] Trade Policy Review: An Open, Sustainable and Assertive Trade Policy, COM(2021) 66 final, p. 4 f. See also ibid. p. 8, 'geopolitical interests'.

[127] ibid, pp. 4, 10, 12. [128] ibid, 12 f.

[129] Charter of Fundamental Rights of the European Union, OJ EU 2012 No. C 326/391, 26 October 2012.

[130] Trade Policy Review, pp. 6, 12 f.

[131] Jacobs, Niels Gheyle, Ferdi de Ville, and Jan Orbie, 'The Hegemonic Politics of Strategic Autonomy and Resilience' (2023) *JCMS* 3–19 at 14 f.

pushed aside in trade policy by invoking the 'EU autonomy exception' from implementing international legal obligations. This exception does not apply to a (trade) policy that is merely seeking to enlarge policy room for more robustness in EU interest representation and enforcement. The constitutional obligation of respecting international legal commitments thus remains valid and relevant to its fullest extent in the trade policy redirection. There is no 'autonomy discount' which would be applicable. As a consequence, only insofar as international legal obligations of the EU are not violated or make available policy space for the Union, in adopting trade policy legislation or implementing measures the EU has leeway to balance the political objective of its strategic autonomy and self-protection against that of support for multilateralism, a task which will likely not be an easy one.[132]

3.2.3.3 Conclusion

The preceding analyses have demonstrated that the constitutional obligation to respect international law and to approach international issues multilaterally explored in Section 3.2.1 comes, first, with a restriction regarding protecting the EU autonomy (meaning that the autonomy of the EU legal order may require non-implementation of international obligations in case of conflict with its essential constitutional characteristics), which, however, is not relevant for the new trade policy reorientation; and, second, a qualification with regard to international legal obligations' internal consequences for the validity of EU legal acts (meaning that the violation of international law does not make EU internal acts null, except under very narrow conditions). The constitutional obligation for respecting international law and multilateralism thus remains a core requirement in determining trade policy and legislating trade instruments, and this is in conformity with Piet Eeckhout's observation that the EU is based on integrating international law into its legal order, as rules such as Article 3 (5) 21 TEU and Article 216 (2) TFEU clearly indicate. The limitations to this integration 'do not undermine the legal integration paradigm', which 'ought to serve as the framework for analysing normative issues regarding the interrelationship between EU law and

[132] Luca Rubini, 'A Delphic Oracle?' What Does the Recent EU Commission's Trade Policy Review Mean?', *EU Law Live*, 24 June 2020, https://eulawlive.com/op-ed-a-delphic-oracle-what-does-the-recent-eu-commissions-trade-policy-review-mean-by-luca-rubini/#.

international law'.[133] The international legal commitments must be respected and cannot be pushed aside for the mere fact of their usual internal irrelevance for assessing the internal legal force of EU acts. Avoiding conflict with international legal commitments is hence a constitutional-level obligation the EU institutions must respect.

For the new legal instruments which the EU legislator adopted in the course of the implementation of the EU's new trade policy (for a brief overview, see Section 2.1.3.), the requirement of international law compliance consequently means that, first, these instruments should, as far as it is compatible with their wording, be interpreted in conformity with international law, be it international treaty or customary law. In that respect, it is necessary to keep in mind that what counts is the content of an international obligation as it is accepted by international actors. Giving international rules a very specific European-style notion, which is not in conformity with the accepted approaches, applications, and conceptualizations of international obligations under international law, in particular by relevant judicial practice, is not helpful in avoiding conflict between EU legislation and international obligations. The CJEU in its approach to international law is often criticized for adopting a peculiar reading to an international legal concept in order to bring EU legal acts into conformity with international obligations.[134] Such approach might be useful to appease an internal EU debate but does not do much to avoid a violation of international law on the international plane. Second, insofar as the new legislation will not merely pay a rather general respect to WTO obligations but explicitly implement particular WTO law commitments or refer to a specific provision, those international rules definitely will be relevant even for assessing the legal validity of the new EU legislation within the EU legal order, because in this situation the conditions for the above-mentioned two exceptions for

[133] Piet Eeckhout, 'The Integration of Public International Law in EU Law: Analytical and Normative Questions', in Piet Eeckhout and Manuel López-Escudero (eds.), *The EU's External Action in Times of Crisis* (Oxford: Hart Publishing, 2016), p. 204.

[134] For this widespread criticism, see Eva Kassoti, 'Between Sollen and Sein: The CJEU's Reliance on International Law in the Interpretation of Economic Agreements Covering Occupied Territories' (2020) 33(2) *Leiden Journal of International Law* 371–389 at 378 et seq; Jed Odermatt, 'Council of the European Union v. Front Populaire Pour la Libération de la Saguia-El-Hamra et du Rio de Oro (Front Polisario): Case C-104/16P' (2017) 111 (3) *American Journal of International Law* 731–738 at 736–738; Guillaume Van der Loo, 'Law and Practice of the EU's Trade Agreements with "Disputed" Territories: A Consistent Approach?', in Inge Govaere and Sacha Garben (eds.), *The Interface Between EU and International Law: Contemporary Reflections* (Oxford: Hart Publishing, 2019), p. 266.

an internal effect of WTO rules (the so-called Nakajima and Fediol exceptions; Section 3.2.2.1) will very likely be met. Apart from these exceptions, as already stated, internally, even if EU legislation does not comply with Union's international obligations under international trade law, this in itself is not sufficient to claim their illegality before EU courts. The legal validity of EU legislative acts within the EU is assessed in view of EU primary law,[135] and not with a view to the EU's international obligations.

A political consequence of this state of constitutional and international conditions for the formulation of EU trade policy is the necessity of a multilateral approach, including attempts to come to multilateral solutions. Before the EU adopts novel trade policy instruments autonomously which tread new paths of law, the obligation to follow multilateralism suggests at least at a political, not necessarily at a legal, level that the EU is expected to pursue its regulatory aspirations for more effective and fairer trade rules on multilateral level first to find solutions on this level. Admittedly, not least with the current state of international relations in a multipolar world, this appears cumbersome and not very promising. Nevertheless, as a corollary, the multilateral approach might mean that the EU addresses its issues with potentially affected trading partners and at least seeks dialogue with them before an autonomous approach is embraced. The concept of multilateralism in international relations implies prior dialogue with affected third countries before novel trade legislation that has a potentially trade distortive effect is enacted, irrespective of whether or not the new legislation is compliant with international law. Hearing the concerns of trade partners gives the chance to reconsider the legislation before adoption, to take care of some issues, which one might not have thought of, and in this way to improve the regulation. Even though this might in the end prove not helpful, it sends a signal of readiness for dialogue and for a still cooperative approach.

3.3 EU Trade Policy Constraints Flowing from Public International Law

After having demonstrated the relevance of respecting the EU's international legal obligations in determining trade policy and implementing it into legislation and new approaches, this section will identify from a general perspective the pertinent international legal rules which have a

[135] CJEU, C-402/05 P and C-415/05 P, *Kadi I*, para. 282.

bearing on the EU's legislative implementation of the assertiveness turn in trade policy without exploring them in detail as this will be done individually in the subsequent chapters on the new tools and instruments the EU has adopted under its new trade policy.

As the new instruments provide tools in the field of trade policy, the most relevant realm of international commitments of the EU which might be affected derive, first of all, from the WTO agreements. WTO rules must be observed in the formulation of EU legislative acts that determine external trade relations. As Article XVI:4 WTO Agreement[136] requires, the EU as a WTO member has to 'ensure the conformity of its laws, regulations and administrative procedures with its obligations' under the diverse WTO agreements. One of the pertinent agreements in that regard is the WTO Dispute Settlement Understanding (DSU)[137] as the EU steps up its enforcement powers in the new tools also with regard to international dispute settlement, for example, by introducing the alternative appeal mechanism MPIA (multi-party interim appeal mechanism)[138] and amending the Trade Enforcement Regulation[139] also in view of the MPIA, or by introducing a new tool in the form of an Anti-Coercion Instrument (ACI)[140] that will offer a varied selection of potential countermeasures to respond to foreign coercive actions, which might serve as an alternative to the formal dispute settlement procedures. Another relevant WTO agreement will be the Agreement on Subsidies and Countervailing Measures (ASCM)[141] as the EU introduces a new legislation against foreign

[136] Agreement Establishing the World Trade Organization, 15 April 1994, 1867 U.N.T.S. 154, 33 I.L.M. 1144 (1994).

[137] Understanding on Rules and Procedures Governing the Settlement of Disputes, Marrakesh Agreement Establishing the World Trade Organization, Annex 2, 1869 U.N.T.S. 401, 33 I.L.M. 1226 (1994).

[138] WTO, Statement on a Mechanism for Developing, Documenting and Sharing Practices and Procedures in the Conduct of WTO Disputes, 'Multi-Party Interim Appeal Arbitration Arrangement Pursuant to Article 25 of the DSU', 30 April 2020, JOB/DSB/1/Add.12.

[139] Regulation (EU) 654/2014 of the European Parliament and of the Council of 15 May 2014 concerning the exercise of the Union's rights for the application and enforcement of international trade rules and amending Council Regulation (EC) No. 3286/94 laying down Community procedures in the field of the common commercial policy in order to ensure the exercise of the Community's rights under international trade rules, in particular those established under the auspices of the World Trade Organization (Trade Enforcement Regulation), OJ EU 2014 No. L 189/50.

[140] Regulation (EU) 2023/2675 of the European Parliament and of the Council of 22 November 2023 on the protection of the Union and its Member States from economic coercion by third countries, OJ EU 2023 No. L 2675, 7 December 2023.

[141] Agreement on Subsidies and Countervailing Measures, 15 April 1994, Marrakesh Agreement Establishing the World Trade Organization, Annex 1A, 1869 U.N.T.S. 14.

subsidies which provides for diverse types of possible redressive measures targeting subsidization by foreign states of undertakings active on the EU internal market. Hence, the ASCM may contain relevant disciplines and obligations which might restrict the leeway of WTO Members in addressing foreign subsidies. Fundamental principles of non-discrimination in WTO law, enshrined, for example, in GATT and General Agreement on Trade in Services (GATS)[142] provisions, may also be violated if the EU, at least in implementing its new tools, adopts measures that cannot be adopted in comparable domestic situations, or subjects foreign goods or services to stricter review procedures and/or substantive rules than exist for like EU goods or services. Further issues with regard to the WTO most-favoured-nation principle might also occur if new tools apply to specific states rather than being generally applicable. Such might become a concern with regard to, for example, the International Procurement Instrument (IPI).[143] Also, the EU regulation on a carbon border adjustment mechanism might come into tension with these WTO core principles, as the regulation will oblige foreign producers to purchase carbon certificates for certain imported goods.

Second, as the EU's new tools may even apply with regard to foreign states with which bilateral trade agreements exist, the pertinent bilateral trade rules also may be relevant in assessing the EU legislation. A particular relevance in that regard belongs to market access, non-discrimination commitments, and, again, dispute settlement rules; EU Free Trade Agreements (FTAs) contain specific dispute settlement mechanisms which may be disregarded where the EU provides for tools that allow an autonomous suspension of its trade concessions in relation to an FTA partner, as it may result from the amended Trade Enforcement Regulation or from the ACI.[144] FTA dispute settlement rules are also

[142] General Agreement on Trade in Services, 15 April 1994, Marrakesh Agreement Establishing the World Trade Organization, Annex 1B, 1869 U.N.T.S. 183, 33 I.L.M. 1167 (1994).

[143] Regulation (EU) 2022/1031 of the European Parliament and of the Council of 23 June 2022 on the access of third-country economic operators, goods and services to the Union's public procurement and concession markets and procedures supporting negotiations on access of Union economic operators, goods and services to the public procurement and concession markets of third countries (IPI Regulation), OJ EU 2022 No. L 173/1.

[144] With regard to the ACI, for example, see Annex I to the Regulation (EU) 2023/2675 of the European Parliament and of the Council of 22 November 2023 on the protection of the Union and its Member States from economic coercion by third countries, OJ EU 2023 No.

relevant for assessing the EU Commission's action plan for stronger enforcement of FTA trade and sustainable development chapters.

Third, general international law may serve as a constraint for the EU's leeway in drafting new legislation that affects its external relations with third countries. The EU measures which might be provided in implementing the legislation that aims at strengthening the enforcement of trade and sustainability commitments in EU FTAs may be problematic in view of the requirements of the VCLT for the suspension of treaty obligations, wholly or in part. Relevant requirements are stipulated, for example, in Article 60 VCLT, which codifies customary international law.[145] Of particular relevance appears to be the (again customary) international law on countermeasures. The EU adopts new legislation in order to respond to third-country behaviour possibly breaching international law. Consequently, the EU may justify its responses by invoking the pertinent rules on countermeasures, which, however, also provide for inherent conditions and restraints the EU then must respect. Besides, the issue arises as to whether general law is applicable despite WTO rules providing *leges speciales*.

Fourth, specific international treaties may be relevant in assessing the leeway the EU has in determining environmentally related instruments with regard to the adopted carbon border adjustment mechanism (CBAM).[146] As mentioned, the CBAM provides for certain imported goods to declare carbon certificates in order to compensate for the cost disadvantages incurred by like domestic goods in the EU as a result of CO_2 pricing with the aim to avoid the effectiveness of EU climate policies being undermined by carbon leakage. Relevant international obligations potentially establishing hurdles against the new piece of legislation may result from the United Nations Framework Convention on Climate Change (UNFCCC)[147] and the Kyoto Protocol to the UNFCCC,[148] as they ban disguised and unnecessary excessive restrictions on trade for climate

L 2675, 7 December 2023, listing the non-performance of international trade commitments as one of the possible countermeasures.

145 ICJ, *Gabcikovo-Nagymaros Project (Hungary v Slovakia)*, ICJ Reports 1997, 7, 38.

146 Regulation (EU) 2023/956 of the European Parliament and of the Council of 10 May 2023 establishing a carbon border adjustment mechanism, OJ EU 2023 No. L 130/52, 16 May 2023.

147 United Nations Framework Convention on Climate Change, A/RES/48/189, 20 January 1994, 1771 U.N.T.S. 107.

148 Kyoto Protocol to the United Nations Framework Convention on Climate Change, 10 December 1997, 2303 U.N.T.S. 162, 37 I.L.M 22.

purposes. The principle of Common But Differentiated Responsibilities (CBDR) enshrined in the UNFCCC and the Paris Agreement[149] may provide further restrictions.

Before the possible conflicts of the pertinent new EU legislation with the above-mentioned specific or general international legal commitments will be looked at in detail in the subsequent chapters, this section will address rather general aspects of these international obligations. Subsection 3.3.1 addresses the question of whether the mere existence of a legislative act may in itself represent a possible breach of these obligations, or whether this will only occur, and induce the pertinent consequences of the EU's international liability under international law,[150] if the legislation is implemented into concrete actions by the EU against third countries, in particular by the Commission as the usually responsible implementing body. Subsection 3.3.2 will present the relevance of the above-mentioned international legal obligations of the EU for its new trade legislation more closely. It will not only survey the relevant international disciplines but will also identify their potential to formulate concrete demands to be met by EU legislation in order to avoid the breach of international law by the new legislation. The concrete constraints for the EU trade policy resulting from the above-mentioned relevant international legal rules will be established.

3.3.1 International Legal Responsibility by Virtue of the Mere Adoption of Legislation

The Commission opines in one staff working document that 'the sole existence of an instrument does not breach any international obligation of the EU',[151] meaning that the mere adoption of legislation will not violate international law and hence will not give rise to international

149 Paris Agreement to the United Nations Framework Convention on Climate Change, 12 December 2015, T.I.A.S. No. 16-1104.

150 In this regard, it may be sufficient to remind that the EU as an international actor is subject to rules of customary international law on responsibility of international organizations, which basically follow those rules applicable to states. As a matter of principle, a breach of international law attributable to the EU gives rise to its responsibility under international law, i.e. to its obligation to make reparation. For this principle in international law, see PCIJ, Advisory Opinion, *Chorzow Case (Merits)*, Series A 1928, No. 17; ICJ, *Reparation for Injuries*, ICJ Reports 1949, 174, 184.

151 See Impact Assessment Report Accompanying the document Proposal for a Regulation of the European Parliament and of the Council on the protection of the Union and its Member States from economic coercion by third countries (Impact Assessment Report), 8 December 2021, SWD(2021) 371 final, 57.

responsibility of the EU therefore. Such perception of international law, however, is far too simplistic. The pertinent ILC Draft Articles on State Responsibility,[152] which reflect customary rules or general principles of international law and have been widely referred to in this capacity by international courts and tribunals as well,[153] including by WTO panels and the AB,[154] refer to international wrongful acts as 'conduct consisting of an action or omission' (Article 2). The same formulation is present in Article 4 ILC Draft Articles on the Responsibility of International Organizations (ILC Draft Articles IO).[155] One can doubt whether a legislative act, being a legally binding text issued by the responsible organ of a state or international organization, does represent anything more than mere words. What the cited provisions require is an 'action'. A domestic legislative text, however, may establish the legal foundation for a State's implementing practice by other, in particular executive organs that soon may follow. The relevant 'conduct' is considered an act under international law when the organ exercises, *inter alia*, 'legislative ... functions' (Article 4 (1) ILC Draft Articles on State Responsibility), which is a clear hint that even the mere existence of an emanation of legislative function, namely the issuing of a binding legislative text, may be sufficient to represent an action causing international responsibility, even though the text in itself does not have real consequences. But, as said, the legislative text is the very basis for real-life consequences in form of implementing measures adopted by the competent executive or administrative authorities. Article 6 (1) ILC Draft Articles IO does not use the same but a broader formulation, as it refers to the 'conduct of an organ [...] of

[152] See Annex to the UN General Assembly Resolution 56/83 of 12 December 2001, A/RES/56/83, 28 January 2002.

[153] James Crawford, 'State Responsibility', in Rüdiger Wolfrum (ed.), *Max Planck Encyclopedia of International Law* (Online edition: Oxford University Press, 2006), https://opil.ouplaw.com/display/10.1093/law:epil/9780199231690/law-9780199231690-e1093?prd=EPIL, para. 65; Alejandro Sánchez, 'What Trade Lawyers Should Know about the ILC Articles on State Responsibility' (2012) 7(6) *GTCJ* 292–299 at 293; Fernando Lusa Bordin, 'Reflections of Customary International Law: The Authority of Codification Conventions and ILC Draft Articles in International Law' (2014) 63(3) *ICLQ* 535–567 at 544–546.

[154] Appellate Body Report, *Canada – Continued Suspension*, WT/DS321/AB/R, 16 October 2008, para. 382; Appellate Body Report, *US – Anti-Dumping and Countervailing Duties*, WT/DS379/AB/R, 11 March 2011, paras. 309–311; Panel Report, *Canada – Dairy*, WT/DS103/R, WT/DS113/R, 17 May 1999, para. 7.77; Panel Report, *US – Gambling*, WT/DS285/R, 10 November 2004, para. 6.128.

[155] See Yearbook of the International Law Commission, 2011, vol. II, Part Two, A/CN.4/Ser.A/2011/Add.1 (Part 2).

an international organization in the performance of functions of that organ'. This may not come as a surprise, as legislative functions are hardly ever present in an international organization. When it comes to the EU, however, this is the case. Anyway, in both instances the exercise of functions of an organ may be sufficient to represent a conduct in the sense of an action subject to the law of international responsibility. The conduct, furthermore, must be internationally wrongful – a breach of an international obligation of the wrongdoer. Thus, the question arises whether, even if a mere legislative act is in principle susceptible of being a relevant 'action', it only may be an internationally wrongful act if there is an international obligation of the wrongdoing international actor which bans the mere adoption of such legislative act, and not only of any measure based on it. In other words: Are there international obligations which may already be violated by the mere adoption of a national legislative act? Indeed, this depends on the content of the international obligation, most importantly on the type of prohibited conduct. Compare, for example, the law on the use of force against the principle of non-intervention. In case of the obligation not to use force under the UN Charter's Article 2 (4) and the respective customary *jus cogens*,[156] the mere use of words or the adoption of mere legislation is not susceptible to breaching this rule, as the forbidden use of force must consist in a positive action that represents usage of some military coercion (armed attack or less grave forms of use of force). In contrast, however, the general duty of non-intervention in the internal affairs of another nation might already be breached by mere oral statements of a foreign state organ that comments in a manner which implies some minimum coercion (by putting pressure, e.g. by announcing consequences for bilateral relations) on internal issues of the other nation, such as the lawfulness of general elections, or the legitimate choice of a state representative; such could be deemed to represent relevant 'actions' that trespass the 'right of every sovereign State to conduct its affairs without outside interference', including respect for political integrity.[157] The required element of

[156] ICJ, *Military and Paramilitary Activities in and against Nicaragua (Merits)*, ICJ Reports 1986, 14, paras. 181 ff.

[157] ibid, paras. 202ff. For the prohibited interference through economic, political, and diplomatic means, see Florian Kriener, 'Intervention, Prohibition of', in Anne Peters and Rüdiger Wolfrum (eds.), *Max Planck Encyclopaedia of Public International Law* (Online edition: Oxford University Press, 2024), https://opil.ouplaw.com/display/10.1093/law:epil/9780199231690/law-9780199231690-e1434, paras. 20 f, 27 ff.

coercion for a breach of non-intervention[158] is met if a state uses some form of pressure by deploying threats or intimidation that is sufficiently serious to compel another state to act or not to act in a certain way, or impede the state's free choice in its political or economic affairs, even if the pressure is not successful.[159] Consequently, the mere adoption of a legislative act might represent an international wrongful act if it provides or announces some element of pressure in response to certain actions in internal affairs, even without the legislative act being implemented. An example might be the passing of a law by a state that declares part of a foreign territory to be own territory and providing political or economic consequences thereof. With regard to the legislative EU acts flowing from the implementation of the new trade policy assertiveness turn, there might be legislation where even the mere adoption could already be sufficient for finding a breach of the international obligation not to intervene. Admittedly, the threshold could be considered as being set high by the ICJ in its Nicaragua decision, as the Court held that in that case the trade embargo could not be regarded as a breach of the non-intervention principle,[160] hence even less so in the case of mere trade countermeasures affecting only a comparatively small part of the overall trade between two states; it depends on the concrete circumstances.[161] Anyway, the rather general statement by the Commission quoted above appears to stand on shaky ground, as the pertinent international obligation at stake will determine whether already a mere legislative act, prior

[158] ICJ, *Military and Paramilitary Activities in and against Nicaragua (Merits)*, ICJ Reports 1986, 14, para. 205: 'The element of coercion [. . .] defines, and indeed forms the very essence of, prohibited intervention'. That economic coercion exists and violates the principle of non-intervention is spelled out e.g. in the UN, Declaration on Principles of International Law concerning Friendly Relations and Cooperation among States in accordance with the Charter of the United Nations, A/Res/2625 (XXV), 24 October 1970, see its Preamble and the third principle.

[159] See Iryna Bogdanova, *Unilateral Sanctions in International Law and the Enforcement of Human Rights* (Leiden: Brill Nijhoff, 2022), p. 76; Thibault Moulin, 'Reviving the Principle of Non-Intervention in Cyberspace: The Path Forward' (2020) 25(3) *Journal of Conflict and Security Law* 423–447 at 440 f; Omri Sender, 'Coercion', in Anne Peters and Rüdiger Wolfrum (ed.), *Max Planck Encyclopaedia of Public International Law* (Online edition: Oxford University Press,), https://opil.ouplaw.com/display/10.1093/law:epil/9780199231690/law-9780199231690-e1749, paras. 2 f.

[160] ICJ, *Military and Paramilitary Activities in and against Nicaragua (Merits)*, ICJ Reports 1986, 14, para. 244 f.

[161] Maziar Jamnejad and Michael Wood, 'The Principle of Non-Intervention' (2009) 22 (2) *Leiden Journal of International Law* 345–381 at 371 f.

to its implementation, is susceptible of breaching it. This is particularly true regarding WTO law.

With regard to obligations under WTO law, the DSU allows to challenge even mere legislative acts of another WTO member if already the existence of a legislative act has a negative consequence for trade relations, for example, by placing foreign goods at a disadvantage, an analysis which is provided and required by, for example, Article III:4 GATT relating to 'laws, regulations'. As developed by GATT 1947 panels and later also accepted by the WTO judiciary,[162] there are basically two types of allegations of breach of WTO commitments: 'as such' claims and 'as applied' claims. Article 3:3 DSU provides that any impairment of any benefits accruing to a WTO member under any WTO rule by measures taken by another WTO member can be made subject to dispute settlement, taking up formulations already present in Article XXIII GATT 1947. Also, the already mentioned Article XVI:4 WTO Agreement stipulates that WTO members have to ensure the conformity of their laws, regulations, and procedures,[163] and not only of their practices derived therefrom, with their WTO obligations. From the formulation of Article 3:3 DSU, the Appellate Body inferred that a measure forms any act or omission attributable to a WTO member which includes 'acts setting forth rules or norms' of general application. The rules in themselves could constitute a measure irrespective of how or whether those are applied in a particular situation. 'This is so because the disciplines [...] are intended to protect not only existing trade but also the security and predictability needed to conduct future trade.'[164] Already GATT 1947 panels held that

> legislation which mandated action inconsistent with the General Agreement could be challenged as such, whereas legislation which merely gave the discretion to the executive authority of a contracting party to act inconsistently with the General Agreement could not be challenged as such; only the actual application of such legislation inconsistent with the General Agreement could be subject to challenge.[165]

[162] Jing Kang, 'The Presumption of Good Faith in the WTO "As Such" Cases: A Reformulation of the Mandatory/Discretionary Distinction as an Analytical Tool' (2012) 46(4) *JWT* 879–912 at 881 ff.

[163] Also, non-binding administrative guidance by a government can be a measure subject to review; see Appellate Body Report, *US – Corrosion-Resistant Steel Sunset Review*, WT/DS244/AB/R, 15 December 2003, para. 85.

[164] ibid, paras. 81–82.

[165] For the quote reflecting a summary of GATT panel approaches in that regard, see Appellate Body Reports, *US – 1916 Act (EU)*, WT/DS136/AB/R, WT/DS162/AB/R, 28 August 2000, para. 88.

This case law introduced the mandatory/discretionary distinction. The WTO judiciary in principle followed this line of case law by allowing the challenge of legal rules without reference to their application, but the WTO judiciary does so without placing the same importance on the aspect of mandatory-ness. The existence of discretion does not automatically preclude the finding of an 'as such' violation.[166] Thus, it is uncontested that any legislative act that mandates a violation of any WTO agreement (covered by the WTO DSU; see its Annex 1) is 'as such' inconsistent with WTO law.[167] What is decisive in that regard is the question of whether the act determines a WTO member's conduct that 'will necessarily be inconsistent with that Member's WTO obligations'.[168] Hence, subject to an 'as such' claim is a rule or norm of general application in itself, independent of any subsequent application. WTO judiciary assesses any measure in light of its 'design, structure/architecture and expected operation',[169] the latter indicating that it is not always necessary to wait for the 'operation' of a measure. That there is no need for WTO members to wait for the application of a rule gives the advantage of starting dispute settlement early in an attempt 'to prevent Members *ex ante* from engaging in certain conduct'.[170] If a general rule does not mandate, or concretely prescribe a subsequent specific action, but grants leeway to an executive or administrative authority, which may pertain to whether a measure is adopted at all, or how a particular measure is concretely shaped in detail (as the legislation might offer a choice of actions to be adopted),[171] or combining both types of leeway, then an 'as such' complaint may be unfounded because in this case it is the concrete application of the discretionary general rule by the administrative actor that must be assessed in view of WTO commitments. It cannot – for the sake of good faith – be assumed that the WTO member's executive will

[166] Simon Lester, 'A Framework for Thinking about the Discretion in the Mandatory/Discretionary Distinction' (2011) 14(2) *JIEL*, 369–402 at 370; Appellate Body Report, *EU – Biodiesel (Argentina)*, WT/DS473/AB/R, 6 October 2016, para. 6.229.

[167] Nicolas Lockhart and Elisabeth Sheargold, 'In Search of Relevant Discretion: The Role of the Mandatory/Discretionary Distinction in WTO Law' (2010) 13 (2) *JIEL* 379–421 at 380.

[168] Appellate Body Report, *US – Zeroing (EC)*, WT/DS294/AB/R, 18 April 2006, para. 189.

[169] See, for example, Appellate Body Reports, *Philippines – Distilled Spirits*, WT/DS396/AB/R, WT/403/AB/R, 21 December 2011, para. 250.

[170] Appellate Body Report, *US – Oil Country Tubular Goods Sunset Reviews*, WT/DS268/AB/R, 29 November 2004, para. 172 (emphasis in the original).

[171] For these basic types of leeway, see Lester, 'A Framework for Thinking' (2011) 375.

use its leeway in a manner inconsistent with its WTO obligations.[172] Consequently, if an executive leeway is granted, a finding of a WTO incompatibility of the legal text itself can only be based on an analysis that demonstrates that the legislation in question does not allow the executive or administrative body to abide by the member's WTO obligations. The latter is the case if the discretion is materially restricted in such a way that the body cannot avoid WTO violation because the exercise of WTO-compatible discretion may be prevented by the legislation, at least in certain circumstances.[173] Also, particular discretionary issues may be precluded by a WTO rule. Even giving the mere possibility of acting in a way not compliant with WTO obligations may breach this obligation.

This insight already shows that this, at first sight, seemingly clear distinction between 'as such' complaints for mandatory legislation and 'as applied' complaints with regard to legislation granting discretion is too simplistic and cannot be used as a threshold issue. It does invite different evidentiary burdens to prove a WTO inconsistency.[174] The Appellate Body indeed rather early held that reviewing a mandatory legislative measure per se does not preclude the possibility that 'a Member could violate its WTO obligations by enacting legislation granting discretion to its authorities to act in violation of its WTO obligation'.[175] The Appellate Body later concluded that there in principle is no bar to 'non-mandatory measures' being challenged as such,[176] and this statement indeed is in conformity with the insight that a WTO member's rules by their mere existence may already negatively affect foreign goods or services. It explicitly confirmed that the 'importance of the mandatory/discretionary distinction may vary from case to case, and has cautioned against applying the distinction in a mechanistic fashion'.[177] The Appellate Body did not find a basis to postulate that only certain types of measures could be challenged as

[172] Appellate Body Report, *US – Section 211 Appropriations Act*, WT/DS176/AB/R, 2 January 2002, para. 259.

[173] See Appellate Body Report, *EU – Biodiesel (Argentina)*, WT/DS473/AB/R, paras. 6.229, 6.281; Appellate Body Report, *US – Carbon* Steel, WT/DS213/AB/R, 28 November 2002, para. 162; Panel Report, *US – Ripe Olives from Spain*, WT/DS577/R, 19 November 2021, para. 7.146.

[174] See Jing Kang, 'The Presumption of Good Faith in the WTO "As Such" Cases' (2012) 886 ff.

[175] Appellate Body Report, *US – Countervailing Measures on Certain EC Products*, WT/DS212/AB/R, 9 December 2002, fn 334 to para. 159.

[176] Appellate Body Report, *US – Zeroing (Japan)*, WT/DS322/AB/R, 9 January 2007, para. 74.

[177] Appellate Body Report, *EU – Biodiesel (Argentina)*, WT/DS473/AB/R, paras. 6.227 ff.

such.[178] Also a panel found that the distinction cannot mean that legislation with discretion could never violate WTO law.[179] Dispute settlement practice shows that sometimes legislation can be challenged even before its entry into force, as pending legislation whose entry into force was automatic at a future date may already, before its legal binding force, have an impact on market actors. This is the case if those actors that plan their trade actions well in advance may be influenced by pending legislation to change their behaviour, which in effect may have a back-effect on the trade opportunities of foreign goods and services. WTO rules such as the prohibition against quantitative restrictions in Article XI GATT or against discrimination in Article III GATT also 'protect expectations of [trade partners] as to the competitive relationship between their products and [...] create the predictability needed to plan future trade'.[180] Hence, the nuanced approach by the WTO judiciary may in the end mean that it is sufficient for a finding of a WTO violation that a rule provides for WTO-inconsistent measures.[181]

This state of WTO case law regarding a member's challengeable measures under WTO dispute settlement rules means that the endeavor of this book of assessing the WTO compatibility of EU legislation implementing the new assertiveness already prior to its application by concrete measures, but done merely on the basis of their legal text, is indeed a feasible exercise of exploring the compatibility of the legal rules with WTO commitments. Even though most of the new legal instruments do grant leeway to the European Commission (as the measures provided therein require, besides specific legal exigencies, also the passing of an EU interest[182] or a balancing test[183] or make a choice of measures available), an early analysis of the new legislation in light of EU international commitments even prior to the Commission's exercise of is discretion allows for, first, determining the relevant WTO commitments of the EU to be observed in the application of a specific legislative act, in particular where new legislation grants a broad degree of discretion in choosing the

[178] ibid. [179] Panel Report, *US – Section 301*, WT/DS152/R, 22 December 1999, para. 7.54.

[180] GATT 1947 Panel Report, *US – Taxes on Petroleum and Certain Imported Substances*, L/6175 – 34S/136, 5 June 1987, para. 5.2.2.

[181] Lockhart and Sheargold, 'In Search of Relevant Discretion' (2010) 421.

[182] See e.g. Art. 4 Trade Enforcement Regulation 654/2014 as amended by Regulation 2021/167, OJ EU 2021 No. L 49/1; Art. 6 (2) IPI Regulation 2022/1031, OJ EU 2022 No. L 173/1.

[183] Art. 6 Regulation 2022/2560 of the European Parliament and the Council of 14 December 2022 on foreign subsidies distorting the internal market, OJ EU 2022 No. L 330/1, 23 December 2022 (Foreign Subsidies Regulation (FSR)).

measures to be imposed.[184] Second, it allows identifying the scope and extent of relevant leeway; third, it allows for clearly deciphering the tensions between WTO law and the new legislation, even if the legislation may not 'as such' be WTO inconsistent. The indication of tensions enables the Commission to consider its pertinent WTO obligations when employing its discretion, with a view to abstain from incompatible measures. Finally, as Lester has rightfully pointed out, legislation that grants discretion nevertheless is clearly 'most problematic' with regard to its compliance with WTO rules if it provides for specific measures (as the only possible action or one of the possible actions) that are likely to violate those rules, as the administrative body may see itself to be pushed to take those measures.[185] The mere existence of relevant legislation laying down the powers to adopt such measures must be seen as WTO incompatible when it has a chilling effect on trade (discriminatory measures may be particularly susceptible to this) or when it could cause trade conflict.[186]

3.3.2 Pertinent Disciplines of International and WTO Law and Their Relevant Obligations

3.3.2.1 WTO Law

As already mentioned, the most significant international obligations of the EU that might be affected by the new legislation in trade policy are those from the WTO agreements, with regard to both substantive obligations on how foreign goods or services might be treated as well as dispute settlement. This is because any unilateral countermeasure adopted by the EU leading to a suspension of concessions entered into by the EU or trade benefits granted to WTO members under WTO agreements might be challenged by the latter as not in compliance with the EU's commitments in that regard.

Concerning the latter, Article 23:1 DSU provides that if a WTO member seeks the redress of a violation of obligations under the WTO agreements, 'they shall have recourse to, and abide by, the rules and procedures of this

[184] With regard to e.g. the ACI Regulation, the analysis of the degree of discretion is important, as it expressly provides the possibility of imposing countermeasures in the form of non-performance of international obligations on trade and tariffs; see Annex I to the Regulation (EU) 2023/2675 on the protection of the Union and its Member States from economic coercion by third countries, OJ EU 2023 No. L 2675.

[185] Lester, 'A Framework for Thinking about the Discretion in the Mandatory/Discretionary Distinction' (2011) 399.

[186] ibid.

Understanding'. Consequently, as the EU aims at enlarging and improving its ability to enforce its trade rights, even autonomously, in particular by the amended rules of its Trade Enforcement Regulation or the adoption of the ACI, these rules might come into conflict with the DSU rules. Article 23:1 DSU quite clearly establishes a conclusive and compulsory jurisdiction of the WTO judiciary to the exclusion of any other means of adversary dispute settlement,[187] insofar as WTO commitments are concerned. Consequently, alternative dispute settlement mechanisms and the unilateral suspension of trade concessions or the adoption of other types of countermeasures taken by the EU very likely may come into tension with the DSU, at least with regard to WTO commitments. Alternative ways of enforcing EU trade rights flowing from WTO agreements may easily come into conflict with Article 23 DSU, as a panel once held that 'any unilateral attempt to obtain these results [i.e. seeking the removal of the WTO inconsistent measure, seeking compensation from the other Member, or suspending concessions or obligations under the WTO Agreement in relation to that Member] would be a violation of Article 23.1 of the DSU'.[188] In view of Petros Mavroidis, '[a]rticle 23(2) DSU imposes an unambiguous obligation on all WTO members to submit their disputes to WTO panels; as a consequence, countermeasures remain an option in the WTO only to the extent that they are multilaterally authorized by the WTO'.[189] Admittedly, this assessment might change if dispute settlement according to WTO DSU rules no longer functions; but this deserves closer inspection, as will be undertaken in Chapter 5. Another question is, of course, whether the general regime for countermeasures provided in the rules on state responsibility (Articles 49 ff ILC Draft Articles on State Responsibility; Articles 51 ff ILC Draft Articles IO),[190] which allows countermeasures in response to a previous violation of any international obligation, is applicable. Furthermore, the legality of

[187] See Panel Report, *US – Section 301*, WT/DS152/R, para. 7.43: 'exclusive dispute resolution'.

[188] Panel Report, *EC – Commercial Vessels*, WT/DS301/R, 22 April 2005, para. 7.196.

[189] Petros Mavroidis, 'Remedies in the WTO Legal System: Between a Rock and a Hard Place' (2000) 11 (4) *EJIL* 763–813 at 766. For the conclusiveness of the WTO DSU, see also Gabrielle Marceau, 'WTO Dispute Settlement and Human Rights' (2002) 13 (4) *JIEL* 753–814 at 768; Joanna Gomula, 'Responsibility and the World Trade Organization', in James Crawford, et al. (eds.), *The Law of International Responsibility* (Oxford: Oxford University Press, 2010), pp. 797 f; Sánchez, 'What Trade Lawyers Should Know about the ILC Draft Articles on State Responsibility' (2012) 294.

[190] In what follows, we will refer only to the ILC Draft Articles on State Responsibility, as the EU's countermeasures will only be directed against states.

countermeasures or reprisals under the ILC Draft Articles on State Responsibility requires a previous violation of international law by the other state. The countermeasures foreseen in the new EU trade legislation, however, do not necessarily require such prior illegal behaviour on the part of the other state. The CBAM and the Foreign Subsidies Regulation (FSR)[191] definitely apply to situations in which there hardly is a prior violation of international law by the third country, as states enjoy considerable regulatory freedom with regard to domestic carbon measures and subsidization of undertakings.

As regards trade rights from EU bilateral agreements, the EU will be able to avoid the stipulations of Article 23 DSU by claiming that the EU countermeasures address the violation by the other party of trade rights resulting from bilateral trade agreements and not from WTO rules.[192] The WTO judiciary indeed opines that the exclusivity of the DSU only applies in case of measures seeking redress for a violation of WTO law and no other trade rights.[193] If an FTA obligation merely replicates a WTO rule, claims will not arise under WTO law, so that Article 23 DSU is seen not to be affected by EU unilateral measures enforcing FTA

[191] Even though the FSR does not provide for countermeasures to be addressed to a state or its economic operators generally, the redressive measures foreseen in its Art. 7 apply to individual undertakings and may thus restrain their market access or non-discriminatory treatment, e.g. by obliging them to reduce market presence or refrain from certain activities.

[192] This is implied by the European Commission with regard to its ACI, as the Commission refers to the violation of general international law by a third country exercising economic coercion upon the EU or its Member States, which does not fall in the remit of the WTO DSU; see Impact Assessment Report Accompanying the document Proposal for a Regulation of the European Parliament and of the Council on the protection of the Union and its Member States from economic coercion by third countries (Impact Assessment Report), 8 December 2021, SWD(2021) 371 final, 15, and recitals 12 and 15 and Art. 5 (2), 8 (1) ACI Regulation (EU) 2023/2675 on the protection of the Union and its Member States from economic coercion by third countries, OJ EU 2023 No. L 2675. While this statement is correct, the problem not addressed by the Commission is the issue that the country affected by EU countermeasures interfering with its WTO trading rights definitely will and successfully can challenge the measure with regard to the EU breach of WTO commitments. Even if the EU countermeasure might be justified by the international law on reprisals under international law (and maybe also under WTO law), these general rules will not prove helpful; the EU still has violated WTO substantive rules and possibly also DSU rules by its unilateral course of action (see Chapter 6).

[193] See Panel Report, *US – Certain EC Products*, WT/DS165/R, para. 6.21; Panel Report, *EC – Commercial Vessels*, WT/DS301/R, 22 April 2005, para. 7.196; Appellate Body Reports, *US/Canada – Continued Suspension*, WT/DS320/AB/R, WT/DS321/AB/R, 16 October 2008, paras. 371–372.

commitments.[194] Things again may be different if an EU countermeasure autonomously adopted by virtue of its amended Trade Enforcement Regulation or by virtue of the ACI is challenged under Article 23 DSU in a case where EU statements could be assessed so as to prove the measures as having in fact also been imposed for a violation of like or similar WTO rules. These issues thus deserve closer attention and will be analyzed in Chapters 5 and 6.

As regards substantive obligations contained in WTO law relevant to the EU's external trade policy, the new legislation might be in tension with fundamental principles of GATT/WTO law, i.e. the most-favoured-nation (MFN) or national treatment (NT) disciplines, as enshrined in Articles I, III GATT 1994 and Articles II, XVII GATS. These non-discrimination obligations prohibit any measure which treats goods and services of a specific WTO member less beneficially than those of another WTO member or domestic like goods and services, respectively, with regard to any laws or regulations or requirements affecting internal sale, offering for sale, purchase, distribution, or use of products (see Article III:4 GATT to which Article I:1 GATT refers). The scope of application of the non-discrimination disciplines is thus very broad and covers all types of domestic legislation which has an effect on the marketing conditions of goods or services. Therefore, the redressive or countermeasures of the kind provided for in the new EU trade legislation (suspension of concessions, additional financial burdens, restraints in sale or offer for sale, and the like) will without a doubt be covered, in principle, by the WTO non-discrimination disciplines so that the latter's stipulations have to be respected by the EU. The yardstick for a less beneficial treatment is the alteration of the conditions of competition to the detriment of trading opportunities of another WTO member.[195] The possible violation of the MFN can be seen in the employment of measures against a specific

[194] Pamela Apaza Lanyi and Armin Steinbach, 'Limiting Jurisdictional Fragmentation in International Trade Disputes' (2014) 5(2) *Journal of International Dispute Settlement* 372–405 at 397; James Flett, 'Referring PTA Disputes to the WTO Dispute Settlement System', in Andreas Dür and Manfred Elsig (eds.), *Trade Cooperation: The Purpose, Design and Effects of Preferential Trade Agreements* (Cambridge: Cambridge University Press, 2015), pp. 557 f.

[195] For the protection of 'equal competitive opportunities for like products'/ 'effective equality of opportunities' under MFN and under NT, see Peter van den Bossche and Werner Zdouc, *The Law and Policy of the WTO*, 5th ed. (Cambridge: Cambridge University Press, 2022) 352, 435; for a comprehensive analysis of WTO MFN and NT, see Wolfgang Weiß, *WTO Law and Domestic Regulation* (2020) 122 f, 149 f. For the relevant WTO judiciary, see only Appellate Body Report, *EC – Seal Products*, WT/DS401/AB/R, 22 May 2014, para. 5.101.

WTO member, whereas other WTO members may not become addressees of measures or are not at all covered by the scope of a legislation. Admittedly, a complaint based on such discrimination might successfully be submitted only once a specific measure has been adopted, as the new legislation 'as such' may not necessarily imply discrimination; only the application of new legislation allowing for redressive measures in concrete circumstances can be perceived to be discriminatory. Nevertheless, there might be legislation that still could be challenged as such, merely on the basis of its formulation. The IPI, for example, might become subject of an 'as such' complaint, as it carves out from its scope of application covered procurement from WTO members with whom procurement obligations had been entered into through the GPA or bilateral FTAs,[196] whereas other WTO members may become subject to IPI measures and complain about the discriminatory character of the IPI legislation. Even though non-discrimination disciplines do not apply to certain government procurement due to Article III:8 (a) GATT,[197] still there might be cases of procurement such as concession contracts which do not fall under the Article III:8 (a) GATT exception. Then, of course, the question becomes relevant whether Article XXIV GATT laying down the requirements for regional trade exceptions may justify the departure from the MFN rule in case of the exclusion of FTA parties with respect to covered procurement, albeit not that of GPA parties. As the very reason for entering into FTAs is the granting of more beneficial treatment to the other party, the exclusion of FTA partners may be considered as a necessary consequence flowing from the reciprocal market access public procurement commitments entered into through the FTAs. Accordingly, as it will be explained in more detail in Section 8.4.2, even if the restrictive WTO jurisprudence may at first be considered an impediment, Article XXIV GATT may serve as a successful justification in case of the exclusion of FTA covered procurement. Similarly, exempting FTA partners from import restrictions that were adopted in pursuance of respected policy objectives such as environment or public health protection may lead to the import restriction not meeting the justification requirements of Article XX GATT, because the exemption for FTA partners turns the

[196] For the scope of application of the IPI, see recitals 7 and 10, Art. 1 (1) and the definition of non-covered procurement in Art. 2 (1) k) IPI Regulation.

[197] There is general agreement that the carve-out of government procurement from Arts. III:2, 4 GATT NT disciplines through its paragraph 8 a) also applies to Art. I:1 GATT on MFN; for more see Section 8.4.2.

measure into unjustifiable and arbitrary discrimination in the sense of the chapeau of Article XX GATT, as the exemption goes against the objective of the measure. Consequently, the Article XX GATT justification requirements are not met.[198]

A much more severe NT problem might arise with regard to the FSR, because like domestic service suppliers having received domestic state aids from an EU Member State appear not to be subject to the same or similar review rules. Even though FSR investigations emulate the EU domestic state aids procedures under Article 108 TFEU,[199] the redressive measures provided for in Article 7 FSR Regulation, as well as the applicable substantive rules, are different from those under EU state aids law and might prove more restrictive, and even more so when looking at genuine EU subsidies. These issues will be analyzed in more detail in Chapter 9.

Also pertinent are the disciplines on tariffs and charges as well as the ban on border measures under Articles II and XI GATT, which might be violated by the CBAM. We will assess this in detail in Chapter 10.

Another issue of concern with regard to substantive WTO commitments is the potential clash between the WTO ASCM and the new legislative instruments such as the IPI and the FSR. These debates are addressed in Chapters 8 and 9.

3.3.2.2 EU FTA Provisions

As the EU has concluded dozens of trade agreements or other treaties such as association or cooperation agreements that contain trade chapters, the EU's new legislative tools may also stand in conflict with those agreements. Besides substantive commitments, such as non-discrimination obligations or specific market access rules, the bilateral dispute settlement chapters which many of these treaties contain may be

[198] This can be learnt from the Appellate Body Report, *Brazil – Retreaded Tyres*, WT/DS332/AB/R, 3 December 2007, paras. 228 ff, where the Appellate Body also added that the discrimination does not necessarily result from Mercosur rules. In the report for the same dispute, WT/DS332/R, 12 June 2007, paras. 7.271–7.281, the panel had opined that the exception for FTA (Mercosur) partners was motivated by Brazil's compliance with a Mercosur arbitral tribunal ruling and hence was not arbitrary, and was consequently reversed.

[199] Francois-Charles Laprévote and Wanjie Lin, 'Between State Aid, Trade and Antitrust: The Mixed Procedural Heritage of the Foreign Subsidies Regulation and the Overarching Principle of Non-Discrimination' (2022) 3 *ZEuS* 443–452 at 446 ff; Wolfgang Weiß, 'Ex Officio Third Country Subsidies' Review' (2022) 21(2) *European State Aid Law Quarterly* 132–142 at 136 ff.

violated by countermeasures of the diverse types foreseen in the new legislation. Almost all EU FTAs, in particular those of the latest generation, contain dispute settlement rules, and the prevailing model provides for arbitration, where panels are convened ad hoc whenever a dispute occurs. The rules provide for the arbitral awards usually being final and binding on the parties, and for mechanisms for their implementation.[200] Unilateral countermeasures adopted by the European Commission may collide with the dispute settlement mechanisms providing mutual steps for the solution of conflicts and struggles about the behaviour of the treaty partner. A unilateral determination by the EU of a specific measure of a treaty partner as a breach of FTA rules, on the basis of which the EU adopts countermeasures, might violate the procedures for bilateral dispute settlement in the relevant FTA.

The EU can avoid such problem in several ways. First, it may distinguish its countermeasures from a response to a prior violation of the FTA. The Commission might invoke its right under general international law to adopt reprisals/countermeasures, but this requires the measure of the other party to represent a genuine violation of international law (be it general international law or bilateral commitments different from the FTA) (see Article 49 ILC Draft Articles for the requirement of an 'internationally wrongful act'). Still, the other party may then use the FTA dispute settlement rules to initiate a dispute about the EU's alleged violation of its FTA commitments, and the justification by the EU then requires clear proof of the other party having violated international law. As already mentioned in Section 3.3.2.1, the new EU trade instruments do not all require prior breach of international law by the other state, and therefore the new legislation may be susceptible to breaching FTA commitments if EU countermeasures interfere with their substantive EU commitments – for example, regarding market access or non-discrimination.

Second, if the EU adopts countermeasures as a reaction to a violation of the FTA by the other party, a violation of this FTA's dispute settlement rules by the EU can only occur if these rules preclude recourse to general rules on countermeasures. Whereas the WTO DSU is a clear case of *lex specialis* in the sense of Article 55 ILC Draft Articles, the situation appears to be different with regard to bilateral dispute settlement

[200] For more details on EU FTA dispute settlement, see Cornelia Furculita, *The WTO and the New Generation EU FTA Dispute Settlement Mechanisms: Interacting in a Fragmented and Changing International Trade Law Regime* (Cham: Springer, 2021), pp. 15 f, 20–22, 31 f.

mechanisms, as Chapter 5 will show. The alternative application of general international law rules on countermeasures in the ILC Articles by the EU clearly is possible, all the more so if directed against other breaches of international law. There may, however, be an exception to this: Enforcing FTA Trade and Sustainable Development (TSD) rules may not be allowed under general countermeasure rules, as these TSD chapters do contain their own, very specific provisions on dispute settlement, which again may be deemed to be *lex specialis* that derogates the general rules on state responsibility (we will return to this issue in Chapter 7).

3.3.2.3 *General Public International Law on State Responsibility*

As has already become manifest from the earlier discussion, it is not only specific international economic law but also rules of general public international law which have an impact on the EU's leeway in drafting the new EU trade legislation. A particularly relevant case of general rules is represented by those on reprisals or countermeasures enshrined in the ILC Draft Articles on State Responsibility, which apply as the EU vests itself with the power to adopt countermeasures in response to third-country wrongful behaviour by way of enacting and subsequently implementing the new trade legislation. Insofar as the EU measures adopted in application of the new legislation amount to a breach of WTO or FTA commitments owed to a third country, or might violate the general international law principle of non-intervention, the general rules on countermeasures enshrined in Articles 49 ff ILC Draft Articles may justify the EU countermeasures (except for the already mentioned situation where a different *lex specialis* exists, Article 55 ILC Draft Articles). A precondition thereof, of course, is that the EU countermeasures are a response to a previous breach of international law by the addressee of the EU measures that concerns an international obligation owed to the EU or affects the EU in the sense of Article 42 ILC Draft Articles. Furthermore, Articles 49 ff establish further conditions for a successful claim of a countermeasure as justification of EU's breach of international law, in particular trade rights of the other state.

There is first the direction and intention: Countermeasures may not be taken as a mere revenge but require to be adopted 'in order to induce that State to comply with its obligations' (Article 49 (1) ILC Draft Articles). Thus, countermeasures may not be used for other purposes. This stipulation is reflected in the ACI Regulation, as the countermeasures provided therein serve to induce the cessation of the economic coercion and, where appropriate, the reparation of the injury done to the EU.[201] However, there is a specific problem in that regard with the amended Trade Enforcement Regulation, as this regulation provides for the adoption of countermeasures in case of unavailable WTO dispute settlement on the appeal stage if the other party has not agreed to an alternative interim appeal procedure under Article 25 WTO DSU (see Article 3 aa) Trade Enforcement Regulation 654/2014). This will be explored in detail in Chapter 5.

Second, proportionality has to be respected (see Article 50 ILC Draft Articles), which will have an impact on the type and extent of EU countermeasures foreseen in the EU's amended Trade Enforcement Regulation[202] and in the ACI.[203] Third, Article 52's procedural obligation to first call on the state to meet its obligations (the 'sommation'), to notify of the measures and to offer negotiations must be complied with, as will be analyzed with regard to the EU's amended Trade Enforcement Regulation in Section 5.6 and the Anti-Coercion Regulation in Section 6.3.

Finally, under Article 52 (3) ILC Draft Articles, the EU must not take countermeasures, or must suspend countermeasures already taken, as soon as, and for so long as, the state's wrongful act has ceased and the dispute is pending before a binding dispute settlement institution (and as long as the dispute settlement procedure is implemented in good faith; Article 52 (4) ILC Draft Articles). While this requirement is complied with in Articles 8 (1), 12 (2), (4) ACI Regulation, the requirement may not be sufficiently reflected in Article 7 Trade Enforcement Regulation, as will be shown in Section 5.6.

3.3.2.4 General Public International Law on International Treaties

The VCLT and its special version applying to the treaties concluded by international organizations such as the EU, the VCLTSIO, provide for general rules under which one party to a treaty may suspend its treaty commitments, and these rules may be relevant to justify the EU's suspension of trade concessions (Articles 54 ff VCLTSIO). Article 60 (1)

201 See Art. 11 (2) ACI Regulation. However, the concrete choice of EU response can also consider other objectives such as the 'potential to provide relief to Union economic operators affected' by the coercive measure; see Art. 11 (2) d).

202 Art. 1 b) Regulation 654/2014 provides that the measures taken by the EU are taken with a view to balance the mutual trade commitments. Art. 4 (2) ba) restrains the countermeasures to the extent that the other state has suspended or impaired EU trading rights. See also Art. 4 (2) d).

203 Art. 11 (1) ACI Regulation.

VCLT/VCLTSIO prescribes that a material breach of a bilateral treaty by one party entitles the other to invoke the breach as a ground for terminating or suspending the treaty in whole or in part. Thus, one could opine that EU countermeasures adopted under the new trade legislation might be justified if there is a material breach, which requires, under Article 60 (3) b) VCLT/VCLTSIO, a violation of a provision essential to the accomplishment of the object or purpose of the relevant treaty. Consequently, not any breach of trade rights flowing from a bilateral treaty by a foreign country allows the EU to suspend the said treaty, in contrast to general rules on reprisals, but only essential commitments. Thus, recourse to the rules on countermeasures (which are applicable in parallel to VCLT/VCLTSIO rules; see Articles 73 VCLT and 74 (1) VCLTSIO)[204] is less demanding (procedurally also, perhaps).[205] Still, Article 60 might be attractive for the EU in case recourse to the rules on countermeasures is not possible due to the existence of specific rules in a trade agreement. The prevalence of specific rules may apply in particular to the EU FTAs' TSD chapters, as they contain specific dispute settlement rules which may be seen to provide for the exclusion of general international rules on countermeasures, as mentioned earlier. The weakness of the specific TSD dispute settlement procedures contained in the FTAs concluded until the 2022 novel approach[206] has been deplored widely, as they only provide for non-binding recommendations by the arbitration panel reports and lack the possibility of imposing sanctions in case of non-compliance. Hence, Article 60 VCLT/VCLTSIO could be deemed applicable to allow the suspension of FTAs in response to breaches of TSD commitments by the other party, and so may be the *clausula rebus sic stantibus* in Article 62

[204] See ICJ, *Gabcikovo-Nagymaros Project (Hungary v Slovakia)*, ICJ Reports 1997, 7, 38, 47. On the limits to Art. 60 VCLT's exhaustiveness, see Separate Opinion of Judge Bruno Simma, *Application of the Interim Accord of 13 September 1995 (the former Yugoslav Republic of Macedonia v Greece)*, ICJ Reports 2011, 695, paras. 23 ff.

[205] Whereas countermeasures only require sommation, Art. 65 ff VCLTSIO prescribes a detailed procedure to notify the reasons for suspension, to allow for objections to be raised within three months, and to search for an amicable solution between the parties. There is a debate about the application of the three-month period to situations of an only partial suspension of the treaty; see Frederic Kirgis, 'Some Lingering Questions about Article 60 of the Vienna Convention on the Law of Treaties' (1989) 22(3) *Cornell International Law Journal* 549–573 at 558 ff. For differences between suspension of treaty under Art. 60 VCLT and suspension as countermeasures, see Bruno Simma and Christian Tams, 'Reacting against Treaty Breaches', in Duncan Hollis (ed.), *The Oxford Guide to Treaties*, 2nd ed. (Oxford: Oxford University Press, 2020), pp. 568–594.

[206] European Commission, The power of trade partnerships: together for green and just economic growth, COM(2022) 409 final, 22 June 2022.

VCLT/VCLTSIO. The ACI is not a tool to respond to breaches of TSD chapters by the other party (as such breach usually will lack any coercion), but such breach may be relevant for a countermeasure under Article 3 b) Trade Enforcement Regulation. The first question then, of course, is the applicability of Article 60 VCLT/VCLTSIO, as its paragraph 4 provides that the 'foregoing paragraphs are without prejudice to any provision in the treaty applicable in the event of a breach', which could be understood to express a merely subsidiary character of Article 60 VCLTSIO, in the same way as the general rules on countermeasures stand behind *leges speciales* on dispute settlement. If so, then the pertinent rules on TSD dispute settlement in the FTA prevail, and Article 60 cannot be invoked. One could, however, infer from the wording of Article 60 (4) VCLT/VCLTSIO ('without prejudice') that this rule stands in parallel to more specific treaty rules dealing with the consequences of a breach or the settlement of a related dispute. This is because the wording of Article 60 (4) VCLTSIO resembles that of Article 73 VCLT and 74 (1) VCLTSIO so that one can infer the same legal meaning, and is not drafted in a way similar to Article 55 ILC Articles that clearly provides for prevalence of *lex specialis* ('do not apply where and to the extent that the conditions [. . .] are governed by special rules'). The second question which arises is the issue as to whether TSD breaches amount to a material breach of the FTA. These issues will have to be addressed in detail in Chapter 7 as well.

3.3.2.5 International Climate and Environmental Law

Specific international law on climate change and environment protection also is relevant for the EU's new legislative project with regard to the CBAM. The CBAM will affect imports of particular goods and lead to an additional import burden which may affect not only the tariff and border measure commitments in Articles II and XI GATT and the fiscal non-discrimination obligation under Article III:2 GATT (in case the new financial burden is different to relevant CO_2 charges for like domestic goods) but also particular rules on trade and climate protection enshrined in specific international instruments. Under Article 3 (5) UNFCCC, measures taken to combat climate change, including unilateral ones, should not constitute a means of arbitrary or unjustifiable discrimination or a disguised restriction on international trade. Article 2 (3) of the Kyoto Protocol to the UNFCCC provides that measures shall be implemented in such a way as to minimize adverse effects on international trade. These provisions demonstrate that international climate protection law does not allow for all types of trade restrictions and cannot serve as broad exception clauses. States cannot claim that these rules allow them to freely impede trade for climate or environmental concerns. To the contrary, climate change measures allow for trade impediments only if justified in substance and are not used to disguise other, especially protectionist, intentions. The climate change measures must respect proportionality in their effects on trade. Besides the WTO law requirements for trade barriers adopted out of climate protection motifs under Article XX (b), (g) GATT 1994, the above-mentioned rule of Article 2 (3) Kyoto Protocol may add an additional layer of demands with regard to a necessity standard which is not required under Article XX (g) GATT 1994.

In addition, international climate change law also establishes the need for differential treatment, specifically more favourable treatment to the benefit of developing countries, in particular the least developed ones.[207] The CBDR principle enshrined in the UNFCCC and in the Paris Agreement establishes that even though all states share the common responsibility to counteract global environmental degradation, their responsibility differs. It will be subject to closer scrutiny with regard to its consequences for the CBAM in Chapter 10, were other above-mentioned international legal issues will also be explored in more detail.

3.4 Conclusion

Exploring the external and internal constraints for the EU's trade policy orientation towards a more assertive trade policy, we could demonstrate that the EU's constitutional obligation to respect international law and adopt a multilateral stance restrains the drive for EU autonomy insofar as international obligations of the EU have to be observed by EU legislation, unless core constitutional characteristics of the EU legal order's autonomy are violated. Due to the CJEU case law on EU autonomy, the strict observance for international law is subject to the EU's autonomy which the Court established as a constitutional principle of the EU legal order. Essential characteristics of the EU legal order prevail in case of conflict with international law. Thus, the constitutional obligation to comply with, and hence implement, international law is not an absolute one, in contrast to the respect for the EU's autonomy. Consequently, the Court's emphasis on EU autonomy expresses the limits of the EU's commitment to international law, but this confinement to the internal

[207] Michael A. Mehling, et al., 'Designing Border Carbon Adjustments for Enhanced Climate Action' (2019) 113 (3) *AJIL* 433–481 at 472.

relevance of international law is relevant only insofar as the latter's internal implementation and legal effect on conflicting EU legislation are at stake. On the international level, the EU is bound fully by international law. Given that the EU trade policy's turn towards assertiveness does not protect essential constitutional characteristics of the EU, the protection of the EU's autonomy as an EU internal exception for respecting international law is not relevant for the trade policy reorientation. Thus, the constitutional obligation for respecting international law and multilateralism remains a core requirement in determining trade policy and legislating trade instruments. The international legal commitments must be respected and cannot be pushed aside for the mere fact of their usual internal irrelevance for assessing the internal legal force of EU acts. Avoiding conflict with international legal commitments is hence an important duty the EU institutions must respect in drafting the new EU autonomous trade policy instruments and legislation.

For the new trade instruments and legislation, the requirement of international law compliance consequently means that, first, these instruments should, as much as it is compatible with their wording, be interpreted in conformity with the EU's international legal obligations, irrespective of whether they are treaty or customary law. In this regard, what counts is the substance of an international obligation as interpreted by international actors in compliance with the accepted approaches, applications, and conceptualizations of international obligations under international law, and not peculiar EU style conceptualizations of their notion. Second, insofar as the new legislation does not only generally pay respect to WTO obligations, but explicitly implements or refers to particular WTO norms, those international rules might be relevant even for assessing the internal legal validity of the new EU legislation within the EU legal order. Otherwise, the mere fact that EU legislation is not in conformity with international treaty obligations is not sufficient to claim its illegality before EU courts and, thus, will be irrelevant for assessing the lawfulness of EU legal acts. One has to observe, however, how most recent trends in strengthening the relevance of international law for the lawfulness of EU legal acts[208] will evolve. With regard to customary international law, even though it serves as legal yardstick for EU legal acts irrespective of the issue of direct effect, the CJEU grants considerable leeway to the EU institutions.

[208] See Section 3.2.2.1.

A political consequence of this state of constitutional and international conditions for the formulation of EU trade policy is the necessity of a multilateral approach, including attempts to come to multilateral solutions. Before the EU adopts novel trade policy instruments autonomously, which tread new paths of law, the obligation to follow multilateralism suggests at least at a political, not necessarily at a legal level, the EU is expected to pursue its regulatory aspirations for more effective and fairer trade rules on multilateral level first. Admittedly, not least with the current state of international relations, this appears cumbersome and not very promising. Nevertheless, EU may first address its concerns with potentially affected trading partners and seek dialogue with them before an autonomous approach is embraced. Listening to the concerns of trade partners provides a chance to reconsider the legislation before adoption. This sends a signal of readiness for dialogue and for an enduring cooperative approach.

Within this framework, the present chapter has explored rather general issues to be observed in the subsequent analyses of the international legal compliance of the new trade instruments and legislation with diverse international legal commitments in the remaining chapters of this book. In this respect, we showed that under certain conditions, the mere existence of legislation even prior to and independent from its implementation and application to concrete cases may already prompt the EU's international legal responsibility. We highlighted the pertinent international legal commitments that are highly relevant with regard to the legal assessment of the EU's new legislation. The pertinent disciplines stem not only from WTO dispute settlement and substantive law but also from EU bilateral treaties, general public international law on treaties and responsibility of international organizations, and international climate and environmental law.

PART II

The Tools for Stronger Enforcement of Trade Rights

4 The EU-Led MPIA

An Attempt to Rescue the WTO Dispute Settlement

4.1 Introduction

As previously stated,[1] since 2016 the United States has been blocking the appointment and reappointment of the Appellate Body (AB) Members leading to the complete paralysis of the AB starting with December 2019. While at least three Members are necessary to hear appeals in a dispute, currently there is no AB Member left. Accordingly, the appellate mechanism dubbed as 'the most successful appellate mechanism in international history'[2] is unable to hear appeals lodged by disputing parties, making the adoption of an appealed panel report by the WTO Dispute Settlement Body (DSB) impossible,[3] and hence also its implementation. Therefore, unless disputing parties have reached an alternative arrangement, any dissatisfied disputing party can appeal a panel report into the void, leaving the dispute unresolved until at least three AB Members are appointed and precluding also the possibility to resort to the suspension of concessions or other obligations for the non-implementation of the reports' recommendations and rulings. In June 2022, at the 12th WTO Ministerial Conference, WTO members agreed to start negotiations on WTO reform, including Appellate Body reform, with the hope to table an Appellate Body reform proposal in early

[1] See Chapter 2.

[2] Qualification given by the late James Crawford, '"Back to Square One" if WTO Appeals Body Fails: Judge James Crawford', *Financial Review*, 3 August 2018, www.afr.com/policy/economy/back-to-square-one-if-wto-appeals-body-fails-judge-james-crawford-20180802-h13hz0.

[3] According to Art. 16 (4) DSU, a panel report is adopted by the DSB '*unless* a party to the dispute formally notifies the DSB of its *decision to appeal* or the DSB decides by consensus not to adopt the report' (emphasis added).

2024, at the next Ministerial Conference.[4] This aim appears very difficult to reach given the current state of international affairs which makes dialogue, not to mention agreement, between the United States and China on any reform proposal an almost impossible endeavor.

The AB's paralysis prompted Members to seek alternative solutions. The EU turned to appeal arbitration under Article 25 Dispute Settlement Understanding (DSU)[5] – a temporary alternative first suggested in 2017 by six lawyers.[6] In order to maintain a two-stage WTO dispute settlement process, it first signed bilateral interim appeal arbitration arrangements with Canada in July 2019 and with Norway in October of that same year.[7] The text of these arrangements served as a basis for the negotiations of the EU and 15 other Members,[8] reaching an agreement on the Multi-Party Interim Appeal Arbitration Arrangement (MPIA) in March 2020 and notifying the WTO of it in April 2020.[9]

While in the Annex to its Trade Policy Review the EU acknowledges the US concerns about certain AB approaches and agrees that a meaningful reform of the WTO dispute settlement is needed,[10] the Trade Policy Review under the headline action of strengthening the implementation and enforcement of trade agreements emphasizes the need to address non-compliance through WTO dispute settlement.[11] Furthermore, the EU claims that its 'first priority is the restoring of a fully-functioning dispute

[4] MC12 Outcome Document, WT/MIN(22)/24, paras. 3 f.

[5] Understanding on Rules and Procedures Governing the Settlement of Disputes (DSU), Marrakesh Agreement Establishing the World Trade Organization, Annex 2, 1869 U.N.T.S. 401, 33 I.L.M. 1226 (1994).

[6] Scott Andersen, et al., 'Using Arbitration under Article 25 of the DSU to Ensure the Availability of Appeals' (2017) 17 CTEI Working Papers.

[7] WTO, Communication from Canada and the European Union, 'Interim Appeal Arbitration Pursuant to Article 25 of the DSU', JOB/DSB/1/Add.11, 25 July 2019; WTO, Communication from Norway and the European Union, 'Interim Appeal Arbitration Pursuant to Article 25 of the DSU', JOB/DSB/1/Add.11/Suppl.1, 21 October 2019.

[8] Olga Starshinova, 'Is the MPIA a Solution to the WTO Appellate Body Crisis?' (2021) 55(5) *JWT* 787–804 at 792.

[9] European Commission, 'EU and 15 World Trade Organization Members Establish Contingency Appeal Arrangement for Trade Disputes', 27 March 2020, https://ec.europa.eu/commission/presscorner/detail/en/IP_20_538; WTO, Statement on a Mechanism for Developing, Documenting and Sharing Practices and Procedures in the Conduct of WTO Disputes, 'Multi-Party Interim Appeal Arbitration Arrangement Pursuant to Article 25 of the DSU', 30 April 2020, JOB/DSB/1/Add.12 ('MPIA').

[10] Commission Communication, Trade Policy Review: An Open, Sustainable and Assertive Trade Policy (Trade Policy Review), COM(2021) 66 final, Annex, p. 7.

[11] Trade Policy Review, COM(2021) 66 final, p. 20.

settlement'.[12] In order to be able to continue using the two-stage WTO mechanism for enforcement and implementation without panel reports being appealed into the void, the EU led the efforts to create the MPIA, which has already resulted in successful appeal arbitrations in *Colombia – Frozen Fries*,[13] and was emulated by ad hoc appeal arbitrations in *Turkey – Pharmaceutical Products*.[14]

This chapter will deal with this new arrangement. It will first introduce Article 25 DSU, the conditions that are necessary to be fulfilled in case of its use and assess the usage of arbitration for the appellate stage (Section 4.2). Then, it will present the MPIA, simultaneously assessing its compliance with Article 25 DSU conditions, the similarity with regular appeals, and the innovations that it introduced aiming at rescuing the two-stage WTO dispute settlement (Section 4.3). To establish whether the MPIA can indeed ensure assertive enforcement, respecting EU's commitment to strengthen the enforcement of its trade rights, it will be investigated whether the appeal arbitration is likely to provide security and predictability and high-quality awards. The issue of security and predictability is also essential to unlocking the current AB stalemate. Consequently, especially by considering the recent appeal arbitration awards issued under Article 25 DSU, the potential contribution of the MPIA in this respect will be analyzed (Section 4.4). Section 4.5 will then examine whether this instrument could be enforced within WTO proceedings in case of its breach by an uncooperative attitude of one of the signatories in a concrete dispute; here the relevant jurisprudence and the impossibility to hold regular appeals will be taken into account. Following this, the broader implications for the multilateral trading system and the dispute settlement crisis will be addressed (Section 4.6). The chapter will conclude by summarizing the findings and weighing in on whether the potential benefits of the MPIA are worth taking the risks (Section 4.7).

4.2 Article 25 DSU: Appeal Arbitration and Conditions

Before presenting the MPIA, it is necessary to introduce Article 25 of the DSU, which was used as a legal basis for its creation. In what follows, we

[12] Communication from the European Union, Reinforcing the Deliberative Function of the WTO to Respond to Global Trade Policy Challenges, WT/GC/W/864, 6–7 March 2023.

[13] Award of the Arbitrators, *Colombia – Frozen Fries*, Arbitration Under Article 25 of the DSU, WT/DS591/ARB25, 21 December 2022.

[14] Award of the Arbitrators, *Turkey – Pharmaceutical Products*, WT/DS583/ARB25, 25 July 2022.

explore whether it allows the use of arbitration for the appellate stage and what are the conditions established therein that should be complied with.

According to Article 25.1 DSU, '[e]xpeditious arbitration within the WTO as an *alternative* means of dispute settlement can facilitate the solution of *certain* disputes that concern issues that are *clearly defined* by both parties' (emphasis added). The possibility to use Article 25 DSU as an alternative means within the WTO has also been confirmed by the panel in *US – Certain EC Products*, where it stated that '[t]here is no reason why the WTO assessment of the compatibility of an implementing measure could not be determined by an Article 25 arbitration, as one of the WTO dispute settlement procedures'.[15] However, it is doubtful whether *ex ante* appeal arbitration agreements between parties that would apply to all their potential future disputes concerning undefined issues comply with the condition that the arbitration should be used for 'certain disputes' concerning 'clearly defined' issues. Although it was claimed that agreeing *ex ante* on appeal arbitrations would only concern the issues of law from an appealed panel report that the parties contest could comply with this condition,[16] the disputes would remain uncertain, and it is debatable whether such a broad reading would be justified. This issue of compatibility with the requirements of Article 25.1 DSU will be explored in detail in Section 4.3.

In order to resort to arbitration, the 'mutual agreement of the parties which shall agree on the procedures to be followed' is necessary – an agreement that should be notified sufficiently in advance of the commencement of the proceedings to all the WTO Members (Article 25.2 DSU). Thus, parties are free to depart from the standard DSU proceedings,[17] subject to certain conditions, such as a transparency obligation aiming to allow other Members to establish their course of action in respect to the dispute at hand.[18] The disputing parties shall agree to

[15] Panel Report, *US – Certain EC Products*, WT/DS165/R, 17 July 2000, para. 6.119.

[16] Geraldo Vidigal, 'Living without the Appellate Body: Multilateral, Bilateral and Plurilateral Solutions to the WTO Dispute Settlement Crisis' (2019) 20 *JWIT* 862–890 at 884.

[17] George A. Papaconstantinou and Luigi F. Pedreschi, 'Alternative Dispute Settlement and the Jurisprudential Legacy of the World Trade Organization's Appellate Body' (2022) 56(2) *JWT* 261–282 at 266.

[18] Elisa Baroncini, 'Preserving the Appellate Stage in the WTO Dispute Settlement Mechanism: The EU and the Multi-Party Interim Appeal Arbitration Arrangement' (2019) 29 *The Italian Yearbook of International Law* 33–52 at 36; Elisa Baroncini, 'The EU Approach to Overcome the WTO Dispute Settlement Vacuum: Article 25 DSU Interim Appeal

abide by the arbitral award that shall be notified to the DSB and the Council or Committee of any relevant agreement where any Member may raise any point relating thereto (Article 25.3, second and third sentence DSU). Therefore, although an arbitral award issued under Article 25 DSU is not subject to the DSB adoption, it is still mandatory by virtue of the agreement of the parties,[19] which represents another necessary condition. Moreover, WTO Members can still express their opinion in this regard. Unlike regular dispute settlement proceedings, in which any Member that has a substantial interest in the sense of Article 10.2 DSU can participate as a third party, other Members can become third parties in arbitration proceedings only upon the agreement of the disputing parties (Art. 25.3, first sentence DSU). An arbitration award issued under Article 25 DSU can be implemented according to the rules applicable to any final panel or AB report, being subject to Articles 21 and 22 DSU on surveillance of implementation and compensation and suspension of concessions (Article 25.4 DSU). Arbitration under Article 25 DSU is also subject to Article 1.1 DSU establishing that DSU rules and procedures apply to disputes brought under the covered agreements.[20] Accordingly, while parties have considerable leeway to frame their own rules, they cannot choose other applicable law than the WTO agreements.[21] This is also confirmed by Article 3.5 DSU, which provides that arbitral awards should be consistent with covered agreements and 'shall not nullify or impair benefits accruing to any Member under those agreements, nor impede the attainment of any objective of those agreements'.[22] While Article 27.1 DSU establishes that the Secretariat assists panels, there is no similar express provision with respect to assistance provided to arbitrators selected under Article 25 DSU. Furthermore, the negotiating history

Arbitration as a Bridge between Renovation and Innovation', in Meredith Kolsky Lewis, et al. (eds.), *A Post-WTO International Legal Order. Utopian, Dystopian and Other Scenarios* (Cham: Springer, 2020), p. 119.

19 Also confirmed by the arbitrators in Award of the Arbitrators, *Turkey – Pharmaceutical Products*, WT/DS583/ARB25, para. 3.3.

20 Andersen et al., 'Using Arbitration under Article 25', para. 9.

21 Cornelia Furculita, *The WTO and the New Generation EU FTA Dispute Settlement Mechanisms. Interacting in a Fragmented and Changing International Trade Law Regime* (Cham: Springer, 2021), p. 357.

22 However, Porges argues that Art. 25 DSU could be used to settle issues outside WTO law (Amy Porges, 'Alternative Dispute Settlement in the GATT and the WTO', in Daniel Bethlehem (eds.), *The Oxford Handbook of International Trade Law*, 2nd ed. (Oxford: Oxford University Press, 2022), pp. 1059–1060).

reveals that issues such as financing and administrative and legal support of arbitrators were contentious during the drafting process.[23]

Despite the fact that Article 25 DSU offers an alternative way of WTO dispute settlement, before being considered for appeal proceedings, it was used only once in *US – Section 110(5) of US Copyright Act.*[24] This precedent is less informative in respect to this article's potential because it was used only for the determination of the level of nullification or impairment of benefits after a finding of violation by the panel in its report.[25] Nevertheless, the award from *US – Section 110(5) of US Copyright Act* still provides some findings that are valuable in the context of appeal arbitrations. The arbitrators concluded that '[i]n the absence of a multilateral control [. . .] it is incumbent on the Arbitrators themselves to ensure that it is applied in accordance with the rules and principles governing the WTO system'.[26] In particular, the arbitrators highlighted that the arbitration 'should not be applied so as to circumvent the provisions of Article 22.6 of the DSU'.[27] It seems that arbitrators assumed the responsibility to check the compatibility of the arbitration agreement at issue with the WTO rules, implying that if it circumvented DSU rules, it would have been void.[28] They argued that while it may be claimed that Article 25 DSU represents an alternative only to panel proceedings, the terms of the article may support the view that it 'should be understood as an arbitration mechanism to which Members may have recourse whenever necessary within the WTO framework'.[29] Accordingly, it may be inferred that Article 25 arbitration proceedings can be used for any stage of dispute settlement, including for appeals, especially as long as it is in accordance with DSU's object and purpose – the prompt settlement of a dispute.[30] While the DSU is silent on secretarial support being offered to arbitrators under Article 25 DSU, this aspect did not raise any questions in *US – Section 110(5) of the US Copyright Act*: the USA and the European

23 Kholofelo Kugler, 'Operationalizing MPIA Appeal Arbitrations: Opportunities and Challenges', in Manfred Elsig, et al. (eds.), *International Economic Dispute Settlement: Demise or Transformation* (Cambridge: Cambridge University Press, 2021), pp. 76, 90.

24 Award of the Arbitrators, *US – Section 110(5) of the US Copyright Act*, WT/DS160/ARB25/1, 9 November 2001.

25 ibid, paras. 1.1–1.2. Moreover, compliance is yet to be achieved in this dispute.

26 ibid, para. 2.1.

27 ibid, fn. 22 to para. 2.1.

28 Vidigal, 'Living without the Appellate Body' (2019) 883.

29 Award of the Arbitrators, *US – Section 110(5) of the US Copyright Act*, WT/DS160/ARB25/1, paras. 2.3–2.4.

30 ibid, para. 2.5.

Communities (EC) asked for support for the arbitrators and the WTO Secretariat's Legal Affairs Division granted it without ado.[31]

As it can be seen, arbitral proceedings under Article 25 of the DSU represent an autonomous alternative, which, however, is well integrated into the WTO dispute settlement process[32] through notification requirements to the membership, standard implementation rules, and the applicable law. Moreover, since Article 25 is part of the DSU, Article 23 requiring recourse to DSU rules and procedures when a Member seeks redress of a WTO breach is also fully respected in case of using this alternative.[33] The fact that MPIA participants, including the EU, resorted to a 'within the system' alternative in the AB crisis context is commendable, since it shows their support for the WTO dispute settlement.[34] Hence, even if the EU has other unilateral initiatives the legality of which are questionable under the WTO rules,[35] the MPIA is a demonstration of the participants' will to respect the multilateral trade rules, as they could have designed appeal alternatives outside the system, in violation of Article 23 DSU. Albeit subject to control from arbitrators, Article 25 DSU proceedings cannot be hindered by the DSB consensus either during the process of selection of arbitrators or with respect to the bindingness of the arbitral award. Arbitration under Article 25 DSU is defined by flexibility. Although negotiators might not have designed this article with this particular usage in mind,[36] there is no limitation in its terms that would preclude the use of Article 25 DSU for the appeal stage[37] – a conclusion also supported by the pre-MPIA case law. Furthermore, the disputing Members have the freedom to agree on appellate rules that mirror DSU proceedings.

To conclude, while disputing parties generally enjoy a great degree of flexibility, for the use of appeal arbitration, certain conditions stipulated in Article 25 DSU should be respected: (1) using the alternative for certain disputes concerning clearly defined issues; (2) mutual agreement of the

[31] Kugler, 'Operationalizing MPIA Appeal Arbitrations' (2021), p. 90.

[32] Baroncini, 'Preserving the Appellate Stage' (2019) 36.

[33] Cornelia Furculita, 'The EU's Interim Appeal Arbitration Arrangements: What to Expect?' (2020) https://papers.ssrn.com/sol3/papers.cfm?abstract_id=4787713.

[34] Brad McDonald, 'WTO Dispute Settlement and Rule-Making: One Crisis or Two?' (2021) 55 (3) *JWT* 383–396 at 390.

[35] See, for example, Chapters 5 and 6.

[36] Kugler, 'Operationalizing MPIA Appeal Arbitrations' (2021), 74.

[37] Vidigal, 'Living without the Appellate Body' (2019), 876; Kugler, 'Operationalizing MPIA Appeal Arbitrations' (2021), 74; Starshinova, 'Is the MPIA a Solution?' (2021), 791; Papaconstantinou and Pedreschi, 'Alternative Dispute Settlement' (2022), 266.

parties on the procedures to be followed and to abide by the arbitral award; (3) notification requirements with respect to the arbitration agreement and the award; (4) WTO agreements should be the applicable law and arbitral awards be consistent with them; and (5) arbitration agreements should not circumvent the DSU rules. The creation of an appeal alternative within the WTO system based on Article 25 DSU showcases EU support for trade multilateralism and confirms its intention to comply with international law (whether in the end it really complied with it when designing the MPIA will be explored in more detail in the subsequent sections).

4.3 The MPIA: Introduction, Conformity with the DSU Requirements, and Innovations

This section will introduce the MPIA, assess its compatibility with the conditions established by Article 25 DSU, and present the innovations that the arrangement introduces.

4.3.1 Multi-Party, *Ex Ante*, and Interim Arrangement

The MPIA is structured in three parts: the main part of the arrangement contained in the Communication to the DSB, Annex 1 on the agreed procedures for arbitration, and Annex 2 on the composition of the pool of arbitrators. The MPIA is a *multi-party* arrangement signed by 26 WTO Members as of March 2023, the EU being counted as a single Member. Besides the EU, other important users of the WTO dispute settlement participate, such as China, Brazil, Canada, Mexico,[38] and, most recently, Japan. The most notable absent participant is, however, the United States. Besides it, other important WTO dispute settlement users are missing, for example, India, the United Kingdom, Russia, and Argentina. Although the MPIA has only a few participants relative to the entire WTO membership, it still would have covered about one-fourth of all the disputes brought to the WTO dispute settlement between 1995 and 2019 (based on the number of requests for consultations during this period).[39] Any WTO Member can join the MPIA at any time by notifying the DSB that it

[38] These countries are in the top ten users of the WTO dispute settlement (Peter van den Bossche, 'Is There a Future for the WTO Appellate Body and WTO Dispute Settlement?' (2022) WTI Working Paper No. 01/2022, 21).

[39] Matteo Fiorini, et al., 'WTO Dispute Settlement and the Appellate Body Crisis: Insider Perceptions and Members' Revealed Preferences' (2020) 54(5) *JWT* 667–698 at 680; Bernard M. Hoekman and Petros C. Mavroidis, 'To AB or Not to AB: Dispute Settlement in WTO Reform' (2020) 23 *JIEL* 703–722 at 704.

endorses the arrangement (MPIA, paragraph 12). Similarly, any participating Member may cease its participation by notifying the DSB of its withdrawal, the MPIA continuing to apply to pending disputes on the date of such withdrawal, with any existing appeal agreements remaining in force (MPIA, paragraph 14).

Although the MPIA is concluded between multiple WTO Members, it is not a plurilateral agreement in the sense of Article X:9 Marrakesh Agreement,[40] which requires adoption by consensus of the Membership[41] (whereas the MPIA is signed by its participants; see Article 25.2 DSU). The term 'multi-party' used with respect to the arrangement instead of 'plurilateral' also suggests the will of the participants to dissociate it from plurilateral trade agreements concluded under Article X:9 Marrakesh Agreement. The main part of the arrangement contains the preamble and its general principles, setting only the participants' 'intention to enter into the arbitration agreement' 'in order to render the appeal arbitration procedure operational in particular disputes' (MPIA, paragraph 10). The parties must mutually agree on arbitration and the procedures to be followed (Annex 1 to MPIA, paragraph 1), as Article 25.2 DSU requires, only after a particular dispute between the parties materializes. Hence, the MPIA is an *ex ante* arbitration arrangement between multiple parties to agree on appeal arbitration procedures under Article 25 DSU for the appealed panel reports in disputes between them.[42] The term *arrangement* also indicates that the MPIA is not in itself the arbitration *agreement*. Even though the MPIA has an *ex ante* character, the requirement of Article 25.1 DSU that only certain dispute concerning clearly defined issues should be the subject of arbitration[43] is easily complied with, since arbitration *agreements* are signed only when specific disputes between the parties materialize. Moreover, the arbitration procedures contained in Annex 1, on which parties must agree in every dispute, provide that arbitration appeals will concern only the specific issues raised by the parties, necessary for the resolution of the dispute, and will deal solely with issues of law and panels' legal interpretation (Annex 1 to MPIA, paragraphs 9, 10). Accordingly, each individual

[40] Marrakesh Agreement Establishing the World Trade Organization, 15 April 1994, 1867 U.N.T.S. 154, 33 I.L.M. 1144 (1994).

[41] Furculita, 'The EU's Interim Appeal Arbitration Arrangements' (2020); Joost Pauwelyn, 'The MPIA: What's New (Part III)', IELP Blog, 6 March 2023, https://ielp.worldtradelaw.net/2023/03/the-mpia-whats-new-part-iii.html.

[42] Kugler, 'Operationalizing MPIA Appeal Arbitrations' (2021), p. 77.

[43] See Section 4.2.

arbitration agreement applies to a specific dispute concerning clearly defined issues.

Since the MPIA was created as a solution to the AB crisis, as the title of the arrangement itself suggests, it has only an interim character. Over time, the MPIA and ad hoc arbitration agreements signed between non-MPIA signatories could turn into a de facto permanent solution.[44] Nevertheless, to show that originally participants did not intended to replace the AB with the MPIA and to encroach upon the regular functioning of the WTO dispute settlement system, the MPIA uses strong language to emphasize its temporary nature.[45] Thus, the MPIA in its preamble mentions that it places 'contingency measures' and underlines 'the interim nature' of the arrangement. Furthermore, on several occasions it provides that participants will resort to appeal arbitration only as long as the AB is not able to hear appeals (MPIA, paragraphs 1, 15; Annex 1 to MPIA, paragraph 2), and establishes that solving the AB crisis represents a matter of priority for them.[46] Considering the temporary character of the MPIA and that appeal arbitration will be used only as long as the AB is dysfunctional, the requirements established by jurisprudence that arbitration should not circumvent the DSU rules should be deemed respected.[47] By agreeing to resort to appeal arbitration, as the first MPIA appeal review in *Colombia – Frozen Fries* confirms, participating Members endorse a fully functioning two-level dispute settlement system without the risk that appealed panel reports remain in limbo for an indefinite period. Accordingly, the use of Article 25 DSU for appellate proceedings as long as the AB remains paralyzed contributes to the prompt settlement of disputes and does not circumvent the DSU rules.

Thus, the MPIA is a multi-party and ex ante *arrangement*, complying with the conditions that Article 25 DSU arbitration proceedings should be subject to the mutual agreement of the parties, apply to certain disputes on clearly defined issues, and should not circumvent the DSU rules.

[44] Porges, 'Alternative Dispute Settlement in the GATT and the WTO' (2022), 1062; Julia Qin, 'Turkey – Pharmaceuticals: The First WTO Arbitration for Appellate Review' (2022) 49(4) *LIEI* 415–430 at 426–430, argues that ad hoc appeal arbitration under Art. 25 DSU could become a permanent solution.

[45] Andrea Hamann, 'Living without the WTO Appellate Body: Procedural Developments in International Trade Dispute Settlement' (2021) 20 *The Law and Practice of International Courts and Tribunals* 166–190 at 174.

[46] MPIA, Preamble, recital 3, para. 15.

[47] Vidigal, 'Living without the Appellate Body' (2019) 884.

4.3.2 Appeal Arbitration Procedures under the MPIA

This subsection will analyze the appeal procedures as contemplated by the MPIA in order to further assess its compliance with Article 25 DSU requirements. It will also appraise the similarity of the MPIA procedures to regular appeal reviews. MPIA procedures replicating to a great extent the already familiar rules would signal participants', including EU's commitment to the dispute settlement as enshrined in the DSU and their intention to rescue it, even if with certain reforms.

The appeal arbitration procedures under the MPIA are designed to mirror closely the ordinary appellate review. This becomes evident from the main part of the MPIA, where it is stated that the procedures 'will be based on the substantive and procedural aspects of Appellate Review pursuant to Article 17 of the DSU, in order to keep its core features' (MPIA, paragraph 3), as well as from Annex 1 setting the model proceedings, which establishes that unless otherwise provided in the procedures, 'the arbitration shall be governed, *mutatis mutandis*, by the provisions of the DSU and other rules and procedures applicable to Appellate Review' (Annex 1 to MPIA, paragraph 11). However, in line with the flexibility that arbitration under the DSU entails, participants can depart from the model procedures established in Annex 1 in specific disputes (MPIA, paragraph 11).

Complying with Article 25.2 DSU, requiring to notify WTO Members sufficiently in advance of the commencement of arbitration, the MPIA provides that the appeal arbitration agreements should be notified within sixty days of panel establishment or, in case of pending disputes – thirty days after the date of the MPIA communication (MPIA, paragraph 10). It applies to any future dispute between the participants, at the compliance stage and including pending disputes in which the interim panel report was not issued before the MPIA's communication (MPIA, paragraph 9).[48] To ensure the proper administration of appeal arbitration procedures, the MPIA envisages limited adjustments to the panel proceedings (MPIA, paragraph 8). Thus, according to the model procedures, the parties will request the panel to notify them of the anticipated date of final panel report circulation no later than 45 days prior of that date (Annex 1 to MPIA, paragraph 3). With a view to initiate appeal arbitration

[48] In fn. 3 to this paragraph it is, however, explicitly mentioned that '[t]his is without prejudice to the right of the parties to decide to apply appeal arbitration procedures, such as those contained in Annex 1, to more advanced disputes on an *ad hoc* basis'.

proceedings, no later than ten days before the report's circulation to the entire Membership, any party may request the panel to suspend its proceedings, lift the confidentiality of the report, and transmit the panel records to the arbitrators and the final panel report in the WTO working languages to the parties and third parties (Annex 1 to MPIA, paragraph 4). While parties are free to decide this aspect in case of arbitration procedures, in line with Article 25.3 DSU (see Section 4.2), the model proceedings seeking to closely replicate regular appellate reviews show participants' agreement to allow the participation of third parties having a substantial interest in the matter pursuant to Article 10.2 DSU (Annex 1 to MPIA, paragraph 16). Annex 1 to the MPIA explicitly provides that third parties may make written submissions, shall be given the opportunity to be heard, and that Rule 24 on third parties of the Working Procedures for Appellate Review apply *mutatis mutandis* (Annex 1 to MPIA, paragraph 16). Moreover, since the MPIA refers to third parties in the sense of Article 10.2 DSU, 'any Member' and not just MPIA participants can act as third parties, similar to the participation in regular appeals. This is confirmed by practice, as in *Colombia – Frozen Fries*, besides Brazil, an MPIA signatory, United States and Japan (a non-MPIA signatory at the time) participated as third parties.[49]

Appeal arbitrations are initiated by filing a Notice of Appeal to the WTO Secretariat and notifying other parties and third parties no later than twenty days from the suspension of panel proceedings, the relevant rules from the Working Procedures for Appellate Review being applicable *mutatis mutandis* (Annex 1 to MPIA, paragraph 5). The MPIA not only provides appeal arbitration rules but also contains a limited no-appeal pact (NAP), in which participants appear to relinquish their right to regular appeals until the AB crisis is resolved in case they do not use appeal arbitration proceedings (MPIA, paragraph 2; Annex 1 to MPIA, paragraph 6). The effects of the NAP and their lawfulness are explored in more detail in Section 4.5. In case of appeal arbitration, appellants may still withdraw their appeals at any time during the arbitration, and if no appeal remains, regular panel proceedings resume (Annex 1 to MPIA, paragraph 18).

The appeals are heard by three appeal arbitrators chosen from a pool of ten standing appeal arbitrators (MPIA, paragraph 4; Annex 1 to MPIA, paragraph 7). The pool of arbitrators is composed by consensus after a

[49] Award of the Arbitrators, *Colombia – Frozen Fries*, WT/DS591/ARB25, Annexes D-1, D-2, D-3.

pre-selection process (former AB Members are exempted from this process) and should comprise 'persons of recognised authority, with demonstrated expertise in law, international trade and the subject matter of the covered agreements generally' (MPIA, paragraph 4; Annex 2 to MPIA, paragraphs 3, 4, and footnote 1 to paragraph 1). Hence, the requirements for MPIA arbitrators are the same as for AB Members.[50] The pool of arbitrators was composed in July 2020.[51] Still, it may be modified by the consensus of the participating Members at any time, and in case the AB crisis continues, it will be periodically and partially re-composed two years after the composition (Annex 2 to MPIA, paragraph 5).[52] The selection of arbitrators from the pool of arbitrators for specific disputes is done based on the same rules and methods as for the selection of a division of the AB (MPIA, paragraph 6; Annex 1 to MPIA, paragraph 7). Since the MPIA is set to deal with appealed findings from panel reports, it is conspicuous that the appeal arbitrators apply the WTO agreements complying with the condition with respect to the applicable law. While the AB benefitted from legal and administrative support from the AB Secretariat, the MPIA envisages support from an entirely separate structure from the WTO Secretariat staff and divisions, 'answerable, regarding the substance of their work, only to appeal arbitrators', and the availability of which should be ensured by the WTO Director General (DG) (MPIA, paragraph 7). While initially it was unclear who will be part of this separate structure and how it was going to be financed,[53] in practice it was WTO Secretariat staff from other divisions than Legal Affairs or Rules Divisions supporting the panel in the first instance, paid from the WTO budget.[54] Although the United States has objected at first to the use of

[50] In this respect, see DSU, Art. 17.3.

[51] WTO, Statement on a Mechanism for Developing, Documenting and Sharing Practices and Procedures in the Conduct of WTO Disputes, JOB/DSB/1/Add.12/Suppl.5.

[52] As of March 2023, however, this was not the case.

[53] Simon Lester, 'Who's Going to Pay for Supporting the MPIA?', IELP Blog, 15 June 2020, https://ielp.worldtradelaw.net/2020/06/whos-going-to-pay-for-the-mpia.html; Simon Lester, 'Can Interim Appeal Arbitration Preserve the WTO Dispute System?' (2020) 77 CATO Institute Free Trade Bulletin Hubert A. Stiefel Center for Trade Policy Studies, www.cato.org/free-trade-bulletin/can-interim-appeal-arbitration-preserve-wto-dispute-system#; Caroline Glöckle, 'Bridging the Gap: The MPIA as a Valuable Short-Term Solution to the Impasse of the WTO's Appellate Body?', Völkerrechtsblog, 12 October 2020, https://voelkerrechtsblog.org/bridging-the-gap-the-mpia-as-a-valuable-short-term-solution-to-the-impasse-of-the-wtos-appellate-body/; Kugler, 'Operationalizing MPIA Appeal Arbitrations' (2021), p. 90; Starshinova, 'Is the MPIA a Solution to the WTO Appellate Body Crisis?' (2021) 796.

[54] Pauwelyn, 'The MPIA: What's New (Part III)' (2023).

WTO budget funds 'for a process that is clearly far more than a simple Article 25 arbitration',[55] no similar objections were voiced thereafter.

Under the model procedures, the signatories request appeal arbitrators to issue the award within 90 days following the filing of the Notice of Appeal (Annex 1 to MPIA, paragraph 12), the same maximum time limit that the DSU provides for regular appeals.[56] Complying with the requirements established by Article 25.3 DSU, the model proceedings expressly establish that the parties agree to abide by the arbitration award, which 'shall be notified to, but not adopted by, the DSB and to the Council or Committee of any relevant agreement' (Annex to MPIA, paragraph 15). While not expressly providing that arbitral awards shall be consistent with the covered agreements as stated in Article 3.5 DSU, this becomes evident from the preamble of the MPIA, where it is mentioned that 'awards cannot add to or diminish the rights and obligations provided in the covered agreements' and that it seeks to 'preserve their rights and obligations under the WTO Agreement' (MPIA, Preamble, recitals 4, 6). Finally, replicating Article 25.4 DSU, the proceedings establish that Articles 21 and 22 DSU shall apply *mutatis mutandis* to the appeal arbitration awards (Annex 1 to MPIA, paragraph 17).

Thus, the MPIA complies with the remaining Article 25 DSU conditions, that is, mutual agreement to abide by the arbitral award, notification requirements, applicable law, and conformity of the award with the WTO agreements. Unless participants to particular disputes decide otherwise, the appeal arbitration procedures replicate the regular appellate review with few modifications. Hence, the MPIA allows for the continuity of the familiar two-staged WTO dispute settlement process and shows the MPIA participants', including the EU's, commitment to and support for the DSU rules.

4.3.3 The MPIA's New Features: Timeline, Article 11 Claims, *Obiter Dicta*, and Flexibility

While the MPIA seems to replicate the familiar WTO appellate review, it also introduces some new elements. These innovations seem to address some of the US concerns with respect to the AB's activity, which indicates MPIA participants' engagement in solving the AB crisis and rescuing the

[55] Permanent Mission of the USA to the WTO, 5 June 2020, https://drive.google.com/file/d/1QIhcAoqU8pmdR6nKz0LNmfx8GR6s1lr3/view.

[56] DSU, Art. 17.5.

multilateral dispute settlement system. In what follow, the innovations and the concerns that they seek to address will be presented.

The United States has criticized the AB for routinely violating the 90-day deadline since 2011, stating that it 'has assumed the authority to take whatever time it considers appropriate for individual appeals' without providing a justification for disregarding a clear rule and without having the agreement of the parties to do so.[57] The MPIA indirectly addresses this issue by increasing the number of available adjudicators, the pool of arbitrators consisting of ten arbitrators, whereas the AB had only seven Members. The increase in the number of the appeal adjudicators and the more limited number of disputes that will be dealt with under the MPIA makes it more likely that the 90-days timeline will be respected.[58]

The issue of the deadline is also directly addressed by the MPIA through several innovations. Thus, appeal arbitrators 'may take appropriate organizational measures to streamline the proceedings, without prejudice to the procedural rights and obligations of the parties and due process', such as decisions on page limits, time limits, and deadlines, as well as the length and number of hearings (Annex 1 to MPIA, paragraph 12). Hence, the arbitrators *may* take organizational measures at their own discretion, without the agreement of the parties. Appeal arbitrators from *Colombia – Frozen Fries*, the first MPIA appeal arbitration, as well as from the arbitral appellate review in *Turkey – Pharmaceutical Products*, which largely followed the MPIA model procedures, took several organizational measures. They streamlined the procedures by taking such measures as imposing word limits on the length of the written submissions, suggesting what to include in submissions, requiring an executive summary of written submissions to be annexed to the final awards, time limits on opening and closing oral statements, number of hearings, and sending questions to the parties and third parties in advance of the hearing.[59] The arbitrators in *Colombia – Frozen Fries* sent a pre-arbitration letter in which

[57] USTR, The President's 2018 Trade Policy Agenda, https://ustr.gov/sites/default/files/files/Press/Reports/2018/AR/2018%20Annual%20Report%20I.pdf, p. 24; USTR, Report on the Appellate Body of the World Trade Organization, February 2020, https://ustr.gov/sites/default/files/Report_on_the_Appellate_Body_of_the_World_Trade_Organization.pdf, p. 26.

[58] Starshinova, 'Is the MPIA a Solution to the WTO Appellate Body Crisis?' (2021) 795.

[59] Award of the Arbitrators, *Turkey – Pharmaceutical Products*, WT/DS583/ARB25, para. 2.2. For more on the limits, see Addendum to the Award (WT/DS583/ARB25/Add.1), Annex A-2, Working Procedures for Arbitration under Article 25 of the DSU, paras. 13–15, 25, 33; Award of the Arbitrators, *Colombia – Frozen Fries*, Annex 2 to Annex A-2, Pre-Arbitration Letter, WT/DS591/ARB25/Add.1, 19 September 2022.

these organizational measures were *inter alia* included.[60] Importantly, both awards were issued within the 90-day deadline.[61]

The arbitrators may also *propose* substantive measures, such as the exclusion of claims based on Article 11 DSU on the objective assessment of the facts, which will be up to the party concerned.[62] Since Article 11 claims involve dealing with panels' assessment of issues of facts, this increased AB's workload,[63] contributing to lengthening the proceedings. Although the decision remains at the discretion of the parties, MPIA participants are WTO Members interested in the success of this new alternative and could follow arbitrators' suggestions,[64] including because of the ambition to attract more participants. *Colombia – Frozen Fries* showcases the capability of this approach to produce results. Thus, at the arbitrators' invitation to refrain from bringing Article 11 claims and to bring only a selective number of claims, Colombia deliberately limited the number of claims on appeal and brought no Article 11 claims.[65] Thus, despite being only recommendatory, the arbitrator's invitation was followed in the first MPIA appeal proceedings, potentially signalling a nascent practice that might alleviate US criticism. The pre-arbitration letter also encouraged parties before bringing claims under Article 11 DSU to consider how this would affect the 90-day timeline for issuing the award if they would be fruitful and impact the substantive outcome of the dispute, whether they are necessary for the resolution of the dispute, and whether the substance of such a claim could be brought under a substantive treaty provision.[66] If, nonetheless, a party decided to bring a claim under Article 11 DSU, that party was requested to detail whether and how the error was raised during panel proceedings, especially during the interim review stage, how the claim is necessary for the

[60] Award of the Arbitrators, *Colombia – Frozen Fries*, Pre-Arbitration Letter, WT/DS591/ARB25/Add.1.

[61] The award of the Arbitrators in *Turkey – Pharmaceutical Products* was issued in 79 days and in *Colombia – Frozen Fries* in 74 days.

[62] MPIA, Annex 1, para. 13. Fn 6 to para. 13 of Annex 1 to the MPIA states that if the party concerned does not agree, this 'shall not prejudice the consideration of the case or the rights of the parties'.

[63] USTR, Report on the Appellate Body of the World Trade Organization, p. 44; Baroncini, 'Preserving the Appellate Stage' (2019) p. 46.

[64] Mariana de Andrade, 'Procedural Innovations in the MPIA: A Way to Strengthen the WTO Dispute Settlement Mechanism?' (2020) *Questions of International Law*, http://www.qil-qdi.org/procedural-innovations-in-the-mpia-a-way-to-strengthen-the-wto-dispute-settlement-mechanism/.

[65] Award of the Arbitrators, *Colombia – Frozen Fries*, WT/DS591/ARB25, para. 4.2.

[66] ibid, Pre-Arbitration Letter, WT/DS591/ARB25/Add.1, pt. 3.

resolution of dispute and is a matter that cannot be brought under a substantive provision, and how it amounts to an 'issue of law' and is not a factual issue.[67] It is difficult to assess the reasons behind Colombia's decision; nevertheless, these requirements could have served as an additional motivation to follow the arbitrators' proposal.

Finally, if the 90-day time period is considered insufficient, the MPIA disputing parties may agree to extend it (Annex 1 to MPIA, paragraph 14). Therefore, the MPIA tries to strike a balance between the arbitrators' duty to complete their work within the required time period and the parties' ability to mitigate delays caused by their own actions.[68] By requiring the agreement of the parties for the extension of the deadline, the MPIA seems to address directly the US criticism that the AB has disregarded the 90-day deadline from Article 17.5 DSU without even obtaining the parties' consent.

The above-mentioned MPIA provision on the possible arbitrators' proposals to the parties to exclude Article 11 claims also addresses the US concern that the AB has exceeded its authority to review legal issues established by Article 17.6 DSU by reviewing panel findings of facts. Article 11 DSU provides that 'a panel should make an objective assessment of the matter before it, including an objective assessment of the facts of the case'. The United States claimed that the AB erroneously interpreted this article to confer upon itself the authority to review factual findings in order to establish that the panel made an objective assessment of the facts.[69] Furthermore, the United States accused the AB for incentivizing parties to re-litigate entire disputes *de novo* during appeals under Article 11 DSU.[70] The MPIA does not preclude appeals based on Article 11 DSU, so that the US concern is not completely addressed. However, as *Colombia – Frozen Fries* demonstrates, it is likely to lead to the decrease of such claims in an attempt to address the existing criticism while allowing the continuation of the existing practice by the Members endorsing it.[71] The US criticism on the AB's approach

[67] ibid, Pre-Arbitration Letter, pt. 3.

[68] Kugler, 'Operationalizing MPIA Appeal Arbitrations' (2021), p. 83.

[69] Report on the Appellate Body of the World Trade Organization, pp. 37–39.

[70] ibid, para 46.

[71] From the informal process on the functioning of the AB facilitated by Ambassador Walker, it can be inferred that there was no convergence yet on how exactly to limit claims based on Article 11 of the DSU during appeals. In one of his reports, Ambassador Walker wrote that '[d]iscussion continues on whether guidance should be provided limiting Article 11 appeals to situations of exceptional circumstances such as "egregious

to issues of facts also relates to the treatment of Member's domestic norms as issues of law in order to determine their consistency with WTO rules, which represents a question of law.[72] The MPIA's model procedures do not contain an innovation per se in this respect. They merely replicate Article 17.6 DSU by stating that 'an appeal shall be limited to issues of law covered in the panel report and legal interpretations developed by the panel' (Annex 1 to MPIA, paragraph 9). The line between issues of law and issues of facts may not always be easily discernable.[73] Nevertheless, by choosing to explicitly repeat this provision, this may show the intention of the parties to limit reviews of issues of facts. There seems to be a certain degree of convergence between the WTO Members that domestic law should be treated as an issue of fact, hence not subject to appeals, and that the AB should not engage in de novo reviews.[74] Accordingly, by reproducing Article 17.6 in the MPIA procedures, parties potentially wanted to reinforce their position. Similarly, the arbitrators in *Turkey – Pharmaceutical Products* emphasized on several occasions that they addressed only issues of law and not of facts unless they pertained to allegations related to the assessment of facts and evidence under a claim made by a disputing party under Article 11 DSU.[75] Furthermore, according to the pre-arbitration letter from *Colombia – Frozen Fries*, as shown above, in case a party decided to bring a claim under Article 11 DSU, it would have needed to explain in what way the alleged panel error was not simply an appreciation of facts.[76] Thus, the arbitrators showcased their awareness of the criticism related to the treatment of issues of facts during the appellate stage, indicating the cautiousness of adjudicators in this respect.

The United States also criticized the AB for its alleged practice of issuing advisory opinions or *obiter dicta*.[77] It claims that in line with the

error" by a Panel.' (Informal Process on Matters Related to the Functioning of the Appellate Body – Report by the Facilitator, H. E. Dr. David Walker (New Zealand), JOB/GC/217, 7 May 2019, para. 1.27).

72 USTR, The President's 2018 Trade Policy Agenda, pp. 27–28.

73 de Andrade, 'Procedural Innovations in the MPIA' (2020).

74 See Report by the Facilitator, H. E. Dr. David Walker (New Zealand), JOB/GC/217, 7 May 2019, paras. 1.24–1.25.

75 Award of the Arbitrators, *Turkey – Pharmaceutical Products*, WT/DS583/ARB25, paras. 6.36, 6.65, 6.129,

76 Award of the Arbitrators, *Colombia – Frozen Fries*, Pre-Arbitration Letter, WT/DS591/ARB25/Add.1, pt. 3.

77 It asserts that in an instance, more than two-thirds of the AB's analysis was *obiter dicta* (USTR, The President's 2018 Trade Policy Agenda, p. 27).

purpose of the dispute settlement to secure a positive solution to a dispute, as prescribed in Article 3.7 DSU, the AB should only make findings that will assist the DSB in making recommendations.[78] This concern is related to the broader claim that the AB engaged in judicial activism and lawmaking. Apparently addressing it, the participants of the MPIA included the following provision in the model procedures: '[t]he arbitrators shall only address those issues that are necessary for the resolution of the dispute. They shall address only those issues that have been raised by the parties, without prejudice to their obligation to rule on jurisdictional issues' (Annex 1 to MPIA, paragraph 10). WTO panels and the AB have already confirmed their ability to exercise judicial economy. However, this express provision from the MPIA is likely to encourage appeal arbitrators to exercise it more often, and provides a clear legal basis for doing so.[79] Moreover, it seems in line with the proposal made by Ambassador Walker in his Draft Decision based on a certain degree of convergence between WTO Members on this issue.[80] With this provision, the MPIA also contributes to reducing the arbitrators' workload and, therefore, helps with respecting the 90-day deadline. In practice, appeal arbitrators have already shown due restraint and emphasized their mandate to consider only issues necessary for the resolution of the dispute. For example, in *Turkey – Pharmaceutical Products*, on many occasions, the arbitrators refrained from treating issues that were not necessary for resolving the dispute, indicating their mindfulness of the mandate that they have received from the parties in the agreed appeal procedures.[81] Notably, in *Colombia – Frozen Fries*, the parties were invited in the pre-arbitration letter to a virtual pre-hearing conference to assist arbitrators in identifying the issues to be addressed at the hearing and to avoid issues that are not necessary for the resolution of the dispute.[82] Therefore, it seems that appeal arbitrators are fully aware of the criticism directed at the AB's activity in this respect and display a distinct, more mindful approach.

[78] USTR, Report on the Appellate Body of the World Trade Organization, pp. 47–54.

[79] de Andrade, 'Procedural Innovations in the MPIA' (2020).

[80] Informal Process on Matters Related to the Functioning of the Appellate Body, JOB/GC/222, 15 October 2019, 6.

[81] Award of the Arbitrators, *Turkey – Pharmaceutical Products*, WT/DS583/ARB25, paras. 3.3, 3.5, 6.50, 6.70, 6.71.

[82] Award of the Arbitrators, *Colombia – Frozen Fries*, Pre-Arbitration Letter, WT/DS591/ARB25/Add.1, para. 1.11

Besides these innovations, as they retain the flexibility to depart from the model appeal arbitration procedures contained in the MPIA,[83] the parties to specific disputes could also introduce other novelties to address further issues. For example, in *Canada – Wine (Australia)*[84] and *Canada – Commercial Aircraft*,[85] the agreed appeal procedures contained additional rules on confidential information. In *Costa Rica – Avocados*, the parties agreed that 'the arbitrators shall send advance written questions on the issues that are set to be raised at the meeting or meetings with the parties' and 'may pose additional questions at the meeting',[86] making appeal hearings more akin to panel hearings.[87] *Costa Rica – Avocados*, *Colombia – Frozen Fries*, *China – Goods (EU)*, and *China – IPRs Enforcement (EU)* appeal arbitrations agreements also established the 'immediate transmission of the final panel report, on a provisional basis' apparently seeking to offer arbitrators more time to analyze the panel report, helping them to comply with the 90-day deadline.[88] Due to the flexibility that the parties enjoy under the MPIA and the already established practice to modify the agreed procedures according to the parties' needs, other innovations should be expected, including potential innovations addressing criticism related to AB practices or interpretations, such as the appeal arbitrators' interpretation of standard of review under Article 17.6 (ii) Anti-Dumping Agreement (ADA)[89], detailed in the following section. Accordingly, the MPIA could present a sort of 'laboratory' for testing different procedural rules and interpretations of substantive norms in specific disputes.

[83] MPIA, para. 11.

[84] *Canada – Wine (Australia)*, Agreed Procedures for Arbitration under Article 25 of the DSU, WT/DS537/15, 3 June 2020, paras. 4, 5, 11.

[85] *Canada – Commercial Aircraft*, Agreed Procedures for Arbitration under Article 25 of the DSU, WT/DS522/20, 3 June 2020, paras. 4, 5, 11.

[86] *Costa Rica – Avocados*, Agreed Procedures for Arbitration under Article 25 of the DSU, WT/DS524/5/Rev.1, 2 December 2021, para. 11.

[87] Starshinova, 'Is the MPIA a Solution to the WTO Appellate Body Crisis?' (2021) 790.

[88] *Costa Rica – Avocados*, Agreed Procedures for Arbitration under Article 25 of the DSU, WT/DS522/20, para. 4 (i); *Colombia – Frozen Fries*, Agreed Procedures for Arbitration under Article 25 of the DSU, WT/DS591/3/Rev.1, 22 April 2021, para. 4 (i); *China – Goods (EU)*, Agreed Procedures for Arbitration under Article 25 of the DSU, WT/DS610/10, 7 July 2023, para. 4 (i); *China – IPRs Enforcement (EU)*, Agreed Procedures for Arbitration under Article 25 of the DSU, WT/DS611/7, 7 July 2023, para. 4 (i); Simon Lester, 'Tweaking the MPIA Procedures', IELP Blog, https://ielp.worldtradelaw.net/2021/12/tweaking-the-mpia-procedures.html.

[89] Agreement on the Implementation of Article VI of GATT 1994, Anti-Dumping Agreement, 15 April 1994, 1868 U.N.T.S. 201.

To conclude, the MPIA introduced innovations, reproduced certain DSU provisions aiming to address to a certain degree several issues criticized by the United States, and enabled other potential innovations. Hence, the MPIA does not only serve as a workaround in the context of the current AB deadlock; it also represents an attempt to resolve it. It demonstrates the EU's and other participants' continuing commitment to the multilateral dispute settlement and their endeavor to rescue it.

4.4 MPIA Arbitration Awards: Security, Predictability, and High-Quality Awards

As the EU still prefers enforcing its trading rights on international level through the WTO mechanism, in order not to undermine the assertiveness of the multilateral trade dispute settlement, any alternative mechanism such as the MPIA should allow for a comparable way of enforcing trading rights in terms of quality, security, and predictability, as it used to be before the AB crisis. Endorsing an appeal alternative that could provide security, predictability, and awards of a quality similar to AB reports would show the EU's and other MPIA participants' commitment to a two-stage multilateral dispute settlement, as envisaged by the relevant WTO rules. Moreover, the EU's intention to strengthen the implementation and enforcement of trade agreements would be undermined if the alternative did not result in arbitration awards at least somewhat comparable to AB reports in terms of quality, security, and predictability. Without an appeal alternative providing high-quality awards, the EU would enhance enforcement through means representing a less robust multilateral dispute settlement mechanism. Furthermore, security and predictability, associated with coherence across the legal findings of the WTO adjudicators, have been named an essential element to the success of the WTO dispute settlement system.[90] Therefore, for the MPIA not to weaken the multilateral dispute settlement system, to which the EU is committed, it should offer an increased degree of coherence. At the same time, as it will be shown, coherence has been a contentious issue during the AB crisis. Hence, a more peculiar approach to it might have the

[90] James Bacchus and Simon Lester, 'The Rule of Precedent and the Role of the Appellate Body' (2020) 54(2) *JWT* 183–198 at 195; Henry Gao, 'Finding a Rule-Based Solution to the Appellate Body Crisis: Looking beyond the Multiparty Interim Appeal Arbitration Arrangement' (2021) 24 *JIEL* 534–550 at 538–539.

potential to contribute to rescuing the WTO dispute settlement. Accordingly, the MPIA will need to provide a certain degree of security and predictability while at the same time also alleviating US concerns in an attempt to resolve the crisis.

Since the MPIA provides a default set of procedural rules to be followed in case of appeals, participants would have a broad idea of what follows.[91] Furthermore, as concluded in Section 4.3.2, due to the fact that the appeal arbitration proceedings largely emulate regular appeals, the process would also be generally familiar to the disputing parties. Therefore, the MPIA offers a certain degree of security and predictability in terms of procedures. Article 3.2 DSU establishes that '[t]he dispute settlement system of the WTO is a central element in providing security and predictability to the multilateral trading system'. Under Article 3.2 DSU, 'security and predictability' also entails consistent legal reasoning over time in different cases.[92] The AB famously stated that '[e]nsuring "security and predictability" in the dispute settlement system, as contemplated in Article 3.2 of the DSU, implies that, absent cogent reasons, an adjudicatory body will resolve the same legal question in the same way in a subsequent case'.[93] However, treating past reports as precedents has also been one of the main US criticisms behind the paralysis of the AB. While the United States has criticized the AB's approach, it stated that this does not mean that 'a prior panel or Appellate Body interpretation is without any value [. . .] to the extent that a panel finds the reasoning in a prior report persuasive, the panel may refer to that reasoning'.[94] Thus, while coherence is necessary to ensure security and predictability, it might not be desirable to *always* follow the existing case law.

Possible fragmentation of the case law has been one of the main concerns related to the MPIA.[95] Unlike the interim appeal arbitration agreements concluded by the EU with Canada and Norway, which required that appeal arbitration awards 'be deemed to constitute Appellate Body reports adopted by the DSB for the purposes of

[91] Angshuman Hazarika and Pieter Van Vaerenbergh, "One Rule to Rule Them All': Rules for Article 25 DSU Arbitration' (2019) 36(5) *Journal of International Arbitration* 595–628 at 597.

[92] Bacchus and Lester, 'The Rule of Precedent' (2020) 188.

[93] Appellate Body Report, *US – Stainless Steel (Mexico)*, WT/DS344/AB/R, 30 April 2008, para. 160, fn. 13 referring to international writings and case law of other international fora.

[94] USTR, Report on the Appellate Body of the World Trade Organization, p. 57.

[95] Kugler, 'Operationalizing MPIA Appeal Arbitrations' (2021), p. 87; Papaconstantinou and Pedreschi, 'Alternative Dispute Settlement' (2022) 269–271.

interpretation of the covered agreements',[96] the MPIA contains no provision that would determine which value to attach to past awards. Thus, these earlier arrangements seemed to recognize the interpretative value of the appeal arbitration awards and implicitly also the authority of the AB jurisprudence for future disputes.[97] Nevertheless, the MPIA mentions that 'consistency and predictability' in interpretations is 'of significant value to Members' and also refers to the promotion of 'consistency and coherence'.[98] Thus, it expressly uses such terms as 'consistency' and 'coherence', which are absent from the DSU. The inclusion of these terms is most likely not accidental, showing parties' endorsement of coherent jurisprudence but without providing particular guidance on the treatment of past reports.[99] Furthermore, it provides that the principle of collegiality will be applicable to the decision-making of arbitrators (MPIA, paragraph 5; Annex 1 to MPIA, paragraph 8). Accordingly, the MPIA expressly provides that 'in order to promote consistency and coherence in decision-making', the ten members of the pool of arbitrators 'will discuss among themselves matters of interpretation, practice and procedure, to the extent practicable' (MPIA, paragraph 5).[100] Nevertheless, the MPIA also explicitly establishes in the model rules that appeal arbitrators retain the 'exclusive responsibility and freedom [. . .] with respect to such decisions and their quality' (Annex 1 to MPIA, paragraph 8). Therefore, despite the principle of collegiality, the three arbitrators sitting on a dispute are free to depart from the interpretation endorsed by other appeal arbitrators, if they consider it necessary. All ten arbitrators selected in the pool of arbitrators have extensive experience in WTO law, having adjudicated disputes as panelists or arbitrators,[101] having

[96] WTO, Communication from Canada and the European Union, 'Interim Appeal Arbitration Pursuant to Article 25 of the DSU', JOB/DSB/1/Add.11, para. 8; WTO, Communication from Norway and the European Union, 'Interim Appeal Arbitration Pursuant to Article 25 of the DSU', JOB/DSB/1/Add.11/Suppl.1, para. 8.

[97] Vidigal, 'Living without the Appellate Body' (2019) 886; Furculita, 'The EU's Interim Appeal Arbitration Arrangements' (2020).

[98] MPIA, Preamble, recital 6; MPIA, Annex 1, para. 5

[99] Starshinova, 'Is the MPIA a Solution to the WTO Appellate Body Crisis?' (2021) 801; de Andrade, 'Procedural Innovations in the MPIA' (2020).

[100] Thomas Graham, former AB Member from the United States, criticized this practice listing the 'over-emphasis on "collegiality" that shaded into peer pressure to conform' as one of the things that struck him (Thomas R. Graham, 'The Rise (and Demise?) of the WTO Appellate Body', 5 March 2020, https://worldtradelaw.typepad.com/files/t.graham.greenwaldlecture.final_.pdf, p. 8).

[101] Thomas Cottier, Switzerland; Mateo Diego-Fernandez Andrade, Mexico; José Alfredo Graça Lima, Brazil; Valerie Hughes, Canada; Alejandro Jara, Chile; Claudia Orozco,

served in the WTO Secretariat,[102] working in academia on trade-related issues,[103] or having worked for national governments in WTO-related areas.[104] Given their vast experience in WTO law and knowledge of existing practice, it is expected that they will generally pay attention to consistency with past reports. Yet, the fact that participants have not selected former AB Members, unlike envisaged in EU–Canada and EU–Norway interim appeal arbitration arrangements,[105] might signal the participants' readiness for new approaches.

Although the appeal arbitration procedures agreed by the parties in *Turkey – Pharmaceutical Products* did not contain provisions similar to the MPIA on coherence and consistency in interpretation,[106] the arbitrators (two of which are MPIA arbitrators) largely referred to past WTO reports, sought it necessary to specify that their approach was consistent with that of the AB in other dispute,[107] and, when seemingly adopting a different approach, argued that the AB in fact 'did not discuss the proper interpretation of the words' at issue, hence accepting the need to consider the previous AB reports.[108] During a DSB meeting on the issue of implementing the award from this dispute, the United States called for discontinuation of certain AB's interpretations and practices.[109] While appellate arbitrators in *Colombia – Frozen Fries* also cited past WTO

Colombia; and Penelope Ridings, New Zealand: all have experience as panelists or arbitrators under Arts. 22.6 and 21.3(c) DSU.

102 Valerie Hughes (Canada) and Joost Pauwelyn (Belgium) have served as, respectively, former director and legal officer in the AB Secretariat and WTO Legal Affairs Division.

103 Although she has not acted as a panelist or arbitrator and has not worked in the WTO Secretariat or for a national government, Locknie Hsu (Singapore) has extensive academic trade-related experience. Additionally, other arbitrators, e.g. Thomas Cottier (Switzerland) and Joost Pauwelyn (Belgium), also have extensive relevant academic experience.

104 Guohua Yang was Director and Deputy Director General for WTO Legal Affairs within the ministry responsible for WTO cases related to China. He is also a former AB candidate (2016).

105 WTO, Communication from Canada and the European Union, 'Interim Appeal Arbitration Pursuant to Article 25 of the DSU', para. 3, Annex, para. 7; WTO, Communication from Norway and the European Union, 'Interim Appeal Arbitration Pursuant to Article 25 of the DSU', para. 3, Annex, para. 7.

106 It only mentions 'consistency and coherence in decision making in this dispute and in dispute DS595' (*Turkey – Pharmaceutical Products*, Agreed Procedures for Arbitration under Article 25 of the DSU, WT/DS583/10, 25 March 2022, para. 8).

107 Award of the Arbitrators, *Turkey – Pharmaceutical Products*, WT/DS583/ARB25, fn 131 to para. 6.44.

108 ibid, para. 6.48.

109 DSB, Minutes of Meeting Held in the Centre William Rappard, WT/DSB/M/469, 10 October 2022, para. 2.4.

jurisprudence, they referred to a lesser degree to past AB reports.[110] Moreover, in these procedures, without mentioning any AB report, appellate arbitrators departed from the AB's interpretation of Article 17.6(ii) ADA according to which only a single correct interpretation is allowed – an alleged 'erroneous' interpretation of a substantive WTO provision that also served as a reason for the US blockage of the AB.[111] Instead, the appellate arbitrators offered a different interpretation and established that using the same tools of interpretation enshrined in the Vienna Convention on the Law of Treaties (VCLT),[112] different interpreters may arrive at different 'correct' interpretations, especially in the context of the ADA and the unique character of its Article 17.6(ii).[113] Nevertheless, the appeal arbitrators did not accept the interpretation submitted by Colombia as being a permissible one,[114] indicating that while they offered more leeway to Member States, it is still circumscribed by the final assessment of the arbitrators. Importantly, the United States has endorsed the appeal arbitrators' novel interpretation, mentioning that it has explained for years that 'permissible' in Article 17.6(ii) ADA refers to 'a meaning that could be reached under the Vienna Convention'.[115] Although it remains to be seen if this interpretation will be followed in other disputes, including in MPIA appeal arbitrations, it shows that, unlike the AB, appeal arbitrators are ready to depart from the existing problematic jurisprudence to experiment with interpretations acceptable to the membership and to help with overcoming the current dispute settlement crisis.

The two appeal arbitration awards under Article 25 DSU demonstrate that past jurisprudence most likely will be followed by appeal arbitrators, unless it concerns contested interpretations in need of a review, an approach that could potentially win over the support of WTO

[110] As noted by Pauwelyn, the appeal award in *Colombia – Frozen Fries* refers only to ten AB reports, the average being twenty-two (Pauwelyn, 'The MPIA: What's New (Part III) (2023)'). In contrast, for example, the appeal award from *Turkey – Pharmaceutical Products* refers to twenty-four AB reports.

[111] USTR, Report on the Appellate Body of the World Trade Organization, 95–104.

[112] Vienna Convention on the Law of Treaties, Vienna, 23 May 1969, in force 27 January 1980, 1155 U.N.T.S. 331; (1969) 8 ILM 679; UKTS (1980) 58.

[113] Award of the Arbitrators, *Colombia – Frozen Fries*, paras. 4.13–4.15, fn. 42.

[114] ibid, paras. 4.18–4.24.

[115] Statements by the United States at the Meeting of the WTO Dispute Settlement Body, 27 January 2023, https://ustr.gov/about-us/policy-offices/press-office/press-releases/2023/january/statements-united-states-meeting-wto-dispute-settlement-body.

Members,[116] including the United States. As the United States has noted, 'adherence to the texts as negotiated and agreed by Members – rather than consistency for consistency's sake – assists in providing security and predictability to the multilateral trading system'.[117] Notably, while the reason behind this decision remains unknown, after the first MPIA award, Japan has also decided to join the arrangement[118] and already agreed with China on arbitration procedures under Article 25 DSU in a dispute,[119] suggesting that other Members might follow in its footsteps. However, it might be difficult to issue reports on contentious issues that will appease *all* WTO Members.[120] Thus, if arbitrators generally follow past reports but diverge from the existing jurisprudence in case of contentious interpretations, and even manage to gain the support of the Membership, they could get more WTO Members on board, could help solve the existing crisis, or the MPIA could even become a permanent solution. Accordingly, this EU-led initiative could bolster EU's pronouncement in favour of multilateralism and help in resolving the AB crisis.

However, the question arises whether in practice WTO Members participating in the MPIA will confer on appeal arbitration awards in cases in which they were not parties the same interpretative value as on AB reports, especially since appeal arbitration awards could be perceived as less authoritative by WTO panels and non-participant Members. Thus, MPIA awards could be associated with a lower degree of legitimacy due to the fact that they are issued by arbitrators selected only by participants and not the entire Membership.[121] Moreover, although other Members could participate as third parties in the appeal arbitration proceedings, the Membership has no say in the adoption of the awards, as they have only to be notified to the DSB and are not subject to adoption by this body. Accordingly, MPIA arbitration awards could have less 'precedential

[116] Georgie Juszczyk, 'Legitimacy Crisis at the World Trade Organisation Appellate Body: Other Ways Than the MPIA?' in Jelena Bäumler et al. (eds.), *European Yearbook of International Economic Law 2021* (Cham: Springer 2022), p. 116.

[117] ibid.

[118] Ministry of Foreign Affairs Japan, 'Cabinet Understanding Regarding Participation in the MPIA', 10 March 2023, www.mofa.go.jp/press/release/press6e_000447.html.

[119] *China – AD on Stainless Steel (Japan)*, Agreed Procedures for Arbitration Under Article 25 of the DSU, WT/DS601/6, 13 April 2023.

[120] Papaconstantinou, Pedreschi, 'Alternative Dispute Settlement', 272.

[121] Xiaoling Li, 'DSU Article 25 Appeal Arbitration: A Viable Interim Alternative to the WTO Appellate Body?' (2020) 15 (10) *GTCJ* 461–478 at 468; Starshinova, 'Is the MPIA a Solution to the WTO Appellate Body Crisis?' (2021) 802.

value', but it is not yet clear how much less.[122] Without an AB in place to review the panel reports from disputes involving non-participants, acting as a guardian of coherence, panelists might feel the urge to depart from the reasoning given in other disputes, especially from that contained in appeal arbitral awards by virtue of their potential lower interpretative value. Non-participants might also avoid referring to MPIA jurisprudence in their submissions.[123] Nevertheless, as secretarial support, albeit from different divisions, is offered to both panel and MPIA arbitrators, institutional memory is likely to favour referencing the MPIA awards. Furthermore, if MPIA arbitrators issue persuasive awards that will convince panelists of their soundness and strike a balance to satisfy most WTO Members, the risk of fragmentation caused by the MPIA will be seriously diminished. Thus, although only time will show precisely, it is unlikely that coherence across WTO case law will be seriously affected by the MPIA.

As stated in the introduction to this section, for the MPIA to be a viable alternative for the enforcement of EU's multilateral trade rights and not to undermine the EU's endeavor to strengthen the enforcement of its trade rights, it should also offer appeal arbitration awards of a quality at least comparable to that of AB reports. The appellate stage should bring added value to the dispute settlement process, offering the opportunity to correct possible errors present in panel reports. Given that the MPIA requires the same qualifications for appeal arbitrators as for the AB Members and their vast experience in WTO law,[124] it can be reasonably expected that the awards will be of a comparably high quality.[125] Moreover, this conclusion is further supported by the fact that MPIA appeal arbitrators benefit from the highly qualified support of the WTO Secretariat. In case of both *Turkey – Pharmaceutical Products* and *Colombia – Frozen Fries*, the awards are drafted in a very similar manner to that of AB reports.[126] Thus, the MPIA can be expected to result in high-quality awards.

[122] Lester, 'Can Interim Appeal Arbitration Preserve the WTO Dispute System?' (2020), p. 3.

[123] Furculita, *The WTO and the New Generation EU FTA Dispute Settlement Mechanisms* (2021), p. 127; Kugler, 'Operationalizing MPIA Appeal Arbitrations' (2021), p. 87.

[124] See Section 4.3.2.

[125] Papaconstantinou and Pedreschi, 'Alternative Dispute Settlement' (2022) 273–274.

[126] As Lester put it, in case of *Turkey – Pharmaceutical Products*, '[i]f a WTO lawyer had been in a coma for the last few years, came out of it, and was handed this report with no label on it and no context provided for what had happened to the Appellate Body, I think that lawyer would believe this was a real Appellate Body report'. Simon Lester, 'The

4.5 Enforceability and 'Automaticity' of the MPIA, and Its No-Appeal Pact

Besides security, predictability, and high-quality awards, the MPIA should also ensure an 'automatic' two-stage dispute settlement mechanism similar to that before the paralysis of the AB. While the regular appeal stage under the DSU was an automatic step that could not be blocked when a disputing party appealed the panel report (the United States, nonetheless, hindered all appeals with its AB blockage), the question arises whether the MPIA also provides the same degree of 'automaticity', ensuring that an unwilling party cannot forestall the appeal arbitration procedures. Related to this and not less important, this section will also examine if in case of disregard of the MPIA (especially of the NAP it may enshrine), it could be given effect and be enforced, taking into consideration the constraints established by the WTO rules, the jurisprudence interpreting them, and the current crisis.

As previously stated, the MPIA, being merely an *arrangement*, is setting only the intention of the participants to enter into arbitration agreements when a particular dispute materializes (see Section 4.3.1). To date, an appeal arbitration agreement was signed in every dispute that arose between MPIA participants. Nevertheless, in the future, one of the MPIA parties could refuse to enter into such agreements. There is nothing in the MPIA which indicates that parties committed themselves to sign arbitral agreements. The MPIA could be said to be a 'procedural agreement' akin to sequencing agreements aimed at solving the inconsistency in terms of timelines found in Articles 21.5 and 22.2 DSU.[127] In practice, parties usually comply with such agreements,[128] possibly because of their interest in solving the dispute, fear of emulation by other countries, and potential reputational damages suffered. Considering the MPIA participants' commitment to a two-stage WTO dispute settlement, exhibited precisely through the participation in the MPIA, it is hardly likely that a participant will refuse to sign an appeal arbitration agreement when a specific dispute occurs. Nevertheless, this possibility cannot be ruled out entirely. A perceived failure of the MPIA combined with the

Turkey – Pharmaceutical Products Article 25 (Appellate Review) Award', IELP Blog, 25 July 2022, https://ielp.worldtradelaw.net/2022/07/the-turkey-pharmaceutical-products-article-25-appellate-review-award.html.

127 Starshinova, 'Is the MPIA a Solution to the WTO Appellate Body Crisis?' (2021) 797.

128 Matilda J Brolin, 'Procedural Agreements in WTO Disputes: Addressing the Sequencing Problem' (2016) 85 *Nordic Journal of International Law* 65–88 at 80.

ongoing AB crisis could completely bring down the moral of the Membership and undermine further efforts of reforming the WTO dispute settlement and reviving the AB.

Since the MPIA contains no mandatory and enforceable language that would oblige participants to sign an arbitration agreement, in case a participant refuses to do so, the other party would not be able to benefit from a two-stage dispute settlement process under the MPIA. Even if the other party then tried to enforce the MPIA in separate panel proceedings in which it complained about the breach of the MPIA, it would not be successful in its endeavor, as WTO panels have jurisdiction only over WTO-covered agreements under Article 1.1 DSU.[129] The MPIA, especially the NAP contained therein, could, however, serve as a jurisdictional defence for the other party to be invoked against the refusing participant that tries to appeal a panel report to the AB (and hence into the void), instead of employing the MPIA arrangement. A mere refusal to sign an appeal arbitration agreement according to the MPIA, even if eroding the arrangement's reliability, would be less harmful to the advancement of procedures, but this has to be assessed entirely differently if an uncooperative party files an appeal into the void. In that case, the NAP contained in the main part of the MPIA (paragraph 2), according to which 'the participating Members will not pursue appeals under Articles 16.4 and 17 DSU', would be infringed. If a participant files an appeal contrary to its (alleged) commitment not to do so, it could be accused of acting in bad faith. WTO jurisprudence recognized that there is 'little in the DSU that explicitly limits the rights of WTO Members to bring an action' except Articles 3.7 and 3.10 DSU requiring Members to engage in dispute settlement in good faith.[130] The AB has established in several disputes that Articles 3.7 and 3.10 DSU could be violated when a Member acts contrary to good faith, precluding a panel or AB from ruling on the matter at issue if a party *clearly* relinquished its right to legal action under the DSU, especially by virtue of a mutually agreed solution

[129] Lorand Bartels, 'Applicable Law in WTO Dispute Settlement Proceedings' (2001) 35 *JWT* 499–519 at 502–503; Gabrielle Marceau, 'WTO Dispute Settlement and Human Rights' (2002) 13(4) *EJIL* 753–814 at 814; Joost Pauwelyn, 'How to Win a World Trade Organization Dispute Based on Non-World Trade Organization Law? Questions of Jurisdiction and Merits' (2003) 37(6) *JWT* 997–1030 at 1000; Furculita, *The WTO and the New Generation EU FTA Dispute Settlement Mechanisms* (2021), p. 216.

[130] Appellate Body Report, *EC – Export Subsidies on Sugar*, WT/DS265/AB/R, 28 April 2005, para. 312.

(MAS).[131] Thus, it could be argued that MPIA participants relinquished their right to appeal a panel report under Articles 16.4 and 17.4 DSU. While the WTO jurisprudence does not seem to prevent WTO Members from relinquishing their DSU rights, the relinquishment of the DSU rights should not be 'lightly assumed'.[132] Accordingly, for the relinquishment contained in the NAP to be given effect within WTO dispute settlement, it should adhere to the constraints established by the existing case law. In what follows, this section will assess the enforceability of the MPIA considering the pertinent WTO jurisprudence. It will be shown that, while the NAP contained in the EU-led MPIA does not raise questions with respect to its legality under multilateral trade rules, it does, however, cast doubt with respect to its conformity with the requirements for being recognized within dispute settlement.

The threshold for establishing that a Member relinquished its right has been set at a rather high level,[133] with no relinquishment being confirmed in WTO dispute settlement as of yet. First, it should be established whether the relinquishment contained in the NAP is clear and unambiguous. Unlike the MPIA provision that establishes only the participants' 'intention to enter into the arbitration agreement', the NAP clearly and unambiguously provides that 'the participating Members *will not* pursue appeals' (emphasis added) (MPIA, paragraph 2). Nevertheless, as the NAP is contained in an *arrangement* and MPIA participants still have to sign arbitral agreements, its context might cast doubt on whether parties indeed have *completely* relinquished their right to appeal. Furthermore, the case law establishes some other requirements, namely that compliance with Articles 3.7 and 3.10 DSU 'should be ascertained on the basis of actions taken in relation to, or within the context of, the rules and procedures of the DSU', and that the relinquishment of DSU rights and obligations cannot go 'beyond the settlement of specific disputes'.[134]

[131] Appellate Body Report, *EC – Bananas III (Article 21.5 – Ecuador II / Article 21.5 – US)*, WT/DS27/AB/RW/USA, WT/DS27/AB/RW2/ECU, 26 November 2008, para. 217; Appellate Body Report, *Peru – Agricultural Products*, WT/DS457/AB/R, 20 July 2015, para. 5.25.

[132] Appellate Body Report, *EC – Bananas III (Article 21.5 – Ecuador II / Article 21.5 – US)*, WT/DS27/AB/RW/USA, WT/DS27/AB/RW2/ECU, para. 217; Appellate Body Report, *Peru – Agricultural Products*, WT/DS457/AB/R, para. 5.25; Panel Report, *US – Tariff Measures*, WT/DS543/R, 15 September 2020, para. 7.9.

[133] Panel Report, *US – Tariff Measures*, WT/DS543/R, para. 7.9.

[134] Appellate Body Report, *Peru – Agricultural Products*, WT/DS457/AB/R, para. 5.25 and fn. 106 to para. 5.26; For more on these requirements, their possible meaning, and criticism, see Furculita, *The WTO and the New Generation EU FTA Dispute Settlement Mechanisms* (2021), pp. 241–242.

The former requirement would most likely be complied with by the NAP, since the relinquishment has taken place in the context of an arrangement based on Article 25 DSU. The last requirement, however, could be more problematic. It could be interpreted more broadly to refer to an entire category of disputes,[135] such as disputes between MPIA participants for as long as the AB remains paralyzed. Nonetheless, if this last requirement is construed narrowly to refer only to individual disputes,[136] it will not be respected by the NAP, as it refers generally to all the future disputes between MPIA participants. However, a relinquishment included directly in the arbitration agreements signed for specific disputes would easily comply with this requirement regardless of its interpretation. The model MPIA procedures for the arbitral agreements to be signed once disputes occur also clearly and unequivocally seem to relinquish the right to regular appeals by establishing that subject to the NAP contained in the main MPIA body, 'where the arbitration has not been initiated under these agreed procedures, the parties shall be deemed to have agreed not to appeal the panel report pursuant to Articles 16.4 and 17 of the DSU' (Annex 1 to MPIA, paragraph 6). Moreover, the appeal arbitration agreements are signed in the context of a DSU rule – Article 25.1. Hence, this type of relinquishment of the right to appeal is better tailored to adhere to the constraints established by the WTO jurisprudence, yet this would require an appeal arbitration agreement to be signed first.

It could also be argued that MPIA participants relinquished their right by virtue of a MAS, even outside the claim of a good-faith violation.[137] Nonetheless, it is unlikely that this argument will stand considering the existing WTO jurisprudential interpretations of what it takes for a MAS to be found in case of an uncooperative MPIA participant. The term 'solution' 'refers to the "act of solving a problem"',[138] and it has not been

[135] Joost Pauwelyn, 'Interplay between the WTO Treaty and Other International Legal Instruments and Tribunals: Evolution after 20 Years of WTO Jurisprudence', (2017) https://papers.ssrn.com/sol3/papers.cfm?abstract_id=2731144, 19, fn. 68.

[136] Lukasz Gruszczynski, 'The WTO and FCTC Dispute Settlement Systems: Friends or Foes' (2017) 12 *Asian Journal of WTO and International Health Law and Policy* 105–134 at 123.

[137] In *US – Tariff Measures*, the United States claimed that it reached a MAS together with China when they agreed to hold bilateral negotiations including on matters covered by the dispute brought in front to the WTO panel. The panel considered it as a preliminary issue, since the United States argued that it should not issue findings and recommendations consistent with Art. 12.7 of the DSU (Panel Report, *US – Tariff Measures*, WT/DS543/R, para. 7.4).

[138] Appellate Body Reports, *EC – Bananas III (Article 21.5 – Ecuador II / Article 21.5 – US)*, WT/DS27/AB/RW/USA, WT/DS27/AB/RW2/ECU, para. 212.

settled yet whether agreeing on a 'process'[139] or only showing the intention to agree, such as an agreement indicating the intention to resort to appeal arbitration when disputes materialize, could qualify as a solution. However, the WTO jurisprudence established that for a MAS, both parties should have a '*shared* assessment that they have reached a solution'.[140] In case an MPIA participant refuses to sign an appeal arbitration agreement and appeals a panel report in a dispute with another participant to the inactive AB, this behaviour most likely implies that a solution was not reached. Accordingly, there would be no shared assessment with regard to the existence of a MAS, and it is unlikely that the MPIA could be recognized as offering one.

Lastly, and most importantly, these two ways of giving effect to the potential relinquishments of the right to appeal are mostly theoretical. In practice, if a participant files an appeal, the report would go into the void and there would be no opportunity to raise these arguments related to them during adjudication and no AB to consider them. However, the EU could also invoke the NAP during the DSB meetings and ask for the adoption of the panel report under Article 16.4 DSU despite the fact that it was appealed, on the ground that the AB has no jurisdiction due to the relinquishments of the right to appeal. While it is unlikely that the DSB will accept such an argument considering the consensus rule requiring also the agreement of the appealing state and considering that the DSB might most likely refer this issue of jurisdiction to be decided by the AB itself, in case the EU decides to resort to the imposition of unilateral countermeasures against that state (under Regulation 654/2014[141]; see Chapter 5), its credibility as a self-declared multilateralist might be less affected.

To conclude, the MPIA cannot ensure an automatic two-stage dispute settlement to the same degree as regular appeals to the AB did. In case of non-conformity by a disputing party with the MPIA, the other party(ies) will not be able to enforce the arrangement and the pledge not to use

[139] Panel Report, *US – Tariff Measures*, para. 7.13. [140] ibid, paras. 7.13, 7.19.

[141] Regulation (EU) 654/2014 of the European Parliament and of the Council of 15 May 2014 concerning the exercise of the Union's rights for the application and enforcement of international trade rules and amending Council Regulation (EC) No. 3286/94 laying down Community procedures in the field of the common commercial policy in order to ensure the exercise of the Community's rights under international trade rules, in particular those established under the auspices of the World Trade Organization, OJ EU 2014 No. L 189/50.

regular appeals. Thus, it means that a disputing party will be able to prevent appeal arbitration from happening, albeit the probability of this happening is very low, as the signatories to the MPIA may be deemed to have signed it out of the intention to implement it in case of a materializing dispute. Given the low risk of non-conformity, participants, including the EU, chose to assume it and further benefit from a two-stage dispute settlement process on a regular basis rather than capitulating and accepting that panel reports would be constantly appealed into the void or investing time and other resources for negotiating arbitration agreements on a case-by-case basis for every dispute.[142]

4.6 Broader Implications of the EU-Led MPIA

Since the WTO dispute settlement reverted to the GATT days, where panel reports could be blocked by a party, with the paralysis of the AB,[143] the MPIA has the aim to rescue the system as known since the creation of the WTO. However, the MPIA will likely have broader implications for the multilateral organization and its dispute settlement. Considering that EU's commitment to multilateralism is also enshrined in its constitutional treaties, this section looks into the MPIA's broader implications, particularly whether it supports or rather endangers the WTO dispute settlement. While the MPIA's aim is to save the multilateral two-stage dispute settlement, the question is whether it will not end up doing more harm than good to it.

The MPIA has already shaped how appeal arbitrations under Article 25 DSU take place in case of disputes with non-participating Members, and most likely will continue doing so. Thus, the MPIA serves as a template that can be used by participants in their disputes with the rest of the Membership or in disputes between non-participants only.[144] For example, in *EU – Safeguard Measures on Steel* and *Turkey – Pharmaceutical Products*, the parties – EU and Turkey – agreed on procedures for appeal arbitration under Article 25 DSU, which to a great

[142] Baroncini, 'The EU Approach to Overcome the WTO Dispute Settlement Vacuum' (2020), 121.

[143] Annex to Trade Policy Review: An Open, Sustainable and Assertive Trade Policy, COM (2021) 66 final, pp. 1–2.

[144] Simon Lester, 'Questions about the MPIA and Article 25 Appeal Arbitration', IELP Blog, 1 September 2020, https://ielp.worldtradelaw.net/2020/09/questions-about-the-mpia.html.

extent replicated the MPIA procedures.[145] Furthermore, the parties agreed that the three arbitrators should be selected from a combined list of former AB Members and MPIA appeal arbitrators.[146] In some instances non-participants might even be pressured by participants into agreeing on appeal arbitration procedures reproducing the MPIA ones. In *EU – Cost Adjustment Methodologies II (Russia)*, it was the EU who appealed the panel report into the void and stated that it was ready for appeal arbitration proceedings based on the MPIA and the model arbitration agreement contained in Annex 1 of the MPIA,[147] which, however, did not happen. As it will be shown in the next chapter, the EU amended its Enforcement Regulation to allow the imposition of unilateral countermeasures in case the other disputing party has not agreed to appeal arbitration under Article 25 DSU and the appeal cannot be completed. Accordingly, some Members, especially those less powerful, may be forced into signing appeal arbitration agreements by the EU or other countries threatening with retaliation. Thus, although currently the MPIA covers only disputes between 26 WTO Members, in practice its reach could be considerably wider. Moreover, the successful dispute settlement under the MPIA might encourage non-participating Members reluctant to solve their disputes through appeal arbitration on a permanent basis to use Article 25 DSU for the appellate stage on an ad hoc basis. Still, if appeal arbitration procedures based on the MPIA become more frequent due to pressure, this occurrence will be less indicative of the will of the Membership to solve the current crisis using the arrangement as a model.

Before the first MPIA award was issued, the disputes that could have been solved under the MPIA did not reach the appeal stage, either because

[145] For example, the agreed procedures also contain NAPs and provisions on how to streamline the proceedings (*Turkey – Pharmaceutical Products*, Agreed Procedures for Arbitration under Article 25 of the DSU, WT/DS583/10, 25 March 2022, paras. 6, 12, 13; *European Union – Safeguard Measures on Steel (Turkey)*, Agreed Procedures for Arbitration under Article 25 of the DSU, WT/DS595/10, 25 March 2022, paras. 6, 12, 13).

[146] *Turkey – Pharmaceutical Products*, Agreed Procedures for Arbitration under Article 25 of the DSU, WT/DS583/10, para. 7; *European Union – Safeguard Measures on Steel (Turkey)*, Agreed Procedures for Arbitration under Article 25 of the DSU, WT/DS595/10, 25 March 2022, para. 7. For more, see Simon Lester, 'Arbitrators Selected in DSU Article 25 Arbitration Appeal', IELP Blog, 5 May 2022, https://ielp.worldtradelaw.net/2022/05/arbitrators-selected-in-dsu-article-25-arbitration-appeal.html.

[147] *EU – Cost Adjustment Methodologies II (Russia)*, Notification of an Appeal, WT/DS494/7, 1 September 2020, p. 11.

the complaint was withdrawn,[148] the case was settled,[149] or the report was not appealed.[150] Thus, it could be that MPIA participants and other WTO Members will now more often resort to negotiated solutions and show restraint in appealing panel reports in order to address the US criticism that the appellate stage was used too often, against the initial intention of the WTO drafters.[151] Nevertheless, once there are more appeals solved under the MPIA without States being pressured into it and, as stated in Section 4.4, the interpretations and innovations satisfy Member States, the MPIA could attract new participants and help to solve the AB crisis. However, the MPIA and all the attention dedicated to it might also distract Members from restoring the AB. Additionally, there is the risk, as shown in Section 4.5, resulting from the MPIA lacking full enforceability and automaticity.

Moreover, as stated in Section 4.4, the more successful the MPIA is, the more likely that it will become the permanent route for appeals – this being the greatest risk posed to the multilateral dispute settlement, which seems to concern scholars and Members alike.[152] Yet, in the near future it is unlikely that the MPIA will disincentivize its participants from seeking solutions for the AB crisis, as many WTO Members are still absent, and the United States – the biggest WTO dispute settlement user – has rejected the idea of joining the MPIA in its current form, arguing that the arrangement only perpetuates AB's failings.[153] According to the United States, the MPIA weakens the deadline for appellate reports, contemplates appellate review of panel findings of fact, fails to reflect

[148] *Canada – Commercial Aircraft*, Communication from Brazil, WT/DS522/23 19 February 2021.

[149] *Canada – Wine (Australia)*, Notification of a Mutually Agreed Solution, WT/DS537/18, 18 May 2021.

[150] Panel Report, *Costa Rica –Avocados*, WT/DS524/R, 13 April 2022.

[151] Bacchus and Lester, 'The Rule of Precedent' (2020) 186.

[152] Joost Pauwelyn, 'WTO Dispute Settlement Post 2019: What to Expect?' (2019) 22 *JIEL* 297–321, 313; Glöckle, 'Bridging the Gap' (2020), 3; Li, 'DSU Article 25 Appeal Arbitration' (2020) 475–476; Gao, 'Finding a Rule-Based Solution to the Appellate Body Crisis' (2021) 547; Felicia A. Grey, 'Arbitration as an Alternative Dispute Settlement Mechanism at the WTO' (2021) 12 *Journal of International Dispute Settlement* 477–504 at 502. WTO Members, such as South Africa, also named this risk (Jan Yves Remy, 'Dispute Settlement at the WTO: How Did We Get Here and What's Next for Commonwealth States?' (2020) 166 *The Commonwealth Trade Hot Topics*, p. 6).

[153] Statements by the United States at the 29 June 2020, DSB Meeting, Minutes of Meeting Held in the Centre William Rappard on 29 June 2020, WT/DSB/M/442, 13 October 2020; reiterated during a DSB meeting on *Turkey – Pharmaceutical Products* award (DSB, Minutes of Meeting Held in the Centre William Rappard, WT/DSB/M/469, 10 October 2022, para. 2.4)

the limitation on appellate review to findings necessary to solve the dispute, and promotes the use of precedent by identifying 'coherence' as a guiding principle and thereby also encourages arbitrators to make law.[154] Indeed, the MPIA has not totally written off certain criticized practices (e.g. substantive measures to streamline proceedings and the possibility to extend the deadline remain at the discretion of the parties[155]; it does not preclude Article 11 DSU claims), and it indeed uses the terms 'consistency' and 'coherence', which are absent from the DSU, seemingly explicitly endorsing the approach taken by the AB under Article 3.2 DSU.[156] Thus, despite the innovations introduced by the MPIA aimed at alleviating some of the invoked concerns, it appears that they were not sufficient from the US perspective.[157] Moreover, it seems that the United States has pressured other Members into not becoming MPIA participants.[158] Despite this, in *Turkey – Pharmaceutical Products*, the United States welcomed the arbitration agreement under Article 25 DSU to facilitate the prompt settlement of disputes and asserted that such agreements could present a unique opportunity to explore new approaches,[159] indicating that it could also eventually resort to ad hoc appeal arbitration. Moreover, as already illustrated by the first MPIA appeal award and its interpretation of Article 17.6(ii) ADA praised by the United States, potential practice more in line with the US vision could renew this country's interest in the two-stage dispute settlement proceedings. Thus, it seems plausible that appeal arbitration under Article 25 DSU could interest the United States in the future, especially considering the flexibility it entails, lower institutionalism,[160] and decreased automaticity, leaving open the door to possible blockages by a single party due to enforceability issues. If the MPIA becomes a permanent solution joined by the entire Membership, this might not be the best solution to the crisis, but it would be less problematic than if dispute

[154] ibid. [155] See Section 4.3.3. [156] See Section 4.4.

[157] Alan Wm. Wolff, 'WTO 2025: Restoring Binding Dispute Settlement' Peterson Institute for International Economics Working Papers 22-5, www.piie.com/publications/working-papers/wto-2025-restoring-binding-dispute-settlement, p. 5; Hoekman and Mavroidis, 'To AB or Not to AB' (2020) 719; Starshinova, 'Is the MPIA a Solution to the WTO Appellate Body Crisis?' (2021) 801.

[158] For example, Korea initially signed the MPIA initiative but was notably absent when it was agreed (Baroncini, 'Preserving the Appellate Stage in the WTO Dispute Settlement Mechanism' (2019) 41).

[159] DSB, Minutes of Meeting Held in the Centre William Rappard, WT/DSB/M/469, 10 October 2022, para. 2.4.

[160] Lester, 'Can Interim Appeal Arbitration Preserve the WTO Dispute System?' (2020), p. 4.

settlement becomes 'balkanized'[161] with some Members participating in the MPIA, some using Article 25 on an ad hoc basis, and others appealing panel reports into the void.[162] Fragmentation of dispute settlement could result in fragmented jurisprudence, putting the existence of the entire multilateral system into question.

In conclusion, besides having the purpose to ensure that disputes between participants are not sent into limbo by appeals into the void, the MPIA already has and could have other, broader implications for the multilateral trading system, which the EU as a committed multilateralist should take into account. Albeit there are certainly potential negative implications that it entails, the MPIA could also be the key to the AB deadlock. Therefore, the risks that the EU has taken when it initiated and as it continues to support this arrangement seem justified.

4.7 Conclusion

This chapter dealt with the MPIA, an alternative appeal arbitration mechanism under Article 25 of the DSU created against the backdrop of the AB crisis, and considered it in view of WTO rules, relevant jurisprudence (including the appeal arbitration awards already issued), EU's recent commitment to a more assertive trade policy, and the MPIA's potential negative and positive effects on the multilateral trade dispute settlement.

The present chapter showed that arbitration proceedings are well integrated in the DSU and are characterized by a great degree of flexibility, which allows the use of Article 25 DSU solely for the appeal stage of a dispute as long as the requirements prescribed therein are respected. Moreover, choosing a WTO rule – Article 25 DSU – as the legal basis of an appeal alternative is fully in line with EU's international obligations and is a manifestation of its 'multilateralist DNA'. Nevertheless, certain issues, such as financing and secretarial support in case of using Article 25 DSU, were left unanswered by the DSU, the MPIA, and the pre-MPIA jurisprudence.

The EU-led MPIA was designed as a temporary, ex ante, and multi-party arrangement to agree on appeal arbitration procedures once a dispute materializes, which largely mimics the familiar appellate review rules. It is not a plurilateral agreement in the sense of Article X:9 of the WTO

[161] Wolff, 'Restoring Binding Dispute Settlement' (2022), p. 1.

[162] Hoekman and Mavroidis state that '[w]e are proponents of open plurilateral agreements but not for dispute settlement' (Hoekman and Mavroidis, 'To AB or Not to AB' (2020) 719).

Agreement and will not impinge on the regular activity of the AB if restored. As shown, it also complies with Article 25 DSU requirements. Therefore, by initiating and promoting this arrangement, the EU not only sought an alternative within the WTO but also respected the requirements prescribed by the WTO rules. The MPIA largely replicates the regular appellate review, which is clearly backed by its participants, and it even became clear that in practice, MPIA appeal arbitrators are supported by WTO secretarial staff from other divisions than those providing support to the panels. Nevertheless, the MPIA also contains innovative or not entirely innovative language that seems to target the US criticism to a certain degree in an attempt, at least suitable, to contribute to the resolution of the AB crisis. Some of these innovations were already successfully tested in practice, such as organizational measures to streamline the proceedings to ensure that the awards are issued timely, proposals to exclude Article 11 DSU claims, and measures to ensure that only issues necessary for the resolution of the dispute are considered. Consequently, the efforts of the MPIA participants, including the EU, to save the WTO dispute settlement are evident. Moreover, due to the high degree of flexibility that participants retain, many other innovations could be introduced, the MPIA being able to become a laboratory for testing different approaches. Hence, by initiating and promoting this arrangement, the EU confirmed its support for the existing two-stage WTO dispute settlement and showed its genuine interest in reviving it, even if reformed.

The MPIA is expected to provide a high degree of security and predictability in terms of procedure and substance. In addition, appeal arbitral awards are predicted to be of high quality, especially since they will be issued by highly qualified appeal arbitrators supported by WTO secretarial staff. Consequently, the robustness of the multilateral trade dispute settlement and the EU's intention to strengthen the implementation and enforcement of its trade agreements will be neither significantly affected nor undermined. Nevertheless, as the current scant practice already indicates, MPIA appeal arbitrators could depart from the existing AB jurisprudence, especially from the controversial one that has been highly criticized by WTO Members such as the United States. Such a departure has already resulted in some positive reactions from WTO Members, most notably the United States. If such departures will balance national interests and trade liberalization better than AB reports did, these awards might be welcomed by the Membership, contributing to the exit from the current deadlock. Such a potential positive outcome will depict MPIA participants, especially the EU, as the forerunners of the blueprint that unlocked the AB stalemate. Still, MPIA appeal arbitral awards might have less precedential value than AB reports.

It was also established that the MPIA cannot offer the same degree of automaticity as regular appeals to the AB under former circumstances, since it only confines the intention of the participants to sign appeal arbitration agreements once a dispute occurs. While it is less probable that this will happen, a participant could refuse to sign such an agreement when a dispute materializes, and due to stringent conditions established by the WTO jurisprudence, limited jurisdiction of the panels over WTO-covered agreements, and absence of a functional AB, there would be no possibility to enforce the arrangement, which is in full conformity with the voluntariness of any arbitration, impliedly also demanded by Article 25 DSU. Nevertheless, since the risk of non-compliance is low, for the EU it seems worth assuming it will continue to benefit from a two-stage dispute settlement on a constant basis rather than negotiating appeal arbitration rules with other Members for every single dispute that arises. Moreover, in case of an MPIA participant's refusal to sign an arbitral agreement in a specific dispute and appealing to the AB instead, the invocation of the NAP within the DSB would offer some kind of political support to EU's potential unilateral countermeasures.

Although the MPIA is set to be a temporary multi-party arrangement, its implications might have a wider ambit. It already has and probably will continue to have influence over appeal arbitrations in disputes with non-participating parties. In time, as the US reaction to the first appeal arbitration award already indicates, the MPIA might revive that particular country's interest in solving the AB crisis, and even become the answer to it. Yet, albeit currently less likely, it could likewise divert Members' attention from the AB paralysis and, after more appeals are successfully settled under the MPIA, become a permanent solution – an outcome which is especially worrisome in case only some Members will participate, fragmenting the multilateral dispute settlement.

Finally, the analysis contained in this chapter showed that the EU-led MPIA, which provides the possibility to resort to appeal arbitration in case of disputes between its participants for as long as the AB paralysis continues, contains potential other benefits as well as some risks. Nonetheless, with no better alternative in place within the system, it seems justified for the participants, including the EU as a staunched supporter of multilateralism, to assume these risks. In an attempt of saving the two-stage dispute settlement, the MPIA is a clear manifestation of the support for this system and disapproval of a GATT-like one. In its absence, participants would likely file appeals into the void in their disputes, engaging in conduct that would certainly threaten trade multilateralism and the multilateral dispute settlement no less than the MPIA. With the AB completely paralyzed, the MPIA has given the WTO two-stage dispute settlement another chance and represents an attempt to save it. Accordingly, despite MPIA's potential undesirable consequences, the EU's position as an initiator and promoter of the arrangement is to be praised, considering the extreme circumstances under which it originated.

5 The Amended Trade Enforcement Regulation

Addressing Dispute Settlement Blockages

5.1 Introduction

The so-called Trade Enforcement Regulation 654/2014[1] was adopted in 2014. It governs the exercise of EU rights for the enforcement of international trade rules under WTO law and bilateral trade agreements, provides for the 'appropriate instruments to ensure the effective exercise of the Union's rights under international trade agreements', and allows the Union to suspend concessions or other obligations according to the relevant trade dispute settlement mechanisms.[2] The need for an amendment of the Trade Regulation 654/2014 arose even before the Trade Policy Review of 2021,[3] due to the paralysis of the Appellate Body (AB) and, accordingly, impossibility to enforce EU's trade rights under WTO rules when a panel report is appealed into the void.[4] Thus, at the end of 2019, when the number of AB Members went down to one, being impossible to form a division to hear an appeal, the Commission tabled a proposal for amendments to the Trade Enforcement Regulation 654/2014, which allows the Union to act 'in response to a measure maintained by a third country but dispute settlement through adjudication is blocked or

[1] Regulation (EU) 654/2014 of the European Parliament and of the Council of 15 May 2014 concerning the exercise of the Union's rights for the application and enforcement of international trade rules and amending Council Regulation (EC) No. 3286/94 laying down Community procedures in the field of the common commercial policy in order to ensure the exercise of the Community's rights under international trade rules, in particular those established under the auspices of the World Trade Organization (Trade Enforcement Regulation), OJ EU 2014 No. L 189/50.

[2] Trade Enforcement Regulation, Preamble, recitals 2 and 3.

[3] European Commission, Trade Policy Review: An Open, Sustainable and Assertive Trade Policy (Trade Policy Review), COM(2021) 66 final, 18 February 2021.

[4] For more on the AB crisis, see Chapter 2.

otherwise not available for reasons of non-cooperation of the third country which has adopted the measure'.[5] Thus, the amendments permit the imposition of unilateral countermeasures against WTO Members without waiting for the Dispute Settlement Body's (DSB) authorization, which, as will be shown, is prescribed by the Dispute Settlement Understanding (DSU)[6] rules, and against Free Trade Agreement (FTA) parties, even before a panel report is issued. Moreover, additional amendments were made to widen the scope of the Regulation to allow the imposition of measures in the area of services and trade-related aspects of intellectual property rights. All these amendments are in line with EU's recent turn towards stronger enforcement of international trade rules, but they also question the Union's declared support for international law, especially multilateral trade rules.

This chapter will first introduce the un-amended Trade Enforcement Regulation 654/2014 (Section 5.2), followed by a presentation of the recent amendments and their legislative history (Section 5.3). It will then investigate whether the EU has the flexibility to impose unilaterally countermeasures at the WTO level (Section 5.4) and then at the FTA level (Section 5.5) considering the constraints established by the relevant multilateral and regional rules and taking into consideration also the general international law on countermeasures as codified by the International Law Commission (ILC) Draft Articles on State Responsibility (ILC Draft Articles).[7] It will also assess the compliance of countermeasures taken under the Enforcement Regulation with the requirements established by general public international law (Section 5.6). The chapter will then contemplate the possible influence of the amendments on the multilateral trading system and their other consequences (Section 5.7). Finally, it will conclude by summarizing the findings and appraise the conformity of the amendments to Regulation 654/2014 permitting unilateral actions with EU's multilateral aspirations and commitment to international law (Section 5.8).

[5] Regulation (EU) 2021/167 of the European Parliament and of the Council of 10 February 2021 amending Regulation (EU) No 654/2014 concerning the exercise of the Union's rights for the application and enforcement of international trade rules, OJ EU 2021 No. L 49/1.

[6] Understanding on Rules and Procedures Governing the Settlement of Disputes (DSU), Marrakesh Agreement Establishing the World Trade Organization, Annex 2, 1869 U.N.T.S. 401, 33 I.L.M. 1226 (1994).

[7] Draft Articles on Responsibility of States for Internationally Wrongful Acts with Commentaries (ILC Draft Articles with Commentaries), in Report of the International Law Commission on the Work of Its Fifty-third Session, UN Doc. A/56/10, (2001) *Yearbook of the International Law Commission*, vol. II, Part Two.

5.2 The Un-Amended Trade Enforcement Regulation 654/2014

The Trade Enforcement Regulation 654/2014 was designed to step up the enforcement of the EU's trade agreements since 2014. In line with EU's recent turn towards more assertive trade enforcement, the scope of the Regulation was expanded in 2021 to allow the Union to act in more cases.

The Trade Enforcement Regulation 654/2014 has been regulating the suspension or withdrawal of EU trade concessions – in other words, countermeasures – in relation to third states in well-established cases.[8] Before the 2021 amendments, the Regulation allowed the imposition of countermeasures in case of an authorization or a right to do so after successful adjudication of trade disputes under WTO and, respectively, regional or bilateral agreements; rebalancing of concessions or other obligations according to WTO or other international trade rules on safeguards; and modification of concessions by a WTO member under Article XXVIII of the General Agreement on Tariffs and Trade (GATT),[9] where no compensatory adjustments have been agreed (Article 3 Trade Enforcement Regulation). Accordingly, the Regulation provided for the imposition of countermeasures only when this was permitted under the relevant international trade rules, either after all the dispute settlement procedures were exhausted and necessary authorizations obtained or in other permissible situations in which reaction is allowed by the special rules. As countermeasures that could have been enacted, the Trade Enforcement Regulation listed only actions with respect to trade in goods, namely the suspension of tariff concessions, new or increased customs duties, import or export quantitative restrictions, or suspension of concessions regarding goods, services, or suppliers in the area of public procurement (Article 5 Trade Enforcement Regulation). Therefore, the original text of the Regulation did not allow the imposition of countermeasures with respect to trade in services and intellectual property. The only possibility to address violations in these areas was to cross-retaliate with measures from other sectors, namely trade in goods and public procurement, with respect to which actions were permitted under Regulation 654/2014.[10] Article 10 Regulation and Recital 11 to it provided that the Commission should conduct a review on its scope no later than

[8] Wolfgang Weiß, 'Handelsvergeltungs-VO', in Horst Günter Krenzler, Christoph Herrmann, and Marian Niestedt (eds.), *EU-Außenwirtschafts- und Zollrecht* (München: C.H. Beck, 2022) 112, Erwägungsgründe, mn 1.

[9] General Agreement on Tariffs and Trade, 30 October 1947, 61 Stat. A-11, 55 U.N.T.S. 194.

[10] Weiß, 'Handelsvergeltungs-VO', Art. 5, mn. 2.

three years after the first instance of its implementation or no later than five years from its date of entry into force, whichever is the earlier, particularly with respect to the commercial policy measures that may be adopted under the Regulation and possibility to extend them over measures in the sector of intellectual property rights and additional measures concerning services.

5.3 The 2021 Amendments to Trade Enforcement Regulation 654/2014

In line with the review procedure described in the preceding section, the Commission first considered the Regulation's scope in 2017, when it concluded that there was no need for a modification.[11] In 2019, however, when the Commission conducted a new review, it emerged that there was a need to amend the scope of Regulation 654/2014 because of the paralysis of the AB and the possibility to block dispute settlement procedures under other trade agreements when another country does not cooperate for the mechanism to function properly.[12] Hence, the Commission proposal for the amendment of the scope of Regulation 654/2014 had the aim to offer the EU an instrument for it to be able to protect and enforce its rights in these situations as well.[13]

The Commission's initial proposals have been included in the 2021 amendments, which first address the AB crisis. Currently, with the AB being paralyzed and unable to hear appeals, any disputing WTO Member can block the adoption of a panel report by sending it into the void with an appeal, unless an alternative agreement was set for appellate review, such as that under Article 25 DSU on arbitration. Thus, the newly added Article 3 (aa) provides that the Regulation is now also applicable when following the circulation of a WTO panel report upholding in whole or in part EU's claims, an appeal is filled and it cannot be completed and the

[11] Gisela Grieger, 'Review of EU Enforcement Regulation for Trade Disputes' (2021) EPRS Briefing, www.europarl.europa.eu/RegData/etudes/BRIE/2020/652021/EPRS_BRI(2020)652021_EN.pdf, p. 5.

[12] Report From the Commission to the European Parliament and the Council, Review of the scope of the Regulation No 654/2014 of the European Parliament and of the Council of 15 May 2014, COM(2019) 639 final, 12 December 2019, pp. 1-3.

[13] Proposal for Amending Regulation (EU) No. 654/2014 of the European Parliament and of the Council concerning the Exercise of the Union's rights for the Application and Enforcement of International Trade Rules (Proposal for Amending Regulation 654/2014), COM(2019) 623 final, p. 2.

other disputing country has not agreed to appeal arbitration under Article 25 DSU.[14] Hence, this amendment not only serves as a legal basis for potential unilateral countermeasures; it also represents a threat aimed at incentivizing other WTO Members to participate in the Multi-Party Interim Appeal Arbitration Arrangement (MPIA)[15] or at least enter into ad hoc appeal arbitration arrangements.[16] The MPIA could be said to be 'the carrot', while the Enforcement Regulation is 'the stick', incentivizing indecisive WTO Members to join the former.[17] Without this amendment, there was a risk that the EU would not have been able to enforce its rights, since appealed panel reports are not binding, and for the imposition of countermeasures, WTO rules require the DSB's authorization.[18]

Second, the new Article 3 (ba) enlarged the scope of the Regulation to cover situations in which a third disputing party 'is not taking the steps that are necessary for a dispute settlement procedure to function, including unduly delaying the proceedings amounting to non-cooperation in the process' under other international trade agreements, particularly bilateral or regional ones. This amendment is seemingly set to specifically address potential blockages during the selection process of FTA panels of arbitrators that have famously taken place in the North American Free Trade Agreement (NAFTA) disputes and are also possible under the EU FTA rules, due to the imperfect design of these dispute settlement mechanisms. Most recent FTAs concluded by the EU provide that when arbitrators are not selected by agreement, they should be selected by lot from a pre-established list of candidates.[19] However, under the EU–Korea FTA and

[14] For more on the MPIA and appeal arbitrations under Art. 25 DSU, see Chapter 4.

[15] Statement on a Mechanism for Developing, Documenting and Sharing Practices and Procedures in the Conduct of WTO Disputes, Multi-Party Interim Appeal Arbitration Arrangement Pursuant to Article 25 of the DSU, JOB/DSB/1/Add.12, 30 April 2020.

[16] Wolfgang Weiß, 'The EU's Strategic Autonomy and Rule of Law in External Affairs: What Future for Respect for International Law and Multilateralism in Trade Policy?', in Luis M. Hinojosa-Martínez and Carmela Pérez Bernárdez (eds.), *Enhancing the Rule of Law in the EU´s External Action* (Cheltenham: Edward Elgar, 2023), p. 196 f.

[17] Folkert Graafsma, 'The Revised Enforcement Regulation (No 2021/167) and Some Possible Effects on EU Trade Disputes' (2022) 17 (7)&(8) *GTCJ* 289-299 at 290-291.

[18] Arts. 21(3), (6), 22(8), 23.2(c) DSU.

[19] Free trade Agreement between the European Union and its Member States, of the one part, and the Republic of Korea, of the other part (EU–Korea FTA), OJ EU 2011 No. L 127/6, 14 May 2011, Art. 14.5(2)-(3); Comprehensive Economic and Trade Agreement (CETA) between Canada, of the one part, and the European Union and its Member States, of the other part, OJ EU 2017 No. L 23/11, 14 January 2017, Art. 29.7(2)-(4); Agreement between the European Union and Japan for an Economic Partnership (JEPA), OJ EU 2018 No. L 330/

EU–Singapore FTA the parties can perform the selection only together, leaving open the possibility for one uncooperative party blocking the selection process.[20] Furthermore, under the EU–Korea FTA, if the parties do not manage to agree on a pre-established list of candidates, there are no further rules that would regulate this situation, potentially leading to decades-long blockages, as it happened under NAFTA.[21] In case the lists of candidates are missing or incomplete, even the EU FTAs with more detailed and developed rules on panel selection, such as EU–Canada Comprehensive Economic and Trade Agreement (CETA) and EU–Vietnam FTA, provide opportunities for delays in the process of panel establishment due to vagueness and uncertainty of some rules.[22] Accordingly, the amendment seeks to grant the Union an enforcement tool even when regional or bilateral dispute settlement mechanisms are hindered by other treaty parties. Moreover, the amendment could act as an impetus for EU FTA partners to cooperate in the process of panel establishment. Thus, the 2021 amendments enlarge the scope of Regulation 654/2014 to cover the situations in which 'dispute settlement through adjudication is blocked or otherwise not available for reasons of non-cooperation'.[23] Additionally, when imposing countermeasures in the AB crisis context and in case of blockages by uncooperative parties, in line with the proportionality principle established by the international customary law (Article 51 ILC Draft Articles), the level of such measures shall not exceed the nullification or impairment of the Union's commercial interests caused by the third country's measures.[24]

Following the draft report of the European Parliament Committee on International Trade (INTA), EU legislators agreed to further extend the scope of Regulation 654/2014 to add the possibility to impose trade policy

3, 27 December 2018, Art. 21.8(2)-(4); Free trade Agreement between the European Union and the Republic of Singapore (EU–Singapore FTA), OJ EU 2019 L No. 294/3, 14 November 2019, Art. 14.5(2)-(4); Free Trade Agreement between the European Union and the Socialist Republic of Viet Nam (EU–Vietnam FTA), OJ EU 2020 No. L 186/3, 12 June 2020, Art. 15.7(2)-(4).

[20] For more, see Cornelia Furculita, *The WTO and the New Generation EU FTA Dispute Settlement Mechanisms: Interacting in a Fragmented and Changing International Trade Law Regime* (Cham: Springer, 2021), pp. 101–102.

[21] ibid. [22] ibid.

[23] Regulation (EU) 2021/167 of the European Parliament and of the Council of 10 February 2021 amending Regulation (EU) No 654/2014 concerning the exercise of the Union's rights for the application and enforcement of international trade rules, OJ EU 2021 No. L 49/1 (2021 amendments), 12 February 2021, Preamble, recital 2.

[24] Regulation (EU) 2021/167 amending Regulation (EU) No 654/2014, Art. 1 inserting point (ba) in Art. 4 (2) Regulation 654/2014.

measures covering services and partially trade-related aspects of intellectual property rights and to allow the imposition of measures also in case of modification of concessions or commitments by a WTO Member under Article XXI General Agreement on Trade in Services (GATS)[25] and where compensatory adjustments are not made in conformity with the findings of the arbitration pursuant to this article.[26] Additionally, the amended Regulation 654/2014 required a new review of its scope at the earliest possible or no later than 13 February 2022, including the possible addition of further commercial policy measures suspending concessions or other obligations in the field of trade-related aspects of intellectual property rights.[27] The Commission conducted the required review and concluded in its report that while there are no legal or technical impediments to a further extension in the field of trade-related aspects of intellectual property rights, which would also be beneficial, a legislative proposal is not yet considered opportune, since the last amendment is still very recent.[28]

INTA also suggested introducing another amendment that would have allowed the Commission to adopt trade policy measures in case of a 'clear breach' of international law or a 'clear violation' of trade obligations by a third country which threatened or impaired the EU's commercial interests or jeopardized its strategic autonomy, provided that the Union had appropriately challenged those illegal measures at the WTO or in front of the relevant regional or bilateral dispute settlement body.[29] As argued by the authors in a separate paper, this suggested amendment, which was

[25] General Agreement on Trade in Services, 15 April 1994, Marrakesh Agreement Establishing the World Trade Organization, Annex 1B, 1869 U.N.T.S. 183, 33 I.L.M. 1167 (1994).

[26] Regulation (EU) 2021/167 amending Regulation (EU) No 654/2014, Preamble, recital 9, Art. 1 amending Arts. 1-3, 4-5. Additionally, the Regulation introduces other provisions related to the imposition of potential trade policy measures in the newly added areas, such as a hierarchy of steps to be followed when selecting measures in the field of trade in services or the obligation to inform and conduct stakeholder consultations (amendments of Arts. 5 and 9).

[27] Regulation (EU) 2021/167 amending Regulation (EU) No 654/2014, Preamble, recital 9, Art. 1.

[28] Report from the Commission to the European Parliament and the Council, Review of the scope of the Regulation No 654/2014 of the European Parliament and of the Council of 15 May 2014, COM(2022) 74 final, 1 March 2022, p. 8.

[29] Report on the Proposal for a Regulation of the European Parliament and of the Council amending Regulation (EU) No. 654/2014 of the European Parliament and of the Council concerning the Exercise of the Union's Rights for the Application and Enforcement of International Trade Rules (INTA Report), A9– 0133/2020, 6 July 2020, Amendments 8, 14.

not even claimed to be justified under general international law, was clearly in breach of Article 23 DSU, requiring WTO Members to have recourse to the DSU rules when they seek redress of a WTO violation.[30] This proposed change has not been included in the amended Regulation 654/2014; instead, the Commission promised and thereafter tabled a proposal on an Anti-Coercion Instrument, which, as it will be demonstrated in Chapter 6, has better chances to stand the legality test under the WTO rules, at least 'as such'.

The 2021 amendments are certainly in line with EU's recent turn towards stronger and more assertive enforcement of its trade agreements. The expansion of the scope of the Trade Enforcement Regulation 654/2014 to allow the imposition of trade policy measures in new areas would allow the EU to use these measures to put greater pressure on third countries which engage in violations and even to deter them from engaging in such conduct, making the Union a more credible international actor and demonstrating its intention to exercise its rights in these areas to the full extent.[31] The amendments are also said to reflect EU's commitment to multilateralism and binding dispute settlement, preventing EU's trading partners from thwarting the international rules-based trading system.[32] However, the question arises whether with these amendments the EU is not itself undermining the professed support for international law and multilateralism and whether they are in line with the Union's international commitments, an aspect that will be dealt with in the following sections.

5.4 The Legality of the 2021 Amendments Addressing the AB Crisis

As explained, the amended Trade Enforcement Regulation 654/2014 allows the imposition of countermeasures in case of ongoing, albeit obstructed, WTO dispute settlement proceedings. In what follows, this section will analyze the legality of this amendment under the WTO rules and whether potential unilateral countermeasures could be justified under public international law.

[30] Wolfgang Weiß and Cornelia Furculita, 'The EU in Search for Stronger Enforcement Rules: Assessing the Proposed Amendments to Trade Enforcement Regulation 654/2014' (2020) 23(4) *JIEL* 865–884 at 879.

[31] Review of the scope of the Regulation No 654/2014 of the European Parliament and of the Council of 15 May 2014, COM(2022) 74 final, p. 7.

[32] Grieger, 'Review of EU Enforcement Regulation for Trade Disputes' (2021), p. 2.

5.4.1 Article 23 DSU and Article 52 (4) ILC Draft Articles on State Responsibility

For the amendment addressing the AB crisis, the relevant article within the WTO is Article 23 DSU. As the following discussion will show, the Commission also invokes Article 52 (4) ILC Draft Articles on State Responsibility. Accordingly, these articles, as well as the relationship between them, will be analyzed here to establish the legality of the amendment in question under EU's international commitments.[33]

As stated in Chapter 3, Article 23.1 DSU establishes that when a WTO Member seeks redress of a WTO violation, it shall have recourse to, and abide by, the rules and procedures contained in the DSU. According to the WTO case law, this article stresses the primacy of the multilateral dispute settlement system, to the exclusion of unilateral measures.[34] Doctrinal writings also confirm that the *raison d'être* of Article 23.1 DSU is to prevent Members from adopting unilateral measures without making use of the WTO multilateral dispute settlement mechanism.[35] The 2021 amendments do allow, however, unilateral actions while the dispute settlement proceedings have not been technically finalized, contrary to the DSU. The first paragraph of Article 23 DSU states the general prohibition on unilateralism, while '[s]ubparagraphs (a), (b) and (c) of Article 23.2 articulate specific and clearly-defined forms of prohibited unilateral action'.[36] Article 23.2 (a) establishes that Members shall not make a determination to the effect that a violation has occurred, benefits have been nullified or impaired, or the attainment of any objective of the covered agreements has been impeded, except through recourse to dispute settlement under the DSU, and shall make any such determination consistent with the findings contained in the panel or AB report adopted by the DSB or an arbitration award issued under the DSU. In case a panel report is

[33] This section draws on Weiß and Furculita, 'The EU in Search for Stronger Enforcement Rules' (2020).

[34] Panel Report, *US – Shrimp*, WT/DS58/R, 15 May 1998, para. 7.43; Decision by the Arbitrators, *EC – Bananas III (United States) (Article 22.6 – EC)*, WT/DS27/ARB, 9 April 1999, para. 4.12; Panel Report, *Canada – Aircraft Credits and Guarantees*, WT/DS222/R, 28 January 2002, para. 7.170.

[35] Erich Vranes, 'Jurisdiction and Applicable Law in WTO Dispute Settlement' (2005) 48 *German Yearbook of International Law* 265–290 at 287; Makane Moïse Mbengue, 'The Settlement of Trade Disputes: Is There a Monopoly for the WTO?' (2016) 15 *The Law and Practice of International Courts and Tribunals* 207–248 at 223.

[36] Appellate Body Report, *US – Certain EC Products*, WT/DS165/AB/R, 11 December 2000, para. 111.

appealed into the void, it cannot be adopted by the DSB and is not final.[37] Therefore, if the EU imposes unilateral countermeasures under the amended Trade Enforcement Regulation 654/2014 when a panel report is appealed into the void, it would act against Article 23.2 (a) DSU. Moreover, Article 23.2 (c) DSU expressly establishes that Members shall follow the DSU procedures for the determination of the level of suspension of concessions or other obligations and obtain the DSB authorization before suspending concessions or other obligations under the WTO agreements. In *US – Certain EC Products* the panel expressly stated that 'Article 23.2(c) prohibits *any* suspensions of concessions or other obligations [. . .], prior to a relevant DSB authorization'[38] (emphasis added). By taking countermeasures against WTO alleged violations without the DSB authorization, the EU would clearly act in breach of Article 23.2 (c) DSU. Furthermore, if imposing unilateral countermeasures without the DSB authorization, the EU might not follow the Article 22 DSU principles and procedures on the suspension of concessions detailing the necessary sequence of sectors in which the suspension should take place.[39]

Looking at the scant practice under the un-amended Trade Enforcement Regulation, one could expect that the newly added Article 3 (aa) may be rarely used, too. However, for imposing countermeasures under Article 3 (a), the EU has to wait for a final WTO report, most often compliance proceedings and proceedings on the level of the suspension of concessions and other obligations,[40] before receiving the DSB authorization. The fact that the majority of WTO disputes are settled or discontinued before reaching the stage of retaliation, even when authorized countermeasures are rarely applied,[41] contributes to the scant usage of the un-amended Trade Enforcement Regulation. In contrast, Article 3 (aa) applies in case of appeals into the void, which as the record shows parties do not shy away from lodging. Accordingly, it can be expected that there will be more instances in which Article 3 (aa) could be used compared to Article 3 (a). Even if Article 3 (aa) Trade Enforcement Regulation is not applied in practice, as already argued in Chapter 3, it still violates 'as such' Article 23 DSU. The mandatory/discretionary distinction will be

[37] DSU, Art. 16.4.

[38] Panel Report, *US – Certain EC Products*, WT/DS165/R, 17 July 2000, para. 6.37.

[39] Graafsma, 'The Revised Enforcement Regulation (No 2021/167)' (2022) 295.

[40] Geraldo Vidigal, 'Why Is There So Little Litigation under Free Trade Agreements? Retaliation and Adjudication in International Dispute Settlement' (2017) 20 *JIEL* 927–950 at 947.

[41] ibid, 946–948.

useful for establishing the 'as such' conformity of legislation with the WTO law, albeit discretion in itself may not be sufficient to preclude such a violation.[42] Thus, it is needed to establish the degree of leeway that the Commission enjoys when deciding whether or not to adopt unilateral measures and what measures to adopt. As explained by recent WTO jurisprudence, the legislation analyzed should either *require* a violation or otherwise *restrict in a material way* the Member's discretion to act consistently with WTO agreements.[43] The Trade Enforcement Regulation establishes that the Commission 'shall' adopt implementing acts '[w]here action is *necessary* to safeguard the Union's *interests*' (emphasis added).[44] Hence, the Commission enjoys discretion in establishing the Union's interests and whether action is necessary to safeguard them, and it is not required to impose unilateral countermeasures against the obligation contained in Article 23 DSU. Still, discretionary legislation could violate 'as such' WTO law, especially when it explicitly provides a WTO-inconsistent action.[45] The Regulation expressly lists in Article 5 (1) that the Commission can resort to the suspension of tariff concessions and the imposition of new or increased customs duties, including the imposition of custom duties beyond the most-favoured-nation (MFN) level, the introduction or increase of quantitative restrictions on imports or exports of goods, the suspension of obligations regarding trade in services, trade-related aspects of intellectual property, or public procurement, and the imposition of restrictions on trade in services or intellectual property rights. Thus, in case the Commission decides to act, all the actions that the Regulation explicitly lists would be against Article 23.2 (c) DSU, as they concern the suspension of concessions or obligations under WTO agreements without the DSB authorization. Furthermore, these actions could also violate other substantive WTO obligations, such as Articles I, II, XI GATT and Articles XVI,

[42] Simon Lester, 'A Framework for Thinking about the Discretion in the Mandatory/ Discretionary Distinction' (2011) 14(2) *JIEL* 369–402 at 370; Panel Report, *US – Section 301*, WT/DS152/R, 22 December 1999, para. 7.53; Panel Report, *Brazil – Aircraft (Article 21.5 – Canada II)*, WT/DS46/RW2, 26 July 2001, paras. 5.9, 5.12; Appellate Body Report, *US – Corrosion-Resistant Steel Sunset Review*, WT/DS244/AB/R, 15 December 2003, para. 93; Appellate Body Report, *EU - Biodiesel*, WT/DS473/AB/R, 6 October 2016, para. 6.227.

[43] Appellate Body Report, *EU – Biodiesel*, WT/DS473/AB/R, paras. 6.229, 6.281; Panel Report, *US – Olives*, WT/DS577/R, 19 November 2021, para. 7.146. Referring to older Appellate Body Reports from *US – Corrosion-Resistant Steel Sunset Review*, WT/DS244/AB/R, 15 December 2003, para. 100 and *US – Carbon Steel*, WT/DS/213/AB/R, 28 November 2002, para. 162.

[44] Trade Enforcement Regulation, Art. 4 (1).

[45] Lester, 'A Framework for Thinking' (2011) 399.

XVII GATS.[46] Consequently, it can be concluded that the Trade Enforcement Regulation could also be found 'as such' in violation of Article 23 DSU and even other substantive WTO provisions.

The Commission, however, does not even allege that the Trade Enforcement Regulation is in conformity with Article 23 DSU. Instead, it opines that in the context of the AB crisis, the general public international law can be used as a valid legal basis for unilateral countermeasures. It argues that under customary rules of international law, as codified by the ILC Draft Articles, the EU is allowed, under conditions such as proportionality and prior notice, to take countermeasures to curb the breach of its rights and to obtain reparation.[47] When tabling the proposal for amending Regulation 654/2014, the Commission stated that under Article 50 (2) (a) ILC Draft Articles, a party is not relieved from fulfilling its obligations under any applicable dispute settlement procedure, the rules on dispute settlement being *lex specialis* in relation to the provisions of general international law on countermeasures according to Article 55 ILC Draft Articles.[48] However, the Commission claims that the possibility to resort to countermeasures under general rules, specifically Article 52 (4) ILC Draft Articles, revives when the 'responsible party fails to cooperate in good faith in the dispute settlement procedures, thereby preventing the injured party from completing such procedures'.[49] Article 52 (4) read in conjunction with Article 52 (3) ILC Draft Articles establishes that, notwithstanding binding dispute settlement rules, the possibility to impose countermeasures arises if the responsible State fails to implement the dispute settlement procedures in good faith. Accordingly, the Commission seems to claim that Article 52 (4) ILC Draft Articles containing conditions relating to the resort to countermeasures under general international law is applicable in case of breaches of international trade treaties, despite the fact that they contain special rules.

By virtue of Article 55 ILC Draft Articles, general rules contained in the articles do not apply where and to the extent that the conditions for the existence of an internationally wrongful act or its legal consequences are determined by special rules of international law.[50] Thus, the ILC Draft Articles apply in a residual way, and the extent to which the relevant

[46] Graafsma, 'The Revised Enforcement Regulation (No 2021/167)' (2022) 298.
[47] Proposal for Amending Regulation (EU) No. 654/2014, COM(2019) 623 final, p. 4.
[48] ibid. [49] ibid.
[50] ILC Draft Articles with Commentaries, Commentary to Article 55, para. 2.

general rules are displaced depends on the special rules.[51] According to the Commentaries to the ILC Draft Articles, in case of the WTO DSU it is clear from its language 'that only the consequences specified are to flow'.[52] Thus, while the ILC Draft Articles may remain pertinent in a residual way for other aspects, which are outside the scope of the present chapter, it seems that the general rules on countermeasures, such as the ones contained in Article 52 ILC Draft Articles, have been displaced by the more special DSU rules on the same matter. Additionally, scholars seem to largely agree that while the WTO is not a self-contained regime and the ILC Draft Articles could be residually pertinent with respect to other aspects, the WTO rules on countermeasures have displaced the more general customary rules on this particular aspect.[53] The 'fall-back' doctrine could, nevertheless, render the ILC Draft Articles rules on countermeasures relevant even in this case – a potential justification treated in detail in the next section.

The Commission could try arguing that the DSU is silent as to the consequences of a disputing party acting in bad faith by blocking the dispute settlement procedures,[54] and adopt a reading of the DSU that does not preclude the residual applicability of Article 52 (4) ILC Draft Articles, with the effect of permitting countermeasures even in the wake of a pending WTO appeal. Even if admitting that Article 52 (4) ILC Draft Articles has not been displaced by the more special DSU rules on countermeasures, the legal approach presented by the Commission raises at least two questions. First, is this reading of the relationship between DSU rules and the ILC Draft Articles compatible with the WTO judiciary's approach

[51] ibid, paras. 2, 3; Gabrielle Marceau and Julian Wyatt, 'Dispute Settlement Regimes Intermingled: Regional Trade Agreements and the WTO' (2010) 1(1) *Journal of International Dispute Settlement* 67–95 at 76.

[52] ILC Draft Articles with Commentaries, Commentary to Article 55, para. 3.

[53] Petros C. Mavroidis, 'Remedies in the WTO Legal System: Between a Rock and a Hard Place' (2000) 11(4) *EJIL* 763–813 at 766; Gabrielle Marceau, 'WTO Dispute Settlement and Human Rights' (2002) 13 (4) *JIEL* 753–814 at 768; Joanna Gomula, 'Responsibility and the World Trade Organization', in James Crawford, et al. (eds.), *The Law of International Responsibility* (Oxford: Oxford University Press, 2010), p. 797; Alejandro Sánchez, 'What Trade Lawyers Should Know about the ILC Articles on State Responsibility' (2012) 7 (6) *GTCJ* 292–299 at 294; James Crawford, *State Responsibility: The General Part* (New York: Cambridge University Press, 2013), pp. 710–711; Tom Ruys, 'Sanctions, Retorsions and Countermeasures: Concepts and International Legal Framework', in Larissa van den Herik (ed.), *Research Handbook on UN Sanctions and International Law* (Cheltenham: Edward Elgar Publishing, 2017) p. 44.

[54] Although, as shown in this section, the DSU (Arts. 3.7 and 3.10) prescribes the obligation of the Members to engage in dispute settlement in good faith.

to countermeasures? Second, can one blame any WTO Member that appeals a panel report into the void under current circumstances to act in bad faith? Only if one can answer both questions in the affirmative can the argumentation by the Commission stand.

As to the first issue: One may infer from Articles 50 (2) and 52 (3) ILC Draft Articles a choice for a disputing party between taking countermeasures or initiating dispute settlement procedures, unless the special rules provide otherwise.[55] As shown, Article 23 DSU, as *lex specialis*, clearly prohibits unilateral actions in case of disputes on WTO violations, thereby displacing the general customary rule contained in Article 52 (3) ILC Draft Articles. As mentioned, this has been confirmed by the panel in *US – Certain EC Products* when stating that '[u]nder international law, these types of countermeasures are now subject to requirements, such as those identified by the International Law Commission in its work on state responsibility [...] However, in WTO, countermeasures [...] are strictly regulated and can take place only within the framework of the WTO/DSU.'[56] Moreover, it is highly doubtful whether WTO adjudicators would accept the ILC Draft Articles as a defense in a potential dispute on the legality of EU countermeasures taken without DSB authorization. The WTO panels and the AB used the ILC Draft Articles and other sources of general international law for the purpose of interpretation and determination of the meaning of WTO rules and to support their already adopted views.[57] WTO panels and the AB have not expressly ruled out the possibility to use the ILC Draft Articles to determine issues not regulated by the WTO law.[58] However, they have not directly applied them or any other

[55] Third Report on State Responsibility, by Mr. James Crawford, Special Rapporteur, DOCUMENT A/CN.4/507 and Add. 1–4, para. 300, fn. 576.

[56] Panel Report, *US – Certain EC Products*, WT/DS165/R, fn. 100 to para. 6.23.

[57] Petros C. Mavroidis, *The Sources of WTO Law and Their Interpretation* (Cheltenham: Edward Elgar Publishing, 2022) pp. 42–43. See, for example, Decision by the Arbitrators, *Brazil – Aircraft (Article 22.6 – Brazil)*, WT/DS46/ARB, 28 August 2000, paras. 3.42-3.44; Appellate Body Report, *US – Cotton Yarn*, WT/DS192/AB/R, 8 October 2001, para. 120; Appellate Body Report, *US – Line Pipe*, WT/DS202/AB/R, 15 February 2002, paras. 251–260; Decision by Arbitrator, *US – FSC (Article 22.6 – US)*, WT/DS108/ARB, 30 August 2002, para. 5.26, fn. 52; Appellate Body Report, *Canada – Continued Suspension*, WT/DS321/AB/R, 16 October 2008, para. 382. It seems that the AB treated the references to the ILC Draft Articles in the WTO jurisprudence as instances of interpretation under Art. 31(3)(c) Vienna Convention on the Law of Treaties (VCLT), Vienna, 23 May 1969, in force 27 January 1980, 1155 UNTS 331; (1969) 8 ILM 679; UKTS (1980) 58 (Appellate Body Report, *US – Anti-Dumping and Countervailing Duties (China)*, WT/DS379/AB/R, 11 March 2011, paras. 313–316).

[58] Sánchez, 'What Trade Lawyers Should Know about the ILC Articles on State Responsibility' (2012) 299; Joachim Åhman, 'Exploring Border Areas between the Law of

general rules on state responsibility either. When invoking the ILC Draft Articles, WTO adjudicators did so without providing a legal basis[59] and have never explicitly confirmed the direct applicability of ILC Draft Articles, avoiding answering this question to this day.[60] The WTO panels and the AB are, generally, known for their reticence to apply non-WTO law as a substantive defense for an alleged violation of WTO rules.[61] Therefore, the potential invocation of the ILC Draft Articles within WTO dispute settlement proceedings as a substantive defense in case of unilateral measures taken against a WTO Member that appealed a panel report into the void under the amended Trade Enforcement Regulation 654/2014 will most likely be unsuccessful.

As to the second issue: Even if ILC Draft Articles were applicable within WTO proceedings to the detriment of the more special DSU rules, the Commission's argument presupposes that an appeal to a dysfunctional AB has to be classified as being contrary to good faith, as prescribed by Article 52 (4) ILC Articles. The principle of good faith, considered both a customary norm and a general principle of international law, is an abstract and vague one,[62] being more difficult to define it rather than illustrating it in examples.[63] According to the commentaries to Article 52 (4) ILC Draft Articles, the remedy of countermeasures revives if a party is

State Responsibility and WTO Law' (2020) 54 (2) *JWT* 219–238 at 223. Ventouratou claims that WTO adjudicators have already directly applied the ILC Draft Articles in limited instances, although in the cited cases the adjudicators seem to refer to the Articles to support their adopted view. In this respect, see Anna Ventouratou, 'The Law on State Responsibility and the World Trade Organization' (2021) 22 *JWIT* 759–803 at 777–779.

59 Ventouratou, 'The Law on State Responsibility and the World Trade Organization' (2021) 785.

60 See, for example, how the AB avoided this question in Appellate Body Report, *Peru – Agricultural Products*, WT/DS457/AB/R, 20 July 2015, paras. 5.21–5.28.

61 For this debate, see Joost Pauwelyn, 'How to Win a World Trade Organization Dispute Based on Non-World Trade Organization Law? Questions of Jurisdiction and Merits' (2003) 37(6) *JWT* 997–1030; Lorand Bartels, 'Jurisdiction and Applicable Law in the WTO' (2016) SIEL Working Paper No. 2016/18, pp. 1–21; Wolfgang Weiß, *WTO Law and Domestic Regulation* (München: Hart/Beck/Nomos, 2020), pp. 412–419.

62 Robert Kolb, 'Principles as Sources of International Law (with Special Reference to Good Faith)' (2006) 53(1) *Netherlands International Law Review* 1–36 at 13; Andrew D. Mitchell, 'Good Faith in WTO Dispute Settlement' (2006) 7 *Melbourne Journal of International Law* 339–371 at 340; Andreas R. Ziegler and Jorun Baumgartner, 'Good Faith as a General Principle of (International) Law', in Andrew D. Mitchell, M. Sornarajah, and Tania Voon (eds.), *Good Faith and International Economic Law* (New York: Oxford University Press, 2015), pp. 9–11.

63 Mitchell, 'Good Faith in WTO Dispute Settlement' (2006) citing Bin Cheng, *General Principles of Law as Applied by International Courts and Tribunals* (London: Grotius Publications Limited, 1987), p. 105.

not acting in good faith, such a situation occurring when, for example, a party does not appear in the process, does not comply with a provisional measures order, refuses to accept a final decision of the court or tribunal, fails to cooperate in the establishment of the relevant tribunal, or fails to appear before the tribunal once it is established.[64] The argument that any WTO Member appealing a panel report into the void would be acting against good faith because of the blockage of the appointment of AB Members by the United States is not convincing. Under Article 16.4 DSU, the parties to the dispute have the right to appeal the panel report, the provision indicating no limitation for doing so.[65] Thus, WTO Members appealing panel reports act according to their DSU rights notwithstanding the AB crisis. While the United States could be held responsible for blocking the appointment and reappointment of the AB Members (for more on this, see later in this section), the rest of the WTO Members should not be charged for this. Theoretically, the AB as an institution still exists, and any appeal can be heard again as soon as the AB Members positions are filled. Neither can one argue that WTO Members that appeal a panel report are abusing their right to appeal. Admittedly, no right is *a priori* absolute, and the recognition of its recourse could be refused in certain circumstances on the grounds that it has been abused.[66] An allegation of the breach of good faith could be considered not only under Article 52 (4) ILC Articles but could also be invoked under the more special rules contained in Articles 3.7 and 3.10 DSU, which are manifestations of the good-faith principle.[67] However, WTO adjudicators, the International Court of Justice (ICJ), and other international courts and tribunals have showed caution and restraint in finding an abuse of rights or process.[68] There is a presumption of good

64 ILC Draft Articles with Commentaries, Commentary to Article 52, para. 9.

65 Appellate Body Report, *EU – Fatty Alcohols (Indonesia)*, WT/DS442/AB/R, 5 September 2017, para. 5.175.

66 Hersch Lauterpacht, *The Development of International Law by the International Court* (London: Stevens & Sons Limited, 1958), p. 164; Ziegler and Baumgartner, 'Good Faith as a General Principle of (International) Law' (2015), p. 30.

67 Appellate Body Report, *EC – Export Subsidies on Sugar*, WT/DS265/AB/R, 28 April 2005, para. 312; Appellate Body Report, *Peru – Agricultural Products*, WT/DS457/AB/R, paras. 5.18–5.19.

68 Mitchell, 'Good Faith in WTO Dispute Settlement' (2006) 371; Ziegler and Baumgartner, 'Good Faith as a General Principle of (International) Law' (2015), p. 33; Freya Baetens, 'Abuse of Process and Abuse of Rights before the ICJ: Ever More Popular, Ever Less Successful?', *EJIL:Talk!*, 15 October 2019, www.ejiltalk.org/abuse-of-process-and-abuse-of-rights-before-the-icj-ever-more-popular-ever-less-successful/.

faith,[69] for the rebuttal of which an abuse to be found is necessary to show convincing evidence of the use of a norm in a manner other than the one in which it was intended and with an unreasonable, arbitrary, malicious, frivolous purpose or for causing harm or obtaining an illegitimate advantage.[70] It appears difficult, if not almost impossible to show that a WTO Member used its right to appeal with a different purpose than to obtain the modification or reversal of legal findings of a panel in its favour, which is expressly permitted under the DSU and is the *raison d'être* of the appeal mechanism in the DSU. While all WTO Members are certainly aware that their appeals would send a panel report into limbo until the crisis is resolved and unless disputing parties agree to appeal arbitration, they cannot be charged for not renouncing a right they are legally entitled to because of reasons that are not attributable to them. A WTO Member can always argue that it appealed the panel report with the sincere hope that the appeal will be heard once a way out of the AB crisis is found.

The EU might also be in a bad position to blame others for acting in bad faith, since the Union itself appealed first into the void the panel report in *EU – Cost Adjustment Methodologies II (Russia)*,[71] followed by another appeal from Russia.[72] As the EU's notification of the appeal states, the EU is aware that there are insufficient AB Members to hear appeals, but that it stands ready to move to appeal arbitration proceedings pursuant to Article 25 DSU.[73] However, WTO Members are not obliged to follow such an invitation – a choice also made by Russia. An appeal arbitral agreement is subject to the *mutual agreement* of the parties according to Article 25.2 DSU.[74] Deciding not to exercise this possibility is not a breach

[69] Appellate Body Report, *Mexico – Corn Syrup (Article 21.5 – US)*, WT/DS132/AB/RW, 22 October 2001, para. 74; Mitchell, 'Good Faith in WTO Dispute Settlement' (2006) 344.

[70] Mitchell, 'Good Faith in WTO Dispute Settlement' (2006) 350; Ziegler and Baumgartner, 'Good Faith as a General Principle of (International) Law' (2015), p. 33; Steven Reinhold, 'Good Faith in International Law' (2013) Bonn Research Papers on Public International Law Paper No. 2/2013, p. 12; Baetens, 'Abuse of Process and Abuse of Rights before the ICJ'.

[71] Notification of an Appeal by the European Union Under Article 16.4 and Article 17.1 of the Understanding on Rules and Procedures Governing the Settlement of Disputes (DSU), and Under Rule 20(1) of the Working Procedures for Appellate Review, *EU – Cost Adjustment Methodologies II (Russia)*, WT/DS494/7, 1 September 2020, p. 11.

[72] Notification of an Other Appeal by the Russian Federation Under Article 16.4 and Article 17 of the Understanding on Rules and Procedures Governing the Settlement of Disputes (DSU), and Under Rule 23(1) of the Working Procedures for Appellate Review, *EU – Cost Adjustment Methodologies II (Russia)*, WT/DS494/8, 8 September 2020.

[73] Notification of an Appeal by the EU, *EU – Cost Adjustment Methodologies II (Russia)*, p. 11.

[74] For more on the conditions of Art. 25 of the DSU, see Chapter 4.

of law or a breach of trust.[75] Moreover, when the EU appealed the report, there was no appeal arbitration arrangement in sight, a behaviour which according to the Union's reasoning would amount to a breach of the good-faith obligation prescribed by Article 52 (4) ILC Draft Articles and would even entitle the Russian Federation to impose unilateral countermeasures against the EU. The newly introduced Article 3 (aa) of the Trade Enforcement Regulation 654/2014 also does not take into account a conceivable situation in which the EU's counterparty would agree to subject the same dispute to a bilateral mechanism, where possible, instead of making use of WTO proceedings, which would enable the imposition of countermeasures according to the relevant bilateral rules.[76]

The appraisal of the US behaviour, however, could lead to a different outcome. The argument that the United States acted in bad faith because of its blockage of the appointments and reappointments of the AB Members on grounds unrelated to the personal qualifications of the candidates might be upheld.[77] Proving bad faith is usually a difficult task. Yet, in this case, the US actions clearly fall under one of the examples of bad faith given by the Commentaries to the ICL Draft Articles.[78] The United States still considers itself entitled to appeal panel reports and is still available for negotiations on mutually agreed solutions for the disputes, which is 'clearly to be preferred' under Article 3.7 DSU. For example, in *US – Carbon Steel (India) (Article 21.5 – India)*, the United States notified the DSB of its decision to appeal the report but did not file a notice of appeal or an appellant submission (to be submitted once an AB division is established), and then the parties communicated that they will continue to engage in good-faith discussions to seek a positive solution to this dispute.[79] Similarly, in other cases, the United States has been only notifying its decision to appeal, without filing notices of appeal and appellant submissions, often mentioning that due to the impossibility

[75] Caroline Glöckle, 'Die Ungewisse Zukunft des WTO Appellate Body' (2020) 9 *Europäische Zeitschrift für Wirtschaftsrecht* 356–364 at 364.

[76] For more on the relationship between the WTO and the EU FTAs dispute settlement mechanisms, see Furculita, *The WTO and the New Generation EU FTA Dispute Settlement Mechanisms* (2021).

[77] Ernst-Ulrich Petersmann, 'How Should WTO Members React to Their WTO Crises?' (2019) 18 (3) *WTRev* 503–525 at 507.

[78] ILC Draft Articles with Commentaries, Commentary to Article 52, para. 9.

[79] Joint Communication from India and the United States, *US – Carbon Steel (India) (Article 21.5 – India)*, WT/DS436/22, 16 January 2020.

to form an AB division, the parties are to determine the way forward in the disputes.[80] In certain cases it explicitly stated that such a way forward may represent engaging in good offices, conciliation, or mediation pursuant to Article 5 DSU, without mentioning Article 25 DSU arbitration proceedings.[81] However, in none of these notifications of appeals did the United States acknowledge that the appeals cannot be completed because of its blockage. Thus, the United States seems to force other parties to go back to the negotiating table or resort to alternative dispute resolution methods by deciding to appeal into the void while blocking the appointments and reappointments of the AB Members. Hence, its position could amount to taking advantage of the paralysis that it has generated. This could also be seen as a violation of the good-faith obligation on the part of the United States because it could be argued that it pursued the blockage with the malevolent purpose of replacing the judicial settlement of disputes with diplomatic negotiations or alternative dispute resolution means helping the parties to reach an agreement. This contradicts the fundamental idea of the DSU. A negotiated solution under the pressure exercised by a big economic power in this situation is different than the peaceful agreement that is always permitted by the DSU in the shadow of a pending dispute settlement procedure. Therefore, the United States uses DSU rules in a manner in which they were not intended to, which could qualify as bad faith.[82] While the invocation of Article 52 (4) ILC Draft Articles against the United States has better chances to be maintained, it is still expected that it will not be even considered as a substantive defence within WTO proceedings.

5.4.2 The Fall-Back Doctrine

Although the Commission has not expressly mentioned the fall-back doctrine when justifying the 2021 amendments in the WTO context,

[80] For example, Notification of an Appeal by the United States Under Article 16 of the Understanding on Rules and Procedures Governing the Settlement of Disputes, *United States – Tariff Measures On Certain Goods from China*, WT/DS543/10, 27 October 2020; Notification of an Appeal by the United States Under Article 16 of the Understanding on Rules and Procedures Governing the Settlement of Disputes, *United States – Anti-dumping and Countervailing Duties on Certain Products and the Use of Facts Available*, WT/DS539/9, 22 March 202.

[81] For example, Notification of an Appeal by the United States under Article 16 of the Understanding on Rules and Procedures Governing the Settlement of Disputes, *United States – Certain Measures on Steel and Aluminium Products (Norway)*, WT/DS552/16, 30 January 2023.

[82] Mitchell, 'Good Faith in WTO Dispute Settlement' (2006) 350.

the present section will analyze whether this potential justification has better chances to be endorsed than the invocation of Article 52 (4) ILC Draft Articles.

According to the fall-back doctrine, even *lex specialis* rules do not completely contract out of general international law on the same matter, which continues to be applicable in case of failure of the special regime, when 'instead of enhancing the effectiveness of the relevant obligations the regime serves to dilute existing standards'.[83] Thus, while the WTO special rules on remedies shall be applied exclusively to disputes between Members, the question raised is whether they are also final.[84] For the doctrine to be successfully invoked by the EU, (1) the doctrine should indeed have the status of general international law – that is, customary law; (2) it should be relevant for the AB crisis; and (3) it should be considered as a justification by the WTO adjudicators. The last aspect – the question of the applicability of general international law within WTO proceedings – was already treated in the previous section. Thus, unless WTO adjudicators change their approach, it is unlikely that non-WTO law will be considered as a justification for a WTO violation. In what follows, the remaining two issues will be considered.

During the GATT era, the fall-back doctrine was used as a justification for unilateral countermeasures imposed when the dispute settlement proceedings were blocked by another disputing party due to the rule of positive consensus.[85] The doctrine was used by powerful countries, such as the United States, to legitimize their unilateral actions.[86] The European Communities, however, considered it to be against the special regime established by the GATT 1947,[87] which did not even provide such a clear prohibition against unilateral actions as the one contained in Article 23 DSU. Accordingly, were the EU to invoke the fall-back doctrine

[83] Report of the Study Group of the International Law Commission, 'Fragmentation of International Law: Difficulties Arising from the Diversification and Expansion of International Law' (ILC Report on Fragmentation), A/CN.4/L.682, 13 April 2006, para. 137 citing Prosper Weil, 'Towards Relative Normativity in International Law' (1983) 77 *AJIL* 413–442.

[84] The ILC Report on Fragmentation states that 'Crawford left open, however, whether "exclusivity" here meant exclusive and final replacement of the general law or merely its substitution at an initial stage with the possibility of "fall-back" if the self-contained regime had, as Riphagen had put it, "failed"' (ILC Report on Fragmentation, para. 150).

[85] Javier Fernández Pons, 'Self-Help and the World Trade Organization', in Paolo Mengozzi (ed.), *International Trade Law on the 50th Anniversary of the Multilateral Trade System* (Milano: Giuffrè, 1999), p. 70.

[86] ibid, pp. 73–74. [87] ibid, p. 72.

against the background of the AB crisis, it would mean that it changed its position in this respect. Despite the fact that two Special Rapporteurs (Riphagen and Arangio-Ruiz) were in favour of a fall-back to general remedies when a special system fails, this question has not been ultimately treated in the ILC Draft Articles or the commentaries to it.[88] The Draft Committee of the ILC considered that the link between countermeasures and dispute settlement would be the good-faith obligation, subject to the *lex specialis* rule.[89] While some authors refer to this doctrine,[90] there is no agreement between international scholars with respect to it. Accordingly, the status of the fall-back doctrine as a customary norm does not seem to be established yet. In contrast, Article 52 (4) ILC Draft Articles provides a clear legal basis for imposing countermeasures (also invoked by the EU Commission) recognized as international customary law.

Even scholars in favour of the fall-back doctrine recognize that by including Article 23 DSU, WTO Members clearly excluded the possibility to resort unilaterally to countermeasures governed by the DSU.[91] Indeed, the inclusion of Article 23 DSU during the Uruguay Round was determined by the GATT-era unilateralism, in order to prevent Members from creating the same situation under WTO rules.[92] Therefore, recourse to general international law for the imposition of unilateral countermeasures would go against the initial will of the WTO drafters. The proponents of the fall-back doctrine consider the use of countermeasures outside the WTO system only when WTO dispute settlement procedures were exhausted and authorized measures failed to induce compliance.[93] They do not envisage the use of the fall-back doctrine and the imposition of

[88] ILC Report on Fragmentation, para. 152 (4).

[89] Mariano Garcia-Rubio, 'Unilateral Measures as a Means of Forcible Execution of WTO Recommendations and Decisions', in Laura Forlati and Linos-Alexandre Sicilianos (eds.), *Economic Sanctions in International Law* (Leiden: Brill Nijhoff, 2004), p. 471.

[90] Fernández Pons, 'Self-Help and the World Trade Organization' (1999), pp. 72 ff.; Garcia-Rubio, 'Unilateral Measures' (2004), p. 449; Bruno Simma and Dirk Pulkowski, 'Of Planets and the Universe: Self-Contained Regimes in International Law' (2006) 17 (3) *EJIL* 483–529; Bruno Simma and Dirk Pulkowski, 'Leges Speciales and Self-Contained Regimes', in James Crawford, et al. (eds.), *The Law of International Responsibility* (Oxford: Oxford University Press, 2010), pp. 149–150.

[91] Fernández Pons, 'Self-Help and the World Trade Organization' (1999), p. 76; Garcia-Rubio, 'Unilateral Measures' (2004), pp. 466–467; Simma and Pulkowski, 'Of Planets and the Universe' (2006) 521.

[92] Fernández Pons, 'Self-Help and the World Trade Organization' (1999), p. 74.

[93] ibid, p. 86; Garcia-Rubio, 'Unilateral Measures' (2004), p. 449; Simma and Pulkowski, 'Of Planets and the Universe' (2006) 522.

unilateral measures while a WTO dispute is still pending, unlike prescribed by the Trade Enforcement Regulation 654/2014. The supporters of the use of the fall-back doctrine in WTO disputes claim that when WTO special remedies are ineffective against a recalcitrant Member, resorting to countermeasures *outside* the WTO system would be possible, such as the suspension of a bilateral treaty.[94] Thus, there was no discussion about imposing countermeasures envisaged under the DSU without the DSB authorization.

Still, the fall-back to general rules of international law on countermeasures has also been proposed in case the special system fails.[95] Even if there was an agreement that in case of a failure of the special regime, the right to countermeasures under general international law revives, it is far from clear what such a failure would represent.[96] Yet, it becomes evident that the answer to this will depend on the nature of the special regime.[97] Would the AB crisis amount to a procedural failure of the WTO dispute settlement system? According to the ILC Report on Fragmentation, '[a] dispute-settlement mechanism under the regime may function so slowly or so inefficiently that damage continues to be caused without a reasonable prospect of a just settlement in sight' and then '[a]t some such point the regime will have "failed"'.[98] On one hand, it could be argued by the EU that because of the AB paralysis there is no reasonable prospect of a settlement in sight in the near future and that the WTO dispute settlement failed, especially since prompt settlement is essential to the effective functioning of the WTO (Article 3.3 DSU). On the other hand, it could be said that the WTO dispute settlement system has not failed yet, since un-appealed panel reports and potential arbitral appeal awards issued under the MPIA can be enforced, and when the system is restored, appeals filed will be heard. Moreover, the disputing parties can still use negotiations, good offices, conciliation, or mediation to settle a dispute (Article 5 DSU), 'a solution mutually acceptable to the parties to a dispute and consistent with the covered agreements' being clearly preferred (Article 3.7 DSU). Therefore, even if the EU could try arguing that the WTO dispute settlement system fails when a panel report is sent into limbo, due to the unsettled status of the fall-back doctrine as

[94] Garcia-Rubio, 'Unilateral Measures' (2004), p. 468; Simma and Pulkowski, 'Of Planets and the Universe' (2006) 522–523; Simma and Pulkowski, 'Leges Speciales and Self-Contained Regimes' (2010), p. 157.

[95] ILC Report on Fragmentation, paras. 186–190; Simma and Pulkowski, 'Of Planets and the Universe' (2006) 485, 509.

[96] ILC Report on Fragmentation, para. 186. [97] ibid. [98] ibid, para. 187.

international customary law and high likelihood that it would not be considered within WTO proceedings, it is less likely that the invocation of this doctrine will justify the violation of Article 23 DSU.

5.5 The Legality of the 2021 Amendment Addressing Potential Dispute Settlement Blockages under EU FTAs

In contrast to the situation under WTO law, the legal assessment of the 2021 amendments with regard to regional or bilateral dispute settlement mechanisms in EU FTAs might prove more beneficial for the EU.[99] Since, as discussed in the previous section, the status of the fall-back doctrine as a customary norm of international law is highly questionable, in what follows only the invocation of Article 52 (4) ILC Draft Articles under the FTA rules will be considered.

The EU's invocation of Article 52 (4) ILC Draft Articles when a party blocks the panel formation under bilateral trade agreements is more likely to be in conformity with international law, as these agreements do not express the exclusivity of the dispute settlement procedures and of the special remedies as in the case of the DSU.[100] For example, the FTAs with South Korea, Singapore, Vietnam, the EU–Japan Economic Partnership Agreement (JEPA), and CETA contain rather weak clauses according to which the dispute settlement provisions of these agreements apply to any dispute concerning their interpretation or application, without stating the exclusivity of these rules.[101] There is no similar clause to Article 23 DSU that would expressly require FTA parties to have exclusive recourse to FTA rules, including on remedies, in case of FTA disputes. To the contrary, all the mentioned agreements provide a choice of forum clause according to which recourse to the dispute settlement mechanism is without prejudice to recourse to dispute settlement under the WTO or any other instrument.[102] The FTA rules on temporary remedies used in case the responding party fails to comply with a final report also do not

[99] This section draws on Weiß and Furculita, 'The EU in Search for Stronger Enforcement Rules' (2020).

[100] The only exclusion relates to the TSD dispute settlement provisions in FTAs; see Chapter 7 for a detailed discussion.

[101] EU–Korea FTA, Art. 14.2; CETA, Art. 29.2; EU–Singapore FTA, Art. 14.2; EU–Vietnam FTA, Art. 15.2; JEPA, Art. 21.2.

[102] EU–Korea FTA, Art. 14.2; CETA, Art. 29.2; EU–Singapore FTA, Art. 14.2; EU–Vietnam FTA, Art. 15.2; JEPA, Art. 21.2

expressly preclude the suspension of obligations in other instances,[103] such as when a disputing party blocks the establishment of a panel. Since there is no exclusivity of FTA rules on dispute settlement and remedies, the argument that in this respect the general rules of international law, such as the ILC Draft Articles, can be applied residually has better chances to stand as a justification.[104]

While the ILC agreed that dispute settlement should be pursued, the question with respect to the extent to which compliance with dispute settlement procedures should be a prerequisite for initiating countermeasures was highly controversial in the Commission.[105] In its final version, Article 52 (3) ILC Draft Articles embodies the compromise that there is no requirement to resort to available dispute settlement mechanisms as a first step. Countermeasures should not be taken or, if taken, suspended only if the international wrongful act has ceased *and* the dispute is pending before a court or tribunal with authority to issue binding decisions.[106] Due to the use of the conjunction 'and', which is also confirmed by the drafting history,[107] it becomes clear that these conditions are cumulative. Otherwise, a state can choose between initiating dispute settlement proceedings and imposing unilateral countermeasures.[108] As the more special FTA law does not seem to preclude resort to general rules on countermeasures, the EU has the right to choose between taking countermeasures and initiating FTA dispute settlement procedures under the ILC Draft Articles. Compared to this, the newly added Article 3 (ba) Trade Enforcement Regulation 654/2014 is more restrictive, as it implicitly requires the initiation of dispute settlement procedures before allowing countermeasures. The obligation not to take or, if taken, to suspend countermeasures when the cumulative

[103] EU–Korea FTA, Art. 14.19; CETA, Art. 29.3; EU–Singapore FTA, Art. 14.21; EU–Vietnam FTA, Art. 15.24; JEPA, Art. 21.27.

[104] Except with regard to the specific provisions on dispute settlement in TSD chapters, see Chapter 7. Marco Bronckers and Giovanni Gruni, 'Retooling the Sustainability Standards in EU Free Trade Agreements' (2021) 24 *JIEL* 25–51 at 41.

[105] Third Report on State Responsibility, by Mr. James Crawford, Special Rapporteur, DOCUMENT A/CN.4/507 and Add. 1–4, 5 March, 15 June, 10 and 18 July and 4 August 2000, para. 299; Crawford, *State Responsibility* (2013), p. 702.

[106] Laurence Boisson de Chazournes, 'Remarks', The State of State Responsibility (2002) *ASIL Proceedings of the 96th Annual Meeting* 169–172 at 170.

[107] Third Report on State Responsibility, by Mr. James Crawford, Special Rapporteur, DOCUMENT A/CN.4/507 and Add. 1–4, para. 298.

[108] As mentioned in Section 5.4.1, this choice can be inferred from Arts. 50 (2) and 52 (3) of the ILC Draft Articles.

conditions of Article 52 (3) ILC Articles are met would not be applicable if a disputing party acts in bad faith, since Article 52 (4) explicitly states that '[p]aragraph 3 does not apply if the responsible State fails to implement the dispute settlement procedures in good faith'. The question of whether a party acts in bad faith when frustrating the bilateral procedures is easier to answer in the affirmative, as the parties to a bilateral or regional treaty are much more clearly bound by their duty of loyalty. As a frustration of a bilateral procedure would emanate directly from them, the allegation of breach of good faith is much easier to substantiate. The failure to cooperate in the establishment of the relevant panel is an explicit example of bad faith mentioned in the ILC articles.[109]

Unilateral countermeasures could, nevertheless, violate substantive FTA norms, such as those on market commitments or non-discrimination. Thus, even if an FTA party is not bound by the exclusive character of FTA procedural rules, the question remains open if an FTA panel accepts justifications based on general public international law. Therefore, the acceptance of ILC Draft Articles as a defence against a violation of substantive FTA norms will depend on the openness of FTA panels to consider and apply rules of general public international law.

5.6 Compliance with ILC Draft Articles Conditions

Even if resort to Article 52 (4) ILC Draft Articles is considered a valid legal basis in the WTO or FTA context, countermeasures imposed under it should comply with the conditions established by these Articles.

As already mentioned in Chapter 3, according to Article 49 (1) ILC Draft Articles, unilateral countermeasures under general public international law can only be taken against a wrongdoer to induce compliance. Accordingly, this article establishes the prerequisites for countermeasures, specifically the prevalence of an international wrongful act, and other requirements, namely against whom countermeasures should be imposed, and what should be their purpose.[110] Article 3 (aa) Trade Enforcement Regulation, however, violates this last condition, as it allows resort to countermeasures also as a means to prevent the filing of an appeal into the void and as an incentive to participate in the MPIA, and not merely as an instrument to induce the wrongdoer to comply with its obligations, as required by Article 49 (1) ILC Draft Articles. This is

[109] ILC Draft Articles with Commentaries, Commentary to Article 52, para. 9.

[110] ibid, Commentary to Article 49, paras. 2, 3, 4, 8.

because the countermeasure is adopted if the other party, after having appealed to the (currently inactive) WTO AB, does not subscribe to the MPIA. In this context, countermeasures are not used to induce the other state to comply with its WTO obligations but to enforce participation in the alternative appeal mechanism with regard to which no obligation exists.

The principle of proportionality enshrined in Article 51 of the same Articles is reflected in Article 4 (2) (ba) Trade Enforcement Regulation. Article 52 (1) ILC Draft Articles requires a state before taking countermeasures to call upon the responsible state to fulfill its obligation, notify about the decision to take countermeasures, and offer to negotiate. Since both paragraphs (aa) and (ba) of Article 3 Trade Enforcement Regulation are used only after disputes are initiated, which are preceded by negotiations, this requirement could be considered complied with. But the Regulation contains no express requirement with respect to the call on fulfillment of obligations and notification of the country subject to countermeasures. The Commission, nevertheless, in a 2021 Declaration on compliance with international law – an instrument without binding legal force but of political value – affirms that before resorting to countermeasures under Article 3 (aa), it 'will call upon the WTO Member concerned to implement the panel's findings and recommendations, notify that WTO Member of the Union's intention to take countermeasures and reiterate its openness to negotiate'.[111] Still, the Declaration is silent about compliance with these requirements in case of using Article 3 (ba). Thus, it remains to be seen whether in practice these requirements are respected.

Finally, as stated in the previous section, Article 52 (3) ILC Draft Articles establishes that countermeasures must not be taken or, if taken, must be suspended if the international wrongful act has ceased *and* the dispute is pending before a court or tribunal with authority to issue binding decisions. If the EU's argument that its countermeasures are taken under Article 52 (4) ILC Draft Articles is accepted, then it would derogate from Article 52 (3). If the alleged bad faith discontinues and the disputing party returns to good-faith dispute settlement, then the requirement needs to be complied with. The requirement of Article 52 (3) ILC Draft Articles, however, may not be fully complied with by Article 7 Trade Enforcement Regulation. Even though Article 7 provides for the suspension of the EU

[111] Commission declaration on compliance with international law, OJ EU 2021 No. C 49/03.

countermeasure in certain situations, there is no clause that applies to a situation where a state ceases its wrongful acts and returns to good will dispute settlement (i.e. stops blocking bilateral dispute settlement). Article 7 (2) a) provides for suspension only if 'a third country whose measures were found to be in breach of international trade rules in a dispute settlement procedure brings itself into compliance, or where a mutually satisfactory solution has otherwise been reached'. This does not cover the situation where the third country ceases its wrongful measures while the settlement procedure is pending (but blocked, e.g. by lack of cooperation) and changes its mind by returning in good faith to the settlement procedures. Then, under Article 52 (3) ILC Draft Articles, the EU must suspend its measures, but cannot do so under its Trade Enforcement Regulation, as its Article 7 does not cover this situation; Article 7 (2) a) provides for the Commission to suspend its countermeasure(s) only when the third country had already been found to act in breach of trade rules by dispute settlement. The Trade Enforcement Regulation provides in Article 7 (2) a) that the Commission must repeal an implementing act 'when a third country whose measures *were found* to be in breach of international trade rules *in a dispute settlement procedure* brings itself into compliance, or where a mutually satisfactory solution has otherwise been reached' (emphasis added). Article 7 (2) a) Trade Enforcement Regulation would be applicable in case of a WTO panel sent into the void by the other disputing party if it terminates the alleged inconsistent measure and agrees on a way forward for dispute settlement procedures, as there would be measures *found* in breach by a WTO panel. In contrast, if an uncooperative EU FTA partner ceases the wrongful act and returns to good-faith dispute settlement before a breach is found in dispute settlement procedures (due to the fact that the settlement is still pending and ongoing), the Trade Enforcement Regulation provides no legal basis for the suspension of countermeasures. Without prior findings by a panel/arbitration, the requirements of Article 7 (2) a) are not met, and consequently the Commission does not have power to suspend the countermeasures adopted under Article 3 (ba) Trade Enforcement Regulation. The above-mentioned Commission declaration on compliance with international law does not cover this situation, as it relates only to WTO dispute settlement problems but not to the comparable situation for bilateral or other dispute settlement mechanisms, for which EU countermeasures were adopted by virtue of Article 3 (ba) Trade Enforcement Regulation. While the Commission's Declaration on compliance with international law states that it 'will act in accordance with the requirements of the international law on countermeasures' when taking measures under Article 3 (aa) Trade Enforcement Regulation, it is silent with respect to compliance when adopting measures under paragraph (ba) of its Article 3. Accordingly, if an EU FTA partner ceases its alleged wrongful act and starts implementing the dispute settlement procedures in good faith before a panel issues its findings, the Commission would have no legal basis in Article 7 Trade Enforcement Regulation to act in conformity with Article 52 (3) ILC Draft Articles requirement, unless the disputing parties report to have reached a mutually agreed solution. For the new situation addressed in Article 3 (ba) Trade Enforcement Regulation, the case when suspension is required by international law under Article 52 (3) ILC Draft Articles did not find entrance into Article 7 Trade Enforcement Regulation to enable the Commission to suspend its countermeasures. Thus, the Commission under EU law does not have the power in such a situation to suspend its countermeasures, even though international law of responsibility so requires. The EU then cannot successfully claim justification for continuing its countermeasures.

Article 7 (2) Trade Enforcement Regulation finally ensures compliance with Article 53 ILC Draft Articles, which requires that countermeasures be terminated as soon as the responsible state complies with its obligations.

Thus, even if the EU's argument based on Article 52 (4) ILC Draft Articles is accepted, countermeasures taken under paragraphs (aa) and (ba) of Article 3 Trade Enforcement Regulation may still be against the requirements established by the general public international law.

5.7 Broader Implications of the 2021 Amendments of Trade Enforcement Regulation 654/2014

Beyond the mere legal issues, the extension of the scope of the Trade Enforcement Regulation 654/2014 would have broader political implications.[112] First of all, the 2021 amendment that seeks to offer the EU a tool to enforce its WTO rights in the context of the AB crisis might have other negative effects on the multilateral trading system besides non-conformity with the rules.

[112] This section draws on Weiß and Furculita, 'The EU in Search for Stronger Enforcement Rules' (2020).

While the ability to enforce the Union's trade rights might outweigh the risk of the Regulation being found inconsistent with the WTO rules,[113] the costs might be higher than that. This approach to multilateral dispute settlement is likely to invite other Members to resort to unilateral retaliation in such situations. For example, in January 2022, Brazil (another MPIA participant) has also adopted a Provisional Measure authorizing the Foreign Trade Chamber to retaliate against WTO Members that file appeals into the void.[114] In these circumstances, the weaker states are the most disadvantaged ones, as they are not able to credibly threaten more powerful players to ensure compliance and would have to give in to the pressure exercised by others. While big players like the EU or Brazil can use the mere threat of retaliation to push weaker states into participating in the MPIA, ad hoc interim appeal arbitrations, or accepting panel reports instead of appealing into the void,[115] the same might not be true in case of disputes between equally powerful states,[116] which would most likely not give in easily despite the exercised pressure. There is a risk that powerful states will retaliate and counter-retaliate, the conflicts escalating to trade wars.[117] Moreover, one of the main benefits of the DSU is that retaliation would be capped in compliance proceedings under Article 22 DSU,[118] avoiding the imposition of excessive measures. If other WTO Members engage in establishing unilaterally the extent of the suspension of concessions taken against the EU, the Union industry might support significant unwarranted costs. Most importantly, the EU risks to be accused of undermining the WTO dispute settlement

[113] Trung Nguyen, 'The Procedural Inconsistency of the Envisaged EU Enforcement Regulation with the EU's WTO Obligations', *OpinioJuris*, 30 October 2020, http://opiniojuris.org/2020/10/30/the-procedural-inconsistency-of-the-envisaged-eu-enforcement-regulation-with-the-eus-wto-obligations/.

[114] Ministry of Foreign Affairs of Brazil, Joint press release by the Ministry of Foreign Affairs, the Ministry of Economy and the Ministry of Agriculture, Livestock and Supply – Provisional Measure authorizes Brazil to suspend concessions to WTO Members filing an 'empty appeal', 28 January 2022, www.gov.br/mre/en/contact-us/press-area/press-releases/joint-press-release-by-the-ministry-of-foreign-affairs-the-ministry-of-economy-and-the-ministry-of-agriculture-livestock-and-supply-2013-provisional-measure-brazil-to-suspend-concessions-to-wto-members-filing-an-2018empty-appeal2019.

[115] Terence P. Stewart, 'European Union Moves to Authorize Retaliation Where There Is No Alternative to the Appellate Body Pursued', *Current Thoughts on Trade*, 19 December 2019, https://currentthoughtsontrade.com/2019/12/19/european-union-moves-to-authorize-retaliation-in-disputes-where-there-is-no-alternative-to-the-appellate-body-pursued/.

[116] Joost Pauwelyn, 'WTO Dispute Settlement Post 2019: What to Expect?' (2019) 22 *JIEL* 297–321 at 308.

[117] ibid. [118] ibid, 307.

mechanism with its unilateral measures, making its claim of being a convinced multilateralist contradictory to its actions. With the amendments to Regulation 654/2014, the EU could be said to have come closer to states that only commit to multilateralism if it is in their own interest. Such a step taken by such a big economic and political player as the EU is also a sign that the longer the crisis stays unresolved, the higher is the risk to the viability of the WTO.[119] Last, the EU could be accused of hypocrisy, as it also appeals panel reports into the void.[120] Despite the listed potential negative implications for the multilateral trading system, given the current context, it is hard to accuse the EU of bad faith when it amended Regulation 654/2014.[121]

In practice, the amendment adopted in the context of the AB crisis might have a deterrent effect and be rarely used. As noted in the first review of the Regulation after the amendments were adopted, 'the mere possibility to use it may have produced the necessary encouragement for the responding third country in question to allow a binding resolution of the WTO dispute'.[122] Nevertheless, as stated earlier in this chapter, even if never used, this amendment could violate 'as such' WTO norms. Even though the EU could argue that it made a choice in favour of the lesser evil, since it plans to use unilateral measures for the sole purpose of upholding the binding multilateral dispute settlement mechanism that results in final panel reports or appeal arbitration awards,[123] this can neither excuse the violations of international, in particular WTO law, nor avoid the counterargument that the EU countermeasures under the amended Trade Enforcement Regulation might be excessive and are not subject to the pertinent safeguards provided for in the DSU or the MPIA. Therefore, the amendment directed towards the AB crisis would question

[119] Ahmed Essa Al-Sulaiti, 'WTO Members Can Save Their "Crown Jewel": A View from the Arab World' (2022) 56 (1) *JWT* 27–50 at 29.

[120] See Notification of an Appeal by the European Union Under Article 16.4 and Article 17.1 of the Understanding on Rules and Procedures Governing the Settlement of Disputes (DSU), and Under Rule 20(1) of the Working Procedures for Appellate Review, *EU – Cost Adjustment Methodologies II (Russia)*, WT/DS494/7, 1 September 2020, p. 11.

[121] Weihuan Zhou, 'WTO Dispute Settlement Mechanism without the Appellate Body: Some Observations on the US-China Trade Deal' (2020) 20 (4) UNSW Law Research Paper, p. 5.

[122] Review of the scope of the Regulation No 654/2014 of the European Parliament and of the Council of 15 May 2014, COM(2022) 74 final, pp. 4–5.

[123] Nicolas Lamp, 'Making WTO Dispute Settlement Work without the Appellate Body: How the Threat of Unilateral Retaliation Could Be Used to Incentivize the Adoption of Panel Reports', IELP Blog, 3 December 2019, https://ielp.worldtradelaw.net/2019/12/making-wto-dispute-settlement-work-without-the-appellate-body-how-the-threat-of-unilateral-retaliati.html.

EU's multilateralist stance, but it could defend it by arguing that the proposal is, in fact, upholding the multilateral dispute settlement system. Still, the EU should assume the risks that its amended Trade Enforcement Regulation poses for the multilateral trading system and its self-declared status of a convinced multilateralist.

As to the implications of the amendment related to the blockage of the dispute settlement procedures under the FTAs, which, as shown in the previous section, might be legally justified, it could also lead to an escalation of a conflict, involving retaliation followed by counter-retaliations in response. Moreover, similar to the suspension of concessions and other obligations under WTO rules, the level of the suspension under FTA rules shall be equivalent to the nullification or impairment caused by the violation, which can be established within compliance proceedings.[124] By suspending concessions and other obligations unilaterally rather than under the FTA rules, the risk that it will surpass the level of nullification or impairment caused by the violation and will bring about more harm than allowed is higher. Thereupon, resorting to unilateral retaliation might harm the EU's friendly relationship with its FTA partners and could endanger the future successful implementation of the agreement. Nevertheless, the state against which retaliation would be imposed under the novel Article 3 (ba) Trade Enforcement Regulation 654/2014 would be the first one blocking the well-functioning of the dispute settlement proceedings and acting in a manner to inflict harm on the relationship with the EU and the implementation of the FTA.

5.8 Conclusion

In line with the EU's turn towards stronger enforcement, the Trade Enforcement Regulation 654/2014 was amended to allow the imposition of countermeasures not only after the dispute settlement procedures under the relevant international trade agreements are exhausted and necessary authorizations obtained but also for reasons of non-cooperation by other WTO Members or treaty parties blocking the dispute settlement procedures. Thus, the amended Regulation allows the Union to impose unilateral countermeasures when a WTO panel report is sent into limbo by an appeal and there is no functional AB to hear it and also, for example, when an FTA party refuses to cooperate to establish a panel.

124 EU–Korea FTA, Art. 14.11(4); CETA, Art. 29.14 (5); EU–Singapore FTA, Art. 14.12 (3); EU–Vietnam FTA, Art. 15.5 (3); JEPA, Art. 21.22 (6).

In accordance with EU's endeavour to ensure stronger enforcement of its trade rights, the Trade Enforcement Regulation 654/2014 was further amended to allow the imposition of measures in the fields of trade in services and trade-related aspects of intellectual property rights. While the 2021 amendments authorize the EU to enforce its rights more assertively and to use the Trade Enforcement Regulation also to deter third countries from engaging in illegal conduct or blocking of the dispute settlement mechanisms established by international trade agreements, the extension of the scope of the Regulation to allow the imposition of unilateral measures in case of dispute settlement blockages raises questions with respect to its legality under the relevant international trade agreements. Thus, although the amendments are said to support binding international adjudication under international trade agreements and multilateralism, they also might challenge EU's professed commitment to international law and its self-declared status of a multilateralist.

Unilateral countermeasures imposed in case of appealed WTO panel reports sent into limbo under the newly added Article 3 (aa) Trade Enforcement Regulation are clearly against the obligations contained in Article 23 DSU. Even if this amendment is never applied in practice, it can also be found 'as such' violating WTO norms. Furthermore, contrary to the Commission's claim, the general customary international law on countermeasures has been displaced by the more special rules contained in the DSU. Although the EU argues that Article 52 (4) ILC Draft Articles establishing the right to countermeasures when the responsible party fails to cooperate in good faith with respect to dispute settlement procedures was not displaced by the DSU rules, two other conditions necessary for its use as a justification would be difficult to comply with. First, most likely WTO adjudicators will not consider the ILC Draft Articles as a defence for a WTO violation. Second, a plea accusing WTO Members other than the United States of acting in bad faith with respect to the WTO dispute settlement mechanism because of the paralysis of the AB is unlikely to be upheld within WTO proceedings. While the EU could claim that a fall-back on the general international rules on countermeasures is allowed due to the failure of the WTO dispute settlement system, because of the unsettled status of the fall-back doctrine as international customary law and high probability that it would not be considered within WTO proceedings, the invocation of this doctrine will most likely also be unsuccessful in justifying the violation of Article 23 DSU. In contrast, the 2021 amendments are more likely to be found consistent with the FTA rules, as Article 52 (4) ILC Draft Articles could be used as a legal basis when an FTA party blocks the dispute settlement procedures against its good-faith obligation. Still, the successful use of this justification depends on the openness of FTA panelists to applying public general international law.

Finally, the 2021 amendments of the Trade Enforcement Regulation 654/2014 clearly have implications beyond their legality under international trade agreements. The potential negative effects of the amendment addressing non-cooperative behaviour of FTA parties during dispute settlement procedures, however, are to be assumed by those parties. Whilst (aside from violating multilateral rules) the amended Trade Enforcement Regulation would negatively impact the multilateral trading system, it could also be argued that it shows support for the multilateral dispute settlement. Nevertheless, the EU should be aware of all the risks that the 2021 amendments entail, including the potential erosion of the credibility of its status of a convinced multilateralist.

6 The Anti-Coercion Instrument

Is There a Place for Unilateralism under International Rules?

6.1 Introduction

Another new tool under the assertiveness turn in EU trade policy is the Anti-Coercion Instrument (ACI),[1] which serves the aim of protecting from unfair trading practices. This legislative tool has its origins in the process of amending the Trade Enforcement Regulation, during which the Parliament and several Member States raised concerns about the lack of a legal instrument to allow the EU to act against illegal unilateral trade measures used by third countries. Thus, the INTA Committee proposed that the Trade Enforcement Regulation included the possibility to allow the EU to respond with countermeasures in case of a 'clear breach of international law or a clear violation of trade obligations' threatening or impairing the Union's commercial interests or jeopardizing its strategic autonomy, provided that the EU has challenged the alleged illegal measures in front of the relevant dispute settlement bodies.[2] Thereupon, the Commission President von der Leyen, in her Letter of Intent to the President of the Parliament and the President in office of the Council from 16 September 2020, mentioned the 'instrument to deter and counteract coercive actions by third countries' as a key new initiative for 2021. These led to a Joint Declaration being made by the Commission, the Council, and the European Parliament, which asserted the

[1] Regulation 2023/2675 of the European Parliament and of the Council on the Protection of the Union and its Member States from Economic Coercion by Third Countries, OJ EU 2023 No. L 2675 (ACI Regulation).

[2] Report on the Proposal for a Regulation of the European Parliament and of the Council amending Regulation (EU) No. 654/2014 of the European Parliament and of the Council concerning the Exercise of the Union's Rights for the Application and Enforcement of International Trade Rules (INTA Report), 6 July 2020, A9–0133/2020.

Commission's intention to table a legislative proposal for an ACI. The Council and the European Parliament (EP) also declared their commitment to consider the proposal in a timely manner.[3]

The need for an ACI emerged in the context of the rising geopolitical tensions, international trade being increasingly 'weaponised'.[4] The concerns materialized after the US investigation under the Section 301 of the US Trade Act of 1974 into France's digital services tax, which did not lead to the imposition of restrictive measures but exerted certain pressure on policymakers.[5] In 2021, China imposed blocks on Lithuania's exports and pressured companies in third countries into stopping doing business with Lithuania after the Baltic state announced the opening of mutual diplomatic offices with Taiwan. This case is said to confirm the need of an ACI to remedy a legislative gap. Given that the EU has exclusive competence in the area of common commercial policy (CCP), and Member States cannot act alone in case of economic coercion aimed against the Union, such an instrument is sought at the Union's level.[6] Thereupon, in December 2021, the EU Commission proposed a new tool to oppose economic coercion exercised by third countries, and in June 2023 the European Parliament (EP) and the Council reached a final political agreement, the ACI being published in December 2023.

The present chapter will, after describing the ACI Regulation in detail (Section 6.2), analyze its conformity under international law rules (Section 6.3), both with regard to customary law (Section 6.3.1) and special trade regimes (Sections 6.3.2 and 6.3.3). Our exploration pertains to the instrument itself, as well as possible future measures adopted under it, and takes into account relevant international jurisprudence and academic literature. Due to the research focus on trade policy and not on

[3] Joint Declaration of the Commission, the Council and the European Parliament on an instrument to deter and counteract coercive actions by third countries, 2021/C 49/01, OJ EU 2021 No. C 49, 12 February 2021.

[4] As stated by the Executive Vice-President and Commissioner for Trade, Valdis Dombrovskis, 'EU Strengthens Protection against Economic Coercion', 8 December 2021, https://ec.europa.eu/commission/presscorner/detail/en/ip_21_6642.

[5] Impact Assessment Report Accompanying the document Proposal for a Regulation of the European Parliament and of the Council on the protection of the Union and its Member States from economic coercion by third countries (Impact Assessment Report), SWD(2021) 371 final, 8 December 2021, p. 5.

[6] ACI Regulation, Preamble, recital 10; Xavier Fernández Pons, 'The European Commission's Proposed Anti-Coercion Instrument from an International Law Perspective' (2023) CIDOB, www.cidob.org/en/articulos/monografias/la_estrategia_geoeconomica_de_china/the_european_commission_s_proposed_anti_coercion_instrument_from_an_international_law_perspective, 57–63 at 60.

smart sanctions, the analysis will be confined only to measures which apply to states and not natural or legal persons. Finally, the potential broader costs and benefits of taking unilateral countermeasures as a reaction to the increased weaponization of international trade will be weighed (Section 6.4).

6.2 The Content of the ACI

With the ACI, the EU purportedly seeks to protect its own interests and that of the Member States by being able to respond to economic coercion applied by third countries in a 'uniform and structured' manner.[7] While the instrument's main aim is described to be acting as a deterrent, meaning that the Commission hopes that the mere existence of the ACI will prevent third countries from engaging in economic coercion, in the event of failure to dissuade third countries from engaging or continuing such conduct, countermeasures will be used as a last resort.[8]

Article 2 ACI Regulation establishes its scope of application, notably in case of 'economic coercion' against the EU or its Member States. The first paragraph prescribes two cumulative conditions that should be met for the presence of economic coercion to be determined. Thus, the Regulation applies when (1) a third country applies or threatens to apply measures affecting trade or investment; and (2) it does so with the aim 'to prevent or obtain the cessation, modification or adoption of a particular act by the Union or a Member State', 'interfer[ing] in the legitimate sovereign choices of the Union or a Member State'. Additionally, the Regulation provides in Article 2 (2) several aspects that shall be 'take[n] into account' in determining whether the conditions for economic coercion are met: (1) 'the intensity, severity, frequency, duration, breadth and magnitude of the third country's measure, including its impact on trade or investment relations with the Union, and the pressure arising from it on the Union or a Member State'; (2) 'whether the third country is engaging in a pattern of interference seeking to prevent or obtain particular acts from the Union, a Member State or another third country'; (3) 'the extent to which the third-country measure encroaches upon an

[7] Dombrovskis, 'EU Strengthens Protection against Economic Coercion'.

[8] Proposal for a Regulation of the European Parliament and of the Council on the protection of the Union and its Member States from economic coercion by third countries, COM(2021) 775 final, 8 December 2021, Explanatory Memorandum, pp. 1, 6; ACI Regulation, Preamble, recital 8.

area of the Union's or a Member State's sovereignty'; (4) 'whether the third country is acting on the basis of a legitimate concern that is internationally recognised'; and (5) 'whether and in what manner the third country, before the imposition or application of the third-country measure, made serious attempts, in good faith, to settle the matter through international coordination or adjudication, either bilaterally or within an international forum'.

In accordance with the Impact Assessment Report accompanying the ACI Proposal, the definition for 'economic coercion' in Article 2 (1) ACI Regulation has a broad scope, encompassing various forms in terms of intensity, formality, and nature.[9] Thus, the coercive measures can be explicit, such as those taken under Section 301 of the US Trade Act of 1974, based on which the United States can adopt trade-restrictive measures against a country allegedly taking measures that are unreasonable and unfairly harming US companies' interests, even in the absence of a breach of international law. However, the coercive measures can also have a more disguised nature and be based on a seemingly legitimate instrument but which is abusively used, such as discriminatory sanitary or phytosanitary measures introduced because of a coercive intention instead of health reasons. The definition also covers any other possible action satisfying the conditions, including silent measures and boycotts by private companies under the unofficial direction of the third country's government with the intention to influence another government's policies.[10] Extraterritorial sanctions that fall under the EU Blocking Statute[11] seeking to protect EU individuals and companies from having to comply with the extraterritorial sanctions of a third country can also fall under the ACI, but only when these sanctions simultaneously coerce the home government of the economic operators.[12] The broadness of the definition also stems from the fact that the interference can take place in any area of competence of the EU or its Member States and not only with respect to trade and investment policy. Furthermore, measures affecting trade or investment taken by third countries through entities controlled or directed by them and present in the Union (thereby actions attributable

[9] Impact Assessment Report, p. 7. [10] Impact Assessment Report, p. 9.

[11] Council Regulation (EC) No 2271/96 of 22 November 1996 protecting against the effects of the extraterritorial application of legislation adopted by a third country, and actions based thereon or resulting therefrom, OJ EU 1996 No. L 309, Consolidated text, 7 August 2018.

[12] Impact Assessment Report, pp. 9–10.

to a State under Article 8 of the ILC Draft Articles on State Responsibility[13]) could also qualify, provided that they exert coercion on the Union or its Member States.[14] Nevertheless, the ACI preamble provides that coercion constitutes an international wrongful act only when it reaches 'a certain qualitative or quantitative threshold', ensuring that 'only economic coercion with a sufficiently serious impact or, where the economic coercion consists in a threat, that only a credible threat' falls under the Regulation.[15]

The process prescribed by the ACI starts with the examination whether a third country's measure meets the condition for economic coercion set in Article 2, initiated by the Commission on its own or following duly substantiated information received from another source (Article 4 (1), (2)). The Commission shall notify in a timely manner the country concerned about the start of examinations and relevant developments regarding ongoing or launched examinations (Article 4 (3)). The examination finalizes with a decision proposal to the Council for an implementing act determining and reasoning whether the conditions set in Article 2 are met, prior to which the Commission may invite the country in question to submit its observations (Article 5 (1), (3)). Where appropriate, the Commission shall also propose that the Council determine that the third country be requested to repair the injury caused by coercion to the Union (Article 5 (2)). The Council shall decide by qualified majority vote (QMV) (including for amending the proposal) on the presence of economic coercion, and then the third country shall be notified, requested to cease the measure immediately, and, if decided by the Council, be requested to repair the injury caused in a reasonable period of time (Article 5 (2), (5), (9)). The Parliament is to be informed already about the result of the examination, as well as about the acts adopted by the Council (Article 5 (4), (8)). After the adoption of the decision, the Commission 'shall provide adequate opportunity for' consultations with the third country pursuing the end of the coercion and, where requested, the reparation of the injury via such means as negotiations, mediation, conciliation, good offices, or international adjudication (Article 6 (1)). Without prejudice to these means, after having consulted the Council, the Commission should seek

[13] Draft Articles on Responsibility of States for Internationally Wrongful Acts with Commentaries (ILC Draft Articles with Commentaries), in Report of the International Law Commission on the Work of Its Fifty-third Session, UN Doc. A/56/10, (2001) *Yearbook of the International Law Commission*, vol. II, Part Two.

[14] ACI Regulation, Preamble, recitals 7, 16.

[15] ACI Regulation, Preamble, recital 15.

cessation of economic coercion by raising the matter to any pertinent international forum (Article 6 (2)).

While the Regulation clearly favours encouraging the cessation of the coercion and, if requested, reparation of injury through other means, as a last resort, the Commission would impose countermeasures, called 'response measures' (Article 8 (1)). Such measures are to be taken by the Commission through implementing acts designating the specific measure to be taken and the date for application, when it is necessary to protect Union's or Member States' interests and rights and the action is in the interest of the Union in light of the available options (Article 8 (1)). Thus, the Commission will be the one to decide on the adoption of countermeasures under the ACI, but it is obliged to respect certain clear obligations regarding appropriateness in light of given criteria and the choice of measures (Article 8 (2), (3)). In adopting the implementing act, the Commission shall respect the comitology procedures set in Article 18 ACI.[16] While under the usual Comitology rules the Commission can go forward if the examination committee does not adopt an opinion, Article 18 (2) takes care that the mere non-adoption of an opinion blocks the Commission, but then, under Article 5 (4) subparagraph 3 Comitology Regulation,[17] the appeal committee can be referred to, and then the Council can block the implementing draft only by QMV which is a very high bar.[18]

The concerned country should be notified about the countermeasures, called to end the coercion and repair the injury caused (where the Council so requested), and being offered to negotiate a solution (Article 8 (7)). In cases of urgency and where necessary for the effectiveness of the measure, the Union could act immediately (Article 8 (10)). Annex I to the Regulation contains a list with the types of measures that can be applied by the Commission (Article 8 (2)) and which are binding on

[16] Regulation (EU) No 182/2011 of the European Parliament and of the Council of 16 February 2011 laying down the rules and general principles concerning mechanisms for control by Member States of the Commission's exercise of implementing powers, OJ EU 2011 No. 55/13, 28 February 2011, Art. 3.

[17] Regulation (EU) No 182/2011 of the European Parliament and of the Council of 16 February 2011 laying down the rules and general principles concerning mechanisms for control by Member States of the Commission's exercise of implementing powers, OJ EU 2011 No. L 55/13, 28 February 2011.

[18] For critcisim see Iana Dreyer, 'Ostrich Policy: The EU's Anti-coercion Instrument Risks Becoming a Damp Squib' (2022) *Borderlex*, 1 February 2022, https://borderlex.net/2022/02/01/comment-ostrich-policy-the-eus-anti-coercion-instrument-risks-becoming-a-damp-squib/.

it; in contrast to the proposal, the Commission cannot alter Annex I. Response measures may consist of the non-performance of international obligations towards a third country insofar as the measure of that country constitutes an international wrongful act (Article 8 (4)). The Commission may apply countermeasures of general application or against natural or legal persons subject to certain substantive and procedural conditions (Articles 8 (3) and 10). A measure can be taken against a natural or legal person that engages or may engage in activities covered by Article 207 Treaty on the Functioning of the European Union (TFEU)[19] and is connected or linked to the government of the third country concerned (Articles 8 (3), (10)). The final version of the ACI sets out very detailed criteria for determining the required connection. Due to our present focus on trade policy, this chapter will only consider the legality of response measures adopted against states.[20]

The ACI establishes the selection and design criteria for countermeasures in Article 11. Accordingly, countermeasures shall be proportionate to the level of injury, be selected and designed by giving regard to the determinations and criteria considered during the process of determining the presence of economic coercion, as well as the Union's interest, and follow other criteria: effectiveness, the avoidance or minimization of negative impacts on affected Union actors, on the investment environments, on promotion of economic growth and employment, and on Union policies or objectives, potential to provide relief, avoidance of disproportionate administrative complexities and costs, measures taken by other countries, and any other relevant criteria established in international law (Article 11 (2)). When other countermeasures are insufficient and after considering other criteria, the Commission may also apply intra-Union measures on foreign direct investment or trade in services provided by persons owned or controlled by persons of the third country (Article 11 (4)). The ACI ensures that countermeasures are not taken for longer periods than necessary. Thus, for example, when the third country suspends the coercion and an agreement is reached to submit the matter to binding international adjudication, the Commission shall also suspend the countermeasures via an implementing act (Article 12 (2), second

[19] Consolidated version of the Treaty on the Functioning of the European Union, OJ EU 2012 No. C 326/47, 26 October 2012.

[20] International responsibility of individuals is expressly left out from the ILC Draft Articles, being a more recent development, mostly applied in the field of international criminal law; see comments to Art. 58 ILC Draft Articles.

subparagraph). Moreover, the countermeasures should be terminated by means of an implementing act when the coercion has ceased and the injury has been repaired, if requested (might also be terminated if injury has not been repaired but coercion has ceased), a mutually agreed solution was reached, a binding decision by a third-party international adjudication covering the matter of the economic coercion requires withdrawal, or when it is in the Union's interest (Article 12 (4)). In addition, countermeasures may be suspended or amended on duly justified grounds, such as ensuring consistency with EU's international obligations (Article 12 (5)).

6.3 Legality under International Law

This section will analyze the conformity of the ACI and potential countermeasures which it authorizes with the customary rule on countermeasures, multilateral, and bilateral special rules. This becomes even more important considering that Article 1 (3) ACI provides that 'any action taken under this Regulation shall be consistent with international law'.

6.3.1 Customary Rules on Countermeasures

6.3.1.1 Countermeasures against an International Wrongful Act

The Commission argues the legality of the ACI in light of the international customary rules on countermeasures.[21] Indeed, according to Article 49 ILC Draft Articles on State Responsibility, which codify customary rules of international law,[22] within certain limits, a state can make use of immediate countermeasures against another state that engages in *unlawful* activity. When an act qualifies as countermeasure taken according to the Draft Articles, the wrongfulness of that act is precluded under Article 22 ILC Draft Articles. In line with Article 1 (3) ACI, Article 8 (4) ACI, read in conjunction with recital (13) of the Preamble explicitly referring the mentioned Articles 22 and 49 from ILC Draft Articles, also

[21] ACI Regulation, Preamble, recitals (5), (13).

[22] James Crawford, 'State Responsibility', in Rüdiger Wolfrum (ed.), *The Max Planck Encyclopedia of International Law* (Oxford: Oxford University Press, 2006), https://opil.ouplaw.com/display/10.1093/law:epil/9780199231690/law-9780199231690-e1093?prd=EPIL, para. 65; Alejandro Sánchez, 'What Trade Lawyers Should Know about the ILC Articles on State Responsibility' (2012) 7 (6) *GTCJ* 292–299; Lori Fisler Damrosch, 'The Legitimacy of Economic Sanctions as Countermeasures for Wrongful Acts' (2019) 37 *Berkeley Journal of International Law* 250–264 at 259; ACI Regulation, Preamble, recital (4a).

rightly limits response measures consisting of the non-performance of international obligations against only international wrongful acts. Based on the text of the Articles 1(1) and 2 (1) ACI Regulation, it becomes clear that the EU's countermeasures will address *economic coercion*, which is found in case of the application or threat of application by a third country of measures affecting trade or investment that *interfere* in the Union's or a Member State's *legitimate sovereign choices*, allegedly in violation of international principle of non-intervention. The ACI preamble explicitly states:

> Coercion is prohibited and therefore a wrongful act under international law when a country deploys measures such as trade or investment restrictions in order to obtain from another country an action or inaction which that country is not internationally obliged to perform under international law and which falls within its sovereignty, and when the coercion reaches a certain qualitative or quantitative threshold.[23]

Thus, it seems that the Commission assumes that economic coercion covered by the ACI Regulation breaches the international principle of non-interference in any case,[24] irrespective of whether it would in and of itself violate other international rules such as WTO, Free Trade Agreements (FTAs), bilateral investment treaties (BITs), or friendship treaties. Thus, according to the Commission, there would always be an international wrongful act to respond to with ACI response measures that otherwise would be illegal.

When the threat or the use of force is used to influence the sovereign choices of a state, this would clearly constitute a violation of the international law. Article 2 (4) UN Charter[25] codifies the prohibition against the threat or use of force against the territorial integrity or political independence of any state. Although there were discussions on whether the term 'force' could also encompass economic force,[26] UN Member

[23] ACI Regulation, Preamble, recital (15).

[24] Mariana de Andrade, 'The EU's Anti-Coercion Instrument: Balancing Ambiguity', IELP Blog, 13 November 2022, https://ielp.worldtradelaw.net/2022/11/guest-post-the-eus-anti-coercion-instrument-balancing-ambiguity.html; Deepak Raju, 'Proposed EU Regulation to Address Third Country Coercion – What Is Coercion?', *EJIL: Talk!*, 6 January 2022, www.ejiltalk.org/proposed-eu-regulation-to-address-third-country-coercion-what-is-coercion/.

[25] Charter of the United Nations, 24 October 1945, 1 U.N.T.S. XVI.

[26] Barry E. Carter, 'Economic Sanctions', in Rüdiger Wolfrum (ed.), *Max Planck Encyclopedia of Public International Law* (Oxford: Oxford University Press, 2011), https://opil.ouplaw.com/view/10.1093/law:epil/9780199231690/law-9780199231690-e1521?prd=OPIL; Natalino Ronzitti, 'Sanctions as Instruments of Coercive Diplomacy: An International Law

States seem to have accepted that Article 2 (4) UN Charter does not cover economic coercion, an opinion also shared by most scholars.[27] The customary law on the prohibition of the threat or the use of force does not seem to have a broader coverage to encompass economic coercion either. However, the interference in the internal affairs of another state could constitute a violation of the non-interference or non-intervention principle analyzed in the following section.

In case of economic coercion, the EU could resort to mere retorsions – that is, international *lawful* acts adopted in response to internationally wrongful *or* lawful acts.[28] The legality of potential retorsions is not questioned under international law, and the EU would be clearly allowed to resort to them provided that there is also an internal EU legal basis for doing so. However, Annex I to the ACI Regulation on potential Union response measures refers only to the 'non-performance of applicable international obligations' which, if not justified, would be unlawful. Furthermore, Article 8 (2) ACI provides that the Commission shall determine the appropriate response measures from Annex I. Accordingly, it seems that there is currently no internal legal basis for imposing mere retorsions against economic coercion, an ACI amendment being commendable. As mentioned, the ACI requires that response measures consisting of the non-performance of international obligations, specifically an illegal conduct under international law, be used only if the coercive measure of the third country consists of an internationally wrongful act (Article 8 (4)). Nevertheless, as already argued, the EU seems to assume that economic coercion covered breaches the non-intervention principle, and the question of legality of the third-country measures is not a factor to be considered in the examination (Article 2). The question of conformity with international law is only taken into account in the decision-making of the Council about whether reparation is to be required (Article 5 (2), second subparagraph) and in the determination of which type of countermeasures to be adopted by the EU (Article 11 (2) (h)).

Perspective', in Natalino Ronzitti (ed.), *Coercive Diplomacy, Sanctions and International Law* (Leiden: Brill Neijhoff, 2016), p. 2.

27 Teoman M. Hagemeyer-Witzleb, *The International Law of Economic Warfare* (Heidelberg: Springer, 2020), pp. 86–96.

28 ILC Draft Articles with Commentaries, Commentary on Chapter II Countermeasures, para. 3; Ronzitti, 'Sanctions as Instruments of Coercive Diplomacy' (2016), p. 13; Tom Ruys, 'Sanctions, Retortions and Countermeasures: Concepts and International Legal Framework', in L. van der Herik (ed.), *Research Handbook on UN Sanctions and International Law* (Cheltenham: Edward Elgar, 2017), p. 24.

Therefore, in order to safeguard the lawfulness of the EU's anti-coercion measures under customary international law, it should be established if and when a third-country measure of economic coercion represents an international wrongful act in violation of the international principle of non-intervention and whether EU's interpretation is accurate.

6.3.1.2 *The International Wrongful Act: Violation of the Principle of Non-Intervention*

According to the International Court of Justice (ICJ), in the *Nicaragua Case* 'the principle of non-intervention involves the right of every sovereign State to conduct its affairs without outside interference'.[29] It stems from the sovereign equality of states, internal self-determination, and political independence.[30] The principle of non-interference has been recognized as customary law,[31] including by the ICJ.[32] Some authors have even argued that it might be *ius cogens*;[33] however, this does not seem to be the case.[34] It was mentioned in the eighteenth-century scholarly works of Christian Wolff and Emer de Vattel, but it is not clear how much it was reflected in the practice of the states at that time.[35] The principle figures in many UN non-binding resolutions and declarations from the 1960s to the 1980s, as

[29] ICJ, Military and Paramilitary Activities in and against Nicaragua (Nicar.v. U.S.), Judgment, ICJ Reports 1986, 14, para. 202 (*Nicaragua Case*).

[30] Mohamed S. Helal, 'On Coercion in International Law' (2019) 52(1) *International Law and Politics* 1–122 at 53; Dire Tladi, 'The Duty Not to Intervene in Matters within Domestic Jurisdiction', in Jorge E. Viñuales (ed.), *The UN Friendly Relations Declaration at 50: An Assessment of the Fundamental Principles of International Law* (Cambridge: Cambridge University Press, 2020), pp. 87, 90.

[31] Florian Kriener, 'Intervention, Prohibition of', in Anne Peters and Rüdiger Wolfrum (ed.), *Max Planck Encyclopedia of Public International Law* (Oxford: Oxford University Press, 2024), https://opil.ouplaw.com/display/10.1093/law:epil/9780199231690/law-9780199231690-e1434, paras. 3, 42; Hagemeyer-Witzleb, *The International Law of Economic Warfare* (2020), p. 97; Tladi, 'The Duty Not to Intervene in Matters Within Domestic Jurisdiction' (2020), p. 90.

[32] ICJ, *Nicaragua Case*, para. 202; ICJ, *Nicaragua Case*, Dissenting Opinion of Judge Sir Robert Jennings, pp. 534–535.

[33] For example,
Philip Kunig, 'Prohibition of Intervention', in Rüdiger Wolfrum (ed.), *Max Planck Encyclopedia of Public International Law* (Oxford: Oxford University Press, 2012), Vol VI, 289–299, para. 7.

[34] Niki Aloupi, 'The Right to Non-intervention and Non-interference' (2015) 4(3) *Cambridge Journal of International and Comparative Law* 566–587 at 587.

[35] Maziar Jamnejad and Michael Wood, 'The Principle of Non-intervention' (2009) 22(2) *Leiden Journal of International Law* 345–381 at 349; Helal, 'On Coercion in International Law' (2019) 50.

well as regional treaties and other instruments.[36] Some of the most notable resolutions are the Declaration on the Inadmissibility of Intervention from 1965,[37] the Declaration on Friendly Relations from 1970,[38] which is also mentioned in the ACI's Preamble,[39] and the Declaration on the Inadmissibility of Intervention and Interference from 1981.[40] The 1965 and 1970 Declarations *inter alia* provide that '[n]o State may use or encourage the use of *economic*, political or any other type of measures *to coerce* another State in order to obtain from it the subordination of the exercise of its sovereign rights or to secure from it advantages of any kind' (emphasis added). The 1981 Declaration lists several duties that arise out of the principle of non-intervention, including a state's duty to refrain from intervention 'in the conduct of its international relations in the *economic*, social, technical and *trade* fields' (emphasis added). Hence, all these resolutions also refer to economic interference.

While it has been codified in numerous instruments and its status of customary law is established, the exact content of the principle is less clear.[41] The ICJ's judgment in the *Nicaragua Case* is usually used as a starting point for identifying the elements of prohibited intervention. Thus, the Court said that:

> [T]he principle forbids all States or groups of States to intervene directly or indirectly in internal or external affairs of other States. A prohibited intervention must accordingly be one bearing on matters in which each State is permitted, by the principle of State sovereignty to decide freely. [...] Intervention is wrongful when it uses methods of *coercion* in regard to such choices, which must remain

[36] Including the 1947 General Agreement on Tariffs and Trade Contracting Parties (Thirty-Eighth Session), Ministerial Declaration, 29 November 1982, L/5424, para. 7 (iii). For more, see Danae Azaria, 'Trade Countermeasures for Breaches of International Law Outside the WTO' (2022) *International & Comparative Law Quarterly* 1–35 at 27–28.

[37] Declaration on the Inadmissibility of Intervention in the Domestic Affairs of States and the Protection of Their Independence and Sovereignty, G.A. Res. 2131(XX), U.N. Doc. A/RES/20/2131, 2 December 1965.

[38] Declaration of Principles of International Law Concerning Friendly Relations and Cooperation among States in accordance with the Charter of the United Nations, G.A. Res 2625 (XV), U.N. Doc. A/RES/25/2625, 24 October 1970.

[39] ACI Regulation, Preamble, recital (5).

[40] Declaration on the Inadmissibility of Intervention and Interference in the Internal Affairs of States, G.A. Res. 36/103, U.N. Doc A/RES/36/103, 9 December 1981.

[41] Kriener, 'Intervention, Prohibition of' (2024), para. 3; Aloupi, 'The Right to Non-intervention and Non-interference' (2015), 570; Antonios Tzanakopoulos, 'The Right to be Free from Economic Coercion' (2015) 4(3) *Cambridge Journal of International and Comparative Law* 616–633 at 623; Helal, 'On Coercion in International Law' (2019) 47.

free ones. The element of *coercion*, which defines, and indeed forms the very essence of, prohibited intervention [. . .] (emphasis added).[42]

Based on this judgment, and finding also support in UN Resolutions, most scholars, identify two elements: (1) an unlawful intervention, the essence of which is coercion; and (2) bearing on the matters in which states decide freely, the so-called *domaine réservé*.[43] While the 1981 Declaration does not mention the 'coercion' element, apparently giving a less strict definition, it most likely did not achieve the status of customary law.[44]

The second element, namely intervention in the *domaine réservé*, seems less controversial.[45] It refers to areas where a state can act freely, as it has not undertaken international obligations, and therefore those areas remain within its sovereign realm.[46] The areas in which a state can decide are very varied. The ICJ in the *Nicaragua Case* states that one of the choices that remain unfettered is 'the choice of a political, economic, social and cultural system, and the formulation of foreign policy'.[47] Nevertheless, the precise limits of the *domaine réservé* cannot be universally defined, as they will vary depending on each state's international obligations.[48] Hence, each state can restrict the width of its *domaine réservé* by undertaking international obligations. The coercive measures that the ACI seeks to address seem to comprise this element, as the Regulation will apply only when they interfere within the '*legitimate sovereign choices* of the Union or a Member State' (emphasis added).[49] Accordingly, while the Regulation does not limit the areas in which the interference can take place, with this expression it seems that legislators intended to allow countermeasures only in case the intervention encroaches upon the fields in which the EU or a Member State have the right to take decisions freely. There is no indication whatsoever in the text that the Union intends to use the

[42] ICJ, *Nicaragua Case*, para. 205.

[43] Jamnejad and Wood, 'The Principle of Non-intervention' (2009) 371. Helal, 'On Coercion in International Law' (2019) 60–61; Hagemeyer-Witzleb, *The International Law of Economic Warfare* (2020), p. 97; Raju, 'Proposed EU Regulation'.

[44] Hagemeyer-Witzleb, The International Law of Economic Warfare (2020), pp. 100–101.

[45] It can, however, raise some difficult questions, such as establishing whether a particular area lies within the *domaine réservé* of a state (Kriener, 'Intervention, Prohibition of' (2024), paras. 3 ff).

[46] Helal, 'On Coercion in International Law' (2019) 65; Raju, 'Proposed EU Regulation'.

[47] ICJ, *Nicaragua Case*, para. 205.

[48] Helal, 'On Coercion in International Law' (2019) 67; Hagemeyer-Witzleb, *The International Law of Economic Warfare* (2020), p. 98.

[49] ACI Regulation, Art. 2 (1).

Regulation to act against a third state when that state imposes countermeasures against EU's initial illegal acts.

The first element, namely unlawful intervention, the very essence of which is coercion, is the one that is surrounded by most uncertainty. The question arises whether economic coercion could amount to prohibited intervention under customary law. Despite the broad approach taken in the UN resolutions, in which the principle of non-intervention covers also economic coercion, many of these resolutions were adopted by divided votes and do not seem to currently reflect the law.[50] Although some authors expressed support for the broader interpretation of the non-intervention principle to include economic coercion,[51] there seems to be an agreement that the practice of states shows that it has not solidified into customary law yet, and even if it did, the extent of the covered economic coercion is unclear.[52] The countermeasures imposed under the ACI Regulation could therefore be illegal under customary rules of international law if there is no breach of the international principle of non-intervention by the alleged measures of economic coercion to respond to under Article 49 of the ILC Draft Articles on State Responsibility. Thus, in case of a narrow construct of the principle of non-intervention, the wrongfulness of the EU's actions taken according to the ACI would not be precluded under customary rules on countermeasures. While the EU could try to advance a broader interpretation of the non-interference principle, it is less likely that the international community would accept it, considering the broad use of economic coercion.

In case *economic* intervention in the *domaine réservé* is considered covered by the customary principle of non-intervention, it would have

[50] Jamnejad and Wood, 'The Principle of Non-intervention' (2009) 351–354.

[51] Vaughan Lowe and Antonios Tzanakopoulos, 'Economic Warfare', in Rüdiger Wolfrum (ed.), *Max Planck Encyclopedia of Public International Law* (Oxford: Oxford University Press, 2013), https://opil.ouplaw.com/view/10.1093/law:epil/9780199231690/law-9780199231690-e292; Tzanakopoulos, 'The Right to Be Free from Economic Coercion' (2015) 623; Hagemeyer-Witzleb, *The International Law of Economic Warfare* (2020), p. 104; Tladi, 'The Duty Not to Intervene in Matters within Domestic Jurisdiction' (2020), p. 100.

[52] Kriener, 'Intervention, Prohibition of' (2024), paras. 19 ff, 27 ff; Kunig, 'Prohibition of Intervention,' (2012), paras. 25, 26; Carter, 'Economic Sanctions' (2015), para. 30; Ruys, 'Sanctions, Retortions and Countermeasures' (2017), p. 27; Hagemeyer-Witzleb, *The International Law of Economic Warfare* (2020), p. 104; Dapo Akande, Payam Akhavan, and Eirik Bjorge, 'Economic Sanctions, International Law, and Crimes against Humanity: Venezuela's Referral to the International Criminal Court' (2021) *American Journal of International Law* 1–25 at 6–7; Helal, however, argues that this is the case when economic coercion is only used as the primary sanction, not together with other sanctions (Helal, 'On Coercion in International Law' (2019) 104).

to reach a certain threshold to amount to *coercion*. One difficulty in this case lies in the fine line between coercion and diplomacy – or, in other words, pressure and persuasion. Using economic measures to obtain some objectives, such as the signing of an agreement, is part and parcel of regular trade negotiations.[53] Considering every economic measure that could influence the decisions of another state as coercion – for example, in favor of signing a treaty – would render many manifestations of diplomacy unlawful under international law. Accordingly, only serious and grave economic intervention, such as trade boycotts or port blockages, should have the potential to amount to coercion.

Many authors take a subjectivist approach towards establishing the existence of coercion, arguing that the main benchmark should be the intention of the states, specifically to influence the free will of other states.[54] The ACI Regulation also seems to place emphasis on the reasons behind the measures when establishing whether they would qualify as economic coercion, as it allows the imposition of countermeasures only against measures seeking 'to prevent or obtain the cessation, modification or adoption of a particular act by the Union or a Member State' (Article 2 (1)). However, establishing the real reasons behind a measure imposed by a third state can often be difficult. Although there could be indications in the domestic legislation adopting those measures, preparatory documents, or officials' declarations in this regard, such evidence might be absent. The Impact Assessment Report accompanying the ACI proposal mentioned that the instrument would also address coercion which would be 'unquestionably existing' because of the 'impulse' behind it.[55] Nevertheless, it did not explain how this 'impulse' would be established. It seems that the determination of the intention behind the measures of third states will be left at the discretion of EU's authority; a determination that will most likely be contested by the alleged coercive states. As mentioned in the Commentaries to the ILC Draft Articles, '[a] State which resorts to countermeasures based on its unilateral assessment of the situation does so at its own risk and may incur responsibility

[53] Carter, 'Economic Sanctions' (2015).

[54] Andreas F. Lowenfeld, *International Economic Law* (Oxford: Oxford University Press, 2008), p. 850; Carter, 'Economic Sanctions' (2015), para. 3; Tladi, 'The Duty Not to Intervene in Matters within Domestic Jurisdiction' (2020), p. 92. On the distincion between 'subjective' and 'objective' criteria, see Hagemeyer-Witzleb, *The International Law of Economic Warfare* (2020), pp. 102–103.

[55] Impact Assessment Report, p. 7.

for its own wrongful conduct in the event of an incorrect assessment'.[56] Moreover, there is often more than one reason behind a restrictive measure,[57] making it complicated to differentiate between them. Hence, it might be difficult for the EU to prove the legality of its actions under international rules on countermeasures when applying this criterion.

There are other authors that maintain that to amount to unlawful intervention, coercion shall be established based on a more 'objective' criterion: the measure's impact on the coerced state.[58] Lastly, there are some that advocate for taking into account an array of criteria for establishing the presence of coercion. For example, Kunig argues that besides motivation, other criteria should be 'the intensity of the measures taken, the result actually reached, and the relationship between the means and the object'.[59] The ACI, although using 'the intention' as one of the two main elements, also lists a number of additional criteria that should be *taken into account* for establishing the presence of these necessary elements. Thus, the ACI also takes into account 'objective' criteria, such as 'the extent to which the third-country measure encroaches' upon a sovereign area, the intensity, severity, frequency, duration, breadth, magnitude of the measure and the pressure arising out of it, the presence of a pattern of interference, and whether the third country tried to settle the matter through coordination or adjudication.[60] Although Baetens and Bronckers state that the criteria listed in the ACI suggest that only grave economic coercion will elicit EU action,[61] the ACI main text mandates that all these criteria only *be taken into account*; it does not prescribe their exact role, nor does it prohibit reaching the conclusion that there is economic coercion out of subsuming other criteria.[62] Nevertheless, while the Commission in its Impact Report accompanying the ACI proposal stated that coercion may take various forms on a broad spectrum of intensity,[63] the Preamble of the final adopted version clarifies that the criteria that the Commission should take into account 'would ensure that

[56] ILC Draft Articles with Commentaries, Commentary on Art. 49, para. 3.

[57] Lowenfeld, *International Economic Law* (2008), p. 850.

[58] Evan J. Criddle, 'Humanitarian Financial Intervention' (2013) 24 *EJIL* 583–615 at 591; Hagemeyer-Witzleb, *The International Law of Economic Warfare* (2020), p. 102; Helal, 'On Coercion in International Law' (2019) 76–77 argues why this approach is erroneous.

[59] Kunig, 'Prohibition of Intervention' (2012), para. 25.

[60] ACI Regulation, Art. 2 (2).

[61] Freya Baetens, Marco Bronckers, 'The EU's Anti-Coercion Instrument: A Big Stick for Big Targets' (2022) *EJIL: Talk!*, 19 January 2022, www.ejiltalk.org/the-eus-anti-coercion-instrument-a-big-stick-for-big-targets/.

[62] Raju, 'Proposed EU Regulation'.

[63] Impact Assessment Report, p. 7.

only economic coercion with a sufficiently serious impact or, where the economic coercion consists in a threat, that only a credible threat, falls under this Regulation'.[64] As stated in Section 1.3, preambles represent context that help in establishing the ordinary meaning of a provision. Accordingly, by taking into account the cited preambular language, the Commission should pay utmost care when applying this instrument and consider that conditions of Article 2 (1) ACI Regulation are met only in case of serious and grave instances of interference and only then submit a proposal to the Council, not least also for the reason to remain within the confines of international law as demanded by Article 1 (3) ACI. In addition, considering the potential significant negative impact of response measures to Union's and Member's economies,[65] it is expected that the Council will also act as a guardian against using the ACI in cases of economic diplomacy and will not be able to adopt the determination under Article 5 ACI by QMV. The exact meaning of serious or 'extreme' cases of economic interference remains obscure.[66] While the withdrawal of a financial aim might not amount to economic coercion,[67] a total trade embargo on all imports and exports or a total blockade having a significant impact on the target economy[68] are significantly more likely to amount to economic coercion. Albeit not addressing the issue of conformity with the non-interference principle, the WTO panel in *Saudi Arabia – Intellectual Property Rights* relevantly points that a total severance of the economic ties consisting of closing all land, sea, and air ports and preventing crossing into Saudi territories, airspace and territorial waters as in the case at issue can be characterized as 'an exceptional and serious crisis in the relations between two or more States'.[69] Still, simple trade boycotts or embargoes do not automatically qualify as economic coercion, as other conditions should be met, such as the interference in the *domaine réservé*, while some even claim that the very existence of the state should be threatened by them.[70] In the *Nicaragua Case*, the ICJ confirms

[64] ACI Regulation, Preamble, recital (15). [65] For more, see Section 6.4.

[66] Hagemeyer-Witzleb, *The International Law of Economic Warfare* (2020), pp. 104–105.

[67] Kunig, 'Prohibition of Intervention' (2012), para. 26; Jamnejad and Wood, 'The Principle of Non-intervention' (2009) 371.

[68] Markus Krajewski, *Völkerrecht* (Baden-Baden: Nomos, 2017), p. 177.

[69] Panel Report, *Saudi Arabia – Measures Concerning the Protection of Intellectual Property Rights*, WT/DS567/R, 16 June 2020, para. 7.262.

[70] See Hagemeyer-Witzleb, *The International Law of Economic Warfare* (2020), p. 102 citing Ignaz Seidl-Hohenveldern, *International Economic Law: General Course on Public International Law* (Leiden: Martinus Nijhoff Publishers, 1986).

that even a total embargo does not necessarily breach the non-interference principle,[71] a conclusion often used in support of arguing that the principle of non-interference does not cover even very severe forms of economic coercion. Nevertheless, the ICJ conclusion does not preclude that in other scenarios a total embargo could amount to a breach of the principle.[72]

Finally, besides the controversy surrounding the question of intensity of intervention, some academic writings argue that for an unlawful intervention, the measures should be illegal per se.[73] The ICJ's judgment in *Nicaragua Case* is often brought in support of this. The Court considered *inter alia* the legality of the cessation of economic aid, reductions in the import quota, and a trade embargo and implicitly seems to have drawn a distinction between lawful and unlawful acts under other international rules.[74] If for a finding of violation of the principle of non-interference the measures should be illegal per se, then countermeasures under the ACI Regulation would not be always justified under international rules on countermeasures, as the instrument does not seek to address only measures of third states that are illegal under international law rules in and of themselves.[75] The legality of measures outside the principle of non-interference is not mentioned as an aspect that shall be taken into account when determining whether the conditions for economic coercion are met.[76] Under such narrower interpretation, the principle of non-interference would not be violated and there would be no wrongful act to lawfully respond to with countermeasures. In case EU's potential response measures address coercive measures that are illegal in and of themselves under other international law norms – for example, under international trade and investment treaties – finding a breach of the non-interference principle would be more likely, but in that case the question could, and perhaps even must, be raised in the pertinent forum. In case of breaches of WTO agreements, as will be shown, this will raise questions about the legality of the EU redressive measures under these special multilateral rules.[77]

[71] ICJ, *Nicaragua Case*, para. 245.

[72] Jamnejad and Wood, 'The Principle of Non-intervention' (2009) 371.

[73] Ronzitti, 'Sanctions as Instruments of Coercive Diplomacy' (2016), p. 6; Helal, for example, argues that to amount to unlawful intervention, the means should also be unlawful (Helal, 'On Coercion in International Law' (2019) 81).

[74] ICJ, *Nicaragua Case*, para. 245.

[75] ACI Regulation, Art. 2 (1).

[76] ACI Regulation, Art. 2 (2).

[77] See Section 6.3.2.1.

To conclude, it is not entirely clear if the principle of non-intervention also covers economic coercion under customary international law, and in case it does, it is ambiguous what the requirements are for a breach to be found. Due to the fact that there is no international court with universal jurisdiction, the ICJ's jurisdiction being subject to the consent of disputing states,[78] there could be no one to solve these dilemmas. Although the EU could choose to take advantage of this situation, as a responsible and credible international actor committed to the international rule of law, it should try to act in conformity with its international obligations. The ACI's language if read in light of its preamble seems to be in line with both the subjective and objective criteria proposed by international scholars in terms of the type of economic coercion that could be covered by the non-interference principle. To maximize its chances to act according to Article 1 (3) ACI, the EU should also in practice respond only to serious and grave cases of interference such as total embargoes and total severance of economic ties.

As already alluded to, even if the principle of non-intervention might not be violated by the coercive economic measures of a third country, these coercive measures could still be violating treaty law, such as WTO, FTAs, BITs, or even bilateral friendship treaties. Thus, there might be other breaches of international law to which the EU could react with lawful countermeasures under Article 49 ILC Draft Articles. However, in case of treaty law, such as WTO, FTAs, or BITs, containing their own rules on dispute settlement, it should be analyzed whether such customary rules are not displaced by the more special rules, an aspect analyzed in Section 6.3.2.

6.3.1.3 *Conformity with the Conditions and Limitations for Countermeasures under the ILC Draft Articles*

If the EU is considered entitled to adopt countermeasures under the ILC Draft Articles, the imposition shall respect the conditions and limitations established therein. As mentioned in Section 3.3.2.3, countermeasures may not be used for purposes other than to induce compliance and, where appropriate, to repare the injury, a condition that ACI Regulation seems to respect as it repeatedly and explicitly mentions that the objective of response measures is to deter or desist third countries from economic coercion and, where appropriate, to seek reparation of the injury

[78] Fernández Pons, 'The European Commission's Proposed Anti-Coercion Instrument from an International Law Perspective' (2023) 59.

caused by such coercion.[79] However, according to Article 11 (2) (d) ACI Regulation, when choosing and designing an EU response measure, the Commission can also consider other secondary objectives such as the 'potential to provide relief to Union economic operators affected by the economic coercion', which, however, does not seem to contravene the main objective of the measures. In compliance with Article 53 ILC Draft Articles requiring the termination of countermeasures as soon as the responsible state complies with its obligations of cessation and reparation,[80] Article 12 (4) (a) ACI Regulation provides that EU's response measures must be terminated when the economic coercion ceases and, where appropriate, the injury has been repaired. The ACI Regulation also complies with Article 52 ILC Draft Articles notification and summation requirements by including them in Article 8 (7) and by using countermeasures only as a last line of defence, initially engaging with the coercing country through other means, including negotiations. Notwithstanding these obligations, in line with Article 52 (2) ILC Draft Articles, the EU can impose urgent countermeasures on duly justified imperative grounds to avoid irreparable damage to the Union or its Member States.[81] As will be explained in more detail in Section 6.3.3, the proposal also respects Article 52 (3), applying when the wrongful act ceases and the dispute is submitted to an international court or tribunal.[82] Furthermore, in line with Article 52 (3) requiring the suspension of countermeasures for as long as dispute settlement procedures are implemented in good faith, Article 12 (2), third subparagraph ACI provides that in case adjudication requires implementation by the third country, 'the Commission shall suspend the application of the Union response measures provided that the third country is engaged in the implementation of that adjudication decision or settlement'.[83] Another requirement is the proportionality principle with which the ACI Regulation complies in Article 11 (1) by almost replicating Article 51 ILC Draft Articles. Therefore, despite the questionable legality under the customary rules on countermeasures of potential EU measures adopted according to the ACI Regulation in response to alleged breaches of the principle of non-intervention, the Regulation was largely drafted with the conditions and limitations contained in the ILC Draft Articles in mind.

[79] ACI Regulation, Arts. 1 (2), 6, 8 (1).

[80] ILC Draft Articles with Commentaries, Commentary on Art. 53, para. 1.

[81] ACI Regulation, Art. 8 (10). [82] See Section 6.3.3.

[83] See ILC Draft Articles with Commentaries, Commentary on Art. 53, para. 7.

6.3.2 Legality under the Multilateral Trade Regime

Although the Commission justifies its potential anti-coercion measures under customary rules of international law on countermeasures, those rules might be displaced by the more special rules. Furthermore, even though they would not be displaced, anti-coercion measures still could violate multilateral, regional, or bilateral trade rules, as the justification provided by customary law might not be given regard within dispute settlement proceedings under special regimes. In conformity with Article 1 (3) requiring consistency with international law, the ACI's Preamble states that '(WTO) is the cornerstone of the rules-based multilateral trading system. Therefore, it is important that the Union continue to support that system, with the WTO at its core, and to use its dispute settlement system where appropriate'.[84] However, the question is whether that is indeed the case.

6.3.2.1 Article 23 DSU

Since WTO DSU rules are *leges speciales* to general rules on countermeasures, it is necessary to see first whether they are applicable to the case at hand, in which situation general customary rules on countermeasure contained in the ILC Draft Articles would be displaced.[85]

As already explored, Article 23.1 DSU establishes the general obligation that disputes arising from WTO law should only be settled according to the DSU disciplines.[86] The ACI Regulation allows the imposition of unilateral measures, including the suspension of concessions and obligations contained in WTO agreements, such as the imposition of restrictions on the import and export of goods or measures affecting trade in services.[87] Therefore, it could be perceived as allowing the imposition of the same countermeasures, for the imposition of which the EU would have to follow the multilateral WTO rules. Since the ACI allows the imposition various response measures, only the legality of those that relate to the suspension of WTO concessions and obligations would be questioned under Article 23 DSU.

Article 23.1 DSU mandates the use of the WTO dispute settlement to the exclusion of the customary rules on unilateral self-help codified in the ILC Draft Articles; however, it does so only in respect to disputes arising out of the WTO rules. The WTO jurisprudence reinforces that

[84] ACI Regulation, Preamble, recital (12). [85] See Sections 3.3.2.3 and 5.4.1.
[86] See Sections 3.3.2.1 and 5.4.1. [87] ACI Regulation, Annex I.

the general obligation contained in Article 23.1 applies when a WTO Member seeks redress for a *WTO violation*.[88] Similarly, Article 23.2 (a) DSU contains the more specific prohibition on unilateral determinations of *inconsistency with WTO rules* prior to exhaustion of DSU proceedings.[89] Article 23.2 (c) DSU prohibits any suspensions of concessions or other obligations without Dispute Settlement Body (DSB) authorization, which as clarified by the jurisprudence, are 'taken as measures seeking to redress a *WTO violation*' (emphasis added).[90] The panel in *US – Certain EC Products* expressly stated that 'the criterion for determining whether Article 23 is applicable is whether the Member that imposed the measure was "seeking the redress of" a WTO violation'.[91] This approach was also confirmed in the *EC – Commercial Vessels* case where the panel said that 'the phrase "seek the redress of a violation . . ." covers any act of a Member *in response to what it considers to be a violation of a WTO obligation* by another Member' (emphasis added).[92]

The ACI Regulation, however, does not necessarily deal with cases related to alleged WTO illegalities, as it comprises all sorts of coercive actions and redressive measures.[93] In fact, as shown in the previous section, the purpose is to deal with measures of economic coercion, which comprises cases which presumably violate customary international law rules, namely the principle of non-interference, regardless of whether these measures simultaneously violate WTO rules, FTAs, BITs, or bilateral friendship treaties.[94] Nevertheless, since economic coercion is exemplified through trade restrictions, it is highly likely that it would also concern alleged WTO breaches.[95] In this highly likely scenario, according to Article 2 (1) ACI, the EU would respond to it because it interferes with the Unions' or a Member State's legitimate sovereign

[88] Panel Report, *US – Certain EC products*, WT/DS165/R, 17 July 2000, paras 6.19–6.20, upheld by the Appellate Body (WT/DS165/ABR, 11 December 2000), para. 111; Appellate Body Reports, *US/Canada – Continued Suspension*, WT/DS320/ABR, WT/DS321/ABR, 16 October 2008, paras. 371–372.

[89] Panel Report, *US – Section 301*, WT/DS152/R, 22 December 1999, para. 7.59.

[90] Panel Report, *US – Certain EC Products*, WT/DS165/R, para. 6.37.

[91] ibid, para. 6.21.

[92] Panel Report, *EC – Commercial Vessels*, WT/DS301/R, 22 April 2005, para. 7.196. Yet, Marceau and Wyatt submit that 'WTO prohibits trade countermeasures based on unilateral determination, irrespective of the breach they are taken in response to'; Gabrielle Marceau and Julian Wyatt, 'Dispute Settlement Regimes Intermingled: Regional Trade Agreements and the WTO' (2010) 1(1) *Journal of International Dispute Settlement* 67–95 at 76–77.

[93] Impact Assessment Report, fn. 18, p. 23.

[94] For more, see Section 6.3.1.1.

[95] Chien-Huei Wu, 'The EU's Proposed Anti-Coercion Instrument: Legality and Effectiveness' (2023) 57(2) *JWT* 297–316 at 307.

choices and not because it violates WTO substantive rules. Since under the ACI, the EU is allowed to impose countermeasures purportedly addressing breaches of customary international law, the legal claim at issue could theoretically not be based on WTO rules. Hence, the *lex specialis*, in the form of Article 23 DSU, requiring the use of the WTO dispute settlement for disputes on WTO law, might not be considered applicable to the ACI dealing with other breaches of international law. In a similar manner, when FTAs contain their own dispute settlement mechanisms and rules on countermeasures, Article 23.1 of the DSU is not considered violated even when the legal basis of a claim is an FTA norm replicating a WTO norm, due to the fact that the basis is still different and the claims arise not under the WTO-covered agreements but under FTA norms.[96] Therefore, the more general customary rules on countermeasures contained in the ILC Draft Article on State Responsibility would still be the applicable law and could serve as justification for an EU redressive measure.[97] Yet, the EU still bears the risk that its countermeasures might be considered illegal under customary international law because of Union's incorrect unilateral assessment of the wrongfulness of the actions of a third state, with the consequence that the EU will incur international responsibility. Admittedly, there might be no court to judge on this. And with regard to WTO panels, this aspect could not be determined within WTO proceedings due to jurisdictional limitations.[98]

But what if the ACI is challenged by a WTO Member for its alleged violation of Article 23 DSU? Can the possible contention by the EU that its ACI is not directed (only) against WTO violations but against violations of the principle of non-intervention save the ACI from being challenged 'as such' under Article 23 DSU?[99] A WTO panel might not only consider the

[96] Pamela Apaza Lanyi and Armin Steinbach, 'Limiting Jurisdictional Fragmentation in International Trade Disputes' (2014) 5 *Journal of International Dispute Settlement* 372–405 at 397; James Flett, 'Referring PTA Disputes to the WTO Dispute Settlement System', in Andreas Dür and Manfred Elsig (eds.), *Trade Cooperation: The Purpose, Design and Effects of Preferential Trade Agreements*. World Trade Forum (New York: Cambridge University Press, 2015), pp. 557–558.

[97] Art. 55 of the ILC Draft Articles. For more on the relationship between special WTO dispute settlement rules and general customary rules on countermeasures, see Section 5.4.

[98] ILC Draft Articles with Commentaries, Commentary on Art. 49, para. 3.

[99] That legislation even prior to its application can violate WTO rules as such was shown in Section 3.3.1.

statutory language but could also take into consideration other aspects, as it did in *US – Section 301* case, such as an administrative act accompanying the legislation, US statements before the panel, and US practice.[100] Thus, despite the fact that the statutory language gives no reason to find an 'as such' violation of Article 23 DSU by the ACI (as the instrument does not specifically mention breach of WTO rules as a condition for EU redressive measures), the panel could find other evidence that would overturn this conclusion. For example, the legislative history of the ACI could be invoked as proof that with this instrument the EU is in fact seeking to regularly address WTO breaches. The INTA's proposal for additional amendments to Trade Enforcement Regulation 654/2014[101], the trigger behind the Commission's promise to introduce new anti-coercion legislation, sought to address 'a clear breach of obligations of trade agreements', since '[d]ispute settlement provisions, including in regional or bilateral trade agreements, might not be sufficiently specific or explicit enough'. It also stated that in case of 'a clear breach of international law or a clear violation of trade obligations', the Union should be able to impose countermeasures provided that it has 'appropriately challenged those illegal measures at the WTO or in front of the relevant dispute settlement body'.[102] While INTA amendments would have also covered breaches other than those of WTO or FTA rules, such as those enshrined in bilateral friendship treaties, the Committee seemed especially concerned about the WTO crisis. The proposed mentioned amendment was introduced by INTA 'against the background of the ongoing tension in international trade and the crisis in the WTO'.[103] Thus, the initial intention behind the amendment was to allow the EU to act unilaterally and immediately in case of breaches of international law, especially WTO law. INTA's proposed amendments were clearly 'as

[100] Panel Report, *US – Section 301*, WT/DS152/R, paras. 7.110–7.130.

[101] Regulation (EU) 654/2014 of the European Parliament and of the Council of 15 May 2014 concerning the exercise of the Union's rights for the application and enforcement of international trade rules and amending Council Regulation (EC) No. 3286/94 laying down Community procedures in the field of the common commercial policy in order to ensure the exercise of the Community's rights under international trade rules, in particular those established under the auspices of the World Trade Organization (Trade Enforcement Regulation), OJ EU 2014 No. L 189/50.

[102] Report on the Proposal for a Regulation of the European Parliament and of the Council amending Regulation (EU) No. 654/2014 of the European Parliament and of the Council concerning the Exercise of the Union's Rights for the Application and Enforcement of International Trade Rules (INTA Report), Amendments 3, 8, and 14.

[103] ibid, Explanatory Statement, p. 19.

such' in violation of Article 23 DSU.[104] The Commission put effort into designing the ACI in conformity with WTO law, as it significantly departed from these proposed amendments. Hence, in comparison, the ACI has significantly better chances to stand the test of 'as such' legality under the DSU. Still, if, for example, there is extensive ACI practice showing that the EU is regularly using the instrument to adopt countermeasures before it challenges the same measures within WTO dispute settlement, the conclusion could be different.

A separate issue is whether ACI's application in individual instances is compliant with WTO obligations, particularly when the EU imposes unilateral countermeasures violating WTO rules. Thus, if a WTO panel determines that the evidence shows the measure at issue to actually seek the redress of a WTO violation, WTO DSU rules would be applicable and Article 23 DSU could be held to be breached by EU's response measures adopted under the ACI Regulation. For example, in *US – Certain EC Products*, the panel established that '[w]e consider that there is ample evidence before us which demonstrates that when it took the 3 March Measure, the United States was seeking redress for a perceived WTO violation by the European Communities, within the meaning of Article 23.1 of the DSU'.[105] The panel made this determination based on 'ample evidence' consisting of the USTR press release announcing the measure, the request from USTR to the US Customs Service, memoranda of US Customs Service officials, and a press conference by the Deputy USTR, clearly showing that when it took the measure, the US 'was seeking redress for a perceived WTO violation'.[106] Hence, although the imposed unilateral anti-coercion measures could be postulated by the EU to address violations of customary law, the WTO panel could analyze whether and finally confirm that the measure is in fact seeking the redress of a WTO violation. Since economic coercion has a different aim than unfair trade practices,[107] the EU could argue that it seeks to address the influence the coercion has on the Union's sovereign choice, which

[104] For more, see Wolfgang Weiß and Cornelia Furculita, 'The EU in Search for Stronger Enforcement Rules: Assessing the Proposed Amendments to Trade Enforcement Regulation 654/2014' (2020) 23(4) *JIEL* 865–884 at 879–881.

[105] Panel Report, *US – Certain EC Products*, WT/DS165/R, para. 6.24

[106] ibid, paras. 6.25–6.34.

[107] Jonathan Hackenbroich and Pawel Zerka, 'Measured Response: How to Design a European Instrument against Economic Coercion' (2021) European Council on Foreign Relations Policy Brief, 23 June 2021, https://ecfr.eu/publication/measured-response-how-to-design-a-european-instrument-against-economic-coercion/.

does not necessarily relate to trade and is not necessarily a genuine WTO violation. However, if the EU simultaneously challenges the alleged economic coercive measure within WTO proceedings, as it recently happened in the EU's conflict with China in relation to restrictions taken against Lithuania,[108] it might be difficult for the EU to argue that by imposing countermeasures it is not seeking to impose unilateral retaliatory measures against a WTO violation, especially considering the legislative history of the ACI. In such cases the panel could establish based on the available evidence that the EU's measures under the ACI proposal, although not overt, are measures which in fact seek redress against a WTO breach and, therefore, represent a DSU violation. Thus, the conformity of a countermeasure adopted under the ACI with Article 23 DSU will depend on the specific facts of the case, especially the available evidence such as the text of the measure or official statements. Therefore, specific unilateral response measures taken under the ACI might be found illegal under Article 23 DSU. Although Article 1 (3) ACI Regulation requires that actions taken under it be consistent with international law, in the Impact Assessment Report, the Commission itself stated that there can be cases in which the coercive measures are simultaneously in breach of WTO obligations,[109] and affirmed that in these cases 'the EU would continue to take to the WTO any grievances [. . .] if the EU considers those to be at odds with WTO disciplines'.[110] To act in conformity with its multilateral procedural trade obligations and in line with Article 1 (3) ACI Regulation, the EU is required to avoid taking unilateral WTO-inconsistent response measures against coercive measures challengeable under WTO rules and instead take the dispute to WTO adjudication.

6.3.2.2 *WTO Substantive Rules*

The ACI and measures taken under it may raise questions with respect to their legality not only under Article 23 DSU but also under substantive WTO rules, such as the non-performance of tariff concessions, the imposition of new or increased customs duties, or the introduction of quantitative restrictions listed in Annex I to the ACI, or the non-discrimination obligations as third countries affected by ACI response measures are treated differently to others.

[108] See WTO, *China – Measures Concerning Trade in Goods and Services*, DS610/8, 9 December 2022.

[109] Impact Assessment Report, p. 23.

[110] ibid, p. 43.

The first question is whether the ACI could even be considered violating 'as such' substantive WTO norms. As explored in Section 3.3.1, discretion in a legislation would not preclude the finding of an 'as such' violation,[111] the importance of the mandatory/discretionary distinction varying from case to case and not being applicable in an automatic manner.[112] For an 'as such' violation, the legislation in question should *require* a violation of WTO agreements or otherwise *restrict in a material way* the Member's discretion to act in a manner consistent with the agreements.[113] Still, discretionary legislation expressly or necessarily providing for WTO-inconsistent conduct as the only possible action or one of the possible actions could be found 'as such' illegal.[114]

The ACI Regulation establishes that in case of economic coercion, when first-tier actions have not resulted in the cessation of the coercion, it is necessary to protect Union's and its Member States' interests and rights, and action is in the Union's interest, the Commission '*shall* adopt a Union response measures' (Article 8 (1), emphasis added). Accordingly, there is no discretion in whether or not to act if certain conditions are fulfilled. Still, the Commission enjoys discretion in appreciating the existence of the above-mentioned conditions. Furthermore, especially due to the multitude of criteria that should only be 'taken into account',[115] the Commission and the Council also enjoy a certain degree of discretion when proposing and deciding, respectively, about the existence of economic coercion (Article 5 (1), (5)). Thus, the proposal leaves the Commission the discretion to take any action in a particular case, and to decide which one. In case first-tier diplomatic measures are unsuccessful, the ACI entails a high degree of discretion with respect to whether

[111] See again Simon Lester, 'A Framework for Thinking about the Discretion in the Mandatory/Discretionary Distinction' (2011) 14(2) *JIEL* 369–402 at 370.

[112] Panel Report, *US – Section 301*, WT/DS152/R, para. 7.53; Panel Report, *Brazil – Aircraft (Article 21.5 – Canada II)*, T/DS46/RW2, 26 July 2001, paras. 5.9, 5.12; Appellate Body Report, *US – Corrosion-Resistant Steel Sunset Review*, T/DS244/AB/R, 15 December 2003, para. 93; Appellate Body Report, *EU – Biodiesel*, WT/DS473/AB/R, 6 October 2016, para. 6.227.

[113] Appellate Body Report, *EU – Biodiesel*, WT/DS473/AB/R, paras. 6.229, 6.281; Panel Report, *US – Olives*, WT/DS577/R, 19 November 2021, para. 7.146. Referring to older Appellate Body Reports from *US – Corrosion-Resistant Steel Sunset Review*, WT/DS244/AB/R, 15 December 2003, para. 100 and *US – Carbon Steel*, WT/DS/213/AB/R, 28 November 2002, para. 162. For more, see Section 3.3.1.

[114] Nicolas Lockhart and Elisabeth Sheargold, 'In Search of Relevant Discretion: The Role of the Mandatory/Discretionary Distinction in WTO Law' (2010) 13 (2) *JIEL* 379–421 at 410 ff; Lester, 'A Framework for Thinking about the Discretion in the Mandatory/Discretionary Distinction' (2011) 399.

[115] For more, see Section 6.3.1.2.

and which response measures to apply from the Annex I list. There are certain criteria set in Article 11 (2) ACI based on which the Commission shall determine which response measures to adopt (Article 8 (2)). Nevertheless, the assessment of these criteria, such as assessing the effectiveness of measures in inducing cessation of coercion, which is to be given predominant weight together with the criterion of 'avoidance or minimisation of negative impact', is likely to be a discretionary and biased exercise. Hence, since the Commission enjoys a high degree of discretion, it can choose and design measures that are consistent with WTO rules, especially considering that when selecting and designing the measure, it shall *inter alia* take into account 'any relevant criteria established in international law' (Article 11 (2) (h)), thus including those from WTO agreements. Therefore, the Commission is not *required* to act in violation of the WTO norms; in fact, Article 1 (3) requires the Commission to act according to its international commitments. Thus, Commission's discretion is not *restricted in a material way* to only act inconsistently with its WTO obligations. Still, Annex I expressly mentions 'the non-performance of applicable international obligations' and contains explicit potential future measures that on their face are WTO inconsistent (such as the 'imposition of customs duties beyond the most-favoured-nation level' seemingly violating Article I General Agreement on Tariffs and Trade (GATT)[116]), which, unless justified, could potentially lead to a finding of an 'as such' violation. Despite the requirement contained in Article 1 (3), since the Commission considers potential WTO-inconsistent measures justified under customary international law, it might impose them against third countries under the ACI. Therefore, considering the ambiguity around how 'as such' claims are evaluated, it is not entirely clear whether the ACI would be *prima facie* 'as such' consistent under substantive WTO law. Nevertheless, its high degree of discretion considerably increases the ACI's chances to pass the legality test under the substantive WTO norms.

The second issue to be dealt with here relates to whether the EU could also face 'as applied' claims of substantive WTO violations, resulting from the specific application of the ACI, namely when the EU imposes countermeasures after the first-tier measures fail. For example, the imposition of tariffs beyond the most-favored-nation level or the imposition of

[116] General Agreement on Tariffs and Trade 1994, 15 April 1994, Marrakesh Agreement Establishing the World Trade Organization, Annex 1A, 1867 U.N.T.S. 187, 33 I.L.M. 1153 (1994).

quantitative restrictions, permitted under Annex I, could be in violation of Articles I, XI, or XIII GATT,[117] unless they would be justified. However, the assessment of such measures should be done for that particular dispute when the measures are applied.

6.3.2.3 *Justifications for Potential WTO Violations*

In case of violations of WTO rules, the EU would most likely try to justify them by invoking non-WTO and/or WTO law. It seems that the EU intends to justify its potential WTO-breaching future measures under international customary rules on countermeasure. However, justifications based on non-WTO law, specifically customary rules of international law, will most likely not be recognized within WTO proceedings. WTO panels and the AB are known for their reticence in applying non-WTO law within WTO proceedings.[118] Thus, even though ILC Draft Articles on State Responsibility have been used for interpretative purposes, they have never been used by a panel or the AB as applicable law within WTO proceedings.[119] Accordingly, even if international customary norms would indeed allow unilateral countermeasures,[120] they would most likely not serve as a justification for a violation of substantive WTO obligations within WTO proceedings.

Nevertheless, the EU could also try to invoke WTO justifications, such as those under Articles XX or XXI GATT.

(1) Article XXI GATT

In their Joint Communication on a European Economic Security Strategy, the Commission and the High Representative talk about economic

[117] Annex I to the ACI, containing a list of response measures that may be adopted allows the imposition of such measures (letters (a) and (b)).

[118] Weiß and Furculita, 'The EU in Search for Stronger Enforcement Rules' (2020) 875, referring to Joost Pauwelyn, 'How to Win a World Trade Organization Dispute Based on Non-World Trade Organization Law? Questions of Jurisdiction and Merits' (2003) 37(6) *JWT* 997–1030; Lorand Bartels, 'Jurisdiction and Applicable Law in the WTO' (2016) SIEL Working Paper No. 2016/18 1-21; Wolfgang Weiß, *WTO Law and Domestic Regulation* (MünchenOxford, Baden-Baden: Hart/Beck/Nomos, 2020) 412–419. For arguments in favour of considering countermeasures against non-WTO law violations as justifications for WTO law breaches, see Azaria, 'Trade Countermeasures for Breaches of International Law outside the WTO' (2022) 1–35.

[119] Sánchez, 'What Trade Lawyers Should Know about the ILC Articles on State Responsibility' (2012) 292.

[120] For more on whether unilateral response measures against alleged measures of economic coercion would be allowed under general customary international law, see Section 6.3.1.

coercion as a risk to the European economic security, the ACI being identified as a tool for protecting it.[121] The recent practice under Article XXI GATT on national security showcases how geopolitical concerns and economic affairs became increasingly linked.[122] While for decades Article XXI was scarcely mentioned, recent cases involving Article XXI GATT justifications have rapidly proliferated.[123] While the dispute in which the first final panel report was issued concerned the Crimean conflict between Ukraine and Russia,[124] a dozen of other disputes followed concerning issues related to the economic security of a country. For example, the most notable dispute is *US – Steel and Aluminium Products* initiated by seven complainants and concerning additional customs duties imposed on steel and aluminium products allegedly because their import affected the US economy and thus threatened its national security.[125] In view of this recent practice and the fact that the EU portrays ACI as a tool for protecting its economic security, it would not be surprising if the EU would also try to invoke Article XXI GATT as a justification for its anti-coercion measures in violation of GATT obligations. Article XXI is also applicable to the Agreement on Trade Related Investment Measures[126] (TRIMs) and the Agreement on Trade Facilitation.[127,128] Additionally, the

[121] Joint Communication to the European Parliament, the European Council and the Council on "European Economic Security Strategy", JOIN(2023) 20 final, 20 June 2023.

[122] Tatiana Lacerda Prazeres, 'Trade and National Security: Rising Risks for the WTO' (2020) 19 *WTRev* 137–148 at 143.

[123] Peter Van den Bossche and Sarah Akpofure, 'The Use and Abuse of the National Security Exception under Article XXI(b)(iii) of the GATT 1994' (2020) WTI Working Paper No. 03/2020, pp. 3–4.

[124] Panel Report, *Russia – Traffic in Transit*, WT/DS512/R, 5 April 2019.

[125] DS544, 547, 548, 552, 554, 556, and 564. Some of these claims were terminated by the mutual agreement of the parties (Notification of a mutually agreed solution, *US – Steel and Aluminium Products (India)*, WT/DS547/15, 18 July 2023), suspended (Suspension of Panel Work, *US – Steel and Aluminium Products (Russia)*, WT/DS554/24, 26 June 2023), or otherwise settled (Recourse to Article 25 of the DSU, *US – Steel and Aluminium Products (EU)*, WT/DS548/19, 21 January 2022).

[126] Agreement on Trade-Related Investment Measures (TRIMS), 15 April 1994, Marrakesh Agreement Establishing the World Trade Organization, Annex 1A, 1868 U.N.T.S. 186.

[127] WTO General Council, Agreement on Trade Facilitation, Annex to the Protocol Amending the Marrakesh Agreement Establishing the World Trade Organization, WT/L/940, 28 November 2014, p. 3.

[128] TRIMs, Art. 3 and Agreement on Trade Facilitation, Art. 24.7. According to Van den Bossche and Akpofure, WTO case law on Art. XX GATT suggests that national security exception is not available to justify violations of other agreements not mentioning the exception (Van den Bossche and Akpofure, 'The Use and Abuse of the National Security Exception' (2020), p. 2).

General Agreement on Trade in Services (GATS)[129] and the Agreement on Trade-Related Aspects of Intellectual Property Rights (TRIPS)[130] provide their own national security exceptions (in Article XIV *bis* and, respectively, Article 73), which are worded similarly to Article XXI GATT.

Thus, the EU could try to argue that its measures taken in response to coercion were justified under Article XXI (b) (iii) GATT as actions 'which it considers necessary for the protection of its essential security interests taken in time of war or other emergency in international relations'. EU's decision to raise this justification should not be made lightly and without a well-grounded reasoning. While it could be easily invoked to circumvent multilateral rules,[131] Article XXI GATT deals with aspects that are extremely sensitive, such as wars and other armed conflicts, and should not be used as a carte blanche.[132] Its invocation in other situations, such as for reasons related to economic security,[133] raises increased risks of abuse and potential of eroding the multilateral regime.

Unlike Article XX GATT, the chapeau of Article XXI (b) seems to set a minimal threshold for showing that a measure was 'necessary' for the 'protection of the essential security interests', due to the expression 'which it considers' qualifying these concepts, that would be easier to reach.[134] Yet, Members' discretion is limited by the good-faith

[129] General Agreement on Trade in Services, 15 April 1994, Marrakesh Agreement Establishing the World Trade Organization, Annex 1B, 1869 U.N.T.S. 183, 33 I.L.M. 1167 (1994).

[130] Agreement on Trade-Related Aspects of Intellectual Property Rights, 15 April 1994, Marrakesh Agreement Establishing the World Trade Organization, Annex 1C, 1869 U.N.T.S. 299, 33 I.L.M. 1197 (1994).

[131] Warren Maruyama and Alan Wm. Wolff, 'Saving the WTO from the National Security Exception' (2023) Peterson Institute for International Economics Working Papers 23-3, p. 7.

[132] Prazeres, 'Trade and National Security' (2020) 139, 144.

[133] For example, in *US – Steel and Aluminium* case the United States clearly invoked interests of economic security (Wolfgang Weiß, 'Interpreting Essential Security Exceptions in WTO Law in View of Economic Security Interests', in Wolfgang Weiß and Cornelia Furculita (eds.), *Global Politics and EU Trade Policy: Facing the Challenges to a Multilateral Approach* (Heidelberg: Springer, 2020), p. 258).

[134] Panel Report, *Russia – Traffic in Transit*, WT/DS512/R, 5 April 2019, paras. 7.82, 7.131, 7.146; this panel's interpretation was confirmed in further panel reports from *Saudi Arabia – Intellectual Property Rights* (WT/DS567/R, para. 7.244, interpreting Art. 73 (b) TRIPS Agreement, dispute terminated but panel report un-adopted), *US – Steel and Aluminium Products (Turkey)* (WT/DS564/R, 9 December 2022, paras. 7.129, 7.143, appealed into the void). Since the reports in these two more recent disputes have not been adopted, the debate might not be settled yet. The United States, for example, has repeatedly claimed that '[i]ssues of national security are political matters not susceptible to review or

obligation.[135] Thus, even though the WTO member invoking this justification enjoys a significant level of discretion as Article XXI GATT refers to the Member's assessment, the exercise of said discretion is not outside any judicial control. Considering that economic coercion is usually far from an 'armed conflict, or a situation of breakdown of law and public order', while the 'military interests, or maintenance of law and public order interests' at stake are less obvious in its case, the EU would have to articulate its essential security interests with greater specificity than in more 'characteristic' cases of 'emergency in international law',[136] unless the conflict would seriously escalate to or coercion was exercised in the context of such more characteristic cases. If this requirement is complied with, the 'necessity' test of the measures taken for the protection of its essential security interests only requires them to meet 'a minimum requirement of plausibility in relation to the proffered essential security interests, i.e. that they are not implausible as measures protective of these interests'.[137] Thus, the measure adopted must have an even looser connection to the security interest. While the panel established a minimal threshold, raising tariffs or impeding market access of another country's goods still might not have a sufficiently plausible relation to protecting a genuine security interest.

However, before even reaching the analysis under the chapeau, the panel would have to establish that the measure was 'taken in time of war or other emergency in international relations'.[138] Although the assessment might differ in case of EU anti-coercion measures applied towards Russia in the context of the war against Ukraine,[139] a mere conflict related to the exercise of economic coercion towards the EU or its Members' sovereign choice clearly does not amount to a war and most likely would not qualify as a situation of 'emergency in international law'. In *Russia – Traffic in Transit*, the panel established that an emergency in international relations, subject to objective determination, refers

capable of resolution by WTO dispute settlement' (*US – Steel and Aluminium Products*, WT/DS544/14, WT/DS552/16, WT/DS556/21, WT/DS564/21).

135 Panel Report, *Russia – Traffic in Transit*, WT/DS512/R, para. 7.133.

136 ibid, para. 7.135.

137 ibid, para. 7.138.

138 For more on the order of the analysis, see Panel Report, *US – Origin Marking (Hong Kong, China)*, WT/DS597/R, 21 December 2022, paras. 7.263–7.264.

139 See Prabhash Ranjan, 'Russia-Ukraine War and WTO's National Security Exception' (2023) 58(2) *Foreign Trade Review* 246–258. Panel Report, *US – Origin Marking (Hong Kong, China)*, WT/DS597/R, para. 7.324 seems to imply that third parties could also invoke the war.

'generally to a situation of armed conflict, or of latent armed conflict, or of heightened tension or crisis, or of general instability engulfing or surrounding a state', and that 'political or economic differences between Members are not sufficient, of themselves, to constitute an emergency in international relations'.[140] It was further clarified in *US – Steel and Aluminium* that 'an "emergency in international relations" [...] must be, if not equally grave or severe, at least comparable in its gravity or severity to a "war" in terms of its impact on international relations'.[141] Thus, generally, conflicts related to economic coercion would amount to political or economic differences, unless they are taken in the context of the stated situations or cause grave and severe impairment of the international relations, such as the severance of diplomatic, consular, or economic relations between the parties to the conflict.[142] Hence, the use of national security exceptions as justifications for the EU's WTO-violating anti-coercion measures would be restricted only to instances of critical and serious gravity.

(2) Article XX GATT

The EU could also try to justify its measures under Article XX (a) GATT permitting measures that are 'necessary to protect public morals'. According to the WTO jurisprudence, the term 'public morals' refers to standards of 'right and wrong conduct' belonging to a community or nation.[143] WTO Members enjoy a wide discretion in defining their own public morals, as they are influenced by each Member's prevailing values.[144] When determining a measure's objective and establishing that

[140] ibid, paras. 7.72, 7.75–7.76. While a dynamic interpretative approach could be adopted with respect to the interpretation of such concepts as 'emergency in international relations', it cannot lead to completely different or novel meanings (Weiß, 'Interpreting Essential Security Exceptions in WTO Law', p. 267).

[141] Panel Report, *US – Steel and Aluminium (Turkey)*, WT/DS564/R, para. 7.154.

[142] In *Saudi Arabia – Intellectual Property Rights* (para. 7.259), the panel agreed with the defendant that 'one Member's severance of "all diplomatic and economic ties" with another Member could be regarded as "the ultimate State expression of the existence of an emergency in international relations"'. Also repeated by the panel in *US – Origin Marking (Hong Kong, China)*, WT/DS597/R, para. 7.357.

[143] Panel Report, *China – Publications and Audiovisual Products*, WT/DS363/R, 12 August 2009, para. 7.759; Appellate Body Reports, *EC – Seal Products*, WT/DS400/AB/R, WT/DS401/AB/R, 22 May 2014, para. 5.199; Panel Report, *US – Tariff Measures*, WT/DS543/R, 15 September 2020, para. 7.140.

[144] Panel Report, *China – Publications and Audiovisual Products*, WT/DS363/R, para. 7.763; Appellate Body Reports, *EC – Seal Products*, WT/DS400/AB/R, WT/DS401/AB/R, para. 5.199; Panel Report, *US – Tariff Measures*, WT/DS543/R, para 7.116.

it falls under the concept of 'public morals', a Member can invoke the relevant domestic regulations and legislative history.[145] Considering that the ACI is set to deal with measures that interfere with the EU's or its Member States' sovereign choices, the EU could argue that anti-coercion measures were taken to protect such values as sovereign equality of states and mutual respect among peoples, even along the economic objectives.[146] These values and principles are enshrined in Articles 3 (5) and 21 (1) and (2) Treaty on European Union[147] (TEU) expressly, such as the principle of equality or mutual respect among peoples, or indirectly by requiring strict observance of international law, including of the principles of the UN Charter and Helsinki Final Act.[148] The ACI Regulation, pursuant to Articles 3 (5) and 21 (1) and (2) TEU, also specifically refers to the principles of equality, mutual respect among peoples, and strict observance of international law.[149] Given the broad and dynamic interpretation justifications such as those contained in Article XX GATT receive,[150] and considering that these values are enshrined in EU constitutional treaties and in the ACI's preamble, and are recognized principles of international law, the claim that they represent 'public morals' is likely to be accepted without much debate, especially considering the leeway the concept allows. Even if the specific instrument implementing the measure did not explicitly reference public morals, this should not be determinative for the justification.[151]

Although the values at stake could most probably be defended as constituting public morals, other conditions established in paragraph

[145] Paola Conconi and Tania Voon, '*EC – Seal Products*: The Tension Between Public Morals and International Trade Agreements' (2015) EUI Working Paper RSCAS 2015/70, pp. 16–17; Panel Report, *EC – Seal Products*, WT/DS400/R, WT/DS401/R, 25 November 2013, para. 7.398.

[146] After *EC – Seals*, it is clear that the defendant does not have to establish that the measure was solely motivated by public morals (Conconi and Voon, '*EC – Seal Products*' (2015), p. 7).

[147] Consolidated version of the Treaty on European Union, OJ EU 2012 No. C 326/13, 26 October 2010.

[148] Art. 1 (2) UN Charter mentions the development of 'friendly relations among nations' among UN's purposes, while Art. 2 mentions the principle of sovereign equality of its Members. The principle of sovereign equality and co-operation among States can also be found in the Helsinki Final Act (Principles I, IX).

[149] ACI, Preamble, recitals (1), (2), (4).

[150] Wolfgang Weiß, *WTO Law and Domestic Regulation* (München, Oxford, Baden-Baden: Hart/Beck/Nomos, 2020) 73 f, 230.

[151] Panel Report, *US – Tariff Measures*, WT/DS543/R, para. 7.125.

(a) and the chapeau of Article XX might be more difficult to meet.[152] According to paragraph (a), the measures at issue should be 'designed' – that is, capable – and 'necessary' to protect public morals.[153] While the threshold set for proving that a measure was 'designed' to protect public morals is lower and might not even be a helpful step for the analysis,[154] analyzing whether a measure is 'necessary' represents a 'holistic approach', involving the 'weighing and balancing' of a series of factors: the relative importance of the pursued objective, the restrictiveness of the measure, and the degree of contribution to the objective, followed by an assessment of whether there were potential WTO-consistent or less restrictive alternatives.[155] In view of the inclusion of the interests and values at issue in EU's constitutional treaties, as well as UN Charter and Helsinki Final Act, it is reasonable to expect that the pursued objectives will be qualified as vital and highly important. The assessment of other factors, however, can be performed only once the specific measure is known. Still, for a justification to be accepted, the measure chosen should be connected to the objective pursued and actually contribute to it, including through the products which the measures covered.[156] Thus, the specified products covered by the measures should be connected to the morally wrong conduct or otherwise contribute to the invoked objectives.[157] One might contend that measures such as raising tariffs for the products do not contribute to protecting the public morals at stake, but assessing such a claim, of course, depends on the facts of the case.

Finally, if the measure is considered provisionally justified under one of the paragraphs of Article XX GATT, the chapeau requires the measure not be '*applied* in a manner which would constitute a means of arbitrary or unjustifiable discrimination between countries where the same

[152] Art. XX GATT involves a two-tier test: the measure at issue must not only fall under a particular exception contained in the paragraphs (a) to (j) but also should satisfy the chapeau (Appellate Body Report, *US – Gasoline*, WT/DS2/AB/R, 29 April 1996, p. 22).

[153] Appellate Body Report, *Colombia – Textiles*, WT/DS461/AB/R, 7 June 2016, para. 5.68; Panel Report, *US – Tariff Measures*, WT/DS543/R, paras. 7.145–7.153.

[154] Panel Report, *US – Tariff Measures*, WT/DS543/R, para. 7.151. If this initial threshold is not met, further examination would not be required (Appellate Body Report, *Colombia – Textiles*, WT/DS461/AB/R, para. 5.68).

[155] Appellate Body Report, *Colombia – Textiles*, WT/DS461/AB/R, para. 5.77; Appellate Body Report, *China – Publications and Audiovisual Products*, WT/DS363/AB/R, 21 December 2009, para. 244; Panel Report, *US – Tariff Measures*, WT/DS543/R, para. 7.159.

[156] Panel Report, *US – Tariff Measures*, WT/DS543/R, para. 7.178.

[157] The panel in *US – Tariff Measures* has not resolved the issue whether a measure would have to apply only to products that embody the morally offensive conduct to benefit from justification (WT/DS543/R, para. 7.179).

conditions prevail, or a disguised restriction on international trade' (emphasis added). Accordingly, a measure's conformity with the chapeau will depend on how it will be applied in practice. The cause and rationale behind the discrimination caused by the measure would have to bear rational connection to the objective.[158] For example, if a measure is imposed on products of a particular coercive state and not those of others,[159] for its potential to provide relief to EU economic operators (a criterion to be taken into account when selecting and designing a measure under the ACI),[160] without rational connection to the EU's alleged objective, it would not pass the chapeau test.

GATS violations could be similarly justified under Article XIV of the agreement also containing an exception of measures 'necessary to protect public morals or to maintain public order' and providing a chapeau with a similar language to that under Article XX GATT. Thus, the analysis under Article XIV GATS would be similar to that under Article XX GATT, except that it additionally covers measures necessary 'to maintain public order',[161] a difference that should not generally affect the analysis described above, especially since the conclusion that measures are necessary to protect public morals would be sufficient considering the use of the conjunction 'or' suggesting their alternative character.[162]

To conclude, the EU could try to justify its WTO-breaching countermeasures taken under the ACI by invoking non-WTO and/or WTO law. However, successfully doing so would be quite difficult. The justifications based on national security could prevail but only in situations of extremely grave and serious conflicts in international relations with the involvement of both or at least the coercive state. Articles XX (a) GATT and XIV GATS have the best chances to justify WTO-breaching measures if

[158] Appellate Body Report, *Brazil – Retreaded Tyres*, WT/DS332/AB/R, 3 December 2007, para. 227; Appellate Body Report, *US – Tuna II (Mexico) (Article. 21-5 – Mexico)*, WT/DS381/AB/RW, 20 November 2015, para. 7.316.

[159] Since the chapeau refers to the discrimination between countries with the same conditions that are relevant in light of the particular policy objective (Appellate Body Reports, *EC – Seal Products*, WT/DS400/AB/R, WT/DS401/AB/R, paras. 5.299–5.300), we consider that there will be discrimination if countries that engage in economic coercive measures, as defined by the ACI, are treated differently.

[160] ACI Regulation, Art. 11 (2) (d).

[161] Appellate Body Report, *US – Gambling*, WT/DS285/AB/R, 20 August 2005, para. 296.

[162] As sovereign equality and mutual respect among peoples are reflected in EU's law and will likely be recognized as fundamental interests of society, measures under the ACI could be considered, besides being 'necessary to protect public morals', also 'necessary to maintain public order', which would still keep the above analysis intact.

they are drafted with the greatest care and the requirements established therein in mind – requirements that are not formally given consideration in the ACI Regulation. Regardless, the issue that Article 23 DSU had been violated by the unilateral course of action by the EU in defending its WTO rights remains (see Section 6.3.2.1).

6.3.3 Legality under Bilateral and Regional Trade Rules

The ACI having a rather broad scope purportedly does not seek to specifically address breaches of regional/bilateral trade or friendship treaties, but rather general measures of economic coercion, presumably violating the customary principle of non-interference per se.[163] Still, the coercive measures to which the EU would be allowed to respond under the ACI Regulation could also violate provisions of bilateral or regional trade agreements. However, as established in the previous chapter,[164] FTAs do not usually contain provisions similar to Article 23 DSU that would completely displace the customary rules on immediate countermeasures even in cases related to breaches of these agreements. Accordingly, since the parties to these treaties have not committed to make exclusive use of the dispute settlement mechanisms contained for settling FTA disputes, as already established,[165] the EU could argue that it has discretion when deciding whether to initiate disputes under FTA rules or rely on general international rules on countermeasures. However, there is a limitation on this discretion. As mentioned in Sections 3.3.2.3 and 5.5, Article 52 (3) ILC Draft Articles provides that countermeasures shall not be taken and, if already taken, should be suspended when two cumulative conditions are met: the wrongful act was terminated *and* the dispute is pending before an international court or tribunal.[166] The ACI seems in line with these conditions, as it establishes that for the duration of proceedings, the Union's response measure shall be suspended '[w]here the third country and the Union or the Member State concerned have concluded an agreement, including on the basis of an offer from that third country, to submit the matter to binding international third-party adjudication and that third country suspends its economic coercion'.[167] Thus, in the

[163] See Section 6.3.1.1 referring to the ACI Regulation, Preamble, recital (15).
[164] See Section 5.5. [165] See Section 5.5.
[166] See the ILC Draft Articles with Commentaries, Commentary on Art. 52, para. 7: 'Once *the conditions* in paragraph 3 are met, the injured State may not take countermeasures' (emphasis added).
[167] ACI Regulation, Art. 12 (2), second subparagraph.

event of coercive actions violating FTA rules, immediate EU countermeasures would be legal under international law, unless the other party ceases its wrongful act *and* the dispute is submitted to, for example, an FTA panel. Nevertheless, as in case of the Trade Enforcement Regulation,[168] the question arises whether an FTA panel would be more open than the WTO adjudicators in the past and accept justifications invoked by the EU for its unilateral countermeasures based on customary international law for violations of FTA substantive provisions. As all the measures listed in the ACI Regulation, Annex I on Union response measures concern the non-performance of international obligations, such as those related to tariffs, custom duties, quantitative restrictions, or trade in services, they could clearly violate FTA substantive provisions. The successful defence of such provisions, therefore, will depend on whether FTA panels would accept justifications based on customary international law or other FTA justifications. EU FTAs regularly incorporate and, respectively, reproduce Articles XX and XXI GATT.[169] As FTA arbitrators are likely to interpret these provisions in a similar manner to WTO adjudicators due to the requirement to take into account relevant WTO jurisprudence,[170] the conclusions reached in Section 6.3.2.3 on pertinent WTO justifications are also applicable in the bilateral/regional contexts.

Another issue to be addressed in this context is the suspension of bilateral FTA obligations by the EU in response to a coercive measure of a third state that does not affect EU's bilateral trade rights but does affect other aspects of its sovereignty or trade in products to which the FTA is not applicable. In such case, the EU might unilaterally breach FTA rules by adopting ACI countermeasures, and the third state then might bring these before an FTA tribunal. The legal questions then are the same as dealt with earlier: May the FTA tribunal treat general international law on countermeasures as applicable law, and if so, may it accept a defence based on them? Most probably, the legal assessment will come to the same conclusions as mentioned earlier, irrespective of the difference that the coercive measure of the complainant did not breach the FTA.

168 See Section 5.5.

169 See, for example, Comprehensive Economic and Trade Agreement (CETA) between Canada on the one part, and the European Union and its Member States on the other part, OJ EU 2017 No. L 23/11, 14 January 2017, Art. 28.3(1), 28.6; Agreement between the European Union and Japan for an Economic Partnership (JEPA), OJ EU 2018 No. L 330/3, 27 December 2018, Arts. 2.2(1), 8(3), 12(9), 13(8), 1(5); EU–Chile FTA, Arts. 32.1(1), 32.2.

170 For example, CETA, Art. 29.17; JEPA, Art. 21.16; EU–Chile FTA, Art. 31.22.

6.4 Broader Costs and Benefits

Besides the question of its legality under international law, adopting an ACI will entail certain benefits, as well as costs that should be weighed in order to assess the necessity of such an instrument.

The new ACI would indeed provide the Commission with a new tool to react to the increased weaponization of the international trade. It would signal to the international community that the EU does not let others intervene in its sovereign choice and affect its legitimate policy space, and that it will protect the Union's and Member States' interests when necessary.[171] While initially designed to respond to the US Trumponomics, the ACI is currently being discussed more as an instrument against the Chinese Exceptionalism.[172] However, the ACI could also be a useful instrument in relation to Russia in the context of its war against Ukraine.[173] In the words of Bernd Lange, International Trade Committee Chair, 'those who are unable to resolutely confront coercion by third countries will allow others to dictate their policies'.[174] The ACI confers credibility to the EU that it will act in case it is pressured into taking a decision with the help of trade and investment measures.[175] Accordingly, one of the ACI's aims, which has been stressed even more in the final adopted version of the ACI (Article 1 (2)), is to deter other countries from engaging in economic coercive activity, even without being applied. Thus, the Commission hopes that despite its potential negative implications, it will not be used very often, and when used,

[171] Jonathan Hackenbroich, 'Protecting Europe from Economic Coercion: A European Toolbox for Countering Economic Coercion', European Council on Foreign Relations, Policy Brief, 20 October 2020, https://ecfr.eu/publication/defending_europe_economic_sovereignty_new_ways_to_resist_economic_coercion/?amp%3Bqid=9084882#protecting; Impact Assessment Report, p. 7.

[172] See Sections 1.2, 2.2.1, and 2.2.2. For more, see Mathieu Duchâtel, 'Effective Deterrence? The Coming European Anti-Coercion Instrument', Institut Montaigne, 2 December 2022, www.institutmontaigne.org/en/expressions/effective-deterrence-coming-european-anti-coercion-instrument.

[173] For more see Jonathan Hackenbroich, 'Europe's New Economic Statecraft: A Strong Anti-Coercion Instrument', European Council on Foreign Relations, 1 April 2022, https://ecfr.eu/article/europes-new-economic-statecraft-a-strong-anti-coercion-instrument/.

[174] Bernd Lange, 'Comment: How to Make the EU's Anti-coercion Instrument Work', Borderlex, 7 December 2021, https://borderlex.net/2021/12/07/comment-how-to-make-the-eus-anti-coercion-instrument-work/.

[175] Hackenbroich, 'Protecting Europe from Economic Coercion'; AFEP, 'Comments on the Preliminary Impact Assessment Roadmap', French Association of Private Enterprises, March 2021, www.afep.com/wp-content/uploads/2021/05/AFEP-comments-on-IIA-roadmap-for-an-anti-coercition-instrument.pdf, p. 3.

the first step employing diplomatic means will be successful, so that those implications will be mostly avoided.[176] The ACI's deterrent effect stems no less from its broad coverage of the forms of coercion to be addressed, the varied selection of potential countermeasures available, as well as the possibility to react swiftly strengthened by the short deadlines set for the examination (Article 4 (2): four months), determination (Article 5 (1): six months), and Council decision-making (Article 5 (6): eight weeks), although the process is lengthier in case the imposition of countermeasures is needed as a second step.

While the ACI clearly entails certain benefits, the potential costs associated with it might not be worth taking the risks. As will be seen further in this Section, the Commission addresses some of the risks in the proposal and the Impact Assessment Report (such as the threat posed to multilateralism and the risk of escalation through retaliation), showing that it is aware of them. Considering that the legality of the ACI and, in particular, of the measures provided in Annex I under international law rules is questionable, as the non-performance of trading commitments might quite easily come into conflict with EU's WTO or FTA obligations, it could harm multilateralism and the international rules-based order. While the Commission contends that the ACI is in line with international law, even in the event of a finding of violation, the EU could still try to argue that it is forced to protect itself and its interests when others are attacking it and the rules-based order.[177] Although this could be contested, the EU seems to suggest that as a 'good' geopolitical trade actor, it is only taking defensive actions,[178] which, however, is not an argument providing for a legal justification or mere excuse in itself. EU's obligations under international law must remain unaffected in any situation, and even more so when and insofar as other countries respect their obligations.[179] Seemingly addressing the risk that the ACI could threaten multilateralism, the Commission contends that Article 7 ACI Regulation

[176] Impact Assessment Report, p. 21.

[177] Hackenbroich and Zerka, 'Measured Response' (2021).

[178] Sjorre Couvreur, et al., 'The Good Geopolitical Trade Actor? The European Unions Discursive Justification of the Anti-Coercion Instrument' (2022) Special Issue *Perspectivas Journal of Political Science* 68–81 at 76

[179] National Board of Trade Sweden, 'Comments on the Commission's Roadmap for a Mechanism to Deter and Counteract Coercive Action by Non-EU Countries', 17 March 2021, https://ec.europa.eu/info/law/better-regulation/have-your-say/initiatives/12803-Trade-mechanism-to-deter-counteract-coercive-action-by-non-EU-countries/F2000578_en, p. 3.

encouraging international cooperation promotes a multilateral solution.[180] Furthermore, as already stated in Section 6.3.2, the ACI acknowledges in its preamble the importance of the WTO for the rules-based multilateral trading system.[181] Nevertheless, even the adoption of the ACI could erode the credibility of the EU as a staunch supporter of WTO multilateral rules.[182] Even though the Regulation seeks to counter economic coercion in general, as stated in Section 6.3.2.1, it might be argued by other states that with it the EU is in fact circumventing the existing WTO rules, all the more so as the EU came up with a defensive argument based on customary international law. Furthermore, as argued in Section 6.3.2.2, it is likely that specific countermeasures will also violate WTO substantive rules, contributing to the further erosion of the multilateral rules. Finally, resorting to unilateral trade measures to deal with economic coercion could make the EU less interested in reforming the WTO to address such issues, leading to the risk of further WTO redundancy. At least in view of other WTO members, the EU's unilateral capacities may undermine their readiness to positively contribute to WTO reform.

As the ACI could be perceived as protectionist, with the EU contributing even more to the increased weaponization of international trade to which it reacts, the Union could be accused of hypocrisy.[183] Furthermore, the EU actions might invite other countries to engage in similar conduct, thereby turning international trade and investment regimes into fields of war. For example, G7 nations have already launched the Coordination Platform on Economic Coercion to increase their 'collective assessment, preparedness, deterrence and response to economic coercion', and intend to use their existing domestic tools, 'review their effectiveness and develop new ones as needed to deter and counter the use of coercive economic measures'.[184] As shown, the ACI entails a high degree of discretion. While the EU might use cautiously the instrument and react only when third countries put illegal pressure on it, others might adopt legislation entailing a high degree of discretion and adopt measures

[180] ACI Proposal, Explanatory Memorandum, p. 8.

[181] ACI Regulation, Preamble, recital (12).

[182] Weiß and Furculita, 'The EU in Search for Stronger Enforcement Rules' (2020), 884.

[183] ibid, 878, 880.

[184] 'G7 Leaders' Statement on Economic Resilience and Economic Security', 20 May 2023, www.whitehouse.gov/briefing-room/statements-releases/2023/05/20/g7-leaders-statement-on-economic-resilience-and-economic-security/.

against EU alleged coercive measures.[185] For example, the EU has been accused of using economic pressure by imposing certain conditions for trade aid under its GSP+ scheme to influence policies of third countries.[186] Therefore, third countries could also resort to countermeasures against the EU and try to justify them under customary rules of international law, claiming that the EU infringes the principle of non-intervention.

Moreover, although the ACI would allow the EU to protect itself and its Member States, implementing measures under the ACI could still result in damage caused to them and European industries. First, EU companies could be negatively affected, as, due to value chains, they may be dependent on goods, services, or suppliers from third countries to which anti-coercion measures are applied.[187] This risk, however, should be taken into account by the Commission when selecting and designing response measures, as the criterion of 'avoidance or minimisation of negative impact', including on Union actors, is one of the two criteria to be given predominant weight.[188] There is also an increased risk that by imposing countermeasures the dispute will escalate into a 'trade war' through retaliation against the EU. For example, China would most likely respond with retaliation.[189] While the Commission specifically addresses this risk and argues that such an action would not be permitted, since EU's measures would be lawful, the legality of EU's response measures is questionable and disputable, as the preceding discussion has shown. Moreover, the third state against which the EU would take response measures could have a distinct reading of EU's actions and regard them as being illegal. The Commission further argues that countermeasures do not necessarily bring about retaliatory measures, and when they do, in many cases the one or two exchanges of measures are followed by a solution being reached.[190] However, as the empirical study cited in support shows, this is especially true for countries with a certain economical

185 During the consultation process, Sweden also pointed to the risk of others adopting similar measures (National Board of Trade Sweden, 'Comments' (2021), p. 3.

186 Baetens, Bronckers, 'The EU's Anti-Coercion Instrument'; Couvreur, et al., 'The Good Geopolitical Trade Actor?' (2022) 75, 78–79.

187 National Board of Trade Sweden, 'The EU Proposal for an Anti-Coercion Instrument' (2022), p. 5.

188 ACI Regulation, Article 11 (2) (b).

189 Henry S. Gao, 'Will the European Union's New Anti-Coercion Instrument Work with China? (2022) *Research Collection Yong Pung How School of Law* 1–3 at 2.

190 Impact Assessment Report, p. 41.

weight, such as the EU.[191] Accordingly, the EU is hoping that its economical weight can pressure others into stopping economic coercive actions. While the EU could rely on its power and size and could invite other powerful actors to follow its lead, smaller developing countries cannot adopt legislation with the same effect without fearing retaliation. Hence, there is a risk that international law will become ruled by the law of might,[192] with the EU contributing to this. Finally, even if the dispute does not escalate, the countermeasures imposed by the EU could ricochet and result in collateral damage to the EU businesses and consumers.[193] Furthermore, if the EU decides to confront big powers such as the United States or China by imposing anti-coercion measures – a decision that might not be taken lightly[194] – the Union's expectations might still not be met in these cases. Such big players are in no less powerful positions than the EU, so that responsive measures could spiral without subsequent diplomatic solutions being reached. Therefore, the Commission's argument that EU's anti-coercion measures would encourage the third country to work towards reaching a solution is not entirely convincing. This justification seems plausible only with respect to smaller states.

Considering that the economic coercion the ACI seeks to confront could encroach upon any area of EU's or its Member States' competence, it has an increased geopolitical character, which is unusual for European trade instruments. Accordingly, the ACI does not only deal with pure trade matters; it also touches upon aspects that traditionally fall under foreign policy.[195] While foreign policy tools are subject to the unanimity rule, under the ACI, the Council decides on the existence of economic coercion by QMV (Article 5 (5)). Furthermore, even though it can oppose

[191] ibid, p. 41, fn. 86, citing Dursun Peksen and Jin Jeong, 'Coercive Diplomacy and Economic Sanctions Reciprocity: Explaining Targets' Counter-Sanctions' (2021) *Defence and Peace Economics* 1–17.

[192] Rachel Brewster, 'Can International Trade Law Recover? WTO Dispute Settlement: Can We Go Back Again?' (2019) 113 *AJIL Unbound* 61–66 at 65; Weiß and Furculita, 'The EU in Search for Stronger Enforcement Rules' (2020), 880.

[193] Außenhandelsvereinigung des deutschen Einzelhandels e.V., 'Instrument to Deter and Counteract Coercive Actions by Third Countries. Inception Impact Assessment' (2021); European Commission, 'Detailed Results of the Open Public Consultation on an EU Anti-Coercion Instrument', https://content.mlex.com/Attachments/2021-09-08_35902J3VEN821YO7/Anti-coercion%20tool_public%20consultation%20report_EU.pdf, p. 3.

[194] For more, see Wu, 'The EU's Proposed Anti-Coercion Instrument' (2023) 313.

[195] While the legal basis for the foreign investment screening mechanism is also Art. 207 TFEU, it is still governed by the consensus rule, respecting Member States' competence (Dreyer, 'Ostrich Policy'); Crochet, 'The EU Anti-Coercion Mechanism', p. 9.

the Commission's proposals on the Union's response measures by not delivering an opinion in the comitology committee, the Commission's right to appeal to the appeal committee means that in effect the Council could oppose the adoption of a countermeasure by the high bar of a qualified majority voting against it within the appeals committee.[196] Thus, what has started as an initiative of the EP would finally lead to the strengthening of the Commission's position, which could be accused of a 'power grab'. Therefore, the ACI could cause polemics not only at the international level but also at the EU level.

Finally, despite all the above critique, one can accept that the ACI provides the legislative mandate for the EU executive to be able to take any action with a view to bring the coercive state to the negotiation table. Therefore, the adoption of the ACI Regulation was necessary for providing a legal basis to act at the EU level. However, the EU executive must take utmost care that it acts only and truly in line with the EU's international obligations, a requirement of Article 1 (3) ACI, which in practice will not be easy to respect, as the remaining scope of application of the ACI in the area of trade and investment may be effectively limited to those areas and relations which are not subject to WTO and specific bilateral or regional rules. In contrast, if the EU resorts to last-tier measures violating its international obligations to react to economic coercion,[197] it would recognize that the world is turning towards increased unilateralism, and the Union together with it – a point from which it might be more difficult to return to multilateralism and international cooperation.

6.5 Conclusion

In an attempt to respond to the recent increased unilateralism in international trade law, the EU adopted the ACI allowing, as a measure of last resort, the imposition of its own unilateral response measures on states allegedly engaging in economic coercion against the Union or its Members. While the ACI comes to remedy an internal legislative gap, as shown in this chapter, its legality under international law is highly questionable, all the more so as the response measures to be adopted

[196] For more, see Section 6.2.

[197] Baetens and Brockers argue that the ACI 'needs to be adequately equipped to handle its challenges' (Freya Baetens and Marco Bronckers, 'The EU's Anti-Coercion Instrument: A Big Stick for Big Targets' (2021) *EJIL: Talk!*, 19 January 2022, www.ejiltalk.org/the-eus-anti-coercion-instrument-a-big-stick-for-big-targets/.

will mainly relate to the suspension of trading relations which are grossly subject to WTO or specific bilateral treaties.

The Commission bases the instrument on customary international law on countermeasures as a response to the alleged violation of the international principle of non-interference. However, as argued in Section 6.3.1.2, it is not entirely clear if and which economic coercion would constitute a violation of the non-intervention principle for the EU to have an international wrongful act to respond to with lawful countermeasures. As an international actor committed to the international rule of law and in order to increase its chances to act in line with Article 1 (3) ACI requiring that actions be consistent with international law, the EU should respond with last-resort measures only to serious and grave cases of interference and take utmost care to comply with the conditions and limitations imposed on countermeasures under the ILC Draft Articles.

Considering that anti-coercion measures might be imposed against economic coercion violating also multilateral, regional, or bilateral trade rules, the question arises whether these special regimes displace the general rules on countermeasures. Furthermore, anti-coercion measures could be in violation of substantive trade rules. As shown, the ACI was diligently designed not to be a blatant 'as such' violation of Article 23 DSU, but WTO panels could still find evidence other than the statutory language of the Regulation to reach a different conclusion, for example by considering the legislative history of the instrument. Furthermore, the assessment of the Regulation under Article 23 DSU is likely to be different, particularly in instances concerning EU's unilateral measures against coercion simultaneously alleged as violating WTO rules. Accordingly, in these cases, the EU is advised to avoid taking unilateral WTO-inconsistent measures and take the dispute to WTO adjudication. The ACI is likely to be 'as such' legal under WTO substantive rules; however, in case the EU suspends WTO obligations as provided in Annex I to the Regulation to respond to economic coercion, these measures would also violate pertinent substantive WTO rules unless justified. As argued, general customary norms are less likely to be applied within WTO proceedings, while WTO justifications, such as Articles XXI (b) (iii) and XX (a) GATT, would be possible only in case of critical and serious instances of impairment of international relations and, respectively, in case of consideration of the strict conditions that the ACI does not currently give regard to. Despite this, the issue of violating Article 23 DSU by EU's unilateral measure remains. In case of regional and bilateral regimes the ACI's assessment under FTA substantive rules is similar to that under WTO rules, but the legality under procedural rules was shown to be less controversial.

Finally, the Regulation was argued to entail many other potential risks for the EU economy and companies, but especially for multilateralism. Accordingly, the EU is advised to act within the confines established by pertinent international law to avoid contributing to the unilateral weaponization of international trade, the exact phenomenon it seeks to counter. Thus, we propose, for the sake of clarification, that the ACI's main text be amended so that only serious and grave cases of interferences could qualify as economic coercion, and to completely avoid the imposition of response measures in case of simultaneous alleged breaches of more special trade rules, unless trade justifications can lawfully be invoked in the bilateral context to justify substantive violations. Furthermore, the ACI could also explicitly allow the imposition of lawful international measures to provide an internal legal basis for them.

7 Enforcement of the FTA TSD Chapters

Newfound Strength?

7.1 Introduction

The EU's pragmatist turn towards increased robustness, and thus increased enforcement, does not only refer to traditional market access commitments; it also covers the sustainable development chapters included in EU's free trade agreements (FTAs). As established,[1] sustainability figures in one of the three core objectives of the new assertive trade policy were brought about by the EU's Trade Policy Review of 2021.[2] Therein, the strengthening of the enforcement of the trade and sustainable development (TSD) commitments based on the complaints made to the Chief Trade Enforcement Officer (CTEO)[3] and the recent review of the 2008 '15-point Action Plan'[4] on the effective implementation and enforcement of the TSD FTA chapters are mentioned as actions to be taken under one of the six areas to deliver the three core objectives of the Trade Policy Review.[5] As a result, in June 2022 the Commission unveiled its new plan to enhance the contribution of EU trade agreements to sustainable development, focusing *inter alia* on more assertive enforcement of FTA TSD chapters, including through sanctions and extending the dispute settlement compliance stage to the TSD

[1] See Section 2.1.3.

[2] The second objective is entitled 'Shaping Global Rules for a More Sustainable and Fairer Globalisation' (European Commission, Trade Policy Review: An Open, Sustainable and Assertive Trade Policy, COM(2021) 66 final, 18 February 2021, p. 10).

[3] For more on this, see Section 7.3.2.

[4] Non-paper of the Commission services, Feedback and Way Forward on Improving the Implementation and Enforcement of Trade and Sustainable Development Chapters in EU Free Trade Agreements, 26 February 2018, (15-Point Action Plan).

[5] European Commission, Trade Policy Review: An Open, Sustainable and Assertive Trade Policy, COM(2021) 66 final, p. 13.

chapter.[6] Accordingly, the Commission is stepping up the enforcement of its FTA TSD chapters – an advancement that, as will be shown, has been long called for by the EP, some Member States, representatives of civil society, as well as numerous scholars.

In what follows, this chapter will first describe the relevant context (Section 7.2), specifically EU's cooperative approach to TSD enforcement used before the most recent action plan (Section 7.2.1), as well as the calls for stronger enforcement and the long-lasting debate on whether remedies, such as countermeasures, should be available for the enforcement of TSD commitments (Section 7.2.2). It will then consider the latest developments related to the new robustness of EU's approach towards enforcement of the FTA TSD chapters (Section 7.3), in particular the labour dispute under the EU–Korea FTA[7] (Section 7.3.1) and EU's latest steps towards this direction, especially its new TSD action plan (Section 7.3.2). The chapter will then examine whether the desired higher robustness and stronger enforcement can be achieved with the help of public international law tools when sanctions are not available (Section 7.4). Thus, it will be investigated whether the European Commission can resort to countermeasures against alleged TSD violations under the customary norms on countermeasures contained in the International Law Commission Draft Articles on State Responsibility (ILC Draft Articles),[8] even without an express authorization contained in FTAs (Section 7.4.1). Further, it will be analyzed whether Article 60 (1) of the Vienna Convention on the Law of Treaties (VCLT)[9]/ Vienna Convention on the Law of Treaties between States and International Organizations or between International Organizations (VCLTSIO)[10] and the 'essential elements' clauses usually contained in framework agreements could be referred to as a legal basis for the

[6] European Commission, The Power of Trade Partnerships: Together for Green and Just Economic Growth, COM(2022) 409 final, 22 June 2022.

[7] Free Trade Agreement between the European Union and its Member States, of the one part, and the Republic of Korea, of the other part (EU–Korea FTA), OJ EU 2011 No. L 127/6, 14 May 2011.

[8] Draft Articles on Responsibility of States for Internationally Wrongful Acts with Commentaries (ILC Draft Articles with Commentaries), in Report of the International Law Commission on the Work of Its Fifty-third Session, UN Doc. A/56/10, (2001) *Yearbook of the International Law Commission*, vol. II, Part Two.

[9] Vienna Convention on the Law of Treaties, Vienna, 23 May 1969, in force 27 January 1980, 1155 U.N.T.S. 331, (1969) 8 ILM 679, UKTS (1980) 58.

[10] Vienna Convention on the Law of Treaties between States and International Organizations or between International Organizations, 21 March 1986, not yet in force, 25 ILM 543 (1986), UN Doc. A/CONF.129/15.

termination or suspension of the liberalization of trade in total or in part in case of a TSD violation, as suggested by the Court of Justice of the European Union (CJEU) in Opinion 2/15[11] (Section 7.4.2). Finally, the chapter will present other pertinent political considerations related to EU's New TSD Enforcement approach (Section 7.5) and will close with a summing up of the conclusions reached throughout the chapter and weigh in on the latest developments in strengthening the enforcement of EU's FTA TSD chapters (Section 7.6).

7.2 Relevant Context

7.2.1 EU's Former Cooperative Approach towards FTA TSD Enforcement

The EU has long realized the possibility of using trade policy instruments to promote sustainable development around the world.[12] The importance of promoting sustainability in EU's FTAs has for long figured in Commission's Communications.[13] EU–CARIFORUM Economic Partnership Agreement (EPA)[14] was the first agreement to include TSD commitments. Since 2011, after the EU–Korea FTA, TSD chapters have been incorporated in all EU's trade agreements.[15] However, in order for EU's sustainable development–related values to be promoted not only on paper but also in practice, implementation and enforcement mechanisms are necessary. Until EU's most recent revision of its approach towards TSD enforcement, the Commission included in its FTAs special

[11] CJEU, Opinion 2/15, Free Trade Agreement between the European Union and the Republic of Singapore, ECLI:EU:C:2017:376, 16 May 2017.

[12] See Sections 2.1.1 and 2.1.3.

[13] Commission's Communications 'Global Europe: Competing in the World – A Contribution to the EU's Growth and Jobs Strategy' COM(2006) 567 final, pp. 2, 8, 9; 'Trade, Growth and Development: Tailoring Trade and Investment Policy for Countries Most in Need', COM(2012) 22 final, pp. 3 ff.; 'Trade for All: Towards a More Responsible Trade and Investment Policy' COM(2015) 497 final, pp. 10 ff.

[14] Economic Partnership Agreement between the CARIFORUM States, of the one part, and the European Community and its Member States, of the other part, OJ EU 2008 No. L 289/3, 30 October 2008.

[15] Thus, the EU is currently implementing 11 agreements with TSD chapters. For an analysis of TSD chapters in EU FTAs since 2011, see Jean Baptiste Velut, et al., 'Comparative Analysis of Trade and Sustainable Development Provisions in Free Trade Agreements' (2022) *Trade Policy Hub*, London School of Economics and Political Science Consulting, www.lse.ac.uk/business/consulting/assets/documents/TSD-Final-Report-Feb-2022.pdf.

cooperative dispute settlement mechanisms dedicated to solving matters arising under the TSD chapters. The only exception was the EU–CARIFORUM EPA, which permits recourse to the general dispute settlement in case of TSD breaches (albeit explicitly excluding the possibility to suspend trade concessions).[16] In what follows, the present section will describe the cooperative approach that the EU adopted towards FTA TSD enforcement before the June 2022 revision, which is present in such agreements as EU–Korea FTA, EU–Canada Trade Agreement (CETA)[17], or EU–Japan Economic Partnership Agreement (JEPA)[18]. As will be shown, these special mechanisms diverge from the general FTA dispute settlement mechanisms in terms of civil society involvement, degree of cooperation required between the parties, monitoring of the implementation of the panel of experts reports, as well as the availability of sanctions.

Under the TSD special dispute settlement mechanisms from FTAs concluded until 2022, in the event of disagreement, parties must engage in government consultations as a first step,[19] which under some FTAs could be further discussed in the intergovernmental TSD committees comprising senior officials of the parties.[20] In several FTAs, the Domestic Advisory Groups (DAGs), composed of domestic independent representative organizations of civil society, could also provide advice to the TSD Committees.[21] When parties do not manage to solve the dispute, at the request of one of them, a panel of experts with knowledge or expertise in labour or environmental law may be convened to examine the matter.[22] Within a certain time frame the panel should issue a report to the parties,

[16] EU–CARIFORUM EPA, Art. 213 (2); For more on the EU–CARIFORUM EPA, see Axel Marx, et al., *Dispute Settlement in the Trade and Sustainable Development Chapters of EU Trade Agreements* (2017) Leuven Centre for Global Governance Studies, https://ghum.kuleuven.be/ggs/publications/books/final-report-9-february-def.pdf, pp. 24–25.

[17] Comprehensive Economic and Trade Agreement (CETA) between Canada, of the one part, and the European Union and its Member States, of the other part, OJ EU 2017 No. L 11/23, 14 January 2017.

[18] Agreement between the European Union and Japan for an Economic Partnership (JEPA), OJ EU 2018 No. L 330/3, 27 December 2018.

[19] EU–Korea FTA, Art. 13.14; CETA, Art. 23.9; JEPA, Art. 16.17.

[20] EU–Korea FTA, Arts. 13.12, 13.14 (3); CETA, Art. 23.9 (4); Free Trade Agreement between the European Union and the Socialist Republic of Viet Nam (EU–Vietnam FTA), OJ EU 2020 No. L 186/3, 12 June 2020, Art. 13.6 (4).

[21] EU–Korea FTA, Art. 13.14 (4); EU–Vietnam FTA, Art. 13.6 (5); Association Agreement between the European Union and the European Atomic Energy Community and their Member States, of the one part, and the Republic of Moldova, of the other part (EU–Moldova AA), OJ EU 2014 No. L 260/4, 30 August 2018, Art. 378 (5).

[22] EU–Korea FTA, Art. 13.15 (1); CETA, Art. 23.10 (1); EU–Vietnam FTA, Art. 13.7 (1).

usually made public, containing its findings and recommendations.[23] The panel may receive submissions from stakeholders, such as DAGs or international organizations.[24] After the panel issues a report in which it determines that a party has not conformed with its obligations, the parties may be required to discuss and identify appropriate measures or actions taking into account the panel's recommendations,[25] or to make best efforts to accommodate the advice or recommendations of the panel.[26] In some agreements the parties may also decide upon a mutually satisfactory plan.[27] Therefore, under the FTAs concluded before the most recent TSD review, the recommendations contained in the panels of experts' reports do not have a binding character.[28] Parties are only required to take into account the recommendations during discussions or to make best efforts to accommodate them, but there is no mandate to strictly follow them. Moreover, the EU–UK Trade and Cooperation Agreement (TCA)[29] explicitly provides that 'if the Panel makes recommendations in its report, the respondent Party does not need to follow these recommendations in ensuring conformity with this Agreement'.[30] The

[23] JEPA, Art. 16.18 (5); EU–Vietnam FTA, Art. 13.17 (8); Free trade Agreement between the European Union and the Republic of Singapore (EU–Singapore FTA), OJ EU 2019 No. L 294/3, 14 November 2019, Art. 12.17 (8); Association Agreement between the European Union and the European Atomic Energy Community and their Member States, of the one part, and Georgia, of the other part (EU–Georgia AA), OJ EU 2014 No. L 261/4, 30 August 2014, Art. 243 (7).

[24] EU–Korea FTA, Art. 13.15 (2); JEPA, Art. 16.18 (3).

[25] Agreement establishing an Association between the European Union and its Member States, on the one hand, and Central America on the other (EU–Central American AA), OJ EU 2012 No. L 346/3, 15 December 2012, Art. 301 (3); Art. 285 (4); JEPA, Art. 16.18 (6); EU–Vietnam FTA, Art. 13.17 (9); EU–Singapore FTA, Art. 12.17 (9).

[26] EU–Korea FTA, Art. 13.15 (2); Association Agreement between the European Union and its Member States, of the one part, and Ukraine, of the other part (EU–UA AA), OJ EU 2014 No. L 161/3, 29 May 2014, Art. 301 (2).

[27] For example, CETA, Art. 24.15 (11); Trade Agreement between the European Union and its Member States, of the one part, and Colombia and Peru, of the other part, OJ EU 2012 No. L 354/3, 21 December 2012, Protocol of Accession to the Trade Agreement between the European Union and its Member States, of the one part, and Colombia and Peru, of the other part, to take account of the accession of Ecuador, OJ EU 2016 No. L 356/3, 24 December 2016, (EU–Colombia/Peru/Ecuador FTA), Art. 285 (4); EU–Central America AA, Art. 301 (3).

[28] Denise Prévost and Iveta Alexovičová, 'Mind the Compliance Gap: Managing Trustworthy Partnerships for Sustainable Development in the European Union's Free Trade Agreements' (2019) 6 (3) *International Journal of Public Law and Policy* 236–269 at 250.

[29] Trade and Cooperation Agreement between the European Union and the European Atomic Energy Community, of the one part, and the United Kingdom of Great Britain and Northern Ireland, of the other part (EU–UK TCA), OJ EU 2021 No. L 149/10, 30 April 2021.

[30] EU–UK TCA, Art. 409 (9).

defendant could also be required to inform the TSD Committee or the DAGs about the actions it intends to take.[31] The monitoring of the implementation of the panel's recommendations is the responsibility of the TSD Committees and civil society mechanisms, such as DAGs or Civil Society Fora (composed of representatives of civil society organizations established in both parties, including those participating in DAGs), which are allowed to submit observations to the responsible Committees.[32] Unlike the general dispute settlement mechanisms, the special TSD ones do not provide compliance-stage rules that would require the party found in violation to implement the panel report within a certain time frame and report about it, subject to panel review. Moreover, the EU FTAs concluded before June 2022 do not allow the imposition of trade remedies in case of non-compliance with the recommendations of the panel of experts. Accordingly, EU's previous model of TSD enforcement has been relying on the pressure that the EU can exert using its leverage, as well as on the pressure exerted by civil society bodies.[33] Yet, the EU–UK TCA represents an exception, indicating EU's readiness to move away from its approach based on cooperation already at that point in time by allowing remedies in case of disputes on the interpretation and application of the non-regression chapters on labour, social standards, environment, and climate,[34] and permitting parties to take rebalancing measures to tackle situations in which significant divergences between the parties arise in the areas of sustainable development.[35]

Thus, with limited exceptions, the EU's former approach to enforcement in its FTA TSD chapters has been based solely on increased

[31] CETA, Art. 24.15 (11); JEPA, Art.16.8 (6); EU–Moldova AA, Art. 379 (8).

[32] CETA, Art; JEPA, Art.16.8 (6); EU–Singapore FTA, Art. 12.17 (9); EU–Georgia AA, Art. 243 (8).

[33] Nevertheless, as Prévost and Alexovičová note, the 'shaming' mechanism provided in EU FTAs is less effective, since TSD Committees meet rather seldom and there are no rules on publishing the minutes of the meetings (Prévost and Alexovičová, 'Mind the Compliance Gap' (2019) 250–251). Pacheco Restrepo points to the Peru forest protection dispute as an example of how pressure during consultations can be successful (Yilly Vanessa Pacheco Restrepo, 'Enforcement Practice Under Preferential Trade Agreements: Environmental Consultations and Submissions on Environmental Enforcement Matters in the US–Peru TPA' (2019) 46 (3) *LIEI* 247–262 at 260). Zamfir also marks the limited use of pressure from civil society on less democratic governments (Ionel Zamfir, 'Labour Rights in EU Trade Agreements towards Stronger Enforcement' (2022) EPRS Briefing, www.europarl.europa.eu/RegData/etudes/BRIE/2022/698800/EPRS_BRI(2022)698800_EN.pdf, p. 11).

[34] EU–UK TCA, Art. 410. Velut et al., 'Comparative Analysis' (2022), p. 63, fn. 123. The TCA is, however, a specific agreement focused on level playing field, taking into consideration the closeness of the EU and UK markets and their regulatory integration.

[35] EU–UK TCA, Art. 411.

cooperation, discussions, involvement of civil society at different stages of dispute settlement, and potential reputational pressure, without the possibility to resort to sanctions as in case of general FTA dispute settlement. This model has been termed a 'managerial', 'cooperative', or 'cooperation-based' one, including by the Commission itself,[36] which, unlike the sanction-oriented model, does not rely on the assumption that sanctions – which create costs and remove benefits – are needed for compliance.[37] EU FTA TSD chapters that are in force contain many broad provisions formulated in a hortatory and co-operative language aimed at raising the existing standards of labour and environmental protection in the parties and sometimes only 'best efforts' commitments to ratify ILO conventions.[38] Due to the aspirational nature of these commitments, their enforcement with the help of a sanction-based model was claimed to be more difficult.[39]

7.2.2 Stronger Enforcement of FTA TSD Chapters: A Heated Debate That Lasted for Years

Calls for stronger enforcement and increased robustness of TSD chapters have not been made just recently in the context of EU's new trade policy focusing on increased robustness. As will be explained in this section, the lack of teeth of the FTA TSD chapters has long been criticized by the EP, some Member States, several civil society representatives, and multiple academics. The question whether to introduce the possibility to impose sanctions in the event of non-compliance with the recommendations of the panel of experts has been actively discussed in academic writings and

[36] European Commission, The Power of Trade Partnerships, COM(2022) 409 final, p. 11.

[37] Prévost and Alexovičová, 'Mind the Compliance Gap' (2019) 241; Karolina Zurek, 'From "Trade *and* Sustainability" to "Trade *for* Sustainability" in EU External Trade Policy', in A. Bakardjieva Engelbrekt, et al. (eds.), *The European Union in a Changing World Order: Interdisciplinary European Studies* (Cham: Palgrave Macmillan, 2020) 115–143, p. 125; Gesa Kübek, 'Sustainable Development Chapters in EU FTAs and Dispute Settlement: Lessons Learned from Ukraine – Wood Products and Korea – Labour Rights', in Elaine Fahey, Isabella Mancini (eds.), *Understanding the EU as a Good Global Actor: Ambitions, Values and Metrics* (Cheltenham: Edward Elgar, 2022), p. 277.

[38] Marco Bronckers and Giovanni Gruni, 'Retooling the Sustainability Standards in EU Free Trade Agreements' (2021) 24 *JIEL* 25–51 at 26, 33. For how a best-effort commitment to ratify core ILO labour conventions was treated during dispute settlement, see Section 7.3.1.

[39] Gracia Marín Durán, 'Sustainable Development Chapters in EU Free Trade Agreements: Emerging Compliance Issues' (2020) 57 *CMLRev* 1031–1068 at 1063, 1067.

also during Commission consultations – a debate that lasted for years and which will be presented below.

As early as 2010, the EP advocated in favour of allowing recourse to the general FTA dispute settlement mechanism on equal footing with other parts of the agreement and providing fines or temporary suspension of certain benefits in case of aggravated breaches of sustainable development standards.[40] Since then, the issue has been regularly discussed within the European Council and benefitted from the increased attention of the civil society.[41] In 2017, after the signature of CETA, several Member States (the Netherlands, Belgium, Sweden, Luxembourg, Finland), through their trade ministers, expressed calls in favour of strengthening the enforcement of EU's FTA TSD chapters.[42] Given the mounting pressure, the Commission published a Non-Paper in 2017, launching a discussion with all the stakeholders on how to improve the implementation of FTA sustainability chapters and also containing some possible options as a basis for discussions, including using more often the existing TSD mechanism or introducing the possibility to impose sanctions.[43] Despite many calls in favour of the last option, including from NGOs, there were still many in favour of the existing managerial mechanism, such as business associations. Thus, following up, the Commission issued another Non-Paper in 2018 on a '15-point Action Plan', in which it established that there was 'a clear consensus that the implementation of TSD chapters should be stepped-up and improved', but the majority still supported the cooperation-based model of enforcement, and in 'the absence of consensus on a sanctions-based model' it was impossible to move to such an approach.[44] Hence, the Commission services suggested a set of 15 concrete and practicable actions to be taken to revamp the TSD chapters under four headings.[45] The Commission pledged to regularly review together with EU institutions and the stakeholders the effectiveness of the implementation of the TSD chapters and to examine whether further measures are needed, at least within five years.[46]

[40] European Parliament Resolution of 25 November 2010 on Human Rights and Social and Environmental Standards in International Trade Agreements (2009/2219(INI)), para. 22 (c).

[41] Kateřina Hradilová and Ondřej Svoboda, 'Sustainable Development Chapters in the EU Free Trade Agreements: Searching for Effectiveness' (2018) 52 (6) *JWT* 1019–1042 at 1028.

[42] ibid, 1030.

[43] Non-Paper of the Commission Services, Trade and Sustainable Development (TSD) Chapters in EU Free Trade Agreements (FTAs), 11 July 2017, pp. 5–9.

[44] 15-point Action Plan, pp. 2–3. [45] ibid, pp. 4–12. [46] ibid, p. 3.

After the publication of the 15-point Action Plan, the Parliament continued to urge the Commission to consider proposals on how to strengthen the enforcement of TSD commitments,[47] introducing remedies in FTA TSD chapters, such as sanctions, and making certain international treaties, such as the Paris Agreement,[48] essential elements of the FTAs.[49] France and the Netherlands in a 2020 Non-Paper proposed the introduction of staged implementation of tariff reduction linked to the implementation of TSD commitments, including the possibility to withdraw those specific tariff lines in case of TSD breaches and asked for making the Paris Agreement an essential element of the FTAs.[50]

The robustness of TSD dispute settlement mechanisms has also been the subject of numerous academic writings. There are multiple works that have been advocating in favour of subjecting the TSD commitments to the general FTA dispute settlement mechanisms, arguing that TSD commitments should be treated on equal footing with the market access commitments.[51] The main difference between the special cooperation-based and general dispute settlement mechanisms has been the non-binding character of the recommendations contained in the panel reports and, consequently, also the absence of the possibility to impose sanctions in case of non-compliance with those recommendations. Many authors expressed themselves in favour of introducing the possibility to impose sanctions under the special TSD mechanism as a last resort, similar to the sanction-based approach adopted in the US and Canada FTA TSD chapters.[52] The proposal to introduce sanctions was based on the

[47] INTA Report 2020, p. 16; European Parliament Resolution of 7 October 2020 on the Implementation of the Common Commercial Policy – Annual Report 2018 (2019/2197 (INI)), para. 49.

[48] Paris Agreement to the United Nations Framework Convention on Climate Change, 12 December 2015, T.I.A.S. No. 16-1104.

[49] European Parliament Resolution of 9 June 2021 on the EU Biodiversity Strategy for 2030: Bringing nature back into our lives (2020/2273(INI)), paras. 169, 172.

[50] Non-paper from the Netherlands and France on Trade, Social Economic Effects and Sustainable Development, 8 May 2020.

[51] Marco Bronckers and Giovanni Gruni, 'Taking the Enforcement of Labour Standards in the EU's Free Trade Agreements Seriously' (2019) 56 *CMLRev* 1591–1622 at 1610; Peter-Tobias Stoll, Henner Gött, and Patrick Abel, 'Model Labour Chapter for European Union Trade Agreements' (2020) *Friedrich Ebert Stiftung*, http://library.fes.de/pdf-files/bueros/singapur/16089.pdf; Bronckers and Gruni, 'Retooling the Sustainability Standards' (2021) 36–37.

[52] For example, Axel Marx, Franz Ebert, and Nicolas Hachez, 'Dispute Settlement for Labour Provisions in EU Free Trade Agreements: Rethinking Current Approaches' (2017) 5(4) *Politics and Governance* 49–59 at 50; Paolo Mazzotti, 'Stepping Up the Enforcement of Trade and Sustainable Development Chapters in the European Union's Free Trade Agreements:

idea that they would make the enforcement of the TSD commitments contained in FTAs more credible.[53] Those against, however, argued that sanctions are counterproductive, as they could harm bilateral collaborative relations necessary for achieving regulatory convergence,[54] and could go against sustainability, by hurting the most vulnerable and contributing to social injustice.[55] Furthermore, sanctions have been said to be usually acceptable only with respect to less aspirational substantive TSD norms, which could make more difficult the signature of FTAs with deeper commitments, and are considered by some as inappropriate, due to the difficulty of quantifying the damage caused by TSD breaches.[56] Even in the ILO context, sanctions are rarely used, the focus being on reporting and following up on recommendations.[57] Additionally, sanctions are generally known for entailing such negative effects as hurting also the country imposing it, increasing the risk of counter-retaliation, and being less effective in the hands of smaller economies.[58]

Although sanctions are clearly not ideal, they may be a necessary last option when all other efforts fail. There seems to be no evidence that

Reconsidering the Debate on Sanctions' (2021) *European Law Institute*, www.europeanlawinstitute.eu/fileadmin/user_upload/p_eli/YLA_Award/Submission_ELI_Young_Lawyers_Award_Paolo_Mazzotti_2021.pdf; Bronckers and Gruni, 'Retooling the Sustainability Standards' (2021) 37–39. On the US model, see Kathleen Claussen, 'Reimagining Trade-Plus Compliance: The Labor Story' (2020) 23 *JIEL* 25–43 at 33.

53 Clara Portela, 'Enforcing Respect for Labour Standards with Targeted Sanctions' (2018) *Friedrich Ebert Stiftung*, http://library.fes.de/pdf-files/bueros/singapur/14689.pdf; James Harrison, et al., 'Labour Standards Provisions in EU Free Trade Agreements: Reflections on the European Commission's Reform Agenda' (2019) 18(4) *WTRev* 635–657 at 652; Zurek, 'From "Trade *and* Sustainability" to "Trade *for* Sustainability"' (2020), p. 125.

54 Prévost and Alexovičová, 'Mind the Compliance Gap' (2019) 255.

55 ibid, 241; Jan Orbie, 'EU Trade Policy Meets Geopolitics: What about Trade Justice?' (2021) 26(2) *EFARev* 197–202 at 200; Ji Sun Han, 'The EU-Korea Labour Dispute: A Critical Analysis of the EU's Approach' (2021) 26(4) *EFARev* 531–552 at 549.

56 15-point Action Plan, p. 3; Sam Lowe, 'The EU Should Reconsider Its Approach to Trade and Sustainable Development' (2019) Centre for European Reform, www.cer.eu/sites/default/files/insight_SL_31.10.19.pdf, p.4; Bronckers and Gruni, 'Taking the Enforcement' (2019) 1616; Bronckers and Gruni, 'Retooling the Sustainability Standards' (2021) 33; Demy van 't Wout, 'The Enforceability of the Trade and Sustainable Development Chapters of the European Union's Free Trade Agreements' (2022) 20 *Asia Europe Journal* 81–98.

57 Laurence Boisson de Chazournes and Jaemin Lee, 'The European Union–Korea Free Trade Agreement Sustainable Development Proceeding: Reflections on a Ground-Breaking Dispute' (2022) 23 *JWIT* 329–346 at 342.

58 Marín Durán, 'Sustainable Development Chapters in EU Free Trade Agreements' (2020) 1059; Bronckers and Gruni, 'Retooling the Sustainability Standards' (2021) 39. While under the GSP the withdrawal of benefits is allowed, the EU has been reluctant to resort to such measures.

broader yet vaguer TSD commitments produce more meaningful outcomes, while financial penalties can be imposed and quantified when, for example, EU Member States fail to comply with environmental norms.[59] Moreover, in spite of these counterarguments, the possibility to impose sanctions has been available in case of breaches of other FTA chapters, and the EU does allow the withdrawal of tariff concessions, which is a form of sanctions, in case of violations of sustainable development standards under its Generalized Scheme of Preferences (GSP).[60] Therefore, avoiding any type of sanction towards TSD chapters seems unwarranted.[61] Furthermore, including the possibility to impose sanctions does not entail frequently making use of it in practice.[62] As an argument against allowing sanctions, the US unsuccessful claim against Guatemala under the Dominican Republic – Central America FTA (CAFTA-DR) has been often brought as an example.[63] However, the usefulness of this example for the present debate is questionable, as the reason behind this outcome was the US failure to prove that Guatemala's actions were taken 'in a manner affecting trade'.[64] Hence, this case does not provide the necessary evidence to speak in favour or against using sanctions in case of non-compliance with panel of experts' recommendations. Despite the disadvantages that sanctions entail when employed for enforcing sustainability commitments, the proposal to insert them in EU FTA TSD chapters has gained more traction, and, as will be shown, their

[59] Bronckers and Gruni, 'Retooling the Sustainability Standards' (2021) 33, 39, 44.

[60] Regulation (EU) No 978/2012 of the European Parliament and of the Council of 25 October 2012 applying a scheme of generalised tariff preferences and repealing Council Regulation (EC) No 732/2008, OJ EU 2012 No. L 303/1, 31 October 2012.

[61] For more, see Mazzotti, 'Stepping Up the Enforcement' (2021), pp. 13–14; Bronckers and Gruni, 'Retooling the Sustainability Standards' (2021) 39–40.

[62] The general FTA dispute settlement mechanisms have also been used in some instances, despite the possibility to impose sanctions.

[63] Final Report of the Panel, In the Matter of Guatemala – Issues Relating to the Obligations Under Article 16.2.1(a) of the CAFTA-DR, 14 June 2017, https://ustr.gov/sites/default/files/files/agreements/FTA/CAFTA-DR/Guatemala%20Final%20Report%20of%20the%20Panel.pdf.

[64] Harrison, et al., 'Labour Standards Provisions' (2019) 653; Mattia Colli Vignarelli, 'The European Commission Trade Policy Review: The Effectiveness of Sustainable Development Chapters in EU FTAs' (2021) 6(1) *European Papers* 1–5 at 4. To avoid the same situation in future disputes, the United States addressed this issue in the Agreement between the United States of America, the United Mexican States, and Canada (USMCA), in force 1 July 2020, and made it a rebuttable presumption that a labour measure affects trade and investment. Additionally, it added special provisions, including on a special dispute settlement process, to tackle freedom of association violations in specific workplaces (Velut, et al., 'Comparative Analysis' (2022), p. 23).

introduction was considered anew and resulted in a partial change of EU's approach. Beside the proposal to allow sanctions in the form of suspension of trade concessions and obligations, scholars have additionally tabled other proposals to make EU FTA TSD chapters more robust, which received less attention, such as the introduction of financial penalties and targeted sanctions,[65] allowing private complaints,[66] or tightening up the language of the commitments.[67]

Along the calls for amending the TSD chapters to ensure stronger enforcement, the Commission has also been asked not to shy away from using the existing mechanisms. For example, under EU–Korea FTA, the Civil Society Forum has raised the question of ratification of four fundamental International Labor Organization (ILO) conventions by Korea multiple times since 2012.[68] Yet, the Commission triggered the dispute settlement mechanism only in December 2018 – when the first dispute under EU FTA TSD chapters, described in detail in Section 3.1, was initiated.

Thus, for years the Commission has been called to strengthen the enforcement of the FTA TSD chapters, either through suggested amendments or through pleas not to hesitate to use its cooperative model. The introduction of sanctions, however, proved to be a contentious issue, showing that even if it were possible, due to their potential negative consequences, a state should use them carefully and only *exceptionally* – as a last resort when other means fail.

7.3 New Robustness of EU's Approach towards FTA TSD Chapters

Before this section explores in more detail the recent shift in the Commission's approach towards FTA TSD chapters, we will first shed

65 Portela, 'Enforcing Respect for Labour Standards' (2018), pp. 10–13; Bronckers and Gruni, 'Taking the Enforcement' (2019) 1616–1617; Stoll, Gött, and Abel, 'Model Labour Chapter' (2020), pp. 36–37; Bronckers and Gruni, 'Retooling the Sustainability Standards' (2021) 45–48; The Greens/European Free Alliance (EFA) Group in the EP examined the possibility of introducing bans on goods produced by means of forced or child labour, including under EU FTA rules. Nevertheless, the paper suggested that a separate dedicate instrument addressing this issue would be preferable. ('Towards an Import Ban on Forced Labor and Modern Slavery', Discussion paper commissioned by the Greens/EFA Group in the European Parliament, February 2021, www.annacavazzini.eu/wp-content/uploads/Towards_an_EU_import_ban_on_forced_labour_and_modern_slavery_February.pdf).

66 Bronckers and Gruni, 'Taking the Enforcement' (2019) 1598–1609; Stoll, Gött, and Abel, 'Model Labour Chapter' (2020), p. 38.

67 Bronckers and Gruni, 'Taking the Enforcement' (2019) 50.

68 Hradilová and Svoboda, 'Sustainable Development Chapters' (2018) 1027.

light on the EU–Korea TSD FTA dispute, as the analysis of the arbitration panel report delivers insights into the qualities of the existing settlement mechanisms and indicates ways for improvement.

7.3.1 The Labour Dispute under EU–Korea FTA

As South Korea had not ratified four out of eight fundamental ILO labour conventions, the Commission made continuous efforts to achieve progress through consultations since the start of the implementation of the FTA, constantly raising this issue during TSD Committee meetings and mentioning it in the Civil Society Forum's statements.[69] Although some improvement was reported on certain issues,[70] due to lack of progress in other areas, eight years after the EU–Korea FTA's entry into force, in December 2018, the Commission requested consultations under the TSD chapter. This marked the first time the EU initiated dispute settlement procedures under its FTA TSD chapters and under its FTAs in general. With this dispute the Commission finally responded to the calls to use more assertively the existing tools and displayed its readiness to step up the enforcement of the TSD chapters.[71] Furthermore, this dispute illustrated how the proactive DAGs, which have a strong collaborative potential and initially could have been blamed for weakening the TSD dispute settlement, in the case at hand prompted the EU to act and initiate proceedings under the EU–Korea FTA TSD chapter.[72] Additionally, it furnishes evidence on how the cooperative approach works in practice, despite the absence of possibility to impose sanctions.

In its request to establish a panel, the EU made two sets of claims: (1) concerning four measures in the form of specific provisions of Korea's Trade Union and Labour Relations Adjustment Act (TULRAA), which the EU claimed that are inconsistent with the commitment contained in Article 13.4.3 EU–Korea FTA, namely to respect, promote, and realize, in parties' laws and practices, the principles concerning fundamental

[69] María J. García, 'Sanctioning Capacity in Trade and Sustainability Chapters in EU Trade Agreements: The EU–Korea Case' (2022) 10(1) *Politics and Governance* 58–67at 62.

[70] Aleydis Nissen, 'Not That Assertive: The EU's Take on Enforcement of Labour Obligations in Its Free Trade Agreement with South Korea' (2022) 33 *EJIL* 607–630 at 610.

[71] Still, Nissen, for example, criticizes the EU for not raising certain controversial issues, such as those related to Korea's export sectors (Nissen, 'Not That Assertive' (2022) 624–625).

[72] Tonia Novitz, 'The Role of the EU in Making "Sustainable" Labour Linkages in Contemporary Trade: Is Being "Assertive" also "Good"?', in Elaine Fahey and Isabella Mancini (eds.), *Understanding the EU as a Good Global Actor* (Cheltenham: Edward Elgar, 2022), p. 129.

rights; and (2) concerning Korea's insufficient efforts towards the ratification of the core ILO Conventions, since the last sentence of Article 13.4.3 FTA provides that 'the Parties will make continued and sustained efforts towards ratifying the fundamental ILO Conventions'.[73]

Since Korea raised a jurisdictional objection on the grounds that the scope of the TSD chapter was limited only to 'trade-related aspects of labour', the panel needed to establish first whether it had jurisdiction. Article 13.2.1 EU–Korea FTA provides that '[e]xcept as otherwise provided in this Chapter, this Chapter applies to measures [...] affecting trade-related aspects of labour, and environmental issues'. After examining the ordinary meaning of the terms of Article 13.4.3 read in their context and in light of the object and purpose of Chapter 13, the panel established that the phrase 'except as otherwise provided' from Article 13.2.1 clearly applied to this article.[74] Hence, there was no need to show that the measures considered were affecting trade-related aspects of labour under Article 13.4.3. This conclusion is in stark contrast to the one reached by the panel in US–Guatemala dispute under CAFTA–DR FTA, where the US claim was unsuccessful because of the failure to show that the measure was taken in a manner affecting trade.[75] Furthermore, the panel established that the CAFTA–DR panel report was not pertinent to the EU–Korea case, as the provision dealt with in that dispute had a different wording and, especially, context.[76] The panel did not stop there; it further stated that its findings did not entail that the measures in question were not connected to trade. In fact, it established that fundamental labour rights are 'inherently related' to trade under the EU–Korea FTA.[77] The panel's findings in respect to the 'affecting trade' test are probably the most notable ones,[78] solidifying the EU's pursuit of sustainable development

[73] Report of the Panel of Experts (EU–Korea FTA Panel Report), Panel of Experts Proceeding Constituted under Article 13.15 of the EU-Korea Free Trade Agreement, 20 January 2021, para. 55. The Report is available at https://policy.trade.ec.europa.eu/enforcement-and-protection/dispute-settlement/bilateral-disputes/korea-labour-commitments_en.

[74] ibid, paras. 63, 68.

[75] Rebecca Walker, 'The "Trade-Related" Conundrum of the EU–Korea FTA Expert Panel: Are FTAs a Novel Forum to Enforce Sustainable Development Goals?', International Institute for Sustainable Development, 7 October 2021, www.iisd.org/itn/en/2021/10/07/the-trade-related-conundrum-of-the-eu-korea-fta-expert-panel-are-ftas-a-novel-forum-to-enforce-sustainable-development-goals//.

[76] EU–Korea FTA Panel Report, ibid, paras. 90–93.

[77] ibid, paras. 94–95.

[78] A view also shared by Aleydis Nissen, 'And So It Begins: Trade and Sustainable Development Recommendations by a Panel of Experts under a European Union Free Trade Agreement' (2021) 7 *International Labor Rights Case Law* 257–262 at 258.

through FTAs.[79] Sanction-based mechanisms have been criticized for usually establishing a high threshold for proving that measures are 'affecting trade'.[80] Thus, the panel created a new approach in the EU–Korea FTA dispute, different from the one adopted under CAFTA–DR,[81] potentially alleviating concerns that it would be difficult to comply with the burden of proof necessary for labour claims to succeed in a TSD dispute settlement.[82] Consequently, after this report, policy makers and scholars may be less skeptical with respect to initiating TSD disputes under EU FTAs and less keen on pursuing long-lasting discussions.

In respect to the claims on conformity with the first sentence of Article 13.4.3 EU–Korea FTA, the panel found that several TULRAA provisions did not comply with it.[83] With respect to the claim under the last sentence of Article 13.4.3, the panel concluded that it 'does not set a specific target date or a particular milestone for the ratification process: the provision merely states that the Parties should make 'continued and sustained efforts towards ratification'.[84] Considering this finding and that the obligation at issue was not of result but of effort, the panel established that although Korea's efforts were 'less than optimal', and 'there is still much to be done', they satisfied the legal threshold of the provision.[85] This finding was criticized for providing incentives to EU's partners to delay the ratification of ILO Conventions for as much as ten years if there are at least some efforts being made.[86] Therefore, it could be said that the panel established a precedent for an interpretation of the last sentence of Article 13.4.3 that is narrower than what the EU hoped for, offering a justification for the calls to use more stringent language in TSD chapters, particularly introducing time-bound commitments and milestones, in order to improve their enforceability.[87]

[79] Tonia Novitz, 'Enforceable Social Clauses in Trade Agreements with "Bite"? Implications of the EU–South Korea Panel of Experts Report of 20 January 2021' (2021) 6 European Trade Union Institute Policy Brief, www.etui.org/publications/enforceable-social-clauses-trade-agreements-bite, p. 4.

[80] Prévost and Alexovičová, 'Mind the Compliance Gap' (2019) 242.

[81] Walker, 'The "Trade-Related" Conundrum' (2021).

[82] However, there are authors criticizing this broad approach adopted by the panel. See, for example, Desiree LeClercq, 'The Panel Report under the EU-Korea Trade Agreement Concerning Labor Practices: What Are the Purposes of Trade Agreements as They Relate to the ILO's Fundamental Labor Rights?', IELP Blog, 8 February 2021, https://ielp.worldtradelaw.net/2021/02/guest-post-the-panel-report-under-the-eu-korea-trade-agreement-concerning-labor-practices-what-are-t.html.

[83] EU–Korea FTA Panel Report, paras. 175, 196, 208, 227.

[84] ibid, para. 276.

[85] ibid, paras. 288, 291, 292.

[86] Sun Han, 'The EU-Korea Labour Dispute' (2021) 543.

[87] For example, see Position Paper of the Green MEPs of the International Trade Committee on the Review of the 15-Point Action Plan, www.greens-efa.eu/files/assets/docs/20220428_inta_green_position_paper_on_tsd_def.pdf, p. 8.

Although under Article 13.15.2 EU–Korea FTA the parties are only required to 'make their best efforts to accommodate advice or recommendations of the Panel of Experts', the progress in implementing the panel report has already been mentioned as evidence of the effectiveness of the cooperation-based approach by business associations and even the Commission itself.[88] South Korea ratified three fundamental ILO conventions in April 2021, which entered into force in April 2022. The Commission seems to credit the TSD enforcement for these ratifications.[89]Although the Korean government claimed that the consultations with the EU had no impact on the ratification process,[90] it initiated the formal procedure for ratifications after unsuccessful consultations with the EU in January 2019 and after receiving a letter from the Commissioner Malmström in which the intention to request the establishment of a panel in the event of no substantive progress by Korea was made clear.[91] Thus, although EU's claim that Korea has not complied with the obligation contained in the last sentence of Article 13.4.3 failed, three fundamental ILO conventions have already been ratified – a process that started even before the report was issued in January 2021. Considering that it took Korea almost a decade to ratify the three conventions despite EU's calls and only after the initiation of dispute settlement procedures, this could be an indication that EU's long-awaited decisiveness to initiate TSD proceedings was behind this progress. Convention No. 105 on Abolishment of Forced Labour[92] remains to be ratified; because for its ratification process an 'additional review of Korea's penal system and social consensus building process are needed',[93] but according to the panel, it should still 'be completed in an expeditious manner'.[94] The ratification of the ILO Convention No. 105, as a

[88] European Commission, 'Panel of Experts Confirms Republic of Korea Is in Breach of Labour Commitments Under Our Trade Agreement', 25 January 2021, https://ec.europa.eu/commission/presscorner/detail/en/ip_21_203; LSE Consulting, 'Open public consultation on the Trade and Sustainable Development (TSD) Review', Summary Report, December 2021, https://circabc.europa.eu/ui/group/e9d50ad8-e41f-4379-839a-fdfe08f0aa96/library/95aafa87-8d69-4f1e-9ce6-a4e5416ba444/details, p. 8.

[89] In this respect, see Sabine Weyand, Director General of DG Trade, on Twitter: 'Enforcement of our TSD chapter EU-Korea in practice', quoting Valdis Dombrovskis, Trade Commissioner, https://twitter.com/WeyandSabine/status/1365222408454627334.

[90] 'Panel of Experts Proceeding Established under Article 13.15 of the Korea-EU Free Trade Agreement', Contents of the Hearing of 8 and 9 October 2020, https://circabc.europa.eu/rest/download/cea833d8-f8b6-4089-9841-86f8b1330928?ticket=, p. 24.

[91] Sun Han, 'The EU-Korea Labour Dispute' (2021) 536–537.

[92] ILO, Abolition of Forced Labour Convention, C105, 25 June 1957, 320 U.N.T.S 291.

[93] For more on the reasons why the ratification of ILO Convention No. 105 is more problematic in South Korea, see Nissen, 'Not That Assertive' (2022) 619–620.

[94] EU–Korea FTA Panel Report, paras. 289–290.

result, remains under the monitoring of the TSD Committee.[95] South Korea also adopted and promulgated amendments to the TULRAA while the panel's report was still pending, which entered into force in July 2021, potentially showcasing the effect of the pressure put on Korea by the dispute settlement proceedings initiated by the EU.[96] Even though the conformity of these amendments with Article 13.4.3 EU–Korea FTA was not considered by the panel due to their timing, and thus they might not fully reflect panel's recommendations,[97] the EU commended Republic of Korea for them.[98] Accordingly, even with a big economic power like Korea,[99] the EU managed to exert the necessary pressure through the cooperative TSD model to achieve desired changes. Seemingly successful in quickly achieving important results, there are still some pending changes needed for Korea to be in full compliance with panel's recommendations, besides the concerns expressed with respect to the lack of ratification of the ILO Convention No. 105.[100]

To conclude, the EU–Korea labour dispute is a landmark dispute which could be generally considered a victory for the cooperation-based dispute settlement model. Although it does not entail the possibility to impose sanctions, progress with respect to FTA TSD implementation was noted even before the panel of experts' report was issued. Although sanctions might still be considered necessary in case the ILO Convention No 105 is not ratified in the future or the EU considers that Korea's TULRAA does not otherwise comply with the panel's report, the dispute showed that the EU's cooperative approach also has teeth, as long as the EU does not abstain from initiating dispute settlement procedures.

7.3.2 Strengthening the Enforcement of the FTA TSD Chapters: The New Action Plan

Following the continuous calls to strengthen the TSD chapters' enforcement, with its renewed trade policy and even before, the EU Commission started to act towards this direction.

[95] This question was already raised during the 7th Committee on Trade and Sustainable Development Joint Minutes, 13–14 April 2021, https://circabc.europa.eu/rest/download/2e6ac3df-18ba-4328-9571-4225c7f86468?ticket=, p. 2; and also during the 9th EU–Korea Trade Committee Joint Minutes, 29 April 2021, https://circabc.europa.eu/rest/download/4a29db81-a6ed-4626-9624-07a343d33dcc?ticket=, p. 2.

[96] Sun Han, 'The EU-Korea Labour Dispute' (2021), p. 542.

[97] ibid.

[98] 9th EU–Korea Trade Committee Joint Minutes, p. 1.

[99] Nissen, 'Not That Assertive' (2022) 625.

[100] EU–Korea Free Trade Agreement 8th session of the Committee on Trade and Sustainable Development, Joint Minutes, Seoul, 15–16 September 2022, https://circabc.europa.eu/rest/download/3d1d9557-4318-45b1-b277-77da4eaba260?ticket=.

In July 2020, the Commission appointed the CTEO, which *inter alia* monitors and is responsible of the enforcement of TSD chapters, a step welcomed by the EP and other stakeholders.[101] The Commission also created, under the leadership of the CTEO, the Single Entry Point (SEP), which is a complaint system for EU stakeholders having two complaint forms, one of them specifically dedicated to TSD/GSP complaints. Since stakeholders made little use of the SEP in the first two years of its existence, in parallel to the TSD review, the Commission also recently updated the Operating Guidelines clarifying that DAGs can also submit collective complaints and that an EU-based complainant can represent the TSD-related concerns of an entity located in a partner country.[102] Nevertheless, SEP still offers discretion to the Commission services on whether enforcement actions will be commenced.[103]

As announced in the Trade Policy Review, the Commission has conducted an early review of its 15-point Action Plan, covering different aspects of FTA TSD implementation and enforcement, including the possibility to allow sanctions for non-compliance. During the consultations, as well as in 2017, business associations and companies seemed to favour the cooperation-based approach, highlighting the potential negative features of sanctions.[104] In contrast, for many NGOs, trade unions, public authorities, and environmental organizations the cooperation-based approach was deemed insufficient and, hence, suggested the introduction of sanctions (i.e. countermeasures, expansion of the 'essential elements' clause, financial penalties).[105] As it can be seen, as well as during the consultations following the 2017 Non-paper, opinions were split between stakeholders, but the number of sanctions advocators has increased. As a result, the Commission tabled a new action plan on TSD Chapters in the summer of 2022 containing a novel approach towards FTA TSD enforcement, which embodies a compromise. In line with many proposals[106] and also the earlier announcement of Trade

[101] European Parliament resolution of 7 October 2020 on the implementation of the common commercial policy – Annual Report 2018 (2019/2197(INI)), para. 63; LSE Consulting, 'Open Public Consultation', December 2021, p. 9.

[102] European Commission, The power of trade partnerships, COM(2022) 409 final, p. 9.

[103] In this respect, see European Commission, Operating guidelines for the Single Entry Point and complaints mechanism for the enforcement of EU trade agreements and arrangements, 22 June 2022, https://trade.ec.europa.eu/access-to-markets/en/form-assets/operational_guidelines.pdf.

[104] LSE Consulting, 'Open Public Consultation', pp. 8–9, 11.

[105] ibid, pp. 9, 11–12.

[106] European Commission, The power of trade partnerships: together for green and just economic growth, COM(2022) 409 final, 22 June 2022.

Commissioner Valdis Dombrovskis,[107] the new FTA TSD enforcement model entails the possibility to impose sanctions, but only as a last resort and solely in serious instances of non-compliance with ILO fundamental labour principles and rights at work, and in case of violations materially defeating the object and purpose of the Paris Agreement on Climate Change, reinforcing them as essential elements of the trade agreements.[108] Accordingly, the Commission finally responded to the calls to allow the imposition of sanctions for FTA TSD violations, albeit only in certain instances, displaying certain cautiousness that can be explained by the potential disadvantages that sanctions entail. Additionally, the recent TSD review seems to have partly responded to the calls to subject TSD commitments to the same dispute settlement rules as market access aspects. Thus, under the new approach, panel recommendations have binding character, and the party in violation will have to implement them in a certain period of time and promptly notify about how it will proceed in order to achieve that, subject to panel review.[109] Accordingly, like disputes on market access commitments, FTA TSD disputes will be covered by compliance stage rules. Hence, sanctions will be imposed only following a panel of experts' report and further failure to bring a measure into compliance after compliance proceedings. Apparently, in an attempt to prevent conclusions similar to those from the EU–Korea FTA dispute, where EU's claim related to the ratification of ILO Conventions failed because of the vague treaty language, the Commission intends to negotiate, where appropriate, 'detailed and time-bound roadmaps with milestones'.[110] Thus, the Commission also contemplates improving the enforceability of the FTA TSD commitments by including more stringent language. Additionally, the new TSD approach involves being more proactive in the cooperation with partners, intensifying the country-specific approach, reinforcing the role of the civil society including by extending the remit of the DAGs beyond TSD, mainstreaming sustainability throughout the entire FTAs, and increasing the monitoring of the implementation of TSD commitments by involving more the Member States, European and national parliaments, INTA's

[107] European Parliament: EVP Dombrovskis speech at the hearing for the Commissioner-Designate for Trade, 2 October 2020, www.europarl.europa.eu/news/en/press-room/20201001IPR88310/hearing-of-executive-vice-president-valdis-dombrovskis-on-trade-portfolio.

[108] European Commission, The power of trade partnerships, COM(2022) 409 final, p. 11. Additionally, the Commission pledged to evaluate the possibility of including the Convention on Biological Diversity in this new approach.

[109] ibid, p. 11. [110] ibid, p. 7.

Monitoring Groups, and the civil society.[111] Therefore, the TSD review resulted in a mixed enforcement model, by enhancing the cooperation-based one but adding further elements from a sanction-based model.

While some aspects of the updated approach, or, as the Commission notes, 'the majority of those that relate to the implementation of TSD commitments and the reinforcement of the role of civil society', can be immediately applied in practice, including in trade agreements already in force, the rest will be proposed for all future negotiations and 'reflected in the ongoing negotiations *as appropriate*' (emphasis added).[112] Accordingly, only actions related to the monitoring of the implementation (but not enforcement), such as working together with EU Delegations that have direct contact with local governments and DAGs or supporting the involvement of the EP interacting with parliaments of partners countries, and those to the reinforcement of the role of civil society, for instance related to strengthening the role of the EU DAGs or ensuring an inclusive consultation process with civil society throughout all stages of a lifecycle of an FTA, could be applied to already existing FTAs. In contrast, actions related to more assertive enforcement through general dispute settlement and trade sanctions would have to be implemented only with respect to future negotiations of FTAs or during the review of the existing ones. Thus, the new TSD Chapter action plan will most likely be reflected to different degrees in different FTAs for which negotiations are ongoing, since the Commission's capacity to integrate it depends on the stage of completion of the negotiations.[113] For example, the EU–New Zealand FTA[114] incorporates the new approach, while the EU–Chile FTA[115] politically concluded on 9 December 2022 does not as of yet follow suit. In the latter case, the parties issued a joint statement according to which they will initiate a review once the interim FTA enters into force, including on the possibility to allow resort to sanctions and to make the Paris Agreement an essential element.[116] In addition, it cannot

[111] ibid, p. 4. [112] ibid, p. 12.

[113] Institute for European Environmental Policy, 'IEEP's Assessment of the New EU Trade and Sustainable Development Action Plan', 23 June 2022, https://ieep.eu/news/ieeps-assessment-of-the-new-eu-trade-and-sustainable-development-action-plan/.

[114] Free Trade Agreement between the European Union and New Zealand (EU–New Zealand FTA), 9 July 2023.

[115] EU–Chile FTA, https://policy.trade.ec.europa.eu/eu-trade-relationships-country-and-region/countries-and-regions/chile/eu-chile-agreement/text-agreement_en.

[116] Joint Statement on Trade and Sustainable Development by the European Union and Chile, 2 December 2022,https://circabc.europa.eu/rest/download/96cafa19-80fe-4455-b63b-ea36adf2635a?ticket=.

be excluded that EU's potential FTA partners will not accept this new approach.[117] Moreover, the Commission does not mention anything about renegotiating existing FTAs to update them according to its most recent approach. The Council has welcomed the new approach proposed by the Commission, called for quick actions in this respect, and even invited the Commission to use the review clauses and, if relevant, joint committees to align the existing FTAs with the new approach.[118] Until successful revision of existing FTAs takes place, however, these agreements will still rely exclusively on the cooperative approach.

The EU–New Zealand FTA, the first trade agreement concluded approximately a week after the new approach was unveiled, already reflects the new TSD approach.[119] Moreover, it could be said to go even further by completely renouncing the special TSD dispute settlement mechanism, the general dispute settlement mechanism covering also disputes arising out of the TSD chapter, with only some provisions specifically dedicated to such disputes.[120]Thus, as communicated by the Commission in its new action plan, the TSD enforcement is further aligned with the general dispute settlement mechanism by extending the compliance stage to TSD disputes but also by extending the rest of the rules, with only a few rules being exceptionally dedicated to the TSD disputes. It shall be seen if other new FTAs will take a similar approach. In line with the announced TSD review, the EU–New Zealand FTA allows the imposition of trade remedies when compliance with a final report issued in certain cases is not possible, if the party complained against does not notify about any measure taken to comply, or the panel finds that such a measure does not exist or is still inconsistent.[121] In particular, it does so in case of disputes related to violations of ILO core labour rights or the obligation to refrain from any action or omission that materially defeats the object and purpose of

[117] For example, Ceretelli states that the inclusion of this model could be problematic in the FTAs with India and Indonesia (Carlotta Ceretelli, 'EU–New Zealand FTA: Towards a New approach in the Enforcement of Trade and Sustainable Development Obligations', *EJIL: Talk!*, 28 September 2022, www.ejiltalk.org/eu-new-zealand-fta-towards-a-new-approach-in-the-enforcement-of-trade-and-sustainable-development-obligations/).

[118] Council of the European Union, Conclusions on the Trade and Sustainability Review, Brussels, 17 October 2022, www.consilium.europa.eu/en/press/press-releases/2022/10/17/council-conclusions-on-the-trade-and-sustainability-review/.

[119] European Commission, 'EU–New Zealand Trade Agreement: Unlocking Sustainable Economic Growth', 30 June 2022, https://ec.europa.eu/commission/presscorner/detail/en/ip_22_4158.

[120] EU–New Zealand FTA, Chapter 26.

[121] ibid, Art. 26.16 (1), (2).

the Paris Agreement.[122] The remedies prescribed are the same as in case of the rest of FTA violations, namely a mutually acceptable compensation or, if no compensation is requested or agreed, the suspension of obligations.[123] The level of suspension of obligations can also be subject to panel review if the party complained against considers that it exceeds the permitted level.[124] As envisaged under the new TSD approach and as already foreseen in the EU–UK TCA,[125] under the EU–New Zealand FTA the role of the DAGs and Civil Society Forum is extended to cover the implementation of the entire agreement, not only that of the TSD chapter.[126] In relation to the TSD enforcement, under the EU–New Zealand FTA, the DAGs and Civil Society Forum have functions similar to those under the older FTAs: for example, providing advice during consultations, being notified about measures taken to comply with the panel report, and submitting observations to the TSD Committee monitoring the implementation of the report.[127] Accordingly, the EU–New Zealand FTA embodies a mixed model of TSD enforcement still containing elements of the cooperative one but at the same time pivoting towards the sanctions-based model.

Although the possibility of adopting sanctions in certain instances of FTA TSD violations was included only following the 2022 TSD review, the EU already had an internal legal basis for imposing them, without the need for further amending Trade Enforcement Regulation 654/2014.[128] Article 3 (b) of the Regulation establishes that it applies following FTA adjudication 'when the Union has *the right* to suspend concessions or other obligations under such agreements' (emphasis added). Thus, since under the trade agreements reflecting the Commission's new TSD approach the EU will have the right to impose countermeasures in limited instances, it will be able to use Regulation 654/2014 as an internal legal basis. This is also confirmed by Regulation 2021/167 amending the Trade Enforcement Regulation, which provides in Recital (10) in respect

[122] ibid, Art. 26.16 (2). [123] ibid, Art.26.16 (1) and (3). [124] ibid, Art. 26.16 (6).

[125] EU–UK TCA, Arts. 12-14. [126] EU–New Zealand FTA, Arts. 20.6, 24.6, 24.7.

[127] ibid, Arts. 26.3 (6), 26.13 (3).

[128] Regulation (EU) 654/2014 of the European Parliament and of the Council of 15 May 2014 concerning the exercise of the Union's rights for the application and enforcement of international trade rules and amending Council Regulation (EC) No. 3286/94 laying down Community procedures in the field of the common commercial policy in order to ensure the exercise of the Community's rights under international trade rules, in particular those established under the auspices of the World Trade Organization (Trade Enforcement Regulation), OJ EU 2014 No. L 189/50.

of the TSD chapters that the Regulation applies to countermeasures taken in response to a TSD violation, '*if and to the extent* that such measures *are permitted* and are warranted by the circumstances' (emphasis added).[129] In a 2021 Declaration on amended Enforcement Regulation 654/2014 the Commission stated that it 'will pay equal attention to alleged breaches of the trade and sustainable development provisions of EU trade agreements as to alleged breaches of market access systems', and that the processing of alleged TSD breaches 'will be fully integrated into the system'.[130] Accordingly, Regulation 2021/167 confirms that the Trade Enforcement Regulation applies to the TSD chapters but allows for countermeasures only when bilateral agreements provide a legal basis for doing so,[131] which under the former cooperation-based model is absent and consequently may only be found in general international law (see Section 7.4).

Thus, the Commission clearly made substantial steps towards strengthening the enforcement of its FTA TSD chapters with its new TSD policy. Its most recent TSD action plan brought changes that were long-awaited by many, such as the introduction of sanctions that can be imposed in limited instances and treating the TSD and market access commitments more uniformly. As a result, under the Commission's new action plan and as illustrated by the EU–New Zealand FTA, the new approach towards FTA TSD enforcement combines elements of both cooperative- and sanction- based models. Nevertheless, the cooperative dispute settlement model present in all EU's already concluded FTAs will remain dominant until the majority is revised, while the possibility to impose sanctions under FTAs embracing the new approach will still cover only limited instances. Thus, the calls for even stronger enforcement could still be expected, and the debate about introducing sanctions in respect to other violations might continue. Moreover, even though the EU–Korea FTA dispute showed that compliance can be achieved without sanctions, the question of TSD enforcement under the cooperation-based model remains pertinent.

[129] Regulation (EU) 2021/167 of the European Parliament and of the Council of 10 February 2021 Amending Regulation (EU) No 654/2014 Concerning the Exercise of the Union's Rights for the Application and Enforcement of International Trade Rules, OJ EU 2021 No. L 49, 12 February 2021, pp. 1–5.

[130] Declaration of the Commission, OJ EU 2021 No. C 49/5, 12 February 2021.

[131] Léo Gargne, 'Sustainable Development in Preferential Trade Agreements (PTAs)', in Michael Faure (ed.), *Elgar Encyclopedia of Environmental Law* (Cheltenham: Edward Elgar Publishing, 2021), vol. 11, p. 473.

7.4 The Tools Available for Use in Case of Non-Compliance with the Panel of Experts' Report

7.4.1 Resort to Unilateral Countermeasures under Public International Law Rules

The FTA TSD dispute settlement model based exclusively on cooperation will still be present in all EU's FTAs concluded until June 2022, unless renegotiated, and sanctions will be available only with respect to a limited number of cases under FTAs that incorporate the new approach (which could also be to different degrees.) The question, therefore, arises whether the CTEO could use the Trade Enforcement Regulation 654/2014 for imposing countermeasures under international customary rules contained in the ILC Draft Articles on State Responsibility even without an express legal basis found in the FTAs.

As stated in the previous section, the Trade Enforcement Regulation 654/2014, even after the recent amendments, allows the imposition of countermeasures in case of FTA violations only when the Union has the right to do so 'under such agreements'.[132] Accordingly, for using the Trade Enforcement Regulation as a tool of TSD enforcement, the FTAs themselves should confer the right to impose countermeasures. However, as mentioned, such right is not provided by the cooperation-based mechanisms included in the TSD chapters of the FTAs concluded before June 2022, while the new TSD action plan envisages the possibility to impose sanctions only in specific instances.

In view of the present authors, the imposition of countermeasures under customary law in case of FTA TSD violations does not seem possible. This is because the EU's FTA TSD chapters establish special rules on countermeasures in the sense of Article 55 ILC Draft Articles, thereby displacing the more general customary rules,[133] which otherwise would have allowed a choice between taking countermeasures and initiating dispute settlement procedures.[134] Unlike the general dispute settlement mechanisms of the FTAs that do not contain exclusive clauses similar to

[132] Trade Enforcement Regulation, Art. 3 (b). This approach is further confirmed by Recital 10 of the Regulation 2021/167 amending the Trade Enforcement Regulation, mentioned in Section 7.3.2.

[133] Wolfgang Weiß and Cornelia Furculita, 'The EU in Search for Stronger Enforcement Rules: Assessing the Proposed Amendments to Trade Enforcement Regulation 654/2014' (2020) 23 *JIEL* 865–884 at 881–882. Opinion also shared by Marín Durán, 'Sustainable Development Chapters in EU Free Trade Agreements' (2020) 1047.

[134] See Chapter 5.

Article 23 DSU, the special TSD dispute settlement mechanisms from EU FTAs in force, except EU–Central America AA and EU–Colombia/Peru/ Ecuador FTA, expressly provide that for matters arising under the TSD chapters the parties should '*only*' have recourse to the procedures provided in those chapters.[135] In line with Article 31 VCLT, it is necessary to establish the ordinary meaning of these provisions, in their context and in light of the TSD chapters' object and purpose. The adverb 'only' clearly suggests that no other rules and procedures than those from the TSD chapters can be used in case of disputes, thereby precluding reliance on the residual customary law. However, Bronckers and Gruni argue that such an interpretation puts too much emphasis on the word 'only', and that these provisions indicate nothing more than that the EU's FTA TSD chapters are merely special in respect to the general FTA dispute settlement mechanisms.[136] Indeed, establishing the extent to which one regime is special in respect to the general rules could be a difficult task.[137] The interpretation advanced here, nonetheless, does not rely on the word 'only' read in isolation, but also on other FTA TSD provisions representing its context and highlighting the cooperative approach, especially on those related to the panel of experts' reports according to which parties are only required to discuss and identify appropriate measures, make best efforts to accommodate, or design a mutually satisfactory plan.[138] These provisions exhibiting the lack of binding character of the recommendations indicate that the intention of the parties was to preclude the use of countermeasures in case of non-compliance with the recommendations, and to exclusively rely instead on cooperative mechanisms. Furthermore, some TSD chapters from FTAs concluded before June 2022 contain provisions on their objectives, which highlight the

135 EU–Korea FTA, Art. 13.16; CETA, Arts. 23.11 (1), 24.16 (1); JEPA, Art. 16.17 (1); EU–Vietnam FTA, Art. 13.16 (1); EU–Singapore FTA, Art. 12.16 (1); EU–UA AA, Art. 300 (7); EU–Moldova AA, Art. 378 (1); EU–Georgia AA, Art. 242 (1). However, the EU–UK TCA, in Arts. 389, 396, 407, provides that by way of derogation from the Part dedicated to general dispute settlement, 'the Parties shall have recourse *exclusively* to the procedures established' for the TSD chapters, which seems to be used interchangeably with 'only'.

136 Bronckers and Gruni, 'Retooling the Sustainability Standards' (2021) 40–41.

137 The extent to which special regimes are *lex specialis* is often a contentious issue (Bruno Simma and Dirk Pulkowski, 'Of Planets and the Universe: Self-Contained Regimes in International Law' (2006) 17 (3) *EJIL* 483–529 at 507 ff; Alejandro Sánchez, 'What Trade Lawyers Should Know about the ILC Articles on State Responsibility' (2012) 7 (6) *GTCJ* 292–299 at 294).

138 See Section 7.2.2.

importance of cooperation,[139] confirming that EU's former approach is based on it to achieve compliance and not on sanctions. Thus, the interpretation of the clauses requiring the parties to only have recourse to the TSD procedures in their context and in light of their object and purpose establishes their TSD procedures' exclusive character, confirming also the conclusion that the EU FTA TSD chapters in question displace the customary law for the imposition of countermeasures. Moreover, this conclusion is also confirmed by the supplementary means of interpretation under Article 32 VCLT. If EU tried to argue that the more special FTA TSD chapters have not displaced the customary rules on countermeasures, this would go against its position stated in official internal documents, such as those of the EU Parliament and Council proposing to introduce the possibility to impose sanctions,[140] Commission's 2017 and 2018 Non-Papers, or the Commission's new action plan. In the 2017 Non-Paper it is expressly mentioned that the EU's approach towards TSD chapters 'does not include sanctions'. The Commission also has expressly recognized in the 2018 Non-Paper that 'negotiating partners have been clear that they would not accept a broad scope combined with trade sanctions'. Most recently, the Commission confirmed in its new action plan containing its most recent approach that 'the EU's approach to TSD did not contemplate the use of sanctions in the case of non-compliance with the panel report'.[141] It is widely accepted that one party's official documents related to the application of the treaty can constitute 'subsequent practice in the application of the treaties' under Article 32 VCLT, which may serve as supplementary means of interpretation to confirm the meaning resulting from the application of Article 31 VCLT.[142] Additionally, in light of its public recognition that sanctions are not available under the cooperative model, EU's potential contention that it could make use of the customary rules on countermeasures would be devoid of any credibility and could

[139] See, for example, EU–Korea FTA, Art. 13.1 (2); CETA, Arts. 23.1 (1), 24 (2); JEPA, Art. 16.1 (2); EU–Singapore FTA, Art. 12.1 (2).

[140] See Section 7.2.2.

[141] European Commission, The power of trade partnerships, COM(2022) 409 final, p. 11.

[142] ILC, Draft Conclusions on Subsequent Agreements and Subsequent Practice in Relation to the Interpretation of Treaties, with Commentaries (2018) *Yearbook of the ILC*, 2018, vol. II, Part Two 16-116, Conclusion 2, Commentary, paras. (8)–(9), pp. 20–21 in conjunction with Conclusion 4, Commentary, para. (18), p. 32; Oliver Dörr, 'Article 32 Supplementary Means of Interpretation', in Oliver Dörr and Kirsten Schmalenbach (eds.), *Vienna Convention on the Law of Treaties: A Commentary*, 2nd ed. (Heidelberg: Springer, 2018), p. 627, para 26.

have political consequences: EU's reputation as a good-faith trade negotiator would be affected.

Although EU–Central America AA and EU–Colombia/Peru/Ecuador FTA TSD chapters do not contain exclusive clauses that would provide that for matters arising under the TSD chapter the parties should only have recourse to TSD procedures, the legal situation is the same. For a determination of the special character of these TSD procedures in the meaning of Article 55 ILC Draft Articles, the presence of clauses similar to those contained in the EU FTAs analyzed above is not mandatory.[143] Their special character can be established through other means. These agreements expressly mention that their TSD chapters embody a 'cooperative approach'.[144] Considering this express mentioning, as well as other evidence of the parties' will to rely solely on cooperative mechanisms and not sanctions, which was also mentioned above in the process of interpretation of the exclusive clauses of other FTAs (i.e. the provisions indicating the lack of binding character of recommendations and EU internal documents), it is reasonable to deduce that EU–Central America AA and EU–Colombia/Peru/Ecuador FTA TSD chapters also exclude the residual application of customary rules on countermeasures. This conclusion is reinforced by the writings of many scholars who label EU's approach in its FTA TSD chapters as a 'cooperative approach', defining it as not entailing sanctions and contrasting it with other sanction-based mechanisms.[145] Thus, the EU most likely uses this expression in EU–Central America AA and EU–Colombia/Peru/Ecuador FTA TSD chapters with the same meaning.

The EU–New Zealand FTA, reflecting EU's novel TSD approach, contains no special TSD dispute settlement mechanism and, hence, no exclusive clause that would provide that TSD disputes should be settled using it. The agreement only specifies that the FTA article on trade remedies applies in the specific situations described in the previous sections. This provision alone does not seem to legally preclude potential invocation of

[143] ILC Draft Articles with Commentaries, Commentary on Art. 55, para. (1).

[144] EU–Central America AA, Art. 284 (3); EU–Colombia/Peru/Ecuador FTA, Art. 286.

[145] See, for example, Jean-Frédéric Morin and Myriam Rochette, 'Transatlantic Convergence of PTAs' Environmental Clauses' (2017) *Business and Politics*, www.chaire-epi.ulaval.ca/sites/chaire-epi.ulaval.ca/files/publications/morin_and_rochette.pdf, pp. 12 ff, 35; Hradilová and Svoboda, 'Sustainable Development Chapters' (2018) 1029; Prévost and Alexovičová, 'Mind the Compliance Gap' (2019) 241, 245, 252; Marín Durán, 'Sustainable Development Chapters in EU Free Trade Agreements' (2020) 1058; Zurek, 'From "Trade *and* Sustainability" to "Trade *for* Sustainability"' (2020), pp. 124–125.

residual customary international norms on countermeasures. However, by stating in its official Communication that under the new approach it proposes the possibility of trade sanctions in specific instances, the Commission implicitly confirms that in other instances such possibility is absent. Had the EU wanted to allow the imposition of sanctions in other instances, it would have explicitly listed them. Once again, an unlikely contention on the EU's side that it could rely on general public international law for the imposition of countermeasures in other instances than those explicitly mentioned in the EU–New Zealand FTA would seriously damage its credibility and would not be reasonable.

Consequently, under EU's TSD cooperative models included in the FTAs concluded before June 2022, there is no room for countermeasures in case of non-compliance with panel of experts' reports either under EU law or under customary international law on countermeasures. Hence, in these cases, the EU will have to use the cooperative mechanisms, which, as the EU–Korea dispute (analyzed in Section 7.3.1) demonstrated, are not toothless. However, in case the EU wants to resort to sanctions against its partners' non-compliance with TSD obligations, an express provision in FTAs for doing so is necessary. Accordingly, the Commission's new action plan envisaging the possibility to impose sanctions is welcome also from a perspective of compliance with EU's international commitments. The imposition of countermeasures based on the ILC Draft Articles in other TSD-related instances than those for which trade remedies are explicitly allowed under the new model would not be permissible under EU law and undesirable under public international law.

7.4.2 Article 60 (1) VCLT/VCLTSIO, the 'Essential Elements' Clauses, and Article 62 (1) VCLT/VCLTSIO

The Commission's recent action plan on FTA TSD chapters explicitly mentions the possibility of sanctions in instances of serious violations of core TSD commitments, specifically ILO fundamental principles and rights at work and the Paris Agreement, reinforcing them as essential elements of the trade agreements. The question, however, arises whether the parties could use Article 60 (1) VCLT/VCLTSIO and the 'essential elements' clauses contained in the framework agreements accompanying older FTAs as legal bases for sanctions in case of violations related to the TSD chapters embracing exclusively the cooperation-based model.

In its Opinion 2/15, the CJEU found that a breach of the provisions concerning social protection of workers and environmental protection set out in EU–Singapore FTA authorizes the other Party, in accordance with Article 60 (1) VCLT, to terminate or suspend the liberalization provided for in the other provisions of the envisaged agreement.[146] As EU FTAs embracing the cooperative model contain special TSD dispute settlement rules, it could be argued that they displace not only the customary rules on countermeasures codified in the ILC Draft Articles, as demonstrated in the previous section, but also the general customary rules providing consequences in case of breaches codified in Article 60 (1) VCLT/VCLTSIO. Moreover, Article 60 (4) of the VCLT/VCLTSIO, which states that '[t]he foregoing paragraphs are without prejudice to any provision in the treaty applicable in the event of a breach', confirms its residual character, not affecting the more special rules contained in the treaty applicable in the event of a breach.[147] Thus, the Court's findings are doubtful.[148] In contrast to the CJEU's Opinion, Advocate General (AG) Sharpston argued in her Opinion that '[u]nlike the "essential elements" clauses [. . .] breach of the labour and environmental standards [. . .] does not give the other Party the right to suspend trade benefits resulting from the EUSFTA'.[149] Disagreements between the AG and the CJEU are rare occurrences that cannot be overlooked, warranting a certain degree of caution before taking the CJEU's opinion for granted.[150] This reticence is also backed by various documents of the Commission, Council, and other Member States which recognize the absence of the possibility to impose sanctions for TSD breaches (see Section 7.2.2). Furthermore, CJEU's Opinion has been met with criticism by many scholars.[151]

Even if CJEU's Opinion 2/15 is followed and Article 60 (1) VCLT/VCLTSIO is an option for TSD enforcement, it entitles one of the parties to

[146] CJEU, Opinion 2/15, para. 161.

[147] Mark E. Villiger, *Commentary on the 1969 Vienna Convention on the Law of Treaties* (Leiden: Martinus Nijhoff Publishers, 2009) 746, para 22; Thomas Giegerich 'Article 60: Termination or Suspension of the Operation of a Treaty as a Consequence of Its Breach', in Oliver Dörr and Kirsten Schmalenbach (eds.), *Vienna Convention on the Law of Treaties: A Commentary*, 2nd ed. (Heidelberg: Springer, 2018), pp. 1116–1117, paras. 68–69.

[148] Weiß and Furculita, 'The EU in Search for Stronger Enforcement Rules' (2020) 882.

[149] AG Opinion in Opinion 2/15, 21 December 2016, paras. 490–491.

[150] Zurek, 'From "Trade *and* Sustainability" to "Trade *for* Sustainability"', p. 136.

[151] Marín Durán, 'Sustainable Development Chapters in EU Free Trade Agreements' (2020) 1046; Zurek, 'From "Trade *and* Sustainability" to "Trade *for* Sustainability"' (2020), p. 138. Ankersmith praises CJEU's conclusion from an environmental and social point of view but argues that certain practicalities in this respect 'may cause less enthusiasm' (Laurens Ankersmit, 'Opinion 2/15: Adding Some Spice to the Trade & Environment Debate', European Law Blog, 15 June 2017, https://europeanlawblog.eu/2017/06/15/opinion-215-adding-some-spice-to-the-trade-environment-debate/).

terminate the treaty or suspend its operation in whole or in part only in case of a 'material breach'. According to Article 60 (3) (b) VCLT/VCLTSIO, a 'material breach' implies a violation of 'a provision essential to the accomplishment of the object or purpose of the treaty'. In Opinion 2/15 the CJEU simply states that the EU–Singapore FTA TSD chapter 'plays an essential role in the envisaged agreement',[152] without justifying its statement in any way. Without the treaty explicitly establishing so, it could be a challenging task for a party to show that a provision is essential for achieving the treaty's purpose, the view of a state being 'nearly inevitably subjective'.[153] EU FTAs concluded before the EU–UK TCA, which establishes that the Paris Agreement and the United Nations Framework Convention on Climate Change (UNFCCC)[154] process are essential elements of the TCA and any supplementing agreements,[155] do not contain any express provision that would qualify TSD provisions as essential elements. Since Article 60 (1) VCLT/VCLTSIO has been displaced by the more special TSD rules (and even if this was not the case), the requirement contained in Article 60 (3) (b) VCLT/VCLTSIO would be difficult to comply with; its self-standing use as a basis for imposing sanctions against TSD breaches has little chance to pass the test of legality. However, it was argued that 'essential elements' clauses covering respect for human rights together with the conditionality clauses protecting the fulfillment of these rights contained in the framework agreements accompanying the FTAs could serve as a legal basis for the termination or suspension of the FTAs in case of TSD breaches. These clauses of the framework agreements seem to emulate Article 60 (1) VCLT/VCLTSIO and thereby establish its application to the FTAs with the effect of enabling their termination or suspension; nevertheless, they would do so only in specific instances of human rights breaches, as will be shown now.

Respect for human rights has figured as an 'essential element' in EU's bilateral preferential agreements since the early 1990s.[156] Until recently,

[152] CJEU, Opinion 2/15, para. 162.

[153] Isabelle Buffard and Karl Zemanek, 'The Object and Purpose of a Treaty: An Enigma?' (1998) 3 *Austrian Review of International and European Law* 311–345 at 342–343; Malgosia Fitzmaurice, 'Material Breach of Treaty: Some Legal Issues' (2001) 6 *Austrian Review of International and European Law* 3–44 at 9.

[154] United Nations Framework Convention on Climate Change, 9 May 1992, S. Treaty Doc No. 102-38, 1771 U.N.T.S.

[155] EU–UK TCA, Art. 771 in conjunction with Art. 764 (1).

[156] Bronckers and Gruni, 'Taking the Enforcement' (2019) 1613.

they have been commonly included in the Framework Agreements accompanying EU's FTAs that contain TSD chapters.[157] Thus, these Agreements usually contain a clause designating respect for human rights as an essential element and another conditional one dedicated to the fulfillment of the obligations, which clarifies that in the event of serious breaches of that clause, the termination and suspension of that agreement is possible.[158] While EU FTAs have been usually linked to these framework agreements, making possible the use of the 'essential elements' clauses in respect to FTAs *mutatis mutandis*,[159] this is not always the case. For example, whereas the EU–Canada Strategic Partnership Agreement (SPA) could also be *suspended* in case of a particularly serious and substantial violation of the 'essential elements' clause,[160] this is not applicable to CETA. EU–Canada SPA establishes that 'a particularly serious and substantial violation of human rights [. . .] could also serve as grounds for the *termination* of [. . .] (CETA)' (emphasis added).[161] Thus, a breach of the 'essential elements' clause would allow only the

[157] In the absence of framework agreements, such clauses are included in the agreement containing the free trade provisions (Ionel Zamfir, 'Human Rights in EU Trade Agreements: The Human Rights Clause and Its Application' (2019) *European Parliamentary Research Service*, www.europarl.europa.eu/RegData/etudes/BRIE/2019/637975/EPRS_BRI(2019)637975_EN.pdf, p. 4). For example, the AAs with Ukraine, Moldova, and Georgia provide the 'essential elements' clauses directly in the agreement containing provisions for a Deep and Comprehensive Free Trade Area (EU–UA AA, Art. 2; EU–Moldova AA, Art. 2.1; EU–Georgia AA, Art. 2.1).

[158] Such framework agreements accompanying FTAs have been regularly adopted since 2009 (Portela, 'Enforcing Respect for Labour Standards with Targeted Sanctions' (2018), p. 1). Framework Agreement between the European Union and its Member States, on the one part, and the Republic of Korea, on the other part (EU–Korea Framework Agreement), OJ EU 2013 No. L 20/2, Arts.1 (1), 45 (3), 45 (4), and the Joint Interpretative Declaration Concerning Articles 45 and 46; Strategic Partnership Agreement between the European Union and its Member States, of the one part, and Canada, of the other part (EU–Canada SPA), OJ EU 2016 No. L 329/45, Arts. 2, 28 (3) and (6); Strategic Partnership Agreement between the European Union and its Member States, of the one part, and Japan, of the other part (EU–Japan SPA), OJ EU 2018 No. L 216/4, Arts. 2 (1), 43 (4) and (5); Partnership and Cooperation Agreement between the European Union and its Member States, of the one part, and the Republic of Singapore, of the other part (EU–Singapore PCA), OJ EU 2018 L189/2, Arts. 1 (1), 44 (1) and (4); Framework Agreement on Comprehensive Partnership and Cooperation between the European Union and its Member States, of the one part, and the Socialist Republic of Viet Nam, of the other part (EU–Vietnam Framework Agreement), OJ EU 2016 No. L 329/8, Arts. 1 (1), 57 (4), and Joint Declaration on Article 57.

[159] EU–Korea FTA, Art. 15.14 (2); EU–Singapore FTA, Art. 16.18 (1); EU–Vietnam FTA, Art. 17.22 (2).

[160] EU–Canada SPA, Art. 28 (6) (a).

[161] EU–Canada SPA, Art. 28 (7).

termination of CETA, making it a 'nuclear option'.[162] Furthermore, there is no linkage between the SPA and the EPA with Japan, the former making no reference to the latter. Thus, the 'essential elements' clause from the EU–Japan SPA can be invoked only with respect to it, but not the EU–Japan EPA. This different approach is explained by Japan's insistence on it, due to the difference between the parties' legal systems, particularly the existence of the death penalty in Japan.[163] Accordingly, the 'essential elements' and conditionality clauses are available only to a limited extent or not at all in case of EU FTAs signed with such important partners as Canada and Japan.

Even when the conditionality clauses from the framework agreements covering the respect for human rights as essential elements allow the suspension or the termination of the FTAs, the main question remains whether labour obligations, and which of them, can be deemed to reflect human rights.[164] ILO Conventions on core labour rights, which are included in EU's FTAs as minimum-level standards, are the only TSD obligations that could be perceived as falling under the notion of 'human rights'.[165] Nevertheless, AG Sharpston clearly differentiated between the FTA TSD obligations and the 'essential elements' clauses, suggesting that there is no overlap between the two.[166] There is also no practice that

[162] Lorand Bartels, 'Human Rights, Labour Standards, and Environmental Standards in CETA', in Stefan Griller, Walter Obwexer, and Erich Vranes (eds.), *Mega-Regional Trade Agreements: CETA, TTIP, and TiSA: New Orientations for EU External Economic Relations* (Oxford: Oxford University Press, 2017), p. 210.

[163] Yuki Moritani, 'The Partnership Agreements with Japan as a Part of Structural Foreign Policy' (2020) 2 (1) *The Greater European Journal* 72–78 at 74; Yumiko Nakanishi, 'Significance of the Strategic Partnership Agreement Between the European Union and Japan in International Order', in Yumiko Nakanishi and Olivia Tambou (eds.), *The EU-Japan Relationship*, Collection Open Access Book (Blogdroiteuropeen, 2020), https://blogdroiteuropeen.com/wp-content/uploads/2020/12/eu-japan-relationship-v3-4.pdf, p. 22.

[164] Jin Woo Kim and Ann-Evelyn Luyten, 'Op-Ed: Could the EU's Chief Trade Enforcement Officer Enforce Sustainable Development Commitments Under EU Trade Agreements against Non-Compliant Third Countries?', *EU Law Live*, 13 May 2020, https://eulawlive.com/op-ed-could-the-eus-chief-trade-enforcement-officer-enforce-sustainable-development-commitments-under-eu-trade-agreements-against-non-compliant-third-countries-by-ann-evel/#.

[165] Lorand Bartels, 'Human Rights and Sustainable Development Obligations in EU Free Trade Agreements' (2013) 40 (4) *LIEI* 297–313 at 310; Portela, 'Enforcing Respect for Labour Standards with Targeted Sanctions' (2018), p. 2; Bronckers, Gruni, 'Taking the Enforcement' (2019) 1613.

[166] Weiß and Furculita, 'The EU in Search for Stronger Enforcement Rules', 883, referring to AG Opinion in Opinion 2/15, paras. 490–491.

would support this approach, as no FTA was ever suspended or terminated as a result of the activation of the human rights conditionality clauses in case of core labour standards violations.[167] The European Communities suspended the Cooperation Agreement with Yugoslavia,[168] but this was done by virtue of Article 62 VLCT in view of the war there (sustained by the CJEU),[169] and occasionally imposed trade sanctions for human rights violations even without a 'human rights clause'.[170] When the EU, nevertheless, activated its human rights conditionality clauses, this was only with regard to EU development aid and cooperation, and only in situations of serious political gravity, such as civil wars or coups d'état or situations entailing grave breaches of human rights (but not labour rights).[171] This practice is indicative of the seriousness of the situations that would warrant the invocation of EU's conditionality clauses. The gravity of the situations to which the human rights conditionality applies is also evoked by the treaty language. For example, in EU–Korea Framework Agreement, it applies only in cases of 'special urgency', which consist of 'a particularly serious and substantial violation of an essential element of the Agreement'.[172] The EU–Canada SPA goes even further and specifies in Article 28.3 that for a situation to constitute a 'particularly serious and substantial violation', 'its gravity and nature would have to be of an exceptional sort such as a coup d'État or grave crimes that threaten the peace, security and well-being of the international community'. Thus, the SPA with Canada marks a shift in EU's practice, excluding the possibility to invoke the 'essential elements'

[167] Portela, 'Enforcing Respect for Labour Standards with Targeted Sanctions' (2018), p. IX.

[168] Cooperation Agreement between the European Economic Community and the Socialist Federal Republic of Yugoslavia, OJ EU 1983 NO. L 41/2, no longer in force.

[169] CJEU, Case C-162/96, *Racke v Hauptzollamt Mainz* [1998] I-03655, paras. 53–56.

[170] For example, it did so against Myanmar; see Council Common Position 2007/750/CFSP of 19 November 2007 amending Common Position 2006/318/CFSP renewing restrictive measures against Burma/Myanmar, OJ EU 2007 No. L 308/1. For more, see Bruno de Witte, 'The EU and the International Legal Order: The Case of Human Rights', in Malcolm Evans and Panos Koutrakos (eds.), *Beyond the Established Legal Orders: Policy Interconnections between the EU and the Rest of the World* (Oxford: Hart Publishing 2011), p. 142.

[171] See, for example, Council Common Position 2005/792/CFSP of 14 November 2005 concerning restrictive measures against Uzbekistan, OJ EU 2005 No. L 299/72, suspending technical meetings under the EU–Uzbekistan Partnership and Cooperation Agreement; CJEU, C-268/94, *Portugal v Council* [1996] I-06177, para. 27. Portela and Zamfir also note that all activations, except that against Uzbekistan, were taken against parties to the Cotonou Partnership Agreement (Portela, 'Enforcing Respect for Labour Standards with Targeted Sanctions' (2018), p. 2; Zamfir, 'Human Rights in EU Trade Agreements' (2019), p. 9).

[172] EU–Korea Framework Agreement, Joint Interpretative Declaration Concerning Articles 45 and 46.

clauses from framework agreements to suspend the trade agreement (i.e. CETA) with respect to mere human rights violations without consequences for peace and security, as its Article 28.7 requires 'a particularly serious and substantial violation of human rights' in the above sense.[173] Furthermore, in the EU–Korea labour dispute, the Commission hesitated to invoke the 'essential elements' clause, affirming its reluctance to use human rights conditionality for core labour rights.[174] Considering the limitations described herein, the 'essential elements' and conditionality clauses from framework agreements could be used only in a few instances to enforce FTA labour commitments.[175] Moreover, even when this were possible, the suspension or termination of an FTA would most likely be perceived as undesirable, including for the EU,[176] since even from the sustainability perspective it could no longer use the agreement as a platform to promote its values.

Furthermore, one may consider using Article 62 (1) VCLT/VCLTSIO in case of a TSD breach allowing withdrawal from, termination, or suspension of a treaty in case of a 'fundamental change of circumstances which has occurred with regard to those existing at the time of the conclusion of a treaty, and which was not foreseen by the parties', 'the existence of those circumstances constituted an essential basis of the consent of the parties to be bound by the treaty', and 'the effect of the change is radically to transform the extent of obligations still to be performed under the treaty'. For the successful invocation of this article, all these conditions should be cumulatively met.[177] First of all, it might be difficult to argue that a TSD breach represents a fundamental change of *circumstances*, as it rather refers to the treaty obligations themselves.[178] Still, Article 62 2 (b) VCLT and 62 (3) VCLTSIO expressly prohibit the invocation of a fundamental change of circumstances in case of a treaty breach only by the wrongdoer itself, but not by an innocent party.[179] The EU would also need to demonstrate that compliance with the TSD obligation allegedly breached was essential for the consent of *both* parties and

[173] Bronckers and Gruni, 'Taking the Enforcement' (2019) 1614.

[174] Weiß and Furculita, 'The EU in Search for Stronger Enforcement Rules' (2020) 883.

[175] ibid.

[176] Louis Koen and Davy Rammila, 'The EU-Korea Panel Report: A Watershed Moment for the Trade-Labor Nexus or Mere Symbolic Victory?' (2021) 7 (2) *Journal of International Trade, Logistics and Law* 53–58 at 57.

[177] Villiger, *Commentary* (2009), p. 770, para. 8; Giegerich, 'Article 60' (2018), p. 1154, para. 31.

[178] Villiger, *Commentary* (2009), p. 771, para. 10.

[179] Giegerich, 'Article 60', p. 1170, para. 81.

without it the parties would not have entered into the treaty.[180] Furthermore, it is unlikely that a TSD breach would radically transform the extent of all other FTA obligations. Decisively, it would be impossible to argue that such a change was unforeseen, as parties clearly foresaw the possibility that one of them could breach a TSD obligation, hence provided a dispute resolution mechanism to raise claims of TSD violations in this respect. Such an interpretation is also confirmed by the drafting history of Article 62 VCLT, an earlier version explicitly establishing that 'changes of circumstances which the parties have foreseen and for the consequences of which they have made provision in the treaty itself' cannot be used as a ground for treaty termination or withdrawal.[181] Thus, it could be said that the condition that it was not 'foreseen' by the parties is an expression of the *lex specialis* maxim.[182] Therefore, Article 62 (1) VCLT/VCLTSIO is similarly unlikely to serve as a legal basis for imposing sanctions in case of TSD breaches. The rare instances of the EU applying Article 62 VCLT to justify the suspension of trade relations again concerned situations of severe atrocities and civil war.[183]

Considering the limitations related to the invocation of the Articles 60 (1) and 62 (1) VCLT/VCLTSIO and the 'essential elements' clauses from framework agreements to impose sanctions in case of TSD violations, the Commission's new plan to expressly include provisions in relevant agreements to allow the imposition of sanctions as a last resort in case of violations of ILO core labour rights and the Paris Agreement, reinforcing them as essential elements will clearly improve their enforceability, in line with Commission's pledge to do so. Thus, this recent advancement is to be appreciated not only from the perspective of climate and labour rights protection but also from the perspective of legal clarity. In case of the new approach, the enforceability of the obligation to respect ILO core labour rights and the Paris Agreement, as essential elements of the FTAs, will not be affected by the answers to such questions as whether customary international law can be used in case of non-compliance or whether labour commitments can be deemed to reflect human rights. Therefore, expressly specifying that certain climate- or labour-related agreements constitute essential elements of the FTAs is a welcome development from the point of view of EU's public international law commitments as well, allowing it to balance its 'open' but at the same time 'strategic' autonomy.

[180] ibid, 1163, para. 60. [181] ibid, 1162, para. 54. [182] ibid.

[183] CJEU, Case C-162/96, *Racke v Hauptzollamt Mainz*, paras. 53–56, with regard to the suspension of the Cooperation Agreement with the Socialist Republic of Yugoslavia.

7.5 Political Considerations

The EU's new approach to TSD enforcement is welcome not only from the perspective of compatibility with international law in case it wants to use sanctions against TSD violations. It also sends a strong message to Union's partners that FTA TSD commitments should not only remain on the paper but are to be implemented in practice. Therefore, FTAs including this new approach might be more successful in achieving palpable results, hoping that even without application, the mere credible threat of sanctions would incentivize parties to comply.[184] Nevertheless, signing agreements embracing this new approach might be a more difficult task to complete, the signing of FTAs being challenging even without it. Furthermore, in case the other party refuses to include EU's novel TSD enforcement approach, it is not clear whether the EU would still pursue the FTA TSD chapter with an exclusively cooperation-based approach or refuse to sign the agreement altogether. Accordingly, the implications of the more assertive TSD enforcement could go way beyond the chapters that it concerns.

7.6 Conclusion

EU FTAs regularly include TSD chapters. In agreements concluded until recently, however, these chapters contain a so-called managerial or cooperative approach to enforcement, meaning that they rely exclusively on cooperation and do not permit the imposition of sanctions. Thus, while some stakeholders supported this approach with suggested improvements, many others had been long calling for a change that would make it considerably more robust. Responding to these calls, the Commission made important steps towards improving FTA TSD enforcement: the recent willingness to use the special TSD dispute settlement mechanisms under EU–Korea FTA, the creation and appointment of the CTEO, the launch of the SEP, and, most importantly, conducting a review of its TSD action plan, which resulted in a new TSD enforcement model.

These recent developments can already be praised. Thus, by commencing the labour dispute under the EU–Korea FTA, the Commission clearly showed its intention to use the existing tools to step up the enforcement of the TSD chapters. Furthermore, the dispute showed a lower threshold necessary for successful claims on fundamental labour rights than the

[184] Harrison, et al., 'Labour Standards Provisions in EU Free Trade Agreements' (2019) 652.

PART III

The Tools for Assertive Representation of EU Interests

8 The IPI Regulation

A 'Level Playing Field' for European Economic Operators in Foreign Public Procurement Markets within International Law Confines?

8.1 Introduction

Public procurement generally refers to the process by which governments directly or through other entities, such as state-owned enterprises, purchase goods, services, and works.[1] Public procurement usually accounts for 10–20 per cent of a country's GDP;[2] in case of the EU reaching about 14 per cent,[3] thus representing an important sector of the economy. As the Commission claims, the EU's public procurement market is much more open than that of other states, including that of other major economies that are parties to the revised WTO Agreement on Government Procurement (GPA 2012, hereinafter GPA),[4] such as the United States or Japan.[5] Although the EU's de jure openness might not

[1] For definitions of the term 'public procurement', see European Commission (https://single-market-economy.ec.europa.eu/single-market/public-procurement_en) and OECD (www.oecd.org/gov/public-procurement/).

[2] Roderick Edward Noël Harte, 'International Procurement Instrument' (2017) EPRS Briefing, www.europarl.europa.eu/RegData/etudes/BRIE/2017/614610/EPRS_BRI(2017)614610_EN.pdf, p. 2.

[3] European Commission, 'Public Procurement', https://single-market-economy.ec.europa.eu/single-market/public-procurement_en; BusinessEurope, 'BusinessEurope's Views on an International Procurement Instrument', Position Paper, 20 May 2020, www.businesseurope.eu/sites/buseur/files/media/position_papers/rex/2020-05-20_views_on_an_international_procurement_instrument.pdf.

[4] Revised Agreement on Government Procurement (GPA), 30 March 2012, Marrakesh Agreement Establishing the World Trade Organization, Annex 4(b), 1915 U.N.T.S. 103. The GPA is a plurilateral WTO agreement, meaning that not all WTO Members are parties to it. Currently the agreement has 21 parties (counting the EU as one party), comprising 48 WTO Members, 11 other Members being in the process of accession (WTO, Agreement on Government Procurement, www.wto.org/english/tratop_e/gproc_e/gp_gpa_e.htm).

[5] Kamala Dawar, 'The 2016 European Union International Procurement Instrument's Amendments to the 2012 Buy European Proposal: A Retrospective Assessment of Its

be matched by how open the market is de facto,[6] it still does not offer the EU the desired leverage in public procurement negotiations with third countries.

While the Union has been long advocating for more open public procurement markets within the context of the GPA and its bilateral agreements,[7] the results that it has achieved so far are not satisfactory: Major economies such as Brazil, China, and India are not yet parties to the GPA, nor have they signed bilateral agreements with the EU that would open their public procurement markets. The Chinese procurement market causes the most frustrations due to its obstacles;[8] meantime, Chinese companies, including state-owned ones, are winning important tenders in the EU.[9] Moreover, the GPA also does not cover the entire procurement markets of its signatories, as they are able to specify what are the derogations and limitations to their commitments in their individual annexes, such as thresholds for contracts to be covered, list of authorities and entities concerned, goods explicitly excluded from the coverage, or services explicitly included under it.[10] European companies

Prospects' (2016) 50(5) *JWT* 845–866 at 846; Harte, 'International Procurement Instrument', p. 2.

6 Patrick Messerlin, 'The Beauty of Public Procurement in TTIP' (2016) ECIPE Bulletin No. 1/2016, p. 1.

7 Billy A. Melo Araujo, *The EU Deep Trade Agenda: Law and Policy* (New York: Oxford University Press, 2016), p. 213.

8 Joint Communication to the European Parliament, the European Council and the Council, 'EU-China – A Strategic Outlook', Strasbourg, 12 March 2019, JOIN(2019) 5 final, p. 7; Yelter Bollen, Ferdi De Ville, and Jan Orbie, 'EU Trade Policy: Persistent Liberalisation, Contentious Protectionism' (2016) 38(3) *JEI* 279–294 at 286. 'Some of the strongest barriers to foreign participation in China are erected through procurement' (Agatha Kratz and Janka Oertel, 'Home Advantage: How China's Protected Market Threatens Europe's Economic Power', European Council on Foreign Relations, Policy Brief, 15 April 2021, https://ecfr.eu/publication/home-advantage-how-chinas-protected-market-threatens-europes-economic-power/).

9 For example, a Chinese state-owned construction company has built the Peljesac Bridge in Croatia – one of Europe's longest bridges (Stefan Kirchner, 'More Fairness in Global Procurement: The European Union's Future International Procurement Instrument Moves Closer to Reality' (2021), https://papers.ssrn.com/sol3/papers.cfm?abstract_id=3913595), while the China Railway Rolling Stock Corporation was selected as the best bidder for a major rolling stock tender (40–80 electric regional trains) in Romania (BusinessEurope, 'BusinessEurope's Views on an International Procurement Instrument', p. 3).

10 Dawar, 'The 2016 European Union International Procurement Instrument's Amendments' (2016) 855; Melo Araujo, *The EU Deep Trade Agenda* (2016), p. 210; Mandy Meng Fang, 'Shades of Green: Mapping the Parameters of the GATT Article III:8 (a) Government Procurement Derogation in the Renewable Energy Transition' (2019) 20 *JWIT* 553–576 at 558.

often face obstacles in foreign procurement markets, such as lack of publication of notices, requirements of national establishment, including that of joint ventures, 'buy national' provisions, licensing, heavy subsidization of other companies, or import bans on foreign goods for public procurement purposes,[11] prompting the EU Commission to conclude that European companies are amongst the most discriminated in public procurement markets worldwide.[12] As a result, after decade-long discussions, in 2022, the EU adopted the International Procurement Instrument (IPI) (Regulation (EU) 2022/1031),[13] allowing it to impose restrictive measures against companies originating in third countries that seriously and constantly restrict the access of EU economic operators to their procurement markets. Accordingly, the instrument seeks to ensure access and a level playing field for EU companies in third countries' markets, strengthening the EU's position in public procurement negotiations.[14]

Thus, in what follows, this chapter will first describe the legislative history of the IPI (Section 8.2) and will briefly introduce the instrument as it has finally been adopted by the EU legislator (Section 8.3). Then it will assess it in view of the confines established by WTO law (Section 8.4) and by the EU's FTAs (Section 8.5). Finally, the potential broader implications of the instrument for the EU's trade relations with affected third countries will be assessed (Section 8.6), and the conclusions will be presented (Section 8.7).

8.2 The Thorny Road towards an Adopted IPI

Although the IPI was adopted in 2022 as part of EU's recent turn towards increased robustness and a 'level playing field' (which more

[11] 'EU-China – A Strategic Outlook', JOIN(2019) 5 final, p. 6; BusinessEurope, 'BusinessEurope's Views on an International Procurement Instrument', p. 3; Marcin Szczepański, 'EU International Procurement Instrument' (2022) *EPRS*, www.europarl.europa.eu/RegData/etudes/ATAG/2022/729459/EPRS_ATA(2022)729459_EN.pdf, p. 3.

[12] European Commission, 'International Procurement Instrument', *Factsheet*, https://trade.ec.europa.eu/doclib/docs/2019/march/tradoc_157728.pdf.

[13] Regulation (EU) 2022/1031 of the European Parliament and of the Council of 23 June 2022 on the access of third-country economic operators, goods and services to the Union's public procurement and concession markets and procedures supporting negotiations on access of Union economic operators, goods and services to the public procurement and concession markets of third countries (IPI Regulation), OJ EU 2022 No. L 173/1.

[14] Erik Brattberg and Philippe Le Corre, 'The EU and China in 2020: More Competition Ahead' (2020) *Carnegie Endowment for International Peace*, https://carnegieendowment.org/files/1-31-20_Brattberg_Le_Corre_EU_China.pdf.

assertively advances EU's interests and values), its finalization being mentioned in 2021 Commission's Communication on the Trade Policy Review as an urgent action,[15] the idea behind it is far from new. The first IPI Proposal was tabled by the European Commission in 2012.[16] The proposal targeted only non-covered goods or services, referring to the goods or services originating in countries with which the EU has no international agreement in the field of public procurement, including the GPA or an FTA, or goods and services that do not fall under the coverage of the procurement commitments from an international agreement.[17] It proposed two distinct procedures, a decentralized and centralized one, that would have allowed the imposition of restrictions in case of lack of 'substantial reciprocity in market opening' between the EU and the third country concerned.[18] Under the decentralized procedure, a procuring authority/entity could have requested the Commission's approval of the exclusion of tenders in case of contracts above a certain threshold and when the value of the non-covered goods or services exceeded 50 per cent of the total value of the goods or services constituting the tender.[19] Under the centralized procedures, the Commission would have initiated an investigation into alleged restrictive procurement measures, and in case of a positive finding, it would have initiated consultations with a view of (further) opening the third country's public procurement market.[20] In case of unsuccessful consultations, the Commission could have either excluded the tender of which more than 50 per cent of the total value was made up of non-covered goods or services originating in the concerned country or could have imposed a price penalty on the part of the tender consisting of those non-covered goods or services.[21]

[15] European Commission Communication, 'Trade Policy Review: An Open, Sustainable and Assertive Trade Policy', 18 February 2021, COM(2021) 66 final, p. 21.

[16] European Commission, Proposal for a Regulation of the European Parliament and of the Council on the Access of Third-Country Goods and Services to the Union's Internal Market in Public Procurement and Procedures Supporting Negotiations on Access of Union Goods and Services to the Public Procurement Markets of Third Countries, Brussels (The 2012 IPI Proposal), 21 March 2012, COM(2012) 124 final.

[17] ibid, Art. 2 (1) (e).

[18] The proposal explained that it referred to the situation 'where restrictive procurement measures result in serious and recurring discriminations of Union economic operators, goods and services' and also provided aspects to be taken into account when establishing the presence of such a situation (ibid, Art. 6 (4), second paragraph, (5)).

[19] ibid, Art. 6 (1). [20] ibid, Arts. 8, 9. [21] ibid, Art. 10 (2).

The 2012 IPI proposal proved to be controversial, including in the Commission.[22] Although not without certain debates and essential amendments suggested, the EP approved the proposal and mandated its rapporteur to negotiate with the Council.[23] But it was the Council that blocked its adoption, as some Member States, such as Germany, the Netherlands, the United Kingdom, and Sweden, had reservations about it, especially its potential protectionist character.[24] In 2016, a revised proposal was tabled, incorporating some of the suggested amendments by the EP and the Council and simplifying the procedures perceived as being too burdensome for the domestic authorities and posing the risk of fragmentation of the EU's single market.[25] Thus, the 2016 IPI proposal provided only for a centralized procedure, under which the Commission could have initiated investigations, and if the findings had indicated the presence of 'restrictive and/or discriminatory procurement measures or practices' against EU goods, services and economic operators, the Commission would have initiated consultations.[26] If consultations had not lead to changes, in case of contracts with an estimated value equal to or above EUR 5 million exclusive of VAT, the proposal foresaw only the possibility of imposing price adjustment measures on tenders submitted by companies originating in the countries in question, unless the bidders demonstrated that less than 50 per cent of the total value of their tender was made up of non-covered goods and services originating in that third country.[27] The price adjustment measures would have consisted of a penalty up to 20 per cent of the price of the tender, which would not have impeded the participation of the concerned bidder and would not have affected the actual price to be paid.[28] The 2016 IPI proposal introduced *inter alia* exceptions for products originating in least developed and vulnerable developing countries subject to the GSP+ scheme or the

[22] Commissioners of several Member States deemed the proposal protectionist (Bollen, De Ville, Orbie, 'EU Trade Policy' (2016) 286).

[23] Harte, 'International Procurement Instrument' (2017), p. 5. [24] ibid, p. 5.

[25] Dawar, 'The 2016 European Union International Procurement Instrument's Amendments' (2016) 849–850; Szczepański, 'EU International Procurement Instrument' (2022), p. 1.

[26] European Commission, Amended Proposal for a Regulation of the European Parliament and of the Council on the Access of Third-Country Goods and Services to the Union's Internal Market in Public Procurement and Procedures Supporting Negotiations on Access of Union Goods and Services to the Public Procurement Markets of Third Countries (2016 IPI Proposal), 29 January 2016, COM(2016) 34 final, Arts. 6, 7.

[27] ibid, Explanatory Memorandum, p. 3, Arts. 6, 8, 11 (1).

[28] ibid, Arts. 8 (2), 11 (1) paragraph 3.

'Everything but Arms' arrangement and for Small and Medium Enterprises (SMEs).[29] It also expressly provided that it would have applied only to restrictive or discriminatory procurement measures of a third country in respect to non-covered procurement, 'without prejudice to any international obligations of the Union'.[30] However, Member States were still divided in the Council, and an agreement on the proposal was not reached.

In 2019, discussions on the IPI gained new momentum. The Commission's Communication 'EU-China – A Strategic Outlook' mentioned that the EU needs to adapt to the changing economic realities and strengthen its domestic policy, listing the adoption of the IPI Regulation and issuance of guidance on the participation of third-country bidders and goods in the EU procurement market as two out of ten necessary actions to tackle the Chinese phenomenon.[31] In the Guidance, the Commission mentioned that economic operators from third countries which do not have any agreement opening the EU public procurement market or whose goods and services are not covered by such an agreement can be excluded from procurement procedures.[32] Even the more reluctant Member States, such as Germany, became supportive of the instrument.[33] In early 2021, the Portuguese Presidency of the Council presented a new IPI draft based on the 2016 proposal, *inter alia* adding the possibility to exclude bidders as a restrictive measures, and in June 2022, the IPI was adopted as Regulation 2022/1031.

Accordingly, it took the Council a decade to change its position and break the deadlock. It has abandoned its claims that the instrument might be perceived as being protectionist – a change in attitude that can be explained by the changing landscape of international trade. The increase during the last years in protectionist procurement measures adopted by other countries, such as China, Brazil, or Russia, has likely incentivized the EU to take action. Due to this, but also after COVID, Brexit, and Trump's consideration to withdraw from the GPA, the idea of having a tool to tackle closed procurement markets started to be perceived as being more legitimate.[34]

[29] ibid, Arts. 4, 5. [30] ibid, Art. 1 (4).

[31] 'EU-China – A Strategic Outlook', JOIN(2019) 5 final, pp. 2, 7, 8.

[32] Communication from the Commission, Guidance on the Participation of Third Country Bidders and Goods in the EU Procurement Market, 24 July 2019, C(2019) 5494 final, p. 6.

[33] Brattberg and Le Corre, 'The EU and China in 2020' (2020), p. 6.

[34] Marc Gabriel, Andreas Schulz, and Alice Manzini, 'Proposal for an International Procurement Instrument: The Undiscovered (Third) Country' (2020) *Public Procurement Law*

8.3 The IPI Regulation

Similar to the 2012 and 2016 proposals, the IPI Regulation provides in its Article 1 (1), (3) that it establishes measures only with respect to non-covered procurement, being without prejudice to any international obligation of the Union. Additionally, it explicitly establishes in the preamble that measures adopted under it can only apply to economic operators, goods, and services originating in countries that are not parties to the GPA or bilateral or multilateral agreements that include commitments on access to public procurement or concession markets, or to economic operators, goods, and services from countries that are parties to such agreements, but only with respect to procurement not covered by them, emphasizing and clarifying its relationship with these international agreements (recital 10 and Article 2 (1) (k) IPI Regulation). Accordingly, IPI Regulation measures would not apply to GPA and FTA parties, but only to the extent that the EU has undertaken in these agreements market access commitments specifically in the field of public procurement or concessions.

Similar to the 2012 proposed centralized procedure that was kept under the 2016 proposal, under the IPI Regulation, the Commission, on its own initiative or upon a substantiated complaint of an interested party or a Member State, may initiate an investigation into an alleged third-country measure or practice that results in a serious and recurrent impairment of access of European economic operators, goods, or services to the public procurement market of that country ('measure or practice') by publishing a notice (Articles 2 (1) (i), 5 (1)). Upon publication, the Commission will have to invite the third country to submit its views and relevant information and to enter into consultations to terminate or remedy the alleged practice or measure (Article 5 (2)). If such measure or practice is not maintained or does not have the described result, the investigations should be terminated; and if the third country in question takes corrective measures or undertakes commitments towards the Union to end or phase them out, the investigation should be suspended (Article 5 (5), (6)). The investigation and consultations should be concluded within maximum nine months, a period which can be extended by five months, upon which the Commission should publish the report setting the main findings and the proposed course of action, also presenting it to the EP and the Council (Article 5 (3), (4)).

Review 335–342 at 335; Szczepański, 'EU International Procurement Instrument' (2022), p. 2.

When, following the investigation, the Commission concludes that a third country's practice or measure covered by the IPI Regulation exists (i.e. a measure that results in a serious and recurrent impairment of access of Union economic operators, goods, or services to the public procurement or concession markets of that third country), it should adopt an IPI measure if it considers to be in the Union's interest based on the assessment of various interests taken as a whole, including that of economic operators (Article 6 (1), (2)). For IPI measures to be applied to public procurement procedures, the Regulation introduces different thresholds for goods and services versus works and concessions: an estimated value equal to or above EUR 5 million net of VAT versus EUR 15 million net of VAT (Article 6 (4)), a differentiation absent from the 2012 and 2016 drafts. Article 6 (6), (7) IPI Regulation prescribes two different types of IPI measures. First is the imposition of a score adjustment on tenders submitted by economic operators originating in the third countries concerned, applying only for the purpose of evaluation and ranking of the tenders, without an effect on the actual price to be paid. Second is the exclusion of tenders submitted by such economic operators. Hence, similar to the 2012 proposal, and unlike the 2016 one, the IPI Regulation envisages the possibility to remove altogether the bids of certain bidders. However, unlike the 2012 and 2016 proposals, the main criterion for the application of both types of measures is the origin of the bidders and not the bids. Additionally, the score adjustment can be be applied not only to the score of the tender regarding the assessment of the price (as in the 2012 and 2016 proposals)[35] but also to qualitative criteria. This means that the percentage value of the adjustment could be set up to 100 per cent of the evaluation score in cases where the price or cost is the only contract award criterion (meaning that for the assessment of the tender the price will be doubled), and up to 50 per cent in other cases (Article 6 (8) IPI Regulation). The two types of IPI measures are put by the Regulation on equal footing, there being no specific preference for one over the other in a particular situation.[36] But when choosing a measure, the Commission should take into account criteria such as the proportionality of the measure and the availability of alternative sources

[35] The increase in score will not affect the price if the tenderer nevertheless wins the contract; see IPI Regulation, recital 21 and Art. 6 (7) s. 2.

[36] Daniel Caspary, 'Opinion: International Procurement Instrument – the end of the waiting game', *Borderlex*, 31 March 2022, https://borderlex.net/2022/03/31/opinion-international-procurement-instrument-the-end-of-the-waiting-game/.

of supply for the goods and services concerned (Article 6 (3), (9)). An IPI measure expires five years after its entry into force, unless it is withdrawn or suspended due to the third country taking satisfactory corrective actions or undertaking (further) commitments, or unless extended for a duration of another five years (Article 6 (10), (11)).

While under the 2012 and 2016 proposals the application of restrictive measures would have also been determined based on whether more than 50 per cent of the value of the tender consists of non-covered goods (see Section 8.2), the application of restrictive measures under the IPI Regulation is not affected by such a condition. Instead, Article 8 (1) IPI Regulation imposes obligations upon the successful tenderers: (1) not to subcontract more than 50 per cent of the total value of the contract to economic operators originating in the third country; (2) to ensure that non-covered goods and services represent no more than 50 per cent of the total value of a contract covering the supply of goods; (3) to provide, upon request, adequate evidence with respect to points (1) and (2) to contracting authorities or entities; and (4) in the event of non-compliance with (1) and (2), to pay a proportionate charge of 10–30 per cent of the total value of the contract. Thus, the administrative burden, as well as the burden supported by the bidders, has been greatly reduced, as only the successful ones bear obligations and, upon request, are mandated to provide evidence in this respect.

Article 7 (1) further reduces the administrative burden, as the Commission, upon a justified request by a Member State, may adopt a list of local authorities that are exempted from the application of the Regulation, paying due regard to the fair distribution among Member States. The exemptions may be granted only for authorities within administrative units with a population below 50,000 inhabitants and when the value of contracts above the established thresholds awarded in the past three years by authorities and entities that are not exempted exceeds 80 per cent of the total value of contracts above the thresholds awarded in the requesting Member State (Article 7 (1), (2)). Accordingly, central governments and administrations of big municipalities will always apply IPI measures.[37] Article 4 IPI Regulation prevents the initiation of an investigation in respect to the least developed countries benefitting from the 'Everything but Arms' arrangement, thereby avoiding hindering the

[37] Rhodri Williams, 'A New EU International Procurement Instrument (IPI)', *Henderson Chambers*, 13 April 2022, www.hendersonchambers.co.uk/2022/04/13/alerter-by-rhodri-williams-qc-a-new-eu-international-procurement-instrument-ipi/.

economic growth of these countries. Additionally, contracting authorities and entities may, on exceptional basis, decide not to apply an IPI measure when the economic operators from third countries subject to IPI measures are the only ones meeting the tender requirements, or because of overriding reasons relating to public interest, such as public health or environmental protection (Article 9 (1)). This last exception would have clearly covered the procurement of masks from third countries during the COVID pandemic. Finally, the Regulation should be reviewed no later than four years after the adoption of an implementing act and every five years thereafter (Article 14).

8.4 The IPI and the WTO Constraints

The IPI Regulation establishes measures only with respect to so-called non-covered procurement. In the concrete words of Article 2 (1) (k) IPI Regulation, non-covered procurement means procurement for which the EU 'has not undertaken *market access commitments* in an international agreement *in the field of public procurement or concessions*' (emphasis added), but not market access commitments undertaken in the context of General Agreement on Tariffs and Trade (GATT)[38] or that of other WTO agreements. Therefore, measures adopted under the IPI Regulation would not be applicable to economic operators, goods, or services from GPA parties as long as the procurement in question is covered by market access commitments assumed by the EU under the GPA. Already back in 2012, when the Commission tabled its first proposal, it argued that the EU stands by its international commitments.[39] However, the question of the IPI Regulation's compatibility with the EU's WTO commitments goes further than the GPA, since IPI measures may also fall under other WTO agreements, such as the GATT, the General Agreement on Trade in Services (GATS),[40] the Agreement on Subsidies and Countervailing

[38] General Agreement on Tariffs and Trade 1994, 15 April 1994, Marrakesh Agreement Establishing the World Trade Organization, Annex 1A, 1867 U.N.T.S. 187, 33 I.L.M. 1153 (1994).

[39] European Commission, 'External Public Procurement Initiative – Frequently Asked Questions', 21 March 2012, https://ec.europa.eu/commission/presscorner/detail/en/MEMO_12_201.

[40] General Agreement on Trade in Services, 15 April 1994, Marrakesh Agreement Establishing the World Trade Organization, Annex 1B, 1869 U.N.T.S. 183, 33 I.L.M. 1167 (1994).

Measures (ASCM),[41] and the Dispute Settlement Understanding (DSU).[42] It is striking that the compatibility with international law that the IPI Regulation pursues by carving certain procurement out of its scope of application is reduced to 'market access commitments in an international agreement *in the field of public procurement or concessions*' (emphasis added), as if there could be no other international legal commitments (also under WTO law) applicable to procurement or concessions covered by the IPI Regulation, such as general market commitments included in the GATT like national treatment (NT) obligations. However, similarly to other recent legislation adopted in the implementation of the EU's trade policy assertiveness turn, there is a general provision addressing the conformity of the measures taken[43] under the regulation with international law. Article 1 (3) IPI Regulation stipulates that the regulation 'shall be without prejudice to any international obligations of the Union or to measures that Member States or their contracting authorities or contracting entities may take in accordance with the acts referred to in paragraph 2'. This general disclaimer, however, is not further implemented in the language of the regulation's provisions. It may be seen as requiring the EU Commission, when implementing the regulation, to abstain from measures if they are in conflict with other international law, including the above-mentioned general WTO rules. This issue, however, has not been clarified in the regulation. Recital 4 postulates that the public procurement derogations of Articles III:8 GATT and Article XIII:1 GATS protect IPI measures from the 'main multilateral WTO disciplines'. However, as will be shown, these rules are a carve-out only for specific types of procurement from NT obligations and do not fully comprise the scope of the IPI Regulation; nor are they a general procurement waiver. Therefore, it is necessary to research the potential clashes of the IPI Regulation with WTO rules. This section will look into the confines established by the WTO agreements and will assess the IPI Regulation's

[41] Agreement on Subsidies and Countervailing Measures, 15 April 1994, Marrakesh Agreement Establishing the World Trade Organization, Annex 1A, 1869 U.N.T.S. 14.

[42] Understanding on Rules and Procedures Governing the Settlement of Disputes, Marrakesh Agreement Establishing the World Trade Organization, Annex 2, 1869 U.N.T.S. 401, 33 I.L.M. 1226 (1994).

[43] For general disclaimers as to conformity with international law, see e.g. Art. 44 (9) Foreign Subsidies Regulation (see Chapter 9), according to which any investigation pursuant to the regulation 'shall not be carried out and measures shall not be imposed or maintained where such investigation or measures would be contrary' to the EU international obligations.

compatibility with them, particularly that of the measures and obligations on successful tenderers, which might be challenged sooner or later within WTO proceedings.

The subsequent analysis will begin with the most obvious tension between the IPI measures and WTO rules: their compatibility with WTO non-discrimination obligations, as the implementation of the IPI Regulation will lead to measures specifically addressing certain countries and to disincentives for the affected foreign goods or services as compared to other like foreign or domestic goods or services. Hence, the IPI may violate the most-favoured-nation (MFN) obligation – and even beyond, as some scholars already held, the IPI could violate the NT of GATT and GATS.[44] The subsequent section will not start with the MFN obligation but with the NT commitments, because the pertinent rules and the derogations therefrom for certain forms of procurement are much more elaborate and had been subject to greater clarification in WTO jurisprudence than with regard to the MFN obligation.

8.4.1 National Treatment Obligations under the GATT and GATS

In what follows we will briefly argue that GATT and GATS NT provisions will be violated by IPI measures, before we go into the more complex issue of whether and how far the NT obligations cover public procurement. The sequence of analysis hence is reversing the logical order, because the latter complex issue would not have to be raised if the IPI did not pose problems with regard to the NT disciplines.[45]

8.4.1.1 Violation of National Treatment: Articles III:4 GATT and XVII GATS

Due to their closeness of structure and wording,[46] the NT principles of GATT and GATS will be assessed in the same section. According to Article III:4 GATT, foreign products 'shall be accorded treatment no less favourable than that accorded to like products of national origin in respect of all laws, regulations and requirements affecting their internal sale, offering for sale, purchase, transportation, distribution or use'.

[44] Dawar, 'The 2016 European Union International Procurement Instrument's Amendments' (2016); Gabriel, Schulz, and Manzini, 'Proposal for an International Procurement Instrument' (2020).

[45] As will be shown in Section 8.4.1.2, Art. III:8 GATT is not a justification for a measure that would otherwise be inconsistent with Art. III:4 GATT but limits the scope of Art. III:4 GATT.

[46] See Wolfgang Weiß, *WTO Law and Domestic Regulation* (München: Hart/Beck/Nomos, 2020), pp. 147 f.

As shown in the previous section, the measures envisaged under the IPI Regulation, namely the exclusion of tenders of economic operators originating in targeted third countries or the imposition of a score adjustment on their tenders, do not focus per se on the origin of the goods supplied but on the origin of the bidders (unlike the 2012 and 2016 proposals).[47] However, as the Regulation itself states, the measures have the aim 'to restrict the access of economic operators, goods or services from a third country to public procurement procedures'.[48] Based on the market situation and available information, it could be argued that economic operators originating in targeted third countries usually submit tenders consisting mainly of imported goods from those countries, which as a result are treated less favourably than domestic goods. Additionally, the obligation imposed on successful tenderers that goods or services supplied or provided in the execution of a contract for the supply of goods and originating in a third country subject to IPI measures represent no more than 50 per cent of the total value of the contract or otherwise face a proportionate charge clearly forces *all* successful economic operators to use less imported products from targeted countries, treating them differently than the domestic ones.

A breach of Article III:4 GATT requires first of all that goods are like. The likeness of the products affected under Article III:4 is usually assessed based on the examination of all the evidence related to the criteria established by the existing jurisprudence (physical properties, end-uses, consumers' tastes and habits, tariff classifications).[49] As the products' treatment to be compared under the assessment of likeness will be foreign versus domestic products to be procured in the same procurement procedure run by a domestic contracting authority, one can easily assume that in almost all cases, those goods will share the abovementioned characteristics in order to qualify for the procurement criteria; at least they will be in a competitive relationship. What is more, in case of the potential IPI restrictive measures and obligations on the successful tenderers, the difference in treatment between foreign and domestic products concerned would be based exclusively on the origin of the product or economic operators; it would not rely on any other criterion, such as physical characteristics or end-use. When the difference in treatment is determined by factors unrelated to the definition of likeness, such as the origin of a product or the seller, the products at issue can be

[47] See Section 8.2. [48] IPI Regulation, Art. 6 (6).

[49] Appellate Body Report, *EC – Asbestos*, WT/DS135/AB/R, 12 March 2001, para. 109.

hypothetically treated as 'like' for the purpose of Article III:4 GATT.[50] The IPI Regulation clearly also represents a 'regulation' in the sense of Article III:4 GATT, by prescribing mandatory procurement rules and regulating the conduct of the Commission, Member States, contracting authorities and entities, and economic operators in specific cases.[51] It also affects 'the internal sale, offering of sale, purchase' of products originating in targeted foreign countries, since it concerns the access to and conditions of procurement of these products on the EU market and might adversely modify the competition between domestic and imported products.[52] Thus, the IPI measures would also lead to less beneficial treatment accorded to foreign like goods. By limiting the supply volume of goods originating in third countries subject to IPI measures, the obligation on successful bidders would clearly modify the conditions of competition in the EU procurement market in favour of domestic products,[53] foreign products from those countries being undoubtedly treated de jure less favourably. If shown that in practice the tenders submitted by economic operators originating in countries subject to IPI measures usually consist to a greater extent of products originating in those countries, the potential exclusion or imposition of score adjustments on these tenders could

[50] Panel Report, *Argentina – Hides and Leather*, WT/DS155/R, 19 December 2000, para. 11.169 and fn. 463 to it. Although the panel stated this in relation to Art. III:2 of the GATT, this can also be applied to the analysis of 'likeness' under Art. III:4, since 'to the extent that the imported and domestic products compared are found "like" within the meaning of the first sentence of Article III:2, they can also be deemed to meet the likeness requirement under Article III:4' (Panel Report, *Thailand – Cigarettes (Philippines)*, WT/DS371/R, 15 November 2010, para. 7.662). Additionally, existing jurisprudence confirms that this 'hypothetical' test can be used for the assessment of likeness under Art. III:4 GATT (Panel Report, *India – Autos*, WT/DS146/R, 21 December 2001, para. 7.174; Panel Report, *Canada – Wheat Exports and Grain Imports*, WT/DS276/R, 6 April 2004, fn. 246 to para. 6.164; Panel Report, *China – Publications and Audiovisual Products*, WT/DS363/R, 12 August 2008, para. 7.1446). The Appellate Body, in principle, has confirmed the lawfulness of such approach by the panels but has formulated some limits, in particular with likeness in GATS; see Appellate Body Report, *Argentina – Financial Services*, WT/DS453/AB/R, 14 April 2016, para. 6.38 f.

[51] According to the panel in *India – Solar Cells*, 'the definition of "regulation" likewise refers to a "rule prescribed for controlling some matter, or for the regulating of conduct"' (Panel Report, *India – Solar Cells*, WT/DS456/R, 24 February 2016, para. 7.308).

[52] On the scope of the term 'affecting', see Panel Report, *Canada – Autos*, WT/DS139/R, WT/DS142/R, 11 February 2000, para. 10.80; Panel Report, *China – Publications and Audiovisual Products*, WT/DS363/R, para. 7.1450.

[53] For more on the concept of 'less favourable treatment', see Appellate Body Report, *Korea – Beef*, WT/DS161/AB/R, WT/DS169/AB/R, 11 December 2000, para. 144; Appellate Body Report, *Dominican Republic – Cigarettes*, WT/DS302/AB/R, 25 April 2005, para. 96; Weiß, *WTO Law and Domestic Regulation* (2020), pp. 132 ff, 149 ff.

modify the conditions of competition on the EU public procurement market in favour of domestic products, discriminating de facto against the imported products in question. Thus, all elements for a violation of Article III:4 GATT could be met in case of the examined IPI provisions.

The same conclusion can be found with regard to the NT discipline of Article XVII GATS. For the sectors inscribed in EU's Schedule of Commitments and subject to any conditions and qualifications set out therein,[54] GATS NT obligation in Article XVII:1 demands that 'each Member shall accord to services and service suppliers of any other Member, in respect of all measures affecting the supply of services, treatment no less favourable than that it accords to its own like services and service suppliers'. The IPI measures and obligations on successful tenderers will most likely negatively affect the supply of services by economic operators originating in third countries subject to such measures (especially through Mode 1 of supply – cross-border trade, Article I:2 GATS). Since the IPI measures differentiate between service suppliers and the obligations on successful tenderers between both services and service suppliers solely based on their origin,[55] the 'like service and service suppliers' requirement can be considered hypothetically complied with,[56] even more so as the criterion of likeness under GATS is construed in the same way as under GATT to relate in particular to services in competitive relationship.[57] Additionally, the imposition of a score adjustment on tenders submitted by service suppliers originating in certain third countries, minimizing their chances to be awarded the public contract, as well as the complete exclusion of such tenders, depriving the foreign supplier of any opportunity to compete with other tenders,[58] clearly modify the conditions of competition to the detriment of the suppliers from those countries. Moreover, the obligations on successful tenderers would certainly modify the conditions of competition in favour of other services and service suppliers than those originating in countries concerned by IPI measures, including domestic ones, as the successful

[54] WTO Members may limit at their own discretion the extent to which they grant market access or national treatment to services that they list in their Schedule of Commitments by inscribing certain limitations (Panel Report, *China – Publications and Audiovisual Products*, WT/DS363/R, para. 7.950).

[55] IPI Regulation, Arts. 6 (6), 8 (1).

[56] Panel Report, *China – Publications and Audiovisual Products*, WT/DS363/R, paras. 7.975–7.976.

[57] Panel Report, *EU – Certain Measures Relating to the Energy Sector*, WT/DS476/R, 10 August 2018, paras. 7.1400 ff.

[58] Panel Report, *China – Publications and Audiovisual Products*, WT/DS363/R, para. 7.979.

tenderers would be stimulated to avoid subcontracting to foreign suppliers and supplying foreign services from concerned countries. Thus, foreign like services and service suppliers from countries subject to IPI measures will be 'treated less favourably'.[59] Accordingly, unless covered by an exception or derogation from the scope of Articles III:4 GATT and XVII GATS, the IPI provisions are to be found in violation of these articles.

8.4.1.2 Derogation from National Treatment: Article III:8 (a) GATT and Its Reach

As already mentioned, the IPI Regulation's disclaimer as to respect for the EU's international obligations in Article 1 (3)) is far from clear and shows that the EU might not have considered that the main multilateral WTO agreements do cover governmental procurement despite the existence of scope derogations because the AB's interpretations have conceived them quite narrowly. The EU argues that the IPI Regulation is excluded from the scope of coverage of the NT obligations by Article III:8 GATT and Article XIII GATS (recital 4), the latter to be analyzed in Section 8.4.1.3. Indeed, Article III:8 GATT on government procurement limits the scope of the NT obligation contained in Article III,[60] by providing that

> [t]he provisions of this Article shall not apply to laws, regulations or requirements governing the procurement by governmental agencies of products purchased for governmental purposes and not with a view to commercial resale or with a view to use in the production of goods for commercial sale.

In what follows we will explore the inherent limitations of the NT government procurement derogations; and insofar as these limitations apply, the IPI measures provided in the IPI Regulation might not be always carved out from NT disciplines. The problem lies, as will be shown, in the non-congruence between the scope of application of the IPI Regulation and the derogations on the reach of the NT derogations.

[59] The notion of 'treatment no less favourable' implies the modification of conditions of competition according to Art. XVII:3 of the GATS, as is the case with Art. III:4 GATT. Panel Report, *China – Publications and Audiovisual Products*, WT/DS363/R, paras. 7.978, 7.1130; Panel Report, *China – Electronic Payment Services*, WT/DS413/R, 16 July 2012, para. 7.687; Appellate Body Report, *Argentina – Financial Services*, WT/DS453/AB/R, 14 April 2016, para. 6.103; Weiß, *WTO Law and Domestic Regulation* (2020) 149 ff.

[60] Panel Report, *Canada – FIT Program*, WT/DS412/R, WT/DS426/R, 19 December 2012, fn. 263 to para. 7.113. It is not a justification for measures that would otherwise violate the NT obligation contained in Art. III GATT (Appellate Body Report, *Canada – FIT Program*, WT/DS412/AB/R, WT/DS426/AB/R, 6 May 2013, para. 5.56).

Under Article III:8 GATT, certain types of procurement are excluded from the scope of coverage of the NT obligation of Article III GATT, subject to the specific conditions of paragraph 8 (a).[61] Many commentators have generally assumed that any government procurement falls outside the scope of the GATT (and GATS) obligations.[62] This assumption, however, has been clearly rebutted by the relevant WTO jurisprudence. After Article III:8 (a) GATT had remained dormant for over six decades, in the last few years it has been dealt with in three disputes: *Canada – FIT Program*,[63] *India – Solar Cells*,[64] and, most recently, in an Appeal Arbitration Report in *Turkey – Pharmaceutical Products (EU)*,[65] which showed that its ambit might be much narrower than what initially was thought by many scholars and WTO Members. The adjudicators interpreted this provision quite narrowly, sending a clear message that public procurement not covered by the GPA is still subject to the NT obligation, unless falling under the strict confines of Article III:8 (a) GATT.[66] The narrow interpretation has been criticized for excessively reducing Members' flexibility in adopting public procurement measures, leading to potential absurd results, and disregarding the object and purpose of the provision.[67]

61 Arwel Davies, 'The GATT Article III:8(a) Procurement Derogation and *Canada – Renewable Energy*' (2015) 18 (3) *JIEL* 543–554 at 549; Dawar, 'The 2016 European Union International Procurement Instrument's Amendments' (2016) 849. Also confirmed by the Award of the Arbitrators, *Turkey – Pharmaceutical Products (EU)*, WT/DS583/ARB25, 25 July 2022, para. 6.30.

62 Alan Yanovich, '*Canada – Renewable Energy* and *Canada – FIT Program*: Debunking the Myth that the GATT 1994 Provides Carte Blanche to Discriminate in Government Procurement' (2013) *GTCJ* 8 (11) & (12) 430–434 at 434; Davies, 'The GATT Article III:8(a)' (2015) 549; Frank Hoffmeister, 'The EU Public Procurement Regime on Third-Country Bidders: Setting the Cursor Between Openness and Reciprocity', in Harri Kalimo and Max S. Jansson (eds.), *EU Economic Law in a Time of Crisis* (Cheltenham: Edward Elgar Publishing, 2016), p. 77; Sandeep Thomas Chandy and Anupal Dasgupta, 'Government Procurement Outside the GPA: A Developing Country View' (2019) 14 (7) & (8) *GTCJ* 383–390 at 384.

63 Panel Report, *Canada – FIT Program*, WT/DS412/R, WT/DS426/R; Appellate Body Report, *Canada – FIT Program*, WT/DS412/AB/R, WT/DS426/AB/R.

64 Panel Report, *India – Solar Cells*, WT/DS456/R; Appellate Body Report, *India – Solar Cells*, WT/DS456/AB/R, 16 September 2016.

65 Award of the Arbitrators, *Turkey – Pharmaceutical Products (EU)*, WT/DS583/ARB25.

66 Yanovich, '*Canada – Renewable Energy* and *Canada – FIT Program*' (2013) 434; Kamala Dawar, 'Government Procurement in the WTO: A Case for Greater Integration' (2016) 15 (4) *WTRev* 645–670 at 647; Fang, 'Shades of Green', 553.

67 Davies, 'The GATT Article III:8(a)', 549–550; Fang, 'Shades of Green' (2019) 573–574; Vincent Dalpé, 'Canada – Feed-In Tariff: Are FITs Desirable, or Even Legal? A Case Comment' (2014) 27(1) *Quebec Journal of International Law* 87–112 at 95; Rika Koch, *Green Public Procurement Under WTO Law: Experience of the EU and Prospects for Switzerland* (Cham: Springer, 2020), p. 59. But there are also supporters of a narrower interpretation, e.g. Jan Bohanes and Karolyn Salcedo, 'Overview of WTO Jurisprudence in 2013', in Christoph

Moreover, an excessively narrow interpretation was said to disregard the negotiating history. The Havana Charter for an International Trade Organization[68] drafted by the United States initially subjected public procurement to the NT obligation, but this was too contentious, and ultimately Article III:8 (a) GATT was added to carve public procurement out.[69] However, as a narrow approach has been endorsed in all three disputes dealing with Article III:8 (a) GATT, including most recently in Article 25 DSU appeal arbitration proceedings in *Turkey – Pharmaceutical Products (EU)*,[70] it is most likely that it will be followed in a potential dispute against the IPI Regulation. Furthermore, as will be argued further in this section, the most criticized aspect of the interpretation would not unduly disqualify IPI provisions from the public procurement derogation. Therefore, the present chapter will assess whether and how far the IPI provisions could be covered by Article III:8 (a) GATT and, thus, excluded from the scope of Article III:4 GATT NT obligation in light of this pertinent jurisprudence.

In order for measures to be covered by the derogation contained in Article III:8 (a) GATT, several cumulative elements must be met: (1) the challenged measures are 'laws, regulations or requirements governing procurement'; (2) the procurement is 'by governmental agencies'; (3) the procurement is of 'products purchased for governmental purposes'; and (4) the products purchased are not procured 'with a view to commercial resale or with a view to use in the production of goods for commercial sale'.[71]

The IPI provisions qualify as 'laws and regulations governing procurement'. By excluding or imposing a score adjustment on certain tenders in procurement procedures and by imposing an obligation on tenderers that were successful in procurement procedures, there is an 'articulated connection' between these provisions and the procurement,

Herrmann, Markus Krajewski, and Jörg Philipp Terhechte (eds.), *European Yearbook of International Economic Law 2015* (Cham: Springer, 2015), vol. 6, p. 368.

[68] Havana Charter for an International Trade Organization, 24 March 1948, United Nations Conference on Trade and Employment, Final Act and Related Documents, UN Doc. E/CONF.2/78.

[69] Sue Arrowsmith, *Government Procurement in the WTO* (The Hague: Kluwer Law International, 2003), p. 50; Davies, 'The GATT Article III:8(a)' (2015) 547; Fang, 'Shades of Green' (2019) 560; Koch, *Green Public Procurement under WTO Law* (2020), p. 55.

[70] See Award of the Arbitrators, *Turkey – Pharmaceutical Products (EU)*, WT/DS583/ARB25, paras. 6.42–6.43.

[71] Appellate Body Report, *India – Solar Cells*, WT/DS456/AB/R, para. 5.42; Award of the Arbitrators, *Turkey – Pharmaceutical Products (EU)*, WT/DS583/ARB25, paras. 6.31–6.32.

which can be considered as being 'undertaken within a binding structure of laws, regulations, or requirements', as demanded by WTO case law.[72]

In order for an entity to qualify as a 'governmental agency' in the sense of Article III:8 (a) GATT, it would have to act 'for or on behalf of government' and perform governmental functions within the competences conferred on it.[73] Under the IPI Regulation, procurement is made by 'contracting authorities and entities', which, by virtue of reference in Articles 1 (2), 2 (1) (f) (g) IPI Regulation, are defined in Directives 2014/23/EU,[74] 2014/24/EU,[75] and 2014/25/EU.[76] Thus, 'contracting authorities' means (1) the state; (2) regional or local authorities of the administrative units; (3) bodies governed by public law, which have legal personality, are established for meeting needs of general interest, without having an industrial or commercial character, and which are financed (for the most part) or subject to management supervision by the State, regional or local authorities, or other bodies governed by public law, or have an administrative managerial or supervisory board, the members of which are appointed by those authorities and bodies; or (4) associations formed by one or more such authorities or bodies.[77] All these authorities either represent the government at the national or regional level or are subject to its dominant influence and control, acting on the behalf of it. They also seem to perform governmental functions of general interest.

However, the interpretation of the aforesaid requirement 'established for the specific purpose of meeting needs in the general interest, not having an industrial or commercial character' is less clear, specifically with respect to the test for determining the main activity of a body. It is

[72] Appellate Body Report, *Canada – FIT Program*, WT/DS426/AB/R, para. 5.58; Panel Report, *India – Solar Cells*, WT/DS456/R, para. 7.142.

[73] Appellate Body Report, *Canada – FIT Program*, WT/DS426/AB/R, paras. 5.60–5.61; Panel Report, *India – Solar Cells*, WT/DS456/R, para. 7.149.

[74] Directive 2014/23/EU of the European Parliament and of the Council of 26 February 2014 on the Award of Concession Contracts, OJ EU 2014 No. L 94, 28 March 2014, p. 1.

[75] Directive 2014/24/EU of the European Parliament and of the Council of 26 February 2014 on Public Procurement and Repealing Directive 2004/18/EC, OJ EU 2014 No. L 94, 28 March 2014, p. 65.

[76] Directive 2014/25/EU of the European Parliament and of the Council of 26 February 2014 on Procurement by Entities Operating in the Water, Energy, Transport and Postal Services Sectors and Repealing Directive 2004/17/EC, OJ EU 2014 No. L 94, 28 March 2014, p. 243.

[77] Directive 2014/23/EU, Art. 6; Directive 2014/24/EU, Art. 2; Directive 2014/25/EU, Art. 3. For a list of concrete examples of contracting authorities, see Constant de Konink, Thierry Ronse, and William Timmermans, *European Public Procurement Law: The Public Sector Procurement Directive Explained through 30 Years of Case Law by the Court of Justice of the European Union*, 2nd ed. (Alphen aan den Rijn: Wolters Kluwer, 2015), p. 68.

possible that even the 'attribution of a (marginal, non-market) activity in the general interest could suffice to classify the entity as a body governed by public law' under the mentioned EU Directives.[78] This could also call into question the applicability of Article III:8 (a) GATT, since the WTO jurisprudence has not yet elucidated the relative proportion of other activities to those related to governmental functions that an entity can perform and still be considered a 'governmental agency'. Contracting entities can be contracting authorities, public undertakings (over which contracting authorities may exercise directly or indirectly a dominant influence by virtue of their ownership, financial participation, or the rules which govern these undertakings), or other entities operating on the basis of special or exclusive rights granted by a competent authority of a Member State, without a competitive and public procedure,[79] that pursue one or more of the following activities: the supply of gas (which falls under GATT and not GATS),[80] heat, electricity, and water, as well as the provision or operation of fixed networks intended to provide these services to the public; the provision or operation of networks in the field of transport services; the provision of airports and maritime or inland ports or other terminal facilities to carriers by air, sea, or inland waterway; postal services; and the extraction of oil and gas and exploration for, or extraction of, coal or other solid fuel.[81] Consequently, it could be said that contracting entities act for or on behalf of a governmental authority and perform typical governmental functions of public interest.[82] Energy-related activities, for example, were considered a governmental function by the panel in *India – Solar Cells*,[83] in a finding on which the AB has expressed no view.[84]

[78] Albert Sanchez-Graells, 'Article 2. Definitions', in Roberto Caranta and Albert Sanchez-Graells (eds.), *European Public Procurement: Commentary on Directive 2014/24/EU* (Cheltenham: Edward Elgar, 2021), para. 2.13. In this respect, see CJEU, C-44/96, *Mannesmann Anlagenbau Austria AG and Others v Strohal Rotationsdruck GesmbH*, ECLI:EU:C:1998:4, para. 25.

[79] Directive 2014/23/EU, Art. 7; Directive 2014/25/EU, Art. 4.

[80] See Panel Report, *EU – Certain Measures Relating to the Energy Sector*, WT/DS476/R, 10 August 2018, para. 7.268. GATS may be relevant insofar as there are services involved in the sale of goods, such as selling or transportation, which themselves are challenged for their GATS conformity. In this respect, see Appellate Body Report, *Canada – Automotive Industry*, WT/DS139/AB/R, WT/DS146/AB/R, 31 May 2000, para. 157 ff.

[81] Directive 2014/23/EU, Art. 7, Annex II; Directive 2014/25/EU, Arts. 4, 8-14; CJEU, C-393/06, *Ing. Aigner, Wasser-Wärme-Umwelt, GmbH v Fernwärme Wien GmbH*, ECLI:EU:C:2008:213, paras. 23–33.

[82] Koch, *Green Public Procurement under WTO Law* (2020), p. 122.

[83] Panel Report, *India – Solar Cells*, WT/DS456/R, para. 7.151.

[84] Appellate Body Report, *India – Solar Cells*, WT/DS456/AB/R, para. 5.44.

According to the existing jurisprudence, the scope of the expression 'products purchased' in Article III:8 (a) GATT is informed by the scope of the term 'products' as used in other paragraphs of Article III, referring, therefore, to the products subject to discrimination. Thus, the AB established that the product purchased should *always* be in a competitive relationship with the product discriminated against.[85] This requirement was the one that brought about the criticism regarding the AB's approach towards Article III:8 (a) GATT, as it disqualifies domestic requirements for inputs from the derogation, leading to potential findings of violation by national measures that were likely not intended to be covered by NT obligations.[86] This requirement, however, is unlikely to prove problematic for the IPI Regulation, since the IPI measures and the obligations on successful tenderers directly concern products treated less favourably that are in a competitive relationship with the products purchased. They do not establish conditions for the inputs such as domestic content requirements.

Yet, the type of transaction through which the procurement shall take place in order to be covered by Article III:8 (a) might be more challenging for the IPI Regulation. The text of this paragraph suggests that the terms 'procurement' and 'purchase' are distinct, the latter referring to the specific type of transaction through which procurement is put into effect.[87] Therefore, other types of transactions, such as lease or rent, do not fall under the scope of the GATT NT derogation for procurement.[88] Concession contracts do not fall under the purchase context of procurement either, as these contractual arrangements are different from procurement due to their long-term nature, their complex remuneration mechanism, and their use of private finances. The procuring entity does not purchase goods or services but rather the fulfilment of governmental tasks in exchange for specific rights instead of a financial remuneration,[89] so that concession contracts are also not covered by the GATT

[85] Appellate Body Report, *Canada – FIT Program*, WT/DS426/AB/R, paras. 5.63, 5.79, 5.84; Appellate Body Report, *India – Solar Cells*, WT/DS456/AB/R, paras. 5.22, 5.24, 5.25, 5.36.

[86] Yanovich, '*Canada – Renewable Energy* and *Canada – FIT Program*' (2013) 430; Fang, 'Shades of Green' (2019) 573–576; Koch, *Green Public Procurement under WTO Law* (2020), pp. 58–59.

[87] Appellate Body Report, *Canada – FIT Program*, WT/DS426/AB/R, para. 5.59; Appellate Body Report, *India – Solar Cells*, WT/DS456/AB/R, para. 5.35; Award of the Arbitrators, *Turkey – Pharmaceutical Products (EU)*, WT/DS583/ARB25, para. 6.42.

[88] Award of the Arbitrators, *Turkey – Pharmaceutical Products (EU)*, WT/DS583/ARB25, paras. 6.42–6.43.

[89] Sue Arrowsmith, 'Reviewing the GPA: The Role and Development of the Plurilateral Agreement after Doha' (2002) *JIEL* 761–790 at 784 f.

NT derogation (nor by the GATS derogation analyzed in the following section). The IPI Regulation, nevertheless, applies to procurement through purchase, lease, rental, or hire-purchase, with or without an option to buy, and also to concessions.[90] Accordingly, in case of the application of the IPI Regulation to procurement through other means than purchase, the analyzed provisions are likely to be found in violation of Article III:4 GATT, unless they can be seen as procurement of services and hence may be covered by the derogation of Article XIII GATS.[91]

In order for the products to be considered purchased for 'governmental purpose', they should be 'consumed by government or [. . .] provided by government to recipients in the discharge of its public functions' and there should be a rational relationship between that product and the governmental function.[92] 'The additional reference to "governmental" in relation to "purposes" must go beyond simply requiring some governmental aim or objective with respect to purchases by governmental agencies.'[93] Although it is the procurement of products purchased that shall be directed at the fulfillment of a governmental purpose, it has not yet been fully clarified whether the purpose of the measure that allegedly violates the NT obligation should also be assessed against this element.[94] However, if the purposes of such measures would be also taken into account, it would most likely be found that discriminatory treatment was not necessary for a governmental purpose, rendering the derogation contained in Article III:8 (a) meaningless and against the principle of effective interpretation. Thus, it is submitted here that the products

[90] IPI Regulation, Art. 1 (2) read in conjunction with Directive 2014/24/EU, Art. 2 (1) (8) and Directive 2014/25/EU, Art. 2 (4). Prior to the last EU procurement reform, concession contracts were not subject to procurement rules; Wolfgang Weiß, 'WTO Procurement Rules: In Particular the Government Procurement Agreement (GPA) and Services of General Interest', in Markus Krajewski (ed.), *Services of General Interest Beyond the Single Market: External and International Law Dimensions* (The Hague: T.M.C Asser Press, 2015), p. 70.

[91] The supply of services in the meaning of Art. I GATS includes rental or lease of equipment and other goods; see the Services Sectoral Classification List MTN.GNS/W/120/, for example, with respect to Heading 1 Business Services, Section E on Rental/Leasing Services without Operators.

[92] Appellate Body Report, *Canada – FIT Program*, WT/DS426/AB/R, para. 5.68.

[93] ibid, WT/DS426/AB/R, para. 5.66.

[94] Without expressing a view on the element of 'governmental purpose', the panel in *India – Solar Cells* nevertheless mentioned the purpose of the measures at issue (Panel Report, *India – Solar Cells*, WT/DS456/R, para. 7.157). Fang also refers to the purpose of the local content requirement and not that of the procurement of the product purchased and describes the 'governmental purpose' as 'another "good faith" layer that could catch protection-motivated measures' (Fang, 'Shades of Green' (2019) 566).

purchased are the ones to be directed towards fulfilling governmental purposes and not the measures in violation of Article III:4 GATT. Although the scope of a public function will have to be determined in every specific case,[95] the procurement of goods intended for the pursuit of certain activities, such as those in connection to the supply of gas, heat, electricity, etc.,[96] is more likely to be considered as being provided by the government to recipients in the discharge of its public functions. Nonetheless, the IPI Regulation also covers procurement of products, 'whether or not [...] they are intended for a public purpose'.[97] Consequently, it is irrelevant for the scope of the Regulation whether the products or services are purchased for a 'governmental purpose',[98] EU public procurement having the aim to avoid the risk of giving preference to national tenderers whenever a contract is awarded by a contracting authority.[99] Hence, when products purchased are not intended to be consumed or provided by the government in the discharge of its public functions, the IPI Regulation might not benefit from the Article III:8 (a) GATT derogation and be in violation of the NT treatment obligation from Article III:4 GATT.

Finally, the products purchased should not be procured 'with a view to commercial resale or with a view to use in the production of goods for commercial sale', which formulates a self-standing, cumulative fourth condition; it is not an explanation to the preceding formulation 'governmental purposes'.[100] In the definition of the AB, this requirement means that the good should not be resold or used in the production of goods sold at arm's length, the assessment being made with regard to the entire transaction.[101] The AB also pointed out that procurement, nevertheless, also includes the situation where procured goods are used by the government in the provision of services to recipients in discharge of public functions.[102] The IPI Regulation, however, applies to the procurement of products by contracting authorities and entities, whether it is for the

[95] Appellate Body Report, *Canada – FIT Program*, WT/DS426/AB/R, para. 5.68.

[96] The procurement by entities operating in the water, energy, transport, and postal services sectors is governed by Directive 2014/25/EU.

[97] Directive 2014/24/EU, Art. 1 (2) read in conjunction with IPI Regulation, Art. 1 (2).

[98] See also Koch, *Green Public Procurement under WTO Law* (2020), p. 113.

[99] CJEU, C-271/08, *European Commission v Federal Republic of Germany*, ECLI:EU:C:2010:426, para. 73; Roberto Caranta, 'Article 1. Subject-Matter and Scope', in Roberto Caranta and Albert Sanchez-Graells (eds.), *European Public Procurement. Commentary on Directive 2014/24/EU* (Cheltenham: Edward Elgar 2021), para. 1.13.

[100] Appellate Body Report, *Canada – FIT Program*, WT/DS426/AB/R, para. 5.69.

[101] ibid, paras. 5.71–5.73.

[102] ibid, paras. 5.68, 5.74.

purpose of fulfilling the task of meeting general interests or for commercial purposes,[103] thus including for commercial resale or using them in the production of goods for commercial sale. Thus, only in case of procurement of products which are not commercially sold or not used in the production of goods for commercial resale will the IPI Regulation be able to benefit from the derogation of Article III:8 (a) GATT.

8.4.1.3 Derogation from National Treatment: Article XIII GATS and Its Reach

A textually comparable NT derogation to Article III:8 GATT is contained in Article XIII GATS with regard to services. Article XIII:1 states that the NT obligation 'shall not apply to laws, regulations or requirements governing the procurement by governmental agencies of services purchased for governmental purposes and not with a view to commercial resale or with a view to use in the supply of services for commercial sale'. Since Article XIII:1 GATS largely mirrors the language of Article III:8 (a) GATT, it is reasonable to expect that similar interpretations would be applicable,[104] all the more as, generally speaking, the WTO jurisprudence on GATS non-discrimination provisions closely follows interpretations adopted for the comparable GATT obligation.[105] Thus, our earlier findings with regard to the GATT derogation apply here as well: The IPI Regulation covering also procurement of services through types of transactions other than purchase, for purposes other than governmental, which could be commercially resold or used in the supply of services for commercial sale would not benefit in such situations from the derogation contained in Article XIII:1 GATS. And this would apply even though, admittedly, the term 'purchase' in Article XIII GATS could have a broader meaning than under Article III:8 GATT considering the context provided by the GATS. Thus, the 'supply of services' in the sense of Article I:2 GATS covers not only purchases of services (which may have the form of lease or rent contracts) but also other forms of acquiring the right of performance or use of a service (like entrance or usage fees). Accordingly, the 'supply of services' is defined in Article XXVIII(b) GATS to include 'the production,

[103] IPI Regulation, Art. 1.2 in conjunction with Directive 2014/24/EU, Arts. 2 (4), (5); CJEU, C-44/96, *Mannesmann Anlagenbau Austria*, para. 32; Christopher Bovis, 'The Principles of Public Procurement Regulation', in Christopher Bovis (ed.), *Research Handbook on EU Public Procurement Law* (Cheltenham: Edward Elgar, 2016), p. 41.

[104] Yanovich, '*Canada – Renewable Energy* and *Canada – FIT Program*' (2013) 434.

[105] See Weiß, *WTO Law and Domestic Regulation* (München: Hart/Beck/Nomos, 2020) 147 ff.

distribution, marketing, sale and delivery of a service'. The question whether concession-type arrangements can be considered 'procurement' in the sense of Article XIII GATS is of particular importance in the present context, especially since Directive 2014/23/EU is dedicated to procurement by means of works or services concessions.[106] As also mentioned earlier in the context of Article III:8 (a) GATT analysis, concessions cannot be considered 'procurement' by a governmental agency for the purpose of Article XIII:1 GATS either. Under the mentioned Directive, the concessionaire has the right to exploit the works and services and bears an operating risk;[107] it is the one that derives income and also has a certain degree of control over them and not the governmental agency;[108] and the concession arrangement takes place by means that are not remotely comparable to purchase.

8.4.1.4 *Conclusion on Compliance with WTO National Treatment Obligations*

Although Articles III:8 (a) GATT and XIII:1 GATS serve as a derogation from the NT obligations contained in those agreements, they can do so only when several cumulative elements are met, some of which have been interpreted quite narrowly by the WTO adjudicators. Whether the examined IPI provisions meet those elements must be assessed on a case-by-case basis. Still, in comparison, the scope of the IPI Regulation is broader than the reach of the NT derogations, as the IPI Regulation applies also to procurement (of both goods and services) through other types of transactions than purchase; it applies to procurement not only for governmental purpose but also to procurement of products or services with a view to commercial resale or use in the production of another good or supply of other services for commercial sale. Hence, in these instances, the Regulation will most probably violate Articles III:4 GATT or XVII:1 GATS. For the EU to better balance its international commitments and 'strategic autonomy' in the field of public procurement, the scope of the IPI Regulation could have been refined so that it applies solely to procurement meeting the elements contained in Articles III:8 (a) GATT and XIII:1 GATS derogations.

[106] Directive 2014/23/EU, Arts. 1 (1), 5 (1). [107] ibid, Art. 5 (1).

[108] These elements are indicative of the presence of 'procurement' by a governmental agency (Award of the Arbitrators, *Turkey – Pharmaceutical Products (EU)*, WT/DS583/ARB25, paras. 6.63, 6.68).

8.4.2 Most-Favoured-Nation Obligations under the GATT and GATS

As already alluded to, the MFN obligation enshrined in GATT and GATS may also be violated by the IPI Regulation, unless there is a derogation dedicated to government procurement. This section will first analyze whether Article I:1 GATT could be violated and only then will consider whether the IPI Regulation could benefit from a derogation or justification, the latter question being relevant only if the former is answered positively.

According to Article I:1 GATT,

> [. . .] with respect to all matters referred to in paragraphs 2 and 4 of Article III, any advantage, favour, privilege or immunity granted by any contracting party to any product originating in or destined for any other country shall be accorded immediately and unconditionally to the like product originating in or destined for the territories of all other contracting parties.

Since the IPI Regulation distinguishes between different imported products based solely on their or their suppliers' origin, as in case of NT obligations considered in the previous section, their likeness can be hypothetically assumed for the purpose of Article I:1 GATT.[109] The potential IPI measures and obligations on successful tenderers clearly distort the competition conditions between like imported products to the disadvantage of those originating in third countries concerned by the measures,[110] thereby granting an advantage to products originating in other countries. The extension of this advantage would be subject to conditions related to the situation and conduct of the third country at issue, namely the elimination or remedy of the impairment of access for Union economic operators, goods, or services to public procurement or concession markets of that third country.[111] Accordingly, the Regulation does not extend an advantage 'immediately and unconditionally' to like products from third countries subject to IPI measures.[112]

Furthermore, the initial exclusion of FTA partners and GPA parties with respect to covered procurement from the application of the IPI Regulation could even be perceived as an 'as such' violation of the MFN principle, unless subject to an exception. Whether it could be considered an 'as such' violation depends on the degree of flexibility that the EU

[109] Panel Report, *Colombia – Ports of Entry*, WT/DS366/R, 27 April 2009, paras. 7.355–7.356; Panel Report, *US – Poultry (China)*, WT/DS392/R, 29 September 2009, paras. 7.426, 7.432.

[110] Appellate Body Report, *EC – Seal Products*, WT/DS400/AB/R, WT/DS401/AB/R, 22 May 2014, para. 5.87.

[111] IPI Regulation, Art. 6 (10).

[112] Panel Report, *Canada – Autos*, WT/DS139/R, WT/DS142/R, paras. 10.23–10.25.

enjoys.[113] For a measure to be 'as such' inconsistent, the regulation would have to *require* a breach of WTO agreements or otherwise *restrict in a material way* the EU's discretion to act in a WTO-consistent manner.[114] The Commission seems to enjoy a fairly high degree of discretion, in particular deciding whether to initiate an investigation and if it is in the interest of the Union to adopt an IPI measure.[115] So, it could be said that due to Commission's considerable discretion, it is not required to act inconsistently, nor are its actions restricted in such a way as to prevent it to act consistently with WTO law. Therefore, it is likely that 'as such' the IPI Regulation would not constitute a WTO breach.

The question, nevertheless, arises whether government procurement is in any case covered by or is carved out of the scope of Article I:1 GATT, precluding both potential 'as applied' and 'as such' findings of violation. There is no express provision to establish a government procurement derogation from MFN in the GATT. However, Article I:1 cross-references to paragraphs 2 and 4 of Article III:4 to set its scope. Although not incontestable,[116] there seems to be a general agreement that by carving out government procurement from paragraphs 2 and 4 of Article III GATT through paragraph 8 (a) it was likewise simultaneously carved out from the scope of Article I:1 GATT.[117] This interpretation seems supported by the scant relevant WTO jurisprudence. According to the panel in *EC – Commercial Vessels*, a dispute related to Article III:8 (b) GATT, 'the "matters referred to in paragraphs 2 and 4 of Article III" cannot be interpreted without regard to limitations that may exist regarding the scope of the substantive obligations provided for in these paragraph'.[118] Another argument reads that the MFN obligation does not even cover procurement, as procurement is not mentioned in Article I:1 GATT.[119]

113 For more, see Section 3.3.1.

114 Appellate Body Report, *EU – Biodiesel*, WT/DS473/AB/R, 6 October 2016, paras. 6.229, 6.281; Panel Report, *US – Olives*, WT/DS577/R, 19 November 2021, para. 7.146. Referring to older Appellate Body Reports from *US – Corrosion-Resistant Steel Sunset Review*, WT/DS244/AB/R, 15 December 2003, para. 100 and *US – Carbon Steel*, WT/DS/213/AB/R, 28 November 2002, para. 162.

115 IPI Regulation, Arts. 5 (1), 6 (1), (2).

116 Dawar, 'Government Procurement in the WTO' (2016) 658–662.

117 Arrowsmith, *Government Procurement in the WTO* (2003), pp. 61–63; Chandy, Dasgupta, 'Government Procurement Outside the GPA' (2019) 387–388; Koch, *Green Public Procurement Under WTO Law* (2020), pp. 56–57.

118 Panel Report, *EC – Commercial Vessels*, WT/DS301/R, 22 April 2005, para. 7.83.

119 Peter Trepte, 'The Agreement on Government Procurement', in Patrick F. J. Macrory, et al. (eds.), *The World Trade Organization: Legal, Economic and Political Analysis* (New York: Springer, 2005), p. 1126.

The GATS MFN obligation in Article II:1 GATS uses wording similar to Articles I:1 GATT (MFN) and XVII:1 GATS (NT), requiring each Member to accord 'immediately and unconditionally to services and service suppliers of any other Member treatment no less favourable than that it accords to like services and service suppliers of any other country'. On that account, similar interpretations have been issued.[120] Considering that the IPI measures and obligations upon successful tenderers distinguish between different imported services and service suppliers based only on their origin, thereby distorting the conditions of competition to the detriment of those originating in countries affected by the IPI measures, it can be considered that they treat less favourably those services and suppliers than the like counterparts from other Members.[121] Hence, the IPI Regulation could also be in violation of Article II:1 GATS, and this is particularly relevant, as the scope of the GATS MFN obligation is far broader than that of the GATS NT obligation, since the former applies independent from WTO Member's GATS schedules, which means that any discriminatory service treatment is in breach of GATS. But there is a clear derogation, as Article XIII:1 GATS, in contrast to Article III:8 GATT, explicitly provides for the governmental procurement carve-out also with regard to MFN.

Still, even if the scope of the MFN obligations contained in GATT and GATS is limited by government procurement derogations, as shown in the previous section, they only apply in the specific situation when all the necessary conditions are met. As demonstrated earlier, the potential IPI measures and obligations on successful tenderers will not always meet them. Consequently, the IPI Regulation might violate the MFN obligation of Articles I:1 GATT and II:1 GATS if applied in certain situations.

Then, of course, in cases of procurement not meeting all the conditions for Article III:8 GATT derogation to apply, the question becomes relevant whether Article XXIV GATT laying down the requirements for regional trade exceptions may justify the departure from the MFN rules in case of the exclusion of FTA-covered procurement. Granting more beneficial treatment to an FTA partner is the essence of regional trade agreements so that, as a consequence, the formation of an FTA justifies derogation

[120] See, for example, Appellate Body Report, *Argentina – Financial Services*, WT/DS453/AB/R, 14 April 2016, paras. 6.38, 6.106.

[121] Regarding the analysis of likeness, one can easily refer to the above under Art. II GATS, as the likeness analysis in both provisions is addressing the same requirement of competitiveness; see Appellate Body Report, *Argentina – Financial Services*, WT/DS453/AB/R, paras. 6.25, 629 ff.

from the MFN rule. As it is well known, however, the Appellate Body is understood to require that the formation of a free trade area is only capable of justifying a more favourable treatment to participating members compared to the trade conditions with non-participating WTO members if the formation of the free trade area 'would be prevented if the introduction of the measures concerned were not allowed'.[122] The measure concerned here is a better treatment of a party to an FTA with regard to procurement not covered by the scope of Article III:8 GATT. The carve-out of FTA partners by the IPI Regulation is not a measure adopted by the EU in the wake of entering into diverse FTAs but was adopted later. Nevertheless, the fact that the IPI Regulation results in an a priori better treatment offered to an FTA party, in contrast to other WTO members, may be seen to represent a necessary consequence of entering into procurement disciplines with trade partners in bilateral FTAs. Hence, the carve-out of FTA partners from the scope of the IPI Regulation that provides for measures in case of an unbalanced market access for EU undertakings, goods, and services will not be the subject of a successful challenge. The MFN exception resulting from Article XXIV GATT will cover this distinctive treatment of FTA partners because the difference in treatment of FTA partners compared to other WTO members merely results from the balanced, reciprocal market access as effectuated by mutual FTA public procurement obligations. Of course, Article XXIV GATT cannot justify any type of more beneficial treatment of FTA partners. For example, introducing national tax benefits for domestic goods and those of FTA partners, but not for other WTO members, breaches Article I:1 GATT;[123] Article XXIV GATT cannot serve as justification for this discrimination because the tax benefit is a unilateral measure and has nothing to do with the more progressive and mutual trade liberalization agreed upon between the partners of an FTA. Accordingly, unless the existing restrictive jurisprudence does not pose an impediment, the exclusion of FTA-covered procurement might benefit from the justification of Article XXIV GATT, but the same would not be applicable to the exclusion of GPA signatories with respect to covered procurement.

[122] Peter van den Bossche and Werner Zdouc, *The Law and Policy of the WTO*, 5th ed. (Cambridge: Cambridge University Press, 2022), p. 737, referring to Appellate Body Report, *Turkey – Textiles*, WT/DS34/AB/R, 22 October 1999, para. 58 concluding this with regard to the EU–Turkey customs union.

[123] See Panel Report, *Brazil – Taxation (EU)*, WT/DS472/R, WT/DS497/DS/R, 30 August 2017, paras. 7.1044–7.1048, upheld by Appellate Body Report, *Brazil – Taxation (EU)*, WT/DS472/AB/R, WTDS/497/AB/R, 13 December 2018, para. 5.415.

Accordingly, in case the conditions of government procurement derogations are not met, the exclusion of GPA parties regarding covered procurement would still violate the MFN obligations.

On these grounds, especially because of the a priori exclusion of GPA parties with respect to covered procurement, with a view to EU's international commitments, a careful drafting of the IPI Regulation with the conditions from Articles III:8 (a) GATT and XIII:1 GATS in mind would have been important from the perspective of not only the NT obligations but also the MFN ones. But as the IPI Regulation now stands, the Commission must pay utmost attention in its implementation of this regulation not to apply it to non-covered procurement in situations that are beyond the government procurement derogations from non-discrimination obligations in GATT and GATS, as indicated in Section 8.4.1.4. Otherwise, the EU will breach a WTO non-discrimination obligation.

8.4.3 The Agreement on Subsidies and Countervailing Measures

It was claimed that the IPI Regulation might not only violate non-discrimination GATT and GATS obligations but could also be incompatible with EU's commitments under the WTO ASCM.[124] Although the ASCM does not expressly refer to government procurement, it does refer to the purchase of goods by the government. Moreover, the existing WTO jurisprudence has confirmed that government procurement does not lie outside the WTO subsidies disciplines.[125]

A subsidy is deemed to exist when there is (1) a financial contribution by a government or any public body (or income or price support) (2) which confers a benefit.[126] The government procurement covered by the IPI Regulation would likely qualify as being made 'by a government or public body', as the procuring entities could be considered as 'possessing, exercising, or being vested with governmental authority', especially due to the fact that they exercise public functions and represent governments or are subject to their control or dominant influence.[127] The question,

[124] Dawar, 'The 2016 European Union International Procurement Instrument's Amendments' (2016) 861.

[125] Appellate Body Report, *Canada – FIT Program*, WT/DS426/AB/R, paras. 5.116–5.246.

[126] ASCM, Art. 1.1; Appellate Body Report, *US – Carbon Steel (India)*, WT/DS436/AB/R, 8 December 2014, para. 4.8.

[127] On the notion of 'government or any public body' within the meaning of Art. 1.1 ASCM, see Appellate Body Report, *US – Anti-Dumping and Countervailing Duties (China)*, WT/DS379/AB/R, 11 March 2011. For more on the procuring entities, see Sections 8.4.1.2 and 8.4.1.3.

however, arises if and what type of a financial contribution would be found in case of the imposition of restrictive IPI measures and the obligations on the successful tenderers. Article 1.1 (a) (1) ASCM sets an exhaustive list of the types of transactions that constitute financial contributions under the SCM Agreement.[128] Since potential IPI measures could be alleged to be capable of conferring a benefit during public procurement procedures to other economic operators by excluding or imposing a score adjustment on tenders of operators originating in third countries subject to the measures, when covered government procurement of goods takes place through purchase,[129] it could be argued that the relevant type of financial contribution is the 'purchase of goods' by the government in the sense of Article 1.1 (a) (1) (iii) ASCM, as the successful tenderers from the country not subject to IPI measures would not have won the contract otherwise.[130] It is to be noted that government purchase of *services* does not constitute a financial contribution.[131]

As for obligations on successful tenderers, although regulating government procurement, they could be claimed to confer a benefit on economic operators and goods not originating in third countries subject to IPI measures only *after* a contract was awarded. Hence, these IPI provisions impose obligations to be respected *after* the 'purchase of goods' by a government, meaning that they would not be able to *thereby* confer a benefit as required by Article 1.1 (b) ASCM. In case the successful tenderers do not observe the obligations, they will have to pay a charge of 10–30 per cent of the total value of the contract. While such a charge might encourage the use of goods originating in other countries than those subject to IPI measures and to subcontract only to economic operators from those countries,[132] these measures do not seem to fall under any

[128] Appellate Body Report, *US – Large Civil Aircraft (2nd complaint)*, WT/DS353/AB/R, 12 March 2012, para. 614.

[129] On the coverage of other types of transactions by the IPI Regulation see Sections 8.4.1.2 and 8.4.1.3.

[130] For another case in which government procurement was analyzed as a 'purchase of goods', see Appellate Body Report, *Canada – FIT Program*, WT/DS426/AB/R, paras. 5.127–5.128.

[131] Appellate Body Report, *US – Large Civil Aircraft (2nd complaint)*, para. 619; Simon Lester, Bryan Mercurio, and Arwel Davies, *World Trade Law: Text, Materials and Commentary*, 3rd ed. (Oxford: Hart Publishing, 2018), p. 457; Dawar, 'Government Procurement in the WTO' (2016) 652; David Collins, 'Government Procurement with Strings Attached: The Uneven Control of Offsets by the World Trade Organization and Regional Trade Agreements' (2018) 8 *Asian Journal of International Law* 301–321 at 311.

[132] It is to be noted that the obligations do not encourage the use of domestic over imported products in the sense of Art. 3.1 (b) ASCM on prohibited subsidies, as the use of other

other type of financial contribution listed by Article 1.1 (a) (1) ASCM. Consequently, these obligations cannot be deemed to be subsidies according to the ASCM and will not be further treated in the remainder of this section.

In case of IPI measures, for a subsidy to be found, the conferral of the benefit through the purchase of goods by the government would have to be proven. A benefit is generally found when it is granted on more advantageous terms compared to those available to the recipient on the market.[133] Article 14 ASCM provides relevant context to the interpretation of benefit under Article 1.1 (b),[134] according to which 'purchase of goods by a government shall not be considered as conferring a benefit unless [. . .] the purchase is made for more than adequate remuneration'. Thus, the determination of a benefit in case of government procurement (of goods) procedures via purchase that were subject to IPI measures would require a comparison between the actual remuneration and a market-based benchmark or proxy.[135] Therefore, theoretically, it could be found that the IPI measures, imposing a score adjustment on or excluding the tenders of certain economic operators, lead to a remuneration paid to the successful tenderer (not subject to the measures) that was higher than what was available on the relevant market. The crux of the analysis would be the establishment of the relevant benchmark, which is a controversial issue in WTO panel and AB reports,[136] especially considering that government procurement often relates to markets where the governmental intervention is significant.[137] When the private

imported products than those originating in third countries subject to IPI measure would similarly be free of any additional charge. Dawar contended with respect to a provision contained in the 2016 IPI proposal, namely the imposition of IPI measures on tenders unless the bidders demonstrated that less than 50 per cent of the total value of their tender was made up of non-covered goods and services originating in a certain country, that it could have been considered a prohibited subsidy (Dawar, 'The 2016 European Union International Procurement Instrument's Amendments' (2016) 861). However, that provision is no longer present in the IPI Regulation.

133 Panel Report, *Canada – Aircraft*, WT/DS70/R, 14 April 1999, para. 9.112; Appellate Body Report, *Canada – FIT Program*, WT/DS426/AB/R, para. 5.169.

134 Appellate Body Report, *Canada – FIT Program*, WT/DS426/AB/R, paras. 5.163–5.165.

135 ibid, para. 5.165.

136 Not only did the panel and AB reach different conclusions on the issue of 'relevant market' in *Canada – FIT Program*, but there was also a dissenting opinion expressed in the Panel Report. For more, see Elizabeth Whitsitt, 'A Modest Victory at the WTO for Ontario's FIT Program' (2013) 20(1) *University of California, Davis Journal of International Law and Policy* 75–103.

137 Aaron Cosbey and Petros C. Mavroidis, 'A Turquoise Mess: Green Subsidies, Blue Industrial Policy and Renewable Energy: The Case for Redrafting the Subsidies

prices of the goods in the country of provision are distorted, resorting to an out-of-country or a constructed benchmark is possible, provided that the necessary adjustments are made to reflect the conditions in the market of purchase.[138] As shown by existing jurisprudence, when needed, it might be fairly complicated to find relevant out-of-country benchmarks, since it could be necessary to find markets similarly distorted by governmental intervention.[139] Hence, the analysis of the 'benefit', particularly establishing what is the benchmark for comparison, is a fact-intensive exercise that nevertheless would need to be established on a case-by-case basis.

Even if a benefit was found and the characterization of IPI measures as subsidies was established, the ASCM regulates only subsidies that are 'specific'.[140] Since IPI measures do not seem to be prohibited subsidies according to Article 3 ASCM, which are presumed to be specific, it would have to be proven that these subsidies are specific to an enterprise or industry, or a group of enterprises or industries, within the jurisdiction of the granting authority. While the IPI measures might be deemed subsidies that do not rely on objective criteria as they distinguish between economic operators based on their origin,[141] in all likelihood the benefit conferred would be 'broadly available and widely used'

Agreement of the WTO' (2014) EUI Robert Schuman Centre for Advanced Studies Working Paper 2014/17, p. 7; Collins, 'Government Procurement with Strings Attached' (2018) 313. Another layer of difficulty was added by the AB when it established that supply-side factors also must be taken into account. The AB distinguished, however, between two situations – when the government intervention creates the market versus other government interventions on existing markets – stating that the former situation does not in and of itself give rise to a subsidy, while the latter may amount to subsidies (Appellate Body Report, *Canada – FIT Program*, WT/DS426/AB/R, paras. 5.171–5.172, 5.188). For criticism on AB's approach, see Cosbey and Mavroidis, 'A Turquoise Mess' (2014), pp. 11–12.

[138] Appellate Body Report, *US – Softwood Lumber IV*, WT/DS257/AB/R, 19 January 2004, para. 103; Appellate Body Report, *Canada – FIT Program*, WT/DS426/AB/R, para. 5.184.

[139] Appellate Body Report, *Canada – FIT Program*, WT/DS426/AB/R, para. 5.227; for criticism, see Simon Lester, 'The AB's "Benefit" Reasoning in the Renewable Energy/Feed-in Tariff Case', IELP Blog, 7 May 2013, https://worldtradelaw.typepad.com/ielpblog/2013/05/the-abs-benefit-reasoning-the-feed-in-tariff-case.html.

[140] ASCM, Art. 1.2.

[141] According to Art. 2.1 (b) ASCM, there is no specificity if the automatic eligibility for and amount of a subsidy is governed by objective criteria or conditions, which, according to fn. 2, 'mean criteria or conditions which are neutral, which do not favour certain enterprises over others, and which are economic in nature and horizontal in application'.

throughout the European market,[142] without limiting the access to particular enterprises, industry, or a group of enterprises or industries.[143] For this reason, the IPI measures would most likely fall outside the scope of coverage of the WTO ASCM disciplines.

To conclude, although it has been alleged in respect to the 2016 IPI proposal that it could be incompatible with the ASCM disciplines, this section showed that the IPI Regulation, particularly the obligations imposed on successful tenderers and the IPI measures, either do not constitute specific subsidies or could be subsidies that fall outside the scope of regulation of the SCM Agreement. Respectively, at least in regards to WTO subsidies rules, the EU should be considered as adhering to its international commitments.

8.4.4 The Dispute Settlement Understanding

A further possible clash between the IPI Regulation and WTO law might relate to the DSU, particularly Article 23.1 DSU mandating recourse to DSU rules and proceedings when seeking redress of a WTO violation.

The adoption of IPI measures by the EU would be based on the Commission's finding of a 'third-country measure or practice' (Article 2.1 (i) IPI Regulation). Thus, the analysis of the Commission must explore first whether there is an impairment of EU undertakings' access to the foreign procurement market. Such impairment might be based on a discriminatory practice against EU goods or service providers not in conformity with non-discrimination obligations under GATT or GATS. As shown in Sections 8.4.1.2 and 8.4.1.3, the GATT/GATS procurement derogations from non-discrimination obligations are qualified by specific exigencies, which might not be met by a third-country measure or practice, such as in case of procurement of concession contracts. In such cases, the discrimination against EU undertakings in foreign procurement would impair the EU's trading rights under the WTO agreements. Hence, the Commission adopting IPI measures based on the IPI Regulation would impliedly address a preceding 'impairment' of EU benefits under WTO agreements by the third country. Consequently, there may be situations where the assessment of the EU Commission

[142] According to the panel in *US – Upland Cotton*, such subsidies are not subject to the ASCM's disciplines (Panel Report, *US – Upland Cotton*, WT/DS267/R, 8 September 2004, para. 7.1143).

[143] For a detailed analysis of the meaning of these concepts, see Appellate Body Report, *US – Anti-Dumping and Countervailing Duties (China)*, WT/DS379/AB/R, para. 373.

required under the IPI Regulation entails a prior finding of a violation of WTO obligations by the other party, which under Article 23.1 DSU shall be subject to DSU rules, and not to unilateral assessment and subsequent measures adopted autonomously by the EU. A unilateral response by the EU to such breach by adopting an IPI measure would signify also a violation of Article 23.2 DSU that prohibits

> [...] mak[ing] a determination to the effect that a violation has occurred, that benefits have been nullified or impaired [...], except through recourse to dispute settlement in accordance with the rules and procedures of this Understanding, and shall make any such determination consistent with the findings contained in the panel or Appellate Body report adopted by the DSB or an arbitration award rendered under this Understanding.

However, in order for Article 23.2 DSU to be violated, the panel in *US – Certain EC Products* expressly required that 'the criterion for determining whether Article 23 is applicable is whether the Member that imposed the measure was "seeking the redress of a WTO violation"'.[144] As the EU in adopting IPI measures would not seek addressing a previous WTO breach by the third country, but an impairment against EU undertakings' access to the procurement market, formally the EU would not seek redress of a WTO violation, as it seemingly would not perceive it as one. The EU does not and will not allege that it addresses WTO breaches with its IPI measures. Therefore, it might be difficult to claim that the IPI Regulation is seeking 'as such' the redress of a WTO violation in cases of third countries' measures and practices not covered by Article III:8 GATT, all the more since the EU does not consider the IPI Regulation to violate Article III:4 GATT. At the same time, an 'as applied' claim of Article 23 DSU violation is unlikely to materialize in case the EU takes IPI measures against third-country measures and practices not covered by NT procurement derogations, since the complainant would not be interested in bringing such a claim because it would impliedly denounce its own measures.

Thus, while theoretically the IPI Regulation could breach Article 23 DSU, it is less likely that the EU will face such a claim, and similarly unlikely that it would be successful. Nevertheless, for the EU to act as a responsible supporter of multilateralism, it should avoid taking unilateral IPI measures in cases of third-country measures or practice that could violate WTO rules.

[144] Panel Report, *US – Certain EC Products*, WT/DS165/R, 17 July 2000, para. VI.91.

8.5 The IPI and EU FTAs

Besides core WTO obligations, the IPI could also come into tension with corresponding FTA provisions which contain similar language.

EU FTAs regularly incorporate Article III GATT *mutatis mutandis*,[145] thus including paragraph 8 (a). They do not have any other specific provision that would exclude procurement from the coverage of the general NT obligation outside the governmental procurement chapter. However, the EU would not apply IPI measures against economic operators, goods, or services originating in a third country that is an FTA party to the extent that market access commitments on procurement and concessions were made. Therefore, in such an instance an FTA partner would not have a reason for initiating FTA proceedings in this respect. Still, as recital (10) of the IPI Regulation states, it does apply to 'economic operators, goods or services from countries that are parties to such agreements but only with respect to public procurement procedures for goods, services or concessions *that are not covered by those agreements*' (emphasis added). So, if admittedly the EU applied IPI measures against an FTA partner in cases related to non-covered procurement, FTA provisions incorporating NT obligations could be violated. Accordingly, the analysis under Article III:8 (a) GATT contained in Section 8.4.1.2 is also pertinent in the FTA context. As EU FTA panelists are usually required to take into account relevant WTO jurisprudence,[146] similar interpretations could be expected, unless panelists reach a different conclusion by arguing, for example, that general NT obligations should be interpreted differently by taking into account the context offered by the FTA Government Procurement chapters with its special NT obligation. Thus, to avoid potential claims of FTA violations, the IPI Regulation also for this reason should have been drafted to meet the conditions of Article III:8 (a) GATT.

[145] For example, Free Trade Agreement between the European Union and its Member States, of the one part, and the Republic of Korea, of the other part, OJ EU 2011 No. L 127/6, 14 May 2011, Art. 2.8; Comprehensive Economic and Trade Agreement (CETA) between Canada, of the one part, and the European Union and its Member States, of the other part, OJ EU 2017 No. L 11/23, 14 January 2017, Art. 2.3 (1); Free Trade Agreement between the European Union and the Republic of Singapore, OJ EU 2019 L No. 294/3, 14 November 2019, Art. 2.3; Free Trade Agreement between the European Union and New Zealand (EU–New Zealand FTA), 9 July 2023, Art. 2.4.

[146] For example, CETA, Art 29.17; Agreement between the European Union and Japan for an Economic Partnership, OJ EU 2018 No. L 330/3, 27 December 2018, Art 21.16; Free Trade Agreement between the European Union and the Socialist Republic of Viet Nam, OJ EU 2020 No. L 186/3, 12 June 2020, Art 15.21.

8.6 Broader Implications

Not only the legality of the IPI Regulation under EU's international commitments might have consequences for the EU and its economic operators. The Regulation is likely to entail additional implications, which will be considered here.

The purported intention behind this instrument is to incentivize, including economically, third countries that impose measures, procedures, or practices that seriously and repeatedly impair the access of EU economic operators to their procurement markets to open them. Thus, the Regulation also conveys a political message that the EU is not naïve and will not tolerate conduct of third countries that financially affects its economic operators, but will take action to ensure a fairer treatment for them.[147] Although the Regulation attempts, together with other instruments, to contribute to levelling the playing field for EU companies, it might not only fail to achieve this aim (e.g. due to a circumvention by way of using an EU subsidiary of a third-country bidder economically active in the EU) but could even result in worsening the situation for EU companies. Furthermore, on one hand, there are fears that the instrument might be mostly used against smaller economies, with no particular strategic interest for the EU,[148] due to the latter's fear to clash with powerful states. On the other hand, there is a risk that countries subject to IPI measures will resort to retaliation,[149] especially bigger economies, such as China, that might be less prone to give in under the EU's pressure and instead use their own economic weight to pressure EU into terminating those measures. Furthermore, the obligations on successful tenderers, notably the obligation that goods and services supplied in the execution of a supply of goods contract and originating in third countries subject to IPI measures should not amount to more than 50 per cent of the total value of the contract, could similarly affect EU companies,

[147] Bollen, De Ville, and Orbie, 'EU Trade Policy' (2016) 286; Kirchner, 'More Fairness in Global Procurement' (2021), p. 5; Szczepański, 'EU International Procurement Instrument' (2022), p. 2.

[148] Melo Araujo, *The EU Deep Trade Agenda* (2016), p. 217.

[149] Pedro Telles, 'SME Related Impacts, Thresholds and National Legislation', in *Detailed Appraisal of the European Commission's Impact Assessment: Third Countries' Reciprocal Access to EU Public Procurement* (2013) European Parliamentary Research Service, www.europarl.europa.eu/RegData/etudes/BRIE/2014/508963/EPRS_BRI(2014)508963_REV1_EN.pdf, p. 110; Dawar, 'The 2016 European Union International Procurement Instrument's Amendments' (2016) 849; Gabriel, Schulz, and Manzini, 'Proposal for an International Procurement Instrument' (2020) 341.

especially considering the global supply chains. Finally, although the IPI Regulation, compared to its drafts, has greatly reduced the administrative burden on both authorities and bidders, there are still many obligations that put additional weight on both authorities and companies.[150] Nevertheless, according to the Regulation, these potential negative implications should be taken into account by the Commission when establishing whether the adoption of an IPI measure is in the interest of the Union.[151] When, based on all the information available, the Commission concludes that it is not in the EU's interest, it shall not adopt IPI measures (Article 6 (2) IPI Regulation). Therefore, the IPI Regulation provides the mechanism through which unwanted consequences can be avoided, but this wholly depends on the Commission's assessment of EU interest.

Another concern related to the IPI Regulation is that the EU is engaging in the same conduct that it seeks to curtail, namely economic protectionism.[152] Thus, the EU could lose its credibility when advocating for increased openness of public procurement markets and be accused (once again) of hypocrisy.[153] As mentioned in Section 8.2, initially big economic players, such as Germany, were concerned about the risk that the instrument will be perceived as being protectionist and did not support earlier proposals. However, in light of the increased protectionism and weaponization of international trade, their position has changed, and the IPI Regulation started to be viewed as being a necessary tool. EU's propensity to adopt tools that would allow it to react to external challenges instead of remaining idle to potential threats to its economy, including in the area of public procurement, is understandable. However, in order not to undermine its claims of support for

[150] For example, contracting authorities and entities still must verify the economic operators' origin, which upon request shall submit relevant information and documentation (Art. 3 (3) IPI Regulation), or see the reporting obligations of contracting authorities and entities described in Art. 13 (1), (2) IPI Regulation.

[151] The Regulation explicitly states that the determination of whether the adoption of IPI measures is in the Union's interest should be based on the appreciation of 'all the various interests taken as a whole, including the interests of the Union's economic operators' (Art. 6 (2) IPI Regulation). 'The objective of limiting any unnecessary administrative burden for contracting authorities and contracting entities as well as economic operators should also be taken into account' (Preamble, Recital 20 IPI Regulation).

[152] Dawar, 'The 2016 European Union International Procurement Instrument's Amendments' (2016) 849; Melo Araujo, *The EU Deep Trade Agenda* (2016), p. 216.

[153] Melo Araujo, *The EU Deep Trade Agenda* (2016), p. 216.

multilateralism, the EU should have designed the IPI more carefully with its international commitments in mind, which, as shown in the previous section, most likely was not fully the case.

In sum, the IPI, meant to induce other countries to open their procurement markets, might have negative consequences that should be taken into account and evaluated by the Commission in its decision-making on IPI measures. The EU's trustworthiness as a committed multilateralist would have benefitted from a full conformity with its international obligations.

8.7 Conclusion

As the EU alleges that its public procurement markets are much more open than that of other countries, especially that of economies such as China, with no leverage in negotiations to obtain further openings, it adopted the IPI Regulation seeking to strengthen its negotiation position and to obtain access and ensure a level playing field for the Union's companies.

As shown, the road towards an adopted IPI Regulation was a thorny one, with two earlier proposals in 2012 and 2016 being turned down by the Council, which was *inter alia* concerned with the legislation's potential protectionist character. Nonetheless, in light of the changing context and in line with EU's trade policy review and new 'open strategic autonomy', the Council changed its attitude, and a revised proposal was adopted in 2022. The IPI Regulation 2022/1031 could result in the imposition of IPI measures and obligations on successful tenderers, which limit the access of economic operators, goods, and services originating in certain third countries to the EU's public procurement markets.

Although the Regulation only applies to non-covered procurement – that is, procurement which is outside the scope of the GPA and EU FTA public procurement chapters – its compatibility with multilateral trade rules goes further than that, since public procurement is not entirely exempted from the disciplines of other WTO agreements. Thus, even though the Regulation states that it shall be without prejudice to EU's international obligations, the Union seems to erroneously presume that all public procurement falls outside the coverage of the main WTO disciplines.

It has been argued that the IPI measures and obligations on successful tenderers are likely to violate non-discrimination obligations in the fields of goods and services (Articles I:1, III:4 GATT and II:1, XVII GATS), unless covered by an exception or derogation. As demonstrated also by the controversial yet already established WTO jurisprudence, Articles III:8 (a) GATT and XIII:1 GATS do exclude certain types of public procurement from these non-discrimination obligations, but only when the pertinent requirements are complied with by the procurement in question. Whether the elements of these public procurement derogations are met must be assessed on a case-by-case basis, but it was shown that the IPI Regulation applies to public procurement that does not always meet those elements. Thus, the IPI Regulation also covers public procurement of products and services through types of transactions other than purchase; the procurement of products or services not being intended for governmental purpose; and with a view to commercial resale or use in the production of goods or supply of service for commercial sale. When the IPI measures and obligations on successful tenderers concern at least a type of such procurement, they would not benefit from the derogations. Thus, the chapter arrives at the conclusion that in order to stay within the confines of its international obligations, the EU should have taken into account the elements of Articles III:8 (a) GATT and XIII:1 GATS when designing the IPI Regulation more clearly. Furthermore, compliance with these elements is also important in the context of EU FTAs, as they incorporate Article III GATT. The Commission, when implementing the IPI Regulation, thus has to take utmost care that IPI measures are not adopted in situations that are not covered by the above non-discrimination derogations or by an exception, such as that contained in Article XXIV GATT. Additionally, the chapter showed a minimal risk for a violation of Article 23 DSU by the IPI. Accordingly, the definition of the 'third-country measure or practice' should be refined so that IPI measures are not imposed when foreign measures or practices are not covered by public procurement derogations from non-discrimination obligations, and instead initiate WTO proceedings in case of alleged third country's breach of WTO obligations.

Despite the fact that it was claimed elsewhere that earlier IPI proposals could be incompatible with EU's obligations under the ASCM, it was established herein that IPI obligations on successful tenderers would not constitute specific subsidies, while IPI measures could qualify as subsidies that would, nevertheless, fall outside the scope of WTO subsidies disciplines. As a result, the IPI Regulation should be considered in conformity with the ASCM.

Lastly, whereas the IPI Regulation aims at opening more public procurement markets for EU companies, it could, in fact, lead to adverse consequences. Even so, the instrument was shown to include a mechanism that would allow the Commission to decide against the imposition of IPI measures when, based on various aspects, it concludes that it is not in the Union's interest to do so, thereby avoiding unwanted negative repercussions. The need for an instrument to allow the Union to react to the challenging context, including in the area of international procurement, is reasonable. Still, as the EU risks to be accused of being protectionist with respect to its own public procurement markets while allegedly seeking to open that of other countries with the IPI Regulation, in order for it to remain true to its multilateralist DNA and a credible international actor, it should better balance its international commitments and 'strategic autonomy'.

9 The Foreign Subsidies Regulation

The Way Forward to Competitive Equality and Exterritoriality of EU Competition Law?

9.1 Introduction

Another new instrument that the EU legislative meanwhile has adopted in the wake of the new assertive trade policy is the Regulation 2022/2560 on Foreign Subsidies distorting the Internal Market[1] (hereinafter FSR). This regulation allows the EU to protect its interests against unfair behaviour of its trade partners by aiming at ensuring a level playing field in the EU as regards competition between foreign or EU companies active on the EU internal market that received subsidies from third countries and EU companies that did not. The EU and its Member States became ever more concerned about distortions of competition on the EU internal market resulting from third countries' subsidization. Economic analyses demonstrate that states are increasingly making use of subsidies to substitute for protectionism, and do not shy away from granting subsidies to undertakings operating abroad; the rise of foreign direct investments increased the incentives for granting subsidies, in particular to foster transnational mergers.[2] Third countries provide public funds in order to finance economic activities in the EU market, which may distort competition in the internal market and undermine the level playing field

[1] Regulation 2022/2560 of the European Parliament and the Council of 14 December 2022 on foreign Subsidies distorting the internal market, OJ EU 2022 No. L 330/1, 23 December 2022.

[2] Fredrik Erixon, et al., *The New Wave of Defensive Trade Policy Measures in the European Union*, ECIPE Occasional Paper No 04/2022, p. 69 ff; Gary Hufbauer, Thomas Moll, and Luca Rubbini, 'Investment Subsidies for Cross-Border M&A', United States Council Foundation Occasional Paper No. 2, April 2008, www.uscib.org/docs/usc_foundation_investment_subsidies.pdf, pp. 3 ff; Malorie Schaus, 'EU Trade Policy in Light of the New Industrial Strategy' (2021) 56 *Intereconomics* 144–149 at 146 f; Marios Tokas, 'Playing the Game: The EU's Proposed Regulation on Foreign Subsidies' (2022) 56 (5) *JWT* 779–802 at 780.

in the EU (see recitals 2, 4, and 6 FSR). Furthermore, subsidies are cherished as a useful policy tool to steer the required societal and economic transformations in order to address climate change and other pressing needs.[3] As foreign subsidies may improve the competitive position of their recipient commercially active in the internal market, third-country subsidies are capable of negatively affecting the equality of competitive conditions in the EU, for example by enabling a beneficiary to submit unduly advantageous tenders to engage in a merger or to purchase a company. Hence, the regulation covers unfair competition also in case of investment in EU companies or in public procurement procedures in the EU.

Therefore, the new regulation establishes a framework to address the distortions as it provides for investigation procedures and for remedies against them (Article 1 FSR). The European Commission is bestowed with the power to investigate foreign subsidies granted to undertakings active in the EU and, in case of distortions, to adopt redressive measures to address these distortive effects. The scope of application of the regulation covers any commercial activity of an undertaking in the EU that benefits from foreign subsidies (Chapter 2 FSR). Particular rules are enshrined for beneficiaries that take part in mergers and other types of concentrations (Chapter 3 FSR) or in public procurement (Chapter 4 FSR), as participating undertakings must meet specific notification requirements (see Articles 20 and 28 FSR). Thus, the regulation provides for three tools, or slightly different procedures, two of which are notification-based to investigate concentrations and tenders in public procurement. Concentrations must be notified where the acquired company, one of the merging parties, or a joint venture generates an EU turnover of at least €500 million and the transaction involves a combined aggregate foreign financial contribution of more than €50 million. In case of tenders, notification is required if a bid involves a foreign financial contribution of at least €4 million per third country, where the estimated contract value is at least €250 million. The third tool is a general one in which the Commission may investigate all other commercial activities in all market situations in the EU that may have been distorted by foreign subsidies. As the new regulation subjects third-country subsidies to review procedures, the regulation leads to rather intense scrutiny in the EU over companies benefitting from third-country subsidies.

[3] Erixon, et al., *The New Wave of Defensive Trade Policy Measures in the European Union*, p. 62.

The new regulation has also provoked criticism with regard to its compliance with international legal obligations of the EU. One aspect is the relation of the new redressive measures to the countermeasures available for the EU under the WTO Agreement on Subsidies and Countervailing Measures (ASCM).[4] As the ASCM may be conclusive in its treatment of foreign subsidies due to Article 32.1 ASCM, the EU may not be in a position to introduce additional or divergent measures. FSR even confirms the respect for Article 32.2 ASCM and for the EU's international commitments. Nevertheless, a collision of FSR implementation with international rules is possible, as the perception of what international law requires may vary. It is far from clear how far the scope of the ASCM and its conclusive character actually goes. This deserves closer inspection in Section 9.3.1.

Another concern is related to the non-discrimination rules under the WTO agreements. Even though Article III:8 (b) GATT,[5] by and large, excludes the payment of subsidies from the scope of GATT national treatment (NT) (apart from the non-discriminatory taxation requirement of Article III:2 GATT),[6] this is not the case with regard to subsidized services and the NT obligation of Article XVII GATS.[7] Article XV GATS is not a carve-out of subsidization of services from the GATS disciplines. The review of foreign subsidies granted to foreign service providers active in the internal market under Article 9 ff FSR might be assessed as discriminatory, an issue which will be dealt with more closely in Section 9.3.2.

Finally, the introduction of a foreign subsidies review could also collide with specific commitments in bilateral trade or in association or cooperation agreements that contain disciplines on subsidies, including particular review mechanisms which at least partly go far beyond the WTO ASCM disciplines, cover services, and lay down very specific (so-called WTO-plus) commitments. The unilateral introduction of foreign subsidies review processes by the EU might conflict with those. (Admittedly, an issue might be the different scope of applications, as the subsidy

[4] Agreement on Subsidies and Countervailing Measures, 15 April 1994, Marrakesh Agreement Establishing the World Trade Organization, Annex 1A, 1869 U.N.T.S. 14.

[5] General Agreement on Tariffs and Trade 1994, 15 April 1994, Marrakesh Agreement Establishing the World Trade Organization, Annex 1A, 1867 U.N.T.S. 187, 33 I.L.M. 1153 (1994).

[6] For more detail in that regard, see Appellate Body Report, *Brazil – Taxation*, WT/DS472/AB/R, WT/DS497/AB/R, 13 December 2018, paras. 5.102 ff.

[7] General Agreement on Trade in Services, 15 April 1994, Marrakesh Agreement Establishing the World Trade Organization, Annex 1B, 1869 U.N.T.S. 183, 33 I.L.M. 1167 (1994).

disciplines in the FTA might be limited to addressing trade effects between the EU and the respective third country instead of effects within the internal market.) We will address the FSR's compatibility with bilateral obligations in Section 9.4.

Before Sections 9.3 and 9.4 can explore these issues of compatibility of the FSR with the EU's international obligations in more detail and scrutinize the EU's leeway in legislating unilateral responses to third-country subsidies, the specific rules of the FSR have to be introduced in more detail. Section 9.2 will provide the necessary overview of the FSR's core provisions, with a particular focus on a comparison to EU state aid and EU anti-subsidy law. Particularly EU state aid review can be expected to be used by trade partners as a reference point in complaints about undue discrimination against them brought about by the FSR.

9.2 The Foreign Subsidies Regulation: Need and Core Content

9.2.1 The Gap-Filling Function of the Foreign Subsidies Regulation

In the Commission's view, the need for rules to address foreign subsidies results from the limited scope of EU state aid rules in Article 107 f TFEU, as they do not cover third-country subsidies; furthermore, EU merger control and public procurement rules do not deal with any competition issues caused by foreign subsidization, as merger control reviews the effect of concentrations on competition, and public procurement rules do not allow for considering foreign subsidies and their effects on tenders.[8] Remedies to address trade distortions, however, already exist with regard to the import of subsidized products. In this regard, current trade defense rules in the Basic Anti-Subsidy Regulation 2016/1037 (hereinafter BASR)[9] provide for countervailing measures in order to offset any specific foreign subsidy that was granted, directly or indirectly, for the manufacture, production, export, or transport of any product the release of which into free circulation in the Union causes material injury to a domestic industry in the EU (Articles 1, 4, 15 BASR). Accordingly, the EU

[8] Simone Ritzek-Seidl, 'The Regulation on Foreign Subsidies Distorting the Internal Market: Outline of the Provisional Agreement' (2022) 3 *ZEuS* 423–430 at 424; Till Müller-Ibold, 'The Draft Foreign Subsidies Regulation' (2022) 3 *ZEuS* 431–442 at 432. For more on the regulatory gaps contended by the European Commission, see White Paper on levelling the playing field as regards foreign subsidies, COM(2020) 253 final, 17 June 2020, p. 9 ff.

[9] Regulation (EU) 2016/1037 of the European Parliament and of the Council on protection against subsidised imports from countries not members of the European Union, OJ EU 2016 No. L 176/55, 30 June 2016, as amended.

can adopt countervailing duties or alternatively accept satisfactory voluntary offers from undertakings (Articles 15, 13 BASR). These rules implement the ASCM and apply to imported goods only; hence, prior to the FSR, there were indeed no EU rules addressing foreign subsidized services, investments, or financial flows.[10] The practice of subsidizing also service providers and undertakings doing business abroad, however, became ever more proliferate among nations in past years.[11] Also insofar as foreign subsidies might impact the competition in the company purchase market and in public procurement, there are no rules, as the EU Merger Regulation and the EU procurement law do not address them. Distortions on the market for merger transaction are not considered by the Merger Regulation,[12] nor is the receipt of foreign subsidies in the EU procurement regulations.[13]

Therefore, the Commission proposed the new regulation addressing competition distortions resulting from foreign subsidies in order to close the regulatory gap and to provide the means to respond to foreign subsidies beyond the reach of the ASCM and the BASR.[14] The Commission did so not least for the reason that any attempt in developing further the WTO multilateral subsidies rules would have to take a long road.[15] Despite its trade policy roots, the FSR is not only an application of the EU's open strategic autonomy but also an instrument of EU competition and internal market policy to effectuate a 'strong, open and competitive internal market' where undertakings compete on merits (see recital 1 FSR). Accordingly, the regulation is based on both the EU trade policy competence of Article 207 TFEU and on Article 114 TFEU for the internal market. The subsequent analysis will show that the FSR not only completes the EU's competition law (as the FSR is directed towards counteracting competition distortions caused by foreign subsidies) but also amends its trade defense instruments, which can particularly be

[10] See recital 5 FSR; see also recital 4 of the Commission Proposal for a Regulation of the European Parliament and of the Council on foreign subsidies distorting the internal market, COM(2021) 223 final, 5 May 2021.

[11] Tokas, 'Playing the Game' (2022) 780.

[12] Tabea Bauermeister, 'A Tool to Investigate M&A Transactions with Regard to Foreign Financial Contributions' (2022) 3 *ZEuS* 477–486 at 479 f.

[13] Caspar Ebrecht, 'Foreign Subsidies Regulation and EU International Procurement' (2022) 3 *ZEuS* 487–494 at 490.

[14] See the Explanatory Memorandum to the Commission Proposal for a Regulation of the European Parliament and of the Council on foreign subsidies distorting the internal market, COM(2021) 223 final, 5 May 2021, p. 2 ff.

[15] ibid.

deduced from the wealth of powers for the Commission to adopt substantially diverse decisions on remedies. The FSR rightly has been characterized as a 'unique blend of familiar concepts and rules' drawing on concepts from EU state aid, antitrust, and trade defense law.[16] Nevertheless, the mixture is unique, and the EU presents a novel, 'ground-breaking'[17] instrument to address foreign subsidization.

9.2.2 Core Content of the Foreign Subsidies Regulation

In order to address the competition distortion of foreign subsidies, the FSR provides three tools that build upon specific rules and procedures, besides the FSR's general and common procedural provisions in Chapters 1 and 5, Articles 1–8 and 34–43. The two specific notification-based tools relate to situations of concentration, specifically mergers or acquisitions (Chapter 3 on concentrations, Articles 19–26), and to participation in public procurement in the EU (Chapter 3, Articles 27–33). In these two specific situations, undertakings are required to notify notifiable concentrations to the European Commission and notifiable foreign contributions to the pertinent contracting authority, respectively, in order to allow for an *ex ante* review of foreign subsidies' distortive effects (see Article 21 in connection with Article 20 (3) and Article 29 in connection with Article 28 (1) FSR). The generally applicable tool of *ex officio* review allows for a review in all market situations and is set out in Chapter 2, Articles 9–18, which also provide some general review rules.

The new powers enshrined in the FSR in order to redress competition distortions *ex officio* allow the Commission to adopt decisions that either accept commitments of the subsidized undertakings or impose 'redressive measures' in order to fully remedy an actual or potential distortion on the internal market resulting from third-country subsidies (see Articles 7, 11 (2) FSR). The envisaged commitments or possible measures are very broad in their substance. They comprise behavioural as well as structural remedies against competition distortion. The Commission's *ex officio* review procedure is two-phased, same as under state aid, and

[16] Francois-Charles Laprévote and Wanjie Lin, 'Between State Aid, Trade and Antitrust: The Mixed Procedural Heritage of the Foreign Subsidies Regulation and the Overarching Principle of Non-Discrimination' (2022) 3 *ZEuS* 443–452 at 443.

[17] ibid. 452. In the words of Margarete Vestager, Vice-President of the European Commission, 'This new regulation [. . .] will make us the first trading bloc in the world with tools against harmful subsidies, from both inside the Single Market and from Non-EU countries'; Statement on the Commission proposal, see https://ec.europa.eu/commission/presscorner/detail/en/speech_21_2286.

consists of a preliminary and an in-depth investigation. The Commission enjoys a rather broad decision-making power at the end of the latter: After having assessed the necessary information, the Commission may decide not to raise objections, adopt redressive measures, or accept commitments (Article 11 (2) to (4) FSR). Redressive measures and commitments may take diverse shapes and pertain mainly to behavioural or structural measures. According to Article 7 (4) FSR, commitments or redressive measures may *inter alia* (the list presented there is not exhaustive) oblige an undertaking to offer fair, reasonable, and non-discriminatory (FRAND) access to infrastructures, license assets acquired under FRAND conditions, reduce its capacity or market presence, refrain from certain investments or divest certain assets, make publicly available certain results of research and development, undo a merger or acquisition, or repay the foreign subsidy, inclusive of interests. In case of procurement or concentration, the Commission can adopt a negative decision only in the form of a prohibition of the concentration (Article 25 (3) c) FSR) or of the award of contract (Article 31 (2) FSR), besides accecpting commitments. In addition, the Commission can impose reporting and transparency requirements (Article 7 (5) FSR).

Such decisions cannot be taken after a preliminary investigation, which can only lead either to the opening of an in-depth investigation or to a decision to close the file and inform the undertaking concerned (Article 10 (3), (4) FSR). Compared to EU state aid review, in foreign subsidies review under the FSR, the Commission has quite a broad leeway when it comes to the substantive content of a decision. Under state aid law, the Commission can, after the in-depth investigation, adopt either a positive or a negative decision on the state aid measure's compatibility with the EU internal market (the positive decision may be subject to conditions; Article 9 (4) State Aid Procedure Regulation 2015/1589[18]); furthermore, a recovery decision may follow. The FSR requires a much more complex assessment. According to Article 7 (3) FSR, the Commission must ensure that the (potential) distortion caused by the foreign subsidy in the internal market is 'fully and effectively' remedied, considering also the requirement of the Article 6 FSR balancing test. The latter test allows the Commission ('may') to balance between the negative and positive effects of the foreign subsidy. The balancing test is set up very broadly,

[18] Council Regulation (EU) 2015/1589 laying down detailed rules for the application of Article 108 of the Treaty on the Functioning of the European Union, OJ EU 2015 No. L 248/9, 24 September 2015, as amended.

as – beyond positive effects on economic activity – other positive effects in relation to EU policy objectives also must be considered.

The difference between the FSR decision-making powers and those in state aid review, particularly with regard to the broad discretion granted to the Commission in the FSR to tailor the redressive measures, can be explained by the different objects of the foreign subsidies review compared to state aid review. While EU state aid review focuses on either approving or prohibiting national state aid, foreign subsidy review is concerned with offsetting the adverse effects of foreign subsidies on the competition in the internal market. The content of an effective measure required for this purpose depends on the kind of subsidy measure and its effects on the competition in the internal market. Furthermore, different from EU state aid law, under foreign subsidies review, the Commission cannot effectively prohibit a third state to grant subsidies but can only adopt decisions on compensatory measures addressed to companies, which must be tailored precisely to the distortion of competition caused by the subsidy. In order to do this, the Commission needs a wide margin of manoeuver in its decision-making powers to adjust the content of the remedy accordingly. The Impact Assessment of the FSR proposal stated that the redressive measures 'are based on measures applied in EU State aid control', as the potentially distortive impact of foreign subsidies was deemed similar to that of state aid. The same Impact Assessment document, however, had to admit that, as the reimbursement of a foreign subsidy to the granting authority in a third country is almost impossible to monitor and enforce outside the EU, redressive measures under the FSR have to prefer 'behavioral or structural remedies', as they are more effective in this context.[19] In contrast, in EU state aid law, behavioural or structural remedies are adopted comparatively rarely.[20] Also, the prohibition of intended acquisitions facilitated by foreign subsidies will be more common as a redressive measure than under state aid rules, since acquisitions financed by state aid hardly occur in the EU.[21]

[19] See also Raymond Luja, 'The Foreign Subsidies Regulation: Countering State Aid beyond the European Union' (2021) 20 *European State Aid Law Quarterly* 187–199 at 191.

[20] Commission Staff Working Document, Impact Assessment Accompanying the Proposal for a Regulation of the European Parliament and of the Council on foreign subsidies distorting the internal market, SWD(2021) 99 final, 5 May 2021, p. 48, refers to remedial measures under the Rescue and Restructuring Guidelines, the financial sectoral guidelines or the COVID-19 Temporary Framework.

[21] ibid 76.

Hence, the powers of the Commission under the FSR go significantly beyond its powers under EU state aid law.[22] Given that the redressive measures in the foreign subsidies review can reshape competitive relations, the Commission enjoys considerable steering power.

These Commission powers build upon an investigation that has to explore, slight distinctions in procedural frameworks aside, three common concepts: the existence of a foreign subsidy, the causation of a distortion in competition in the EU internal market, and the compensation of these negative effects by positive effects for the EU economy and its relevant policy objectives.[23] If the Commission finally finds a competitive distortion caused by a foreign subsidy which is not offset by its positive effects, the Commission then has to determine how the redressive measures or offered commitments have to be shaped in order to fully and effectively remedy the distortion (Article 7 (3) FSR).[24] In the procurement and merger situation, the review will only result in a decision prohibiting the award of contract (Article 31 (2) FSR) or the concentration (Article 25(3) c) FSR). The second concept of the Commission's analysis, namely the elaboration of a distortion of competition and the causality of a foreign subsidy for it, is a rather genuine assessment which has little to do with state aid review. Its uniqueness was implicitly confirmed by the Statement of the Commission on clarifications regarding the application of Article 4 FSR on the existence of a distortion and on the broad balancing test of Article 6 FSR, which goes beyond merely balancing the economic positives and negatives. This is because the Commission therein promised to clarify the application of these concepts within twelve months from 12 July 2023, the date of application of the FSR (see Article 54 (2) FSR),[25] which in essence prepares for the application guidelines foreseen in Article 46 FSR to be adopted by 12 January 2026. Compared to these complex analyses required from the Commission under the FSR, under state aid, the main questions to be explored is whether a state aid exists and, if so, whether it is compatible with the internal market under Article 107 (2), (3) TFEU. The first issue, as to

[22] See also Laprévote and Lin, 'Between State Aid, Trade and Antitrust' (2022) 452.

[23] Ritzek-Seidl, 'The Regulation on Foreign Subsidies Distorting the Internal Market' (2022) 425 f.

[24] See Morris Schonberg, 'The EU Foreign Subsidies Regulation: Substantive Assessment Issues and Open Questions' (2022) 21(2) *European State Aid Law Quarterly* 143–152 at 143 f.

[25] Statement of the European Commission on clarifications as regards the application of Regulation 2022/2560, pursuant to Article 46 thereof, OJ EU 2022 No. C 491/8, 23 December 2022.

whether state aid exists, is by and large limited to an analysis of whether there is a specific benefit granted to an undertaking. The distortion of competition which is an additional requirement under Article 107 (1) TFEU then follows as a regular consequence of the financial benefit given to an undertaking, as it strengthens its position in competition in the EU compared to normal market conditions;[26] thus, state aid review is based on a presumption that a benefit causes distortion of competition.[27] This distortion subsequently will be assessed in some detail in the examination of the compatibility requirements for state aid enshrined in Articles 107 (2) and (3) TFEU, which admittedly grant considerable leeway to the Commission.

The third concept of the FSR's test, the balancing exercise, has only a remote resemblance in state aid law. In state aid, the focus of the compatibility assessment is comparatively clear: The state aid measure must address a market failure to demonstrate the need for state intervention; state aid must have an incentive effect, be appropriate, and not go beyond what is necessary for its remedy. Furthermore, the Commission has to assess whether and how far the state aid measure contributes to an objective of common interest determined by the Commission,[28] and whether the positive effects outweigh the negative economic effects of the state aid.[29] Even under Article 107 (3) c) TFEU, for which the Court of Justice of the European Union (CJEU) recently held that this rule does not make the compatibility of aid dependent on its pursuing an objective of common interest,[30] there still is the requirement that state aid is needed for developing an economic activity. Compared to this, the balancing test of Article 6 FSR, which allows for the inclusion of any positive effects,

[26] See e.g. CJEU, Case C-39/94, *Syndicat français de l'Express international (SFEI) and others v La Poste and others* [1996] ECR I-03547, paras. 60–62.

[27] Commission Notice on the Notion of State Aid, OJ EU 2016 No. C 262/1, paras. 187–190; Schonberg, 'The EU Foreign Subsidies Regulation' (2022) 147; Tokas, 'Playing the Game' (2022) 784.

[28] See Claire Micheau, 'Control of State Aid: A Policy Specific Area of EU Administrative Law', in Herwig Hofmann, Gerhard Rowe, and Alexander Türk (eds.), *Specialized Administrative Law of the EU* (Oxford: Oxford University Press, 2018), p. 465 f; Schonberg, 'The EU Foreign Subsidies Regulation' (2022) 147.

[29] The required balancing under state aid law pivotally focuses on balancing the positive versus negative economic effects as a state aid measure is assessed with a view to its effects on the internal market; see CJEU, Case C-594/18, *Hinkley Point* [2020] ECLI:EU:C:2020:742, para. 101: 'Article 107(3)(c) TFEU entails the Commission taking into account the negative effects of the State aid on competition and trade between Member States, but does not require any negative effects other than those to be taken into account.'

[30] CJEU, Case C-594/18, *Hinkley Point*, para. 20.

appears much broader and grants even greater leeway to the Commission. And the core difference between state aid law that provides for justifications of distortion and the FSR that does not provide justifications (only limited safe harbours in Article 4 (2), (4) FSR), but a mere balancing test whose role is not yet clear, remains.

Also, compared to the EU BASR, which provides for countervailing duties, the FSR is rather specific, even though at first view the BASR aims at something similar as the FSR: offsetting subsidies (see Article 1 BASR). Under the BASR, however, this is done by levying a duty that compensates for the damage to EU industry caused by the foreign subsidy. Countervailing duties are the only remedy the BASR provides in its Articles 12 and 15 in case of distortive effects (in the form of injury under Article 8 BASR, particularly in view of the price effects caused by the import of subsidized goods, but also of their broader economic effects on EU industry). In contrast to EU state aid law, subsidization by a foreign country cannot be prohibited under the BASR, nor can subsidized goods be banned.

9.3 The Foreign Subsidies Regulation and WTO Law

Even though Article 44 (9) FSR is intended to bring the FSR into conformity with the EU's international obligations by providing that the FSR shall not prevent the EU from fulfilling its international obligations, the compliance of the FSR with international law cannot be taken for granted. As has already been alluded, in case of a legislative instrument that grants considerable powers to the Commission (as does the FSR), compliance with the exigencies of international law may depend on the way these powers are used and implemented.[31] And as mentioned in Section 9.1, the FSR in itself, prior to any implementation, may already breach commitments the EU entered into under WTO law, but possibly also under bilateral agreements. If so, under Article 44 (9) FSR, the FSR would not be applicable in those situations. Still, the Commission might apply the FSR due to a misapprehension of international law.

First, we will explore the pertinent EU obligations stemming from WTO law that could be violated by the FSR. Among them, the compliance with obligations flowing from the ASCM is the one most debated.

[31] For the mandatory vs discretionary distinction in assessing a breach of international commitments, see Section 3.3.1.

9.3.1 International Commitments under the WTO ASCM

Concerns about the compliance of the FSR with WTO law arise with regard to the compatibility of the redressive measures foreseen in the FSR with Article 32.1 ASCM. This article provides that '[n]o specific action against a subsidy of another Member can be taken except in accordance with the provisions of GATT 1994, as interpreted by this Agreement', so that specific measures against a subsidy only be taken in accordance with the provisions of the ASCM. As mentioned, Article 44 (9) FSR confirms the EU's commitment to fulfil its international obligations, in particular under the ASCM, as it provides that 'no action shall be taken under this Regulation which would amount to a specific action against a subsidy within the meaning of Article 32.1 [ASCM]' granted by a WTO member. Article 44 (9) FSR also explicitly provides that 'no investigation [under the FSR] shall be carried out' nor any 'measures be imposed or maintained' that would breach international commitments. Consequently, one might opine that there does not exist any issue with regard to the ASCM's prevalence over unilateral measures of any WTO member. The Commission on the occasion of the adoption of the FSR confirmed its position that the FSR was in line with EU's international obligation, in particular with the ASCM.[32]

The problem with the ASCM's prevalence starts already with the different type of countermeasures acceptable under ASCM compared to the FSR. Under the ASCM, only provisional or definitive countervailing duties on imports of subsidized goods, price undertakings, or multilateral countermeasures adopted under the WTO dispute settlement system are permissible against actionable or prohibited subsidies (see Articles 4, 17, 19 ASCM). The FSR, however, allows the Commission to adopt completely different measures, such as prohibition against certain investments or mergers or an obligation to repay the subsidies. Even where commitments of undertakings are foreseen, they may be different from price undertakings, provided for in Article 18.1 b) ASCM, as the former comprise completely diverse types of commitments (Article 7 (4) FSR). A further problem might result from a broad scope of the ASCM with regard to not only subsidized goods but also subsidization of goods production, thus limiting the remaining scope for EU

[32] Statement of the European Commission on multilateral rules to address distortive foreign subsidies on the occasion of the adoption of Regulation (EU) 2022/2560, OJ EU 2022 No. C 491/7, 23 December 2022.

responses to subsidization under the FSR beyond what the EU might expect.

Consequently, it has first to be analyzed whether there is an overlap of the scope of application between the FSR and the ASCM – and if so, the extent of it. Article 32.1 ASCM is only applicable to subsidies according to Article 1 ASCM. The definition of a subsidy under Article 1 ASCM, by and large, coincides with the one from the FSR that follows the notion of subsidy in the anti-subsidy rules[33] and not the one in the state aid rules (the criterion of a budgetary burden / use of state resources is missing).[34] Consequently, there may be an overlap between the scopes of the FSR and the ASCM. As already mentioned, the FSR, however, provides in Article 44 (9) that an investigation pursuant to this regulation 'shall not be carried out and measures shall not be imposed or maintained where such investigation or measures would be contrary' to the EU international obligations. 'In particular, no action shall be taken under this Regulation which would amount to a specific action against a subsidy within the meaning of Article 32.1 of the [ASCM].' Hence, the issue arises as to in which situations the application of the FSR would lead to measures amounting to specific action under Article 32.1 ASCM.

9.3.1.1 *Purview of the ASCM: Trade in Goods, Not Only Importation*

This prompts the question of whether the imposition of the remedies provided in the FSR that are different from those of the ASCM might amount to 'specific action against a subsidy'. One might contend that the countermeasures provided for in the ASCM are useless insofar as they apply only in case of import of goods and do not address investment, merger, or procurement situations (which are covered by FSR). Hence, one could opine that there is no overlap, and thus the measures under the FSR cannot be understood to represent specific actions against a subsidy. Indeed, the ASCM provides for countermeasures only with a view to imported goods. In order to adopt ASCM countermeasures, a WTO member has to determine 'that, through the effects of the subsidy, the subsidized imports are causing injury' (Article 19.1 ASCM). The determination of injury is to be 'based on positive evidence and involve an

[33] See White Paper on levelling the playing field as regards foreign subsidies, COM(2020) 253 final, p. 41.

[34] Christian Koenig and Bernhard von Wendland, *The Art of Regulation: Competition in Europe – Wealth and Wariness* (Cheltenham: Edward Elgar, 2017), p. 174 f; Schonberg, 'The EU Foreign Subsidies Regulation (2022) 145; Tokas, 'Playing the Game' (2022) 782.

objective examination of both (a) the volume of the subsidized imports and the effect of the subsidized imports on prices in the domestic market for like products', and (b) the 'consequent impact' of these imports on domestic producers (Article 15.1 ASCM). Thus, under the ASCM, the subsidy's effect on imports, its prices, and domestic producers is relevant, not other effects, as, for example, on the competitive position of the beneficiary in the EU. Accordingly, the Commission argues that the ASCM only covers 'subsidised imports' of goods from third countries and does 'not apply to subsidies related to trade in services and in relation to the establishment and operation of undertakings in the EU which are backed by foreign subsidies and which do not entail any trade in goods'.[35] From this statement one may infer that the ASCM covers all aspects of competition distortion by subsidies granted to undertakings trading goods in the EU. The Commission in its White Paper had stated that the FSR should not cover foreign subsidies provided for goods and agricultural products imported into the EU, as they were seen to be covered by EU trade defence rules.[36] The FSR, however, does apply also to enterprises importing goods, as it applies to any type of economic activity; see its recitals 1 and 2 and Article 1 (2): 'engaging in an economic activity'. Article 44 (2) FSR leaves the application of the EU's BASR unaffected,[37] which means that the latter and the FSR apply in parallel.[38]

Admittedly, the countermeasures under the ASCM only apply to a specific situation. The measures ('action against a subsidy') referred to in Article 32.1 ASCM do not allow for an effective remedy against all types of distortions of competition caused by third-country subsidies. The remedies foreseen in the ASCM are linked to the process of importing goods. The definition of subsidy, however, in Article 1.1 ASCM covers almost all types and means of subsidization, irrespective of the type of economic activity the beneficiary pursues. Article 1.1 does not confine the notion of subsidies to activities pertaining only to trading goods; it could include subsidies for the provision of services, or for purchasing other companies; the provision of services is mentioned in Article 1.1 a) (1) (iii) ASCM. Nevertheless, it appears to be quite clear that the ASCM does not pertain to subsidization of services provision. This is because Article XVI GATT

[35] White Paper on levelling the playing field as regards foreign subsidies, COM(2020) 253 final, p. 41 f.

[36] ibid, p. 13, fn 24.

[37] Also, recital 5 FSR does not provide for an exemption from its scope of application for enterprises active in goods trade.

[38] Laprévote and Wanjie Lin, 'Between State Aid, Trade and Antitrust' (2022) 446.

refers to 'export of goods', and the ASCM is part of Annex 1A to the WTO Agreement dealing with rules on goods trade. Furthermore, the issue of regulating subsidization in the services sector is subject to further arrangements (see Article XV GATS), so that the WTO members held the view that the scope of the ASCM does not cover subsidization of services. Consequently, the effects of foreign subsidies on services, investment, or procurement appear to be outside the scope of the ASCM.

The scope of the ASCM with regard to subsidization in the area of goods trade, however, is broader than the scope of available countermeasures provided for in the ASCM that are related only to the import of goods. The definition of actionable subsidies in Article 5 ASCM refers to adverse effects flowing from subsidization of goods production and does not relate only to subsidized goods crossing the border. The Appellate Body clearly held that 'Article 32.1 of the SCM Agreement refers to specific action against "a subsidy", not action against the imported subsidized product or a responsible entity'.[39] Thus, the fundamental question emerges whether, despite the lack of effective measures at the level of the ASCM outside the realm of importing subsidized goods, WTO members are still not allowed to take unilateral measures different from those under the ASCM against third-country subsidies affecting production of goods. As mentioned, Article 32.1 ASCM confines the lawful measures against third-country subsidies to those actions that are in accordance with the GATT 1994 and the ASCM, and the latter does not provide for measures such as those foreseen in the FSR. Indeed, it is the function of Article 32.1 ASCM to limit the range of actions that a WTO Member may unilaterally take to counter subsidization. Thus, in the words of the Appellate Body,

> (e)xcluding from [. . .] Article 32.1 of the SCM Agreement actions that do not come into direct contact with the imported good or the entity responsible for the [. . .] subsidized good, would undermine that function. [. . .] there is no requirement that the measure must come into direct contact with the imported product, or entities connected to, or responsible for, the imported good such as the importer, exporter, or foreign producer. We also agree with the Panel that the test should focus on [. . .] subsidization as *practices* [. . .] there is no express requirement that the measure must act against the imported [. . .] product, or entities responsible for that product.[40]

[39] See Appellate Body Report, *US – Offset Act (Byrd Amendment)*, WT/DS217/AB/R, WT/DS234/AB/R, 16 January 2003, para. 251.

[40] Appellate Body Report, WT/DS217/AB/R, WT/DS234/AB/R, *US – Offset Act (Byrd Amendment)*, paras. 252 f. Emphasis in the original.

GATT and the ASCM allow for only four responses to a subsidy (countervailing duties, provisional measures, price undertakings, and countermeasures under the Dispute Settlement Understanding (DSU)[41]), so that no other responses to subsidization are permissible.[42] Article 32.1 ASCM 'limits the range of actions a WTO Member may take unilaterally to counter subsidization. Restricting available unilateral actions against subsidization to those expressly provided for [. . .] is consistent with this function.'[43] In view of this determination of the ASCM scope, there is no doubt that the measures foreseen in the FSR are measures directed against foreign subsidization in the goods (trade or production) sector, as the FSR measures aim at levelling 'the playing field' by taking measures dissuading foreign subsidization.[44] Hence, Article 32.1 ASCM is a barrier to the application of the redressive measures provided for in the FSR against companies active in goods trade but which do not use the subsidies they receive for lowering the prices of their imports, but rather for other ways of distorting competition in the internal market. This may be the case, for example, when a subsidy to an ailing producer maintains its market presence.

In sum, one must conclude that the scope of the FSR partly overlaps with that of the ASCM and that Article 32.1 ASCM bans all types of unilateral measures against subsidization of companies active in goods trade, except those provided in the ASCM. Not least due to its Article 44 (9), the FSR remedies cannot be applied with regard to beneficiaries of foreign subsidies economically active in the EU goods' trade sector as redressive measures under the FSR in that regard represent a 'specific action against a subsidy within the meaning of Article 32.1' ASCM. The ASCM covers all types of subsidization in the goods sector and hence bans any remedies not provided for in the ASCM. The EU has to respect this in order to avoid conflict with its ASCM commitments. FSR redressive measures must not be applied to counteract any form of foreign subsidization of undertakings active in the goods' trade sector in the internal market.

[41] Understanding on Rules and Procedures Governing the Settlement of Disputes, Marrakesh Agreement Establishing the World Trade Organization, Annex 2, 1869 U.N.T.S. 401, 33 I.L.M. 1226 (1994).

[42] See Appellate Body Report, *US – Offset Act (Byrd Amendment)*, WT/DS217/AB/R, WT/DS234/AB/R, para. 269.

[43] ibid, para. 271.

[44] Victor Crochet and Marcus Gustafsson, 'Lawful Remedy or Illegal Response? Resolving the Issue of Foreign Subsidization under WTO Law' (2021) 20(3) *WTRev* 343–366 at 352 ff.

9.3.1.2 *ASCM and Transnational Subsidization*

The overlap between the FSR and the ASCM identified in the preceding section presupposes that the notion of subsidy is the same and that the ASCM also covers transnational subsidization. If there is a difference in scope in that regard, the ban against other remedies due to Article 32.1 ASCM might not cover transnational subsidization.

The issue relates to the notion of subsidy with regard to a territorial requirement of covered subsidization. In other words: Does a subsidy under the ASCM require a *territorial link* between subsidy and benefit, specifically between the granting state and the beneficiary that must reside in the former? If so, the ASCM would not apply to instances of cross-border subsidization. Article 32.1 ASCM and Article 44 (9) FSR hence would not bar the Commission from adopting redressive measures against cross-border subsidies granted to goods producers active in the EU.

In any case, the FSR has a broad scope. The subsidies covered by the FSR are both subsidies that a non-EU state grants to an undertaking resident there or in a third country and doing business in the EU, as well as subsidies that a non-EU state grants to undertakings resident in the EU and doing business there. According to Article 1 (2) FSR, as already mentioned, the regulation applies to third-country subsidies granted to 'an undertaking [. . .] engaging in an economic activity in the internal market'. Hence, where the undertaking is resident is irrelevant, just as the issue of jurisdiction or country of production is irrelevant. What counts is the economic activity in the EU and the fact that the enterprise receives a benefit from a foreign country related to that business activity, irrespective of whether the contribution is granted directly or indirectly (see recital 11 FSR). The latter implies that cross-border subsidization is also covered.[45] With regard to Article 1 ASCM, however, it has not yet been conclusively clarified whether the notion of subsidy constitutively requires that the recipient of the subsidy resides in the territory of the state granting the subsidy. It is heavily debated whether the ASCM

[45] Cross-border subsidization is used here to denote not only situations of transnational production subsidization in which the beneficiary resident in the WTO member granting the subsidy produces a good abroad (see in that regard Marc Benitah, *WTO Law of Subsidies: A Comprehensive Approach* (Alphen aan den Rijn: Kluwer Law International, 2019), p. 605 f) but also those in which the beneficiary is resident in a third country. It also covers the scenario described by Benitah, p. 606 f (Korean company receiving subsidy from Korea to allow cheap production of goods by its subsidiary in Mexico destined for import to the United States), where he confirms applicability of the ASCM.

disciplines cross-border subsidization and, if so, for which situations exactly.[46] Whereas Article 1.1 ASCM can be considered to cover subsidies regardless of the location of the recipient,[47] a different hint in that regard can be found in Article 2 ASCM on specificity, where the beneficiary enterprise is linked to 'the jurisdiction of the granting authority' (note that the term 'jurisdiction' is used; thus, it could include personal jurisdiction based on nationality).[48] From this, read in conjunction with Article 1.2 ASCM, one might infer that third-country subsidies granted to beneficiaries *outside* their jurisdiction are not covered by the remedies provided for in the ASCM, as they are not held to be specific in the sense of Articles 2.1 and 2.2 ASCM[49] – a conclusion which might be seen to be confirmed by the negotiating history of the ASCM.[50] Thus, cross-border subsidization would not come under the purview of the ASCM (with the exception of prohibited subsidies under Article 3 ASCM).[51] Against such allegations, one may contend that the requirement of specificity is not part of the notion of subsidy in Article 1.1 ASCM (relevant for Article 32.1 ASCM), and that the notion of subsidy can be separated from the issue of remedies acceptable under the ASCM.[52] Article 32.1 ASCM is contained in Part X of the ASCM that is applicable to all types of subsidies, whereas specificity is required only for the applicability of Parts II, III, and V (argumentum e Article 1.2 ASCM). One can find a hint in WTO case law to the effect that specificity is not part of the definition of subsidy, as the purpose of the definition of specificity in Article 2 ASCM 'is not to identify the elements of the subsidy as set out in Article 1.1, but to

[46] Crochet and Gustafsson, 'Lawful Remedy or Illegal Response?' (2021) 345; Csongor István Nagy, 'Foreign Subsidies, Distortions and Acquisitions: Can the Playing Field Be Levelled?' (2021) 2(1) *Central European Journal of Comparative Law* 147–162 at 149.

[47] Victor Crochet and Vineet Hedge, 'China's "Going Global" Policy: Transnational Production Subsidies under the WTO SCM' (2020) 23(4) *JIEL* 841–863 at 849. Art. 1.1 ASCM contains the phrase 'within the territory of a Member', which, however, clearly refers to the granting public body and is not a territorial confinement of the subsidy; see Nagy, 'Foreign Subsidies, Distortions and Acquisitions' (2021) 153.

[48] Lorand Bartels, 'Does WTO Law Really Not Regulate "Foreign Subsidies"?', *Linklaters*, 22 June 2020, www.linklaters.com/en/insights/blogs/tradelinks/2020/june/does-wto-law-really-not-regulate-foreign-subsidies; Nagy, 'Foreign Subsidies, Distortions and Acquisitions' (2021) 153. But see Crochet and Gustafsson, 'Lawful Remedy or Illegal Response?' (2021) 350.

[49] See Benitah, *WTO Law of Subsidies* (2019), p. 605, fn. 1447.

[50] Tokas, 'Playing the Game' (2022) 799 f.

[51] For such conclusion, see Crochet and Hedge, 'China's "Going Global" Policy' (2020) 852 f; Tokas, 'Playing the Game' (2022) 801.

[52] See Crochet and Gustafsson 'Lawful Remedy or Illegal Response?' (2021) 349, 352 f.

establish whether the availability of the subsidy is limited'.[53] Consequently, even if one read Article 2 ASCM to require territoriality of the subsidization for a subsidy to be specific and for taking actions, this would not be required for the application of Article 32.1 ASCM. There is scarce WTO practice on the issue as to whether subsidies granted by a WTO member to undertakings established in another country are also covered by the notion of subsidy under the ASCM. An affirmative example is the *Brazil – Aircraft* case, in which Brazil's subsidy to foreign aircraft buyers in the form of direct transfers was held by the panel to be subsidies within the scope of the ASCM.[54] The Commission in a recent case did attribute the subsidy paid by China (China paid a subsidy to a Chinese company and its Egypt-based subsidiary that exported goods to the EU) to Egypt for the purpose of the applicability of the ASCM against Egypt (i.e. the goods produced there by the subsidiary) that had welcomed Chinese-subsidized investments.[55] This apparently implies that the Commission considered such attribution necessary in order to confirm that the cross-border subsidy is covered by the ASCM. Hence, it appears that the Commission seems to assume that the notion of subsidy under the ASCM contains a territoriality requirement, reflecting the approach of Articles 2 and 3 of the BASR to stipulate a territorial link between subsidization and beneficiary in the country of origin or export.[56] Despite this, the Commission had no difficulty circumventing it by applying the

[53] Appellate Body Report, *US – Anti-Dumping and Countervailing Duties (China)*, WT/DS379/AB/R, 11 March 2011, para. 413.

[54] Panel Report, *Brazil – Aircraft*, WT/DS46/R, 14 April 1999, paras. 4.40 ff, 7.13 f.

[55] See Commission Implementing Regulation 2020/776 imposing definitive countervailing duties on imports of certain woven and/or stitched glass fiber fabrics originating in the People's Republic of China and Egypt, OJ EU 2020 No. L 189/1, 15 June 2020, paras. 674 ff, and Commission Implementing Regulation 2020/870 imposing a definitive countervailing duty and definitively collecting the provisional countervailing duty imposed on imports of continuous filament glass fiber products originating in Egypt, and levying the definitive countervailing duty on the registered imports of continuous filament glass fiber products originating in Egypt, OJ EU 2020 No. L 201/10, 25 June 2020, para. 72 ff. The admissibility of this approach under WTO law is questioned by Crochet and Hedge, 'China's "Going Global" Policy' (2020) 860; Simon Evenett, Juhi Dion Sud, and Edwin Vermulst, 'The European Union's New Move against China: Countervailing Chinese Outward Foreign Direct Investment' (2020) 15(9) *GTCJ* 413–422 at 418 ff; Patricia Trapp, 'Das Weißbuch der Kommission zur Gewährleistung fairer Wettbewerbsbedingungen bei Subventionen aus Drittstaaten' (2020) 22 *EuZW* 964–970.

[56] Crochet and Hedge, 'China's "Going Global" Policy' (2020) 859; see also Tokas, 'Playing the Game' (2022) 798. Also, the Commission's Staff Working Document, Impact Assessment, Accompanying the Proposal for a Regulation of the European Parliament and of the Council on foreign subsidies distorting the internal market, SWD(2021) 99 final, p. 39,

rules of attribution (Article 11 ILC Draft Articles on State Responsibility[57]), which effectively results in the application of ASCM disciplines also to foreign subsidies in cross-border situations. The approach by the Commission was ultimately confirmed by the EU General Court. The Court opined that, irrespective of Article 11 ILC Draft Articles, under EU anti-subsidy law, a financial contribution that does not come directly from the government of the country of origin or export can nevertheless be attributed to it. The Court additionally held that such attribution also conforms to the notion of subsidy under the ASCM.[58] Either by way of attribution or by implying that cross-border subsidization is covered by the ASCM, the result is the same: The notion of subsidy, at least in Article 32.1 ASCM, includes cross-border subsidies; there is no territoriality or residence requirement.

If, in contrast, one does not want to share this broad approach in construing the scope of the ASCM, but follows the narrow reading, which requires the beneficiary of a subsidy to be resident in the granting state for Article 32.1 ASCM to apply, Article 44 (9) FSR in conjunction with Article 32.1 ASCM would ban the application of the FSR only for those third-country cases where a foreign subsidy is granted to a company residing there. Accordingly, third-country subsidies granted to EU-based undertakings or undertakings based in another country doing business in the EU (situations also covered by the FSR) would not fall under the notion of subsidy in the sense of the ASCM. In the latter cases then, the EU would be free to establish rules of scrutiny in that regard and to provide unilaterally for remedial or countervailing measures (but subject to general WTO principles such as non-discrimination; see Section 9.3.2). Limiting the scope of the ASCM in such a narrow way would allow a country to circumvent quite easily the threat of becoming a target of countervailing measures under ASCM rules simply by ensuring that the home undertakings establish legally independent subsidiaries in the target market or in another jurisdiction, with these subsidiaries receiving

limited the applicability of the BASR to subsidies granted to companies in the territory of the granting state.

[57] Draft Articles on Responsibility of States for Internationally Wrongful Acts with Commentaries (ILC Draft Articles with Commentaries), in Report of the International Law Commission on the Work of Its Fifty-third Session, UN Doc. A/56/10, (2001) Yearbook of the International Law Commission, vol. II, Part Two.

[58] General Court (GC), Case T-480/20, *Hengshi Egypt Fiberglass Fabrics and Jushi Egypt for Fiberglass Industry v Commission*, [2023] ECLI:EU:T:2023:90, paras. 84, 101 ff. For the irrelevance of Art. 11 ILC Draft Articles, see ibid. para. 103.

the subsidy directly. Therefore, it is also preferable from this angle to interpret the ASCM to cover cross-border subsidization, in line with the argumentation given by the EU General Court holding that economic and legal constructs that undermine the EU BASR's effectiveness and purpose, which the Court interpreted in accordance with the ASCM,[59] cannot be accepted.[60] Consequently, Article 32.1 ASCM and Article 44 (9) FSR ban the implementation of the FSR in cross-border situations as well. Thus, under the FSR, the EU must not counteract any form of foreign subsidization of undertakings active in the goods' trade sector in the internal market, as demonstrated in Section 9.3.1.1.

9.3.1.3 *Justification for Breach of ASCM?*

Even in those cases in which the application of the FSR might run afoul the ASCM, one might contend that the breach was justifiable by applying Article XX GATT to a violation of Article 32.1 ASCM. As there is a need for allowing countermeasures to address foreign subsidies for which the ASCM does not provide useful remedies, in order to safeguard the negotiated balance of the ASCM (which consists in allowing subsidization, but also offering actions against them in accordance with the agreed rules),[61] and as Article 32.1 ASCM refers to measures 'in accordance with the provisions of GATT 1994', one might consider applying the justification grounds of Article XX GATT to a breach of the ASCM as well; all the more as footnote 56 to the ASCM reads that Article 32.1 ASCM is 'not intended to preclude action under other relevant provisions of GATT 1994'. The Appellate Body has adopted a careful approach in making Article XX GATT available to justify violations of other WTO agreements.[62] Nevertheless, one might apply Article XX GATT to justify a breach of Article 32.1 ASCM.[63] Assuming, for the sake of argument, that there is sufficient basis for allowing recourse to Article XX GATT also for breach of the ASCM, the pertinent justification ground listed in Article XX GATT could be the public morals exception (letter a). This exception appears to

[59] Parallel interpretation of the ASCM and the EU Basic Anti-Subsidy Regulation is a persistent practice of the EU Courts; see GC, Case T-300/16, [2019] *Jindal Saw and Jindal Saw Italia v Commission*, EU:T:2019:235, para. 101; GC, Case T-480/20, *Hengshi Egypt Fiberglass Fabrics*, para. 100.

[60] GC, Case T-480/20, *Hengshi Egypt Fiberglass Fabrics*, paras. 92 ff.

[61] Crochet and Gustafsson, 'Lawful Remedy or Illegal Response?' (2021) 354.

[62] See Wolfgang Weiß, *WTO Law and Domestic Regulation* (MünchenOxford, Baden-Baden: Hart/Beck/Nomos, 2020), pp. 243 ff.

[63] Crochet and Gustafsson, 'Lawful Remedy or Illegal Response?' (2021) 355.

be the only one that could cover the EU's striving for fair competition and prevention of economic distortions.[64] The problem with this justification ground, however, are the conditions of Article XX GATT chapeau, whose requirements must also be met as the last step in the assessment of a contested measure's justification under one of the justifications enshrined in Article XX GATT.[65] The chapeau of Article XX GATT requires that the measures to be justified 'are not applied in a manner which would constitute a means of arbitrary or unjustifiable discrimination [. . .] or a disguised restriction on international trade'.[66] The chapeau's requirements focus on the way a contested measure is applied, and they are of highest importance in the concluding assessment of a contested measure's conformity, because fewer than a handful of measures where Article XX GATT had been invoked as justification before the WTO judiciary were able to finally meet them.[67]

With regard to foreign subsidies control by the EU, there appears to be an unjustifiable discrimination. First, clearly there is discrimination: Even though the EU subjects national subsidies from EU Member States (i.e. state aid in EU parlance) to scrutiny as well, the applicable rules are more relaxed. Under EU state aid law, there exists, for example, a General Block Exemption Regulation (GBER) which – subject to specific conditions – allows certain national subsidies granted by the EU Member States;[68] the provision of Article 4 (2) FSR (according to which a subsidy whose total amount to an undertaking does not exceed €4 million over three years is unlikely to distort the internal market) does not cover all the exempted cases foreseen in the GBER, even more so as Article 4 (2) FSR does not lay down an exception,[69] but only a statement of unlikeliness of

[64] See Panel Report, *US – Tariff Measures (China)*, WT/DS543/R, 15 September 2020, para. 7.113 ff, according to which the notion of public morals could include even economic concerns, which cannot be relevant under other justification grounds. See also Crochet and Gustafsson, 'Lawful Remedy or Illegal Response?' (2021) 360.

[65] For the sequence of steps in the analysis of a justification under Art. XX GATT, see Peter Van den Bossche and Werner Zdouc, *Law and Policy of the WTO*, 5th ed. (Cambridge: Cambridge University Press, 2022), pp. 601 f.

[66] For more detail on the chapeau's interpretation, see Crochet and Gustafsson, 'Lawful Remedy or Illegal Response?' (2021) 361 ff; Van den Bossche and Zdouc, *Law and Policy of the WTO* (2022), pp. 648–656; Weiß, *WTO Law and Domestic Regulation* (2020), pp. 269 ff.

[67] See Van den Bossche and Zdouc, *Law and Policy of the WTO* (2022), pp. 646 f; Weiß, *WTO Law and Domestic Regulation* (2020), p. 229, fn. 1.

[68] Commission Regulation 651/2014 declaring certain categories of aid compatible with the internal market, OJ EU 2014 No. L 187/1, 26 June 2014, with further amendments.

[69] A *de minimis* clause is contained in Art. 4 (3) FSR incorporating the state aid *de minimis* rule. But this is the only state aid exception that has been transplanted into the FSR, besides

market distortion.[70] Furthermore, in EU state aid law, Article 107 (2) and (3) TFEU provides for exceptions that enable the Commission to allow the EU Member States the pursuit of certain policy objectives. In the FSR, however, there are no such broadly drafted exception clauses. Even Article 4 (4) FSR reflecting Article 107 (2) b) TFEU contains a meaningful difference: Whereas Article 107 (2) b) TFEU commands the conformity of compensations for natural disasters or exceptional occurrences with the internal market, Article 4 (4) FSR only foresees that such compensation 'may be considered not to distort the internal market', giving broader leeway to the Commission. Admittedly, the FSR provides for a balancing test enabling the Commission to balance the anticompetitive effects of the subsidy against their positive effects on the development of the relevant economic activity on the internal market, allowing also the consideration of other (non-economic) positive effects on EU policy objectives (Article 6 FSR). This is different from the assessment of national state aid under EU law, both with regard to their scope (national policy implementation of EU policies versus 'relevant economic activity') and their legal consequences (exception, and hence clearance, of a domestic measure under state aid review, versus consideration of the result of the balancing exercise in the adoption of a redressive measure as under the FSR), leading to less beneficial treatment of foreign subsidies compared to EU Member States' state aid because the former are subject to an assessment that implies greater leeway for the Commission. Of even more concern is the fact that subsidies granted by the EU itself or based on EU programs are not subject to state aid control by the Commission.[71]

Art. 4 (4) FSR which will soon be adressed. A further state aid exception that does not have a counterpart in the FSR is the Commission Decision 2011/21/EU of 20 December 2011 on the application of Article 106(2) of the TFEU to State aid in the form of public service compensation granted to certain undertakings entrusted with the operation of services of general economic interest, OJ EU 2012 No. L 7/3, 11 January 2012.

[70] Luja, 'The Foreign Subsidies Regulation' (2021) 190.

[71] EU subsidies can be based, outside agricultural policy, on Arts. 162 or 177 Treaty on the Functioning of the European Union (TFEU). EU state aid rules, in particular the Commission's supervision, are not fully applicable to genuine EU subsidies; see Commission Notice on the notion of State aid as referred to in Article 107(1) of the Treaty on the Functioning of the European Union, OJ EU 2016 No. C 262/1, 19 July 2016, paras. 44 ff; Art. 81 (2) Regulation 1305/2013, OJ EU 2013 No. L 347/487, 17 December 2013, on support for rural development by the European Agricultural Fund for Rural Development, and recital 30 of Regulation (EU) 2021/695 of the EP and the Council establishing Horizon Europe – the Framework Pogramme for Research and Innovation, laying down its rules for participation and dissemination, OJ EU 2021 No. L 170/1, 12 May 2021.

Second, this discrimination is unjustifiable in the sense of the chapeau. All of these differences between the foreign subsidies control in the FSR and state aid review under EU law are not only grave but have deliberately been introduced by the EU into the FSR. Furthermore, they reflect a lack of consistency in dealing with competition distortions from domestic (EU and national) subsidies compared to the standards for foreign subsidies. The EU has not offered any explanation for the different standards for combating competition distortion, nor do the differences in procedural and substantive standards have any rational connection to the FSR's objective of counteracting competition distortion.[72] Consequently, they result in unjustifiable discrimination in the sense of Article XX GATT chapeau against foreign-country subsidies, as the latter will become subject to EU control according to the new rules, which is more intense than with regard to EU Member States' state aid, and even more so when compared to aid from genuine EU funds. It is this deliberate distinction between domestic and foreign situations and the lack of consistency in the treatment of foreign compared to domestic services or goods that lead the WTO judiciary to find unjustifiable discrimination when assessing the chapeau of the exception provisions.[73] Therefore, even if Article XX GATT were available as a justification for violation of the ASCM, it would not be helpful. Consequently, there is no justification for a breach of Article 32.1 ASCM by the FSR.

9.3.2 WTO Non-Discrimination Disciplines

The issue of discrimination against comparable foreign situations is relevant also beyond the ASCM, namely with regard to those redressive measures under the FSR that clearly do not collide with the ASCM as they address subsidization in the services sector. In this respect, the general WTO non-discrimination obligation becomes relevant[74] and is applied to

[72] According to Appellate Body Report, *US – Tuna II (Mexico) (Article. 21.5 – Mexico)*, WT/DS381/AB/RW, 20 November 2015, para. 7.316: 'discrimination will be arbitrary or unjustifiable when the reasons given for the discrimination "bear no rational connection to the objective"'.

[73] Weiß, *WTO Law and Domestic Regulation* (2020), p. 274 f. For the importance of the deliberate nature and the rationale for the difference in treatment, and the consistency in approaches under the chapeau's requirements, see Van den Bossche and Zdouc, *Law and Policy of the WTO* (2022), pp. 651, 653, 655.

[74] Whereas GATT Art. III:8 (b) excludes subsidies from the scope of the GATT NT obligation, there is no such provision with regard to GATS and services trade, not least for the lack of specific subsidies disciplines in the area of trade in services, which to negotiate actually is provided for in Art. XV GATS. From their lack one cannot derive that subsidization issues

fully comparable situations as the FSR – like EU state aid law – aims at ensuring a level playing field on the EU internal market. As will be shown here, with regard to WTO non-discrimination, another violation of WTO law is at stake, with the consequence that Article 44 (9) FSR prohibits investigations and measures under the FSR.

Redressive measures adopted under the FSR have the capacity of discriminating against foreign service providers and hence violate Article XVII GATS, because like domestic service suppliers having received EU subsidies or domestic state aid from an EU Member State are not subject to the FSR nor to similar review rules. One could even consider discrimination among WTO members in breach of the most-favoured-nation obligation, Article II GATS, as the measures under the FSR may in practice be specifically targeted against specific states such as China,[75] even though its formal scope appears non-discriminatory. The redressive measures under the FSR treat the supply of (covered)[76] services from abroad less beneficially than the domestic supply of like services by beneficiaries of EU Member State subsidies under the internal EU state aid rules, as any redressive measure adopted by the Commission against beneficiaries of third-country subsidies modifies the conditions of competition on the EU internal market to the latter's disadvantage. And not only redressive measures, but already the commencement of an investigation against foreign undertakings themselves may discriminate as the non-discrimination obligation also applies to discrimination in procedural laws or evidence rules.[77] Even though the investigations provided under the FSR emulate the procedures provided for the EU review of domestic state aid under Article 108 TFEU,[78] the commitments and redressive measures provided for in Article 7 FSR as well as the applicable

are fully excluded from GATS disciplines; see Pietro Poretti, 'Waiting for Godot: Subsidy Disciplines in Services Trade', in Marion Panizzon, Nicole Pohl, and Pierre Sauvé (eds.), *GATS and the Regulation of International Trade in Services* (Cambridge: Cambridge University Press, 2008), p. 467.

[75] See Crochet and Gustafsson 'Lawful Remedy or Illegal Response?' (2021) 357 f.

[76] The NT discipline of Art. XVII GATS only applies to those sectors where the EU and its Members entered into specific commitments and only insofar as the EU did not reserve specific rights or expressed limitations in their schedule of commitments; Poretti, 'Waiting for Godot' (2008), pp. 468 f.

[77] See Laprévote and Lin, 'Between State Aid, Trade and Antitrust' (2022) 451, referring to GATT panel *US – Section 337 Tariff Act*; Appellate Body Report, *US – Gasoline*, WT/DS2/AB/R, 29 April 1996, pp. 26 ff.

[78] Laprévote and Lin, 'Between State Aid, Trade and Antitrust' (2022) 446 ff; Wolfgang Weiß, 'Ex Officio Third Country Subsidies' Review' (2022) 21(2) *European State Aid Law Quarterly* 132–142 at 136 ff.

substantive rules are different compared to those under EU state aid law, allowing even the claim of the FSR being an 'as such' violation of WTO rules.[79] This is because the measures under the FSR restrain the undertakings' market access and non-discriminatory treatment when they are obliged to reduce their market presence or to refrain from certain activities, as the latter might prove more restrictive than the consequences of EU state aid procedures and related remedies, and even more so when looking at genuine EU subsidies. Thus, less beneficial treatment results, first, from the fact that comparable domestic subsidization within the EU by its Member States is subject to more beneficial substantive rules, for example by applicability of the exceptions contained in the GBER to domestic subsidies. This was already explained earlier with a view to the – albeit different[80] – discrimination standard of Article XX's chapeau (see Section 9.3.1.3). Second, whereas state aid law only foresees prohibition of state aid and recovery as remedies against unlawful aid, the FSR provides for completely different, more onerous redressive measures (repayment being just one option, subject to conditions under Article 7 (6) FSR); neither are they capped at the amount of the original subsidy granted.[81] Thirdly, besides more onerous decision-making powers, the FSR procedures grant the Commission more robust investigative powers.[82] Hence, the alleged levelling of the competitive conditions aimed for by the FSR results in different conditions for doing business in the EU for domestic service suppliers benefitting from domestic subsidies compared to foreign service suppliers benefitting from foreign subsidies. Additionally, as mentioned in Section 9.3.1.3, the subsidies granted by the EU itself or by EU programs to companies residing in the EU are not subject to state aid control by the Commission at all, which results in discrimination against foreign-country subsidies as the latter are subject to EU control under the new rules.[83]

79 For a discussion of the 'as such' versus 'as applied' distinction in assessing a WTO violation, see Section 3.3.1.

80 The non-discrimination standard of the NT obligation under Art. III GATT and Art. XVII GATS of course is not the same as under the chapeaus of Art. XX GATT and Art. XIV GATS, as the chapeaus only ban arbitrary, unjustifiable discrimination. The mere existence of discrimination does not bar justification under Art. XX GATT/Art. XIV GATS, but the latter require the mentioned qualifiers. See Appellate Body Report, *EC – Seal Products*, WT/DS400/AB/R, WT/DS401/AB/R, 22 May 2014, para. 5.298.

81 Laprévote and Lin, 'Between State Aid, Trade and Antitrust' (2022) 452.

82 See Section 9.2.2; Weiß, 'Ex Officio Third Country Subsidies' Review' (2022) 140–142.

83 See also Laprévote and Lin, 'Between State Aid, Trade and Antitrust' (2022) 451.

This difference is not covered by an 'asymmetric impact' exception. The Appellate Body once stated that an asymmetric impact on foreign goods compared to domestic goods following from the application of domestic rules to both domestic and foreign producers in itself is not sufficient for establishing discrimination, unless the detrimental effects are related to the foreign origin of the product.[84] This interpretation of non-discrimination, even if it still was good law (it later was reinterpreted by the Appellate Body and finally dismissed),[85] does not apply here, because the FSR establishes a regime specifically addressing foreign situations (producers receiving foreign subsidies). There is no asymmetric impact, but a very genuine less beneficial treatment emanating from a legislation specifically adopted to address foreign situations.

Regarding the scope of the GATS NT obligation, one must recall that foreign services providers are not only those based in another WTO member but may also be providers resident in the EU. Article XXVIII (2) (g) and (m)(ii) GATS explicitly defines service suppliers of a WTO Member to include suppliers incorporated or otherwise established elsewhere (outside the WTO member) as long as they are owned or controlled by the nationals of the WTO member. As the FSR applies to any undertaking active in the internal market, it applies to any undertaking regardless of its country of control or ownership.[86] Article XXVIII (f) GATS provides that 'services of another Member' are services supplied by its own service providers. Consequently, the personal scope of the FSR corresponds to the notion of service supplying undertakings in GATS.

The breach of the Article XVII GATS non-discrimination obligation cannot be justified by recourse to the public morals exception in Article XIV a) GATS. As already explained in Section 9.3.1.3 with regard to Article XX GATT, the chapeau of Article XIV GATS requires a non-arbitrary, justifiable discrimination in order for a discriminatory treatment to be justified under Article XIV GATS. The requirements of the chapeau of Article XVI GATS are the same as under Article XX GATT.[87] As mentioned, EU subsidies and programs themselves deliberately are not, at least not fully, subject to the same considerable scrutiny by the Commission, in

[84] Appellate Body Report, *Dominican Republic – Import and Sale of Cigarettes*, WT/DS302/AB/R, 25 April 2005, para. 96. With regard to the FSR, see Nagy, 'Foreign Subsidies, Distortions and Acquisitions' (2021) 157 f.

[85] See Weiß, *WTO Law and Domestic Regulation* (2020), pp. 161 ff.

[86] Laprévote and Lin, 'Between State Aid, Trade and Antitrust' (2022) 451.

[87] For the parallel interpretation of Art. XX GATT and Art. XIV GATS, see Weiß, *WTO Law and Domestic Regulation* (2020), pp. 230 ff.

contrast to foreign ones under the FSR. The deliberate discrimination furthermore is not justifiable, as the EU operates two different approaches in addressing competition distortions flowing from subsidies, which reflects their inconsistencies. Alternatively, one might assess the FSR to constitute a disguised restriction on international trade, which is also inconsistent with the chapeau of Article XVI GATS. Either way, the FSR will not stand the requirements of the chapeau. Hence, there is no sound basis for an EU recourse to Article XIV GATS for justifying a discriminatory EU regulation.

Another eventual breach of non-discrimination exists with regard to Article IV Agreement on Government Procurement 2012 (GPA 2012),[88] under which the EU is obliged to accord immediately and unconditionally to the goods and services of any other Party and to the suppliers of any other Party treatment no less favourable than the treatment the EU accords to its domestic goods, services, and suppliers. In view of the specific scrutiny for third-country bidders the FSR brings about in its Chapter 4 on public procurement procedures (which also applies to those WTO Members party to the GPA 2012 and may lead to a decision prohibiting the award of the contract, see Article 31 (2) FSR), this non-discriminatory treatment is not ensured. The less beneficial treatment results from the lack of consideration of genuine EU subsidies. Even with regard to national state aid from EU Members, the pertinent Article 69 (4) Directive 2014/24/EU[89] allowing for the exclusion of recipients of illegal (in contrast to legal) state aid does not correspond to the scope of the powers the Commission possesses to act against unduly advantageous tenders from beneficiaries of (also legal) foreign subsidies under the FSR.

9.3.3 Conclusion on WTO Law Conformity

The above-mentioned deliberations have shown that even though possible violations of WTO law by the FSR can be established only in certain contexts and circumstances (with regard to ASCM, insofar as the FSR covers subsidization in the goods sector beyond importation of goods; with regard to GPA 2012 and GATS NT obligations, only insofar as the procurement concerned is covered by the EU commitments, or the EU has assumed commitments for service liberalization, respectively), the FSR

88 Revised Agreement on Government Procurement (GPA), 30 March 2012, Marrakesh Agreement Establishing the World Trade Organization, Annex 4(b), 1915 U.N.T.S. 103.

89 Directive 2014/24/EU of the EP and the Council of 26 February 2014 on public procurement, OJ EU 2014 No. L 94/65, 28 March 2014.

can lead to the commencement of investigations and the adoption of redressive measures not in conformity with the EU's WTO obligations. As Article 44 (9) FSR prohibits even the initiation of investigations and not only the final adoption of measures that contradict the EU's international obligations, the purview for the Commission to lawfully implement the FSR and adopt the measures foreseen therein appears rather narrow. It may be applicable only for services and procurements not covered by WTO law.

9.4 The Foreign Subsidies Regulation and Bilateral Subsidy Commitments

As the redressive measures based on the FSR can be adopted by the EU unilaterally, the rules in the FSR on foreign subsidies might also collide with specific subsidy provisions the EU entered into with other states in EU Free Trade or Association/Cooperation Agreements. This is particularly so if their rules provide for specific institutions or procedures to assess subsidies for their conformity with agreed standards.[90] Then, establishing a unilateral review mechanism as the EU does in the FSR very probably comes into conflict with these bilateral rules (see Section 3.3.2.2) Consequently, the Commission would not be allowed to apply the FSR with regard to those states with which it entered into these commitments, by virtue of Article 44 (9) FSR. The subsequent analysis will address this issue in an exemplary approach, as not all (even of the most recent) individual EU agreements can be assessed here, as their subsidies chapters contain rather diverse provisions.[91] Thus, the analysis will be limited to the most important agreements having relevant commitments and serving as role-models for other comparable agreements. As it has been observed, as a general rule, the more explicit and demanding the subsidy commitments in the EU's agreements are, the closer an agreement is meant to align a third state to the EU internal market and its rules,[92] and

[90] See also Müller-Ibold, 'The Draft Foreign Subsidies Regulation' (2022) 438.

[91] For the reasons, see Felix Neumann, *Export des Europäischen Beihilfenrechts. Eine Analyse der Europäisierung des internationalen Subventionsrechts durch bilaterale Handelsabkommen* (Cham: Springer, 2019), pp. 182–184.

[92] Frank Hoffmeister, 'Securing a Level Playing Field through EU Free Trade Agreements: From Traditional Competition Chapters to a Dedicated Title in the EU-UK Trade and Cooperation Agreement', in Alexander Heger and Sascha Gourdet (eds.), *Fairen Wettbewerb in der Europäischen Union sichern* (Baden-Baden: Nomos, 2022), p. 131.

the more recently an agreement has been concluded; older agreements before 2006 – with the exception of the Agreement on the European Economic Area (EEA Agreement)[93] – by and large contain rather general subsidies disciplines with which the FSR very likely will not come into conflict.[94] Besides, the present analysis will not deal (again) with the breach of FTA non-discrimination commitments that reflect the WTO obligations, which has been analyzed in the preceding section.

9.4.1 EU–UK Trade and Cooperation Agreement

The most elaborate disciplines on subsidies are contained in the EU–UK Trade and Cooperation Agreement (TCA),[95] in its Title XI on 'A level playing field for open and fair competition and sustainable development', from Articles 363 to 375 TCA. Title XI, in essence, is about ensuring equal standards in areas sensitive to economic policy and social law (i.e. a 'level playing field'), thus restraining regulatory competition between the EU and the United Kingdom. These rules are intended to ensure that the level playing field between Brussels and London remains comparable and that the British do not set lower standards in the areas of (*inter alia*) competition. Title XI's Chapter 3 on subsidies lays down the substantive rules on subsidies providing, for example, definitions, particular rules on services of public economic interest, as well as on prohibited subsidies and subsidies subject to conditions, the substance of which closely resembles EU state aid policies developed by the European Commission under Articles 107 and 108 TFEU[96] and differs considerably from the FSR rules. For example, the exceptions from the notion of subsidy in the TCA are closer to EU state aid law than in the FSR, which in Article 4 (4), as mentioned above, only enshrines a kind of carve-out for compensations for natural disasters and exceptional occurrences, whereas Article 364 (1) TCA

[93] Decision of the Council and the Commission of 13 December 1993 on the conclusion of the Agreement on the European Economic Area between the European Communities, their Member States and the Republic of Austria, the Republic of Finland, the Republic of Iceland, the Principality of Liechtenstein, the Kingdom of Norway, the Kingdom of Sweden and the Swiss Confederation, OJ EU 1994 No. L 1/4, 3 January 1994.

[94] For an analysis of the subsidies provisions in the older agreements, see Neumann, *Export des Europäischen Beihilfenrechts* (2019), pp. 28 ff.

[95] Trade and Cooperation Agreement between the European Union and the European Atomic Energy Community, of the one part, and the United Kingdom of Great Britain and Northern Ireland, of the other part, OJ EU 2021 No. L 149/1, 30 April 2021.

[96] See e.g. Article 367 (2)-(7), (13)-(15) TCA and Piet Eeckhout, 'Brexit after the Negotiation of the Trade and Cooperation Agreement: Who Takes Back Control of What?' (2021) 68 *Revista de Derecho Comunitario Europeo* 11–22 at 13.

provides for a clear exception in that regard and goes beyond this in Articles 364 (4)-(6) and 365 TCA.

In addition, the parties in Article 371 TCA committed to establishing or maintaining 'an operationally independent authority or body with an appropriate role in its subsidy control regime. That independent authority or body shall have the necessary guarantees of independence in exercising its operational functions and shall act impartially.' Article 371 (2) provides for cooperation between the parties' respective independent authorities or bodies 'on issues of common interest within their respective functions, including the application of Articles 363 to 369' TCA.

Furthermore, the Chapter contains monitoring and enforcement rules and mechanisms (Articles 368 ff TCA), *inter alia* foreseeing consultations in case of negative effects (Article 370 TCA), recovery of illegal subsidies (Article 373 TCA), remedial measures (Article 374), and dispute settlement (Article 375). These rules stipulate that a party may first request explanations if a subsidy granted by the other party has a negative effect on trade and investment between the parties (Article 370 (1) TCA). Then follow consultations in the Trade Specialised Committee on Level Playing Field for Open and Fair Competition (Article 370 (4) TCA), in order to reach a 'mutually satisfactory solution' (Article 370 (5) TCA). Article 374 (3) TCA allows the imposition of remedial measures within sixty days if a subsidy actually has or could have a '*significant* negative effect on trade or investment between the Parties' (emphasis added). The remedial measure is subject to arbitration (Article 374 (9) TCA). The arbitration has no suspensive effect, which means that despite pending arbitration, the party can proceed and adopt the remedial measures. If the arbitration tribunal finds against the respondent party, this party shall within thirty days deliver a notification to the other party of any measure taken to comply with the ruling (Article 374 (11) TCA). The TCA does not provide whether a negative ruling requires the other party to terminate its remedial measures.

There is also a general rebalancing mechanism for the whole of Title XI, applicable to all of its chapters, in Article 411 TCA, whereby a party may implement 'appropriate rebalancing measures' whenever 'significant divergences' in the areas covered by Title XI (i.e. subsidy control) arise which lead to 'material impacts on trade or investment between the Parties' (Article 411 (2) TCA). These measures require prior notification, consultation (Article 411 (3) lit. a) TCA), and prior arbitration within thirty days. The respondent party may call for the intervention of an arbitration tribunal. If the arbitration tribunal does not deliver its ruling within thirty days, the rebalancing measures can be adopted, which then can be answered by countermeasures by the other party (Article 411 (3) lit. c) TCA). This mechanism allows each side to directly sanction a more than insignificant deviation from the TCA subsidy standards.

Hence, the TCA establishes very detailed review and counteraction mechanisms with regard to the parties' subsidies and their effect on the 'trade and investment between the Parties'. This prompts the question whether the FSR and its implementation with regard to the United Kingdom being a foreign country now would collide with these bilateral obligations. The first issue in that regard is the scope of application, as the FSR addresses fair competition in the internal market, whereas the subsidies rules in the TCA aim at fair competition between the EU and the United Kingdom. The difference in wording, however, does not amount to a difference in meaning as far as commerce in the internal market is concerned. UK subsidies can negatively affect the trade with the EU only with regard to goods that are traded within the EU. If the TCA would only cover the competition between EU and the United Kingdom on third or world markets outside the parties' own markets, then the scope of the TCA subsidy rules would be considerably restricted, in contradiction to the parties' intention. Consequently, the phrase 'trade and investment between the Parties' also includes the competition between EU and UK products on the internal market of the EU.

As the purviews overlap, the adoption of unilateral measures enabled under the FSR might collide with the TCA subsidy obligations regarding review procedures.[97] If a UK subsidy to a UK company active in the EU threatens the fair competition in the EU in the sense of the FSR, then under the TCA, the Commission may request explanations and then consultations within a TCA committee. The FSR, in contrast, provides for investigations. Investigations, explanations, and consultations all may go hand in hand, so that there need not be a conflict; the procedures

[97] Of course, regarding timing, the TCA subsidy control and the FSR review can also take place at different points in time, which then might exclude conflict. Whereas TCA control may commence as soon as a UK subsidy is granted or intended, the FSR runs an *ex post* system of control. Hence, there may be FSR investigations pertaining to past UK subsidization to companies even before TCA disciplines were applicable (due to Art. 53 (1) FSR) or to UK subsidies that at the time when granted did not affect the EU internal market, as the recipient was not present in the internal market. Once the recipient decides to enter the EU internal market, then past UK subsidies may become subject to investigations under the FSR.

may be followed in conformity with each other, all the more as the request for explanations and consultations appears not to be obligatory. Recital 60 FSR is not helpful here, as it merely states that 'where a bilateral agreement between the Union and a third country provides for a consultation mechanism that covers foreign subsidies distorting the internal market falling within the scope of this Regulation, such a consultation mechanism could be used to facilitate the third-country dialogue. The dialogue with the third-country should not preclude the Commission from opening or continuing reviews under this Regulation.' Hence, no mention is made of the problem that unilateral measures by the EU might have the capacity for violating bilateral mechanisms of subsidy control. This recital merely recommends, first, the use of consultation mechanisms foreseen in bilateral agreements to engage in the third-country dialogue provided in Article 37 FSR, in case of repeated distortive subsidies or redressive measures adopted against a certain foreign state; and second, to facilitate this dialogue by having recourse to the consultation commitments. Thus, recital 60 does not provide for a simultaneity of FSR investigations and bilaterally foreseen consultations, nor does the power of the Commission to request information from a third country under Article 13 (6) FSR.

After the investigations, remedial measures may then be adopted under Article 374 TCA if there is a 'significant negative effect' on the trade between the parties. The threshold for redressive measures under the FSR is lower, as any distortion of competition suffices for adopting redressive measures, unless outweighed by positive effects in the balancing test (argumentum ex Article 11 (4) b FSR). Thus, if the EU deliberates adopting measures under the FSR, it should respect also the material prerequisites of the TCA. Another issue is timing. Whereas the adoption of redressive measures under the FSR may take eighteen months or more, the TCA provides for remedial measures within sixty days, followed by arbitration within thirty days. Once measures under the TCA have been adopted, no measures under the FSR should follow, apart from countermeasures under Article 411 (3) TCA.

In sum, a conflict between TCA and FSR can be avoided if the TCA's requirements under Article 374 TCA are respected. In effect, this means that the FSR is useless with a view to subsidization in the United Kingdom.

A different issue are the unilateral notification obligations enshrined in Articles 21, 29 FSR. As mentioned, the TCA foresees an UK institution to control UK subsidies in conformity with the stipulations laid down in Article 363 ff TCA. As the EU in the FSR provides for new notification obligations also for UK undertakings active in concentration and procurement situations in the internal market, the EU interferes with the relevant UK institution's jurisdiction as laid down in Article 371 TCA. Claiming unilateral EU enforcement powers over the same subsidies whose surveillance had been attributed in the TCA to a UK authority violates the due respect for the institutional setup for UK subsidy control erected in the TCA.

9.4.2 EEA Agreement

A much older bilateral treaty is the EEA Agreement between the EU and its Member States and the EFTA Countries Liechtenstein, Norway, and Iceland (EEA Agreement).[98] The EEA Agreement in its Part IV, Chapter 2 on State Aid (Articles 61 ff) contains subsidies provisions that emulate the EU's rules on state aid. Thus, state aid is prohibited 'in so far as it affects trade between the Contracting Parties' (Article 61 (1) EEA), which again must include possible competition distortions in the internal market effectuated by commercial activities of EFTA undertakings. Under these rules, state aid is subject to a constant review as to its compatibility with the EEA agreement. And for the European Free Trade Association (EFTA) states, this review is carried out by the EFTA Surveillance Authority according to the rules set out in a particular agreement between the EFTA States establishing the EFTA Surveillance Authority that has the powers and functions laid down in Protocol 26 (Article 62 (1) b) EEA). Article 62 (2) EEA even provides for a 'uniform surveillance in the field of State aid throughout the territory covered by this Agreement' by the European Commission and the EFTA Surveillance Authority acting cooperatively in accordance with Protocol 27. Article 64 EEA provides for dispute settlement in case one of the surveillance authorities considers the implementation of these rules by the other not in conformity with 'equal conditions of competition' within the Parties' territories. First, an exchange of views must take place before the Party affected can adopt interim remedies for the resulting competition distortion. Second, consultations must be held in the EEA Joint Committee with a view to finding a solution. Finally, after three months, when a solution has not been found, and if a distortion of competition affecting trade between the Parties is caused or threatened to be caused, the interim measures may be replaced with definitive measures. Thus, these rules do

[98] Agreement on the European Economic Area, OJ EU 1994 No. L 1/3, 3 January 1994.

not make room for a unilateral control by the European Commission of national state aid granted by EFTA countries with a view to their competitive effects on the internal market. The EEA provides for different procedural steps and for consultations within an EEA treaty body before final measures can be adopted. One could consider, of course, that the mere introduction of an investigation under the FSR may not breach the EEA obligations of the EU, and that the adoption of interim measures under Article 12 FSR may be in line with interim measures after the exchange of views allowed by Article 64 (1) EEA. Still, the second step foreseen in the EEA (i.e. consultations in the EEA Joint Committee) cannot be emulated under the FSR investigation rules. Consequently, as claiming enforcement powers over the same subsidies whose surveillance had been attributed in the EEA to the EEA Joint Committee and EFTA Surveillance Authority would bring the EU in a position that breaches international commitments under the EEA,[99] by virtue of Article 44 (9) FSR, even initiating an FSR investigation against an EFTA undertaking is not allowed. The same must apply to the notification requirements under Chapters 3 and 4 of the FSR, as their application to EFTA undertakings would also contradict the allocation of the surveillance of EFTA subsidies to the EFTA surveillance authority, and not the European Commission.

9.4.3 Association Agreement with Ukraine

The Association Agreement with Ukraine (EU–UA AA)[100] is an example of the deep and comprehensive free trade agreements that the EU concluded with certain third countries in its neighborhood. The EU–UA AA contains some provisions on subsidies that to a very large part reflect the EU's state aid rules in Article 107 TFEU, a fact that is rather uniquely replicated in Articles 262 (3) e) and 264 EU–UA AA. Article 262 (3) e) imports the EU rules on exceptions as laid down in the EU block exemption regulations and sectoral and horizontal EU state aid rules. Article 264 provides that in the interpretation of the EU–UA AA's substantive state aid rules, the criteria arising from the application of Articles 106, 107, and 93 TFEU, including the relevant jurisprudence of the CJEU, as well as relevant EU secondary legislation, frameworks, guidelines, and other administrative acts in force, must be used as sources of interpretation. These rules are a particular confirmation of the EU–UA AA's

[99] Müller-Ibold, 'The Draft Foreign Subsidies Regulation' (2022) 438.

[100] Association Agreement between the European Union and its Member States, of the one part, and Ukraine, of the other part (EU–UA AA), OJ EU 2014 No. L 161/3, 29 May 2014.

objective of Ukraine's incremental and partial integration into the EU internal market.[101] Procedurally, the state aid review in the Ukraine had been attributed in the EU–UA AA to a newly established 'operationally independent authority which is entrusted with the powers necessary for the full application of Article 262' (Article 267 (1) EU–UA AA). This authority has the power to authorize state aid schemes and individual aid grants in conformity with the substantive criteria as well as the power to order the recovery of unlawful state aid. In case of a dispute between the EU and Ukraine over the latter's implementation of its commitments (including those flowing from the state aid chapter), the EU–UA AA provides for dispute settlement by an ad hoc arbitration panel (Article 306), preceded by consultation. Before the panel can decide, the interpretation of those provisions that emulate EU state aid law must be referred to the CJEU (Article 322), whose ruling is binding on the arbitration panel.

As regards the compatibility of the EU FSR with the EU–UA AA, the legal assessment is the same as in the case of the EEA presented earlier. As is the case in the EEA, a specific Ukrainian authority is provided for in the EU–UA AA that has the obligation to surveil state aid granted in Ukraine. This competence would be undermined if the EU unilaterally choses to claim review powers over the same subsidies, all the more so as the CJEU has also been made part of a dispute settlement between EU and Ukraine regarding EU state aid rules. Consequently, by virtue of Article 44 (9) FSR, even initiating an FSR investigation against a Ukrainian company having received Ukrainian subsidies is not allowed. The same must apply to the notification requirements under Chapters 3 and 4 of the FSR, as their application to Ukrainian undertakings would also contradict the allocation of the surveillance competence to the Ukrainian authority.

This result will also apply to other Association Agreements entered into by the EU that oblige the other party to establish a domestic review authority that scrutinizes domestic subsidization of undertakings, as in case of the agreement with Moldova.[102] Also in that regard, the fact that the EU agreed with the other party to attribute domestic subsidization review to a specific authority of the other party implies that the EU's unilateral review of the same subsidies under the FSR is in conflict with this provision.

[101] Cf. Simon Guilliard, *Beihilfenkontrolle zwischen Supranationalität und Intergouvernementalität. Unter besonderer Berücksichtigung des Brexit* (Baden-Baden: Nomos, 2022), p. 414.

[102] See Article 339 ff Association Agreement between the European Union and the European Atomic Energy Community and their Member States, of the one part, and the Republic of Moldova, of the other part (EU–Moldova AA), OJ EU 2014 No. L 260/4, 30 August 2018.

9.4.4 Stabilisation and Association Agreements with the Western Balkan Countries

Also the Stabilisation and Association Agreements (SAA) which the EU and its Member States entered into with the Western Balkan states, such as with Serbia,[103] provide for disciplines on state aid,[104] but compared to the aforementioned agreements, these rules are rather general. Article 73 of the SAA with Serbia addresses both anticompetitive behaviour of undertakings as well as state aid, with regard to which the EU principles have to be respected (Article 73 (1) and (2) SAA Serbia). Again, the establishment of an 'operationally independent authority' is foreseen, 'which is entrusted with the powers necessary for the full application' of state aid rules and must have, *inter alia*, the powers to authorize State aid schemes and individual aid grants in conformity, as well as the powers to order the recovery of State aid (see Article 73 (4) SAA Serbia). Irrespective of this attribution of review competence to the domestic authority, the EU may, if it considers a 'particular practice ... incompatible' with the state aid commitments of the other party, 'take appropriate measures after consultation within the Stabilisation and Association Council or after 30 working days following referral for such consultation' (see Article 73 (10) SAA Serbia). Consequently, the SAA allows for EU unilateral measures despite the competence attributed to the domestic authority, but requires first consultation with the SAA Council or at least the lapse of a waiting period of thirty working days after referring an alleged incompatibility to consultation with the SAA Council. Therefore, the EU may apply the FSR only after it referred the case to consultation and waited for thirty working days. But sincere compatibility problems again exist with regard to the FSR notification requirements enshrined in Articles 21 and 29 FSR. As the state aid review is attributed to a domestic authority, and as the consultations have to be initiated before the EU may adopt unilateral steps, the notification obligations provided for in the FSR must not be applied with regard to Serbian companies having benefitted from Serbian subsidies, unless the EU is ready to breach international commitments.[105]

[103] Stabilisation and Association Agreement between the European Communities and their Member States of the one part, and the Republic of Serbia, of the other part, OJ EU 2013 No. L 278/16, 18 October 2013.

[104] See e.g. Art. 73 of the SAA with Serbia, OJ EU 2013 No. L 278/16.

[105] Müller-Ibold, 'The Draft Foreign Subsidies Regulation' (2022) 439.

9.4.5 CETA and JEPA

More recent EU free trade agreements of the fourth generation that have been entered into include the one with Canada – the Comprehensive Economic and Trade Agreement (CETA), which is not yet fully in force but to a large extent preliminary applicable since September 2017.[106] This bilateral agreement contains in its Chapter 7 some rules on subsidies, which more or less simply confirm the pertinent WTO rules. What is important in our context, however, is the general consultation commitment entered into in Article 7.3 CETA. It applies not only to GATT/ASCM subsidies, specifically subsidies in the goods trade sector (see Section 9.3.1.1), but also with regard to 'government support related to trade in services' (i.e. to subsidies outside the scope of the ASCM), and foresees consultations if one Party considers that a subsidy or support 'may adversely affect its interests'. The responding Party shall then accord full and sympathetic consideration to that request. While the consultations are running, a Party may seek additional information on a subsidy or particular instance of government support related to trade in services provided by the other Party, including its policy objective, its amount, and any measures taken to limit the potential distortive effect on trade. Based on the consultations, the responding Party shall endeavour to eliminate or minimize any adverse effects of the subsidy, or the particular instance of government support related to trade in services, on the requesting Party's interests. These rules establish a particular consultation mechanism, and the general dispute settlement provisions of Chapter 29 CETA are not applicable (Article 7.9 CETA). As far as subsidies in the services sector are concerned to which the FSR remedies may be applied (as the primacy of the ASCM does not apply insofar), redressive measures under the FSR cannot be adopted while consultations are running. Apart from this restriction, nothing in the CETA prohibits the application of the FSR to subsidies from Canada.[107]

The subsidies commitments in the Economic Partnership Agreement between the EU and Japan (JEPA),[108] a most recently concluded agreement of the fourth generation, in its Chapter 12 reflect, by and large, those in

[106] Comprehensive Economic and Trade Agreement (CETA) between Canada, of the one part, and the European Union and its Member States, of the other part, OJ EU 2017 No. L 11/23, 14 January 2017.

[107] See also Müller-Ibold, 'The Draft Foreign Subsidies Regulation' (2022) 439 f.

[108] Agreement between the European Union and Japan for an Economic Partnership, OJ EU 2018 No. L 330/3, 27 December 2018.

the CETA. But there is an additional clause in Article 12.6 (5) JEPA regarding consultations. Specifically, after the sentence (comparable to what one finds in CETA) '[i]f the requesting Party, after the consultations, still considers that the subsidy has or could have a significant negative effect on its trade or investment interests under this Chapter, the requested Party shall accord sympathetic consideration to the concerns of the requesting Party', the parties added a new clause: 'Any solution shall be considered feasible and acceptable by the requested Party.' This could mean that the EU may, even after consultations had been held, not have recourse to unilateral measures as provided under the FSR unless prior exchange with the government of Japan had been taken place about the feasibility and acceptability of the redressive measures intended by the European Commission. This obligation may not only require an additional procedural step but is capable of restricting the substantive leeway of the Commission about the shape of the redressive measure under the FSR addressing the competition distortion.

9.4.6 Conclusion on Conformity with Bilateral Subsidies Commitments

The above analyses of EU bilateral commitments demonstrated that some of the EU's bilateral agreements add another layer of restrictions to the application of the FSR as regards specific trade partners with which WTO-plus subsidies disciplines had been entered into. As these contain deepened subsidy disciplines that also provide for procedures and institutions addressing the consequences of their violation and domestic subsidies review of the EU's trade partner, Article 44 (9) FSR then requires the non-application of the FSR in relation to these trade partners, as could be shown with regard to the United Kingdom, the EFTA states, Ukraine, Moldova, and the Western Balkan countries.[109] Avoiding a violation of international law requires that not only investigations and the adoption of measures under the FSR must be omitted with regard to companies from those states but also the legal obligation for relevant undertakings to submit notifications under Chapters 3 and 4 (Articles 21 and 29) of the FSR cannot be applied without violating bilateral commitments.[110] With regard to the latter, the wording of Article 44 (9) FSR proves insufficient, as it only addresses the EU's and its institutions' commitments and

[109] This is not a conclusive list of relevant bilateral agreements.

[110] See also Müller-Ibold, 'The Draft Foreign Subsidies Regulation' (2022) 439.

rights, but not the imposition of duties for undertakings by the FSR that contradict the EU's international agreements.

9.5 The Political Implications of the Foreign Subsidies Regulation

Besides the above legal problems of the FSR in view of the EU's international commitments, the present analysis must be complemented by considering the further political implications of the EU's approach for its multilateral objectives. The FSR is the expression of a new trade policy assertiveness turn that exhorts its trade partners to comply with EU rules by threatening EU unilateral measures provided in a new tool. Even though its scope of application appears rather limited due to its commitment to respect its international obligations under Article 44 (9) FSR, whose consequences were explored in this chapter, the lack of clarity on the exact scope of the rather broad 'disclaimer of international law compliance' enshrined therein does little to mitigate the inherent threat of unilateral EU measures. The new legislation has not been drafted with a sufficiently careful consideration of the compatibility of its measures with multilateral obligations, which, however, would have been necessary for the EU's international credibility. One way for the EU to reaffirm its continued interest in respecting international rules would have been to prescribe more specifically to which situations the new legislation applies and to which it does not in view of the EU's international commitments, not least with regard to those trade partners with which bilateral agreements containing specific subsidies disciplines had been concluded. Another way would have been to coordinate the FSR with its main trading partners or at least to enter into a dialogue with them to explain the EU's concerns to ensure a level playing field in the internal market even against distortions by foreign subsidization. This has not happened, apart from some discussions in WTO bodies. Consequently, it is the Commission's discretion and assessment of international legal obligations that will be decisive in the implementation and application of the FSR. It is the Commission that is in the position to establish whether the investigation of a particular situation of subsidization or the adoption of redressive measures in a given case would be contrary to international obligations of the EU. As the application of the new legislation then greatly depends on the Commission's good faith in the assessment, and as the Commission might come with ingenious interpretations of WTO law, it cannot be taken for granted that the Commission will not apply the new rules to cases where redressive measures violate WTO law or bilateral commitments of the EU. Due to the Commission's broad leeway, there is a need for greater scrutiny over its application of these rather vague rules.[111]

The unilateral introduction without international dialogue is likely to increase other WTO Members' resistance to the new rules.[112] This in turn may lead to a retaliatory spiral that will backfire negatively in terms of EU companies' market access abroad,[113] all the more so as the companies potentially particularly affected by the control of foreign subsidies, and hence vulnerable to the resulting redressive measures, may originate from large economies such as China, the United States, and the United Kingdom that can afford retaliation both economically and politically.[114] Furthermore, even if the Commission in its application of the FSR succeeds in limiting redressive measures to those cases where EU measures are compliant with international law, the mere existence of this new piece of legislation invites other WTO members to emulate the novel EU practice, which might further damage the already endangered international trading system, to the detriment of the EU's long-term efforts at WTO reform and the EU's economic progress. The Commission expects its WTO partners to establish their own internal state aid control system.[115] This appears naïve. The other countries will rather follow the EU in erecting a comparable external subsidies scrutiny mechanism, without necessarily subjecting their own companies to domestic aid control. The Commission opines that retaliatory measures would likely violate the WTO non-discrimination obligation if a third country does not have in place an equivalent control mechanism for their domestic subsidies.[116] This opinion, however, loses sight of the fact that, first, the basis of comparison for a WTO member's complaint against the EU is the treatment of recipients of foreign subsidies versus those of EU/Member State aid on the internal market (so that the issue as to whether a complainant runs a comparable subsidies control domestically is

[111] See Wolfgang Weiß, 'The EU's Strategic Autonomy in Times of Politicization of International Trade: The Future of Commission Accountability' (2023) 14(Suppl 3) *Global Policy* 54–64.

[112] Crochet and Gustafsson, 'Lawful Remedy or Illegal Response?' (2021) 365 f.

[113] See Evenett, Sud, and Vermulst, 'The European Union's New Move against China' (2020) 417 f.

[114] For these countries' companies' specific potential to become addressees of FSR measures, see Erixon, et al., *The New Wave of Defensive Trade Policy Measures in the European Union*, p. 70 ff.

[115] Commission proposal, COM(2021) 223 final, p. 56.

[116] ibid.

irrelevant in this respect); and, second, the EU's own domestic mechanism also has considerable loopholes, as analyzed in Section 9.3.2. As the EU significantly increases its and its Member States' state aid in order to strongly incentivize a quick green transformation of its economy and bring forward the technological capacities needed for that (such as the production of microchips, semiconductors, and batteries which will also feed into the EU's exporting sectors),[117] foreign countries will easily identify targets for their retaliatory measures.[118] The experiences with China are far from being affirmative of the EU's hopes for taking a leadership role that others will follow: Some years ago, China established a domestic Fair Competition Review System,[119] which, even though it resembles some aspects of EU state aid law, is far from being effective in its domestic subsidy control. This is because this system operates on the basis of an '*ex post* self-review mechanism',[120] does not provide for a duty to recover unlawful aid, and is run by the Anti-Monopoly Enforcement Agency merely on the basis of complaints.[121]

9.6 Conclusion

The FSR fills a gap in the EU's competition policy and trade defence arsenal as it allows the EU to balance the distortive effects on the EU internal market caused by foreign subsidization. Despite this, its application may collide with international legal commitments of the EU, and Article 44 (9) FSR consequently works as a considerable restraint on the FSR implementation by the Commission. As demonstrated in this chapter, the conflict with WTO law exists as regards the ASCM (insofar as FSR addressed subsidization to undertakings active in the goods sector), as well as with the GPA 2012 and GATS NT provisions due to the fact that foreign services and service providers are treated less beneficially compared to domestic recipients of state aid and EU aid. Consequently, the

[117] See most recently the EU's Green Deal Industrial Plan for the Net-Zero Age, Communication from the European Commission, COM(2023)62 final.

[118] Erixon, et al., *The New Wave of Defensive Trade Policy Measures in the European Union*, p. 78 f.

[119] For the Provisional Implementation Rules issued in October 2017 related to state aid, see Shuping Lyu, Caroline Buts, and Marc Jegers, 'Comparing China's Fair Competition Review System to EU State Aid Control' (2019) 18(1) *European State Aid Law Quarterly* 37–60 at 52 ff.

[120] Lyu, Buts, and Jegers, 'Comparing China's Fair Competition Review System to EU State Aid Control' (2019) 46.

[121] Guilliard, *Beihilfenkontrolle zwischen Supranationalität und Intergouvernementalität* (2022), p. 322.

FSR may finally, by and large, be applicable only to services and procurements not covered by WTO law. In addition, as regards EU bilateral agreements which contain WTO-plus subsidies disciplines that also provide for procedures and institutions addressing the consequences of their violation and domestic subsidies review, Article 44 (9) FSR requires the non-application of the FSR in relation to these trade partners. This applies also to the notification requirements under Chapters 3 and 4 of the FSR. With regard to the latter, the wording of Article 44 (9) FSR appears incomplete. The novelty of the EU's new instrument will also very likely lead to the type of imitation by others the EU might not have hoped for: the establishment of comparable external subsidies scrutiny mechanisms against foreign competitors, without subjecting domestic companies to similarly effective control. The FSR thus prompts the fear of another spiral of discriminatory treatment instead of a global level playing field. Thus, the Commission must take utmost care in its implementation that those negative consequences of the FSR do not materialize.

10 Carbon Border Adjustment Mechanism

In Tension with EU's International Trade and Climate Commitments

10.1 Introduction

Although the idea of a carbon border adjustment mechanism (CBAM) is not a novel one and has been long advocated by some academics, civil society representatives, and even EU Member States,[1] the CBAM Regulation was only adopted in May 2023.[2] The CBAM's stated overarching aim is to address the risk of 'carbon leakage', which can be defined as an increase in emissions abroad as a result of carbon-intensive industries losing market share to the benefit of competitors from jurisdictions with no or less stringent carbon emissions constraints in the short term and, because of the shift of production to jurisdictions with such regimes, in the long term.[3] The CBAM will apply carbon pricing to imported products

[1] Chiara Galiffa and Ignacio Garcia Bercero, 'How WTO-Consistent Tools Can Ensure the Decarbonization of Emission-Intensive Industrial Sectors' (2022) 116 *AJIL Unbound*, Symposium on Carbon Border Adjustments, 196–201 at 197.

[2] Regulation (EU) 2023/956 of the European Parliament and of the Council of 10 May 2023 establishing a carbon border adjustment mechanism (CBAM Regulation), OJ EU 2023 No. L 130/52, 16 May 2023.

[3] CBAM Regulation, Preamble, recitals (9), (10); Sarah Davidson Ladly, 'Border Carbon Adjustments, WTO-Law and the Principle of Common but Differentiated Responsibilities' (2012) 12(1) *International Environmental Agreements: Politics, Law and Economics* 63–84 at 66; Galiffa and Garcia Bercero, 'How WTO-Consistent Tools Can Ensure the Decarbonization of Emission-Intensive Industrial Sectors' (2022) 196; Ilaria Espa, 'Reconciling the Climate/Industrial Interplay of CBAMs: What Role For the WTO?' (2022) 116 *AJIL Unbound*, Symposium on Carbon Border Adjustments, 208–212 at 208; Timothy Meyer, 'Taxing, Regulating, And Trading Carbon: An Introduction to the Symposium' (2022) 116 *AJIL Unbound*, Symposium on Carbon Border Adjustments, 191–195 at 192; Gisselman et al. also identify a potential 'reverse' (positive) leakage as a result of transfer of innovative technology from countries with ambitious policies to other countries, which is nevertheless outside the scope of this chapter (Fredrik Gisselman, et al., 'Border Carbon Adjustments. An analysis of Trade Related Aspects and the Way Forward' (2020) *National*

from certain sectors; a mechanism that is allegedly equivalent to the EU's Emissions Trading System (ETS)[4] – a 'cap & trade' mechanism limiting the total greenhouse gas (GHG) emissions, allowing producers in certain emission-intensive sectors to buy and trade carbon permits at market prices.[5] Accordingly, the newly adopted regulation contributes, intentionally or incidentally, to ensuring a level playing field between domestic and imported products. Considering CBAM's aim of addressing 'carbon leakage' and potential of ensuring a level playing field, it clearly seeks to more assertively represent EU's interests and values, thereupon being one of the instruments treated in this part of the book.

After the transition period, the CBAM is set to progressively replace the existing ETS system of allocation of free allowances, which will be gradually phased out by the end of 2033.[6] The EU's ETS has been addressing the risk of carbon leakage by distributing allowances free of charge to sectors deemed to have a high risk of carbon leakage, thereby reducing the carbon price that installations in these sectors have to pay. In practice, however, free allowances send a weak price signal to EU industries compared to full auctioning, diminishing the incentive to decarbonize production processes.[7] While initially the carbon prices were too low to justify the need of a CBAM, in time prices grew manifold, constantly reaching new heights since December 2020,[8] making carbon

Board of Trade Sweden, www.kommerskollegium.se/contentassets/7a09d4cdb83a46feaf0c6ae6e5b02fff/border-carbon-adjustments_final_.pdf, p. 22).

4 Directive 2003/87/EC of the European Parliament and of the Council of 13 October 2003 establishing a scheme for greenhouse gas emission allowance trading within the Community and amending Council Directive 96/61/EC (ETS Directive), OJ EU L 275, 25 October 2003, as amended by Directive (EU) 2023/959 of the European Parliament, OJ EU 2023 No. L 130/134, 16 May 2023; CBAM Regulation, Preamble, Recitals (12), (15), (23), Art. 1 (2).

5 Galiffa and Garcia Bercero, 'How WTO-Consistent Tools Can Ensure the Decarbonization of Emission-Intensive Industrial Sectors' (2022) 196.

6 CBAM Regulation, Art. 1 (3) in conjunction with amended ETS Directive, Art. 10a (1a).

7 CBAM Regulation, Preamble, Recital (11), Impact Assessment Report Accompanying the Document Proposal for a Regulation of the European Parliament and of the Council Establishing a Carbon Border Adjustment Mechanism (Impact Assessment Report), 14 July 2021, SWD(2021) 643 final, Part 1/2, p. 9; Gracia Marín Durán, 'Carbon Border Adjustments: Ensuring Compatibility with the International Climate And Trade Regimes' (2022) 16 *UCL Research Paper Series*, p. 5.

8 The price for a carbon permit started at approximately 16 EUR in 2005 and until December 2020 it fluctuated but never above the point of 30 EUR. In February 2023, by comparison, the price went over 100 EUR (in this respect, see Trading Economics, 'EU Carbon Permits', https://tradingeconomics.com/commodity/carbon).

leakage more likely.[9] Moreover, in 2019, the Commission adopted the 'Green Deal' Communication, in which it proposed to increase the EU's GHG emissions reductions target to 55 per cent by 2030 compared to the 1990 level and to achieve net-zero GHG emissions.[10] These targets were translated into legal obligations with the adoption of the Regulation on European Climate Law.[11] In July 2021, the Commission adopted a package of proposals, termed 'Fit for 55', aimed at ensuring that the EU's freshly set targets are achieved, which included the CBAM proposal. In light of these new ambitions, the gap between the targets set by the EU and those of most of the EU partners will further widen and carbon prices are likely to stay high or continue to grow, increasing the risk of carbon leakage. Thus, the CBAM is said to address this risk that might undermine EU's climate ambitions,[12] which are also in line with the commitment to sustainable development enshrined in its constitutional treaties.[13]

Chapter 10 will present the CBAM Regulation and its aims (Section 10.2), including its 'levelling the playing field' aim or (maybe) effect that, as will be shown, the Commission attempts, for good reasons, to downplay by avoiding mentioning it. The CBAM, being a climate instrument, needs to be in conformity with EU's international climate commitments. Therefore, its consistency with the principle of Common But Differentiated Responsibilities (CBDR) will be assessed (Section 10.3). As the idea of a CBAM had been contested earlier also on account of its possible tensions with WTO rules, the chapter will continue with the analysis of the compatibility of the Regulation with core WTO obligations (Section 10.4). Then, it will proceed with an appraisal of whether such violations could be justified under WTO-relevant rules, including whether these justifications would permit offering special treatment to

[9] Jana Titievskaia, Henrique Morgado Simões, and Alina Dobreva 'EU Carbon Border Adjustment Mechanism Implications for Climate and Competitiveness' (2022) *EPRS*, p. 2.

[10] Communication from the Commission to the European Parliament, the European Council, the Council, the European Economic and Social Committee and the Committee of the Regions, 'The European Green Deal', 11 December 2019, COM(2019) 640 final, pp. 2, 4.

[11] Regulation (EU) 2021/1119 of the European Parliament and of the Council of 30 June 2021 establishing the framework for achieving climate neutrality and amending Regulations (EC) No 401/2009 and (EU) 2018/1999 ('European Climate Law'), OJ EU 2021 No. L 243/1, 9 July 2021.

[12] CBAM Regulation, Preamble, recitals (1), (4), (5), (8), (9).

[13] For more, see Eva Pander Maat, 'The Carbon Border Adjustment Mechanism and the Challenge of Being a "Good" Climate and Trade Actor', in Elaine Fahey and Isabella Mancini (eds.), *Understanding the EU as a Good Global Actor: Ambitions, Values and Metrics* (Cheltenham: Edward Elgar Publishing, 2022), p. 142.

developing countries, in line with the CBDR principle (Section 10.5). As the instrument could also conflict with EU FTA rules, the CBAM's compatibility with them will be considered (Section 10.6). For the assessment of consistency with international trade rules, due to space constraints and to avoid an excessively intricate analysis, the chapter will focus on the main approach of the CBAM towards material goods and not electricity. The employment of such a unilateral tool as the CBAM raises concerns about its legality under international law, but more general implications will also be considered in this chapter (Section 10.7). Lastly, based on the results obtained, the chapter will conclude by weighing in on whether the CBAM is in consonance with EU's commitment to international law and its multilateral stance (Section 10.8).

10.2 Description and Aims

10.2.1 Presenting the CBAM Regulation

The CBAM imposes an obligation on importers of particular goods, certain precursors, as well as some downstream products from certain carbon-intensive sectors listed in its Annex I (initially cement, electricity, fertilizers, iron and steel, aluminium, and hydrogen) to declare embedded emissions and purchase CBAM certificates upon the importation of these goods, thereby seeking to mirror the EU ETS but with certain adaptations and differences (Articles 1 (1), (2) and 2 (1) CBAM Regulation). Embedded emissions cover both direct emissions released during the production process of goods as well as indirect emissions from the production of electricity consumed during production processes; however, initially, the latter are taken into account only for a reduced number of sectors (Articles 3 (22), (34) and 7 (1)).[14]

Under the CBAM, covered goods should be imported into the Union's customs territory only by an authorised CBAM declarant – a person lodging a customs import declaration prior to importing goods in its own name or the person in whose name such a declaration is lodged – which is authorised at its place of establishment by the competent authority designated by the Member State in question (Articles 3 (16), (17), 4, 5 (1), and 17 (1)),[15] and included in the CBAM registry containing

[14] Annex II contains a list of goods for which only direct emissions are to be taken into account (currently iron and steel, aluminium, and hydrogen).

[15] For the detailed process of authorization, see Art. 17 CBAM Regulation.

relevant data on them by this authority (Articles 5 (4) and 17 (4)). The CBAM Registry, established by the Commission, contains relevant data on authorised declarants, CBAM certificates, operators, and installations in third countries (Articles 14 and 16). The applications for authorizations shall be submitted by importers established in the EU or, in case of importers outside the EU, by indirect customs representatives (Article 5 (1), (2)). Thus, the administrative burden will be carried by importers, which could be EU customs brokers or EU entities set up by third-country producers.[16] The CBAM Regulation, however, does not apply to goods originating in countries or territories included in the Annex III list, which are fully integrated into or linked to the EU ETS, provided that there are no rebates beyond those under the EU ETS (Article 2 (4), (6)).[17] Additionally, consignments and goods from travellers' personal luggage with negligible value (less than 150 EUR) are also excluded from the scope (Article 2 (3)).[18]

Each year, by 31 May, authorized declarants are mandated to submit a CBAM declaration through the CBAM registry for the previous year containing information about the total quantity of imported covered goods, the total embedded emissions expressed in metric tonnes of CO_2 emissions per tonne of each type of goods or per megawatt-hour of electricity, the total number of CBAM certificates corresponding to the total embedded emissions after reducing and adjusting it accordingly, and copies of verification reports issued by accredited verifiers (Article 6 (1), (2)). A CBAM certificate has an electronic format and corresponds to one tonne of embedded emissions (Article 3 (24)). These certificates are sold by a Member State to authorised declarants established therein on a common central platform established and managed by the Commission at the average price for each week of the closing prices on the common auction platform of EU ETS allowances or, in case of no auctions in a given week, the average price during the last week in which auctions took place (Articles 20 (1), (2) and 21 (1)). By 31 May of each year and for the first time in 2027 for 2026, authorised declarants shall surrender via the CBAM

[16] Titievskaia, Morgado Simões, and Dobreva, 'EU Carbon Border Adjustment Mechanism', p. 5.

[17] According to Annex III, the following countries are currently excluded: Iceland, Liechtenstein, Norway (already part of the EU ETS), and Switzerland (its ETS is linked to the EU ETS). The Commission may adopt implementing acts to amend the list (CBAM Regulation, Art. 2 (11)).

[18] In connection with Council Regulation (EC) No 1186/2009 of 16 November 2009 setting up a Community system of reliefs from customs duty, OJ EU 2009 No. L 324/23, 10 December 2009, Art. 23.

registry a number of CBAM certificates available on their account corresponding to the amount of declared and verified embedded emissions (Article 22 (1)). Additionally, they shall ensure that the number of CBAM certificates on their account in the CBAM registry corresponds to at least 80 per cent of the embedded emissions at the end of each quarter (Article 22 (2)). After their surrender, upon request from declarants submitted by 30 June of each year, the Commission should repurchase the excess certificates remaining on the account of a declarant in the CBAM registry through the common central platform for the price paid at the time of purchase, but not more than one-third of the total certificates purchased by a declarant during the previous calendar year (Article 23 (1)-(3)); the remaining certificates are cancelled on 1 July of each year without any compensation (Article 24). Besides the fact that the CBAM provides a separate mechanism from the EU ETS scheme for the operationalization of CBAM obligations, there are some important differences between the obligations imposed by the EU ETS and by the CBAM. Thus, unlike the allowances under the former, CBAM certificates are not tradable on European secondary markets and expire relatively fast in order to keep up with the EU ETS carbon permits prices (Preamble, recital (24)).[19] Moreover, while the CBAM would charge authorised declarants for the amount of carbon embedded in the imported products, the EU ETS imposes an obligation to buy allowances based on emissions per installations (Preamble, recital (25)). While, according to the Commission's initial proposal, most CBAM-generated revenues would have been directed towards the EU budget, in particular for addressing the consequences of the COVID-19 pandemic,[20] the adopted CBAM Regulation provides in its preamble with respect to low- and middle-income third countries that 'the Union should continue to support those countries through the Union budget, especially Least Developed Countries (LDCs), in order to contribute to ensuring their adaptation to the obligations under this Regulation', and that it is 'working towards introducing a new own resource based on the revenues generated by the sale of CBAM certificate' (Preamble, recital (74)). Nevertheless, the introduction of such a resource remains pending for now.

[19] Joachim Englisch and Tatiana Falcão, 'EU Carbon Border Adjustments and WTO Law, Part One' (2021) 51(10) *Environmental Law Reporter* 10857–10882 at 10860.

[20] Proposal for a Regulation of the European Parliament and of the Council establishing a carbon border adjustment mechanism (CBAM Proposal), COM/2021/564 final, Explanatory Memorandum, p. 11.

The CBAM declarations can be reviewed within four years after the year in which the declaration should have been submitted by the Commission, which has the oversight role during this process, or by the competent authorities, which must communicate the initiation and results to the Commission (Article 19 (1), (2)). If a CBAM declaration is not submitted or the declared number of CBAM certificates is incorrect, the Commission preliminary determines the number of CBAM certificates based on the available information at the latest by the end of the year following that in which the CBAM declaration should have been submitted or by the end of the fourth year following the submission of the incorrect declaration (Article 19 (4)). If the competent domestic authorities consider the number of CBAM certificates incorrect – a decision that may be appealed – the authority can adjust it based on the information submitted by the Commission and request the surrender of additional certificates within one month or decide to take no action; in case the authority concludes that the amount is in excess, it shall be repurchased at the price paid by the declarant (Articles 19 (5), (6) and 23 (3)). Failure to surrender the necessary number of CBAM certificates is liable to a penalty identical to the penalty for excess emissions under the EU ETS, which, however, does not release the declarants in question from their obligations (Article 26 (1), (3), (4)) .[21] The Commission will have to take action to address circumvention practices (Article 27).

Embedded emissions in goods, except electricity, are determined based on actual emissions calculated pursuant to the method contained in Annex IV to the Regulation (Article 7 (2)). If, however, they cannot be adequately determined, the amount of embedded emissions should be calculated using default values set at the average emission intensity of each exporting country for each of the covered goods increased by a proportionate mark-up established in the implementing acts of the CBAM Regulation. In the absence of reliable data from an exporting country, the default values should be determined using the average emission intensity of a fixed percentage of the worst-performing installations producing that type of good, to be determined in the implementing acts (Article 7 (2); Annex IV, 4.1). Embedded indirect emissions, however, shall be determined from the outset using default values calculated, on average, of either the emission factor of the Union or country of origin electricity grid or the CO_2 emission factor of price-setting sources

[21] Additionally, according to Art. 26 (5), in case of disregard of penalty, payment may be secured by means prescribed under national law.

in the country of origin, of the electricity used in the production process, unless authorised declarants demonstrate that they meet the criteria for using actual emissions: a direct technical link between installations and electricity generation source or a power purchase agreement between the installation and the electricity producer for an amount equivalent to that for which the use of a specific value is claimed (Article 7 (4), Annex IV, 4.3, 6). The number of CBAM certificates is to be adjusted to reflect the extent to which EU ETS free allowances were allocated (Article 31 (1)), and declarants may claim reductions in the number of CBAM certificates to be surrendered to take account of the carbon price already effectively paid for the emissions in the country of origin (Article 9 (1)). Authorised declarants are mandated to ensure that the declared embedded emissions are verified according to the principles set in Annex VI of the Regulation by verifiers accredited by Member States' national accreditation bodies (Article 8 (1)).[22] Third-country operators and installations, however, can ask the Commission to register information on them in the CBAM registry (Article 10 (1)), in which case the declarant can use the already verified information disclosed to it (Article 8 (2)). Registered operators must determine the embedded emissions by type of goods produced at the installation and ensure that the information on embedded emissions is verified by accredited verifiers (Article 10 (5) (a), (b)).

The rules described above, however, would only be applicable after the transitional period, which will last from 1 October 2023 to 31 December 2025 (Article 32 (1)), allowing business and authorities to adjust.[23] During this period each importer or indirect customs representative will have to submit to the Commission only a quarterly report containing information on the quantity of imported goods, total actual embedded emissions, total indirect emissions, and the carbon price due in the country of origin, or otherwise face a proportionate and dissuasive penalty (Article 35 (1), (2), and (5)). Before the end of the transitional period, the Commission shall present a report to the European Parliament (EP) and Council assessing *inter alia* the possibility to extend the scope of the Regulation to embedded emissions in other sectors with the aim of

[22] Accredited verifiers are deemed those accredited under the ETS scheme (see Commission Implementing Regulation (EU) 2018/2067 of 19 December 2018 on the verification of data and on the accreditation of verifiers pursuant to Directive 2003/87/EC of the European Parliament and of the Council, OJ L 334/94, Art. 3 (3)) or other verifiers specifically accredited under the CBAM Regulation (CBAM Regulation, Art. 18 (1), (2)).

[23] Galiffa and Garcia Bercero, 'How WTO-Consistent Tools Can Ensure the Decarbonization of Emission-Intensive Industrial Sectors' (2022) 199.

including all goods covered by the ETS by 2030, especially organic chemicals and polymers, the emissions from the transport of covered goods, indirect emissions in all covered goods, or other inputs, as well as the progress made in international discussions on climate action and the impact on imports from developing countries and LDCs (Article 30 (2)). In addition, before the end of the transitional period the Commission must present a report containing products further down the value chains to be included in the scope (Article 30 (3)). Furthermore, after the transition period, every two years, the Commission will assess the CBAM's effectiveness in addressing the risk of carbon leakage in case of EU goods exported to third countries without carbon pricing and, where appropriate, present a WTO-compliant legislative proposal to address it (Article 30 (5)). Finally, after the transition period, as part of the annual report, the Commission must evaluate on 'how the financing under that Regulation has contributed to the decarbonization of the manufacturing industry in LDCs' (Article 30 (8)).

10.2.2 EU's Interests and Values: Environmental Protection and a 'Level Playing Field'

As stated, the CBAM's declared main aim is to address the risk of carbon leakage, which might increase considering the EU's new ambitious climate goals. Thus, with CBAM the EU is more assertively representing its interests and values in terms of environmental protection and tackling climate change. However, the CBAM also has other secondary and ancillary aims or maybe effects, especially addressing the competition between domestic and imported carbon-intensive products on the EU market, thereby advancing its interest of competitive equality and ensuring a level playing field for the EU industry.

Although the CBAM is set to address the risk of carbon leakage replacing the existing mechanism granting free allowances, the level of this risk and effectiveness of CBAM in tackling it are less straightforward. Economic studies have reached different results with respect to the extent of carbon leakage from countries with higher climate standards absent protecting measures.[24] The Commission itself in its Impact Assessment Report acknowledges the disparity between the results of *ex*

[24] Sam Lowe, 'Should the EU Tax Imported CO_2?' (2019) *Insight Centre for European Reform*, www.cer.eu/sites/default/files/insight_SL_24.9_19.pdf, p. 2 ; Gracia Marín Durán, 'EU Carbon Border Adjustment Mechanism: Key Issues Going Forward' (2021) 26(4) *EFARev* 499–506 at 502; Pander Maat, 'The Carbon Border Adjustment Mechanism' (2022), p. 143.

ante and *ex post* economic analyses, the last indicating that there is no substantial evidence of carbon leakage.[25] However, it claims that these results can be explained by the successful prevention of carbon leakage before CBAM by the EU's current mechanism of allocating free allowances.[26]

The CBAM, nevertheless, might also have other positive effects in terms of climate protection. First, the Regulation aspires to create incentives for third countries to adopt more stringent rules on carbon emissions and even to fully integrate into or link to the EU ETS their existing carbon pricing systems.[27] Thus, the Commission hopes that the CBAM will bring about the so-called Brussels effect, referring to the EU exporting its rules to other parts of the world resulting in unilateral regulatory globalization.[28] The CBAM Regulation in its preamble (recital (72)) expressly states that a 'Climate Club' should be created between countries with carbon pricing instruments 'to promote the implementation of ambitious climate policies in all countries'. In a Commission's publication, albeit not representing its official position, the CBAM's potential regulatory incentive for third countries to introduce their own carbon pricing mechanisms is mentioned as a key feature, the instruments's purpose being 'behavior-changing'.[29] However, it might also be the case that importers will simply engage in reshuffling exports so that products with lower carbon content reach the EU market while those with higher content go to other markets.[30] Second, the phase-out of free allowances might also encourage *domestic* producers to decarbonize further. Third, the CBAM might boost the consumption of less carbon-intensive products.[31]

Moreover, the Regulation could make it easier for EU producers to accept increased climate ambitions knowing that they will compete on

25 Impact Assessment Report, Part 1/2, p. 7.

26 ibid. As the Commission states, this argument is also supported by the OECD.

27 ibid, p. 15; Gary Clyde Hufbauer, Jisun Kim, and Jeffrey J. Schott, 'Can EU Carbon Border Adjustment Measures Propel WTO Climate Talks?' (2021) Peterson Institute for International Economics Policy Brief, www.piie.com/sites/default/files/documents/pb21-23.pdf, p. 1.

28 For more, see Anu Bradford, 'The Brussels Effect' (2012) 107(1) *Northwestern University Review* 1–67 at 3; Anu Bradford, *The Brussels Effect: How the European Union Rules the World* (New York: Oxford University Press, 2020), p. 1.

29 James Flett, 'The European Union Carbon Border Adjustment Mechanism and Its Consistency with World Trade Organization Law', in European Commission, *70 Years of EU Law: A Union for Its Citizens* (Brussels: Bietlot, 2022), p. 287.

30 Titievskaia, Morgado Simões, and Dobreva, 'EU Carbon Border Adjustment Mechanism', p. 5.

31 Impact Assessment Report, Part 1/2, p. 68.

equal footing with imported products. In fact, levelling the playing field is closely connected to the aim of preventing carbon leakage. If competition weighs in favour of cheaper imported products from countries with lower climate goals and less strict carbon rules, it becomes more likely that EU producers will move production oversees. The logic behind the CBAM is that carbon leakage prevention is equal to ensuring a level playing field between domestic and imported carbon-intensive products. In her 2020 State of the Union Address, President von der Leyen stated that the CBAM should motivate foreign producers to decarbonize while ensuring that the EU levels the playing field in a WTO-compatible way.[32] The potential positive impact of the CBAM on competitiveness of EU industries in the covered sectors has also been explicitly recognized by the Commission in the Impact Assessment Report, but not as the main objective.[33] The EP tabled multiple amendments to explicitly add the aim of levelling the playing field,[34] which, however, never reached the adopted version of the CBAM. In light of these considerations, the CBAM is treated in this book along other trade instruments ensuring a level playing field, although the Regulation itself is cautiously silent in this respect, the legislator seemingly being aware that the aim of ensuring a level playing field could jeopardize a potential justification under Article XX General Agreement on Tariffs and Trade (GATT).[35]

The CBAM could bring about accusations of protectionism under the guise of climate protection, as the line between ensuring a level playing field and protectionism is often blurry.[36] The EU could, nevertheless, argue that ensuring competitive equality is a prerequisite for preventing carbon leakage. In order for this argument to stand, it should be apparent from the design of the CBAM that it seeks nothing more than equal carbon pricing.[37] Still, even a well-designed CBAM would likely be

[32] State of the Union Address by President von der Leyen at the European Parliament Plenary, 16 September 2020, https://ec.europa.eu/commission/presscorner/detail/en/SPEECH_20_1655.

[33] Impact Assessment Report, Part 1/2, p. 68.

[34] See Amendments Adopted by the European Parliament on 22 June 2022 on the proposal for a regulation of the European Parliament and of the Council establishing a carbon border adjustment mechanism (EP Amendments), (COM(2021)0564 – C9–0328/2021 – 2021/0214(COD))1, Amendments 7, 10, 11, 16, 31, 262.

[35] General Agreement on Tariffs and Trade 1994, 15 April 1994, Marrakesh Agreement Establishing the World Trade Organization, Annex 1A, 1867 U.N.T.S. 187, 33 I.L.M. 1153 (1994).

[36] Bradford, *The Brussels Effect: How the European Union Rules the World* (2020), p. 241.

[37] Espa, 'Reconciling the Climate/Industrial Interplay of CBAMs' (2022) 209.

accused of green protectionism.[38] In order for the EU to successfully refute such allegations, the CBAM should be in compliance with WTO rules, as these multilateral rules were drafted with the purpose to prevent disguised protectionist trade measures. Accordingly, this chapter will assess whether the CBAM will stand the test under the WTO rules or will be considered a protectionist measure.

10.3 CBAM and the CBDR Principle

Although the question of compatibility of carbon border adjustments with the CBDR principle[39] has received considerably less attention than the question of consistency with WTO rules, CBAM is a trade-related climate measure that should comply with both international trade and climate rules. The United Nations Framework Convention on Climate Change (UNFCCC)[40] implicitly recognizes that parties can resort even unilaterally to trade-related climate measures.[41] In a language evoking the chapeau of Article XX GATT, it provides in Article 3.5 that '[m]easures taken to combat climate change, including unilateral ones, should not constitute a means of *arbitrary or unjustifiable discrimination or a disguised restriction on international trade*' (emphasis added). As these terms are likely to be interpreted in line with the relevant WTO jurisprudence, reference could be made to the pertinent analyses in Section 10.5.1.3. The CBAM does not contain any provision akin to those found in other instruments according to which regulations should be without prejudice to EU's or its Members' international obligation. Nonetheless, while compliance with both international trade and climate rules might prove difficult, as it will be argued, such a possibility should not be discounted, and CBAM should be designed in a manner that would have the highest chances to comply with both sets of rules in order for the EU to live up to its declared status of multilateralist and supporter of international law. This section will particularly assess whether EU's CBAM complies with the CBDR principle, and if not, what changes should be introduced.

38 Michael A. Mehling, et al., 'Designing Border Carbon Adjustments for Enhanced Climate Action' (2019) 113 (3) *AJIL* 433–481 at 441.

39 On the significance of the word 'principle', see Lavanya Rajamani, 'Common but Differentiated Responsibilities', in Michael Faure (ed.), *Elgar Encyclopedia of Environmental Law* (Cheltenham: Edward Elgar Publishing, 2016), p. 293.

40 United Nations Framework Convention on Climate Change, A/RES/48/189, 20 January 1994, 1771 U.N.T.S 107.

41 Marín Durán, 'Carbon Border Adjustments' (2022), p. 6.

The CBDR principle generally recognizes the unequal contribution to climate change and enunciates that the responsibility to combat it should be differentiated based on countries' ability and developmental levels.[42] Thus, the CBDR is generally perceived as requiring the developed countries to undertake more onerous obligations than developing countries, particularly LDCs. Still, the exact formulation of the CBDR principle differs in various international agreements.[43] Nevertheless, as CBAM does not differentiate between countries based on their level of development, it could come into tension with the CBDR principle.

The CBAM Regulation does not expressly refer to the CBDR principle; only the Explanatory Memorandum to the CBAM proposal mentions it *en passant* by stating that under Paris Agreement[44] each Party must prepare its own nationally determined contribution (NDC), reflecting the CBDR.[45] In the Impact Assessment Report the Commission clarified that it considers the CBDR to be respected, as the CBAM obligations do not depend on the level of ambitions or policy choices of a country. It further argues that a blank exemption of LDCs would run counter CBAM's overarching objective of carbon leakage and would be counterproductive for LDCs, since later transition to a greener economy would be more costly.[46] Instead, in its preamble, the Regulation highlights the need to provide 'technical assistance' to developing countries and LDCs 'to support those countries through the Union budget, especially LDCs, in order to contribute to ensuring their adaptation to the obligations under this Regulation', and that the EU works towards introducing its 'own resource based on the sale of CBAM certificates generated revenues' to support climate mitigation, adaptation, and decarbonization in those countries.[47] While it remains to be seen if and how exactly this pledge contained just in the preamble of the CBAM Regulation would be transposed into reality, it seems that the EP's call to finance LDC's efforts towards decarbonization 'with an annual amount corresponding at least to the level of revenues generated by the sale of CBAM certificates'[48] was taken into consideration.

[42] Davidson Ladly, 'Border Carbon Adjustments' (2012) 63; Pander Maat, 'The Carbon Border Adjustment Mechanism' (2022), p. 150.

[43] Davidson Ladly, 'Border Carbon Adjustments' (2012) 65.

[44] Paris Agreement to the United Nations Framework Convention on Climate Change, 12 December 2015, T.I.A.S. No. 16-1104.

[45] CBAM Proposal, Explanatory Memorandum, p. 8. [46] ibid, p. 30.

[47] CBAM Regulation, Preamble, recitals (72), (74).

[48] EP Amendments, Amendments 40, 130.

The CBDR was clearly mentioned for the first time in the 1992 Rio Declaration, referring to two elements: the common responsibility of states for the protection of the environment and the different circumstances that need to be taken into account, in particular the historical contributions to the climate degradation and the ability to address it.[49] Thereupon, the CBDR has been enshrined in numerous almost universal instruments with widespread participation, including the UNFCCC, Kyoto Protocol,[50] and Paris Agreement.[51] Although the CBDR has appeared in multiple agreements, the majority of scholars agree that it has not yet attained the status of customary law or principle of international law.[52] Nevertheless, even if the EU could consider the principle as well as the NDCs as not reflecting a sufficiently ambitious approach,[53] the CBDR is an international obligation for the EU also by virtue of said international agreements to which it is a party and agreed to in the first place. Accordingly, the EU is not entitled to decide on the appropriatness of the NDCs of other countries. Still, the exact content of the obligation flowing from the principle, especially the criteria for differentiating between countries, is ambiguous and represents a contentious issue.[54] This is a particularly challenging aspect considering that some emerging

[49] UN General Assembly, Report of the United Nations Conference on Environment and Development, Rio de Janeiro, 3–14 June 1992, A/CONF.151/26 (Vol. I), Principle 7. An incipient expression was also included in the Stockholm Declaration (The United Nations Conference on the Human Environment, Stockholm, 16 June 1972, UN General Assembly Resolutions 2994/XXVII, 2995/UVII and 2996/XXII, 15 December 1972, Principle 23); Philippe Sands, et al., *Principles of International Environmental Law*, 3rd ed. (Cambridge: Cambridge University Press, 2012), p. 233.

[50] Kyoto Protocol to the United Nations Framework Convention on Climate Change, 10 December 1997, 2303 U.N.T.S. 162, 37 I.L.M 22.

[51] Rajamani, 'Common but Differentiated Responsibilities' (2016), p. 292.

[52] Davidson Ladly, 'Border Carbon Adjustments' (2012) 70; Rajamani, 'Common but Differentiated Responsibilities' (2016), p. 298; Marín Durán, 'Carbon Border Adjustments' (2022), p. 7. Sands also notes that 'state practice is inconclusive as to the precise legal nature and consequence of each formulation' (Sands, et al., *Principles of International Environmental Law* (2012), p. 234).

[53] Flett, 'The European Union Carbon Border Adjustment Mechanism' (2022), p. 271.

[54] Davidson Ladly, 'Border Carbon Adjustments' (2012), 70; Ulrike Will, *Climate Border Adjustments and WTO Law: Extending the EU Emissions Trading System to Imported Goods and Services* (Leiden: Brill Neijhoff, 2019), p. 105; Ingo Venzke and Geraldo Vidigal, 'Are Unilateral Trade Measures in the Climate Crisis the End of Differentiated Responsibilities? The Case of the EU Carbon Border Adjustment Mechanism (CBAM)', in Maarten den Heijer and Harmen van der Wilt (eds.), *Netherlands Yearbook of International Law 2020: Global Solidarity and Common but Differentiated Responsibilities* (The Hague: T.M.C. Asser Press, 2022), vol. 51, p.192; Marín Durán, 'Carbon Border Adjustments' (2022), p. 7.

economies that are considered developing countries, such as China, India, Brazil, and South Africa, are also among world's largest emitters.[55] These countries have already issued a joint statement in which they expressed their 'grave concern' that the CBAM is against the CBDR principle.[56] Similar concerns have been expressed by the United Nations Conference of Trade and Development (UNCTAD).[57]

While for a long time the CBDR seemed to draw a line between developed countries on one hand and developing and least developed countries on the other, the principle has evolved.[58] The CBAM is clearly contrary to the 'binary' approach differentiating between developed and developing countries as enshrined in the UNFCCC and Kyoto Protocol.[59] Nevertheless, the Paris Agreement adopted a more nuanced form of differentiation,[60] which is also more in tune with the current realities. The Paris Agreement provides in Article 2 (2) that it will be implemented to reflect the CBDR principle, but 'in the light of different national circumstances'.[61] Thus, it suggests that the CBDR should have an evolutionary understanding.[62] Under the Paris Agreement, each party self-determined its contributions, tailored to own national circumstances, and distinct approaches were adopted for different issue areas.[63] Hence, every single country, be it developed or developing, undertook responsibilities to reduce carbon emissions. The Paris Agreement does distinguish

[55] See Worldometer, CO_2 Emissions by Country, www.worldometers.info/co2-emissions/co2-emissions-by-country/.

[56] Joint Statement issued at the conclusion of the 30th BASIC Ministerial Meeting on Climate Change hosted by India, 8 April 2021, para. 19.

[57] UNCTAD, 'A European Union Carbon Border Adjustment Mechanism: Implications for Developing Countries' (2021), https://unctad.org/system/files/official-document/osginf2021d2_en.pdf, p. 9.

[58] Mehling, et al., 'Designing Border Carbon Adjustments' (2019) 472; Marín Durán, 'Carbon Border Adjustments' (2022), p. 8.

[59] Marín Durán, 'Carbon Border Adjustments' (2022), p. 10.

[60] Mehling, et al., 'Designing Border Carbon Adjustments' (2019) 472, fn. 287 stating that 'especially through the Kyoto Protocol [. . .] under which only developed countries listed in Annex I of the UNFCCC were obliged to achieve emissions targets'.

[61] According to Rajamani this qualification, which she calls the 'Lima qualifier', was a compromise between China and the United States that 'arguably shifts the interpretation of the CBDRRC principle' (Lavanya Rajamani, 'Ambition and Differentiation in the 2015 Paris Agreement: Interpretative Possibilities and Underlying Politics' (2016) 65 *ICLQ* 493–514 at 508).

[62] Christina Voigt and Felipe Ferreira, 'Dynamic Differentiation: The Principles of CBDR-RC, Progression and Highest Possible Ambition in the Paris Agreement' (2016) 5(2) *Transantional Environmental Law* 285–303 at 294–295.

[63] ibid, 510; Rajamani, 'Common but Differentiated Responsibilities' (2016), p. 299.

between developed and developing countries[64] but does not define these categories, nor does it provide lists of such countries as under the UNFCCC and Kyoto Protocol, allowing them to embrace greater ambitions without progressing to a different category.[65]

This chapter will assess the CBAM in light of this more recent understanding of the CBDR principle, which does not seem to necessarily require a blank exemption from the CBAM obligations of *all* developing countries. Still, contrary to the aforementioned Commission's claim,[66] the CBAM in fact imposes a policy choice in favour of carbon pricing mechanisms, to be able to benefit from reductions in the number of CBAM certificates. Developing countries are free to choose a regulatory mechanism or establish their own carbon prices under the CBAM, but then importers of goods originating in these countries would still have to pay the same price for CBAM certificates as EU producers, with no regard to the different national circumstances of distinct countries. Accordingly, although the CBDR as enshrined in the Paris Agreement does not require a blank exemption of *all* developing countries, certain differentiation would still be necessary. Venzke and Vidigal argue that differentiation should be based on 'objectively justifiable criteria', 'reasoned policy decisions as well as reviewable individual determinations' related to levels of development and to historic and present emissions, regardless of what the exact formula is.[67] Thus, it would be the task of the policymakers to identify such criteria. Even so, the Paris Agreement clearly and explicitly differentiates between developed and developing countries in terms of financial support.[68] Articles 4.5 and 7.13 of the agreement unequivocally establish that 'support shall be provided to *developing* country Parties' (emphasis added) for their mitigation efforts and adaptation actions, respectively, including the achievement of nationally determined contributions. Article 9.1 expressly establishes that '*[d]eveloped* country Parties *shall* provide financial resources' (emphasis added) to assist developing countries, while per Article 9.2, other parties are only 'encouraged' to provide such support. Thus, developing countries should clearly benefit from financial support from developed economies, such as the EU. Thus, the intention to support low- and middle-income countries, especially

64 For example, in Arts. 3, 4.1, 4.4, 4.5, 7.2, 9.1, 9.3, 11.1, 11.3, etc.

65 Rajamani, 'Common but Differentiated Responsibilities' (2016), p. 300; Voigt and Ferreira, 'Dynamic Differentiation' (2016) 294–295.

66 Impact Assessment Report, Part 1/2, p. 30.

67 Venzke and Vidigal, 'Are Unilateral Trade Measures in the Climate Crisis the End of Differentiated Responsibilities?' (2022), p. 215.

68 Voigt and Ferreira, 'Dynamic Differentiation' (2016) 299.

LDCs, also by creating the Union's own instrument based on CBAM-generated revenues is commendable and should be pursued in order to comply with the CBDR principle. Yet, it remains to be seen in practice if and when such an instrument would be adopted and whether it would indeed provide financial support to all developing countries.

While no complete exemption from CBAM obligations of all developing countries seems to be required to comply with the CBDR principles, LDCs and Small Island Developing States (SIDS) are treated as a separate category of countries with a special regime in the Paris Agreement.[69] Most notably, following provisions applicable to all countries, Article 4.6 of the Paris Agreement states that LDCs and SIDS '*may* prepare and communicate strategies, plans and actions for low greenhouse gas emissions development reflecting their special circumstances' (emphasis). Thus, Article 4.6 uses a very permissive language compared to Article 4.2, which establishes that each party '*shall* prepare, communicate and maintain successive nationally determined contributions' (emphasis added), and Article 4.4, which mentions that developed countries '*should* continue taking the lead' (emphasis added) and developing countries '*should* continue enhancing their mitigation efforts' (emphasis added). While differentiation in respect to developing countries remains an unsettled question, there is a general consensus among scholars that to comply with the CBDR principle, LDCs should be fully exempted from the CBAM obligations,[70] all the more so as the EU itself acknowledges that LDCs account for only a small share of CBAM-covered imports.[71] Accordingly, contrary to the Commission's claim, it is unlikely that the exemption of LDCs and SIDS would seriously undermine the CBAM's overarching objective to prevent carbon leakage.[72] At the same time,

[69] Marín Durán, 'Carbon Border Adjustments' (2022), pp. 10–11.

[70] Gisselman, et al., 'Border Carbon Adjustments' (2020), pp. 4, 66; Mehling, et al., 'Designing Border Carbon Adjustments' (2019) 472; Joost Pauwelyn and David Kleimann, 'Trade Related Aspects of a Carbon Border Adjustment Mechanism: A Legal Assessment' (2020) EP Briefing Requested by the INTA Committee, www.europarl.europa.eu/cmsdata/210514/EXPO_BRI(2020)603502_EN.pdf, p. 11; Sam Lowe, 'The EU's Carbon Border Adjustment Mechanism: How to Make it Work for Developing Countries' (2021) Open Society European Policy Institute Policy Brief, www.cer.eu/publications/archive/policy-brief/2021/eus-carbon-border-adjustment-mechanism-how-make-it-work, p. 8 f; Marín Durán, 'Carbon Border Adjustments' (2022), p. 12.

[71] Impact Assessment Report, Part 1/2, p. 12.

[72] Mehling, et al., 'Designing Border Carbon Adjustments' (2019) 472–473; Lowe, 'The EU's Carbon Border Adjustment Mechanism' (2021), p. 1; Marín Durán, 'Carbon Border Adjustments' (2022), p. 12.

the impact of the CBAM on these countries could be significant.[73] The Commission itself notes in the CBAM Impact Assessment Report that 'the relative importance of these exports for LDCs' economies can conversely be quite large'.[74] While the CBAM Regulation requires Commission to report after the transitional period *inter alia* on CBAM's impact on LDCs, it contains no mention whatsoever of their exemption. Even if it were counterproductive for LDCs and SIDs to transit to greener economies later rather than earlier, these countries have the latitude to self-determine what is in their best interest.

To conclude, the CBAM is most likely inconsistent with the international obligation flowing from the CBDR principle as enshrined in the Paris Agreement. To comply, the CBDR should at least provide differentiated financial support to all developing countries and fully exempt from CBAM obligations the LDCs and SIDS. As will be demonstrated later, such an exemption might come into conflict with the most-favoured-nation (MFN) obligation contained in Article I:1 GATT, whose violation, however, could be justified under WTO rules.

10.4 CBAM and Core WTO Obligations

The preamble to the CBAM Regulation contends that it ensures compatibility with the WTO rules,[75] a condition stressed also by von der Leyen when announcing this tool.[76] Nevertheless, this section will verify whether the CBAM complies with core WTO obligations, such as National Treatment (NT), MFN, and the prohibition on quantitative restrictions. The question of the CBAM's WTO compatibility becomes especially relevant considering that India, backed by other developing countries, already announced its intention to challenge the regulation at the WTO.[77]

[73] Especially since the administrative costs for LDCs could be higher considering their limited capacities (Impact Assessment Report, Part 2/2, p. 21; Rafael Leal-Arcas, Manuliza Faktaufon, and Anna Kyprianou, 'A Legal Exploration of the European Union's Carbon Border Adjustment Mechanism' (2022) *European Energy and Environmental Law Review* 223–240 at 233).

[74] For example, exports of aluminium to the EU accounted for nearly 7% of Mozambique's GDP in 2020, and those of iron ore accounted for 10–18% of Mauritania's GDP (Impact Assessment Report, Part 2/2, pp. 19–21).

[75] CBAM Regulation, Preamble, recital (15).

[76] State of the Union Address by President von der Leyen at the European Parliament Plenary, 16 September 2020 https://ec.europa.eu/commission/presscorner/detail/en/SPEECH_20_1655.

[77] Manoj Kumar and Neha Arora, 'India Plans to Challenge EU Carbon Tax at WTO', Reuters, 16 May 2023, www.reuters.com/world/india/india-plans-challenge-eu-carbon-tax-wto-

The EU is certainly aware of the controversy surrounding the adoption of CBAM and its consistency with WTO rules, but purportedly considering that action is necessary and even demanded by its citizens,[78] the EU is likely to advance interpretations of WTO rules that might not be accepted by WTO adjudicators and the majority of the membership. It should be noted that WTO-relevant rules and pertinent jurisprudence provide little clarity as to how border carbon adjustment mechanisms would be treated, making it difficult to predict with certainty whether the CBAM would be found as WTO consistent in a dispute.[79] The analysis is particularly complicated due to the double uncertainty related to the nature of the CBAM that would determine the applicable law: (1) charge or a regulation? and (2) border or internal measure?

10.4.1 CBAM and Its Fiscal Character under Articles II:1 (b), II:2 (a), and III:2 GATT

10.4.1.1 The Appropriate Venues, Their Relationships, and Related Uncertainties

Although it is not a generally agreed-upon conclusion,[80] there seems to be considerable support in the academic literature in favour of considering the CBAM as a measure with a fiscal character, in particular a 'charge' within the meaning of GATT Articles II:1 (b), II:2 (a), and III:2 GATT.[81]

According to the WTO jurisprudence, the term 'charge' denotes a 'pecuniary burden' and a 'liability to pay money'.[82] The obligation to buy and surrender CBAM certificates could thus be considered a charge, as it imposes a pecuniary burden and an obligation to pay money on

sources-2023-05-16/; Ravi Dutta Mishra, 'India Seeks Taiwan, South Africa Backing on Carbon Border Tax', *Mint*, 16 June 2023, www.livemint.com/economy/india-seeks-taiwan-s-africa-backing-on-carbon-border-tax-11686936697768.html.

78 Flett, 'The European Union Carbon Border Adjustment Mechanism' (2022), p. 281.

79 Anna Dias, Stéphanie Seeuws, and Agnieszka Nosowicz, 'EU Border Carbon Adjustment and the WTO: Hand in Hand towards Tackling Climate Change' (2020) 15 (1) *GTCJ* 15–23 at 16; Pauwelyn and Kleimann, 'Trade Related Aspects of a Carbon Border Adjustment Mechanism' (2020), p. 5.

80 Reinhard Quick, 'Carbon Border Adjustment. A Dissenting View on its Alleged GATT-Compatibility' (2020) 4 *ZEuS* 549–597 at 564–565; Mehling, et al., 'Designing Border Carbon Adjustments' (2019) 459; Pander Maat, 'The Carbon Border Adjustment Mechanism' (2022), p. 153. For an opinion in favour of considering it a regulation, see Gisselman, et al., 'Border Carbon Adjustments' (2020), p. 3.

81 Englisch and Falcão, 'EU Carbon Border Adjustments and WTO Law, Part One' (2021) 10866–10867; Venzke and Vidigal, 'Are Unilateral Trade Measures in the Climate Crisis the End of Differentiated Responsibilities?' (2022), p. 197.

82 Panel Report, *Argentina – Hides and Leather*, WT/DS155/R, 19 December 2000, para. 11.143.

importers.[83] The Commission tries to portray the CBAM as a regulatory measure,[84] apparently due to its regulatory purpose to induce change in the behaviour of third countries.[85] The designation by national authorities of a measure as a tax, charge, or regulation is, however, irrelevant for the assessment under WTO rules. Thus, despite its alleged regulatory purpose of inducing change, the CBAM still does impose a pecuniary burden and obligation to purchase certificates on importers. Similarly, the CJEU's conclusion that the obligation to buy allowances under the Aviation Directive 2008/101 does not constitute a duty, tax, fee, or a charge[86] is not determinative for the analysis under WTO law. Nevertheless, decisions of other courts could help WTO adjudicators to establish the ordinary meaning of a term in accordance with Article 31 (1) Vienna Convention on the Law of Treaties (VCLT) [87] when panels consider them informative.[88] Thus, according to the CJEU, the ETS scheme as amended by the Aviation Directive did not constitute a tax or charge on fuel consumption, since it was not intended to generate revenue for public authorities and did not establish 'a basis of assessment and a rate defined in advance, of an amount that must be payable per tonne of fuel consumed for all the flights carried out in a calendar year'.[89] Instead, under the ETS amended scheme, aircraft operators did not necessarily bear costs if they participated in the allowance-trading scheme or could even make profit from transactions with the allowances, and the actual cost was market based.[90] The CBAM, however, differs in both respects, as there is no market for CBAM certificates, nor can they be obtained free of charge or resold to other declarants for profit.[91] Accordingly, the CJEU's decision should not be an impediment to consider the CBAM a charge.

[83] Gisselman, et al., 'Border Carbon Adjustments' (2020), p. 39.

[84] Impact Assessment Report, Part 1/2, p. 27; CBAM Regulation, Preamble, Recitals (15), (20), (73).

[85] Flett, 'The European Union Carbon Border Adjustment Mechanism' (2022), p. 287.

[86] CJEU, Case C-366/10, *Air Transport Association of America and Others v Secretary of State for Energy and Climate Change*, Judgment of the Grand Chamber [2011] ECR I-13755, para. 143.

[87] Vienna Convention on the Law of Treaties, Vienna, 23 May 1969, in force 27 January 1980, 1155 U.N.T.S. 331; (1969) 8 ILM 679; UKTS (1980) 58.

[88] Cornelia Furculita, *The WTO and the New Generation EU FTA Dispute Settlement Mechanisms: Interacting in a Fragmented and Changing International Trade Law Regime* (Cham: Springer, 2021), pp. 314–317.

[89] CJEU, Case C-366/10, *Air Transport Association of America*, para. 143.

[90] ibid, para. 142.

[91] Venzke and Vidigal, 'Are Unilateral Trade Measures in the Climate Crisis the End of Differentiated Responsibilities?' (2022), p. 199.

The next question is whether the CBAM is a border or an internal measure. The difficulty in establishing under which type a measure falls lies in the fact that the moment of collection of the charge is not determinative for its nature; a customs duty could be collected after the importation, and an internal charge could be collected at the border.[92] Rather, what matters is the factor triggering a charge. Thus, if the obligation to pay a charge accrues because of an internal factor, such as because of reselling or using a product internally, it would be considered an internal one.[93] This principle is explicitly enshrined in *Ad* Note to Article III GATT stating that any internal tax or charge 'which applies to an imported product and to the like domestic product and is collected or enforced in the case of the imported product at the time or point of importation' is nevertheless considered an internal tax or other internal charge.

The CBAM may seem to impose obligations on authorized declarants that accrue upon importation of certain products. Accordingly, it could be claimed that the CBAM is a border charge 'imposed on or in connection with the importation in excess' of bound tariffs (the maximum tariffs that a Member may apply to the products listed in that Member's list) in violation of Article II:1 (b) GATT prohibiting such measures.[94] However, the CBAM could fall under the limitation contained in Article II:2 (a) and/or Article III:2 GATT together with *Ad* Note to Article III. Thus, it could be claimed that the CBAM is exempted from the obligation contained in Article II:1 (b)[95] by virtue of falling under Article II:2 (a), which establishes that nothing in Article II shall prevent the imposition at any time on the importation of any product of

> a charge equivalent to an internal tax imposed consistently with the provisions of paragraph 2 of Article III in respect of the like domestic product or in respect of an article from which the imported product has been manufactured or produced in whole or in part.

92 Appellate Body Report, *China – Auto Parts*, WT/DS342/AB/R, 15 December 2008, para. 158.

93 ibid, para. 162.

94 See, for example, James Bacchus, 'Legal Issues with the European Carbon Border Adjustment Mechanism' (2021) CATO Briefing Paper No. 125, www.cato.org/sites/cato.org/files/2021-08/briefing-paper-125.pdf; Sakuya (Yoshida) Sato, 'EU's Carbon Border Adjustment Mechanism: Will It Achieve Its Objective(s)?' (2021) 56(3) *JWT* 383–404 at 396.

95 Such a reading of the relationship between Arts. II:1(b) and II:2(a) was confirmed in Appellate Body Report, *India – Additional Import Duties*, WT/DS360/AB/R, 30 October 2008, para. 153.

Since the CBAM establishes the obligation to buy and surrender CBAM certificates with the purpose to mirror the ETS scheme imposing the obligation on domestic installation to buy or receive emissions allowances, it could also be argued that it would fall under Article III:2 read together with *Ad* Note to Article III, making it an internal charge.[96]

What is less clear, however, is the relationship between Articles II:2 (a) and III:2 GATT read together with *Ad* Note to Article III. Many authors seem to support the interpretation that Article II:2 (a) simply parallels *Ad* Note to Article III, having the same scope.[97] According to such an interpretation, measures adjusted at the border under Article II:2 (a) would be exempted from Article II:1 (b) obligation, as they would be triggered by internal factors and would, therefore, be analyzed under Article III:2.[98] Such an interpretation seems also supported by the panel's reasoning in *Argentina – Hides and Leather*, where it concluded that a measure applied only to imports at the time and point of importation was *equivalent* to a domestic measure and, according to *Ad* Note to Article III, was an internal measure within the meaning of Article III:2 GATT.[99] Thus, the panel used language similar to that of Article II:2 (a) and equated it with a measure falling under *Ad* Note Article III. On the other hand, there are authors that differentiate between the scope of these articles and distinguish between measures akin to customs duties *equivalent* to an international tax falling under Article II:2 (a) that needs to comply with Article III:2 requirements and measures that are an integral part of an internal tax according to *Ad* Note to Article III.[100] Hence, in case of the former, the measures concerned will still remain border measures, while in case of

96 Venzke and Vidigal, 'Are Unilateral Trade Measures in the Climate Crisis the End of Differentiated Responsibilities?' (2022), pp. 197–198.

97 Mehling, et al., 'Designing Border Carbon Adjustments for Enhanced Climate Action' (2019) 458; Gisselman, et al., 'Border Carbon Adjustments' (2020), p. 38; Dias, Seeuws, and Nosowicz, 'EU Border Carbon Adjustment and the WTO' (2020) 16; Quick, 'Carbon Border Adjustment' (2020) 568.

98 Mehling, et al., 'Designing Border Carbon Adjustments for Enhanced Climate Action' (2019) 458; Quick, 'Carbon Border Adjustment' (2020) 568.

99 Panel Report, *Argentina – Hides and Leather*, WT/DS155/R, paras. 11.149-11.154.

100 Joost Pauwelyn, 'Carbon Leakage Measures and Border Tax Adjustments under WTO Law', in Geert Van Calster and Denise Prévost (eds.), *Research Handbook on Environment, Health and the WTO* (Cheltenham: Edward Elgar Publishing, 2013), pp. 474–475; Simon Lester, Bryan Mercurio, and Arwel Davies, *World Trade Law: Text, Materials and Commentary*, 3rd ed. (Oxford: Hart Publishing, 2018), p. 235; Englisch and Falcão, 'EU Carbon Border Adjustments and WTO Law, Part One' (2021) 10864–10865; Venzke and Vidigal, 'Are Unilateral Trade Measures in the Climate Crisis the End of Differentiated Responsibilities?' (2022), p. 197, fn. 42.

the latter they will be considered internal ones. Such an interpretation seems also supported by the statement of the Appellate Body (AB) in *India – Additional Import Duties*: '[w]hether a measure is a "charge" to which Article II:2 (a) applies, *or* an "internal tax or other internal charge" referred to in the *Ad* Note to Article III, has to be decided in the light of the characteristics of the measure and the circumstances of the case' (emphasis added).[101]

The second approach seems to be more in line with the principle of effective interpretation, imparting meaning to the terms of Article II:2 (a): 'a charge *equivalent* to an internal tax' (emphasis added), which stand in contrast to the wording of the Note *Ad* Article III referring to 'any internal tax or other internal charge'. Moreover, in line with Article 31 (1) VCLT, this interpretation is also supported by the context of these provisions, Art. II:2 (a) being part of Article II dedicated to border measures, while Article III covers internal ones.[102] Since the CBAM obligations to buy and surrender CBAM allowances seek to mirror the ETS obligations but do not impose the same obligations as under the ETS scheme,[103] it would most logically be considered a charge *equivalent* to an internal tax under Article II:2 (a) GATT. Still, in a an un-appealed finding with respect to Note *Ad* Article III, the panel in *EC – Asbestos* said that '[w]e therefore consider that the word "comme" cannot be interpreted as requiring an identical measure to be applied to imported products and domestic products if Article III is to apply.'[104] It has also been argued that the CBAM and the ETS are different mechanisms used for collecting the same charge in line with *Ad* Note to Article III.[105] Due to the fact that the CBAM provides an entirely separate and quite distinct mechanism to charge carbon emissions than that used under the ETS scheme, such a conclusion is deemed here an erroneous one. Nevertheless, considering the ambivalent academic views and jurisprudence, the CBAM could be considered under Article II:2 (a) *and/or* Article III:2 GATT. Since the analysis of the CBAM under Article II:2 (a) in any case requires also an assessment of the compatibility with

[101] Appellate Body Report, *India – Additional Import Duties*, WT/DS360/AB/R, fn. 304 to para. 153. Statement also endorsed in Appellate Body Report, *China – Auto Parts*, WT/DS342/AB/R, fn. 233 to para. 171.

[102] Englisch and Falcão, 'EU Carbon Border Adjustments and WTO Law, Part One' (2021) 10865.

[103] For the differences, see Section 10.2.1.

[104] Panel Report, *EC – Asbestos*, WT/DS135/R, 18 September 2000, para. 8.94.

[105] Venzke and Vidigal, 'Are Unilateral Trade Measures in the Climate Crisis the End of Differentiated Responsibilities?' (2022), pp. 197–198.

Article III:2 requirements, in what follows the chapter will proceed with it. Therefore, the conclusions reached in the next section will be pertinent in case of either of the possible interpretations adopted with respect to the relationship between Articles II:2 (a) and III:2 read together with Note *Ad* Article III.

10.4.1.2 CBAM and Article II:2 (a) GATT Requirements

For the CBAM to fall under the limitation contained in Article II:2 (a) GATT, besides being a charge, it shall comply with several additional requirements: (1) to be 'equivalent to an internal tax'; (2) imposed consistently with Article III:2 requirements; and (3) 'in respect of the like domestic product or in respect of an article from which the imported product has been manufactured or produced in whole or in part'.

(1) Equivalent to an Internal Tax

The Commission portrays the CBAM as the equivalent of the ETS. While the ETS clearly has an internal nature, the question is whether it could be considered a 'tax' in the sense of Article II:2 (a) GATT. Unlike Note *Ad* Article III that states 'tax or charge', Article II:2 (a) GATT uses the term 'tax' only with respect to the measure with which the adjusted one should be equivalent. As mentioned earlier, the CJEU already concluded that the ETS does not constitute a tax; however, this conclusion is irrelevant for the interpretation of Article II:2 (a) GATT, unless a panel considers it informative.[106] Some authors used definitions of 'tax' as provided by the *Oxford English Dictionary*, requiring *inter alia* a fixed rate of a compulsory contribution,[107] or that used by the Organisation for Economic Co-operation and Development (OECD) in 1996, according to which taxes are 'compulsory, unrequited payments to general government',[108] claiming that it represents subsequent practice and that it has been referenced in the 1970 GATT Report of the Working Party on Border Tax Adjustments (WP on BTAs).[109,110] As the prices of ETS allowances are determined through auction, allowances can be resold to private parties, and some are allocated for free, the ETS would not qualify as a

106 See Section 10.4.1.1.

107 Sato, 'EU's Carbon Border Adjustment Mechanism' (2021) 396–397.

108 OECD, Definition of Taxes (Note by the Chairman), Negotiating Group on the Multilateral Agreement on Investment (MAI), 19 April 1996, DAFFE/MAI/EG2(96)3.

109 GATT Report of the Working Party, Border Tax Adjustments (WP on BTAs), 2 December 1970, L/3464.

110 Will, *Climate Border Adjustments and WTO Law* (2019), p. 118.

contribution of a fixed rate paid to the government.[111] However, while using the definition provided by the *Oxford English Dictionary* is informative, interpretation should be a holistic exercise, as a treaty shall be interpreted as a whole.[112] The meaning of a term should not be established in abstract, but in its context as required by Article 31 VCLT.[113] The relevance of the 1996 OECD definition is also questionable, since it is not (and due to its later nature could not be) referenced in the 1970 GATT WP on BTAs, the Report only referring to the OECD definition of border tax adjustments and 'taxes occultes'[114] but not to a definition for the term 'tax'.[115] If, nevertheless, a restrictive interpretation were adopted and the CBAM were considered a border charge, it would violate Article II:1 (b) GATT, unless considered an internal tax and/or regulation under Articles III:2 and/or III:4 GATT.

The term 'tax' as used in Article II:2 (a) GATT is, however, likely to be interpreted by WTO adjudicators as encompassing charges as well. Such an interpretation would be supported by the context of the phrase 'internal tax' that is followed by the requirement to be imposed consistently with Article III:2 GATT referring to 'internal taxes *or other internal charges of any kind*' (emphasis added).[116] Indeed, there is no textual indication that parties intended Article II:2 (a) GATT to allow the adjustment of a border charge equivalent only to an internal tax but not a charge, while *Ad* Note Article III GATT permits internal taxes as well as other internal charges that apply to both imported and like domestic products that are collected at the time or point of importation in case of imported products. This interpretation could be further supported by GATT preparatory work, which also uses the term 'duties' besides or instead of the term 'tax' when referring to Article II:2 (a),[117] denoting that the term 'tax'

[111] Sato, 'EU's Carbon Border Adjustment Mechanism' (2021) 397; Will, *Climate Border Adjustments and WTO Law* (2019), pp. 118–120. (According to him, when allowances are resold, at least at the stage of distribution, the government receives a payment, which is not the case when allowances are allocated for free.)

[112] Appellate Body Report, *Korea – Dairy*, WT/DS98/AB/R, 14 December 1999, para. 81

[113] Mark E. Villiger, *Commentary on the 1969 Vienna Convention on the Law of Treaties* (Leiden: Martinus Nijhoff Publishers, 2009), p. 427, para. 10.

[114] In this respect, see OECD Report, Border Tax Adjustments and Tax Structures in OECD Member Countries (1968).

[115] WP on BTAs, paras. 4, 15 (a).

[116] The cross-reference to the entire Art. III:2 GATT without any limitations is also confirmed by *Ad* Note Art. II:2 (a) (Englisch and Falcão, 'EU Carbon Border Adjustments and WTO Law, Part One' (2021) 10867).

[117] See Second Session of the Preparatory Committee of the United Nations Conference on Trade and Employment Amendments Proposed by Australian Delegation, Suggested

encompasses also other charges; and by the AB in *India – Additional Import Duties*, where it found that the measure was not justified under Article II:2 (a) GATT, as it was imposed in 'excess of the sales taxes, value-added taxes, and other local taxes *and charges*' (emphasis added).[118] Thus, the AB implicitly confirmed that the term 'tax' in the sense of Article II:2 (a) GATT has to be interpreted broadly to encompass also charges.[119] Still, even if the term 'tax' encompasses other charges, as already mentioned, a 'charge' signifies a 'pecuniary burden'. However, as long as free allowances are allocated, the ETS might not qualify even under the broader understanding of the 'internal tax' encompassing charges. Thus, without complying with Article II:2 (a) conditions, it could be that before the complete phase-out of free ETS allowances, the CBAM might be found in violation of Article II:1 (b) GATT.

The AB in *India – Additional Import Duties* stated that 'these two concepts – "equivalence" and "consistency with Article III:2" – cannot be interpreted in isolation from each other; they impart meaning to each other and need to be interpreted harmoniously'.[120] Therefore, whether the CBAM, as a charge, is equivalent to the ETS (were it considered an internal tax) will be examined together with the analysis of 'consistency with Article III:2'.

(2) '[I]n respect of the like domestic **product** *or in respect of an article* **from which the imported product has been manufactured or produced in whole or in part'**

Before examining the compliance with Article III:2 GATT requirements, it would be logical to first see if the CBAM can be even considered to be imposed on a *product* or an *article* from which the imported product has been manufactured or produced in whole or in part. Hence, even if the

Addition to Article II of the Draft General Agreement on Tariffs and Trade and Possibly a Corresponding Addition to Article 15 of the Draft Charter, E/PC/T/W/112, 24 May 1947; Second Session of the Preparatory Committee of the United Nations Conference on Trade and Employment, Verbatim Report, Twenty-Sixth Meeting of the Tariff Agreement Committee, E/PC/T/TAC/PV/26, 23 September 1947, p. 21; also mentioned by Englisch and Falcão, 'EU Carbon Border Adjustments and WTO Law, Part One' (2021) 10867.

[118] Appellate Body Report, *India – Additional Import Duties*, WT/DS360/AB/R, para. 221. As noted by Venzke and Vidigal, 'Are Unilateral Trade Measures in the Climate Crisis the End of Differentiated Responsibilities?' (2022), pp. 198–199, fn. 42.

[119] This would not be unusual for WTO jurisprudence. Similarly, the phrase 'like products' has been interpreted differently in terms of its broadness in different WTO provisions. In this respect, see Won-Mog Choi, *'Like Products' in International Trade Law: Towards a Consistent GATT/WTO Jurisprudence* (New York: Oxford University Press, 2003).

[120] Appellate Body Report, *India – Additional Import Duties*, WT/DS360/AB/R, para. 170.

ETS is considered an internal tax within the meaning of Article II:2 (a) GATT, there are other questions left.

First, there is general agreement, confirmation of which is also found in the 1970 WP on BTAs, that only indirect taxes – that is, those that concern products and not producers (the last being considered direct taxes) – are adjustable under both Articles II and III GATT.[121] Accordingly, this question is relevant also in case the CBAM is considered either solely or simultaneously under Article III:2 GATT. The question arises whether it could be considered that the CBAM imposes an indirect tax, especially since it tackles GHG emissions that are not present in the final product. Thus, it could be said that with its obligation to buy and surrender CBAM certificates corresponding to the amount of total embedded *direct* emissions, the Regulation imposes a carbon charge on inputs that are nevertheless consumed during the production process of a product. While WTO rules, such as the non-discrimination obligations do not per se prohibit taxes on non-product-related production processes,[122] the question of their adjustability under Articles II and III GATT is not a straightforward one. As the WP on BTAs noted, there was divergence on the issue of 'taxes occultes' that are 'consumption taxes on capital equipment, auxiliary materials and services used in the transportation and production of other taxable goods', such as taxes on energy.[123] The WTO Secretariat's position has also been ambivalent in this respect.[124]

While Article II:2 (a) clearly covers charges on inputs, it is less clear if it also refers to inputs that would not be physically incorporated into the final product.[125] Some authors argue in favour of the eligibility of carbon taxes for border adjustment so that it corresponds to the rebate of the same tax on the export side, which is allegedly permitted under the rules

[121] WP on BTAs, para. 14.

[122] Flett, 'The European Union Carbon Border Adjustment Mechanism' (2022), p. 280.

[123] ibid, para. 15 (a).

[124] For example, in 2004 the WTO Secretariat stated that taxes and charges on processes cannot be adjusted at the border, while in 2009, in a Report issued together with United Nations Environment Programme (UNEP), it is only mentioned that there is an 'extensive discussion' on whether energy inputs and fossil fuels used in the production process are covered by Art. II:2 (a) (WTO, 'Trade and Environment at the WTO' (2004), www.wto.org/english/tratop_e/envir_e/envir_wto2004_e.pdf, p. 21; Ludivine Tamiotti, et. al, 'Trade and Climate Change' (2009) WTO-UNEP Report, www.wto.org/english/res_e/booksp_e/trade_climate_change_e.pdf, p. 104).

[125] Pauwelyn, 'Carbon Leakage Measures' (2013), p. 478; Gisselman, et al., 'Border Carbon Adjustments' (2020), p. 41; Englisch and Falcão, 'EU Carbon Border Adjustments and WTO Law, Part One' (2021) 10868.

on export subsidies.[126] Some consider that carbon taxes should be considered as being indirect by virtue of being a cost component of the price of the final product.[127] Others refer to the GATT Panel decision in the *US – Superfund* case, where the panel allowed the imposition of a tax on certain imported substances that was equal to the amount of the tax that would have been imposed on the 'chemicals used as materials in the manufacture or production of the imported substance',[128] as a confirmation of border adjustability of charges related to production methods.[129] Still, the *US – Superfund* seems inconclusive, as it did not answer the question whether physical presence of the chemicals in the final product was necessary.[130] Article III:2 GATT provides that imported products 'shall not be subject, directly or *indirectly*, to internal taxes or other internal charges of any kind in excess of those applied, directly or *indirectly*, to like domestic products' (emphasis added). Some authors refer to the word 'indirectly' (used only in this article) and interpret it in favour of adjustability of inputs consumed during production processes.[131] Such an interpretation would be beneficial for the EU's CBAM if it is analyzed

[126] For example, Mitsuo Matsushita, et al., *The World Trade Organization. Law, Practice, and Policy*, 3rd ed. (New York: Oxford University Press, 2015), p. 766; Pauwelyn, 'Carbon Leakage Measures' (2013), pp. 475–476; Zaker Ahmad, *WTO Law and Trade Policy Reform for Low-Carbon Technology Diffusion. Common Concern of Humankind, Carbon Pricing, and Export Credit Support* (Leiden, Boston: Brill 2021), pp. 166–167. Paragraph (g) of Annex I, Agreement on Subsidies and Countervailing Measures, 15 April 1994, Marrakesh Agreement Establishing the World Trade Organization, Annex 1A, 1869 U.N.T.S. 14. (SCM Agreement) on export subsidies suggests that the adjustment upon exports of border 'indirect taxes in excess of those levied in respect of the *production* and *distribution* of like products' (emphasis added), and thus potentially also of production method taxes, is permitted. Furthermore, paragraph (h) of the same Annex explicitly allows the border adjustability upon exports of prior-stage cumulative indirect taxes, even when levied on 'inputs that are consumed in the production of the exported product' (Pauwelyn, 'Carbon Leakage Measures' (2013), p. 479, fn. 85; Joel P. Trachtman, 'WTO Law Constraints on Border Tax Adjustment and Tax Credit Mechanisms to Reduce the Competitive Effects of Carbon Taxes' (2016) Resources for the Future Discussion Paper, https://media.rff.org/documents/RFF-DP-16-03.pdf, p. 40).

[127] Pauwelyn, 'Carbon Leakage Measures' (2013), p. 480; Englisch and Falcão, 'EU Carbon Border Adjustments and WTO Law, Part One' (2021) 10868; Ahmad, *WTO Law and Trade Policy Reform for Low-Carbon Technology Diffusion* (2021), p. 166.

[128] GATT Panel Report, *US – Superfund*, L/6175 – 34S/136, 17 June 1987, para. 5.2.8.

[129] For example, Dias, Seeuws, and Nosowicz, 'EU Border Carbon Adjustment and the WTO' (2020) 17.

[130] WTO, 'Trade and Environment at the WTO' (2004), fn. 222; Pauwelyn, 'Carbon Leakage Measures' (2013), p. 479; Mehling, et al., 'Designing Border Carbon Adjustments' (2019) 458–459; Englisch and Falcão, 'EU Carbon Border Adjustments and WTO Law, Part One' (2021) 10869.

[131] Dias, Seeuws, and Nosowicz, 'EU Border Carbon Adjustment and the WTO' (2020) 16–17.

under Article III:2 GATT alone or under Articles II:2 (a) and III:2 GATT if they are considered to have the same scope.[132]

There are also authors that are against the adjustability of 'taxes occultes'. Proponents of a narrow interpretation often refer to French and Spanish versions which, according to Article 33 (1) VCLT in connection with last paragraph WTO Agreement,[133] are equally authoritative. Thus, instead of the term 'article', these versions use terms that would translate as merchandise ('*marchandise*'/'*mercancia*'), suggesting that it only refers to tangible inputs; furthermore, the French version expressly provides that the merchandise shall be incorporated in the imported product ('*ou une marchandise qui a été incorporée dans l'article importé*').[134] During the preparatory work, in response to a question related to English and French drafts of Article II:2 (a), the Chairman of the Preparatory Committee noted that he does 'not quite see how an article could serve the production and at the same time not enter into the composition of the final product',[135] providing further support for precluding border adjustment of charges on intangible inputs.

Even if a broader interpretation of Article II:2 (a) GATT would be accepted to allow the adjustability of charges on inputs that have no physical presence in the final product, it is highly unlikely that it could also cover indirect emissions released during the production of electricity consumed during the production processes of final goods, that are, nevertheless taken into account when calculating the embedded emissions initially in certain goods, and – after further revisions – expected to be taken into account in case of all covered goods. While in case of direct emissions resulting from the production process of the final product, the carbon charge has a close nexus to that *product* and *articles* from which it was produced, in case of indirect emissions resulting from a previous industrial stage, the carbon charge would hardly qualify as a charge on

[132] See, for example, how Englisch and Falcão argue in favour of a broader interpretation of Art. III:2 that would allow to adjust charges on inputs consumed during the production process (Englisch and Falcão, 'EU Carbon Border Adjustments and WTO Law, Part One' (2021) 10870–10871). For the debate on the relationship between Arts. II:2 (a) and III:2, see section 10.4.1.1.

[133] Marrakesh Agreement Establishing the World Trade Organization, 15 April 1994, 1867 U.N.T.S. 154, 33 I.L.M. 1144 (1994).

[134] Englisch and Falcão, 'EU Carbon Border Adjustments and WTO Law, Part One' (2021) 10870.

[135] Second Session of the Preparatory Committee of the United Nations Conference on Trade and Employment, Verbatim Report, Twenty-Seventh Meeting of the Tariff Agreement Committee, E/PC/T/TAC/PV/27, 24 September 1947, pp. 3–4.

the final *product* or *article* from which it was produced.[136] Thus, the EU cannot invoke Article II:2 (a) GATT as a self-standing limitation to Article II:1 (b) or read together with Article III:2 GATT in respect to CBAM's pricing of indirect emissions.

What exactly a carbon border adjustment mechanism charges has also been surrounded by ambiguity. In a 2011 WTO Staff Working Paper, the authors claimed that a tax on GHG emissions would address outputs and not inputs (whether or not physically present)[137] – an interpretation that would unequivocally disqualify the CBAM from Article II:2 (a) GATT. On the other hand, Howse argues that the phrase 'carbon tax' leads to semantic confusion suggesting that the carbon itself is taxed when in fact carbon taxes are 'applied to products or inputs in products', the physical presence of inputs being irrelevant.[138] In support, Howse refers to the *US – Superfund* case in which the panel stated that 'the tax on certain chemicals, being a tax *directly imposed on products*, was eligible for border tax adjustment independent of the purpose it served' (emphasis added).[139] The obligation on authorized declarants to buy and surrender a number of CBAM certificates corresponding to the total amount of embedded GHG emissions,[140] especially in case of indirect emissions, could hardly be perceived as a charge imposed *directly* on the covered goods. Accordingly, Howse's argument is unlikely to be applicable to the EU's CBAM.

Since only indirect taxes can be adjusted under both Article II:2 (a) and III:2 read together with *Ad* Note Article III GATT, the present analysis is also pertinent in case CBAM is analyzed under the last.

(3) Article III:2 GATT Requirements

Assuming that the CBAM qualifies under the requirements examined in the previous sections, it would still have to be considered 'equivalent' to an internal tax imposed 'consistently with Article III:2 GATT

[136] Pauwelyn, 'Carbon Leakage Measures' (2013), p. 480; Englisch and Falcão, 'EU Carbon Border Adjustments and WTO Law, Part One' (2021) 10871, 10872.

[137] Patrick Low, Gabrielle Marceau, and Julia Reinaud, 'The Interface Between the Trade and Climate Change Regimes: Scoping the Issues' (2011) WTO Staff Working Paper ERSD-2011-1, www.wto.org/english/res_e/reser_e/ersd201101_e.pdf, pp. 5, 8, fn. 9.

[138] Robert Howse, 'Distinguished Essay: Non-tariff Barriers and Climate Policy: Border-Adjusted Taxes and Regulatory Measures as WTO-Compliant Climate Mitigation Strategies', in Christoph Herrmann, et al. (eds.), *European Yearbook of International Economic Law* (Berlin, Heidelberg: Springer, 2015), pp. 6–7.

[139] ibid, p. 7; GATT Panel Report, *US – Superfund*, L/6175 – 34S/136, para. 5.2.4.

[140] CBAM Regulation, Arts. 6 (2) (c), 22 (1).

requirements' in respect to like domestic products. As already stated, according to the jurisprudence, these two requirements must be read together, imparting meaning to each other.[141] Furthermore, the AB established that the analysis of consistency with Article III:2 GATT requirements 'forms an integral part' of the assessment of equivalence between a charge and an import tax.[142] Insofar as Article III:2 GATT is not complied with, a charge imposed upon importation and an internal tax will not be considered equivalent in the sense of Article II:2 (a) GATT.

Article III:2 GATT has two functions: as an element in the analysis under Article II:2 GATT and as a separate rule. As argued, although this chapter considers Article II:2 (a) GATT as the appropriate avenue for the CBAM, it is not precluded that the CBAM could be considered exclusively under Article III:2 GATT if considered an internal tax, in which case the present section will be equally relevant.

Article III:2 GATT contains two different sentences establishing the NT obligation for fiscal measures. While the first sentence contemplates the NT obligation for the category of 'like products' referring to 'perfectly substitutable' products, the second sentence addresses a broader category of products – 'directly competitive or substitutable products', which are nevertheless 'imperfectly substitutable products'.[143] For a violation of Article III:2, first sentence, there are two cumulative questions that should be answered affirmatively: (1) whether imported and domestic products are 'like' and (2) whether imported products are taxed 'in excess' of the domestic ones. If the answer to at least one of these questions is negative, a measure could still violate the second sentence of Article III:2 GATT.

As will be shown, the products covered by the CBAM and the domestic products subject to the ETS if deemed an internal tax will most probably be considered 'like', regardless of their carbon footprint. In order to assess the likeness of products, as already mentioned in a previous chapter,[144] the relevant factors are physical properties, end-uses, consumers' tastes and habits, and tariff classification.[145] The argument that the regulatory

[141] Appellate Body Report, *India – Additional Import Duties*, WT/DS360/AB/R, paras. 170, 180.

[142] ibid, para. 181.

[143] Appellate Body Report, *Korea – Taxes on Alcoholic Beverages*, WT/DS75/AB/R, 18 January 1999, para. 118.

[144] See Chapter 8.

[145] Appellate Body Report, *Japan – Taxes on Alcoholic Beverages*, WT/DS8/AB/R, 4 October 1996, p. 20; Panel Report, *Argentina – Hides and* Leather, WT/DS155/R, para. 11.167; Appellate Body Report, *EC – Asbestos*, WT/DS135/AB/R, 12 March 2001, para. 109.

purpose of a measure, known as the 'aims and effects' test, should inform the assessment of 'likeness' of imported and domestic products has been clearly rejected by WTO jurisprudence.[146] Accordingly, the CBAM's purpose to prevent carbon leakage should not weigh in on the likeness of imported and domestic products.

Production methods and processes are generally irrelevant for the question of 'likeness', unless they leave physical traces.[147] There seem to be no physical differences between the CBAM-covered imported products and the identical domestic counterparts, even if their carbon footprints differ, since the latter leave no physical traces. Identical imported and domestic products are also expected to have the same end-uses. Moreover, as the current tariff classifications do not differentiate between products based on their carbon footprint, it can be assumed that identical imported and domestic products will have the same classification.[148] Thus, these three criteria seem to indicate that CBAM covered products and their domestic counterparts are 'like' in the sense of Article III:2 GATT, first sentence,[149] as they seem perfectly substitutable.

The only criterion that could change this conclusion is consumers' tastes and habits. Thus, the question arises if consumers differentiate between the same products but with different carbon footprints. In *EC – Asbestos*, the AB considered that the health risks associated with chrysotile asbestos fibres that are known to be carcinogenic, which is also reflected in their physical properties, were likely to shape consumers' tastes and habits in respect to these fibres and products containing them.[150]

[146] Appellate Body Report, *Japan – Taxes on Alcoholic Beverages*, WT/DS8/AB/R, pp. 16-18; Appellate Body Report, *EC – Seal Products*, WT/DS400/AB/R, WT/DS400/AB/R, WT/DS401/AB/R, 22 May 2014, para. 5.114. Lester, Mercurio, and Davies, *World Trade Law* (2018), p. 279; Timothy Meyer and Todd N. Tucker, 'A Pragmatic Approach to Carbon Border Measures' (2022) 21 *WTRev* 109–120 at 116. This approach has been criticized by some (Timothy Meyer and Todd N. Tucker, 'Trade and Climate, Law and Politics: A Response' (2022) 21 *WTRev* 127–129 at 127.

[147] Michael A. Mehling and Robert A. Ritz, 'Going Beyond Default Intensities in an EU Carbon Border Adjustment Mechanism' (2020) Energy Policy Research Group Paper, www.jstor.org/stable/resrep30315#metadata_info_tab_contents, p. 9; Quick, 'Carbon Border Adjustment' (2020) 573–574; Weiß, *WTO Law and Domestic Regulation* (München, Oxford, Baden-Baden: Hart/Beck/Nomos, 2020), pp. 187 f.

[148] Quick, 'Carbon Border Adjustment' (2020) 573.

[149] Conclusion generally supported by the academic literature. See, for example, Mehling, et al., 'Designing Border Carbon Adjustments' (2019) 461; Pauwelyn and Kleimann, 'Trade Related Aspects of a Carbon Border Adjustment Mechanism' (2020), p. 9; Englisch and Falcão, 'EU Carbon Border Adjustments and WTO Law, Part One' (2021) 10875; Meyer and Tucker, 'A Pragmatic Approach to Carbon Border Measures' (2022) 116.

[150] Appellate Body Report, *EC – Asbestos*, WT/DS135/AB/R, paras. 114, 122, 130. 136, 142, 145.

The AB reached this conclusion even if the primer consumers of fibres or chrysotile-fibre products could have been manufacturers or other commercial parties.[151] Nevertheless, chrysotile fibres had also a different tariff classification than other considered fibres and shared only a small number of similar end-uses.[152] Still, since the complainant did not submit any evidence with respect to consumers' tastes and habits, the AB warned that 'this is only speculation',[153] emphasizing that what matters is whether there is a competitive relationship between the products.[154] While some authors consider that it is possible that consumers will differentiate between CBAM covered and non-covered products based on their carbon footprint,[155] even more seem to argue that such a conclusion is currently less probable.[156] Thus, compared to the health effects of carcinogenic asbestos fibres, the effects of carbon-intensive products on human health are not following directly from the decision of the consumers to buy them; therefore, potential future indirect health effects are less likely to affect consumers' tastes and habits.[157] Moreover, consumers are usually unaware of the carbon footprint of the CBAM covered commodities that are commonly used in the production of final products, as well as when they are directly sold to them.[158] Furthermore, especially since all other criteria would be pointing towards the 'likeness' of products, it is likely that convincing empirical evidence indicating upon the fact that consumers actually perceive the products as not being 'like' would be necessary. Therefore, it is reasonable to expect that domestic and imported

[151] ibid, paras. 122, 130. [152] ibid, paras. 124, 138, 140. [153] ibid, para. 145.

[154] ibid, paras. 139, 145. Aspect criticized in a separate individual opinion expressed in the report, para. 154.

[155] Howse, 'Distinguished Essay' (2015), p. 8; Gisselman, et al., 'Border Carbon Adjustments' (2020), p. 52; Venzke and Vidigal, 'Are Unilateral Trade Measures in the Climate Crisis the End of Differentiated Responsibilities?' (2022) 203.

[156] Henrik Horn and Petros C. Mavroidis, 'To B(TA) or Not to B(TA)? On the Legality and Desirability of Border Tax Adjustments from a Trade Perspective' (2011) *The World Economy* 1911–1937 at 1917; Mehling, et al., 'Designing Border Carbon Adjustments' (2019) 461; Quick, 'Carbon Border Adjustment' (2020) 573–574; Englisch and Falcão, 'EU Carbon Border Adjustments and WTO Law, Part One' (2021) 10875; Ahmad, *WTO Law and Trade Policy Reform for Low-Carbon Technology Diffusion* (2021), p. 173. For the problems of replacing a market-based likeness test by a consumer choice-related test, see Weiß, *WTO Law and Domestic Regulation* (2020), pp. 189–190; Flett, 'The European Union Carbon Border Adjustment Mechanism' (2022), p. 276.

[157] Horn and Mavroidis, 'To B(TA) or Not to B(TA)?' (2011) 1917; Mehling, et al., 'Designing Border Carbon Adjustments' (2019) 461.

[158] Englisch, Falcão, 'EU Carbon Border Adjustments and WTO Law, Part One' (2021) 10875.

products falling under the CBAM sectors will be considered 'like' within the meaning of the first sentence of Article III:2 GATT.

With respect to the second question, it is generally agreed that even the smallest amount of 'excess' would be too much, there being no *de minimis* standard.[159] The assessment of the CBAM in light of this element depends on what is compared. Thus, it is not yet settled if the entire *group* of imported product should not be taxed on the whole in excess compared to the tax on the entire *group* of domestic products (the 'asymmetric impact test'), or if any *particular* imported product should not be taxed in excess compared to any *particular* domestic one (the 'diagonal test').[160] The price of CBAM certificates is equal to the average auctioning weekly price of the ETS certificates. Furthermore, the required number of CBAM certificates, in goods other than electricity, will be calculated based on actual embedded direct emissions, when they can be adequately determined, and based on default values in case of indirect emissions, importers being able also to claim reductions for carbon prices already paid in the country of origin.[161] Thus, in case of goods for which only direct emissions are to be taken into account, the number of CBAM certificates, as well as the number of ETS allowances should depend on actual GHG emissions and not on the origin of products; and even though domestic installations will still benefit from free allowances until they are fully phased out, during this period the required number of CBAM certificates would be reduced proportionally. Therefore, the proponents of the first approach could argue that de jure imported and domestic products for which only direct emissions are taken into account are taxed the same, unless proven that they are de facto discriminated when on the whole imports have a higher footprint than domestic products.[162] As already stated, in case actual monitoring data cannot be adequately provided, a default value is set at the average emission intensity of each exporting country and for each of the goods listed in Annex I other than electricity, increased by a mark-up.[163] In the *US – Superfund* case, the panel seemed to confirm the legality under Article III:2 GATT, first sentence, in the absence of sufficient actual data, of a rate equal to the amount that would have

[159] Appellate Body Report, *Japan – Taxes on Alcoholic Beverages*, WT/DS8/AB/R, p. 23; Panel Report, *Argentina – Hides and Leather*, WT/DS155/R, para. 11.243.

[160] For a discussion, see Lester, Mercurio, and Davies, *World Trade Law* (2018), p. 279.

[161] CBAM Regulation, Arts. 7.2, 9.1, Annex IV, 4.3.

[162] See, for example, Pauwelyn and Kleimann, 'Trade Related Aspects of a Carbon Border Adjustment Mechanism' (2020), pp. 9–10.

[163] CBAM Regulation, Annex IV, 4.1.

been imposed if the substance were produced using the predominant method of production,[164] without mentioning whether it is in the United States or elsewhere. Furthermore, indirect emissions are to be determined using default values calculated on the average of either the emission factor of the Union electricity grid or of the country of origin electricity grid, or the CO_2 emission factor of price-setting sources in the country of origin, unless the declarant can demonstrate that certain conditions are met.[165] If, however, the predominant method of production in the country of origin of a product has higher carbon emission rates than within EU and/or if the average of the emission factor of the country of origin electricity grid or CO_2 emission factor of price-setting sources in that country is higher than in the EU and these benchmarks are regularly used, a de facto violation of Article III:2 GATT, first sentence, is likely under the asymmetric impact test. Moreover, in case of direct emissions, when reliable data cannot be applied for an exporting country for a type of goods, the secondary default values shall be based on the average emission intensity of the X per cent (the X value to be determined in implementing acts) of the worst-performing EU installations.[166] Thus, when secondary default values are used, all imports from that country will be treated worse than the majority of the EU installations, making the finding of a violation of Article III:2 GATT, first sentence, highly probable.

In case of the adoption of the diagonal test, a finding of a violation of Article III:2 GATT, first sentence, would be unavoidable. Even when actual emissions are used, there would always be an imported product that will have higher carbon embedded emissions than another, less 'dirty' domestic product and will, therefore, be taxed 'in excess'.[167] Same conclusion would almost certainly be reached in case of default values (both in case of primary direct and indirect emissions), as it is unlikely that another country's average will be equal to or even lower than the least carbon-intensive like domestic product in order not to be taxed 'in excess'. Moreover, a violation of Article III:2 GATT, first sentence, would be clearly found in case the default value is set according to the X per cent of the worst-performing EU installations.[168] Considering that the CBAM seems

[164] GATT Panel Report, *US – Superfund*, para. 5.2.9.

[165] CBAM Regulation, Art. 7 (4), Annex IV, 4.3, 6.

[166] CBAM Regulation, Annex IV, 4.1.

[167] Howse, 'Distinguished Essay' (2015), p. 10; Englisch and Falcão, 'EU Carbon Border Adjustments and WTO Law, Part One' (2021) 10878.

[168] Englisch and Falcão, 'EU Carbon Border Adjustments and WTO Law, Part One' (2021) 10878.

to fall under the first sentence of Article III:2 GATT violating it, the analysis under the second sentence of the same article is superfluous.[169]

To conclude, as the requirements of Article III:2 GATT will most likely not be met by the CBAM, especially in case of using default values, it will also not be able to benefit from the limitation contained in Article II:2 (a) GATT. To comply with the requirements of Article III:2 GATT, some authors advice treating imported products similar to the least carbon-intensive like domestic products.[170] Since the price paid by importers in such a case would be much lower than that paid by the majority of domestic installations, the risk of carbon leakage would not be sufficiently addressed. Accordingly, a better approach could be to rely on Article XX GATT justifications for potential violations of Articles II:1 (b) or/and Article III:2 GATT.

10.4.2 CBAM and Its Regulatory Character under Articles III:4 and XI GATT

Although the obligation to buy CBAM certificates, as argued in the previous section, will most likely be considered a charge in the sense of Articles II:1 (b), II:2 (a), and/or Article III:2 GATT, the same measure could also have regulatory aspects treated under Articles III:4 and/or XI:1 GATT.

10.4.2.1 Articles III:4 and XI:1 GATT: Applicability and Relationship

It is well established that a single measure could be subject to the disciplines of both Articles III:2 and III:4 GATT, as the same measure could have multiple aspects.[171] While Article III:2 GATT prohibits discrimination between imported and domestic like products caused by an internal tax, Article III:4 GATT prohibits discrimination between these products caused by internal regulations.[172] According to Article III:4 GATT, imported products 'shall be accorded treatment no less favourable than that accorded to like products of national origin in respect of all laws, regulations and requirements affecting their internal sale, offering for sale, purchase, transportation, distribution or use'. Besides imposing the obligation to buy certificates, the CBAM Regulation – a mandatory piece

[169] For an analysis under the second sentence of Art. III:2 GATT, see Ahmad, *WTO Law and Trade Policy Reform for Low-Carbon Technology Diffusion* (2021), pp. 179–180.

[170] Pauwelyn, 'Carbon Leakage Measures' (2013), p. 493; Mehling, et al., 'Designing Border Carbon Adjustments' (2019) 461; Quick, 'Carbon Border Adjustment' (2020) 574; Englisch and Falcão, 'EU Carbon Border Adjustments and WTO Law, Part One' (2021) 10877.

[171] Appellate Body Report, *Brazil – Taxation*, WT/DS472/AB/R, 11 January 2019, para. 5.53.

[172] ibid, para. 7.33.

of legislation – contains a sophisticated regulatory mechanism described above,[173] imposing additional obligations upon importers and rules governing the operation of certificates, such as the application for an authorization, the submission of a CBAM declaration, ensuring that the amount of declared embedded emissions is verified by an accredited verifier or using verified information from registered installations, the possibility to request the competent authorities to re-purchase a part of excess certificates purchased in a year, and the cancellation of CBAM certificates purchased during the year before the previous calendar year. Thus, it could be argued that the CBAM has also a regulatory aspect besides the fiscal one qualifying as 'laws, regulations and requirements' that could violate Article III:4 GATT.[174]

However, for a regulatory measure to fall under Article III:4, it should be an internal one, as border measures are covered by Article XI GATT. CBAM contains laws, regulations, and requirements only in case of imports of the covered products. To establish whether CBAM regulatory aspects represent border or internal measures, the question of applicability of Note *Ad* Article III arises. When the same measure applies to both domestic and imported products, it is fairly clear that Article III applies, but when there is a measure applied to imports which is related to a domestic measure, such as the CBAM that is related to the ETS, the applicability of Note *Ad* Article III is more controversial.[175] The CBAM regulatory obligations and rules described above, however, apply only to imports; there are no equivalent or even somewhat comparable rules that would apply also to like domestic products, the ETS establishing a totally different mechanism for operationalizing ETS allowances.[176] Accordingly, the CBAM's regulatory aspects could fall under the scope of Article XI:1 GATT prohibiting any 'restrictions other than duties, taxes or other charges, whether made effective through quotas, import or export licences or other measures, [...] by any contracting party on the importation of any product' from other WTO Members. However, exceptionally a single measure could simultaneously be addressed by both Articles III:4 and XI GATT, as the same

[173] For more, see Section 10.2.1.

[174] According to the panel in *India – Solar Cells*, 'the terms "laws or regulations" refer to legally enforceable rules of conduct under the domestic legal system of the WTO Member concerned' (Panel Report, *India – Solar Cells*, WT/DS456/R, 24 February 2016, para. 7.310).

[175] Lester, Mercurio, and Davies, *World Trade Law* (2018), p. 248.

[176] Venzke and Vidigal, 'Are Unilateral Trade Measures in the Climate Crisis the End of Differentiated Responsibilities?' (2022), p. 204.

measure could both affect domestic competitive opportunities and be covered by Article III:4 GATT, and also affect the opportunities of importation itself and fall under Article XI:1 GATT.[177] For a measure to fall under Article III:4, it should affect the products' 'internal sale, offering for sale, purchase, transportation, distribution or use'. The term 'affecting' the products 'internal sale, offering for sale, purchase, transportation, distribution or use' has been interpreted broadly, covering 'not only laws and regulations which directly govern the conditions of sale or purchase but also any laws or regulations which might adversely modify the conditions of competition between domestic and imported products',[178] as well as those that create incentives with respect to the sale, offering for sale, purchase, and use of an imported product.[179] Since it could be argued that the CBAM modifies the internal competition between domestic and imported products[180] while also affecting the importation opportunities of the covered products, in what follows the Regulation will be considered under both Articles III:4 and XI:1 GATT. The analysis under Article III:4 GATT becomes all the more important as the Commission seems to portray the CBAM as an internal regulation.[181]

10.4.2.2 Article III:4 GATT

After establishing whether a measure falls under the scope of Article III:4 GATT, namely qualifying as 'laws, regulations and requirements affecting their internal sale, offering for sale, purchase, transportation, distribution or use', two other elements should be present for a violation to be found: They should accord 'less favourable treatment' to imported products than to 'like' domestic products.

The term 'like' within the meaning of Article III:4 GATT is broader than under Article III:2 GATT, first sentence. It is assessed based on the same four previously named criteria,[182] but it concerns products that are in a

[177] Panel Report, *India – Autos*, WT/DS146/R, 21 December 2001, para. 7.224.

[178] Panel Report, *Canada – Autos*, WT/DS139/R, 11 February 2000, para. 10.80.

[179] Panel Report, *China – Publications and Audiovisual Products*, WT/DS363/R, 12 August 2009, para. 7.1450.

[180] For example, Gisselman, et al., 'Border Carbon Adjustments' (2020), p. 45, argues that carbon border adjustment would fall under Art. III:4 GATT.

[181] The CBAM proposal even uses Art. III:4 GATT wording, such as 'the CBAM should in no case result in more favourable treatment for Union goods compared to goods imported into the customs territory of the Union' (CBAM Regulation, Preamble, recital 12).

[182] See Section 10.4.1.2. Appellate Body Report, *EC – Asbestos*, WT/DS135/AB/R, para. 109.

competitive relationship.[183] This broader interpretation, however, certainly encompasses the narrower one found in the first sentence of Article III:2 GATT. For the analysis of the prospect of non-product-related production processes and methods, such as those related to carbon emissions, to influence the likeness of products, see Section 10.4.1.2 (3). Thus, as the CBAM Regulation has been found most likely to concern imported products identical to domestic ones, except their carbon footprint, it could be expected that it would also be considered to concern 'like' products within the broader meaning of Article III:4 GATT.

The phrase 'treatment no less favourable' has been interpreted as referring to 'effective equality of competitive opportunities' for imported products on the internal market of another WTO Member.[184] The decisive question is whether the conditions of competition are negatively affected, without the need to provide identical treatment.[185] Unlike the jurisprudence under Article III:2, first sentence, it seems generally accepted in the WTO jurisprudence, as well as literature, that under Article III:4, the *group* of imported products should be compared to the *group* of the like domestic products.[186] Thus, it has been argued that the CBAM Regulation imposes more burdensome administrative obligations impacting negatively the competitive opportunities of the group of imported products falling under its scope compared to the group of like domestic products, especially since emissions should be calculated and verified for each type of good in contrast to the ETS that applies to EU installations.[187] This means that, unless relying on default values or on information disclosed by registered operators or installations, importers will need to identify all emissions associated with the imported products by obtaining necessary information from their suppliers, which would likely entail significant administrative costs for the latter, as they will need to assign emissions to individual products.[188] Furthermore, the

[183] Appellate Body Report, *EC – Asbestos*, WT/DS135/AB/R, paras. 98–99.

[184] Appellate Body Reports, *EC – Seal Products*, WT/DS400/AB/R, WT/DS401/AB/R, para. 5.101; Panel Report, *Japan – Film*, WT/DS44/R, 31 March 1998, para. 10.379.

[185] Appellate Body Report, *Korea – Beef*, WT/DS161/AB/R, 11 December 2000, paras. 135–137; Appellate Body Report, *EC – Asbestos*, WT/DS135/AB/R, para. 100.

[186] Appellate Body Report, *EC – Asbestos*, WT/DS135/AB/R, para. 100; Lester, Mercurio, and Davies, *World Trade Law* (2018), p. 288; Giulia Claudia Leonelli, 'Carbon Border Measures, Environmental Effectiveness and WTO Law Compatibility: Is There a Way Forward for the Steel and Aluminium Climate Club?' (2022) *WTRev* 1–14 at 7; Sato, 'EU's Carbon Border Adjustment Mechanism' (2021) 395–396; Flett, 'The European Union Carbon Border Adjustment Mechanism' (2022), pp. 275–276.

[187] Sato, 'EU's Carbon Border Adjustment Mechanism' (2021) 396.

[188] ibid, 389.

rules governing the operation of the CBAM certificates, namely on their shorter validity and being non-tradable, seem less favourable than those applicable to ETS allowances,[189] especially since they might ultimately increase the final price of the imported products.

In *Dominican Republic – Cigarettes*, the AB appeared to find that regulatory distinctions would not amount to 'less favourable treatment',[190] leading some authors to argue that carbon border adjustment having a regulatory purpose would, thus, not violate Article III:4 GATT if analyzed under it.[191] However, it has been subsequently explained by the AB in other disputes that there is no need to further inquire into whether the detrimental impact stems from other factors or circumstances than the foreign origin or exclusively from a legitimate regulatory distinction.[192] Thus, despite some calls included even in a EU Commission publication in favour of taking into account the regulatory intent during the analysis under Article III:4 GATT and not solely under Article XX GATT,[193] such a position finds no support in the existing jurisprudence. While the publication in question suggests applying this approach that has been adopted in the context of NT obligation in the Technical Barriers to Trade (TBT)[194] Agreement, it finds no textual support in the GATT context. As rightly explained by the AB, the TBT agreement contains no separate general exceptions clause similar to Article XX GATT, prompting the interpretation of Article 2.1 TBT on NT accommodating legitimate regulatory distinctions in light of its context.[195] Thus, for the purpose of Article III:4 GATT it is irrelevant that the distinction between imported and domestic products under the CBAM stems from the purpose to prevent carbon leakage.

Certain differences between the CBAM Regulation and the ETS Scheme are explicitly addressed in the Preamble to the first. Thus, the Commission argues that CBAM certificates are non-tradable and expire

[189] ETS allowances are valid indefinitely and can be resold (ETS Directive, Arts. 12, 13).

[190] Appellate Body Report, *Dominica Republic – Cigarettes*, 25 April 2005, WT/DS302/AB/R, para. 98.

[191] See, for example, Howse, 'Distinguished Essay' (2015), p. 12.

[192] Appellate Body Report, *US – Clove Cigarettes*, 4 April 2012, WT/DS406/AB/R, fn. 372 to para. 179; Appellate Body Reports, *EC – Seal Products*, WT/DS400/AB/R, WT/DS401/AB/R, para. 5.105. See also Weiß, *WTO Law and Domestic Regulation* (2020), pp. 160 f.

[193] Flett, 'The European Union Carbon Border Adjustment Mechanism' (2022), pp. 275, 287.

[194] Agreement on Technical Barriers to Trade, Annex 1A to the Marrakesh Agreement, 15 April 1994, 1868 U.N.T.S. 120.

[195] Appellate Body Report, *EC – Seal Products*, WT/DS400/AB/R, WT/DS400/AB/R, WT/DS401/AB/R, paras. 5.123–5.125.

faster in order to preserve the effectiveness of the CBAM as a measure preventing carbon leakage, otherwise if CBAM certificates were carried forward, they would no longer reflect the evolution of EU ETS prices and would thus weaken the incentives to decarbonize between domestic and imported products.[196] Considering the risk of violating the NT obligation enshrined in Article III:4 GATT, but also the need to maintain the purpose of the CBAM to prevent carbon leakage, justification under Article XX GATT, under which regulatory purpose can be taken into account, would be needed.

10.4.2.3 *Article XI:1 GATT*

As the regulatory aspects of the CBAM Regulation could be considered as limiting the imports of the covered products, as argued, it must also be analyzed under Article XI:1 GATT. For a violation of Article XI:1 GATT a measure should meet two elements: (1) to qualify as 'quotas, import or export licences or other measures'; and (2) constitute a prohibition or restriction on the importation or on the exportation or sale for export of any product.[197]

The term 'or other measures' indicates, upon a broad coverage, excluding only fiscal measures or those that are excepted by the second paragraph of Article XI GATT.[198] Thus, the first element would be easily complied with by the regulatory aspects of the CBAM Regulation, which do not fall under any of the letters of Article XI:2 GATT. A 'restriction on the importation' covers measures that have a limiting effect on importation itself, 'generating a disincentive to import'.[199] The limiting effects need not be shown by quantifying them; they can be demonstrated through 'the design, architecture, and revealing structure of the measure'.[200] The mere requirement to obtain authorization before importation is not necessarily in violation of Article XI:1 GATT.[201] It could, however, be argued that the process of authorization is burdensome and a disincentive to importation, as it requires the submission of various information, such as proof of declarant's financial and operational

[196] CBAM Regulation, Preamble, recital 22.

[197] Panel Report, *EU – Energy Package*, WT/DS476/R, 10 August 2018, para. 7.243.

[198] Appellate Body Reports, *Argentina – Import Measures*, WT/DS438/AB/R, 15 January 2015, para. 5.219.

[199] Panel Report, *India – Autos*, WT/DS146/R, paras. 7.269–7.270.

[200] Appellate Body Reports, *Argentina – Import Measures*, WT/DS438/AB/R, para. 5.217.

[201] Venzke and Vidigal, 'Are Unilateral Trade Measures in the Climate Crisis the End of Differentiated Responsibilities?' (2022), p. 205.

capacity to fulfill its obligations under the CBAM Regulation, including by providing a guarantee if the applicant was not established throughout the two financial years preceding the application year, and, if considered necessary by competent authority, the provision of information on the 'profit and loss account and the balance sheet for up to the three last financial years for which the accounts were closed'.[202] Without an authorization, declarants cannot import goods into the Union's customs territory,[203] thereby the CBAM Regulation could clearly limit importation of the covered goods and violate Article XI:1 GATT, requiring justification under Article XX GATT.

10.4.3 CBAM and the Most-Favoured-Nation Principle

The CBAM Regulation could also violate the MFN principle enshrined in Article I:1 GATT by discriminating among imports from different WTO members. The MFN principle applies to both fiscal and non-fiscal measures, whether they are border or behind-the-border measures, as it states that it concerns 'customs duties and charges of any kind imposed on or in connection with importation or exportation', as well as 'all rules and formalities in connection with importation and exportation, and [...] all matters referred to in paragraphs 2 and 4 of Article III'. Thus, regardless of the qualification of the CBAM Regulation under one (or more) of the provisions described in previous sections, it would still be subject to the MFN obligation. Article I:1 GATT requires that 'any advantage, favour, privilege or immunity granted' to products of one WTO Member be accorded 'immediately and unconditionally' to the 'like product' from 'all other Members'.

Several provisions of the CBAM Regulation discriminating between products from different Members could be challenged 'as such' under Article I:1 GATT. The first and the most obvious instance is the exemption from the Regulation's scope of application of the goods originating in countries listed in Annex III which are linked to the EU ETS.[204] While the countries currently listed in this Annex have an FTA in place with the EU, making possible the invocation of Article XXIV GATT as a justification for an MFN violation, the linkage to the EU ETS is not always done by virtue of an FTA but of a Linking Agreement based on the ETS Directive.[205] The

[202] CBAM Regulation, Arts. 5 (5) (f), 17 (5). [203] ibid, Art. 25 (1). [204] ibid, Arts. 4–6.

[205] See, for example, Agreement between the European Union and the Swiss Confederation on the linking of their greenhouse gas emissions trading systems, OJ EU 2017 No. L 322/3, 7 December 2017.

condition for being included in Annex III does not hinge upon the existence of an FTA, the reason behind the exclusion being the link to the EU ETS. In addition, benefitting from Article XXIV GATT justification is less likely even in case of linkage through FTAs, since the EU could have to show that without this CBAM exemption, the formation of the FTA would have been impossible and that this measure was introduced upon formation.[206] Second, CBAM allows reductions in the number of CBAM certificates in case of declarants that already paid for emissions originating in countries with carbon pricing mechanisms.[207] Finally, the Regulation could be even accused of discriminating against countries with more carbon-intensive products.[208]

As to the 'likeness' of imported products from different countries, it would be assessed based on the same four criteria as under Articles III:2 and III:4 GATT.[209] Since under the provisions described earlier, imported products from different countries will be distinguished solely based on their origin, domestic policies of the country of origin, or carbon footprint, it is likely that the same considerations as under Articles III:2 and III:4 GATT will justify the finding that they are 'like products'. Furthermore, when the distinction is origin-based, products can be hypothetically presumed to be 'like'.[210]

A Member can be considered as granting an advantage to a product originating in a country compared to like products from other Members when their competitive opportunities are modified.[211] The regulatory intent behind a measure analyzed under Article I:1 GATT is irrelevant.[212] By excluding goods originating in specific countries from its scope of coverage and offering them the advantage of not having to buy CBAM certificates,[213] the CBAM Regulation clearly modifies the competition in favour of those products, thereby de jure discriminating in their favour. Reductions in the number of CBAM certificates due to the carbon price

206 Appellate Body Report, *Turkey – Textiles*, WT/DS34/AB/R, paras. 45–46, 58.

207 ibid, Art. 9 (1).

208 See, for example, Dias, Seeuws, and Nosowicz, 'EU Border Carbon Adjustment and the WTO' (2020) 18; Sato, 'EU's Carbon Border Adjustment Mechanism' (2021) 398–399.

209 Panel Report, *US – Poultry (China)*, WT/DS392/R, 29 September 2010 paras. 7.424–7.425.

210 Panel Report, *Colombia – Ports of Entry*, WT/DS366/R, 27 April 2009, para. 7.356.

211 Appellate Body Report, *Canada – Autos*, WT/DS139/AB/R, 31 May 2000, para. 79; 3 Appellate Body Reports, *EC – Seal Products*, WT/DS400/AB/R, WT/DS401/AB/R, para. 5.87.

212 Appellate Body Reports, *EC – Seal Products*, WT/DS400/AB/R, WT/DS401/AB/R, paras. 5.90, 5.93; Lester, Mercurio, and Davies, *World Trade Law* (2018), p. 320.

213 Venzke and Vidigal, 'Are Unilateral Trade Measures in the Climate Crisis the End of Differentiated Responsibilities?' (2022), p. 207.

already paid in the country of origin would also amount to lower financial burdens, modifying the competition in favour of products originating in countries with carbon pricing mechanisms (yet not those that have in place regulatory mechanisms).[214] While in these cases the CBAM Regulation clearly distinguishes between imports of different origins, the analysis is less straightforward when considered in the context of the CBAM provisions merely distinguishing between imported products with different carbon footprints, regardless of their origin. The answer to this question would depend on whether WTO adjudicators were to apply an asymmetric impact or diagonal test. In case the first one is applied, namely comparing all imported like products from different countries, and if the majority of products from one country are more carbon intensive, the importers of these products being mandated to pay for a higher number of CBAM certificates than the importers of products with a lower carbon footprint originating mostly from other countries, a de facto discriminatory treatment could be found.[215] In case the diagonal test is used, there will certainly be an individual more carbon-intensive imported product from a Member that would not be accorded the same advantage accorded to another individual like product with a lower carbon footprint from certain other country(ies).[216] The jurisprudence has been ambivalent in this respect. The AB used a diagonal test in *Canada – Autos*.[217] However, in a more recent dispute – *US – Tuna II (Mexico) (Article 21.5 – Mexico)* – the AB used the asymmetric approach, as it compared the treatment of the groups of products.[218] If this more recent approach is adopted, the CBAM differentiation between products with different carbon footprints has better chances to stand the test of Article I:1 GATT.

Finally, the last question is whether the 'advantage' is accorded 'immediately and unconditionally' – in other words, without delay and without conditions.[219] In the GATT dispute *Belgian Family Allowances*, the panel found that legislation discriminating between countries having a given family allowance system and those having a different system or no

[214] ibid. [215] Lester, Mercurio, and Davies, *World Trade Law* (2018), p. 320.
[216] ibid, pp. 320–321.
[217] Appellate Body Report, *Canada – Autos*, WT/DS139/AB/R, paras. 79–80.
[218] Appellate Body Report, *US – Tuna II (Mexico) (Article 21.5 – Mexico)*, WT/DS381/AB/RW, 20 November 2015, para. 7.281.
[219] Appellate Body Reports, *EC – Seal Products*, WT/DS400/AB/R, WT/DS401/AB/R, para. 5.88; Will, *Climate Border Adjustments and WTO Law* (2019), p. 183.

system at all made the granting of an advantage conditional.[220] Thus, the exemption from the coverage of the CBAM Regulation of the countries included in the Annex III list, which are fully integrated into, or linked, to the EU ETS, and the reduction in the number of CBAM certificates to be surrendered taking into account the carbon price paid in other countries would clearly differentiate between countries with different systems to the disadvantage of those that have a regulatory system or no system at all in place to address carbon emissions, making the granting of the advantage dependent on certain conditions. Even in case of countries with carbon pricing mechanisms in place but not integrated into or linked to the ETS, the CBAM would still not comply with the requirement to accord the advantage 'unconditionally', since the CBAM assumes that for a country's mechanism to be considered equivalent to that of the EU, the carbon price should be at the same level or higher, which is not always the case.[221] Many authors have criticized the CBAM for not giving credit to non-pricing carbon policies of other countries.[222] Furthermore, imposing the condition to use only carbon pricing mechanisms in order to benefit from CBAM exemptions or reductions would also be against the Paris Agreement, which seems to grant parties a choice whether to adopt pricing or non-pricing regulatory mechanisms by not imposing any obligation on the adoption of specific mitigation measures.[223] Yet, the

[220] GATT Panel Report, *Belgian Family Allowances*, G/32 – 1S/59, 7 November 1952, para. 3.

[221] CBAM Regulation, Art. 2 (6); Bixuan Wu, 'To Penalize Low Carbon Price or High Carbon Intensity? A Comparison of the EU's CBAM and the U.S. Clean Competition Act', IELP Blog, 1 July 2022, https://ielp.worldtradelaw.net/2022/07/guest-post-to-penalize-low-carbon-price-or-high-carbon-intensity-a-comparison-of-the-eus-cbam-and-th.html. He states that '[a] 2019 IETA report shows that the cost of emissions reduction (shadow prices of CO2) varies significantly among countries, and the cost in the EU tops all other countries'.

[222] Gisselman, et al., 'Border Carbon Adjustments' (2020), pp. 78–79; Leonelli, 'Carbon Border Measures' (2022) 6. On difficulties when taking into account non-pricing mechanisms, see Ilaria Espa, Joseph Francois, and Harro van Asselt, 'The EU Proposal for a Carbon Border Adjustment Mechanism (CBAM): An Analysis under WTO and Climate Change Law' (2022) WTI Working Paper No. 06/2022, p. 25.

[223] Reinhard Quick and Isha Das, 'Can Paris Strike Back? On the Paris Agreement's Inability to Cope with Unilateral Trade-Related Carbon Measures Such as the European Commission's CBAM-Proposal', in Freya Baetens and Stefaan van den Bogaert (eds.), *The EU and the WTO: Ever the Twain Shall Meet. Liber Amicorum Marco Bronckers* (Aalphen aan den Rijn: Wolters Kluwer, 2023), pp. 92–93; Reinhard Quick and Isha Das, 'The EU's CBAM-Regulation Stands in Contrast To Fundamental EU Obligations under the Paris Agreement', IELP Blog, 19 July 2023, https://ielp.worldtradelaw.net/2023/07/guest-post-the-eus-cbam-regulation-stands-in-contrast-to-fundamental-eu-obligations-under-the-paris-.html.

Commission argues that those policies should result in less carbon-intensive goods, and, thus, 'a lesser CBAM obligation'.[224] Some authors also claim that emissions-based criteria for establishing the number of CBAM certificates and thus amount to be paid is also conditional and contrary to the MFN principle.[225] Such a conclusion would be supported by the statement of the panel in *Indonesia – Autos*, according to which Article I:1 GATT requires that the granting of an advantage not 'be made conditional on *any* criteria that is not related to the imported *product itself*' (emphasis added).[226] Under this interpretation, conditions related to production methods, even if origin neutral, would be inconsistent with Article I:1 GATT. Nevertheless, more recent AB jurisprudence seems to have endorsed a narrower interpretation, according to which 'unconditionally' should be interpreted as prohibiting only those conditions that discriminate as to origin and have a detrimental impact on the competitive opportunities of like imported products from any Member.[227] A CBAM distinguishing between products based on their carbon intensity while being origin neutral has better chances to conform with this narrower interpretation of 'unconditionally'.

Finally, an exclusion of developing and/or least developed countries from the scope of the CBAM Regulation to comply with the CBDR principle would clearly confer an advantage on products originating in these countries without granting it 'immediately and unconditionally' to like products from all other WTO Members, thereby being a case of de jure discrimination in violation of Article I:1 GATT,[228] requiring justification. In contrast, offering climate-related financial support to developing countries would most likely fall outside the scope of Article I:1 GATT, as it is not a custom duty, charge, or rule imposed in connection to either importation or exportation, nor an internal tax or other internal charge, or a law, regulation, requirement affecting the internal sale, offering for sale, purchase, transportation, distribution,

[224] Impact Assessment Report, Part 1/2, p. 8.

[225] Will, *Climate Border Adjustments and WTO Law* (2019), p. 184.

[226] Panel Report, *Indonesia – Auto*, WT/DS54/R, WT/DS55/R, WT/DS59/R, WT/DS64/R 2 July 1998, para. 14.143. Also supported by Panel Report, *EC – Tariff Preferences*, WT/DS246/R, 1 December 2003, paras. 7.59–7.60.

[227] Appellate Body Reports, *EC – Seal Products*, WT/DS400/AB/R, WT/DS401/AB/R, para. 5.88. Interpretation first coined in Panel Report, *Canada – Autos*, WT/DS139/R, para. 10.23.

[228] Venzke and Vidigal, 'Are Unilateral Trade Measures in the Climate Crisis the End of Differentiated Responsibilities?' (2022), p. 208; Marín Durán, 'Carbon Border Adjustments' (2022), p. 15.

or use of imported products in the sense of Article III:2 and III:4 GATT.[229]

As Article I:1 GATT will without doubt be violated by certain CBAM provisions and could potentially be violated by others, WTO justifications will be needed to stand the legality test.

10.5 Justifying WTO Violations

As shown in the preceding discussion, regardless of the qualification of the CBAM as a border or internal measures, charge, or regulation, it is likely to violate the relevant WTO norms. Furthermore, compliance with the CBDR principle would lead to a violation of Article I:1 GATT by the CBAM, the question arising whether this principle can be reconciled with international trade law. Accordingly, the EU would almost certainly need to rely on WTO justifications.[230] The most relevant justifications can be found in paragraphs (b) and (g) of Article XX GATT.[231] Additionally, the Enabling Clause could serve as an exception for the violation of the MFN obligation from Article I:1 GATT in case of more favourable treatment accorded to developing countries, LDCs, and SIDs to comply with the CBDR principle.

10.5.1 General Exceptions under Article XX GATT

For a justification under Article XX GATT, a measure must first fall under one of its paragraphs and then satisfy the requirements imposed by the chapeau.[232] Accordingly, in what follows, the chapter will first analyze whether the CBAM could comply with the requirements of paragraphs (b)

[229] Marín Durán, 'Carbon Border Adjustments' (2022), p. 14, fn. 107.

[230] For a criticism of the generally accepted bifurcated approach of WTO judiciary analysing GATT non-discrimination obligations and Article XX GATT separately, see Flett, 'The European Union Carbon Border Adjustment Mechanism' (2022), pp. 274–275, 284, 287.

[231] Art. XX (a) and (d) GATT, justifying measures 'necessary to protect public morals' and 'necessary to secure compliance with laws or regulations which are not inconsistent with the provisions of this Agreement', respectively, could also be invoked. However, as they are more remotely connected to the CBAM, the present chapter will not engage in their assessment. For more on justifying the CBAM under these paragraphs, see Will, *Climate Border Adjustments and WTO Law* (2019), pp. 195–199; Annie Arko, 'A Canadian Border Carbon Adjustment? GATT Compliance and Underexplored Exceptions' (2021) 16 (9) *GTCJ* 446–458 at 451–454.

[232] Appellate Body Report, *US – Gasoline*, WT/DS2/AB/R, 29 April 1996, p. 22. Appellate Body Report, *US – Shrimp*, WT/DS58/AB/R, 12 December 1998, paras. 119–120.

and (g) and then those of the chapeau. It analyzes the two paragraphs separately according to the established traditional approach.[233]

10.5.1.1 *Article XX (b) GATT*

For a measure to fall under paragraph (b) of Article XX GATT, it must first be established that the policy that the measure seeks to implement qualifies as designed 'to protect human, animal or plant life or health' and that the measure is 'necessary' to fulfil that policy objective.[234]

Although not decisive, the EU has been careful to stress that the CBAM is a climate measure in the preambular language of the Regulation.[235] Additionally, it expressly notes that the European Green Deal, in which the CBAM was announced, also aims to 'protect the health and well-being of citizens from environment-related risks and impacts'.[236] This is also supported by the design and structure of the CBAM, as it seeks to charge carbon emissions embedded in imported products, in an attempt to address carbon leakage, thereby leading to a reduction in carbon emissions.[237] Furthermore, as CBAM is part of the 'Fit for 55 Package', it could be said to be part of a 'comprehensive environmental framework of measures put in place to reduce pollution to protect the health' of EU citizens.[238] Considering the wealth of scientific evidence supporting the risk posed by climate change and pollution to human, animal, or plant life and health, it is generally agreed that the CBAM would most likely fall under Article XX (b) GATT.[239] What could make one doubt whether

[233] For calls to assess them concurrently, see Flett, 'The European Union Carbon Border Adjustment Mechanism' (2022), p. 285.

[234] Panel Report, *US – Gasoline*, WT/DS2/R, 29 January 1996, para. 6.20; Panel Report, *EC – Asbestos*, WT/DS135/R, para. 8.184; Panel Report, *EC – Tariff Preferences*, WT/DS246/R, para. 7.198–7.199.

[235] See, for example, CBAM Regulation, Preamble, recitals (1)–(15). The panel in *EC – Tariff Preferences* examined the preambular language of the measure at issue to determine whether its policy objective was the protection of human life or health (Panel Report, *EC – Tariff Preferences*, WT/DS246/R, paras. 7.201–7.202).

[236] CBAM Regulation, Preamble, recital (1).

[237] Venzke and Vidigal, 'Are Unilateral Trade Measures in the Climate Crisis the End of Differentiated Responsibilities?' (2022), p. 210.

[238] The panel in *China – Raw Materials* suggests that it would establish the policy objective of a measure considering the aim of the entire comprehensive framework that it is part of (Panel Reports, *China – Raw Materials*, WT/DS394/R, WT/DS395/R, WT/DS398/R, 5 July 2011, para. 7.511).

[239] Will, *Climate Border Adjustments and WTO Law* (2019), pp. 200–201; Dias, Seeuws, and Nosowicz, 'EU Border Carbon Adjustment and the WTO' (2020) 19; Pauwelyn and Kleimann, 'Trade Related Aspects of a Carbon Border Adjustment Mechanism' (2020), p. 11.

the CBAM falls under letter (b), however, is the issue as to whether the CBAM really contributes to combating climate change. Measures to be justified under letter (b) need at least to be able to make a contribution towards the protection of human life and health, which will be treated in more detail in the assessment of the contribution as part of the subsequent necessity test.

Compliance with the 'necessity' requirement might prove more difficult, however. Thus, the assessment involves 'weighing and balancing' of relevant factors, in particular the importance of interests and values at stake, the extent of the contribution to the measure's objective, and measure's restrictive impact on trade.[240] The more vital or important the interests are, the easier for a measure to be found 'necessary'.[241] Climate change poses risks to the human life and health (for example, the risk of heatwave deaths, floods, and respiratory diseases),[242] which have been recognized as values 'both vital and important in the highest degree'.[243] The reduction of CO_2 emissions has also been found by a WTO panel as having a high importance.[244] Thus, the CBAM would most certainly be recognized as protecting values and interests of the highest degree.

Despite the fact that it would be difficult to prove how the CBAM would counter carbon leakage based on existing data, a panel might conclude that it represents a measure that is 'necessary', since it is 'apt to produce a material contribution to the achievement of its objective' in the future.[245] Furthermore, even if alone the CBAM would not be considered as significantly contributing to the objective of reducing GHG emissions, it could be argued that it is part of a comprehensive legislative framework that is apt to bring a material contribution.[246] As stated by the AB in *Brazil – Retreaded Tyres*, 'measures adopted in order to attenuate global warming and *climate* change [. . .] that may manifest themselves only after

240 Appellate Body Report, *Brazil – Retreaded Tyres*, WT/DS332/AB/R, 3 December 2007, para. 156; Appellate Body Report, *China – Publications and Audiovisual Products*, WT/DS363/AB/R, 21 December 2009, paras. 239, 242.

241 Appellate Body Report, *Colombia – Textiles*, WT/DS461/AB/R, 7 June 2016, para. 5.71.

242 Will, *Climate Border Adjustments and WTO Law* (2019), p. 201.

243 Appellate Body Report, *Brazil – Retreaded Tyres*, WT/DS332/AB/R, para. 179; Also confirmed in Panel Report, *Indonesia – Chicken*, WT/DS484/R, 17 October 2017, para. 7.225.

244 Panel Report, *Brazil – Taxation*, WT/DS472/R, WT/DS497/R, 30 August 2017, para. 7.916.

245 Appellate Body Report, *Brazil – Retreaded Tyres*, WT/DS332/AB/R, para. 151; Appellate Body Report, *China – Publications and Audiovisual Products*, WT/DS363/AB/R, para. 253; Appellate Body Reports, *EC – Seal Products*, WT/DS400/AB/R, WT/DS401/AB/R, para. 5.213.

246 Appellate Body Report, *Brazil – Retreaded Tyres*, WT/DS332/AB/R, para. 154.

a certain period of time – can only be evaluated with the benefit of time' (emphasis added).[247] As mentioned earlier, in order to fall under Article XX (b) GATT, the CBAM should contribute to its environmental objective. For a contribution to be found, there shall be a 'genuine relationship of ends and means' between the measure and the policy objective that it seeks to protect.[248] It might be more difficult to show that CBAM is necessary under Article XX (b) GATT if CBAM revenues were used for the recovery of the EU economy and if export rebates were applied,[249] as these aspects question whether there is indeed a genuine nexus between the measure and its policy objective. Therefore, the decision to forego rules on export rebates for now is welcome,[250] and it is advisable to avoid the introduction of such rules in the future as well. As to the trade restrictiveness of the measure, the CBAM does not prohibit the access of imported products on the EU market; it only imposes the obligation to buy and surrender CBAM certificates and additional administrative burdens related to it. Accordingly, the level of CBAM's trade restrictiveness will most likely not be estimated as tilting towards the highest end, making the finding that it is 'necessary' under Article XX (b) GATT more probable. Since the factors analyzed above should be 'weighed and balanced', which is a holistic exercise, it is very likely that they will support a positive conclusion with respect to the 'necessity' of the CBAM.

Finally, if the 'weighing and balancing' analysis yields a preliminary positive conclusion, the result must be confirmed by establishing that there was no reasonable available less restrictive measure, which is consistent or less inconsistent with GATT provisions and allows the imposing Member to achieve the desired level of protection.[251] The complainant would have the burden of proof to make a prima facie case that there are possible alternatives, in which case the EU would have to show that there is no genuine alternative or that such alternative is not 'reasonably available'.[252] An alternative that the EU has been using to counter

[247] ibid, para. 151. [248] ibid, para. 145.

[249] Mehling, et al., 'Designing Border Carbon Adjustments' (2019) 478; Espa, Francois, and Asselt, 'The EU Proposal for a Carbon Border Adjustment Mechanism (CBAM)' (2022), p. 14.

[250] EP, 'Climate Change: Deal on a More Ambitious Emissions Trading System (ETS)', 18 December 2022, www.europarl.europa.eu/news/en/press-room/20221212IPR64527/climate-change-deal-on-a-more-ambitious-emissions-trading-system-ets.

[251] Appellate Body Report, *Brazil – Retreaded Tyres*, WT/DS332/AB/R, paras. 156, 170; Appellate Body Report, *EC – Asbestos*, WT/DS135/AB/R, paras. 170-172.

[252] Appellate Body Report, *Brazil – Retreaded Tyres*, WT/DS332/AB/R, para. 156; Appellate Body Report, *China – Publications and Audiovisual Products*, WT/DS363/AB/R, para. 319.

the risk of carbon leakage is the use of free allowances; however, this alternative would not achieve the same level of protection, since it weakens the price incentives for installations to further reduce carbon emissions compared to full auctioning.[253] It has been suggested that a less restrictive alternative would be to reach a multilateral negotiated solution.[254] However, potential consultations or negotiations are 'not an appropriate alternative [. . .] to consider because consultations are by definition a process, the results of which are uncertain and therefore not capable of comparison with the measures at issue'.[255] Thus, unless another 'less restrictive alternative' is invoked by the complainant and the EU cannot prove that it is not reasonably available, the CBAM would likely comply with the requirements of paragraph (b) Article XX GATT.

10.5.1.2 Article XX (g) GATT

For a measure to fall under Article XX (g) GATT, it shall relate to 'the conservation of exhaustible natural resources if such measures are made effective in conjunction with restrictions on domestic production or consumption'.

Thus, it should first be shown that clean air or climate represent 'exhaustible natural resources'. The term has been interpreted in a broad and dynamic way, encompassing both living and non-living resources.[256] WTO jurisprudence already established that measures aimed at 'reducing the depletion of clean air' are policies to conserve exhaustible natural resources within the meaning of Article XX (g) GATT.[257] Furthermore, climate change has been recognized as 'a common concern of humankind' in the preamble of the Paris Agreement, and given the vast scientific evidence that emerged in the last decades regarding the phenomenon, it would be reasonable to expect that climate could equally be considered a natural exhaustible resource.[258] Accordingly, there is a general consensus

[253] CBAM Regulation, Preamble, recital (11).

[254] Gisselman, et al., 'Border Carbon Adjustments' (2020), p. 56; Will, *Climate Border Adjustments and WTO Law* (2019), p. 213.

[255] Appellate Body Report, *US – Gambling*, WT/DS285/AB/R, 7 April 2005, para. 317.

[256] Appellate Body Report, *US – Shrimp*, WT/DS58/AB/R, paras. 128–131.

[257] Panel Report, *US – Gasoline*, WT/DS2/R, para. 6.37.

[258] Dias, Seeuws, and Nosowicz, 'EU Border Carbon Adjustment and the WTO' (2020) 16; Quick, 'Carbon Border Adjustment' (2020) 20–21; Venzke and Vidigal, 'Are Unilateral Trade Measures in the Climate Crisis the End of Differentiated Responsibilities?' (2022), pp. 209–210.

in the academic literature that the CBAM would pass this first step of analysis.[259]

Unlike paragraph (b) of Article XX GATT, which requires that the measure be 'necessary' for the achievement of the policy objective, paragraph (g) only provides that it shall 'relate to' to the conservation of natural resources. This standard is considerably more lenient, as it does not involve the weighing and balancing of different factors and the demonstration that there was no reasonably available less restrictive trade alternative when such an alternative is invoked by the complainant. Accordingly, this paragraph is expected to be easier to comply with and a more probable justification. Nevertheless, the EU is free to invoke both paragraphs as justifications for the CBAM. For a measure to 'relate to' the policy objective, it should be 'primarily aimed at'[260] and not 'merely incidentally or inadvertently aimed at' the conservation of natural resources; there must be a 'close and genuine relationship of ends and means' between the measure and the conservation objective,[261] the first being not 'disproportionately wide in its scope and reach' in relation to the last.[262] Although the CBAM would also have a levelling the playing field effect, it could hardly be argued that by targeting carbon intensive sectors and charging imported products based on their GHG embedded emissions that CBAM's aim is not genuinely and closely related to the conservation of climate and clean air. This is further supported by the EU's comprehensive legislative framework aimed at reducing carbon emissions that the CBAM is part of.[263] Finally, refraining from introducing export rebates in the future and directing CBAM-generated revenue to developing countries, LDCs, and SIDs to further their environmental purposes could also help in showing that CBAM 'relates to' the protection of clean air and climate.[264]

[259] Mehling, et al., 'Designing Border Carbon Adjustments' (2019) 472; Marín Durán, 'Carbon Border Adjustments' (2022), p. 467; Gisselman, et al., 'Border Carbon Adjustments' (2020), p. 57; Venzke and Vidigal, 'Are Unilateral Trade Measures in the Climate Crisis the End of Differentiated Responsibilities?' (2022), p. 210.

[260] Appellate Body Report, *US – Gasoline*, WT/DS2/AB/R, p. 18.

[261] Appellate Body Reports, *China – Rare Earths*, WT/DS431/AB/R, WT/DS432/AB/R, WT/DS433/AB/R, 7 August 2014, para. 5.90.

[262] Appellate Body Report, *US – Shrimp*, WT/DS58/AB/R, para. 141.

[263] Although the AB in *Brazil – Retreated Tyres* assessed a measure in the context of its comprehensive legislative framework in an analysis under Art. XX (b) GATT, the authors see no impediment to a similar approach taken under para. (g) of the same article.

[264] Mehling, et al., 'Designing Border Carbon Adjustments' (2019) 472; Marín Durán, 'Carbon Border Adjustments' (2022) 478; Espa, Francois, and Asselt, 'The EU Proposal for a Carbon Border Adjustment Mechanism (CBAM)' (2022), p. 14.

While the relationship between the measure and policy objective is unlikely to be an obstacle for the CBAM's justification under Article XX (g) of the CBAM, it is less clear what the nexus between carbon emissions emitted elsewhere and the Member imposing a measure directed at the protection of clean air and climate, in general, is. The EU's CBAM targets carbon emissions outside its own territory, raising questions about the legality of this measure's alleged extraterritorial character. The AB in *US – Shrimp* famously made a controversial statement in this respect. Although it did not answer 'the question of whether there is an implied jurisdictional limitation in Article XX(g), and if so, the nature or extent of that limitation', it noted that in the case at issue 'there is a *sufficient nexus* between the migratory and endangered marine populations involved and the United States for purposes of Article XX(g)' (emphasis added).[265] Since air pollution anywhere in the world could affect the air quality of any other country, and as climate change directly affects every WTO Member, including the EU, it could credibly claim that it has a 'sufficient nexus' with clean air and climate depleted by carbon emissions to take measures for their protection. The question whether there is an implied jurisdictional limitation in Article XX (g) GATT, however, remained unanswered to this day. Customary international law on extraterritoriality, as relevant rules of international law applicable between the parties under Article 31 (3) (c) VCLT, could be taken into account for the interpretation of this paragraph. Nevertheless, the relevant customary norms seem rather ambiguous and controversial in this respect.[266] First of all, there is ambiguity with respect to the question whether CBAM applies extraterritorially. As CBAM imposes obligations only on imported goods within its territory, the EU is likely to claim that the regulation is based on territorial jurisdiction, albeit with extraterritorial implications as the number of CBAM certificates will be calculated based on the conduct of producers outside the EU. A similar argument was made by the CJEU and Advocate General (AG) Kokott in Case C-366/10,[267] which was heavily

[265] Appellate Body Report, *US – Shrimp*, WT/DS58/AB/R, para. 133.

[266] Christina Voigt, 'Up in the Air: Aviation, the EU Emissions Trading Scheme and the Question of Jurisdiction' (2012) 14 *Cambridge Yearbook of European Legal Studies* 475–506 at 496; Natalie L. Dobson and Cedric Ryngaert, 'Provocative Climate Protection: EU 'Extraterritorial' Regulation of Maritime Emissions' (2017) 66 *ICLQ* 295–333 at 303, 307.

[267] Opinion of Advocate General Kokott, Case C-366/10, *Air Transport Association of America and Others* [2011] ECLI:EU:C:2011:637, paras. 145–147; Judgment of the Court (Grand Chamber), Case C-366/10, *Air Transport Association of America and Others* [2011] ECR I-13755, ECLI:EU:C:2011:864, paras. 124–125.

criticized by other states, leading the EU to ultimately withdraw the alleged extraterritorial element of the measure.[268] Even though this might signal that the approach adopted in the CJEU's decision may not sufficiently reflect customary international law, claiming that exception provisions may not justify measures that have extraterritorial effects actually disguises the real issues behind such claim: It is the issue of allocating regulatory competence either to the country of origin or to the country of destination. This issue of regulatory choice was clearly identified by the panel in *US – Shrimp* that pleaded in favour of the regulatory freedom of country of origin to the detriment of the country of destination, which actually would mean that the country-of-origin regulatory choices would be vested with an extraterritorial effect denied to the country of destination.[269] Hence, in the interest of addressing global problems such as climate change, the combat against which is subject to international instruments, introducing an inherent limitation with extraterritorial effects into WTO justifications does not appear to reflect the overall state of international law. Therefore, against the backdrop of the same controversy surrounding the question of whether extraterritorial elements could be based on the effects doctrine, it has to be welcome that the AB in *US – Shrimp* actually confirmed that a state can exercise its jurisdiction when the effects of a conduct occur in the state claiming jurisdiction.[270] Not least because of the ambiguous state of customary international law on extraterritoriality, the WTO adjudicators are most likely to follow the AB's past findings, which would not represent a hurdle for the CBAM's justification under Article XX (g) GATT.

Still, although the 'necessity' requirement is absent from Article XX (g), as already mentioned in Chapter 3, an additional layer of demands could be added by Article 2 (3) of the Kyoto Protocol, which establishes that '[t]he Parties [. . .] strive to implement policies and measures under this Article in such a way as to minimize adverse effects, including the [. . .]

[268] Joint declaration of the Moscow meeting on inclusion of international civil aviation in the EU-ETS, 22 February 2012, www.ruaviation.com/docs/1/2012/2/22/50/?h.

[269] For more on this, see Weiß, *WTO Law and Domestic Regulation* (2020), pp. 40 ff.

[270] Such controversy relates to the question whether 'effects' doctrine can be used as a ground for jurisdiction, as well as to how exactly to apply it, in particular what type of causality is required between the effects and the state and what should be the scale of effects (Voigt, 'Up in the Air' (2012) 501; Dobson and Ryngaert, 'Provocative Climate Protection' (2017) 327–330).

effects on international trade'. While the WTO judiciary would not be able to enforce this provision that does not fall under its jurisdiction, it could be considered a relevant rule of international law 'applicable in the relations between the parties' to be taken into account during the interpretative process according to Article 31 (3) (c) VCLT. Accordingly, this seemingly easier way of justifying CBAM might be counteracted by raising the justification standard to a type of necessity requirement demanded by the said article of Kyoto Protocol.

Finally, for a measure to fall under Article XX (g), it shall be 'made effective in conjunction with restrictions on domestic production or consumption', which represents a requirement of '*even-handedness* in the imposition of restrictions'.[271] Nevertheless, it does not require 'identity of treatment', otherwise justification of NT violations would be impossible.[272] Domestic restrictions should be 'real' and 'work together' with trade measures so as to conserve exhaustible natural resource.[273] The CBAM works together with the ETS towards the protection of a clean air and of the climate; and even though the ETS does not offer an identical treatment to domestic production compared to the treatment of imports by the CBAM, the ETS still imposes real restrictions on the first. Furthermore, while domestic producers would still benefit from free allowances until they are completely phased out, the CBAM would be applied in an even-handed manner, as the number of CBAM certificates is adjusted to reflect these allowances.[274] Therefore, there is a broad consensus that this test would be easily passed by the EU's CBAM.[275] Consequently, unless Article 2 (3) Kyoto Protocol is considered to add a standard similar to the 'necessary one', the CBAM would most likely be justified under paragraph (g) of Article XX GATT, apart from the chapeau's stipulations to which we now turn.

[271] Appellate Body Report, *US – Gasoline*, WT/DS2/AB/R, p. 20; Appellate Body Report, *US – Shrimp*, WT/DS58/AB/R, para. 144; Appellate Body Reports, *China – Rare Earths*, WT/DS431/AB/R, WT/DS432/AB/R, WT/DS433/AB/R, para. 5.132.

[272] Appellate Body Report, *US – Gasoline*, WT/DS2/AB/R, p. 21.

[273] Appellate Body Reports, *China – Raw Materials*, WT/DS394/R, WT/DS395/R, WT/DS398/R, para. 360; Appellate Body Reports, *China – Rare Earths*, WT/DS431/AB/R, WT/DS432/AB/R, WT/DS433/AB/R paras. 5.93, 5.132, 5.136.

[274] CBAM Regulation, Art. 31; Joachim Englisch and Tatiana Falcão, 'EU Carbon Border Adjustments and WTO Law, Part Two' (2021) 51(11) *Environmental Law Reporter* 10935–10946 at 10941; Marín Durán, 'EU Carbon Border Adjustment Mechanism' (2021) 503–504.

[275] Mehling, et al., 'Designing Border Carbon Adjustments' (2019) 467; Dias, Seeuws, and Nosowicz, 'EU Border Carbon Adjustment and the WTO' (2020) 21.

10.5.1.3 The Chapeau of Article XX GATT

While the likelihood of the CBAM to be provisionally justified under paragraphs (b) and (g) of Article XX is very high, the chapeau test might be more difficult to pass. It establishes the requirement that the measures 'are not applied in a manner which would constitute a means of arbitrary or unjustifiable discrimination between countries where the same conditions prevail, or a disguised restriction on international trade'. Thus, the aim of the chapeau is to prevent the abuse of the general exceptions enshrined in Article XX GATT[276] by ensuring that a measure is truly and even-handedly used for an environmental purpose and does not represent protectionism in disguise.

For the CBAM to comply with the chapeau it must be discerned from its design, architecture, and structure that it is applied consistently to achieve the policy objective listed in the relevant subparagraphs,[277] namely the protection of human, animal, or plant life or health and/or the conservation of clean air and climate. Accordingly, these policy objectives must be at the forefront of the Regulation and not other purposes, such as ensuring a level playing field, which must remain only an incidental and not disguised intentional consequence.[278] Accordingly, the restraint exercised with respect to this consequence, which is not acknowledged in the Regulation, is commendable.

For a measure to be applied in a manner which would represent 'arbitrary or unjustifiable discrimination between countries where the same conditions prevail', three elements should be met: (1) the measure's application must result in discrimination, which, albeit determined by using a different standard than that used under Article III GATT, can be brought about by the same circumstances as under the last;[279] (2) the discrimination must be 'arbitrary or unjustifiable'; and (3) it must occur 'between countries where the same conditions prevail'.[280] As to the first element, the same exemptions analyzed under the MFN obligation, namely exempting states that are fully integrated into or linked to the

[276] Appellate Body Report, *US – Gasoline*, WT/DS2/AB/R, p. 22.

[277] Appellate Body Reports, *EC – Seal Products*, WT/DS400/AB/R, WT/DS401/AB/R, para. 5.302.

[278] On the CBAM's aims, see Section 10.2.2.

[279] Appellate Body Reports, *EC – Seal Products*, WT/DS400/AB/R, WT/DS401/AB/R, para. 5.298.

[280] Appellate Body Report, *US – Shrimp*, WT/DS58/AB/R, para. 150. Whether there is a 'disguised restriction on trade' has been determined by reference to the 'arbitrary or unjustifiable' analysis (see, e.g. Appellate Body Report, *US – Gasoline*, WT/DS2/AB/R, p. 25; Appellate Body Report, *Brazil – Retreaded Tyres*, WT/DS332/AB/R, para. 239). Hence, the chapter will focus on the last.

EU ETS from the CBAM obligations and reducing the number of CBAM certificates in case of declarants originating in countries with carbon pricing mechanisms in place, would also give raise to discrimination relevant for the chapeau of Article XX GATT. Furthermore, to comply with the CBDR principle, LDCs and SIDs would have to be exempted from CBAM obligations, which would equally be perceived as discrimination under the chapeau of Article XX GATT.

According to the AB in *Brazil – Retreaded Tyres*, discrimination is likely to be considered 'arbitrary or unjustifiable' if it 'bears no relationship to the objective of a measure provisionally justified' or even 'goes against the objective'.[281] Exempting states integrated into or linked to the ETS and taking account of the carbon pricing in other countries is clearly related to the objective of carbon leakage prevention and, consequently to climate and clean air protection, and protection of human, animal, or plant life or health. Nevertheless, these provisions could be accused of requiring other Members 'to adopt essentially the same comprehensive regulatory program [. . .] as that in force within that Member's territory', which has been designated as unacceptable in international trade relations and was assessed to represent an unjustified and arbitrary discrimination by the AB in the *US – Shrimp* dispute.[282] As the CBAM does not provide exemptions or reductions to countries with mechanisms 'comparable in effectiveness' to that of the EU, for example regulatory rather than monetary in nature, it could be suspected of being 'more concerned with effectively influencing WTO Members to adopt essentially the same' mechanism as the one adopted by the EU.[283] Thus, the so-called Brussels effect is unlikely to score well under the existing WTO jurisprudence unless WTO adjudicators would accept Commission's argument that non-price regulatory approaches would be given consideration, since, if effective, they would result in less actual emissions and, consequently, lead to lesser CBAM obligations.[284] Adding consideration for regulatory mechanisms of other WTO Members would improve CBAM's chances to pass the chapeau test. Assessing the effectiveness of these non-pricing approaches compared to the EU's approach, which uses not only pricing but also non-price approaches,[285] would be an exercise of heightened difficulty, though not an impossible one, as the comparability of pricing and non-pricing measures is mentioned in the context of the establishment of a

[281] Appellate Body Report, *Brazil – Retreaded Tyres*, WT/DS332/AB/R, para. 232.

[282] Appellate Body Report, *US – Shrimp*, WT/DS58/AB/R, para. 164. [283] ibid, para. 165.

[284] Impact Assessment Report, Part 1/2, p. 8. [285] ibid, p. 26.

'Climate Club' in the CBAM's preamble, and considered by the Members of the G7 Climate Club.[286] In addition, such consideration would also score better under the Paris Agreement seemingly allowing states to choose the type of mechanism to tackle carbon emissions.[287] Moreover, since default values might often be used for calculating the number of CBAM certificates without taking into account actual emissions reflecting other policies,[288] non-pricing mechanisms of other WTO Members could end up being disregarded.[289] Additionally, the inclusion of rules on export rebates in the CBAM should not only be postponed but discarded, as it would be difficult to argue that offering export rebates is related to the CBAM's objective to reduce carbon emissions.[290]

If applying the *Brazil – Retreaded Tyres* test, exempting LDCs and SIDs would be hard to link to the CBAM's policy objective,[291] as this does not contribute to carbon emissions reductions. Such a rigid approach has been criticized for failing to regard that in practice, legislations often have competing objectives.[292] In subsequent disputes, the AB noted that the connection to the policy objective is 'not the sole test' and that 'there could be additional factors' relevant to the chapeau assessment.[293] As no separate test has been established yet for potential legitimate competing objectives, it is difficult to foretell whether an exemption in line with the CBDR principle is likely to be considered 'arbitrary or unjustifiable'. This

[286] CBAM Regulation, Preamble, recital (72). G7 Terms of Reference for the Climate Club, 12 December 2022, para. 7, provides that exchange between members will entail, *inter alia*, 'working towards a common understanding through comparative analysis of the effectiveness and economic impact of such policies, including price-based and *non-price-based* climate change mitigation instruments' (emphasis added).

[287] Quick and Das, 'Can Paris Strike Back?' (2023), pp. 92–93.

[288] See Section 10.2.1 on how embedded (direct and indirect) emissions are calculated.

[289] Espa, Francois, and Asselt, 'The EU Proposal for a Carbon Border Adjustment Mechanism (CBAM)' (2022), p. 24.

[290] Gisselman, et al., 'Border Carbon Adjustments' (2020), p. 59; Mehling, et al., 'Designing Border Carbon Adjustments' (2019) 470; Dias, Seeuws, and Nosowicz, 'EU Border Carbon Adjustment and the WTO' (2020) 22; Espa, Francois, and Asselt, 'The EU Proposal for a Carbon Border Adjustment Mechanism (CBAM)' (2022) p. 14.

[291] Although some authors, like Pauwelyn and Kleimann, argue that such an exemption could be based on environmental grounds, considering that these countries have historically emitted less carbon and that this differentiation is enshrined in Paris Agreement (Pauwelyn and Kleimann, 'Trade Related Aspects of a Carbon Border Adjustment Mechanism' (2020), p. 11).

[292] Venzke and Vidigal, 'Are Unilateral Trade Measures in the Climate Crisis the End of Differentiated Responsibilities?' (2022), pp. 213–214.

[293] Appellate Body Reports, *EC – Seal Products*, WT/DS400/AB/R, WT/DS401/AB/R, para. 5.321; Appellate Body Report, *US – Tuna II (Mexico) (Article. 21.5 – Mexico)*, para. 7.316.

issue can be left open here, as we will argue below that exempting LDCs and SIDs will be acceptable considering that the conditions prevailing in those countries are different, not least in conformity also with the CBDR principle.

Besides the test used in *Brazil – Retreaded Tyres*, the AB determined whether there was 'arbitrary or unjustifiable discrimination' based on the concept of 'due process', particularly whether the procedures in question were transparent, predictable, formal, and whether applicants were offered the opportunity to be heard, respond to arguments, and appeal the decision.[294] The EU's CBAM would most likely comply with these requirements, as it provides formal and predictable proceedings for the application for and granting of authorizations, submission and review of CBAM declarations, surrender of CBAM certificates, as well as penalties.[295] Furthermore, these proceedings contain clear rules on notification of applicants/declarants and their right to appeal decisions.[296] Additionally, in *US – Shrimp*, the AB determined that the failure to engage the complainants and other Members in 'across-the-board negotiations with the objective of concluding bilateral or multilateral agreements' 'before enforcing' the provisionally justified measure on exports of other WTO Members would constitute unjustifiable discrimination.[297] Seriously engaging in negotiations only with some but not all affected Members would also run afoul the chapeau test.[298] The EU could argue that there is currently no international consensus related to carbon pricing in the UNFCCC context, even bringing the Paris Agreement as an example of negotiations that did not result in relevant provisions.[299] However, this argument would most likely not be accepted, as these negotiations did not specifically concern carbon border adjustment,[300] nor has the EU attempted bilateral or multilateral consultations in this

294 Appellate Body Report, *US – Shrimp*, WT/DS58/AB/R, paras. 180–181.

295 CBAM Regulation, Arts. 5, 6, 17, 19, 22, 26.

296 ibid, Arts. 17.3, 17.8, 19.5, 22.3, 26.4, 35 (6) (e).

297 Appellate Body Report, *US – Shrimp*, WT/DS58/AB/R, para. 166.

298 ibid, paras. 171–172. Howse, however, suggests that this might simply be viewed as a finding of discrimination, but that there was no obligation established for exhausting efforts at a cooperative approach. Although he references the AB's report from *US – Gambling*, the last only establishes that consultations cannot represent a viable alternative in the context of the 'necessity' analysis (Howse, 'Distinguished Essay' (2015), p. 17; Appellate Body Report, *US – Gambling*, WT/DS285/AB/R, para. 317).

299 Mehling, et al., 'Designing Border Carbon Adjustments' (2019) 469; Flett, 'The European Union Carbon Border Adjustment Mechanism' (2022), p. 270.

300 ibid.

respect before tabling the CBAM proposal.[301] The EU seems to have bypassed developing and least developed countries, especially China, during negotiations because of the invocation of the CBDR by these countries, and instead has engaged in negotiations with its 'main trading partners'.[302] The recently established G7 Climate Club shows how certain EU Members engaged in discussions on carbon pricing only with some WTO Members.[303] Similarly, in December 2022, the United States sent a proposal to the EU to form the Global Arrangement on Sustainable Steel and Aluminum, allowing them to impose tariffs against metals from other countries produced in environmental harmful ways.[304] These developments are indicative that the EU did not attempt across-the-board negotiations with all WTO Members before pursuing the CBAM, which could hamper its chances to pass the chapeau's test. The CBAM Regulation, in its preamble, encourages the Commission to continue the dialogue with third countries in particular during the transitional period and especially with those affected by it, to inform its decisions during implementation, and calls for the creation of a Climate Club,[305] but this does not entail negotiations on core CBAM rules, nor does it refer to across-the-board negotiations. The EU has also stressed that the adoption of CBAM 'will go together with an intensification of our efforts to cooperate with our trading partners [. . .] both in the WTO and bilaterally'.[306] While it would have been advisable that the EU attempted negotiations before adopting the Regulation, as the AB in *US – Shrimp* seems to require across-the-board negotiations 'before enforcing' the measure to be justified,[307] the EU should pursue them at least before

301 André Sapir and Henrik Horn, 'Political Assessment of Possible Reactions of EU Main Trading Partners to EU Border Carbon Measures' (2020) EP Briefing Requested by the INTA Committee, www.europarl.europa.eu/cmsdata/210515/EXPO_BRI(2020)603503_EN.pdf, p. 10.

302 Flett, 'The European Union Carbon Border Adjustment Mechanism' (2022), p. 271.

303 'G7 Establishes Climate Club to Support Green Transition', *Reuters*, 12 December 2022, www.reuters.com/business/environment/g7-establishes-climate-club-support-green-transition-2022-12-12/.

304 'U.S. Proposes Green Steel Club That Would Levy Tariffs on Outliers', *The New York Times*, 7 December 2022, www.nytimes.com/2022/12/07/business/economy/steel-tariffs-climate-change.html.

305 CBAM Regulation, Preamble, recitals (70), (71).

306 Permanent Mission of the European Union to the World Trade Organization (WTO), '15th Trade Policy Review of the European Union, 5 & 7th June 2023', 5 June 2023, www.eeas.europa.eu/delegations/world-trade-organization-wto/15th-trade-policy-review-european-union-5-7th-june-2023_en?s=69.

307 Appellate Body Report, *US – Shrimp*, WT/DS58/AB/R, para. 166.

the end of the transitional period when the obligation to buy and surrender CBAM certificates becomes applicable.

Lastly, this section will analyze whether a CBDR-related exception could be justified considering the prevailing conditions in the LDCs and SIDS. The AB established in *US – Shrimp* that there is discrimination not only when countries are treated differently under the same conditions but also when countries are treated equally under different conditions.[308] Accordingly, if the prevailing conditions in the LDCs and SIDS were considered to be different than those in other Members, treating them in the same manner would amount to arbitrary and unjustified discrimination under the chapeau of Article XX GATT. It is to be noted, however, that the term 'conditions' refers only to those conditions that relate to the particular policy objective of the relevant Article XX subparagraph.[309] In case of the CBAM then, the relevant conditions are those that relate to the protection of human, animal, or plant life or health from GHG emissions-related risks and to that of clean air and climate. This condition is likely to be satisfied in case of LDCs and SIDS exemption from the CBAM obligation, as their different responsibilities and capabilities in terms of climate protection, as already shown,[310] are explicitly recognized in the Paris Agreement and other environmental treaties.[311] These environmental treaties should especially be taken into account in case of disputes between their parties as 'any relevant rules of international law' under Article 31 (3) (c) VCLT. Such an interpretation of the expression 'between countries were the same conditions prevail' is also supported by the context provided by WTO agreements, as the international trade law concept of Special and Differential Treatment (SDT), offering special rights to developing countries and LDCs, finds expression in various WTO provisions.[312]

308 ibid, para. 165.

309 Appellate Body Reports, *EC – Seal Products*, WT/DS400/AB/R, WT/DS401/AB/R, para. 5.300.

310 See Section 10.3.

311 Marín Durán, 'Carbon Border Adjustments' (2022), p. 20. For a different opinion, see Flett, 'The European Union Carbon Border Adjustment Mechanism' (2022), p. 288.

312 Venzke and Vidigal, 'Are Unilateral Trade Measures in the Climate Crisis the End of Differentiated Responsibilities?' (2022), pp. 217–219. For more on SDT, see Alexander Keck and Patrick Low, 'Special and Differential Treatment in the WTO: Why, When, and How?', in Bernard M. Hoekman and Simon J. Evenett (eds.), *Economic Development and Multilateral Trade Cooperation* (Washington, DC: Palgrave Macmillan, The World Bank, 2006), pp. 147–188. See, for example, Agreement Establishing the World Trade Organization, signed 15 April 1994, in force 1 January 1995, 1867 U.N.T.S. 154, Preamble, recital 1; Decision of 28 November 1979 (L/4903), Differential and More Favourable

To conclude, while the EU's CBAM is likely to be provisionally justified under paragraphs (b) and (g) of Article XX GATT, it might not comply with the conditions of the chapeau. To increase its chances to pass the chapeau's test, the CBAM should consider other countries' regulatory non-pricing carbon measures and avoid the introduction of export rebates in the future. In addition, the EU should attempt a multilateral negotiated solution with all WTO Members before the end of the transitional period. Although the CBAM contains no CBDR-related exception yet, to comply with its international obligations, the EU should include one, especially since it was shown that it could be accommodated under the chapeau of Article XX GATT. Hence, the chapeau of Article XX GATT could be interpreted in a way that permits a harmonious coexistence of international trade law and the environmental principle of CBDR.

10.5.2 The Enabling Clause

The potential addition of an exception from the CBAM obligations for LDCs and SIDS to comply with the CBDR principle could also be justified under the Enabling Clause, which represents an exception to Article I:1 GATT, allowing 'differential and more favourable treatment to developing countries'.[313]

Provided that LDCs are exempted in the context of other general measures in favour of developing countries, such as offering financial support from CBAM revenues to all developing countries (including LDCs and SIDS) as required by the CBDR,[314] such an exemption could benefit from Article 2 (d) Enabling Clause, as it explicitly permits 'special treatment on the least developed among the developing countries in the context of any general or specific measures in favour of developing countries'. Thus, it emphasizes that LDCs form 'an identifiable subcategory of developing countries with "special economic difficulties and ... particular development, financial and trade needs"'.[315] Existing jurisprudence suggests that granting preferential treatment only to LDCs among other developing countries would be permissible, without the need for the preference-granting country to demonstrate that such differentiation is 'non-discriminatory'.[316] As required by paragraphs (a) and (b)

Treatment Reciprocity and Fuller Participation of Developing Countries (Enabling Clause), paras. 1, 2 (d).

[313] Appellate Body Report, *EC – Tariff Preferences*, WT/DS246/AB/R, 7 April 2004, para. 90.

[314] See Section 10.3.

[315] Appellate Body Report, *EC – Tariff Preferences*, WT/DS246/AB/R, para. 172. [316] ibid.

of Article 3 Enabling Clause, an LDC exception from CBAM obligations would not 'raise barriers to or create undue difficulties for the trade of any other contracting parties' and would 'not constitute an impediment to the reduction or elimination of tariffs and other restrictions to trade on a most-favoured-nation basis'. It would likely comply with Article 3 (c) Enabling Clause too, which provides that differential and more favourable treatment 'shall [. . .] respond positively to the development, financial and trade needs of developing countries', meaning that there should be a sufficient nexus between the treatment and the likelihood of alleviating the particular need at issue.[317] By exempting importers of goods originating in LDCs from the obligation to buy and surrender CBAM certificates, the EU would alleviate these countries' trade needs; otherwise, considering their limited administrative capabilities, their exports could be significantly affected.[318]

As argued in Section 10.3, for compliance with the CBDR, the CBAM should also exempt from its obligations importers of goods originating in SIDS. The Enabling Clause does not distinguish the category of SIDS among developing countries, as it does in case of the LDCs. Yet, such an exemption might be justified under other paragraphs of Article 2 Enabling Clause. Article 2 (a) allows preferential, generalized, non-reciprocal, and non-discriminatory[319] *tariff* treatment accorded by developed countries to products from developing countries. Hence, paragraph (a) could represent a justification for SIDS preferential treatment if CBAM were treated as a fiscal measure. Although Article 2 (a) Enabling Clause allows preferential, but 'generalized' and 'non-discriminatory' treatment, distinctions would be considered discriminatory only insofar as they apply to 'similarly-situated beneficiaries'.[320] In contrast, identical treatment should be offered to similarly situated countries that 'have the "development, financial and trade needs" to which the treatment in question is intended to respond'.[321] Therefore, the EU could argue that SIDS and other developing countries are not similarly situated: the first having special 'development financial, and trade needs' eliciting the more favourable treatment offered to the them. For a country to qualify for preferential treatment, objective criteria or standards should be

[317] ibid, para. 164.

[318] Impact Assessment Report, Part 2/2, p. 21; Leal-Arcas, Faktaufon, and Kyprianou, 'A Legal Exploration of the European Union's Carbon Border Adjustment Mechanism' (2022) 233.

[319] Footnote 3 to Article 2 (a) Enabling Clause.

[320] Appellate Body Report, *EC – Tariff Preferences*, WT/DS246/AB/R, para. 153.

[321] ibid, para. 173.

established by the granting country.[322] The Paris Agreement, which explicitly recognizes SIDS as a separate subcategory of developing countries with reduced capabilities that are not expected to take the same mitigation efforts as the developed or even other developing countries,[323] could provide for such a standard.[324] In this way, the Paris Agreement also implicitly recognizes that reduced commitments, such as an exemption from the CBAM obligations, would respond positively to the particular financial, development, and trade needs of the SIDS within the meaning of Article 3 (c) Enabling Clause, there being a sufficient nexus between the different treatment and the likelihood of alleviating their needs. If the CBAM were considered to impose non-tariff measures,[325] the Enabling Clause would fail to justify GATT violations by the SIDS exemptions. The AB in *Brazil – Taxation* established that Article 2 (b) Enabling Clause, providing for differential and more favourable treatment with respect to *non-tariff* measures 'governed by the provisions of instruments multilaterally negotiated under the auspices of the GATT', does not apply with respect to discriminatory treatment of a measure falling under Article III:2 and III:4 GATT.[326] Thus, it is apparent that Article 2 (b) would provide a justification only on the basis of SDT provisions in other WTO Agreements than GATT negotiated under the GATT auspices, such as those from the Agreement on Technical Barriers to Trade[327] (TBT Agreement).[328]

Lastly, according to Article 4 Enabling Clause, to benefit from its exceptions, the EU should comply with the notification requirement,[329] as well as to provide the opportunity for prompt consultations with any

[322] ibid, para. 188.

[323] ibid, para. 163; Paris Agreement, Art. 4.6. For more, see Section 10.3.

[324] Although referring to other multilateral instruments, particularly a UN Declaration and Report, Lorand Bartels also argues in favour of considering SIDS as a special category to be offered more favourable treatment compared to other developing countries (Lorand Bartels, 'The WTO Legality of the EU's GSP+ Arrangement' (2007) 10(4) *JIEL* 869–886 at 884.

[325] For the discussion on the type of measures imposed by the CBAM, see Sections 10.4.1 and 10.4.2.

[326] Appellate Body Report, *Brazil – Taxation*, paras. 5.414–5.415.

[327] Agreement on Technical Barriers to Trade, Marrakesh Agreement Establishing the World Trade Organization, Annex 1A, 15 April 1994, 1868 U.N.T.S. 120.

[328] Venzke and Vidigal, 'Are Unilateral Trade Measures in the Climate Crisis the End of Differentiated Responsibilities?' (2022), pp. 219–220.

[329] For more on the notification requirement see Panel Report, *Brazil – Taxation*, paras. 7.1080, 7.1108; Appellate Body Report, *Brazil – Taxation*, WT/DS472/AB/R, WT/DS497/AB/R, 13 December 2008. paras. 5.375–5.376.

WTO Members with respect to difficulties or other matters that may arise, at their request.

To conclude, the Enabling Clause could also potentially justify a CBDR-related exception, especially with respect to the LDCs. Nevertheless, several other conditions should be complied with by the EU.

10.6 CBAM and FTA Rules

The CBAM might come into tension not only with multilateral trade rules but also with bilateral and regional FTA rules, which often incorporate or reproduce core GATT obligations. As EU FTA adjudicators would likely take into account the WTO jurisprudence during the interpretative process of these provisions, especially in case of FTAs that expressly require them to do so,[330] similar conclusions as the ones reached in the sections on the pertinent GATT provisions could be expected, unless particular wording or provisions allow for a different interpretation. Considering the AB crisis, compliance with FTA norms becomes especially important as using FTA dispute settlement mechanisms, as alternative fora could be an attractive option for EU's partners.[331]

FTAs, which derogate from the MFN treatment, have no corresponding obligation to the one contained in Article I:1 GATT. Thus, FTA parties would not be able to contest the CBAM aspects that might conflict with the MFN obligations under the EU FTA rules. Nonetheless, EU's FTA parties could potentially invoke violations of FTA rules on the elimination or reduction of customs duties on imports according to the agreed

[330] For example, Free Trade Agreement between the European Union and its Member States, of the one part, and the Republic of Korea, of the other part (EU–Korea FTA), OJ EU 2011 No. L 127/6, 14 May 2011, Art. 14.16; Trade Agreement between the European Union and its Member States, of the one part, and Colombia and Peru, of the other part, OJ EU 2012 No. L 354/3, 21 December 2012, Protocol of Accession to the Trade Agreement between the European Union and its Member States, of the one part, and Colombia and Peru, of the other part, to take account of the accession of Ecuador (EU–Colombia/Peru/Ecuador FTA), OJ EU 2016 No. L 356/3, 24 December 2016, Art. 19; Comprehensive Economic and Trade Agreement (CETA) between Canada, of the one part, and the European Union and its Member States, of the other part, OJ EU 2017 No. L 11/23, 14 January 2017, Art. 29.17. In contrast, the EU–CARIFORUM EPA (Economic Partnership Agreement between the CARIFORUM States, of the one part, and the European Community and its Member States, of the other part, OJ EU 2008 No. L 289/3, 30 October 2008) does not contain a similar provision.

[331] For more, see Furculita *WTO and the New Generation EU FTA Dispute Settlement Mechanisms* (2021), pp. 61–193.

tariff schedules[332] or NT obligation, which is regularly enshrined in FTAs by incorporating Article III GATT *mutatis mutandis* (both paragraphs 2 and 4)[333] or by reproducing its text.[334] Still, newer EU FTAs seem to explicitly answer the question whether border tax adjustment would be a border or internal measure, in favour of the last. These FTAs, evoking the language of Article II:2 (a) GATT, clarify that a charge *equivalent* to an internal tax imposed consistently with Article III:2 GATT or the FTA NT obligation does not constitute a customs duty.[335] Thus, it seems that these FTAs align with the interpretation of Article II:2 (a) GATT as simply paralleling *Ad* Note to Article III GATT.[336] Therefore, the EU's CBAM would still likely violate the NT obligations contained in EU's FTAs (either as a charge or a regulation). In addition, regulatory aspects of the CBAM could violate FTA provision incorporating or reproducing Article XI GATT.[337] Nevertheless, EU's FTAs also contain general exception rules, by either incorporating or replicating Article XX GATT,[338] which could provide justifications for the identified violations. Yet, as in case of the GATT, it might be more difficult to comply with the requirements contained in the chapeau.

Along WTO incorporated or reproduced provisions, EU FTAs also contain sustainable development and climate provisions that might be violated independently or provide additional context for the interpretation of the first.[339] For instance, the EU's CBAM might come into tension with the right of each FTA party to regulate, including by establishing or

[332] For example, EU–CARIFORUM EPA, Art. 15; Economic Partnership Agreement between the European Union and its Member States, of the one part, and the SADC EPA States, of the other part (EU–SADC EPA), OJ EU 2016 No. L 250/3, 16 September 2016, Arts. 23 (5), 24.

[333] EU–Korea FTA, Art. 2.8; CETA, Art. 2.3; EU–Chile Interim Trade Agreement, 9 December 2022, https://policy.trade.ec.europa.eu/eu-trade-relationships-country-and-region/countries-and-regions/chile/eu-chile-agreement/text-agreement_en, Art. 2.4.

[334] EU–CARIFORUM EPA, Art. 27; EU–SADC EPA, Art. 40.

[335] CETA, Art. 1.1; EU–Chile Interim Trade Agreement, Art. 2 (c) (i); Free Trade Agreement Between the European Union and New Zealand (EU–New Zealand FTA), 30 June 2022, https://policy.trade.ec.europa.eu/eu-trade-relationships-country-and-region/countries-and-regions/new-zealand/eu-new-zealand-agreement/text-agreement_en, Art. 1.2 (d) (i).

[336] For a detailed discussion on the subject, see Section 10.4.1.1.

[337] EU–Korea FTA, Art. 2.9; EU–Colombia/Peru/Ecuador FTA, Art. 23; EU–SADC EPA, Art. 39; EU–Chile Interim Trade Agreement, Art. 2.11.

[338] EU–Colombia/Peru/Ecuador FTA, Art. 106; CETA, Art. 28.3; EU–SADC EPA, Art. 97.

[339] The EU–New Zealand FTA, for instance, contains a unique provision (Art. 19.6 (4) (c)) according to which each party shall 'promote emissions trading as an effective policy tool for reducing greenhouse gas emissions efficiently'. It could be considered to provide relevant context to establish that EU's CBAM, contrary to AB's conclusion in the *US – Shrimp* case (para. 164), does not represent an instance of arbitrary and unjustified discrimination when it encourages other countries to adopt ETS schemes.

modifying own climate policies as long as they are consistent with each party's commitments assumed under multilateral environmental agreements.[340] Furthermore, developing and LDCs could invoke FTA provisions according to which parties shall effectively implement the UNFCCC and the Paris Agreement,[341] which enshrine the CBDR principle. Furthermore, the EU–Colombia/Peru/Ecuador FTA, for example, expressly mentions that '[t]he Parties are resolved to enhance their efforts regarding climate change [. . .] in accordance with their *common but differentiated responsibilities and respective capabilities*' (emphasis added).[342] Consequently, in certain instances, developing EU FTA parties could initiate FTA proceedings with claims of violations of the FTA provisions enshrining the CBDR principle by the CBAM unless the exigencies of CBDR will be implemented.

In view of the analysis on CBAM's compatibility with FTA rules, to comply with its bilateral commitments, the EU should respect the same principles as already identified in the previous sections. To that end, bilateral rules only further heighten the arguments already made. Nevertheless, particular attention should be given to the specific wording of each particular FTA, since it could influence the analysis of the CBAM's consistency with these bilateral or regional rules.

10.7 Broader Implications

As in case of other instruments analyzed herein, the CBAM will have broader implications besides its mere legality under WTO law, which could be either positive or negative in nature. These implications would pertain to climate change, international trade, European market and stakeholders, and vulnerable countries.

As already stated, the Commission counts on a positive effect of the CBAM on climate change, incentivizing others to adopt more ambitious climate policies, leading to global reductions in GHG emissions.[343] Thus, it hopes to incentivize other countries to adopt similar instruments, especially since CBAM gives credit to third countries' ETS schemes,

[340] EU–Colombia/Peru/Ecuador FTA, Art. 268; EU–SADC EPA, Art. 9; CETA, Art. 24.3; EU–Chile Interim Trade Agreement, Art. 26.2.

[341] For example, Free Trade Agreement between the European Union and the Republic of Singapore (EU–Singapore FTA), OJ EU 2019 No. L 294/3, 14 November 2019, Art. 12.6 (2); EU–Chile Interim Trade Agreement, Art. 26.10 (2) (a).

[342] EU–Colombia/Peru/Ecuador FTA, Art. 275 (2).

[343] For more, see Section 10.2.2.

thereby creating a de facto 'climate club'.[344] Additionally, the Commission anticipates a positive impact on innovation in clean technologies in the EU and elsewhere.[345] Nevertheless, as argued, the CBAM's ability to counter carbon leakage is contested and its effectiveness might be undermined by export reshuffling.[346] Furthermore, while CBAM is likely to prompt multilateral negotiations on the issue,[347] it could equally cause turmoil and tension between countries, compromising a potential successful multilateral outcome. As many countries have criticized the CBAM,[348] these countries could sidestep multilateral negotiations. Still, the CBAM has already induced the adoption of similar mechanisms by third countries as several states, such as Canada and Japan, have already announced that they are planning to adopt carbon adjustment instruments.[349] Furthermore, it already stimulated cooperation among like-minded states with the G7 Climate Club terms being announced and the United States proposing to the EU the already mentioned creation of a Global Arrangement on Sustainable Steel and Aluminum, which would entail imposing charges on less green metals from third countries, such as those from China.[350] However, the adoption of multiple mechanisms with various designs targeting carbon emissions would lead to the fragmentation of the landscape,[351] making it more difficult to navigate for the business and reducing the likelihood of reaching a multilateral solution, since each state will be inclined to favour its own design. Furthermore, as can be seen, the CBAM seems to incentivize other developed countries to adopt similar unilateral instruments or to cooperate between them, while developing countries are

[344] Venzke and Vidigal, 'Are Unilateral Trade Measures in the Climate Crisis the End of Differentiated Responsibilities?' (2022), p. 190.

[345] Impact Assessment Report, Part 1/2, p. 68. [346] For more, see Section 10.2.2.

[347] See, for example, China's calls for multilateral discussions ('WTO: China Calls for Dedicated Multilateral Discussions on EU's CBAM', Third World Network, 16 June 2023, www.twn.my/title2/wto.info/2023/ti230610.htm).

[348] See, for example, the Joint Statement issued at the conclusion of the 30th BASIC Ministerial Meeting on Climate Change hosted by India, 8 April 2021, para. 19.

[349] European Commission, 'Carbon Border Adjustment Mechanism: Questions and Answers', 14 July 2021, https://ec.europa.eu/commission/presscorner/detail/en/qanda_21_3661.

[350] Nikolaus J. Kurmayer, 'Green industry: G7 Sets Out Terms for Global 'Climate Club', 13 December 2022, www.euractiv.com/section/energy-environment/news/green-industry-g7-sets-out-terms-for-global-climate-club/.

[351] Michael Mehling, et al., 'The Form and Substance of International Cooperation on Border Carbon Adjustments' (2022) 116 *AJIL Unbound*, Symposium on Carbon Border Adjustments 213–218 at 213.

showing reluctance, further increasing the divide between the two categories of states. Although the proponents of climate clubs argue that they could represent a bottom-up approach towards cooperation, a multilateral approach would be preferable, all the more so as it is generally agreed that it would be the most effective way of boosting mitigating efforts in addition to the NDCs under the Paris Agreement.[352]

The adoption of the CBAM is anticipated to have implications for the international trade law regime, beyond the issue of its legality. On the positive end, the CBAM being the first instrument of its kind could bring about answers to pressing international trade law questions, such as the long-debated issue of climate-trade nexus.[353] Nonetheless, the mechanism might entail more negative implications. Considering the increased level of 'weaponization' of international trade law, there is a risk of immediate retaliation by those countries that consider it protectionist or unfair without waiting for a final WTO report (especially considering the AB crisis), waging an international trade war and causing welfare damage to the EU.[354] India, for example, already announced plans to adopt its own carbon border tax as a form of retaliation against the EU taking into account also its historic emissions.[355] Likewise, it could create tensions with countries with domestic carbon measures that are not given credit under the CBAM or that result in only limited reductions in the number of CBAM certificates, as, for example, may be the case for China.[356] Considering the strong negative reactions to the EU Aviation Directive, similar reactions could be expected to the CBAM due to their shared features.[357] Furthermore, the EU was already accused of engaging in economic coercion with its CBAM by using trade restrictive measures with the aim of obtaining the adoption of ETS schemes in third

352 Ahmad, *WTO Law and Trade Policy Reform for Low-Carbon Technology Diffusion* (2021), pp. 159–160.

353 Pander Maat, 'The Carbon Border Adjustment Mechanism' (2022), p. 157.

354 This risk was also feared by EU industries (BusinessEurope, 'The 'Fit for 55' Package', November 2021, pp. 2, 18, 19, 20, 22). See also Gabriel Felbermayr and Sonja Peterson, 'Economic Assessment of Carbon Leakage and Carbon Border Adjustment' (2020) EP Briefing Requested by the INTA Committee, www.europarl.europa.eu/RegData/etudes/BRIE/2020/603501/EXPO_BRI(2020)603501_EN.pdf, p. 17.

355 Gireesh Chandra Prasad and Ravi Dutta Mishra, 'India Brews Its Own Carbon Levy to Hit Back at EU Imports', *Mint*, 19 June 2023, www.livemint.com/economy/india-brews-its-own-carbon-levy-to-hit-back-at-eu-imports-11687113102140.html.

356 Lowe, 'Should the EU Tax Imported CO_2?' (2019), p. 6.

357 Sapir, Horn, 'Political Assessment' (2020), p. 17.
Lowe, 'Should the EU Tax Imported CO_2?' (2019), p. 5.

countries.[358] Consequently, the EU risks to be accused of behaving exactly the same way it seeks to counter under the ACI, acting against what it preaches.

CBAM also entails implications for the European market and stakeholders. As argued, it would help creating a level playing field between the imported covered products and the like domestic products.[359] Despite this, European industry (including steel and aluminium) is not supportive of the instrument, as it would make the producers of downstream products, which are more likely SMEs, less competitive on the market facing increased prices of the outputs.[360] The initial scope of the CBAM proposal covers only some processed goods, most end products being excluded for now but subject to further review.[361] As the prices of the covered as well as downstream products are likely to increase, albeit only marginally, stakeholders fear that final consumers, especially from the poorer segments of the population, could be negatively affected.[362] At the same time, EU industries producing covered goods will face increased competition on external markets without carbon pricing, without benefitting any longer from the free allowances which will be gradually phased out.[363] Along these lines, export rebates could be introduced after the transitional period, which, however, as analyzed earlier, will cause tensions with EU's international commitments. Therefore, although at first glance the adoption of the CBAM could be considered being advocated by the EU industries, it is not without negative implications for them either. Last but not least, without complying with the CBDR principle, the CBAM, and especially its high compliance administrative costs, would have negative implications for vulnerable countries[364] such as LDCs and SIDS.

[358] Position expressed by H.E. Mr Pedro Miguel da Costa e Silva, Ambassador, Head of the Mission of the Federative Republic of Brazil to the European Union during the Policy Forum 'Unilateralisation of EU Trade Policies: Asserting Interests or Deserting Principles?', *Unilateralisation and Sustainability*, 27 October 2022.

[359] See Section 10.2.2.

[360] Paul Messad, 'Steel Industry United in Opposing Bloc's Carbon Border Levy', *Euractiv*, 23 December 2022, www.euractiv.com/section/emissions-trading-scheme/news/steel-industry-united-in-opposing-blocs-carbon-border-levy/.

[361] Wester van Gaal, 'EU Negotiators Agree on Historic Carbon Tariff', *EUobserver*, 13 December 2022, https://euobserver.com/green-economy/156534.

[362] Impact Assessment Report, Part 1/2, pp. 71, 73.

[363] Titievskaia, Morgado Simões, and Dobreva, 'EU Carbon Border Adjustment Mechanism' (2022), p. 7.

[364] Impact Assessment Report, Part 2/2, p. 21.

To conclude, even though, as enshrined in international law instruments, climate change represents 'a common concern of human kind',[365] due to CBAM's contested ability to effectively counter carbon leakage and manifold potential negative implications, the EU should have put more effort into trying to negotiate a multilateral solution before pursuing a unilateral instrument.

10.8 Conclusion

The EU's CBAM Regulation advances more assertively EU's interests and values by seeking to combat the risk of carbon leakage, although the degree of the risk itself and the effectiveness of the instrument in preventing it face considerable doubts. CBAM is also hoped to incentivize others to adopt more stringent carbon policies generating the so-called Brussels effect, promoting further decarbonization and the consumption of less carbon-intensive goods within the EU. In addition to potential climate effects, the CBAM also promotes EU's interests in ensuring competitive equality and a level playing field between covered imported and domestic products on the European market. While the assertive representation of these interests could be argued to be a prerequisite for fighting carbon leakage, it could also elicit accusations of green protectionism.

CBAM being a trade-related climate measure raises concerns over its compatibility with both international environmental and trade law commitments. In order for the CBAM to stay within the limits established by international environmental law, the present analysis demonstrated the need to comply with the CBDR principle in accordance with its more recent understanding in the Paris Agreement. The CBAM does not give regard to the distinct national circumstances of different countries as required. To comply with the CBDR, the EU should pursue the announced own resource based on CBAM-generated revenues to provide financial support to all developing countries, but also a full exemption from CBAM obligations to LDCs and SIDS.

When it comes to international trade law, as shown, the CBAM is likely to come into tension with such core WTO GATT obligations as NT, MFN, and the ban on quantitative restrictions. With the caveat that the analysis of the CBAM under WTO rules depends on multiple questions yet to be answered, with no pertinent jurisprudence on comparable mechanisms,

[365] UNFCCC, Preamble, Recital 1. For more on the concept, see Ahmad, *WTO Law and Trade Policy Reform for Low-Carbon Technology Diffusion* (2021), pp. 29–47.

and numerous related ambiguities, the chapter showed that the CBAM is, nevertheless, most likely to be found in violation of WTO core obligations. As argued, this instrument is likely to be considered as imposing a charge, either a border one considered under the limitation to Article II:1 (b) contained in Article II:2 (a) or an internal one analyzed under both Articles II:2 (a) and III:2 GATT, depending on the reading of the relationship between the two articles. Nevertheless, as Article II:2 (a) GATT requires *inter alia* compliance with the requirements of Article III:2 GATT, conformity with the last would be crucial for the analysis in either scenario.

The CBAM could infringe Article II:1 (b) by failing to comply with the requirements of Article II:2 (a) GATT, particularly due to the fact that the ETS might not be considered an *internal tax* and because CBAM targets inputs consumed during the production process. Furthermore, it was shown that the charge would clearly fall outside the scope of Article II:2 (a) GATT in case of products for which indirect emissions should be taken into account. Additionally, the CBAM is also likely to run afoul of Article III:2 GATT requirements, especially in case default values are used for the calculation of embedded emissions. Therefore, it is highly probable that the CBAM is found in violation of Articles III:2 or even II:1 (b) GATT, as the limitation contained in Article II:2 (a) might not cover the instrument. Although CBAM is likely to be considered as imposing a border or internal charge, it has other aspects that seem to have a regulatory nature, which could be assessed under Articles III:4 and/or XI:1 GATT. CBAM's regulatory mechanism could be perceived as providing less favourable treatment to imported products than the ETS to domestic ones, infringing Article III:4 GATT. Additionally, the CBAM's regulatory aspects could be found as limiting the importation of covered goods in violation of Article XI:1 GATT. Nevertheless, all the more so as changes required to the CBAM to comply with these core GATT articles might be considered as rendering the CBAM ineffective in addressing carbon leakage, reliance on a justification based on Article XX GATT could be preferable. Regardless of whether CBAM is considered a charge or a regulation, a border or an internal measure, due to the fact that it discriminates between different countries, it would almost certainly be considered in violation of the MFN principle enshrined in Article I:1 GATT. What is more, even differentiation based on the carbon footprint of different imported products could eventually violate this principle. LDCs and SIDS are currently not exempted from CBAM obligations, but such an exemption would be necessary in order for the EU to comply with the CBDR principle, which in turn might be proclaimed to breach Article I:1 GATT.

Despite many ambiguities related to CBAM's compliance with core WTO obligations, the chapter showed that a justification under Article XX GATT would most likely be needed, also in order to make room for a lawful implementation of the CBDR principle. It was argued that paragraphs (b) and (g) of Article XX GATT could justify CBAM's GATT violations. While it seems more or less undisputable that the CBAM would fall under both of them, the last one might be the preferred venue, due to potential difficulties in connection with the 'necessity' requirement attached to the first. Nevertheless, in case of paragraph (g), an additional layer of complexity could be added by Article 2 (3) of the Kyoto Protocol if considered in the process of interpretation. The test of the chapeau of Article XX GATT might be more difficult to pass. To comply with the chapeau conditions, CBAM should give credit to the carbon regulatory mechanisms of other countries (not only carbon pricing), avoid imposing export rebates also in the future, and seriously engage in multilateral negotiations with all WTO Members at least before the end of the transitional period. Furthermore, the chapeau of Article XX GATT could be conceived in a way that accommodates an environmental measure having due regard to the CBDR principle, thereby reconciling a potential conflict between international trade and environmental regimes. In addition, at least an exemption for the LDCs could be pursued in line with the CBDR principle by recourse to the Enabling Clause.

Bilateral and regional rules enshrined in EU FTAs replicating or incorporating core WTO obligations, such as the NT or prohibition on quantitative restrictions, could equally be violated by the CBAM, and then justified by the corresponding FTA rules on general exceptions. Although the analysis under FTA norms is likely to yield similar outcomes to those reached under the WTO rules, special attention should be dedicated to the exact wording of each FTA. Furthermore, EU FTAs enshrine the parties' right to regulate in sustainable development and environmental chapters, while others even consecrate the CBDR principle, which could also be infringed by the CBAM.

Finally, beyond the legal problems, the analyzed instrument would entail broader implications concerning climate change, international trade, European market and stakeholders, and vulnerable countries. Some implications could be positive, but there are also numerous perilous implications. In light of the incontestable importance of fighting climate change, the adoption of the CBAM should have been pursued but only after at least attempting genuine multilateral negotiations, a multilateral outcome being the most effective in achieving substantial climate change mitigating pledges.

11 Conclusion

11.1 Introduction

This book explored the question of whether the implementation of the new trade policy reorientation of the EU initiated with its 2021 trade policy review that resulted in several new pieces of policy approaches and trade legislation adopted between 2021 and 2023 complies with its international legal commitments and, beyond, with its multilateral orientation rooted in its constitutional essence and long political tradition. As illustrated in the above analyses, the new legislative instruments and approaches significantly expand the European Commission's capacities of effectively responding to trade and other coercive measures of third states and increase the EU's deterrence capabilities.

This final chapter will first put EU's recently acquired assertiveness in its trade policy into perspective (Section 11.2). Then it will summarize and exploit in a concise way the detailed assessments of the interlinkage between the new approaches and trade legislation on the one hand and the EU's international and constitutional obligations on the other, as explored in the previous chapters (Section 11.4). Before doing so, however, the results of our analyses of the constitutional and international legal constraints for the EU's Strategic Autonomy must be recalled (Section 11.3). Finally, we will deliver the core message of the results (Section 11.5) and in a prospective view explore the impact of the new EU instruments and legislation on current debates in the multilateral and bilateral context, in particular with respect to China, as well as relevant shifts brought about by the new trade policy within the EU (Section 11.6).

11.2 The EU Trade Policy's Assertiveness Turn in Perspective

The new trade policy is embedded in the EU's search for Strategic Autonomy and a new geostrategic orientation intending to address current world challenges posed by the crisis of multilateralism, by the need for new rules due to technological and economic progress, and imbalances and lack of reciprocity in the WTO Members' market openness, in particular China's,[1] induced not least by the unilateral practices and geoeconomic approaches of the United States and China.[2] The EU's intention to respond to these challenges stands at the centre of the new trade policy, as it allows the EU to take corresponding measures and actions at all levels of trade policy and thus to defend its values, interests, and trade rights assertively and to secure its independence. As shown in Section 2.1.3, the notion of Open Strategic Autonomy has gradually evolved and finally been invigorated with respect to the EU's capacity for resilience, interest protection, and independence;[3] it received a clear dimension of trade policy capacity building. Besides other facets of the trade policy review, the most significant for the new trade policy and the present research focus is the turn towards robust implementation and enforcement of EU's trade rights and assertive representation of its interests in a level playing field in terms of fair competition by establishing new legislative tools for unilateral measures and introducing new bilateral and international approaches (i.e. the MPIA and the stricter disciplines regarding Trade and Sustainable Development (TSD) enforcement in Free Trade Agreements (FTAs)) in order to remedy the lack of suitable multilateral rules to counter the challenges. Consequently, the new legislation and approaches give the Commission considerable new powers to restrain trade relations with other countries, which imply substantial consequences beyond trade policy for the overall foreign relations with them. The new legislation provides for mechanisms to unilaterally enforce WTO or FTA trade rights even if pertinent dispute settlement mechanisms are

[1] Trade Policy Review, COM(2021) 66 final, Annex, 8, 10, 13.

[2] Milan Babić, Adam Dixon, and Imogen Liu, 'Geoeconomics in a Changing Global Order', in Milan Babić, Adam Dixon, and Imogen Liu (eds.), *The Political Economy of Geoeconomics* (Cham: Palgrave Macmillan, 2022), pp. 12 f.

[3] European Commission, 2022 Strategic Foresight Report Twinning the green and digital transitions in the new geopolitical context, COM(2022) 289 final, 29 June 2022, pp. 8, 12. Suzana Anghel, et. al, 'On the Path to "Strategic Autonomy": The EU in an Evolving Geopolitical Environment' (2020) 652.096 EPRS Study; Milan Babić, Adam Dixon, and Imogen Liu, 'Geoeconomics in a Changing Global Order', in Babić, Dixon, and Liu (eds.), *The Political Economy of Geoeconomics* (2022), p. 11 f.

blocked or unavailable; it allows responding to geoeconomic behaviour by third states, in particular weaponization of trade relations, and establishes instruments which enable redressive measures in case of competition distortion by third-country subsidies or an imbalance in market access in public procurement, in order to ensure a level playing field. Ensuring a level playing field is also an important effect of a CO_2 border adjustment measure directed against undermining the effectiveness of EU climate policies by carbon leakage.

The comprehensive legal examinations and assessments undertaken in this book and summarized in detail in Section 11.4 demonstrate that while the EU in its new trade legislation strives for compliance with its international obligations flowing from WTO law, EU FTA and climate protection rules, and general international law on treaties and countermeasures, there are several areas in which we identified severe problems and even conflict with the EU's pertinent international legal obligations. The legislative instruments collide in several aspects with international law, and its implementation and application to concrete cases must observe certain limitations to avoid the EU derailing into (illegal)[4] protectionism, besides the political problem of counteraction by trade partners and hence conflict escalation. Consequently, the observer's concerns about the new trade policy instruments undermining the credibility of the EU multilateralism, its confession towards international law, WTO reforms, and free trade[5] are more than justified. The EU trade policy reorientation confirms the turn towards a trade policy that places more dominance on EU sustainability and human rights (in particular labour rights) but also security and resilience interests, and less so on traditional liberal free trade.[6] Due to the probable counteractions by third countries affected by measures based on the new legislation, this legislation puts at risk the EU's trading interests and European companies' market access to these countries. On the other hand, the extent of the criticism that the new EU legislation and the new EU approaches to

[4] See Section 3.2.1.

[5] See e.g. Sjorre Couvreur, et al., 'The Good Geopolitical Trade Actor? The European Union's Discursive Justification of the Anti-Coercion Instrument' (2022) *Journal of Political Science* Special Issue 133–147 at 136; Jan Wouters and Akhil Raina, 'The European Union and Global Economic Governance: A Leader without a Roadmap?', in Julien Chaisse (ed.), *Sixty Years of European Integration and Global Power Shifts: Perceptions, Interactions and Lessons* (London: Hart Publishing, 2020), pp. 198 ff.

[6] Johan Eliasson and Patricia Garcia-Duran, 'New Is Old? The EU's Open, Sustainable and Assertive Trade Policy', (2023) 14(Suppl 3) *Global Policy* 9–18 at 10.

TSD chapters in FTAs and dispute settlement contribute to the contestation of multilateral trade rules and to a further demise of rule of law in international relations or to the weaponization of international trade relations clearly appears exaggerated. In that regard, whether the criticism proves right will decisively depend on the way the Commission handles and applies the new tools.

The new EU trade policy is embedded within an advancement of trade policy from which the 'open, assertive and sustainable trade' policy does not fundamentally deviate. The turn of trade policy under the redirection towards more Strategic Autonomy of the EU does not reflect a deep change of ideas or normative stances; however, new directions are indeed taken by the strong focus on assertiveness and autonomous, partly novel capacities for enforcing reciprocity, independence, and a level playing field for companies competing in the EU internal market. Competition distortions can now be more effectively addressed, and the notion of unfairness in trade relations has been significantly expanded by new concepts introduced in the Anti-coercion Instrument (ACI)[7] and the Foreign Subsidies Regulation (FSR).[8] The former broad openness of EU markets is now replaced by a sort of 'qualified openness',[9] and the way towards more geopolitics and geoeconomics in EU trade policy has been unlocked not least by the ACI and the FSR, which give the EU the capacity to use available measures against certain trade partners in pursuit of specific (economic as well as non-economic) objectives addressing imbalances in their trade relations or to defend or even impose EU regulatory preferences. In particular, the ACI has the capacity also to be used in an offensive way, all the more so as the notion of coercive practice by a third country actually is vague. Robust implementation and enforcement of trade rules and international rights of the EU form freshly enhanced directions of the EU's new trade policy which affects all levels of trade policy: multilateral, bilateral, and autonomous. Thus, EU trade partners may observe it as an offensive turn towards significantly more power politics in trade, as EU trade policy is now part of the EU's overall foreign

[7] Regulation (EU) 2023/2675 of the European Parliament and of the Council of 22 November 2023 on the protection of the Union and its Member States from economic coercion by third countries, OJ EU 2023 No. L 2675, 7 December 2023.

[8] Regulation 2022/2560 of the European Parliament and the Council of 14 December 2022 on foreign Subsidies distorting the internal market, OJ EU 2022 No. L 330/1, 23 December 2022.

[9] Luuk Schmitz and Timo Seidl, 'As Open as Possible, as Autonomous as Necessary' (2023) 61 (3) *JCMS* 834–852 at 845.

policy more than ever before.[10] The dividing line between protectionism and assertive enforcement of one own's interest is a very fine one, and it is not only for the EU to determine it.

Still, multilateralism and the WTO as its institutionalisation in international trade relations have an important status in EU trade policy, and the EU trade policy's support and engagement on the international scene were reconfirmed,[11] but its salience has diminished. The cooperation for WTO reform as well as negotiations and conclusions of FTAs are continued. Yet, the assertiveness turn in trade policy shifts the challenges and consequences of the current contests for the WTO and, in particular, for the EU trade relations and its domestic implications to the forefront of EU trade policy.

The search for a greater Strategic Autonomy of the EU's trade policy must, however, remain within the confines set by international law, even though EU autonomy, understood as an EU constitutional principle that stresses the autonomy of the EU legal order vis-à-vis domestic and international law, obliges non-implementation of international legal commitments in case of their conflict with the EU's essential constitutional characteristics as defined by the CJEU case law. Consequently, EU autonomy as a constitutional principle could at first sight be perceived to back the EU's new trade policy turn towards strategic autonomy. At closer inspection, the constitutional principle of EU autonomy showed its neutrality to, even irrelevance for, the trade policy reorientation. As the EU trade policy's assertiveness turn does not protect essential constitutional characteristics of the EU, the protection of EU autonomy as a constitutional principle is not pertinent for the trade policy reorientation. Thus, the constitutional obligation for respecting international law and multilateralism remains a core requirement in and restriction for determining trade policy and legislating trade instruments also in the striving for more EU Strategic Autonomy.

11.3 The Assertiveness Turn and the Constraints for Strategic Autonomy

Consequently, autonomous trade legislation is not relieved from its constitutional constraints, so that the search for a greater strategic

[10] Eliasson and Garcia Duran, 'New Is Old?' (2023) 14.

[11] Trade Policy Review, COM(2021) 66 final, p. 6.

autonomy also in EU trade policy cannot justify any disrespect for international legal obligations of the EU. The constitutional obligation for respecting international law and multilateralism thus remains a core requirement in determining trade policy and legislating trade instruments. The international legal commitments, thus, also must be respected by the new trade legislation and cannot be pushed aside for the mere fact of their usual internal irrelevance for assessing the internal legal force of EU acts. The politically grounded but constitutionally not demanded[12] project for greater strategic autonomy of the EU cannot legitimate or justify the adoption of EU legislative instruments in breach of international law.

The requirement of international law compliance means, first, that the new trade legislation should, as far as compatible with its wording, be interpreted in conformity with international law, irrespective of whether it is international treaty or customary law. In this respect, one must recall that it is the substantive content of an international obligation as accepted by international actors that counts. Giving international rules a very specific EU notion, which is not in conformity with the internationally accepted understandings, applications, and conceptualisations of an international norm, in particular by relevant judicial practice, would not be helpful in avoiding conflict between EU legislation and international obligations. The CJEU in its approach to international law often is criticized for adopting a peculiar reading to an international legal concept in order to bring EU legal acts into conformity with international obligations.[13] A relevant example pertinent for the purposes of this book was

[12] For the sake of clarity, we must add here that this is not to say that the new trade policy lacks constitutional foundation or is even unconstitutional under EU primary law. As the new trade policy contributes to the pursuance of EU values and interests such as sustainability and human rights, it indeed has its constitutional basis, but this is to be discerned from the EU constitutional principle of EU autonomy. Allowing the EU to operate in greater independence from other nations and enforce its interests with greater affirmation is not part of the demands of the constitutional principle of EU autonomy.

[13] For this widespread criticism, see Eva Kassoti, 'Between Sollen and Sein: The CJEU's Reliance on International Law in the Interpretation of Economic Agreements Covering Occupied Territories' (2020) 33(2) *Leiden Journal of International Law* 371–389 at 378 ff.; Jed Odermatt, 'Council of the European Union v. Front Populaire pour la Libération de la Saguia-el-Hamra et du Rio de Oro (Front Polisario). Case C-104/16P' (2017) 111 (3) *AJIL* 731–738 at 736–738; Guillaume Van der Loo, 'Law and Practice of the EU's Trade Agreements with 'Disputed Territories'', in Sacha Garben and Inge Govaere (eds.), *The Interface between EU and International Law: Contemporary Reflections* (Oxford: Hart Publishing, 2019), p. 266.

the statement of the CJEU that a breach of the provisions concerning social protection of workers and environmental protection set out in EU–Singapore FTA authorises the other Party, in accordance with Article 60 (1) Vienna Convention on the Law of Treaties (VCLT)[14] to terminate or suspend the liberalisation provided for in the other provisions of the envisaged agreement.[15] As shown above in Section 7.4.2, the correct perception of the termination's clause requirements in these findings is highly doubtful.

Second, insofar as the new legislation not only pays explicit respect to WTO or other international obligations but even implements or explicitly refers to WTO or other international norms, those rules definitely would become relevant even for assessing the legal validity of the new EU legislation within the EU legal order. In such situation the conditions for direct effect of WTO law or other international rules within the EU's legal order would very likely be met.[16] Furthermore, customary international law may also be relevant for assessing the EU new legislation's lawfulness.[17] The above-detailed analyses, however, have shown that only some of the legislative instruments make explicit reference to international obligations quite generally,[18] and even then they only express respect for them but neither implement WTO or FTA rules nor explicitly refer to specific WTO norms.[19] As shown in Section 3.2.2.1, general inferences that a legal act has to be implemented with due regard for the EU's international commitments are not sufficient to confirm their direct effect. Consequently, the new trade legislation cannot be deemed illegal in the internal legal order of the EU even if the legislation contradicts EU international obligations. Even Article 44 (9) FSR is no exception. This Article in its last sentence reads that 'no action shall be taken under this Regulation which would amount to a specific action against a subsidy within the meaning of Article 32.1 of the Agreement on Subsidies and Countervailing Measures' granted by a WTO member. The provision does not implement said Article of the Agreement on Subsidies and

[14] Vienna Convention on the Law of Treaties, Vienna, 23 May 1969, in force 27 January 1980, 1155 U.N.T.S. 331; (1969) 8 ILM 679; UKTS (1980) 58.

[15] CJEU, Opinion 2/15, para. 161. [16] See Section 3.2.2.1. [17] See Section 3.2.2.1.

[18] See e.g. Article 5 (1) Trade Enforcement Regulation 654/2014; Article 44 (9) FSR.

[19] Art. 2 (6) CBAM Regulation excludes countries with which the EU had entered into agreements on their participation in the EU ETS from the scope of the regulation. In the same way, Article 1 in connection with Article 2 (1) k) IPI Regulation excludes public procurement covered by international agreements from the scope of the IPI Regulation.

Countervailing Measures (ASCM)[20] into EU law but takes care that the FSR is not applied in a way which would imply the adoption of a redressive measure by the EU that violates said Article of the ASCM. Any such measure issued by the Commission is not in conformity with Article 44 (9) FSR and consequently would be void for this reason, but not for its violation of the ASCM.

A political consequence of this state of constitutional and international conditions for the formulation of EU trade policy is the necessity of a multilateral approach, including attempts to come to multilateral solutions. Before the EU adopts novel trade policy instruments autonomously which tread new paths of law, the obligation to follow multilateralism suggests at least at a political, not necessarily at a legal level, that the EU is expected to pursue its regulatory aspirations for more effective and fairer trade rules on multilateral level first to find solutions on this level. Admittedly, not least with the current state of international relations, this appears cumbersome and not very promising. Nevertheless, as a corollary, the multilateral approach might mean that the EU addresses its issues with potentially affected trading partners and at least seeks dialogue with them before an autonomous approach is embraced. The concept of multilateralism in international relations implies prior dialogue with affected third countries before novel trade legislation that has a potentially trade distortive effect is enacted, irrespective of whether the new legislation is compliant with international law or not. Hearing the concerns of trade partners gives the chance to reconsider the legislation before adoption, to take care of some issues which one might not have thought of, and in this way to improve the regulation. Even though this might in the end not result in ameliorations of the legislative texts, it sends a signal of readiness for dialogue and for a still cooperative approach that does not lightly abandon accomplishments in international trade policy.

Our general analysis in Section 3.3 could also explore that while striving for strategic autonomy in trade policy, the EU has to respect international legal commitments stemming from diverse sources. The pertinent international legal disciplines highly relevant with regard to the legal assessment of the EU's new legislation's conformity with international law do not only result from international economic law, namely WTO dispute settlement and substantive WTO law, as well as EU bilateral

[20] Agreement on Subsidies and Countervailing Measures, 15 April 1994, Marrakesh Agreement Establishing the World Trade Organization, Annex 1A, 1869 U.N.T.S. 14.

treaties, but also flow from general public international law on treaties and responsibility of international organisations, as well as from international climate and environmental law. With regard to the EU's international legal responsibility, we could show that under certain conditions, the mere existence of legislation even prior to and independent from its implementation and application to concrete cases may already give rise to concerns. The mere adoption of a legal instrument even prior to its application may be assessed as an 'as such' violation of international law. This assessment depends on the degree of flexibility that the acting body, the European Commission, enjoys in its implementation of the legal instrument.[21] For a regulation to be 'as such' inconsistent, the legislative act would have to require a breach of international agreements or otherwise restrict in a material way the Commission's discretion to act in a manner compliant with international law.[22] The existence of discretion on part of the Commission in itself, however, is not sufficient to preclude an 'as such' violation.[23] A case of an 'as such' violation could be the amended Trade Enforcement Regulation, as it establishes an enforcement mechanism whose mere existence is contrary to the exclusionary character of WTO dispute settlement rules by virtue of Article 23 DSU.[24] Another, albeit less likely case of an 'as such' violation complaint might become the International Procurement Instrument (IPI) Regulation,[25] as it exempts from its scope procurement covered by FTAs and the Government Procurement Agreement (GPA),[26] which gives rise to

[21] For more, see Section 3.3.1.

[22] For the case of WTO law, see: Appellate Body Report, *EU – Biodiesel*, WT/DS473/AB/R, 6 October 2016, paras. 6.229, 6.281; Panel Report, *US – Olives*, WT/DS577/R, 19 November 2021, para. 7.146. Referring to older Appellate Body Reports from *US – Corrosion-Resistant Steel Sunset Review*, WT/DS244/AB/R, 15 December 2003, para. 100 and *US – Carbon Steel*, WT/DS/213/AB/R, 28 November 2002, para. 162.

[23] Simon Lester, 'A Framework for Thinking About the Discretion in the Mandatory/Discretionary Distinction' (2011) 14(2) *JIEL* 369–402 at 370; Panel Report, *US – Section 301*, WT/DS152/R, 22 December 1999, para. 7.53; Panel Report, *Brazil – Aircraft (Article 21.5 – Canada II)*, WT/DS46/RW2, 26 July 2001, paras. 5.9, 5.12; Appellate Body Report, *US – Corrosion-Resistant Steel Sunset Review*, WT/DS244/AB/R, 15 December 2003, para. 93; Appellate Body Report, *EU – Biodiesel*, WT/DS473/AB/R, 6 October 2016, para. 6.227.

[24] For more detail, see Sections 3.3.1 and 5.4.1.

[25] Regulation (EU) 2022/1031 of the European Parliament and of the Council of 23 June 2022 on the access of third-country economic operators, goods and services to the Union's public procurement and concession markets and procedures supporting negotiations on access of Union economic operators, goods and services to the public procurement and concession markets of third countries, OJ EU 2022 No. L 173/1.

[26] Revised Agreement on Government Procurement (GPA), 30 March 2012, Marrakesh Agreement Establishing the World Trade Organization, Annex 4(b), 1915 U.N.T.S. 103.

concerns over violation of the most-favoured-nation (MFN) principle, but only insofar as the carve-out under Article III:8 General Agreement on Tariffs and Trade (GATT)[27] does not apply to procurement covered by the IPI Regulation.[28]

11.4 The Results in a Nutshell

After these preliminaries and overall assessments of the new trade policy in view of its context and constitutional constraints, it is time now to summarize the detailed analyses of the new legislative tools and approaches as presented in Chapters 4 to 10 in this section, before further assessments follow. The first EU initiative that one must see as part of the new trade policy turn is the Multi-Party Interim Appeal Arbitration Arrangement (MPIA),[29] which aims at assertive enforcement of EU's multilateral trade rights stemming from WTO agreements. With this initiative, the EU showed its intention to pursue first a cooperative, multilateral (even though not in a technical sense) approach within the WTO, showcasing its support for this system. As shown in Section 4.3, the MPIA fully complies with the requirements of Article 25 Dispute Settlement Understanding (DSU),[30] replicates regular appellate reviews providing a sense of continuity of the familiar two-stage WTO dispute settlement procedures to its parties, and has already resulted in instances of successful application. In addition, the MPIA introduces several innovations addressing the voiced US concerns with respect to WTO's Appellate Body (AB) activity, such as exceeding the timeline, reviewing issues of facts, and issuing advisory opinions and thereby engaging in judicial activism, and allows the introduction of other novelties by granting increased flexibility to the parties. Accordingly, the MPIA might not only represent a multilateral alternative to the WTO appellate stage; it could also help to solve the crisis by providing new approaches that could

[27] General Agreement on Tariffs and Trade 1994, 15 April 1994, Marrakesh Agreement Establishing the World Trade Organization, Annex 1A, 1867 U.N.T.S. 187, 33 I.L.M. 1153 (1994).

[28] For the scope of application of the IPI Regulation, see recitals 7 and 10, Article 1 (1) and the definition of non-covered procurement in Article 2 (1) k) IPI Regulation 2022/1031, 2022 OJ EU No. L 173/1.

[29] WTO, Statement on a Mechanism for Developing, Documenting and Sharing Practices and Procedures in the Conduct of WTO Disputes, 30 April 2020, JOB/DSB/1/Add.12.

[30] Understanding on Rules and Procedures Governing the Settlement of Disputes (DSU), Marrakesh Agreement Establishing the World Trade Organization, Annex 2, 1869 U.N.T.S. 401, 33 I.L.M. 1226 (1994).

alleviate US concerns (potentially also shared by other countries), demonstrating EU's commitment to rescuing the multilateral dispute settlement. Thus, the MPIA could even represent a viable alternative to the WTO appellate stage without undermining EU's efforts towards more assertive enforcement of its trade rights: It results in awards of a quality comparable to that issued by the AB. MPIA awards are likely to provide an increased degree of coherence with existing case law, as confirmed by existing practice. At the same time, certain departures from problematic past jurisprudence are to be expected, which could even help with unlocking the current dispute settlement crisis or making the MPIA a permanent solution, especially if appeal arbitrators manage to gain the support of the Membership. As demonstrated in Section 4.5, in case of MPIA's disregard by a signatory, other party(ies) would not be able to enforce the arrangement and the pledge not to use regular appeals, diminishing its automaticity. Still, the likelihood of such a possibility is very low considering that the reason behind joining the MPIA is avoiding the lodging of regular appeals 'into the void'. Although the MPIA could be accused of endangering the multilateral dispute settlement by becoming the permanent solution and distracting the attention from solving the crisis, it currently provides a feasible alternative for its parties and WTO members in general.[31] Accordingly, with no better multilateral alternative in sight, this EU-led initiative is to be praised for conforming to EU's commitment to international law and multilateralism.

While the MPIA can be lauded for its promotion of multilateralism, the amended Trade Enforcement Regulation, which allows the imposition of unilateral countermeasures in case a disputing party refuses to join it and a WTO panel report is sent 'into the void', conflicts with the dispute settlement rules of the DSU, as shown in Chapter 5. The amended Trade Enforcement Regulation aims at ensuring that EU's trade rights can be enforced despite the ongoing AB crisis, but it undermines the EU's declared support for international law. The imposition of unilateral countermeasures without the Dispute Settlement Body's (DSB) authorization would violate Article 23 DSU (Section 5.4.1). Even though one might find the United States acting in bad faith, such defence for applying the new rules of the Trade Enforcement Regulation is still unlikely to be considered within WTO Proceedings. Furthermore, Article 23 DSU could also be violated 'as such' even before the application of the newly

[31] See Section 4.6.

introduced provision in question. The legal assessment of the amended Trade Enforcement Regulation for the imposition of unilateral countermeasures when an uncooperative disputing party blocks the dispute settlement procedures under bilateral rules proved to be more in line with EU's commitment towards international law (Section 5.5). Nevertheless, the amended Trade Enforcement Regulation could still violate substantive multilateral and bilateral rules, such as those related to market commitments or non-discrimination. This is because the Trade Enforcement Regulation does not fully comply with all the conditions established by general international law for countermeasures: that of being used for compliance and not as a prevention of appeals into the void or incentive to join the MPIA (Section 5.6). Finally, the Regulation has multiple other negative political implications, such as incentivizing others to follow suit, escalation of trade conflicts, damaged trade relations with other partners, and disadvantaging of small and less powerful states.

The ACI, a Regulation born out of the legislative process of the amended of Trade Enforcement Regulation and allegedly against the context of increased weaponization of international trade, allows to respond with unilateral countermeasures against 'economic coercion'. While the Commission argued the legality of this instrument based on international customary law allowing immediate countermeasures in case of an international wrongful act, as shown in Chapter 6, the wrongfulness of *economic* coercion against the international principle of non-intervention is a debatable subject. Although the EU's broad interpretation of the international principle of non-intervention covering economic coercion is not unfounded, it is not unlikely that the international community would not accept it given the extensive use of economic coercion, thereby impeding such an interpretation to be recognized as customary international law. If, nevertheless, economic coercion is covered by the international principle of non-interference, then a certain threshold should be achieved. As Article 1 (3) ACI requires that acts taken under it be consistent with international law and its Article 8 (4) can be read to limit the non-performance of EU international obligations to instances where the coercive measure of a third state is an international wrongful act, the ACI should only be applied to severe forms of economic coercion constituting an international wrongful act. Despite this, as the ACI allows the imposition of unilateral EU trade countermeasures, it could also come into conflict with multilateral and bilateral trade rules, all the more as they may represent special regimes and hence displace the general rules on countermeasures. Even though the ACI was diligently designed not to be a blatant violation of Article 23 DSU, WTO panels could still find evidence other than the statutory language of the Regulation to reach a different conclusion. Furthermore, as discussed in Chapter 6, in case of a WTO violation, customary international law is unlikely to serve as a justification. Accordingly, the EU is well advised to avoid taking unilateral WTO-inconsistent measures and to take the dispute to WTO adjudication where coercive measures simultaneously violate WTO rules. In case of regional and bilateral regimes, the ACI and measures based on it may conflict with substantive FTA rules, but either FTA-specific justifications or the general rules on countermeasures may provide a legal foundation for the EU's unilateral action, and their legality under procedural rules is less controversial. Hence, in this regard, the ACI is likely to pass the legality test under dispute settlement rules, but its violation of substantive FTA rules will be heavily contested, as it could be difficult for the EU to meet the required conditions of FTA justifications comparable to those contained in Article XX (a) and XXI (b) (iii) GATT, also given that the invocation of the latter might not be in the interest of the EU. Thus, although the ACI might prove a useful (deterring) tool in the current state of international trade regime, the potential costs associated with it (e.g. threat posed to multilateralism, escalation of conflicts, affected international reputation, emulation by other states, further weaponisation of international trade, etc.) might not be worth taking the risk.

Chapter 7 analyzed the EU attempts to strengthen the enforcement of trade agreements with regard to FTA TSD chapters. The new action plan announced in 2022 entails,[32] most importantly, the possibility to impose sanctions as a last resort (and solely in serious instances of non-compliance with International Labour Organization (ILO) fundamental labour principles and rights at work, and in case of violations materially defeating the object and purpose of the Paris Agreement[33]). Furthermore, the compliance stage rules should become the same as for market access commitments (Section 7.3.2). Interestingly, the current cooperation-based TSD dispute settlement model included in FTAs until 2022 resulted in concrete results when looking at the implementation of the panel report

[32] European Commission, The power of trade partnerships: together for green and just economic growth, COM(2022) 409 final, 22 June 2022.

[33] Paris Agreement to the United Nations Framework Convention on Climate Change, 12 December 2015, T.I.A.S. No. 16-1104.

issued in the recent EU–Korea FTA labour dispute,[34] albeit some changes are still pending. As concerns the current cooperative TSD dispute settlement approach, one cannot rely on general rules on countermeasures contained in the ILC Draft Articles in order to allow for the imposition of sanctions, due to the more special FTA TSD rules. The use of sanctions for TSD non-compliance would be possible only in instances expressly allowed by the FTAs also from the perspective of EU law, due to Article 3 (b) of the Trade Enforcement Regulation. Furthermore, contrary to CJEU's Opinion 2/15,[35] Article 60 (1) VCLT/ Vienna Convention on the Law of Treaties between States and International Organizations or between International Organizations (VCLTSIO)[36] and the 'essential elements' clauses from the framework agreements accompanying FTAs are unlikely international legal bases for sanctions in case of violations of FTA TSD commitments with cooperation-based enforcement model, the latter being *lex specialis*. Besides, the strict conditions of Articles 60 (1) and 62 (1) VCLT/VCLTSIO on 'fundamental change of circumstances' would be difficult to comply with. Therefore, the new action plan explicitly envisaging the imposition of sanctions is welcome and brings legal clarity, given the multiple ambiguities related to the invocation of general international law for the use of sanctions in cases of FTA TSD breaches. It allows the EU to successfully combine an 'open' but at the same time 'strategic' autonomy, sending a strong signal to FTA partners that TSD commitments should be implemented in practice.

As mentioned, another core purpose of the trade policy review concerns the assertive representation of EU interests, which EU more narrowly refers to as 'ensuring a level playing field'. Thus, Chapter 8 analyzed the IPI Regulation, which allows Commission to impose restrictive measures (i.e. a score adjustment on or exclusion of tenders) against companies from third countries that seriously and constantly restrict the due access of EU economic operators to their procurement markets. Since the IPI Regulation establishes measures only with respect to

[34] Report of the Panel of Experts (EU–Korea FTA Panel Report), Panel of Experts Proceeding Constituted under Article 13.15 of the EU-Korea Free Trade Agreement, 20 January 2021, https://circabc.europa.eu/ui/group/09242a36-a438-40fd-a7af-fe32e36cbd0e/library/d4276b0f-4ba5-4aac-b86a-d8f65157c38e/details.

[35] CJEU, Opinion 2/15, Free Trade Agreement between the European Union and the Republic of Singapore, ECLI:EU:C:2017:376, 16 May 2017. See Section 11.3.

[36] Vienna Convention on the Law of Treaties between States and International Organizations or between International Organizations, 21 March 1986, not yet in force, 25 ILM 543 (1986), UN Doc. A/CONF.129/15.

procurement for which the EU has not undertaken market access commitments in the field of public procurement or concessions under the GPA or an FTA, it conflicts with WTO non-discrimination obligations, namely national treatment (NT) and the MFN principle enshrined in GATT and General Agreement on Trade in Services (GATS).[37] The EU claims that Articles III:8 (a) GATT and XIII:1 GATS public procurement derogations protect IPI measures from the multilateral WTO disciplines. As shown in Section 8.4, these derogations exempt public procurement only under certain strict conditions, and the scope of the IPI Regulation is broader than the reach of these derogations. Accordingly, the adoption of IPI measures in specific instances of procurement falling outside the derogations' scope but still within the scope of the IPI Regulation most likely violate the WTO NT obligations, and also EU FTAs in case of IPI measures against an FTA partner on procurement not covered by these agreements. The same conclusion applies to the MFN obligation, as GPA signatories benefit from an a priori exemption; the IPI Regulation could even be subject to claims of an 'as such' violation, albeit the high degree of flexibility that the Commission enjoys is likely to render such claim unsuccessful. Therefore, the EU should pay utmost attention in the implementation of the IPI Regulation to apply it only to public procurement covered by the pertinent non-discrimination derogations. Furthermore, the EU should avoid taking unilateral IPI measures in case it responds to third-country measures or practices that allegedly violate WTO rules, as it would conflict with Article 23 DSU. The IPI Regulation could also result in other unwanted implications, such as the worsening of the situation of EU companies and smaller states and conflict escalation; nevertheless, the Regulation allows the Commission to take them into account when deciding whether to act. Accordingly, the legality of the IPI Regulation's application under WTO rules as well as the extent of negative implications will very much depend on the decisions taken by the Commission.

Chapter 9 analyzed another new instrument, the FSR, which advances EU interests of ensuring competitive equality by addressing the internal market competition distortions caused by foreign subsides. Article 44 (9) FSR providing that the Regulation shall not prevent EU from fulfilling its ASCM and other international commitments is not a safe haven to protect

[37] General Agreement on Trade in Services, 15 April 1994, Marrakesh Agreement Establishing the World Trade Organization, Annex 1B, 1869 U.N.T.S. 183, 33 I.L.M. 1167 (1994).

the FSR from any violation of international law, as much depends on the EU's interpretation of said commitments. While the FSR might become subject to 'as such' WTO complaints, assessing its conformity with international law hinges upon the Commission's application and exercise of its broad discretion in decision-making on redressive measures. The potential redressive measures adopted under the FSR first and foremost raise questions about the compatibility with Article 32.1 ASCM, allowing actions against subsidies only in accordance with WTO subsidies disciplines. Provided that the ASCM is interpreted to cover cross-border subsidization, the Regulation conflicts with the ASCM in case of subsidization to undertakings active in the goods sector. The public moral justification provided by Article XX (a) GATT, even if applicable, is unlikely to be successful due to the strict conditions of the chapeau, because unjustifiable discrimination is likely to be found when comparing foreign subsidies control to EU domestic situations (Section 9.3.1.3). Furthermore, the said discrimination will also block the justification of the FSR's conflict with the GPA and the GATS NT provisions flowing from the less favourable treatment granted to foreign services and service providers (Section 9.3.2). Thus, to comply with Article 44 (9) FSR, the Commission should apply the FSR only for services and procurement not covered by WTO law. Another layer of restrictions for the FSR application with respect to specific trade partners is added by EU's bilateral commitments (Section 9.4). In addition, the FSR might lead to other unwanted implications, such as eroding EU's international credibility, retaliatory spiral, restricted access to foreign markets for EU companies, and emulation resulting in further erosion of the multilateral trading system. Thus, considering the great leeway that the Commission enjoys, it is advised to pay utmost attention to international commitments in the Regulation's implementation, and as is the case with the IPI Regulation, the legality of the FSR's application under international law and the extent of negative implications will very much depend on its decision-making under the Regulation.

The last instrument, analyzed in Chapter 10, that assertively represents EU's interests and values both in terms of environmental protection and ensuring a level playing field is the Carbon Border Adjustment Mechanism (CBAM).[38] It seeks to address carbon leakage by imposing

[38] Regulation (EU) 2023/956 of the European Parliament and of the Council of 10 May 2023 establishing a carbon border adjustment mechanism (CBAM Regulation), OJ EU 2023 No. L 130/52, 16 May 2023.

the obligation to buy and surrender CBAM certificates on imported products from certain sectors for direct and indirect embedded emissions. Due to the fact that it does not differentiate between developing, least developed, and developed countries, CBAM most likely conflicts with the Common But Differentiated Responsibilities (CBDR) principle as enshrined most recently in the Paris Agreement (see Section 10.3). To comply with these principles, we recommend differentiated financial support to all developing countries and a full exemption of least developed countries (LDCs) and small island developing states (SIDS). Although the pertinent rules and WTO jurisprudence are inconclusive with respect to the exact category of rules under which CBAM has to be assessed, as shown in Section 10.4, the CBAM likely violates Article II:1 (b) or Article III:2 GATT if considered to be an internal or border charge, as well as Articles III:4 and XI:1 GATT for its aspects with regulatory character. Furthermore, the CBAM most likely violates the MFN principle of Article I:1 GATT, even 'as such', due to the a priori discrimination of different Members, as specific states are exempted from CBAM obligation or subject to reduced duties, or potentially due to the distinction between products with different carbon footprints. Therefore, the EU most likely needs to rely on justifications such as those provided by Article XX (b) and (g) GATT. As shown in detail in Section 10.5, the chapeau test might be more difficult to pass, and we formulated proposals to meet its requirements. It could accommodate a CBDR-related exclusion of LDCs and SIDS, and with respect to LDCs, an exclusion could also be justified by the Enabling Clause.[39] The CBAM could also come into tension with FTA NT commitments and quantitative prohibitions (Section 10.6). Furthermore, EU FTAs also contain climate-related and CBDR-incorporating provisions that might be independently breached by CBAM. On these grounds, bilateral trade rules only emphasize the importance of complying with international climate and trade law obligations. Although CBAM incentivizes others to adopt their own carbon pricing mechanisms and stimulates international cooperation, it similarly causes turmoil, tensions with certain countries, increased litigation, retaliation, and, in contrast to the level playing field intentions, could negatively affect the competitiveness of some European producers (Section 10.7). Therefore, considering the utmost importance of addressing climate change, CBAM should have

[39] Decision of 28 November 1979 (L/4903), Differential and More Favourable Treatment Reciprocity and Fuller Participation of Developing Countries (Enabling Clause).

been pursued with all the pertinent international law in mind and with more effort put into negotiating a multilateral solution.

11.5 Core Messages of the Results

Our analyses indicate that the scrutinized instruments were generally designed with international obligations in mind, as most of them pay general lip service to EU's international commitments. Some of the new tools recognize the potential conflicts with international multilateral and trade norms but rely on the invocation of international customary norms on countermeasures or WTO and FTA derogations and justifications; others try to limit the application of the legislation in a way that pays attention to the due respect for international law. Compared to a potential blatant disregard of international norms, EU's efforts to present its new instruments as compliant with international obligations are to be appreciated. Still, the interpretations accepted by the international community and those advanced by the EU in most analyzed cases seem to diverge completely or with regard to the range of the scope of these justifications.

We identified several cases in which instruments could conflict even 'as such' with both procedural and substantive WTO norms, such as Article 23 DSU and Articles I GATT and II:1 GATS MFN obligations, for example with regard to the Trade Enforcement, IPI, and CBAM Regulations. In our view this prompts the need for legislative modifications to comply with EU constitutional commitments to international law and multilateralism. Even more cases were identified in which the instruments could violate several core WTO norms, such as Article 23 DSU, Articles I, II:1 (b), III:2, III:4, XI GATT, Articles II, XIII:1, XVII GATS, and Article 32.1 ASCM, depending on the way the new tools are applied. Although FTA dispute settlement rules seem more lenient, many of the violated WTO obligations are incorporated in EU's FTAs. Furthermore, many FTAs contain more detailed rules on certain disciplines, such as those on subsidies, calling for non-application of the EU's legislation in those instances.

As had already been mentioned, the Commission has been vested with considerable powers in applying the new instruments, and hence it is able to and must pay the utmost attention to ensure compliance with constitutional principles consecrating respect for EU's international obligations and its dedication to multilateralism. At least the latter requires the Commission in bearing its responsibilities to balance between the positive and negative potential broader – including geopolitical – implications of these instruments when weighing whether and how to act. As argued, the majority of these instruments not only pose the risk of colliding with certain international trade law provisions; they also bear such risks as escalation of trade conflicts, deteriorating the competitiveness and market access of EU companies on external markets, emulation by other states of EU behaviour contributing even more to the weaponization of the international trade regime, disadvantaging small and less powerful states, decreased EU credibility, and further contributing to the erosion of multilateralism.

It has already been mentioned that in our view, there is a need for legislative corrections of the new instruments in order to better reflect the limits established by international commitments. The last opportunity to do so are future reviews of the analyzed legislation. If international customary norms contained in ILC Draft Articles are intended to be used as a justification for departures from multilateral and bilateral international trade provisions, the instruments should be designed with respect for conditions required of countermeasures imposed under those norms. Thus, the Trade Enforcement Regulation should be amended to comply with Article 52 (3) ILC Draft Articles. The legislators should avoid the potential inclusion of additional CBAM rules on export rebates after the end of the transition period. Furthermore, while advancing its climate ambitions, the EU should also not disregard its international commitments enshrined in multilateral international agreements, such as the CBDR principle enshrined *inter alia* in the Paris Agreement, all the more so as its importance is also enshrined in EU's bilateral agreements. It would be difficult to achieve tangible results by causing stir and backlash among countries rather than uniting countries across the world in the critical battle against climate change. Therefore, as argued, the EU should at least attempt a multilateral negotiated approach towards issues such as carbon pricing.

We propose further legislative amendments with regard to the ACI, first, in order to specify not only in preambular language but also in the main text that response measures are allowed only against serious cases of interferences to ensure that the non-performance of EU international obligations takes place only against an internationally wrongful act. Second, the ACI should be amended to completely avoid the imposition of response measures in case of simultaneous alleged breaches of more special trade rules, unless trade justifications can be lawfully invoked in the bilateral context to justify substantive violations. Third, the ACI could be amended to explicitly allow the imposition of internationally lawful measures in order to provide an internal EU legal basis for doing so. The IPI's scope should be modified to reflect the conditions of the pertinent derogations contained in pertinent international trade rules.

Despite our critique, some of the analyzed instruments, in fact, contribute towards the credibility of the EU as an actor committed to its international obligations and multilateralism. As shown, the MPIA sustains its support for trade multilateralism and could contribute to the unlocking of the current stalemate, while EU's current action plan for the FTA TSD enforcement offers the Union a valid legal basis for potential imposition of sanctions, avoiding a problematic invocation of general international law. Lastly, the analyzed instruments' potential negative impact on multilateralism and international rule of law should not be exaggerated, as the EU cannot be accused of flagrant disregard of international law, nor can it be held responsible for the demise of multilateralism. However, it should be more prudent and avoid their further unnecessary erosion, which would contradict its constitutional obligations.

11.6 The EU Trade Policy Turn's Impact on Current Debates

Beside its potential clash with international commitments and support for multilateralism, the EU's turn towards a more assertive trade policy is likely to pose further challenges in multilateral, bilateral, as well as internal contexts, particularly in current debates about reform of international trade rules, which will be briefly presented here to point out further consequences of our findings.

Due to the decision-making in the WTO by consensus, multilateral trade rules have mostly failed for decades to keep up with the world changes and adapt to economic and political developments. Some recent developments, such as the adoption in June 2022 of the first WTO agreement to focus on environment, the Agreement on Fisheries Subsidies[40] (which, however will be operational only once two-thirds of Members deposit their instruments of acceptance, as well as the potential successful outcomes of the 13th Ministerial Conference (MC13) in February

[40] Agreement on Fisheries Subsidies, Ministerial Decision of 17 June 2022, WT/MIN(22)/33 WT/L/1144, 22 June 2022.

2024),[41] could bring hope that the adoption of multilateral rules to address pressing problems such as climate change would be possible. Otherwise, reform proposals among WTO members might finally lead to plurilateral agreements to whose formation the new tools of the EU are capable to contribute.

Currently, it appears that the CBAM Regulation caused the strongest reactions among the newly introduced trade instruments from the EU's trade partners. Thus, while some countries, such as Canada and Japan, are considering the adoption of similar legislation,[42] a result sought by the EU, some intend to use carbon pricing as a way of retaliation,[43] and others, possibly including China, announced the initiation of WTO disputes.[44] Given the interest shown by so many countries, big and small actors alike, a discussion on new WTO rules to address carbon pricing is expected. China has been reported to already make calls for multilateral discussions within the WTO dedicated to the EU's CBAM and other border adjustment tariff schemes considered in the United States, which also may have significant implications for developing countries and the multilateral trading system.[45] Due to its clash with the CBDR principle, the CBAM is also likely to cause discussions within multilateral climate fora, such as within United Nations Climate Conferences. Thus, unilateral instruments such as CBAM can and do spark multilateral discussions on pressing issues. Still, as argued in Section 10.7, due to the divergent views of developed and, especially, big developing countries, such as China and India, that the CBAM has triggered, a broad multilateral agreement on carbon pricing currently seems less probable. Still, attempting a multilateral approach from the start should be the preferred route, rather than pursuing a unilateral approach, which causes tensions, even though it may inspire multilateral discussions.

The MPIA is another instrument that is likely to impact the reform debate regarding multilateral rules, specifically WTO dispute settlement.

[41] For example, WTO, 'Members agree trade policy review enhancement, delivering WTO reform proposal for MC13', www.wto.org/english/news_e/news23_e/tpr_26jul23_e.htm.

[42] See Section 10.7.

[43] For example, India (Gireesh Chandra Prasad and Ravi Dutta Mishra, 'India Brews Its Own Carbon Levy to Hit Back at EU Imports', *Mint*, 19 June 2023, www.livemint.com/economy/india-brews-its-own-carbon-levy-to-hit-back-at-eu-imports-11687113102140.html).

[44] 'China May Take Further Action against CBAM after Upcoming WTO Discussions: Analysts', https://carbon-pulse.com/206454/.

[45] 'WTO: China Calls for Dedicated Multilateral Discussions on EU's CBAM', *Third World Network*, 16 June 2023, www.twn.my/title2/wto.info/2023/ti230610.htm.

It could be said to set the current standard for alternative WTO two-stage dispute settlement that, beside the EU, was embraced by such major Members as China and Japan. As argued in Section 4.4, the MPIA is likely to influence the reform of the WTO dispute settlement process, as Members committed 'to conduct discussions with the view to having a fully and well-functioning dispute settlement system accessible to all Members by 2024' during the 12th Ministerial Conference.[46] Thus, some of the innovations introduced by the MPIA and the current (albeit scant) practice under it could represent in some respects an example of how dispute settlement rules could be reformed.

The FSR, with respect to which concerns were already raised within the WTO,[47] can be expected to also bring forward multilateral discussions about WTO rules on foreign subsidies, all the more as the EU, the United States, and Japan already work on proposals for renewed industrial subsidies' disciplines in the WTO.[48] When the FSR was adopted, the Commission's statement recognized that 'WTO rules may not be sufficiently effective in tackling the negative spillovers of state intervention in the economy' and confirmed its commitment 'to modernising rules on industrial subsidies to enhance the proper functioning of and to promote compliance with the WTO Agreement on Subsidies and Countervailing Measures (ASCM). In this context, the European Commission recalls its ongoing trilateral cooperation with Japan and the United States.'[49] Consequently, the Commission promised to invest time and strength in developing this debate further, and one should not be surprised if its endeavours in that regard would reflect approaches and solutions enshrined in the FSR. Besides, addressing industrial subsidies would add to the much bigger topic of how to handle and amend WTO rules accordingly, as well as the systemic challenges of China's economic system for WTO disciplines (see Section 2.2.2).

Furthermore, the ACI has also already sparked international discussions on countering economic coercion. Thus, while recognizing joint efforts including at the WTO, in May 2023, G7 Leaders expressed their

[46] WTO, 'MC12 Outcome Document', WT/MIN(22)/24 WT/L/1135, 22 June 2022, para. 4.

[47] WTO, 'Members Reiterate Concerns on Lack of Transparency with Subsidy Notifications', www.wto.org/english/news_e/news23_e/scm_02may23_e.htm.

[48] Bernard Hoekman and Douglas Nelson, 'From EU-Japan-US Trilateral to a Plurilateral Initiative on Subsidies' (2021) RSC PP 2021/08.

[49] Statement of the European Commission on multilateral rules to address distortive foreign subsidies on the occasion of the adoption of Regulation (EU) 2022/2560, OJ EU 2022 No. C 491, 23 December 2022, p. 7.

concern over this phenomenon in a statement and launched the Coordination Platform on Economic Coercion to increase their 'collective assessment, preparedness, deterrence and response to economic coercion'.[50] Accordingly, the ACI is likely to have already sparked some initial cooperative mechanisms to deter economic coercive measures, which is likely to lead to other reactions and discussions within multilateral contexts, such as at the WTO. Thus, although Chapter 6 showed that the question of ACI response measure's consistency with general international customary law is still ambiguous, the newly developed tool might have started a discussion that could lead to the development of international law and the clarification of existing uncertainties. Moreover, the issue might also come up during broader discussions on how to deal with issues related to national security, especially economic security, within the WTO.

Bilaterally, the Union's new approach towards FTA TSD enforcement could also pose further challenges for the EU's trade policy. As the EU seeks to open up and diversify trade with other nations by signing multiple bilateral trade agreements while at the same time trying to reduce dependence on the trade ties with China, the value-driven trade policy that aims at strengthening sustainability and human rights standards in international trade relations might hamper its aspirations for more resilience and less dependency with regard to its supply chains. As mentioned in Section 7.5, the EU's new approach towards TSD enforcement could make it more difficult to sign new agreements, as other countries might not be willing to accept it, and it is not clear if the EU would in that case be ready to lower its ambitions and sign FTAs with exclusively cooperation-based TSD enforcement mechanisms. In contrast, China and other trade actors stand ready to engage in more trade with partners across the globe without such conditionalities. Hence, the question arises whether some objectives of the new EU trade policy are not inherently contradictory, thereby potentially affecting the newly elaborated plan for stronger FTA TSD enforcement.

Finally, since internal and external challenges are interconnected, EU's new trade policy has already and is likely to further question the balance of powers among EU institutions. As shown in Chapter 5 on the ACI, the new trade policy tools touch not only upon pure trade matters but also

[50] 'G7 Leaders' Statement on Economic Resilience and Economic Security', 20 May 2023, www.whitehouse.gov/briefing-room/statements-releases/2023/05/20/g7-leaders-statement-on-economic-resilience-and-economic-security/.

upon aspects that traditionally fall under the foreign policy, where the Council would like to enjoy its traditional decision-making powers. Given the extensive powers that the Commission gained under the majority of the analyzed new tools, including by deciding whether and how to act, not only the Council but also the European Parliament (EP) might want to have a say. Accordingly, the question of Commission's accountability and the EP's role is likely to arise, while calls for parliamentary scrutiny can be anticipated. As argued in Section 1.1, increased Commission accountability could be beneficial also from the perspective of conformity with international law, adding an additional filter to ensure that Commission's newly acquired powers are not used to adopt measures violating EU's international commitments.

To conclude, the EU's recent turn towards a more assertive enforcement of its international trade rights and robust representation of its interests and values is likely to pose future multilateral, bilateral, and internal challenges, besides its legality under international law. These challenges, however, might also turn into opportunities and are certainly worth a close inspection in the years to come.

Bibliography

Abdelal, Rawi and Meunier, Sophie, 'Managed Globalization: Doctrine, Practice and Promise' (2010) 17(3) *Journal of European Public Policy*, pp. 350–367.

Ahmad, Zaker, *WTO Law and Trade Policy Reform for Low-Carbon Technology Diffusion: Common Concern of Humankind, Carbon Pricing, and Export Credit Support* (Leiden: Brill, 2021).

Akande, Dapo, Akhavan, Payam, and Bjorge, Eirik, 'Economic Sanctions, International Law, and Crimes against Humanity: Venezuela's Referral to the International Criminal Court' (2021) 115(3) *American Journal of International Law*, pp. 1–25.

Alden, Chris and Large, Daniel, 'On Becoming a Norms Maker: Chinese Foreign Policy, Norms Evolution and the Challenges of Security in Africa' (2015) 221 *The China Quarterly*, pp. 123–142.

Allee, Todd, Elsig, Manfred, and Lugg, Andrew, 'The Ties between WTO and Preferential Trade Agreements' (2017) 20(2) *Journal of International Economic Law*, pp. 333–363.

Aloupi, Niki, 'The Right to Non-intervention and Non-interference' (2015) 4(3) *Cambridge Journal of International and Comparative Law*, pp. 566–587.

Al-Sulaiti, Ahmed Essa, 'WTO Members Can Save Their 'Crown Jewel': A View from the Arab World' (2022) 56(1) *Journal of World Trade*, pp. 27–50.

Andersen, Scott, Friedbacher, Todd, Lau, Christian et al., 'Using Arbitration under Article 25 of the DSU to Ensure the Availability of Appeals' (2017) 17 *Centre for Trade and Economic Integration Working Papers*, pp. 1–10.

Anghel, Suzana, Immenkamp, Beatrix, Lazarou, Elena et al., 'On the Path to "Strategic Autonomy": The EU in an Evolving Geopolitical Environment' (2020) 652(96) *European Parliamentary Research Service Study*, pp. 1–53.

Ankersmit, Laurens, 'Opinion 2/15: Adding Some Spice to the Trade & Environment Debate', European Law Blog, 15 June 2017, https://europeanlawblog.eu/2017/06/15/opinion-215-adding-some-spice-to-the-trade-environment-debate/.

Apaza Lanyi, Pamela and Steinbach, Armin, 'Limiting Jurisdictional Fragmentation in International Trade Disputes' (2014) 5(2) *Journal of International Dispute Settlement*, pp. 372–405.

Arko, Annie, 'A Canadian Border Carbon Adjustment? GATT Compliance and Underexplored Exceptions' (2021) 16(9) *Global Trade and Customs Journal*, pp. 446–458.

Arrowsmith, Sue, *Government Procurement in the WTO* (The Hague: Kluwer Law International, 2003).

Arrowsmith, Sue, 'Reviewing the GPA: The Role and Development of the Plurilateral Agreement after Doha' (2002) *Journal of International Economic Law*, pp. 761–790.

Asteriti, Alessandra, 'Article 21 TEU and the EU's Common Commercial Policy: A Test of Coherence', in Marc Bungenberg, Markus Krajewski, Christian Tams et al. (eds.), *European Yearbook of International Economic Law 2017* (Cham: Springer, 2017), pp. 111–137.

Azaria, Danae, 'Trade Countermeasures for Breaches of International Law Outside the WTO' (2022) *International & Comparative Law Quarterly*, pp. 1–35.

Azoulai, Loïc, 'Structural Principles: Internal and External', in Marise Cremona (ed.), *Structural Principles in EU External Relations Law* (Oxford: Hart Publishing, 2018), pp. 35–66.

Åhman, Joachim, 'Exploring Border Areas between the Law of State Responsibility and WTO Law' (2020) 54(2) *Journal of World Trade*, pp. 219–238.

Babić, Milan, Dixon, Adam, and Liu, Imogen, 'Geoeconomics in a Changing Global Order', in Milan Babić, Adam Dixon, and Imogen Liu (eds.), *The Political Economy of Geoeconomics* (Cham: Palgrave Macmillan, 2022), pp. 1–27.

Bacchus, James, 'Legal Issues with the European Carbon Border Adjustment Mechanism' (2021) CATO Briefing Paper No. 125, www.cato.org/sites/cato.org/files/2021-08/briefing-paper-125.pdf, pp. 1–7.

Bacchus, James and Lester, Simon, 'The Rule of Precedent and the Role of the Appellate Body' (2020) 54(2) *Journal of World Trade*, pp. 183–198.

Baetens, Freya, 'Abuse of Process and Abuse of Rights before the ICJ: Ever More Popular, Ever Less Successful?', *EJIL:Talk!*, 15 October 2019, www.ejiltalk.org/abuse-of-process-and-abuse-of-rights-before-the-icj-ever-more-popular-ever-less-successful/.

Baetens, Freya and Bronckers, Marco, 'The EU's Anti-Coercion Instrument: A Big Stick for Big Targets', EJIL: Talk!, 19 January 2022, www.ejiltalk.org/the-eus-anti-coercion-instrument-a-big-stick-for-big-targets/.

Bakardjieva Engelbrekt, Antonina, Bremberg, Niklas, Michalski, Anna, and Oxelheim, Lars, *The European Union in a Changing World Order* (Cham: Palgrave Macmillan, 2020).

Baldwin, Richard, 'Global Supply Chains: Why They Emerged, Why They Matter, and Where They Are Going' (2012) No. 9103 CEPR Discussion Paper, pp. 13–59.

Baldwin, Robert E., 'The Case for a Multilateral Trade Organization' in Amrita Narlikar, Martin Daunton, and Robert M. Stern (eds.), *Oxford Handbook on the World Trade Organization* (Oxford: Oxford University Press, 2012), pp. 29–39.

Barfield, Claude, *Free Trade, Sovereignty, Democracy. The Future of the World Trade Organization* (Washington, DC: AEI Press, 2001).

Baroncini, Elisa, 'Preserving the Appellate Stage in the WTO Dispute Settlement Mechanism: The EU and the Multi-Party Interim Appeal Arbitration Arrangement' (2019) 29 *The Italian Yearbook of International Law*, pp. 33–52.

Baroncini, Elisa, 'The EU Approach to Overcome the WTO Dispute Settlement Vacuum: Article 25 DSU Interim Appeal Arbitration as a Bridge between Renovation and Innovation', in Meredith Kolsky Lewis, Junji Nakagawa, Rostam J. Neuwirth et al. (eds.), *A Post-WTO International Legal Order. Utopian, Dystopian and Other Scenarios* (Cham: Springer, 2020), pp. 115–132.

Bartels, Lorand, 'Applicable Law in WTO Dispute Settlement Proceedings' (2001) 35 *Journal of World Trade*, pp. 499–519.

Bartels, Lorand, 'The Trade and Development Policy of the European Union' (2007) 18(4) *European Journal of International Law*, pp. 715–756.

Bartels, Lorand, 'The WTO Legality of the EU's GSP+ Arrangement' (2007) 10(4) *Journal of International Economic Law*, pp. 869–886.

Bartels, Lorand, 'Human Rights and Sustainable Development Obligations in EU Free Trade Agreements' (2013) 40(4) *Legal Issues of Economic Integration*, pp. 297–313.

Bartels, Lorand, 'Human Rights, Labour Standards, and Environmental Standards in CETA', in Stefan Griller, Walter Obwexer, and Erich Vranes (eds.), *Mega-Regional Trade Agreements: CETA, TTIP, and TiSA: New Orientations for EU External Economic Relations* (Oxford: Oxford University Press, 2017), pp. 202–215.

Bartels, Lorand, 'Jurisdiction and Applicable Law in the WTO' (2016) Society of International Economic Law Working Paper No. 2016/18, pp. 1–21.

Bartels, Lorand, 'Does WTO Law Really Not Regulate 'Foreign Subsidies'?', *Linklaters*, 22 June 2020, www.linklaters.com/en/insights/blogs/tradelinks/2020/june/does-wto-law-really-not-regulate-foreign-subsidies.

Bauermeister, Tabea, 'A Tool to Investigate M&A Transactions with Regard to Foreign Financial Contributions' (2022) 3 *Zeitschrift für Europarechtliche Studien*, pp. 477–486.

Benitah, Marc, *WTO Law of Subsidies: A Comprehensive Approach* (Alphen aan den Rijn: Kluwer Law International, 2019).

Bhagwati, Jagdish and Patrick, Hugh (eds.), *Aggressive Unilateralism. America's 301 Trade Policy and the World Trading System* (Ann Arbor: University of Michigan Press, 1991).

Bhala, Raj, *Modern GATT Law: A Treatise on the Law and Political Economy of the GATT & Other W.T.O Agreements*, 2nd ed. (London: Sweet & Maxwell, Thomson Reuters, 2013).

Bianchi, Andrea, Peat, Daniel, and Windsor, Matthew (eds.), *Interpretation in International Law* (New York: Oxford University Press, 2015).

Bilal, San and Hoekman, Bernard, 'Introduction: EU Trade and External Policy in Troubled Waters', in San Bilal and Bernard Hoekman (eds.), *Perspectives on the Soft Power of EU Trade Policy* (London: CEPR Press, 2019), pp. 9–14.

Bluth, Christian Johannes, *Europe's Trade Strategy for the Age of Geoeconomic Globalization* (London: CEPR Press, 2021).

Bogdanova, Iryna, *Unilateral Sanctions in International Law and the Enforcement of Human Rights* (Leiden: Brill Nijhoff, 2022).

Bohanes, Jan and Salcedo, Karolyn, *Overview of WTO Jurisprudence in 2013*', in Christoph Herrmann, Markus Krajewski, and Jörg Philipp Terhechte (eds.), *European Yearbook of International Economic Law 2015* (Cham: Springer, 2015), pp. 337–373.

Boisson de Chazournes, Laurence, 'Remarks: The State of State Responsibility', (2002) *American Society of International Law Proceedings of the 96th Annual Meeting*, pp. 169–172.

Boisson de Chazournes, Laurence, and Lee, Jaemin, 'The European Union–Korea Free Trade Agreement Sustainable Development Proceeding: Reflections on a Ground-Breaking Dispute' (2022) 23 *The Journal of World Investment & Trade*, pp. 329–346.

Bollen, Yelter, De Ville, Ferdi, and Orbie, Jan, 'EU Trade Policy: Persistent Liberalisation, Contentious Protectionism' (2016) 38(3) *Journal of European Integration*, pp. 279–294.

Borchert, Ingo, Conconi, Paola, Di Ubaldo, Mattia, and Herghelegiu, Cristina, 'The Pursuit of Non-Trade Policy Objectives in EU Trade Policy' (2020) European University Institute Working Papers, RSCAS 2020/26, pp. 1–37.

Bordin, Fernando Lusa, 'Reflections of Customary International Law: The Authority of Codification Conventions and ILC Draft Articles in International Law' (2014) 63(3) *International & Comparative Law Quarterly*, pp. 535–567.

Bovis, Christopher, 'The Principles of Public Procurement Regulation', in Christopher Bovis (ed.), *Research Handbook on EU Public Procurement Law* (Cheltenham: Edward Elgar, 2016), pp. 35–59.

Bown, Chad P. and Kolb, Melina, 'Trump's Trade War Timeline: An Up-to-Date Guide', 24 March 2023, www.piie.com/blogs/trade-investment-policy-watch/trump-trade-war-china-date-guide.

Bradford, Anu, 'The Brussels Effect' (2012) 107(1) *Northwestern University Review*, pp. 1–67.

Bradford, Anu, *The Brussels Effect: How the European Union Rules the World* (New York: Oxford University Press, 2020).

Brattberg, Erik and Le Corre, Philippe, 'The EU and China in 2020: More Competition Ahead' (2020) Carnegie Endowment for International Peace, https://carnegieendowment.org/files/1-31-20_Brattberg_Le_Corre_EU_China.pdf.

Breton, Thierry, 'A European Sovereignty Fund for an industry "Made in Europe"', Blog of Commissioner Thierry Breton, 15 September 2022, https://ec.europa.eu/commission/presscorner/detail/en/statement_22_5543.

Brewster, Rachel, 'WTO Dispute Settlement: Can we Go Back Again?' (2019) 113 *AJIL Unbound*, pp. 61–66.

Brittain, Stephen, 'Justifying the Teleological Methodology of the European Court of Justice: A Rebuttal' (2016) 55 *Irish Jurist*, pp. 134–165.

Brolin, Matilda J., 'Procedural Agreements in WTO Disputes: Addressing the Sequencing Problem' (2016) 85 *Nordic Journal of International Law*, pp. 65–88.

Bronckers, Marco, 'Trade Conflicts: Whither the WTO?' (2020) *Legal Issues of Economic Integration*, pp. 221–244.

Bronckers, Marco and Gruni, Giovanni 'Taking the Enforcement of Labour Standards in the EU's Free Trade Agreements Seriously' (2019) 56 *Common Market Law Review*, pp. 1591–1622.

Bronckers, Marco and Gruni, Giovanni 'Retooling the Sustainability Standards in EU Free Trade Agreements' (2021) 24 *Journal of International Economic Law*, pp. 25–51.

Buffard, Isabelle and Zemanek, Karl, 'The Object and Purpose of a Treaty: An Enigma?' (1998) 3 *Austrian Review of International and European Law*, pp. 311–345.

BusinessEurope, 'BusinessEurope's Views on an International Procurement Instrument', Position Paper, 20 May 2020, www.businesseurope.eu/sites/buseur/files/media/position_papers/rex/2020-05-20_views_on_an_international_procurement_instrument.pdf.

Callahan, William A., 'Sino-Speak: Chinese Exceptionalism and the Politics of History' (2012) 71(1) *The Journal of Asian Studies*, pp. 33–55.

Cannizarro, Enzo, 'The Value of the EU International Values', in Wybe Douma, Christina Eckes, Peter Van Elsuwege et al. (eds.), *The Evolving Nature of EU External Relations Law* (Berlin: T.M.C. Asser Press, Springer, 2021), pp. 3–18.

Caranta, Roberto, 'Article 1. Subject-Matter and Scope', in Roberto Caranta and Albert Sanchez-Graells (eds.), *European Public Procurement. Commentary on Directive 2014/24/EU* (Cheltenham: Edward Elgar 2021), pp. 1–16.

Carter, Barry E., 'Economic Sanctions', in Rüdiger Wolfrum (ed.), *Max Planck Encyclopedia of Public International Law* (Oxford: Oxford University Press, 2015), https://opil.ouplaw.com/view/10.1093/law:epil/9780199231690/law-9780199231690-e1521?prd=OPIL.

Caspary, Daniel, 'Opinion: International Procurement Instrument – the end of the waiting game', *Borderlex*, 31 March 2022, https://borderlex.net/2022/03/31/opinion-international-procurement-instrument-the-end-of-the-waiting-game/.

Cass, Deborah, Williams, Brett, and Barker, George (eds.), *China and the World Trading System: Entering the New Millennium* (Cambridge: Cambridge University Press, 2003).

Ceretelli, Carlotta, 'EU – New Zealand FTA: Towards a New approach in the Enforcement of Trade and Sustainable Development Obligations', *EJIL:Talk!*, 28 September 2022, www.ejiltalk.org/eu-new-zealand-fta-towards-a-new-approach-in-the-enforcement-of-trade-and-sustainable-development-obligations/.

Chaisse, Julien and Matsushita, Mitsuo, 'China's 'Belt and Road' Initiative: Mapping the World Trade Normative and Strategic Implications' (2018) 52(1) *Journal of World Trade*, pp. 163–185.

Chandra Prasad, Gireesh and Dutta Mishra, Ravi, 'India Brews Its Own Carbon Levy to Hit Back at EU Imports', *Mint*, 19 June 2023, www.livemint.com/economy/india-brews-its-own-carbon-levy-to-hit-back-at-eu-imports-11687113102140.html.

Chandy, Sandeep Thomas and Dasgupta, Anupal, 'Government Procurement Outside the GPA: A Developing Country View' (2019) 14(7 & 8) *Global Trade and Customs Journal*, pp. 383–390.

Charnovitz, Steve, 'Grading Trump's China Trade Strategy', in Marc Bungenberg, Markus Krajewski, Christian Tams et al. (eds.), *European Yearbook of International Economic Law 2019* (Cham: Springer, 2020), pp. 217–256.

Cheng, Bin, *General Principles of Law as Applied by International Courts and Tribunals* (London: Grotius Publications Limited, 1987).

Choer Moraes, Henrique, 'The Turn to Managed Interdependence: A Glimpse into the Future of International Economic Law?' *EJIL:Talk!*, 14 August 2018, www.ejiltalk.org/the-turn-to-managed-interdependence-a-glimpse-into-the-future-of-international-economic-law.

Choer Moraes, Henrique and Wigell, Mikael, 'Balancing Dependence: The Quest for Autonomy and the Rise of Corporate Geoeconomics', in Milan Babić, Adam Dixon, and Imogen Liu (eds.), *The Political Economy of Geoeconomics* (Cham: Palgrave Macmillan, 2022), pp. 29–55.

Choi, Won-Mog, *'Like Products' in International Trade Law. Towards a Consistent GATT/WTO Jurisprudence* (New York: Oxford University Press, 2003).

Claussen, Kathleen, 'Reimagining Trade-Plus Compliance: The Labor Story' (2020) 23 *Journal of International Economic Law*, pp. 25–43.

Colli Vignarelli, Mattia, 'The European Commission Trade Policy Review: The Effectiveness of Sustainable Development Chapters in EU FTAs' (2021) 6(1) *European Papers*, pp. 1–5.

Collins, David, 'Government Procurement with Strings Attached: The Uneven Control of Offsets by the World Trade Organization and Regional Trade Agreements' (2018) 8 *Asian Journal of International Law*, pp. 301–321.

Conconi, Paola and Voon, Tania, 'EC – Seal Products: The Tension between Public Morals and International Trade Agreements' (2015) EUI Working Paper RSCAS 2015/70, pp. 1–19.

Conley, Heather, 'The Birth of a Global Strategy amid Deep Crisis' (2016) 51(3) *The International Spectator*, pp. 12–14.

Cosbey, Aaron and Mavroidis, Petros C., 'A Turquoise Mess: Green Subsidies, Blue Industrial Policy and Renewable Energy: The Case for Redrafting the Subsidies Agreement of the WTO' (2014) EUI Robert Schuman Centre for Advanced Studies Working Paper 2014/17, pp. 1–30.

Couvreur, Sjorre, De Ville, Ferdi, Jacobs, Thomas, and Orbie, Jan, 'The Good Geopolitical Trade Actor? The European Union's Discursive Justification of the Anti-Coercion Instrument' (2022) Special Issue *Perspectivas Journal of Political Science*, pp. 133–147.

Crawford, James, 'State Responsibility', in Rüdiger Wolfrum (ed.), *Max Planck Encyclopedia of International Law* (Oxford: Oxford University Press, 2006), https://opil.ouplaw.com/display/10.1093/law:epil/9780199231690/law-9780199231690-e1093?prd=EPIL.

Cremona, Marise, 'The European Union and Regional Trade Agreements', in Christoph Herrmann and Jörg Philipp Terhechte (eds.), *European Yearbook of International Economic Law 2010* (Cham: Springer, 2010), pp. 245–268.

Cremona, Marise, 'Values in Foreign Policy', in Malcolm Evans and Panos Koutrakos (eds.), *Beyond the Established Legal Orders* (Oxford: Hart Publishing, 2011), pp. 275–317.

Cremona, Marise, *State Responsibility. The General Part* (New York: Cambridge University Press, 2013).

Cremona, Marise, 'A Quiet Revolution: The Changing Nature of the EU's Common Commercial Policy', in Marc Bungenberg, Markus Krajewski, Christian Tams et al. (eds.), *European Yearbook of International Economic Law 2017* (Cham: Springer, 2017), pp. 3–34.

Cremona, Marise, 'A Quiet Revolution: The Common Commercial Policy Six Years after the Treaty of Lisbon' (2017) Report No. 2, Swedish Institute for European Policy Studies, pp. 1–61.

Criddle, Evan J., 'Humanitarian Financial Intervention' (2013) 24 *European Journal of International Law*, pp. 583–615.

Crochet, Victor, 'The EU Anti-Coercion Mechanism: Legitimate Trade Instrument or Hidden "Economic" Sanction', EU Law Live Weekend Edition No. 96, 2 April 2022, pp. 2–13.

Crochet, Victor and Gustafsson, Marcus, 'Lawful Remedy or Illegal Response? Resolving the Issue of Foreign Subsidization under WTO Law' (2021) 20(3) *World Trade Review*, pp. 343–366.

Crochet, Victor and Hedge, Vineet, 'China's "Going Global" Policy: Transnational Production Subsidies under the WTO SCM' (2020) 23(4) *Journal of International Economic Law*, pp. 841–863.

Curran, Louise, Eckhardt, Jappe, and Lee, Jaemin 'The Trade Policy Response to COVID-19 and Its Implications for International Business' (2021) 17(2) *Critical Perspectives on International Business*, pp. 252–320.

Dalpé, Vincent, 'Canada – Feed-In Tariff: Are FITs Desirable, or Even Legal? A Case Comment' (2014) 27(1) *Quebec Journal of International Law*, pp. 87–112.

Daunton, Martin, 'The Inconsistent Quarte: Free Trade Versus Competing Goals', in Amrita Narlikar, Martin Daunton, and Robert M. Stern (eds.), *Oxford Handbook on the World Trade Organization* (New York: Oxford University Press, 2012), pp. 40–63.

Davidson Ladly, Sarah, 'Border Carbon Adjustments, WTO-Law and the Principle of Common but Differentiated Responsibilities' (2012) 12(1) *International Environmental Agreements: Politics, Law and Economics*, pp. 63–84.

Davies, Arwel, 'The GATT Article III:8(a) Procurement Derogation and Canada – Renewable Energy' (2015) 18(3) *Journal of International Economic Law*, pp. 543–554.

Dawar, Kamala, 'Government Procurement in the WTO: A Case for Greater Integration' (2016a) 15(4) *World Trade Review*, pp. 645–670.

Dawar, Kamala, 'The 2016 European Union International Procurement Instrument's Amendments to the 2012 Buy European Proposal: A Retrospective Assessment of Its Prospects' (2016b) 50(5) *Journal of World Trade*, pp. 845–866.

De Andrade, Mariana, 'Procedural Innovations in the MPIA: A Way to Strengthen the WTO Dispute Settlement Mechanism?' (2020) *Questions of International Law*, www.qil-qdi.org/procedural-innovations-in-the-mpia-a-way-to-strengthen-the-wto-dispute-settlement-mechanism/.

De Andrade, Mariana, 'The EU's Anti-Coercion Instrument: Balancing Ambiguity', International Economic Law and Policy Blog, 13 November 2022, https://ielp.worldtradelaw.net/2022/11/guest-post-the-eus-anti-coercion-instrument-balancing-ambiguity.html.

De Bièvre, Dirk, 'EU Regulatory Trade Agenda and the Quest for WTO Trade Enforcement' (2006) 13(6) *Journal of European Public Policy*, pp. 851–866.

De Konink, Constant, Ronse, Thierry, and Timmermans, William, *European Public Procurement Law: The Public Sector Procurement Directive Explained through 30 Years of Case Law by the Court of Justice of the European Union*, 2nd ed. (Alphen aan den Rijn: Wolters Kluwer, 2015).

De Witte, Bruno, 'The EU and the International Legal Order: The Case of Human Rights', in Malcolm Evans, Panos Koutrakos (eds.), *Beyond the Established Legal Orders: Policy Interconnections Between the EU and the Rest of the World* (Oxford: Hart Publishing, 2011), pp. 127–148.

De Witte, Bruno, 'A Selfish Court? The Court of Justice and the Design of International Dispute Settlement Beyond the EU', in Marise Cremona and Anne Thies (eds.), *The European Court of Justice and External Relations Law* (Oxford: Hart Publishing, 2014), pp. 33–46.

Dias, Anna, Seeuws, Stéphanie, and Nosowicz, Agnieszka, 'EU Border Carbon Adjustment and the WTO: Hand in Hand Towards Tackling Climate Change' (2020) 15(1) *Global Trade and Customs Journal*, pp. 15–23.

Dimopoulos, Angelos, 'The Effects of the Lisbon Treaty on the Principles and Objectives of the Common Commercial Policy' (2010) 15(2) *European Foreign Affairs Review*, pp. 153–170.

Dobson, Natalie L. and Ryngaert, Cedric, 'Provocative Climate Protection: EU 'Extraterritorial' Regulation of Maritime Emissions' (2017) 66 *International & Comparative Law Quarterly*, pp. 295–333.

Dörr, Oliver and Schmalenbach, Kirsten (eds.), *Vienna Convention on the Law of Treaties. A Commentary*, 2nd ed. (Heidelberg: Springer, 2018).

Dreyer, Iana, 'Ostrich Policy: The EU's Anti-Coercion Instrument Risks Becoming a Damp Squib' (2022) *Borderlex*, 1 February 2022, https://borderlex.net/2022/02/01/comment-ostrich-policy-the-eus-anti-coercion-instrument-risks-becoming-a-damp-squib/.

Drezner, Daniel, Farrell, Henry, and Newman, Abraham (eds.), *The Uses and Abuses of Weaponized Interdependence* (Washington, DC: Brookings Institution Press, 2021).

Duchâtel, Mathieu, 'Effective Deterrence? The Coming European Anti-Coercion Instrument', *Institut Montaigne*, 2 December 2022, www.institutmontaigne.org/en/expressions/effective-deterrence-coming-european-anti-coercion-instrument.

Dunbar, Rupert, 'Article 3 (5) TEU a Decade On: Revisiting 'Strict Observance of International Law' in the Text and Context of Other EU Values' (2021) 28(4) *Maastricht Journal of European and Comparative Law*, pp. 479–497.

Dutta Mishra, Ravi, 'India Seeks Taiwan, South Africa Backing on Carbon Tax', *Mint*, 16 June 2023, www.livemint.com/economy/india-seeks-taiwan-s-africa-backing-on-carbon-border-tax-11686936697768.html.

Dür, Andreas, Eckhardt, Jappe, and Poletti, Arlo, 'Global Value Chains, the Anti-Globalization Backlash, and EU Trade Policy: A Research Agenda' (2020) 27 *Journal of European Public Policy*, pp. 944–956.

Early, Bryan R. and Cilizoglu, Menevis, 'Economic Sanctions in Flux: Enduring Challenges, New Policies, and Defining the Future Research Agenda' (2020) 21(4) *International Studies Perspectives*, pp. 438–477.

Ebrecht, Caspar, 'Foreign Subsidies Regulation and EU International Procurement' (2022) 3 *Zeitschrift für Europarechtliche Studien*, pp. 487–494.

Eeckhout, Piet, *The European Internal Market and International Trade: A Legal Analysis* (New York: Oxford University Press, 1994).

Eeckhout, Piet, 'The Integration of Public International Law in EU Law: Analytical and Normative Questions', in Piet Eeckhout and Manuel López-Escudero (eds.), *The EU's External Action in Times of Crisis* (Oxford: Hart Publishing, 2016), pp. 189–204.

Eeckhout, Piet, 'Brexit After the Negotiation of the Trade and Cooperation Agreement: Who Takes Back Control of What?' (2021) 68 *Revista de Derecho Comunitario Europeo*, pp. 11–22.

Eliasson, Johan and Garcia-Duran, Patricia, 'New Is Old? The EU's Open, Sustainable and Assertive Trade Policy' (2023) 14(Suppl 3) *Global Policy*, pp. 9–18.

Englisch, Joachim and Falcão, Tatiana, 'EU Carbon Border Adjustments and WTO Law, Part One' (2021a) 51(10) *Environmental Law Reporter*, pp. 10857–10882.

Englisch, Joachim and Falcão, Tatiana, 'EU Carbon Border Adjustments and WTO Law, Part Two' (2021b) 51(11) *Environmental Law Reporter*, pp. 10935–10946.

Erixon, Frederik, Guinea, Oscar, Lamprecht, Philipp et al., 'The New Wave of Defensive Trade Policy Measures in the European Union', European Centre for International Political Economy Occasional Paper No 04/2022.

Espa, Ilaria, 'Reconciling the Climate/Industrial Interplay of CBAMs: What Role for the WTO?' (2022) 116 *American Journal of International Law Unbound*, Symposium on Carbon Border Adjustments, pp. 208–212.

Espa, Ilaria, Francois, Joseph, and van Asselt, Harro, 'The EU Proposal for a Carbon Border Adjustment Mechanism (CBAM): An Analysis under WTO and Climate Change Law' (2022) World Trade Institute Working Paper No. 06/2022, pp. 1–30.

Evenett, Simon J., 'Paper Tiger? EU Trade Enforcement as if Binding Pacts Mattered' (2016) *New Direction, The Foundation for European Reform*, pp. 8–41.

Evenett, Simon J., Sud, Juhi Dion, and Vermulst, Edwin, 'The European Union's New Move Against China: Countervailing Chinese Outward Foreign Direct Investment' (2020) 15(9) *Global Trade and Customs Journal*, pp. 413–422.

Fang, Meng Mandy, 'Shades of Green: Mapping the Parameters of the GATT Article III:8(a) Government Procurement Derogation in the Renewable Energy Transition' (2019) 20 *The Journal of World Investment & Trade*, pp. 553–576.

Fanou, Maria, 'The CETA ICS and the Autonomy of the EU Legal Order in Opinion 1/17' (2020) 22 *Cambridge Yearbook of European Legal Studies*, pp. 106–132.

Farrell, Henry and Newman, Abraham, 'Weaponized Interdependence' (2019) 44(1) *International Security*, pp. 42–79.

Felbermayr, Gabriel, 'A Trumpian Turn in EU Trade Politics and the Silence of Germany', 2018 EconPol Opinion 6, www.econpol.eu/opinion_6.

Felbermayr, Gabriel and Peterson, Sonja, 'Economic Assessment of Carbon Leakage and Carbon Border Adjustment' (2020) EP Briefing Requested by the INTA Committee, www.europarl.europa.eu/RegData/etudes/BRIE/2020/603501/EXPO_BRI(2020)603501_EN.pdf, pp. 5–21.

Felbermayr, Gabriel and Steininger, Marina, 'Trump's Trade Attack on China – Who Will Have the Last Laugh?' (2019) 20(1) *CesIfo Forum 1/2019*, pp. 27–32.

Fernández Pons, Javier, 'Self-Help and the World Trade Organization', in Paolo Mengozzi (ed.), *International Trade Law on the 50th Anniversary of the Multilateral Trade System* (Milano: Giuffrè, 1999), pp. 55-112.

Fernández Pons, Javier, 'The European Commission's Proposed Anti-Coercion Instrument from an International Law Perspective' (2023) *CIDOB*, www.cidob.org/en/articulos/monografias/la_estrategia_geoeconomica_de_china/the_european_commission_s_proposed_anti_coercion_instrument_from_an_international_law_perspective, pp. 57–63.

Fiorini, Matteo, Hoekman, Bernard M., Mavroidis, Petros C. et al., 'WTO Dispute Settlement and the Appellate Body Crisis: Insider Perceptions and Members' Revealed Preferences' (2020) 54(5) *Journal of World Trade*, pp. 667–698.

Fisler Damrosch, Lori, 'The Legitimacy of Economic Sanctions as Countermeasures for Wrongful Acts' (2019) 37 *Berkeley Journal of International Law*, pp. 250–264.

Fitzmaurice, Malgosia, 'Material Breach of Treaty: Some Legal Issues' (2001) 6 *Austrian Review of International and European Law*, pp. 3–44.

Flett, James, 'Referring PTA Disputes to the WTO Dispute Settlement System', in Andreas Dür and Manfred Elsig (eds.), *Trade Cooperation: The Purpose, Design and Effects of Preferential Trade Agreements* (Cambridge: Cambridge University Press, 2015), pp. 555–579.

Flett, James, 'The European Union Carbon Border Adjustment Mechanism and Its Consistency with World Trade Organization Law', in European Commission, *70 Years of EU Law: A Union for its Citizens* (Brussels: Bietlot, 2022), pp. 268–290.

Frankopan, Peter, *The New Silk Roads. The Present and Future of the World* (London: Bloomsbury Publishing, 2018).

Furculita, Cornelia, 'The Time of PTA Dispute Settlement Mechanisms Might Have Come', in Manfred Elsig, Rodrigo Polanco, and Peter Van den Bossche (eds.), *International Economic Dispute Settlement: Demise or Transformation?* (New York: Cambridge University Press, 2021a), pp. 442–469.

Furculita, Cornelia, *The WTO and the New Generation EU FTA Dispute Settlement Mechanisms: Interacting in a Fragmented and Changing International Trade Law Regime* (Cham: Springer, 2021b).

Gabriel, Marc, Schulz, Andreas, and Manzini, Alice, 'Proposal for an International Procurement Instrument: The Undiscovered (Third) Country' (2020) *Public Procurement Law Review*, pp. 335–342.

Galiffa, Chiara and Garcia Bercero, Ignacio, 'How WTO-Consistent Tools Can Ensure the Decarbonization of Emission-Intensive Industrial Sectors' (2022) 116 *American Journal of International Law Unbound*, Symposium on Carbon Border Adjustments, pp. 196–201.

Gao, Henry, 'Finding a Rule-Based Solution to the Appellate Body Crisis: Looking Beyond the Multiparty Interim Appeal Arbitration Arrangement' (2021) 24 *Journal of International Economic Law*, pp. 534–550.

Gao, Henry, 'Will the European Union's New Anti-Coercion Instrument Work with China?' (2022) Research Collection Yong Pung How School of Law, https://ink.library.smu.edu.sg/cgi/viewcontent.cgi?article=6036&context=sol_research, pp. 1–3.

García, María J., 'Sanctioning Capacity in Trade and Sustainability Chapters in EU Trade Agreements: The EU–Korea Case' (2022) 10(1) *Politics and Governance*, pp. 58–67.

Garcia-Duran Huet, Patricia and Eliasson, Leif Johan, 'Was the EU's 2021 Trade Strategy a Critical Juncture?' (2022) *European Foreign Affairs Review*, pp. 563–584.

Garcia-Rubio, Mariano, 'Unilateral Measures as a Means of Forcible Execution of WTO Recommendations and Decisions', in Laura Forlati and Linos-Alexandre Sicilianos (eds.), *Economic Sanctions in International Law* (Leiden, Boston: Brill Nijhoff, 2004), pp. 445–475.

Gargne, Léo, 'Sustainable Development in Preferential Trade Agreements (PTAs)', in Michael Faure (ed.), *Elgar Encyclopedia of Environmental Law* (Cheltenham: Edward Elgar Publishing, 2021), vol. 11, pp. 468–479.

Gavin, Brigid, *The European Union and Globalization: Towards Global Democratic Governance* (Cheltenham: Edward Elgar, 2001).

Gehrke, Tobias, 'EU Open Strategic Autonomy and the Trappings of Geoeconomics' (2022) *European Foreign Affairs Review* Special Issue, pp. 61–78.

Gertz, Geoffrey and Evers, Miles, 'Geoeconomic Competition: Will State Capitalism Win?' (2020) 43(2) *The Washington Quarterly*, pp. 117–136.

Giegerich, Thomas, 'Article 60. Termination or Suspension of the Operation of a Treaty as a Consequence of Its Breach', in Oliver Dörr and Kirsten Schmalenbach (eds.), *Vienna Convention on the Law of Treaties. A Commentary*, 2nd ed. (Heidelberg: Springer, 2018), pp. 1095–1125.

Gisselman, Fredrik et al., 'Border Carbon Adjustments. An analysis of Trade Related Aspects and the Way Forward' (2020) *National Board of Trade Sweden*, www.kommerskollegium.se/contentassets/7a09d4cdb83a46feaf0c6ae6e5b02fff/border-carbon-adjustments_final_.pdf, pp. 1–105.

Glöckle, Caroline, 'Bridging the Gap: The MPIA as a Valuable Short-Term Solution to the Impasse of the WTO's Appellate Body?', *Völkerrechtsblog*, 12 October 2020, https://voelkerrechtsblog.org/bridging-the-gap-the-mpia-as-a-valuable-short-term-solution-to-the-impasse-of-the-wtos-appellate-body/.

Glöckle, Caroline, 'Die Ungewisse Zukunft des WTO Appellate Body' (2020) 9 *Europäische Zeitschrift für Wirtschaftsrecht*, pp. 356–364.

Glöckle, Caroline and Würdemann, Aike, 'Die Appellate Body-Krise der WTO – eine Analyse der US-Kritikpunkte' (2018) 23 *Europäische Zeitschrift für Wirtschaftsrecht*, pp. 976–982.

Glöckle, Caroline and Würdemann, Aike, 'The Atypical Fashion of the US-China 'Phase 1'-Deal: Context, Content and Perspectives' (2020) 23(2) *Zeitschrift für Europarechtliche Studien*, pp. 347–370.

Gomula, Joanna, 'Responsibility and the World Trade Organization', in James Crawford, Alain Pellet, and Simon Olleson (eds.), *The Law of International Responsibility* (Oxford: Oxford University Press, 2010), pp. 791–802.

Govaere, Inge, 'Interconnecting Legal Systems and the Autonomous EU Legal Order', in Inge Govaere and Sacha Garben (eds.), *The Interface between EU and International Law. Contemporary Reflections* (Oxford: Hart Publishing, 2019), pp. 19–43.

Graafsma, Folkert, 'The Revised Enforcement Regulation (No 2021/167) and Some Possible Effects on EU Trade Disputes' (2022) 17(7 & 8) *Global Trade and Customs Journal*, pp. 289–299.

Graham, Thomas R., 'The Rise (and Demise?) of the WTO Appellate Body', 5 March 2020, https://worldtradelaw.typepad.com/files/t.graham.greenwaldlecture.final_.pdf.

Grey, Felicia A., 'Arbitration as an Alternative Dispute Settlement Mechanism at the WTO' (2021) 12 *Journal of International Dispute Settlement*, pp. 477–504.

Grieger, Gisela, 'Review of EU Enforcement Regulation for Trade Disputes' (2021) *European Parliamentary Research Service Briefing*, www.europarl.europa.eu/RegData/etudes/BRIE/2020/652021/EPRS_BRI(2020)652021_EN.pdf.

Gruszczynski, Lukasz, 'The WTO and FCTC Dispute Settlement Systems: Friends or Foes' (2017) 12 *Asian Journal of WTO and International Health Law and Policy*, pp. 105–134.

Guilliard, Simon, *Beihilfenkontrolle zwischen Supranationalität und Intergouvernementalität. Unter besonderer Berücksichtigung des Brexit* (Baden-Baden: Nomos, 2022).

Hackenbroich, Jonathan, 'Protecting Europe from Economic Coercion: A European Toolbox for Countering Economic Coercion', *European Council on Foreign Relations*, Policy Brief, 20 October 2020, https://ecfr.eu/publication/defending_europe_economic_sovereignty_new_ways_to_resist_economic_coercion/?amp%3Bqid=9084882#protecting.

Hackenbroich, Jonathan, 'Europe's New Economic Statecraft: A Strong Anti-Coercion Instrument', *European Council on Foreign Relations*, 1 April 2022, https://ecfr.eu/article/europes-new-economic-statecraft-a-strong-anti-coercion-instrument/.

Hackenbroich, Jonathan and Zerka, Pawel, 'Measured Response: How to Design a European Instrument against Economic Coercion' (2021) *European Council on Foreign Relations*, Policy Brief, 23 June 2021, https://ecfr.eu/publication/measured-response-how-to-design-a-european-instrument-against-economic-coercion/.

Hagemeyer-Witzleb, Teoman M., *The International Law of Economic Warfare* (Heidelberg: Springer, 2020).

Hahn, Michael, 'We'll Always Have Geneva: The Existential Crisis of the US-led Multilateral Trading System and the EU Reactions', in Inge Govaere and Sascha Garben (eds.), *The Interface Between EU and International Law* (Oxford: Hart Publishing, 2019), pp. 269–292.

Hamann, Andrea, 'Living without the WTO Appellate Body: Procedural Developments in International Trade Dispute Settlement' (2021) 20 *The Law and Practice of International Courts and Tribunals*, pp. 166–190.

Hanson, Brian, 'What Happened to Fortress Europe? External Trade Policy Liberalization in the EU' (1998) 52(1) *International Organization*, pp. 55–85.

Harding, Rebecca, and Harding, Jack, *The Weaponization of Trade: The Great Unbalancing of Politics and Economics* (London: London Publishing Partnership, 2017).

Harrison, James et al., 'Labour Standards Provisions in EU Free Trade Agreements: Reflections on the European Commission's Reform Agenda' (2019) 18(4) *World Trade Review*, pp. 635–657.

Harte, Roderick Edward Noël, 'International Procurement Instrument' (2017) *EPRS Briefing*, www.europarl.europa.eu/RegData/etudes/BRIE/2017/614610/EPRS_BRI(2017)614610_EN.pdf.

Hazarika, Angshuman and Van Vaerenbergh, Pieter, "'One Rule to Rule Them All': Rules for Article 25 DSU Arbitration' (2019) 36(5) *Journal of International Arbitration*, pp. 595–628.

Heath, J. Benton, 'The New National Security Challenge to the Economic Order' (2020) 129(4) *Yale Law Journal*, pp. 1020–1098.

Hegde, Vineet, Wouters, Jan, and Raina, Akhil, 'The Demise of the Rules-Based International Economic Order?' (2020) Leuven Centre for Global Governance Studies, Working Paper 224, pp. 1–25.

Helal, Mohamed S., 'On Coercion in International Law' (2019) 52(1) *International Law and Politics*, pp. 1–122.

Hinojosa-Martínez, Luis M. and Pérez-Bernárdez, Carmela (eds.) *Enhancing the Rule of Law in the EU's External Action* (Cheltenham: Elgar Publishing, 2023).

Hiro, Dilip, *After Empire: The Birth of a Multipolar World* (New York: National Books, 2010).

Hoekman, Bernard M. and Mavroidis, Petros C., 'To AB or Not to AB: Dispute Settlement in WTO Reform' (2020) 23 *Journal of International Economic Law*, pp. 703–722.

Hoekman, Bernard and Puccio, Laura, 'EU Trade Policy: Challenges and Opportunities' (2019) 2019/06 Robert Schuman Centre for Advanced Studies Policy, pp. 1–7.

Hoffmeister, Frank, 'The EU Public Procurement Regime on Third-Country Bidders – Setting the Cursor between Openness and Reciprocity', in Harri Kalimo and Max S. Jansson (eds.), *EU Economic Law in a Time of Crisis* (Cheltenham: Edward Elgar Publishing, 2016), pp. 76–88.

Hoffmeister, Frank, 'The Devil Is in the Detail: A First Guide on the EU's New Trade Defence Rules', in Wolfgang Weiß and Cornelia Furculita (eds.), *Global Politics and EU Trade Policy: Facing the Challenges to a Multilateral Approach* (Cham: Springer, 2020), pp. 211–230.

Hoffmeister, Frank, 'Do Ut Des oder Tit for Tat? – Die Europäische Handelspolitik Angesichts Neuer Herausforderungen aus den USA und China', in Christoph Herrmann (ed.), *Die Gemeinsame Handelspolitik im Europäischen Verfassungsverbund* (Baden-Baden: Nomos, 2020), pp. 77–94.

Hoffmeister, Frank, 'Securing a Level Playing Field through EU Free Trade Agreements – from Traditional Competition Chapters to a Dedicated Title in the EU-UK Trade and Cooperation Agreement', in Alexander Heger and Sascha Gourdet (eds.), *Fairen Wettbewerb in der Europäischen Union sichern* (Baden-Baden: Nomos, 2022), pp. 127–144.

Holden, Patrick, 'Regional Integration and Trade in the Era of COVID-19: A First Look', UNU-CRIS Working Paper Series, September 2020, p. 11, https://cris.unu.edu/sites/cris.unu.edu/files/WP20.3%20-%20Holden.pdf.

Hooijmaaijers, Bas, 'China, the BRICS and the Limitations of Reshaping Global Economic Governance' (2021) 34 *The Pacific Review*, pp. 29–55.

Hopeland, Kristen, *Clash of Powers: US–China Rivalry in Global Trade Governance* (Cambridge: Cambridge University Press, 2020).

Horn, Henrik and Mavroidis, Petros C., 'To B(TA) or Not to B(TA)? On the Legality and Desirability of Border Tax Adjustments from a Trade Perspective' (2011) *The World Economy*, pp. 1911–1937.

Horn, Henrik, Mavroidis, Petros C., and Sapir, André, 'Beyond the WTO? An Anatomy of EU and US Preferential Trade Agreements' (2010) 33(11) *The World Economy*, pp. 1565–1588.

Howse, Robert, 'Distinguished Essay: Non-tariff Barriers and Climate Policy: Border-Adjusted Taxes and Regulatory Measures as WTO-Compliant Climate Mitigation Strategies', in Christoph Herrmann, Markus Krajewski, and Jörg Philipp Terhechte (eds.), *European Yearbook of International Economic Law* (Berlin: Springer, 2015), pp. 3–18.

Hradilová, Kateřina and Svoboda, Ondřej, 'Sustainable Development Chapters in the EU Free Trade Agreements: Searching for Effectiveness' (2018) 52(6) *Journal of World Trade*, pp. 1019–1042.

Hufbauer, Gary C., 'China as an Economic Actor on the World Stage: An Overview', in Frederick M. Abbott (ed.), *China in the World Trading System. Defining the Principles of Engagement* (The Hague: Kluwer Law International, 1998), pp. 47–52.

Hufbauer, Gary Clyde, Kim, Jisun, and Schott, Jeffrey J., 'Can EU Carbon Border Adjustment Measures Propel WTO Climate Talks?' (2021) *Peterson Institute for International Economics Policy Brief*, www.piie.com/sites/default/files/documents/pb21-23.pdf, pp. 1–13.

Hufbauer, Gary, Moll, Thomas, and Rubbini, Luca, 'Investment Subsidies for Cross-Border M&A', United States Council Foundation Occasional Paper No. 2, April 2008, www.uscib.org/docs/usc_foundation_investment_subsidies.pdf, pp. 1–31.

Ikenberry, G. John, 'The End of Liberal International Order?' (2018) 94(1) *International Affairs*, pp. 7–23.

Jacobs, Thomas, Gheyle, Niels, De Ville, Ferdi, and Orbie, Jan, 'The Hegemonic Politics of "Strategic Autonomy" and "Resilience": COVID-19 and the Dislocation of EU Trade Policy' (2023) 61(1) *Journal of Common Market Studies*, pp. 3–19.

Jamnejad, Maziar and Wood, Michael, 'The Principle of Non-Intervention' (2009) 22(2) *Leiden Journal of International Law*, pp. 345–381.

Juncos, Ana, 'Resilience as the New EU Foreign Policy Paradigm: A Pragmatist Turn' (2017) 26(1) *European Security*, pp. 1–18.

Kang, Jing, 'The Presumption of Good Faith in the WTO "As Such" Cases: A Reformulation of the Mandatory/Discretionary Distinction as an Analytical Tool' (2012) 46(4) *Journal of World Trade*, pp. 879–912.

Kassoti, Eva, 'Between Sollen and Sein: The CJEU's Reliance on International Law in the Interpretation of Economic Agreements Covering Occupied Territories' (2020) 33(2) *Leiden Journal of International Law*, pp. 371–389.

Kassoti, Eva and Odermatt, Jed, 'The Principle of Autonomy and International Investment Arbitration: Reflections on Opinion 1/17' (2020) 73 *Questions of International Law*, pp. 5–20.

Kassoti, Eva and Wessel, Ramses A., 'The Conclusion of Trade Agreements and the EU's Duty to Respect Human Rights Abroad', in Nuno Cunha Rodrigues (ed.), *Exterritoriality of EU Economic Law: The Application of EU Economic Law Outside the Territory of the EU* (Cham: Springer, 2021), pp. 229–250.

Kassoti, Eva and Wessel, Ramses A., 'The Normative Effect of Article 3 (5) TEU. Observance and Development of International Law by the European Union', in Paula García Andrade (ed.) *Interacciones entre el Derecho de la Union Europea y el Derecho Internacional Público* (Valencia: Tirant lo Blanch, 2023), pp. 19–46.

Keck, Alexander and Low, Patrick, 'Special and Differential Treatment in the WTO: Why, When, and How?', in Bernard M. Hoekman and Simon J. Evenett (eds.), *Economic Development and Multilateral Trade Cooperation* (Washnigton, DC and New York: Palgrave Macmillan and The World Bank, 2006), pp. 147–188.

Khorana, Sangeeta and Garcia, Maria, 'Introduction', in Sangheta Khorana and Maria Garcia (eds.), *Handbook on the EU and International Trade* (Cheltenham: Edward Elgar Publishing, 2018), pp. 1–17.

Kim, Song and Osgood, Iain, 'Firms in Trade and Trade Politics' (2019) *Annual Review of Political Science*, pp. 399–417.

Kirchner, Stefan, 'More Fairness in Global Procurement: The European Union's Future International Procurement Instrument Moves Closer to Reality' (2021), https://papers.ssrn.com/sol3/papers.cfm?abstract_id=3913595.

Kirgis, Frederic, 'Some Lingering Questions About Article 60 of the Vienna Convention on the Law of Treaties' (1989) 22(3) *Cornell International Law Journal*, pp. 549–573.

Klimas, Tadas and Vaičiukaitė, Jūratė, 'The Law of Recitals in European Community Legislation' (2008) 15(1) *ILSA Journal of International and Comparative Law*, pp. 1–33.

Koch, Rika, *Green Public Procurement under WTO Law. Experience of the EU and Prospects for Switzerland* (Cham: Springer, 2020).

Koen, Louis and Rammila, Davy, 'The EU-Korea Panel Report: A Watershed Moment for the Trade-Labor Nexus or Mere Symbolic Victory?' (2021) 7(2) *Journal of International Trade, Logistics and Law*, pp. 53–58.

Koenig, Christian and von Wendland, Bernhard, *The Art of Regulation. Competition in Europe: Wealth and Wariness* (Cheltenham: Edward Elgar, 2017).

Kolb, Robert, 'Principles as Sources of International Law (with Special Reference to Good Faith)' (2006) 53(1) *Netherlands International Law Review*, pp. 1–36.

Konstadinides, Theodore, 'Customary International Law as a Source of EU Law: A Two-Way Fertilization Route?' (2016) 35(1) *Yearbook of European Law*, pp. 513–532.

Koutrakos, Panos, 'More on Autonomy: Opinion 1/17 (CETA)' (2019) 3 *European Law Review*, pp. 293–294.

Krajewski, Markus, 'The Reform of the Common Commercial Policy', in Andrea Biondi and Piet Eeckhout (eds.), *EU Law After Lisbon* (Oxford: Oxford University Press, 2012), pp. 292–311.

Kratz, Agatha and Oertel, Janka, 'Home Advantage: How China's Protected Market Threatens Europe's Economic Power', *European Council on Foreign Relations*, Policy Brief, 15 April 2021, https://ecfr.eu/publication/home-advantage-how-chinas-protected-market-threatens-europes-economic-power/.

Krieger, Heike, Nolte, Georg, and Zimmermann, Andreas (eds.), *The International Rule of Law: Rise or Decline?* (Oxford: Oxford University Press, 2019).

Kriener, Florian, 'Intervention, Prohibition of', in Anne Peters and Rüdiger Wolfrum (eds.), *Max Planck Encyclopaedia of Public International Law* (Oxford: Oxford University Press, 2024), https://opil.ouplaw.com/display/10.1093/law:epil/9780199231690/law-9780199231690-e1434.

Kübek, Gesa, 'Sustainable Development Chapters in EU FTAs and Dispute Settlement: Lessons Learned from Ukraine – Wood Products and Korea – Labour Rights', in Elaine Fahey and Isabella Mancini (eds.), *Understanding the EU as a Good Global Actor. Ambitions, Values and Metrics* (Cheltenham: Edward Elgar, 2022), pp. 277–293.

Kugler, Kholofelo, 'Operationalizing MPIA Appeal Arbitrations: Opportunities and Challenges', in Manfred Elsig, Rodrigo Polanco, and Peter van den Bossche (eds.), *International Economic Dispute Settlement: Demise or Transformation* (Cambridge: Cambridge University Press, 2021), pp. 68–96.

Kuijper, Pieter Jan, 'From Dyestuffs to Kosovo Wine: From Avoidance to Acceptance by the European Community Courts of Customary International Law as Limit to Community Action', in Ige Dekker and Harry Post (eds.), *On the Foundations and Sources of International Law* (The Hague: T.M.C. Asser Press Institute, 2003), pp. 151–172.

Kuijper, Pieter Jan, '"It Shall Contribute to [. . .] the Strict Observance and Development of International Law . . ."', in Allan Rosas, Egils Levits, and Yves Bot (eds.), *The Court of Justice of the EU and the Construction of Europe: Analyses and Perspectives on Sixty Years of Case-law* (The Hague: T.M.C. Asser Press, 2013), pp. 589–612.

Kumar, Manoj and Arora, Neha, 'India Plans to Challenge EU Carbon Tax at WTO', *Reuters*, 17 May 2023, www.reuters.com/world/india/india-plans-challenge-eu-carbon-tax-wto-sources-2023-05-16/.

Kunig, Philip, 'Prohibition of Intervention', in Rüdiger Wolfrum (eds.), *Max Planck Encyclopaedia of Public International Law* (Oxford: Oxford University Press, 2012), vol. 6, pp. 289–299.

Kurmayer, Nikolaus J., 'Green industry: G7 Sets Out Terms for Global "Climate Club"', 13 December 2022, www.euractiv.com/section/energy-environment/news/green-industry-g7-sets-out-terms-for-global-climate-club/.

Lacerda Prazeres, Tatiana, 'Trade and National Security: Rising Risks for the WTO' (2020) 19 *World Trade Review*, pp. 137–148.

Lamp, Nicolas, 'Making WTO Dispute Settlement Work without the Appellate Body: How the Threat of Unilateral Retaliation Could Be Used to Incentivize the Adoption of Panel Reports', International Economic Law and Policy Blog, 3 December 2019, https://ielp.worldtradelaw.net/2019/12/making-wto-dispute-settlement-work-without-the-appellate-body-how-the-threat-of-unilateral-retaliati.html.

Lange, Bernd, 'Comment: How to Make the EU's Anti-coercion Instrument Work', Borderlex, 7 December 2021, https://borderlex.net/2021/12/07/comment-how-to-make-the-eus-anti-coercion-instrument-work/.

Lanz, Rainer and Maurer, Andreas, 'Services and Global Value Chains: Some Evidence on Servicification of Manufacturing and Services Networks' (2015) No. ERSD-2015-03 WTO Staff Working Paper, www.wto.org/english/res_e/reser_e/ersd201503_e.pdf, pp. 1–21.

Laprévote, Francois-Charles and Lin, Wanjie, 'Between State Aid, Trade and Antitrust: The Mixed Procedural Heritage of the Foreign Subsidies Regulation and the Overarching Principle of Non-Discrimination' (2022) 3 *Zeitschrift für Europarechtliche Studien*, pp. 443–452.

Larik, Joris, 'The Kadi Saga as a Tale of "Strict Observance" of International Law' (2014) 61(1) *Netherlands International Law Review*, pp. 23–42.

Lauterpacht, Hersch, *The Development of International Law by the International Court* (London: Stevens & Sons Limited, 1958).

Lavery, Scott, McDaniel, Sean, and Schmid, Davide, 'European Strategic Autonomy', in Milan Babić, Adam Dixon, and Imogen Liu (eds.), *The Political Economy of Geoeconomics* (Cham: Palgrave Macmillan, 2022), pp. 57–80.

Leal-Arcas, Rafael, *EU Trade Law* (Cheltenham: Edward Elgar Publishing, 2019).

Leal-Arcas, Rafael, Faktaufon, Manuliza, and Kyprianou, Anna, 'A Legal Exploration of the European Union's Carbon Border Adjustment Mechanism' (2022) *European Energy and Environmental Law Review*, pp. 223–240.

LeClercq, Desiree, 'The Panel Report under the EU-Korea Trade Agreement Concerning Labor Practices: What Are the Purposes of Trade Agreements as They Relate to the ILO's Fundamental Labor Rights?', International Economic Law and Policy Blog, 8 February 2021, https://ielp.worldtradelaw.net/2021/02/

guest-post-the-panel-report-under-the-eu-korea-trade-agreement-concerning-labor-practices-what-are-t.html.

Lenaerts, Koen, 'Direct Applicability and Direct Effect of International Law in the EU Legal Order', in Inge Govaere, Erwan Lannon, Peter van Elsuwege, and Stanislas Adam (eds.), *The EU in the World: Essays in Honour of Marc Maresceau* (Leiden: Brill Nijhoff, 2014), pp. 45-64.

Lenaerts, Koen and Gutiérrez-Fons, José A., 'To Say What the Law of the EU Is: Methods of Interpretation and the European Court of Justice' (2013) European Union Institute Working Papers AEL 2013/9, pp. 1–48.

Leonelli, Giulia Claudia, 'Carbon Border Measures, Environmental Effectiveness and WTO Law Compatibility: Is There a Way Forward for the Steel and Aluminium Climate Club?' (2022) *World Trade Review*, pp. 1–14.

Lester, Simon, 'A Framework for Thinking about the Discretion in the Mandatory/Discretionary Distinction' (2011) 14(2) *Journal of International Economic Law*, pp. 369–402.

Lester, Simon, 'Can Interim Appeal Arbitration Preserve the WTO Dispute System?' (2020) 77 *CATO Institute Free Trade Bulletin*, Hubert A. Stiefel Center for Trade Policy Studies, www.cato.org/free-trade-bulletin/can-interim-appeal-arbitration-preserve-wto-dispute-system.

Lester, Simon, 'Questions About the MPIA and Article 25 Appeal Arbitration', International Economic Law and Policy Blog, 1 September 2020, https://ielp.worldtradelaw.net/2020/09/questions-about-the-mpia.html.

Lester, Simon, 'Who's Going to Pay for Supporting the MPIA?', International Economic Law and Policy Blog, 15 June 2020, https://ielp.worldtradelaw.net/2020/06/whos-going-to-pay-for-the-mpia.html.

Lester, Simon, Mercurio, Bryan, and Davies, Arwel, *World Trade Law: Text, Materials and Commentary*, 3rd ed. (Oxford: Hart Publishing, 2018).

Li, Xiaoling, 'DSU Article 25 Appeal Arbitration: A Viable Interim Alternative to the WTO Appellate Body?' (2020) 15(10) *Global Trade and Customs Journal*, pp. 461–478.

Lim, Darren and Ferguson, Victor, 'Informal Economic Sanctions: The Political Economy of Chinese Coercion During the THAAD Dispute' (2022) 29(5) *Review of International Political Economy*, pp. 1525–1548.

Lockhart, Nicolas and Sheargold, Elisabeth, 'In Search of Relevant Discretion: The Role of the Mandatory/Discretionary Distinction in WTO Law' (2010) 13(2) *Journal of International Economic Law*, pp. 379–421.

Low, Patrick, Marceau, Gabrielle, and Reinaud, Julia, 'The Interface between the Trade and Climate Change Regimes: Scoping the Issues' (2011) WTO Staff Working Paper ERSD-2011-1, www.wto.org/english/res_e/reser_e/ersd201101_e.pdf, pp. 1–41.

Lowe, Sam, 'The EU Should Reconsider Its Approach to Trade and Sustainable Development' (2019a) *Centre for European Reform*, www.cer.eu/sites/default/files/insight_SL_31.10.19.pdf, pp. 1–4.

Lowe, Sam, 'Should the EU Tax Imported CO_2?' (2019b) *Insight Centre for European Reform*, www.cer.eu/sites/default/files/insight_SL_24.9_19.pdf, pp. 1–6.

Lowe, Sam, 'The EU's Carbon Border Adjustment Mechanism. How to Make it Work for Developing Countries' (2021) Open Society European Policy Institute Policy Brief, www.cer.eu/publications/archive/policy-brief/2021/eus-carbon-border-adjustment-mechanism-how-make-it-work, pp. 1–15.

Lowe, Vaughan and Tzanakopoulos, Antonios, 'Economic Warfare', in Rüdiger Wolfrum (ed.), *Max Planck Encyclopedia of Public International Law* (Oxford: Oxford University Press, 2013), https://opil.ouplaw.com/view/10.1093/law:epil/9780199231690/law-9780199231690-e292.

Lowenfeld, Andreas F., *International Economic Law* (Oxford: Oxford University Press, 2008).

Luja, Raymond, 'The Foreign Subsidies Regulation: Countering State Aid Beyond the European Union' (2021) 20 *European State Aid Law Quarterly*, pp. 187–199.

Lyu Shuping, Buts Caroline and Jegers Marc, 'Comparing China's Fair Competition Review System to EU State Aid Control' (2019) 18(1) *European State Aid Law Quarterly*, pp. 37–60.

Malkin, Anton, 'The Made in China Challenge to US Structural power: Industrial Policy, Intellectual Property and Multinational Corporations' (2018) No. 183 *Centre for International Governance Innovation Papers*, pp. 1–27.

Manners, Ian, 'Normative Power Europe: A Contradiction in Terms?' (2002) *Journal of Common Market Studies*, pp. 235–258.

Marceau, Gabrielle, 'WTO Dispute Settlement and Human Rights' (2002) 13(4) *Journal of International Economic Law*, pp. 753–814.

Marceau, Gabrielle and Wyatt, Julian, 'Dispute Settlement Regimes Intermingled: Regional Trade Agreements and the WTO' (2010) 1(1) *Journal of International Dispute Settlement*, pp. 67–95.

Marín Durán, Gracia, 'Sustainable Development Chapters in EU Free Trade Agreements: Emerging Compliance Issues' (2020) 57 *Common Market Law Review*, pp. 1031–1068.

Marín Durán, Gracia, 'EU Carbon Border Adjustment Mechanism: Key Issues Going Forward' (2021) 26(4) *European Foreign Affairs Review*, pp. 499–506.

Marín Durán, Gracia, 'Carbon Border Adjustments: Ensuring Compatibility with the International Climate and Trade Regimes' (2022) 16 *University College London Research Paper Series*, pp. 1–24.

Martinico, Giuseppe, 'The Autonomy of EU Law. A Joint Celebration of Kadi II and Van Gend en Loos', in Matej Avbelj, Filippo Fontanelli, and Giuseppe Martinico (eds.), *Kadi on Trial: A Multifaceted Analysis of the Kadi Trial* (London: Routledge, 2014), pp. 157–171.

Marx, Axel, Ebert, Franz, Hachez, Nicolas, and Wouters, Jan, 'Dispute Settlement in the Trade and Sustainable Development Chapters of EU Trade Agreements' (2017) *Leuven Centre for Global Governance Studies*, https://ghum.kuleuven.be/ggs/publications/books/final-report-9-february-def.pdf, pp. 13-22.

Marx, Axel, Ebert, Franz, and Hachez, Nicolas, 'Dispute Settlement for Labour Provisions in EU Free Trade Agreements: Rethinking Current Approaches' (2017) 5(4) *Politics and Governance*, pp. 49–59.

Matsushita, Mitsuo, Schoenbaum, Thomas, Mavroidis, Petros C., and Hahn, Michael, *The World Trade Organization: Law, Practice, and Policy*, 3rd ed. (New York: Oxford University Press, 2015).

Mavroidis, Petros C., 'Remedies in the WTO Legal System: Between a Rock and a Hard Place' (2000) 11(4) *European Journal of International Law*, pp. 763–813.

Mavroidis, Petros C., *The Sources of WTO Law and Their Interpretation* (Cheltenham: Edward Elgar Publishing, 2022).

Mazzotti, Paolo, 'Stepping Up the Enforcement of Trade and Sustainable Development Chapters in the European Union's Free Trade Agreements: Reconsidering the Debate on Sanctions' (2021) *European Law Institute*, www.europeanlawinstitute.eu/fileadmin/user_upload/p_eli/YLA_Award/Submission_ELI_Young_Lawyers_Award_Paolo_Mazzotti_2021.pdf.

Mbengue, Makane Moïse, 'Preamble', in Rüdiger Wolfrum (ed.), *The Max Planck Encyclopedia of Public International Law* (Oxford: Oxford University Press, 2008), https://opil.ouplaw.com/view/10.1093/law:epil/9780199231690/law-9780199231690-e1456.

Mbengue, Makane Moïse, 'The Settlement of Trade Disputes: Is There a Monopoly for the WTO?' (2016) 15 *The Law and Practice of International Courts and Tribunals*, pp. 207–248.

McDonald, Brad, 'WTO Dispute Settlement and Rule-Making: One Crisis or Two?' (2021) 55(3) *Journal of World Trade*, pp. 383–396.

Mearsheimer, John J., 'Bound to Fail: The Rise and Fall of the Liberal International Order' (2019) 43(4) *International Security*, pp. 7–50.

Mehling, Michael A. and Ritz, Robert A., 'Going Beyond Default Intensities in an EU Carbon Border Adjustment Mechanism' (2020) Energy Policy Research Group Paper, www.jstor.org/stable/resrep30315#metadata_info_tab_contents, pp. 1–23.

Mehling, Michael A., van Asselt, Harro, Das, Kasturi et al., 'Designing Border Carbon Adjustments for Enhanced Climate Action' (2019) 113(3) *American Journal of International Law*, pp. 433–481.

Mehling, Michael,van Asselt, Harro, Droege, Susanne, and Das, Kasturi, 'The Form and Substance of International Cooperation on Border Carbon Adjustments' (2022) 116 *American Journal of International Law Unbound*, Symposium on Carbon Border Adjustments, pp. 213–218.

Melo Araujo, Billy, *The EU Deep Trade Agenda: Law and Policy* (New York: Oxford University Press, 2016).

Mendez, Mario, *The Legal Effects of EU Agreements. Maximalist Treaty Enforcement and Judicial Avoidance Techniques* (Oxford: Oxford University Press, 2013).

Mendez, Mario, 'The Application of International Law by the CJEU', in Curtis Bradly (ed.), *The Oxford Handbook of Comparative Foreign Relations Law* (New York: Oxford University Press, 2019), pp. 601–624.

Messad, Paul, 'Steel Industry United in Opposing Bloc's Carbon Border Levy', *Euractiv*, 23 December 2022, www.euractiv.com/section/emissions-trading-scheme/news/steel-industry-united-in-opposing-blocs-carbon-border-levy/.

Messerlin, Patrick, 'The Beauty of Public Procurement in TTIP' (2016) European Centre for International Political Economy Bulletin No. 1/2016, pp. 1–3.

Meunier, Sophie, 'Managing Globalization? The EU in International Trade Negotiations' (2007) 45(4) *Journal of Common Market Studies*, pp. 905–926.

Meunier, Sophie, 'The End of Naivety: Assertiveness and New Instruments in EU Trade and Investment Policy' (2022) *European Union Institute Global Governance Programme*, Policy Brief Issue 2022/55, pp. 1–10.

Meunier, Sophie and Nicolaidis, Kalypso, 'The Geopoliticization of European Trade and Investment Policy' (2019) *Journal of Common Market Studies*, pp. 103–113.

Meyer, Timothy, 'Taxing, Regulating, and Trading Carbon: An Introduction to the Symposium' (2022) 116 *American Journal of International Law Unbound*, Symposium on Carbon Border Adjustments, pp. 191–195.

Meyer, Timothy and Tucker, Todd N., 'A Pragmatic Approach to Carbon Border Measures' (2022a) 21 *World Trade Review*, pp. 109–120.

Meyer, Timothy and Tucker, Todd N., 'Trade and Climate, Law and Politics: A Response' (2022b) 21 *World Trade Review*, pp. 127–129.

Micheau, Claire, 'Control of State Aid', in Herwig Hofmann, Gerhard Rowe, and Alexander Türk (eds.), *Specialized Administrative Law of the EU* (Oxford: Oxford University Press, 2018), pp. 451–475.

Mitchell, Andrew D., 'Good Faith in WTO Dispute Settlement' (2006) 7 *Melbourne Journal of International Law*, pp. 339–371.

Moens, Barbara and van der Burchard, Hans, 'Europe First: Brussels Gets Ready to Dump Its Free Trade Ideals', www.politico.eu/article/ursula-von-der-leyen-joe-biden-trade-europe-first-brussels-gets-ready-to-dump-its-free-trade-ideals/.

Moore, Stephen and Laffer, Arthur B., *Trumponomics: Inside the America First Plan to Revive Our Economy* (New York: St. Martin's Press, 2018).

Moreno-Lax, Violeta and Gragl, Paul, 'Beyond Monism, Dualism, Pluralism: The Quest for a (Fully-Fledged) Theoretical Framework' (2016) 35(1) *Yearbook of European Law*, pp. 455–470.

Morin, Jean-Frédéric and Rochette, Myriam 'Transatlantic Convergence of PTAs' Environmental Clauses' (2017) *Business and Politics*, www.chaire-epi.ulaval.ca/sites/chaire-epi.ulaval.ca/files/publications/morin_and_rochette.pdf, pp. 1–38.

Moritani, Yuki, 'The Partnership Agreements with Japan as a Part of Structural Foreign Policy' (2020) 2(1) *The Greater European Journal*, pp. 72–78.

Moulin, Thibault, 'Reviving the Principle of Non-Intervention in Cyberspace: The Path Forward' (2020) 25(3) *Journal of Conflict and Security Law*, pp. 423–447.

Maruyama, Warren and Wolff, Alan Wm., 'Saving the WTO from the National Security Exception' (2023) Peterson Institute for International Economics Working Papers 23-3, pp. 1–22.

Müller, Andreas, 'The Direct Effect of Customary International Law', in Fernando Lusa Bordin, Andreas Th. Müller, and Francisco Pascual-Vives (eds.), *The EU and Customary International Law* (Cambridge: Cambridge University Press, 2022), pp. 210–239.

Müller-Ibold, Till, 'The Draft Foreign Subsidies Regulation' (2022) 3 *Zeitschrift für Europarechtliche Studien*, pp. 431–442.

Nagy, Csongor István, 'Foreign Subsidies, Distortions and Acquisitions. Can the Playing Field Be Levelled?' (2021) 2(1) *Central European Journal of Comparative Law*, pp. 147–162.

Nakanishi, Yumiko, 'Significance of the Strategic Partnership Agreement between the European Union and Japan in International Order', in Yumiko Nakanishi and Olivia Tambou (eds.), *The EU-Japan Relationship, Collection Open Access Book* (Blogdroiteuropeen, 2020), https://blogdroiteuropeen.files.wordpress.com/2020/12/eu-japan-relationship-v3-4.pdf, pp. 20–26.

National Board of Trade Sweden, 'Comments on the Commission's Roadmap for a Mechanism to Deter and Counteract Coercive Action by Non-EU Countries', 17 March 2021, https://ec.europa.eu/info/law/better-regulation/have-your-say/initiatives/12803-Trade-mechanism-to-deter-counteract-coercive-action-by-non-EU-countries/F2000578_en.

National Board of Trade Sweden, 'The EU Proposal for an Anti-Coercion Instrument' (2022), www.kommerskollegium.se/en/publications/reports/2022/the-eu-proposal-for-an-anti-coercion-instrument.

Neframi, Eleftheria, 'Customary International Law and the EU from the Perspective of Article 3 (5) TEU', in Piet Eeckhout and Manuel López-Escudero (eds.), *The EU's External Action in Times of Crisis* (Oxford: Hart Publishing, 2016), pp. 205–222.

Neumann, Felix, *Export des Europäischen Beihilfenrechts. Eine Analyse der Europäisierung des internationalen Subventionsrechts durch bilaterale Handelsabkommen* (Cham: Springer, 2019).

Nguyen, Trung, 'The Procedural Inconsistency of the Envisaged EU Enforcement Regulation with the EU's WTO Obligations', *OpinioJuris*, 30 October 2020, http://opiniojuris.org/2020/10/30/the-procedural-inconsistency-of-the-envisaged-eu-enforcement-regulation-with-the-eus-wto-obligations/.

Nissen, Aleydis, 'And So It Begins: Trade and Sustainable Development Recommendations by a Panel of Experts under a European Union Free Trade Agreement' (2021) 7 *International Labor Rights Case Law*, pp. 257–262.

Nissen, Aleydis, 'Not That Assertive: The EU's Take on Enforcement of Labour Obligations in Its Free Trade Agreement with South Korea' (2022) 33 *European Journal of International Law*, pp. 607–630.

Novitz, Tonia, 'Enforceable Social Clauses in Trade Agreements with 'Bite'? Implications of the EU–South Korea Panel of Experts Report of 20 January 2021' (2021) 6 *European Trade Union Institute Policy Brief*, www.etui.org/publications/enforceable-social-clauses-trade-agreements-bite.

Novitz, Tonia, 'The Role of the EU in Making 'Sustainable' Labour Linkages in Contemporary Trade: Is Being 'Assertive' also 'Good'?', in Elaine Fahey and Isabella Mancini (eds.), *Understanding the EU as a Good Global Actor* (Cheltenham: Edward Elgar, 2022), pp. 124–141.

Odermatt, Jed, 'Council of the European Union v. Front Populaire Pour la Libération de la Saguia-El-Hamra et du Rio de Oro (Front Polisario). Case C-104/16P' (2017) 111(3) *American Journal of International Law*, pp. 731–738.

Odermatt, Jed, *International Law and the European Union* (Cambridge: Cambridge University Press, 2021).

Oh, Seung-Youn, 'China's Race to the Top: Regional and Global Implications of China's Industrial Policy' (2021) 20(2) *World Trade Review*, pp. 169–185

Orbie, Jan, 'EU Trade Policy Meets Geopolitics' (2021) 26(2) *European Foreign Affairs Review*, pp. 197–202.

O'Sullivan, David, 'The European Union and the Multilateral System: Lessons from Past Experience and Future Challenges', European Parliamentary Research Service Briefing PE 689.365, 5 March 2021, www.europarl.europa.eu/RegData/etudes/BRIE/2021/689365/EPRS_BRI(2021)689365_EN.pdf.

Pacheco Restrepo, Yilly Vanessa, 'Enforcement Practice under Preferential Trade Agreements: Environmental Consultations and Submissions on Environmental Enforcement Matters in the US-Peru TPA' (2019) 46(3) *Legal Issues of Economic Integration*, pp. 247–262.

Pander Maat, Eva, 'The Carbon Border Adjustment Mechanism and the Challenge of Being a "Good" Climate and Trade Actor', in Elaine Fahey and Isabella Mancini (eds.), *Understanding the EU as a Good Global Actor: Ambitions, Values and Metrics* (Cheltenham: Edward Elgar Publishing, 2022), pp. 141–157.

Papaconstantinou, George A. and Pedreschi, Luigi F., 'Alternative Dispute Settlement and the Jurisprudential Legacy of the World Trade Organization's Appellate Body' (2022) 56(2) *Journal of World Trade*, pp. 261–282.

Pauwelyn, Joost, 'How to Win a World Trade Organization Dispute Based on Non-World Trade Organization Law? Questions of Jurisdiction and Merits' (2003) 37 (6) *Journal of World Trade*, pp. 997–1030.

Pauwelyn, Joost, 'Carbon Leakage Measures and Border Tax Adjustments under WTO Law', in Geert Van Calster and Denise Prévost (eds.), *Research Handbook on Environment, Health and the WTO* (Cheltenham: Edward Elgar Publishing, 2013), pp. 448–506.

Pauwelyn, Joost, 'Interplay between the WTO Treaty and Other International Legal Instruments and Tribunals: Evolution After 20 Years of WTO Jurisprudence' (2017), https://papers.ssrn.com/sol3/papers.cfm?abstract_id=2731144.

Pauwelyn, Joost, 'WTO Dispute Settlement Post 2019: What to Expect?' (2019) *Journal of International Economic Law*, pp. 297–321.

Pauwelyn, Joost, 'The MPIA: What's New (Part III)', International Economic Law and Policy Blog, 6 March 2023, https://ielp.worldtradelaw.net/2023/03/the-mpia-whats-new-part-iii.html.

Pauwelyn, Joost and Kleimann, David, 'Trade Related Aspects of a Carbon Border Adjustment Mechanism: A Legal Assessment' (2020) European Parliament Briefing Requested by the Committee on International Trade (INTA), www.europarl.europa.eu/cmsdata/210514/EXPO_BRI(2020)603502_EN.pdf, pp. 5–17.

Pechstein, Matthias and Drechsler, Carola, 'Die Auslegung und Fortbildung des Primärrechts', in Karl Riesenhuber (ed.), *Europäische Methodenlehre: Handbuch für Ausbildung und Praxis*, 4 ed. (Berlin: De Gruyter, 2015), pp. 181–208.

Peers, Steve, 'The EU's Accession to the ECHR: The Dream Becomes a Nightmare' (2015) 16(1) *German Law Journal*, pp. 213–222.

Peksen, Dursun and Jeong, Jin, 'Coercive Diplomacy and Economic Sanctions Reciprocity: Explaining Targets' Counter-Sanctions' (2021) *Defence and Peace Economics*, pp. 1–17.

Perdikis, Nicholas and Perdikis, Laurie, 'The Establishment and Development of the European Union and Its Trade Policy', in Sangeeta Khorana and Maria Garcia (eds.), *Handbook on the EU and International Trade* (Cheltenham: Edward Elgar Publishing, 2018), pp. 17–35.

Petersmann, Ernst-Ulrich, 'Participation of the EC in the GATT: International Law and Community Law Aspects', in David O'Keeffe and Henry G. Schermers (eds.), *Mixed Agreements* (Boston: Kluwer Law and Taxation Publishers, 1983), pp. 167–198.

Petersmann, Ernst-Ulrich, 'How Should WTO Members React to Their WTO Crises?' (2019) 18(3) *World Trade Review*, pp. 503–525.

Petersmann, Ernst-Ulrich, 'Multilevel Judicial Protection of "Access to Justice" and the EU's Duty to Contribute to the "Strict Observance and Development of International Law"', in Matej Avbelj, Filippo Fontanelli, and Giuseppe Martinico (eds.), *Kadi on Trial: A Multifaceted Analysis of the Kadi Trial* (London: Routledge, 2014), pp. 187–217.

Pickard, Duncan, 'Judicial Interpretation at the European Court of Justice as a Feature of Supranational Law' (2017) 20 *European Union Law Working Papers*, pp. 1–19.

Poiares Maduro, Miguel, 'Interpreting European Law: Judicial Adjudication in the Context of Constitutional Pluralism' (2007) 1(2) *European Journal of Legal Studies*, pp. 137–152.

Poretti, Pietro, 'Waiting for Godot: Subsidy Disciplines in Services Trade', in Marion Panizzon, Nicole Pohl, and Pierre Sauvé (eds.), *GATS and the Regulation of International Trade in Services* (Cambridge: Cambridge University Press, 2008), pp. 466–488.

Porges, Amy, 'Alternative Dispute Settlement in the GATT and the WTO', in Daniel Bethlehem (eds.), *The Oxford Handbook of International Trade Law*, 2nd ed. (Oxford: Oxford University Press, 2022), pp. 1042–1062.

Portela, Clara, 'Enforcing Respect for Labour Standards with Targeted Sanctions' (2018) *Friedrich Ebert Stiftung*, http://library.fes.de/pdf-files/bueros/singapur/14689.pdf.

Prévost, Denise and Alexovičová, Iveta, 'Mind the Compliance Gap: Managing Trustworthy Partnerships for Sustainable Development in the European Union's Free Trade Agreements' (2019) 6(3) *International Journal of Public Law and Policy*, pp. 236–269.

Qin, Julia, 'Turkey–Pharmaceuticals: The First WTO Arbitration for Appellate Review' (2022) 49(4) *Legal Issues of Economic Integration*, pp. 415-430.

Quick, Reinhard, 'Carbon Border Adjustment: A Dissenting View on Its Alleged GATT-Compatibility' (2020) 4 *Zeitschrift für Europarechtliche Studien*, pp. 549–597.

Quick, Reinhard and Das, Isha, 'Can Paris Strike Back? On the Paris Agreement's Inability to Cope with Unilateral Trade-Related Carbon Measures Such as the European Commission's CBAM-Proposal', in Freya Baetens and Stefaan van den

Bogaert (eds.), *The EU and the WTO: Ever the Twain Shall Meet: Liber Amicorum Marco Bronckers* (Aalphen aan den Rijn: Wolters Kluwer, 2023), pp. 75–102.

Quick, Reinhard and Das, Isha, 'The EU's CBAM-Regulation stands in contrast to fundamental EU-obligations under the Paris Agreement', International Economic Law and Policy Blog, 19 July 2023, https://ielp.worldtradelaw.net/2023/07/guest-post-the-eus-cbam-regulation-stands-in-contrast-to-fundamental-eu-obligations-under-the-paris-.html.

Rajamani, Lavanya, 'Ambition and Differentiation in the 2015 Paris Agreement: Interpretative Possibilities and Underlying Politics' (2016a) 65 *International & Comparative Law Quarterly*, pp. 493–514.

Rajamani, Lavanya, 'Common but Differentiated Responsibilities', in Michael Faure (ed.), *Elgar Encyclopedia of Environmental Law* (Cheltenham: Edward Elgar Publishing, 2016b), pp. 291–302.

Rajput, Aniruddha, 'The BRICS as 'Rising Powers' and the Development of International Law', in Heike Krieger, Georg Nolte, and Andreas Zimmermann (eds.), *International Rule of Law: Rise or Decline?* (New York: Oxford University Press, 2019), pp. 105–124.

Raju, Deepak, 'Proposed EU Regulation to Address Third Country Coercion – What Is Coercion?', *EJIL:Talk!*, 6 January 2022, www.ejiltalk.org/proposed-eu-regulation-to-address-third-country-coercion-what-is-coercion/.

Ranjan, Prabhash, 'Russia-Ukraine War and WTO's National Security Exception' (2023) 58(2) *Foreign Trade Review*, pp. 246–258.

Reinhold, Steven, 'Good Faith in International Law' (2013) Bonn Research Papers on Public International Law Paper No. 2/2013, pp. 1–21.

Remy, Jan Yves, 'Dispute Settlement at the WTO: How Did We Get Here and What's Next for Commonwealth States?' (2020) 166 *The Commonwealth Trade Hot Topics*, pp. 1–8.

Riesenhuber, Karl (ed.), *Europäische Methodenlehre*, 4th ed. (Berlin: De Gruyter, 2021).

Rigod, Boris, 'Global Europe: The EU's New Trade Policy in Its Legal Context' (2012) 18 *Columbia Journal of European Law*, pp. 277–306.

Ritzek-Seidl, Simone, 'The Regulation on Foreign Subsidies Distorting the Internal Market: Outline of the Provisional Agreement' (2022) 3 *Zeitschrift für Europarechtliche Studien*, pp. 423–430.

Roberts, Anthea, Choer Moraes, Henrique, and Ferguson, Victor, 'Toward a Geoeconomic Order in International Trade and Investment' (2019) 22(4) *Journal of International Economic Law*, pp. 655–676.

Ronzitti, Natalino, 'Sanctions as Instruments of Coercive Diplomacy: An International Law Perspective', in Natalino Ronzitti (ed.), *Coercive Diplomacy, Sanctions and International Law* (Leiden: Brill Neijhoff, 2016), pp. 1–32.

Rubini, Luca, '"A Delphic Oracle?" What Does the Recent EU Commission's Trade Policy Review Mean?', *EU Law Live*, 24 June 2020, https://eulawlive.com/op-ed-a-delphic-oracle-what-does-the-recent-eu-commissions-trade-policy-review-mean-by-luca-rubini.

Ruggie, John, 'International Regimes, Transactions, and Change: Embedded Liberalism in the Postwar Economic Order' (1982) 36(2) *International Organization*, pp. 379–415.

Ruiz Fabri, Hélène, 'Is There a Case – Legally and Politically – for Direct Effect of WTO Obligations?' (2014) 25(1) *European Journal of International Law*, pp. 151–173.

Ruys, Tom, 'Sanctions, Retorsions and Countermeasures: Concepts and International Legal Framework', in Larissa van den Herik (ed.), *Research Handbook on UN Sanctions and International Law* (Cheltenham: Edward Elgar Publishing, 2017), pp. 19–51.

Sánchez, Alejandro, 'What Trade Lawyers Should Know About the ILC Articles on State Responsibility' (2012) 7(6) *Global Trade and Customs Journal*, pp. 292–299.

Sanchez-Graells, Albert, 'Article 2: Definitions', in Roberto Caranta and Albert Sanchez-Graells (eds.), *European Public Procurement. Commentary on Directive 2014/24/EU* (Cheltenham: Edward Elgar, 2021).

Sands, Philippe, and Peel, Jacqueline, *Principles of International Environmental Law*, 3rd ed. (Cambridge: Cambridge University Press, 2012).

Sapir, André and Horn, Henrik, 'Political Assessment of Possible Reactions of EU Main Trading Partners to EU Border Carbon Measures' (2020) European Parliament Briefing Requested by the Committee on International Trade (INTA), www.europarl.europa.eu/cmsdata/210515/EXPO_BRI(2020)603503_EN.pdf, pp. 5–14.

Sato, Sakuya (Yoshida), 'EU's Carbon Border Adjustment Mechanism: Will It Achieve Its Objective(s)?' (2021) 56(3) *Journal of World Trade*, pp. 383–404.

Schaus, Malorie, 'EU Trade Policy in Light of the New Industrial Strategy' (2021) 56 *Intereconomics*, pp. 144–149.

Schmitz, Luuk and Seidl, Timo, 'As Open as Possible, as Autonomous as Necessary' (2023) 61(3) *Journal of Common Market Studies*, pp. 834–852.

Schonberg, Morris, 'The EU Foreign Subsidies Regulation: Substantive Assessment Issues and Open Questions' (2022) 21(2) *European State Aid Law Quarterly*, pp. 143–152.

Sender, Omri, 'Coercion', in Anne Peters and Rüdiger Wolfrum (ed.), *Max Planck Encyclopaedia of Public International Law*, Online ed. (Oxford University Press, 2024), https://opil.ouplaw.com/display/10.1093/law:epil/9780199231690/law-9780199231690-e1749.

Shaffer, Gregory, *Emerging Powers and the World Tading System: The Past and Future of International Economic Law* (Cambridge: Cambridge University Press, 2021).

Shaffer, Gregory and Gao, Henry, 'A New Chinese Economic Order?' (2020) 23(3) *Journal of International Economic Law*, pp. 607–635.

Siles-Brügge, Gabriel, *Constructing European Union Trade Policy: A Global Idea of Europe* (London: Palgrave Macmillan, 2014).

Simma, Bruno and Pulkowski, Dirk, 'Of Planets and the Universe: Self-Contained Regimes in International Law' (2006) 17(3) *European Journal of International Law*, pp. 483–529.

Simma, Bruno and Tams, Christian, 'Reacting Against Treaty Breaches', in Duncan Hollis (ed.), *The Oxford Guide to Treaties*, 2nd ed. (Oxford: Oxford University Press, 2020), pp. 568–594.

Starshinova, Olga, 'Is the MPIA a Solution to the WTO Appellate Body Crisis?' (2021) 55(5) *Journal of World Trade*, pp. 787–804.

Stewart, Terence P., 'European Union Moves to Authorize Retaliation Where There Is No Alternative to the Appellate Body Pursued', *Current Thoughts on Trade*, 19 December 2019, https://currentthoughtsontrade.com/2019/12/19/european-union-moves-to-authorize-retaliation-in-disputes-where-there-is-no-alternative-to-the-appellate-body-pursued/.

Stiglitz, Joseph E., *Making Globalization Work* (New York: W. W. Norton & Company, 2006).

Stoll, Peter-Tobias, Gött, Henner, and Abel, Patrick, 'Model Labour Chapter for European Union Trade Agreements' (2020) *Friedrich Ebert Stiftung*, http://library.fes.de/pdf-files/bueros/singapur/16089.pdf.

Sun Han, Ji, 'The EU-Korea Labour Dispute: A Critical Analysis of the EU's Approach' (2021) 26(4) *European Foreign Affairs Review*, pp. 531–552.

Szczepański, Marcin, 'EU International Procurement Instrument' (2022) *European Parliamentary Research Service*, www.europarl.europa.eu/RegData/etudes/ATAG/2022/729459/EPRS_ATA(2022)729459_EN.pdf.

Tamiotti, Ludivine, The, Robert, Kulaçoglu, Vasile et al., 'Trade and Climate Change' (2009) WTO-UNEP Report, www.wto.org/english/res_e/booksp_e/trade_climate_change_e.pdf, pp. 1–166.

Telles, Pedro, 'SME Related Impacts, Thresholds and National Legislation', in *Detailed Appraisal of the European Commission's Impact Assessment: Third Countries' Reciprocal Access to EU Public Procurement* (2013) European Parliamentary Research Service, www.europarl.europa.eu/RegData/etudes/BRIE/2014/508963/EPRS_BRI(2014)508963_REV1_EN.pdf, pp. 100–121.

Titievskaia, Jana, Morgado Simões, Henrique, and Dobreva, Alina, 'EU Carbon Border Adjustment Mechanism Implications for Climate and Competitiveness' (2022) *European Parliament Research Service*, www.europarl.europa.eu/RegData/etudes/BRIE/2022/698889/EPRS_BRI(2022)698889_EN.pdf, pp. 1–11.

Tladi, Dire, 'The Duty Not to Intervene in Matters Within Domestic Jurisdiction', in Jorge E. Viñuales (ed.), *The UN Friendly Relations Declaration at 50: An Assessment of the Fundamental Principles of International Law* (Cambridge: Cambridge University Press, 2020), pp. 87–104.

Tocci, Nathalie, 'The Making of the EU Global Strategy' (2016) 37 *Contemporary Security Policy*, pp. 461–472.

Tokas, Marios, 'Playing the Game: The EU's Proposed Regulation on Foreign Subsidies' (2022) 56(5) *Journal of World Trade*, pp. 779–802.

Trachtman, Joel P., 'WTO Law Constraints on Border Tax Adjustment and Tax Credit Mechanisms to Reduce the Competitive Effects of Carbon Taxes' (2016) Resources for the Future Discussion Paper, https://media.rff.org/documents/RFF-DP-16-03.pdf, pp. 1–42.

Trapp, Patricia, 'Das Weißbuch der Kommission zur Gewährleistung fairer Wettbewerbsbedingungen bei Subventionen aus Drittstaaten' (2020) 22 *Europäische Zeitschrift für Wirtschafsrecht*, pp. 964–970.

Trepte, Peter, 'The Agreement on Government Procurement', in Patrick F. J. Macrory, Arthur E. Appleton, and Michael G. Plummer (eds.), *The World Trade Organization: Legal, Economic and Political Analysis* (New York: Springer, 2005), pp. 1123–1163.

Tzanakopoulos, Antonios, 'The Right to be Free from Economic Coercion' (2015) 4(3) *Cambridge Journal of International and Comparative Law*, pp. 616–633.

Van den Bossche, Peter, 'Is There a Future for the WTO Appellate Body and WTO Dispute Settlement?' (2022) World Trade Institute Working Paper No. 01/2022, pp. 1–27.

Van den Bossche, Peter and Akpofure, Sarah, 'The Use and Abuse of the National Security Exception under Article XXI(b)(iii) of the GATT 1994' (2020) WTI Working Paper No. 03/2020, pp. 1–30.

Van den Bossche, Peter and Zdouc, Werner, *The Law and Policy of the WTO*, 5th ed. (Cambridge: Cambridge University Press, 2022).

Van der Loo, Guillaume, 'Law and Practice of the EU's Trade Agreements with "Disputed" Territories: A Consistent Approach?', in Inge Govaere and Sacha Garben (eds.), *The Interface Between EU and International Law. Contemporary Reflections* (Oxford: Hart Publishing, 2019), pp. 243–268.

Van der Schueren, Paulette, Mizulin, Nikolay, Gergondet, Edourd, and Geraets, Dylan, 'European Commission Unveils its Anti-Coercion Instrument Proposal', *Meyer Brown Legal Update*, 9 December 2021, www.mayerbrown.com/-/media/files/perspectives-events/publications/2021/12/european-commission-unveils-its-anticoercion-instrument-proposal.pdf, pp. 1–7.

van Elsuwege, Pieter, 'The Nexus Between Common Commercial Policy and Human Rights', in Guillaume van der Loo and Michael Hahn (eds.) *The Law and Practice of Common Commercial Policy: The First Ten Years after the Treaty of Lisbon* (Leiden, Boston: Brill Nijhoff, 2021), pp. 416–433.

van Gaal, Wester, 'EU Negotiators Agree on Historic Carbon Tariff', *EUobserver*, 13 December 2022, https://euobserver.com/green-economy/156534.

VanGrasstek, Craig, *Trade and American Leadership: The Paradoxes of Power and Wealth from Alexander Hamilton to Donald Trump* (Cambridge: Cambridge University Press, 2019a).

VanGrasstek, Craig, 'The Trade Policy of the United States under the Trump Administration' (2019b) EUI Working Papers, Robert Schuman Centre for Advanced Studies 2019/11, pp. 1–30.

Van 't Wout, Demy, 'The Enforceability of the Trade and Sustainable Development Chapters of the European Union's Free Trade Agreements' (2022) 20 *Asia Europe Journal*, pp. 81–98.

Velut, Jean Baptiste, Baeza Breinbauer, Daniela, de Bruijne, Marit et al., 'Comparative Analysis of Trade and Sustainable Development Provisions in Free Trade Agreements' (2022) *Trade Policy Hub*, London School of Economics and Political Science Consulting, www.lse.ac.uk/business/consulting/assets/documents/TSD-Final-Report-Feb-2022.pdf.

Ventouratou, Anna, 'The Law on State Responsibility and the World Trade Organization' (2021) 22 *Journal of World Investment & Trade*, pp. 759–803.

Venzke, Ingo and Vidigal, Geraldo, 'Are Unilateral Trade Measures in the Climate Crisis the End of Differentiated Responsibilities? The Case of the EU Carbon Border Adjustment Mechanism (CBAM)', in Maarten den Heijer and Harmen van der Wilt (eds.), *Netherlands Yearbook of International Law 2020: Global Solidarity and Common but Differentiated Responsibilities*, vol. 51 (The Hague: T.M.C. Asser Press, 2022), pp. 187–225.

Verlin Laatikainen, Katie and Smith, Karen E. (eds.), *The European Union at the United Nations: Intersecting Multilateralisms* (Hampshire: Palgrave Macmillan, 2006).

Vermulst, Edwin and Dion Sud, Juhi, 'Are the EU's Trade Defence Instruments WTO Compliant?', in Wolfgang Weiß and Cornelia Furculita (eds.), *Global Politics and EU Trade Policy: Facing the Challenges to a Multilateral Approach* (Cham: Springer, 2020), pp. 231–253.

Vidigal, Geraldo, 'Why Is There So Little Litigation under Free Trade Agreements? Retaliation and Adjudication in International Dispute Settlement' (2017) 20 *Journal of International Economic Law*, pp. 927–950.

Vidigal, Geraldo, 'Westphalia Strikes Back: The 2008 Trade Wars and Threat to the WTO Regime' (2018) 2018/31 Amsterdam Law School Legal Studies Research Paper, pp. 1–57.

Vidigal, Geraldo, 'Living without the Appellate Body: Multilateral, Bilateral and Plurilateral Solutions to the WTO Dispute Settlement Crisis' (2019) 20(6) *Journal of World Investment & Trade*, pp. 862–890.

Vidigal, Geraldo, 'WTO Adjudication and the Security Exception: Something Old, Something New, Something Borrowed – Something Blue?' (2019) 46(3) *Legal Issues of Economic Integration*, pp. 203–224.

Villiger, Mark E., *Commentary on the 1969 Vienna Convention on the Law of Treaties* (Leiden: Martinus Nijhoff Publishers, 2009).

Vogenauer, Stefan, *Die Auslegung von Gesetzen in England und auf dem Kontinent* (Tübingen: Mohr Siebeck, 2001).

Voigt, Christina, 'Up in the Air: Aviation, the EU Emissions Trading Scheme and the Question of Jurisdiction' (2012) 14 *Cambridge Yearbook of European Legal Studies*, pp. 475–506.

Voigt, Christina and Ferreira, Felipe, 'Dynamic Differentiation: The Principles of CBDR-RC, Progression and Highest Possible Ambition in the Paris Agreement' (2016) 5(2) *Transantional Environmental Law*, pp. 285–303.

Vranes, Erich, 'Jurisdiction and Applicable Law in WTO Dispute Settlement' (2005) 48 *German Yearbook of International Law*, pp. 265–290.

Vranes, Erich, 'The Definition of 'Norm Conflict' in International Law and Legal Theory' (2006) 17(2) *European Journal of International Law*, pp. 395–411.

Walker, Rebecca, 'The "Trade-Related" Conundrum of the EU–Korea FTA Expert Panel: Are FTAs a Novel Forum to Enforce Sustainable Development Goals?' (2021) *International Institute for Sustainable Development*, www.iisd.org/itn/en/2021/10/07/the-trade-related-conundrum-of-the-eu-korea-fta-expert-panel-are-ftas-a-novel-forum-to-enforce-sustainable-development-goals/.

Wang, Heng, 'Selective Reshaping: China's Paradigm Shift in International Economic Governance' (2020) 23(3) *Journal of International Economic Law*, pp. 583–606.

Weil, Prosper, 'Towards Relative Normativity in International Law' (1983) 77 *American Journal of International Law*, pp. 413–442.

Weinhardt, Clara, Mau, Karsten, and Hillebrand Pohl, Jens, 'The EU as a Geoeconomic Actor? A Review of Recent European Trade and Investment Policies', in Milan Babić, Adam D. Dixon, and Imogen T. Liu (eds.), *The Political Economy of Geoeconomics* (Cham: Palgrave Macmillan, 2022), pp. 107–136.

Weiß, Wolfgang, 'WTO Procurement Rules: In Particular the Government Procurement Agreement (GPA) and Services of General Interest', in Markus Krajewski (ed.), *Services of General Interest Beyond the Single Market. External and International Law Dimensions* (The Hague: T.M.C Asser Press, 2015), pp. 49–76.

Weiß, Wolfgang, 'EU Multilateral Trade Policy in a Changing, Multipolar World: The Way Forward', in Wolfgang Weiß and Cornelia Furculita (eds.), *Global Politics and EU Trade Policy: Facing the Challenges to a Multilateral Approach* (Cham: Springer, 2020), pp. 17–39.

Weiß, Wolfgang, 'Interpreting Essential Security Exceptions in WTO Law in View of Economic Security Interests', in Wolfgang Weiß and Cornelia Furculita (eds.), *Global Politics and EU Trade Policy: Facing the Challenges to a Multilateral Approach* (Cham: Springer, 2020), pp. 255–284.

Weiß, Wolfgang, 'The CETA Investment Court and EU External Autonomy' (2020) 8(1) *Hungarian Yearbook of International Law and European Law*, pp. 15–39.

Weiß, Wolfgang, *WTO Law and Domestic Regulation* (München, Oxford, Baden-Baden: Hart, Beck, Nomos, 2020).

Weiß, Wolfgang, 'Enhancement of the European Parliament's Monitoring for Better Coherence Between Trade Policy and Non-Trade Policy Objectives (NTPOs)' (2021) 2021/68 Robert Schuman Centre for Advanced Studies Working Paper, https://cadmus.eui.eu/bitstream/handle/1814/72240/RSC%202021_68.pdf?sequence=1&isAllowed=y, pp. 1-19.

Weiß, Wolfgang, 'Ex Officio Third Country Subsidies' Review' (2022) 21(2) *European State Aid Law Quarterly*, pp. 132–142.

Weiß, Wolfgang, 'Handelsvergeltungs-VO', in Horst Günter Krenzler, Christoph Herrmann, and Marian Niestedt (eds.), *EU-Außenwirtschafts-und Zollrecht* (München: C.H. Beck, 2022), p. 112.

Weiß, Wolfgang, 'The EU's Strategic Autonomy in Times of Politicization of International Trade: The Future of Commission Accountability' (2023) 14(Suppl 3) *Global Policy*, pp. 54–64.

Weiß, Wolfgang, 'The EU's Strategic Autonomy and Rule of Law in External Affairs: What Future for Respect for International Law and Multilateralism in Trade Policy?', in Luis M. Hinojosa-Martínez and Carmela Pérez Bernárdez (eds.), *Enhancing the Rule of Law in the EU's External Action* (Cheltenham: Edward Elgar, 2023), pp. 186–215.

Weiß, Wolfgang and Furculita, Cornelia, 'The EU in Search for Stronger Enforcement Rules. Assessing the Proposed Amendments to Trade Enforcement

Regulation 654/2014' (2020) 23(4) *Journal of International Economic Law*, pp. 865–884.

Wessel, Ramses, 'The EU and International Law', in Ramses Wessel and Joris Larik (eds.), *EU External Relations Law: Text, Cases and Materials*, 2nd ed. (Oxford: Hart Publishing, 2020), pp. 139–173.

Wessel, Ramses and Kaspiarovich, Yuliya, 'The Role of Values in EU External Relations, in Elaine Fahey and Isabella Mancini (eds.), *Understanding the EU as a Good Global Actor: Ambitions, Values, and Metrics* (Cheltenham: Edward Elgar Publishing, 2022), pp. 92–106.

Whitsitt, Elizabeth, 'A Modest Victory at the WTO for Ontario's FIT Program' (2013) 20(1) *University of California, Davis Journal of International Law and Policy*, pp. 75–103.

Will, Ulrike, *Climate Border Adjustments and WTO Law: Extending the EU Emissions Trading System to Imported Goods and Services* (Leiden: Brill Neijhoff, 2019).

Williams, Nancy, 'The Resilience of Protectionism in U.S. Trade Policy' (2019) *Boston University Law Review*, pp. 683–719.

Williams, Rhodri, 'A New EU International Procurement Instrument (IPI)', *Henderson Chambers*, 13 April 2022, www.hendersonchambers.co.uk/2022/04/13/alerter-by-rhodri-williams-qc-a-new-eu-international-procurement-instrument-ipi/.

Wolff, Alan Wm., 'WTO 2025: Restoring Binding Dispute Settlement', Peterson Institute for International Economics Working Papers 22-5, www.piie.com/publications/working-papers/wto-2025-restoring-binding-dispute-settlement, pp. 1–35.

Woo Kim, Jin and Luyten, Ann-Evelyn, 'Op-Ed: Could the EU's Chief Trade Enforcement Officer Enforce Sustainable Development Commitments under EU Trade Agreements Against Non-Compliant Third Countries?', *EU Law Live*, 13 May 2020, https://eulawlive.com/op-ed-could-the-eus-chief-trade-enforcement-officer-enforce-sustainable-development-commitments-under-eu-trade-agreements-against-non-compliant-third-countries-by-ann-evel/#.

Woolcock, Stephen, 'EU Policy on Preferential Trade Agreements in the 2000s: A Reorientation Towards Commercial Aims' (2014) 20(6) *European Law Journal*, pp. 718–732.

Woolcock, Stephen, 'Trade Policy: Policy-Making After the Treaty of Lisbon', in Helen Wallace, Mark A. Pollack, and Alasdair R. Young (eds.), *Policy-Making in the European Union*, 7th ed. (New York: Oxford University Press, 2015), pp. 388–406.

World Trade Organization, 'Trade and Environment at the WTO' (2004), www.wto.org/english/tratop_e/envir_e/envir_wto2004_e.pdf, pp. 1–76.

Wouters, Jan, and Raina, Akhil, 'The European Union and Global Economic Governance: A Leader without a Roadmap?', in Julien Chaisse (ed.), *Sixty Years of European Integration and Global Power Shifts: Perceptions, Interactions and Lessons* (London: Hart Publishing, 2020), pp. 193–216.

Wouters, Jan, Odermatt, Jed, and Ramopoulos, Thomas, 'Worlds Apart? Comparing the Approaches of the European Court of Justice and the EU Legislature to International Law', in Marise Cremona and Anne Thies (eds.), *The*

European Court of Justice and External Relations Law: Constitutional Challenges (Oxford: Hart Publishing, 2014), pp. 249–279.

Wouters, Jan, Hoffmeister, Frank, De Baere, Geert, and Ramopoulos, Thomas, *The Law of EU External Relations. Cases, Materials, and Commentary on the EU as an International Legal Actor*, 3rd ed. (New York: Oxford University Press, 2021).

Wu, Bixuan, 'To Penalize Low Carbon Price or High Carbon Intensity? A Comparison of the EU's CBAM and the U.S. Clean Competition Act', International Economic Law and Policy Blog, 1 July 2022, https://ielp.worldtradelaw.net/2022/07/guest-post-to-penalize-low-carbon-price-or-high-carbon-intensity-a-comparison-of-the-eus-cbam-and-th.html.

Wu, Chien-Huei, 'The EU's Proposed Anti-Coercion Instrument: Legality and Effectiveness' (2023) 57(2) *Journal of World Trade*, pp. 297–316.

Wu, Mark, 'The "China, Inc.": Challenge to Global Trade Governance' (2016) 57(2) *Harvard International Law Journal*, pp. 261–324.

Yanovich, Alan, 'Canada – Renewable Energy and Canada – FIT Program – Debunking the Myth that the GATT 1994 Provides Carte Blanche to Discriminate in Government Procurement' (2013) *Global Trade and Customs Journal* 8(11–12), pp. 430–434.

Young, Alaisdair, 'It's the End of EU Trade Policy as We Know It: The Commission's 2021 Trade Policy Review', *Reconnect Online Workshop*, 15 October 2021, https://reconnect-europe.eu/event/reconnect-online-workshop-eu-trade-policy/.

Zamfir, Ionel, 'Human Rights in EU Trade Agreements: The Human Rights Clause and Its Application' (2019) *European Parliamentary Research Service*, www.europarl.europa.eu/RegData/etudes/BRIE/2019/637975/EPRS_BRI(2019)637975_EN.pdf.

Zamfir, Ionel, 'Labour Rights in EU Trade Agreements towards Stronger Enforcement' (2022) *European Parliamentary Research Service Briefing*, www.europarl.europa.eu/RegData/etudes/BRIE/2022/698800/EPRS_BRI(2022)698800_EN.pdf.

Zenglein, Max J. and Holzmann, Anna, 'Evolving Made in China 2025: China's Industrial Policy in the Quest for Global Tech Leadership' (2019) Merics Papers on China No. 8, pp. 7–76.

Zhang, Feng, 'Chinese Exceptionalism in the Intellectual World of China's Foreign Policy' in Rosemary Foot (ed.), *China Across the Divide: The Domestic and Global in Politics and Society* (New York: Oxford University Press, 2013), pp. 43–71.

Zhou, Weihuan, 'WTO Dispute Settlement Mechanism without the Appellate Body: Some Observations on the US-China Trade Deal' (2020) 20(4) *University of New South Wales Law Research Paper*, pp. 1–8.

Zhou, Weihuan, 'Rethinking the (CP)TPP as a Model for Regulation of Chinese State-Owned Enterprises' (2021) 24(3) *Journal of International Economic Law*, pp. 572–590.

Ziegler, Andreas R. and Baumgartner, Jorun, 'Good Faith as a General Principle of (International) Law', in Andrew D. Mitchell, M Sornarajah, and Tania Voon (eds.), *Good Faith and International Economic Law* (New York: Oxford University Press, 2015), pp. 9–36.

Ziegler, Katja, 'Beyond Pluralism and Autonomy: Systemic Harmonization as a Paradigm for the Interaction of EU Law and International Law' (2016) 35(1) *Yearbook of European Law*, pp. 667–711.

Zurek, Karolina, 'From "Trade and Sustainability" to "Trade for Sustainability" in EU External Trade Policy', in Antonina Bakardjieva Engelbrekt, Niklas Bremberg, Anna Michalski, and Lars Oxelheim (eds.), *The European Union in a Changing World Order: Interdisciplinary European Studies* (Cham: Palgrave Macmillan, 2020), pp. 115–143.

Index

For EU product safety concerns, contact us at Calle de José Abascal, 56–1°, 28003 Madrid, Spain or eugpsr@cambridge.org.

www.ingramcontent.com/pod-product-compliance
Lightning Source LLC
LaVergne TN
LVHW021055220926
848484LV00021B/944
* 9 7 8 1 0 0 9 1 9 6 5 3 6 *